Breaker Morant

PETER FITZSIMONS

Breaker Morant

The epic story of the Boer War and Harry 'Breaker' Morant:
drover, horseman, bush poet, murderer or hero?

hachette
AUSTRALIA

Every effort has been made to identify individual photographers and copyright holders where appropriate, but for some photographs this has not been possible. The publishers would be pleased to hear from any copyright holders who have not been acknowledged.

 hachette
AUSTRALIA

Published in Australia and New Zealand in 2020
by Hachette Australia
(an imprint of Hachette Australia Pty Limited)
Level 17, 207 Kent Street, Sydney NSW 2000
www.hachette.com.au

10 9 8 7 6 5 4 3 2 1

A catalogue record for this
book is available from the
National Library of Australia

NATIONAL
LIBRARY
OF AUSTRALIA

ISBN: 978 0 7336 4130 5 (hardback)

Cover design by Luke Causby/Blue Cork
Cover images: 2nd South Australian (Mounted Rifles) Contingent, including Harry 'Breaker' Morant; 5th Contingent, Victorian Mounted Rifles in the Transvaal (AWM P00220, P01866.006)
Author photo courtesy of Peter Morris/Sydney Heads
Maps by Jane Macaulay
Typeset in 11.1/14.1 pt Sabon LT Pro by Bookhouse, Sydney
Printed and bound in Australia by McPherson's Printing Group

MIX
Paper from
responsible sources
FSC
www.fsc.org
FSC® C001695

The paper this book is printed on is certified against the Forest Stewardship Council® Standards. McPherson's Printing Group holds FSC® chain of custody certification SA-COC-005379. FSC® promotes environmentally responsible, socially beneficial and economically viable management of the world's forests.

To my late grandfather, Trooper Frederick Harper Booth,
No. 128 of the 2nd Victorian Mounted Rifles. No less than
120 years on, I hope this book does justice to encapsulate
the truth: the good, the bad and the ugly of both your
experience and that of those you fought with and against.

CONTENTS

LIST OF MAPS

INTRODUCTION

Throughout the whole African army there was nothing but the utmost admiration for the dash and spirit of the hard-riding straight-shooting sons of Australia and New Zealand. In a host which held many brave men there were none braver than they.[1]

War correspondent, Sir Arthur Conan Doyle,
The Great Boer War

Breaker Morant was one of the type the Colonies used to know well years ago – the family 'ne'er-do-well,' sent out here to steady down or go to the devil. The life of the bush exactly suited him; its freedom and unconventionality appealed to the wild, indomitable spirit he inherited from his Irish forebears. He feared neither God nor man, acknowledged no authority, and reckoned that his passions were given him to be gratified. Generous to a fault and lenient to other men's failings, he would lend his last shilling and screen the veriest outlaw.[2]

Wilhelmina (Mina) Rawson, author, columnist
and friend of Breaker Morant

It was on a May day in 2017 that I journeyed to Canberra for the unveiling of the beautifully conceived and executed National Boer War Memorial.

I had voted in favour of its construction when I'd served on the Council of the Australian War Memorial, and had a personal connection. On that Wednesday morning, approaching the newly finished memorial, just a couple of minutes' walk down the boulevard from the Australian War Memorial itself, I was immediately impressed. The essence of the memorial is the larger-than-life bronze statues of four mounted Australian soldiers, on patrol. At the base are a series of bronze plaques, with the moving extracts from the letters of a soldier of the 2nd Victorian Mounted Rifles to his mother.

'At the Sand River we had a terrible fight. The Boers had blown up the bridge and when we crossed they opened fire. The Boers have some very good guns and they make good use of them. We had to fight all day. It was a terrible strain when the shells are screaming amongst you and burst . . . We ride company behind company and if we bunched up at all there would be terrible slaughter . . . everyone admits how terrible artillery fire is, yet no one attempts to move till he is told and no matter how good your horse, you never move to get cover any quicker than the regiment, such is British discipline.'

Those words sounded a little familiar . . .

I looked closer.

Goodness! They were from my grandfather, Trooper Frederick Harper Booth, to my great-grandmother, Maria Sofia Craigie McPherson Dunn Booth.

Grandpa, who lived to the age of 94 and who we all adored, never forgot the horror of the Boer War and when, in 1967, my brother Andrew turned up at his house after cadet parade still in khaki uniform, Grandpa burst into tears at the memory of other fine young men, dressed like him, who never returned to Australian shores. He would have been most honoured to have such words as these preserved in bronze. But, once again, it prompted another brother, James, to say to me, 'It is your family duty to write a book on the Boer War.'

I had always resisted on the grounds that the Boer War was an Imperial war, and while the Australians may have been on the winning side of the conflict, I was never comfortable with a war that was essentially white fellas battling over black fellas' land.

Nevertheless, the more I learnt, the more I came to realise that, horror aside, the Boer War was a foundational conflict in Australian military history and the characters at play were undeniably fascinating, none more than Breaker Morant himself. It also linked nicely with an extraordinary Boer War battle at a place called Elands River I'd heard about many years ago from a history buff by the name of Phil Hore – the first time I realised just how remarkable some of the events in the Boer War were from an Australian perspective.

A further encouragement to do the book was that my researcher and cousin, Angus FitzSimons, proved to be a long-time aficionado of the Breaker Morant story, and was already familiar with the minutiae of the saga, and not just with all the conspiracy theories that abound around it . . .

Even more usefully, he had some strong theories of his own and successfully insisted that this was the book for me. As ever, I owe his work across the board a great debt, even though on a couple of issues – don't get me started – we came to different conclusions! Nevertheless, I could always draw on his intellect and insights, and his passion for the story, which helped breathe life into every page. With his pure pedigree law degree from the University of Sydney, he also understood many of the esoteric details of the legal aspects of this story that defied me.

As to the rest of my team of researchers – down Bunbury way in WA, Barb Kelly trawled as mightily as ever through every document she could get her digital hands on to bring precious and often previously unrevealed detail to the account. She, too, became wonderfully obsessed with the story – Breaker does that to you – and was at her strongest in sifting through endless layers of legend and lies to get down to *what actually happened*. On three aspects she was able to blow away what had been long-accepted fact, and show me it simply wasn't true. As with my books on *Catalpa* and Captain Cook, both her son Lachlan and my son Jake were able to lend valuable assistance throughout. I won't spoil the story here by revealing the details, but when it came to a particular endlessly repeated myth concerning what Breaker Morant and his friend Captain Percy Hunt were doing between late 1900 and early 1901, Lachlan was also able to definitively prove it never happened that way by coming up with facsimiles of original documentation – thus ending a century-long fallacy, started by Breaker Morant himself. (I might note, in passing, how extraordinarily powerful those myths were. I work with the best researchers in the business, and I have never worked on a project where they disagreed more, often with passion, over what happened. It was, nevertheless, through that intellectual jousting that previously hidden truths were teased out. We finished as happy Vegemites because the final, last layer of documentation generally proved it definitively, but it was a long process to trace the byzantine deceptions of the Breaker.)

My warm thanks also to Dr Peter Williams, the Canberra military historian who first started working with me on my book on Gallipoli, and has stayed with me thereafter. He, too – less surprisingly – was a devotee of the Breaker story, and an expert on the Boer War. Time and again his four decades of learning in the field of Australian military history made this book stronger, not the least of which was his ability to instantly call in other experts.

On that subject, I offer my thanks once again to Colonel Renfrey Pearson for finding rare documents in archives in the United Kingdom, and Gregory Blake for his expert advice on all things to do with the weapons of the time. In South Africa, I thank Audrey Portman, Lourens Etchell and most particularly Charles Leach. In Australia, the expertise of Robin Droogleever and Nigel Webster was greatly appreciated.

As ever, and as I always recount at the beginning of my historical writing, I have tried to bring the *story* part of this his*tory* alive, by putting it in the present tense, and constructing it in the manner of a novel, albeit with 2000 footnotes, give or take, as the pinpoint pillars on which the story rests. For the sake of the storytelling, I have occasionally created a direct quote from reported speech in a journal, diary or letter, and changed pronouns and tenses to put that reported speech in the present tense. When the story required generic language – as in the words used when commanding movements in battle, I have taken the liberty of using that dialogue, to help bring the story to life.

Always, my goal has been to determine what were the words used, based on the primary documentary evidence presented, and what the feel of the situation was. For the same reason of remaining faithful to the language of the day, I have stayed with the Imperial system of measurement and used the contemporary spelling, with only the odd exception where it would create too much confusion otherwise.

This is a story that takes place 120 years ago, in an Australia and South Africa where race, or rather any race that was not white, was viewed and named in at best a patronising manner with terms such as 'boy' and 'native'. At worst, and a worst that was common indeed, the terms 'Kaffir' and 'n . . . r' were used to describe African people. These latter terms are used in this book when taken from direct speech or the writing of participants; it is a history that must be reckoned with rather than avoided. I have done my best to use these terms as little as possible without damaging the truth of the story or the true vocabulary of the men and women who lived it. I trust the twenty-first-century reader will understand that my use in no way connotes approval or acceptance of such terms or the underlying racist attitudes that birthed them.

All books used are listed in the Bibliography, but both for the Boer War saga and more particularly the Breaker, I was blessed to have had many authors before me doing *forensic* work on the subject, who I want to doubly acknowledge here.

Any writer on Breaker Morant owes a debt to Arthur Davey, who compiled a fascinating compendium of primary source documents in his *Breaker Morant and the Bushveldt Carbineers* in 1987. That may sound prosaic, but it was a Herculean task to trace so many elusive documents and scraps scattered throughout South Africa and the United Kingdom and finally assemble all the parts of this confounding set of conspiracies and contradictions that other writers had only glimpsed. His book remains fascinating; a detective novel of research that but for him would have slipped from history into myth.

The list of writers who have felt compelled to write about the Breaker is long and illustrious; including Kit Denton, who romanticised and then razed Morant in two wonderful books: the fictional *The Breaker* and the factual *Closed File*, where one can see Denton becoming disillusioned with the legend he helped create. Frank Fox's hot-off-the-press 1903 memoir *Breaker Morant – Bushman and Buccaneer* is the template for the legend of the Breaker, a first draft of history that is still a compelling read almost 120 years later. Another essential volume is *In Search of Breaker Morant* by Margaret Carnegie and Frank Shields, who began looking at the other side of the coin. Their first-hand research unravels some of the Breaker's many whoppers and opens up the can of worms that surrounds every aspect of this strange tale. Not long after beginning this book, I was contacted by Frank Shields himself offering his assistance and counsel, and it proved extremely useful. Just like Ian Jones was with my Ned Kelly book, Frank is *the* living expert, having started his own film and book work on the story in 1972 – he actually personally talked to some of the ancient members of the Bushveldt Carbineers still alive at the time. His vetting of my manuscript proved invaluable even if, inevitably, our conclusions on some matters are different – that is the way of the Breaker. I also salute the late historian Margaret Carnegie, Frank's co-author in their seminal book, and lay a bouquet on her literary grave for having found the previously obscure manuscript of Frederick Ramon de Bertodano in the Zimbabwe archives – I came to rely on it heavily, and for me it is the key to unlocking many Morant mysteries.

My long-time sub-editor meanwhile, Harriet Veitch, took the fine-tooth comb to the whole thing, untangling hopelessly twisted sentences, eliminating many grammatical errors and giving my work a sheen which does not properly belong to it. She has strengthened my stuff for three decades now, and I warmly thank her. In all my books, I give a draft of the near-finished product to my eldest brother, David, who has the best red pen in the business. When his interest flags, it is a fair bet so too will that of the reader, and I generally slash what doesn't grab him, so long as it is not key to the story. In this book, he was as astute as ever, and I record my gratitude. It was also more than useful that he was so familiar with the story of my grandfather because, forty years ago, it was his wife, Merrie, who had so laboriously typed up Grandpa's every letter, now digitised, which was my starting point for understanding his own experience. It was a delight, too, to consult all of my Booth cousins, to weave their wisps of memory of what Grandpa had told them into a more solid account of his experiences. I express my particular appreciation in this exercise to Richard Lander, who not only contributed some of those wisps, but then went painstakingly through the book from first to last, looking for errors.

My thanks also, as ever, to my highly skilled editor Deonie Fiford, who has honoured my request that she preserve most of the oft esoteric – I'm told – way I write, while only occasionally insisting that something come out because it just doesn't work.

I am also grateful to my friend and publisher Matthew Kelly of Hachette, with whom I have worked many times over the last three decades, and who was enthusiastic and supportive throughout, always giving great guidance.

I have loved doing this book, and hope you enjoy it.

Peter FitzSimons
Neutral Bay, Sydney
April 2020

DRAMATIS PERSONAE

My sympathies have always been with the unfortunate man, for I knew and liked him, and moreover one has the feeling that, but for the existence of men of his somewhat ruthless calibre during the eighteenth and nineteenth centuries, the British Empire would not now be the envy of all her neighbours. There were many rough paths to be hewn out of the world between 1750 and 1900, and it was the men of Morant's type who did the work.[1]

Major Claude S. Jarvis, in his book,
Half a Life

One would not rake up old stories were it not that ignorant busybodies were striving to make an Australian hero out of an English scamp.[2]

Windsor and Richmond Gazette, 1904

Lieutenant Harry Morant (Edwin Murrant). Born in 1864 in Bridgewater, Somerset, Morant immigrated to Australia in 1883 where he made a good name for himself as a poet and horse breaker – and a bad name for bad debts and minor scrapes with the law. His usual routine would be to jump from town to town and person to person, usually in Queensland and South Australia. He enlisted in the South Australian Mounted Rifles on 13 January 1900.

Lieutenant Peter Handcock. Born near Bathurst, New South Wales, in 1868, one of eight children. He became a blacksmith and married Bridget Martin in 1888. They had two sons and a daughter. Before joining the Bushveldt Carbineers in 1901, Handcock served with the NSW Mounted Rifles as Farrier Sergeant.

Lieutenant George Witton. Born in 1874 in Warrnambool, Victoria, as one of nine children. Witton came from a farming background. When war began he was a 25-year-old gunner in the Victorian Artillery at Fort Franklin, at the mouth of Port Phillip Bay.

Major Robert Lenehan. The son of Irish parents from Petersham, Sydney, Lenehan was born in 1865. He married in 1899, joined the NSW colonial forces in 1890 and became a solicitor the following year. He sailed for Southern Africa as a Captain with the NSW Mounted Rifles in January 1900.

Lieutenant Henry Picton. Born in London in 1878, Picton was the son of a coachman. He may have served in the French Foreign Legion in the 1890s and was awarded a Distinguished Conduct Medal for service in Southern Africa prior to joining the Bushveldt Carbineers.

Captain Alfred Taylor. Born in 1861 in Dublin, Ireland, as a young man he travelled to Rhodesia where he befriended Lobengula, the king of the Northern Ndebele people. During the First Matabele War in 1893, he was given the task of acting as a guide to Cecil Rhodes. His reputation for harsh treatment of the Rhodesian Natives earned him the name 'Bulala' (killer). In 1896 he was the commanding officer of a portion of Colonel Plumer's column in the Second Matabele War.

Lord Horatio Herbert Kitchener. Fifty years old at the time of the Boer War, Kitchener had joined the British Army in 1871. He saw active service in Egypt and the Sudan, where he acquired a reputation for ruthlessness. During the Boer War he was at first the Chief-of-Staff to Lord Roberts, taking over command of the army in November 1900.

Lord Frederick Roberts. Born in India in 1832, and fighting in half-a-dozen of the British Empire's 'little wars' in India and Africa, he rose rapidly in rank and earned a Victoria Cross. By the time of the Boer War he was Britain's most respected general. In December 1899, at the age of 67, he took over command in Southern African from Sir Redvers Buller, and turned over that command to Kitchener a year later.

General Sir Redvers Buller. Sixty years old when the Boer War began, Buller had, like Roberts, gained prominence in Britain's colonial wars. He earned a Victoria Cross in the Zulu War of 1879 and when the Boer War began was appointed commander of the army in Southern Africa.

Captain Frederick Ramon de Bertodano. Born in New South Wales of an ancient Spanish family, de Bertodano spent several years in Rhodesia with the British Army. Twenty-nine at the outbreak of the Boer War, he became an Intelligence Officer at Army Headquarters.

Major James Thomas. Born in Sydney in 1861, he attended King's School, Parramatta. He studied law at the University of Sydney and opened a practice in Tenterfield, New South Wales, in 1887. A member of the Tenterfield Rifles in peacetime, he sailed to Southern Africa with the first contingent of NSW Citizens' Bushmen in November 1899.

Trooper James Christie. A New Zealand farmer from the district of Clutha, Christie was also a local councillor and part-time schoolteacher. He became bankrupt in 1900, the same year four of his children were killed in a fire. He decided to join the war effort in Southern Africa, and signed up to the Bushveldt Carbineers in April 1901.

Trooper Frederick Harper Booth. After serving with the Victorian Mounted Rifles in the pre-war militia, the 19-year-old grazier from Harkaway joined the 2nd Victorian Mounted Rifles on 28 December 1899, and was on his way to the war on the SS *Euryalus* a scant fortnight later.

Lieutenant James Annat. Born in 1864 in Scotland, at the age of 16 Annat fought with the Gordon Highlanders during the First Boer War, where he was wounded at the Battle of Majuba Hill. He also saw active service in the Zulu War of 1883 and in Canada and the United States of America. Migrating to New South Wales he was an instructor for the colonial forces and a miner. During the Second Boer War he served with the 3rd Queensland Mounted Infantry.

General Sir John French. Born in Kent in 1852, French was in the Royal Navy before becoming a cavalry officer in the British Army. During the Second Boer War he led a cavalry division of 5000 horsemen in several important operations, including the relief of the town of Kimberley.

Emily Hobhouse. Born in Cornwall in 1860, Hobhouse was a welfare campaigner and pacifist. In 1900 she arrived in Southern Africa to investigate conditions in the camps for war-displaced civilians established by the British Army.

The men of Transvaal and the Orange Free State

President Paul Kruger. Born in 1825 in Whittlesea, Cape Colony, Kruger took part in the Great Trek while still a child and, only 12 years old, fought in the Battle of Vegkop against the Matabele. He became the third President of the Southern African Republic (Transvaal) in 1883, leading the war effort during the Second Boer War.

President Martinus Steyn. Steyn was born in Rietfontein in the Orange Free State in 1857. He studied law in the Netherlands and England and opened a practice in Bloemfontein and bought a farm nearby. In 1896 he became President of the Orange Free State.

General Piet Joubert. Born in 1831, Joubert was once Vice-President to Kruger. The Commandant General of all the Transvaal military forces, he led them into battle in Natal for the first five months of the war.

General Jacobus 'Koos' de la Rey. De la Rey, born in 1847, had little formal education. Deeply religious, he married Jacoba Greeff, farmed and raised 12 children. De la Rey became a member of the Transvaal *Volkrad* in 1883 and opposed President Kruger's policies against the Uitlanders.

Christiaan de Wet. Born at Smithfield in the Orange Free State in 1854, de Wet, like most traditional Boers, was a farmer. Fighting as an ordinary burgher at the beginning of the Second Boer War, natural ability saw him rise quickly in rank to command the forces of the Orange Free State in 1900.

Commandant Tom Kelly. Born in Bloemfontein in 1849, Kelly was the son of John Thomas Kelly, from Limerick, Ireland. He bought a farm in the Zoutpansberg, northern Transvaal, where he was also leader of the Zoutpansberg Commando.

Louis Botha. Thirty-seven years old when the war began, Botha was born in Natal. A member of the Transvaal Parliament he, like de la Rey, opposed the harsh line Kruger took with the Uitlanders, one of the causes of the war. In the guerrilla phase of the war he became a prominent general.

Deneys Reitz. Reitz was one of four sons of the Secretary of State for Transvaal. Aged 17 at the start of the war, Reitz fought in almost all the major battles during the conventional phase of the war with the Pretoria Commando. In the latter phase he fought under generals Christiaan de Wet and Jan Smuts.

PROLOGUE

... nothing but breathing the air of Africa, and actually walking through it and beholding its living inhabitants in all the peculiarities of their movements and manners, can communicate those gratifying, and literally indescribable sensations ...[1]

English explorer, William Burchell, who spent many years exploring Southern Africa in the early nineteenth century

Late in the fifteenth century, four years before Columbus caught sight or sound of the Americas, a Portuguese explorer by the name of Bartholomeu Diaz became the first European to see what would one day be known as Cape Town. In the beginning there was just Southern Africa, a vast expanse of mountains, rivers, pastures, jungle and veldt, encompassing nearly half a million square miles and the tribes of the San and Khoikhoi people.

By the mid-1600s, however, the southern tip of the continent had become significant for the fact that the foremost seafaring nation, Holland, had started to use it as their key stopping off point on their way back and forth between Europe and Asia for the spice trade. As that trade became ever more significant a Dutch colony was established, which saw ever more Dutch people flooding in, and pushing the dominant Xhosa tribe to the north.

Throughout the 1700s, the Dutch fastened their grip on Southern Africa, consolidating their colony. The farmers on the frontier were forced to fight the Xhosa, defending *their* land against the Native inhabitants. These Dutch farmers came to be known as 'Boers', a hardy people capable of living off the land while fighting for every inch of it.

Those with a commercial bent could even make a good deal of money, servicing the many ships on their way to not just the Dutch East Indies but also New Holland, with the likes of Captain James Cook, Captain Arthur Phillip and Captain William Bligh among those who brought their ships in to be resupplied.

Nevertheless, by the late 1700s, as Holland lost their part of the War of the First Coalition to the French, Britain began to have its own designs on the Cape area. On Christmas Eve 1805 the British sent the first of a huge fleet of warships into the harbour to prevent the victorious French claiming the most valuable of Holland's overseas territories. A year later the British defeated the Dutch at Blaauwberg – which would soon see the British formally occupy the Cape Colony. In response, many of the Dutch loaded up their ubiquitous 'Cape carts', and embarked on what was effectively a biblical exodus, seeking a new Promised Land. The *Voortrekkers*, as they were known, headed off on their *Grote Trek*, Great Trek, rolling north into the interior, fighting various tribes as they went, not least of which were the Zulu and the Matabele. Their method of fighting was to form 'Commandos', loose military units of irregular troops – farmers becoming soldiers for specific actions, before returning to their usual occupations. Their goal was not simply to kill or subdue the Africans; often, they wanted to take them as slaves.

'Commandos,' one historian will note, 'regularly raided neighboring tribes, killing, looting and seizing children to be brought back to serve as their "apprentices". There was a thriving trade in slaves, with Piet Joubert, the God-fearing commandant-general of the Transvaal [Commandos], being known as a particularly good source of these.'[2]

In fact it was so well known, and so accepted by the Boers, that at one point Piet Joubert's wife, Hendrina, received a letter with a request: 'Please let the general let me have a little Malaboch kaffir . . . I don't mind if it's a boy or a girl. I want one about seven years old.'[3]

(No protests, please. The Bible itself had ordained slavery as quite normal from the moment it had recorded Noah himself saying, 'Cursed be Canaan! The lowest of slaves will he be to his brothers.'[4] If Noah and God don't have a problem with the concept of slavery, why should we argue about the morality of such an ancient practice that suits our present purpose?)

With so many of his younger people taken – those men and women in their prime were the most highly prized – King Khama of Bechuanaland[5] had to write to the Governor of the Cape Colony, Sir Henry Barkly, begging for help: 'The Boers are coming into my country, and I do not like them. Their actions are cruel . . . We are treated like money, they sell us and our children.'[6] King Khama knew it was British policy to eliminate slavery in any place they took over. As Lord Milner had said, 'Our policy . . . is to end slavery in the Transvaal.'[7]

Some Dutch settlers put down roots in a coastal region they christened Natal and were soon joined by further waves of migration from Holland, moving even further north to establish Boer republics known as the *Oranje-Vrystaat*, Orange Free State, and the *Zuid-Afrikaansche Republiek* of Transvaal, just as many British migrants came to settle in the Cape. The area around the Cape continued to grow in importance as it was crucial for controlling the trade route to India, the newest resplendent jewel in the Crown of the British Empire.

So many English settlers came in fact, in an era when the British Empire was expanding as never before, that by 1843 the British had annexed Natal after a brief struggle, seeing many of the *Voortrekkers* pack up to head north once more, while the Native Africans were either pushed into ever smaller areas or began to work for the white settlers. Politically, things became more settled when, in the 1850s, Britain formally recognised the independence of both the Transvaal Republic and the Orange Free State – even though over coming years there continued to be skirmishes between British forces and both the Boers and the Native Africans.

For the most part the British ruling class didn't mind the Boers having that poor land in the remote African interior, until . . .

Until one day in 1867, a 15-year-old lad by the name of Erasmus Stephanus Jacobs is playing by the banks of the Orange River near

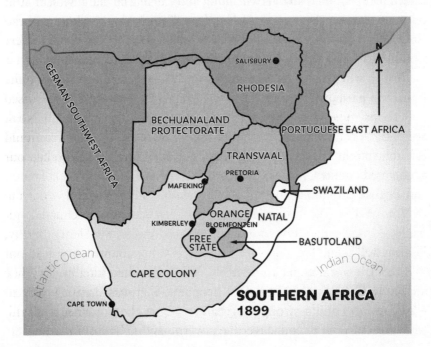

Hopetown on his father's northern Cape farm, throwing *klippies*, stones of a particularly shiny nature, when a passing neighbour, Schalk van Niekerk, asks if he could borrow one of the play stones – a particularly shiny one. Quietly, Schalk is convinced that the stone's hardness, weight and shiny quality means it might be valuable and . . . sure enough. Via a circuitous route, the rock in question comes to Acting Civil Commissioner Lourenzo Boyes at Colesberg who, noting that the stone is capable of cutting glass, pronounces: 'I believe it to be a diamond.'[8]

Mr Richard Southey, the Colonial Secretary, will go a step further, and once it is established that the 'Eureka Diamond' in question is no less than 21.19 carats, states: 'This diamond is the rock upon which the future success of South Africa will be built.'[9]

It doesn't take long for the news to get out, first locally, then nationally and soon enough globally.

Tiny, timid towns like Kimberley – once home to no more than 4000 people – are soon throbbing, thriving with the breath and blood of 50,000 feverish men and women rushing to make their fortune.

Perhaps Britain has been too hasty in consigning such valuable land to the Boers? Of course, problems arise, particularly in the area abutting the western border of the Orange Free State, where the most lucrative of the Kimberley diamonds have been found. Here the incoming tide of crazed prospectors is so overwhelming and causing so many violent land disputes that, on the request of Nicolaas Waterboer – the leader of the Griqua people – the diamond fields are annexed as the 'Griqualand West Colony' by Great Britain to restore order. Waterboer's reckoning is that the British will give his tribe protection from the crazed prospectors and a place in parliament.

Perhaps, now that the Earl of Carnarvon – the British Colonial Secretary – thinks about it, the Orange Free State and the Transvaal Republic might like to join with Natal and the Cape Colony to become a federated country, just as Canada had done in 1867 with their French and English provinces?

Nee.

No.

Very well then.

If the Transvaal won't come freely, it will be taken forcibly. In 1877 the British Governor of Natal, Sir Theophilus Shepstone, sent his 'forces' – 25 Troopers and a stroppy Sergeant – across the border and all the way to Pretoria to announce to the 'government' of Transvaal that their republic had been annexed. Against a government and a republic that existed more in the mind than on the map, it was enough.

Still, the Transvaal Boers form the distinct impression the British might be stretched too thinly to hold what they have and, in December 1880, the revolt that will be known as the First Boer War begins.

Yet it is far from the gentlemen's conflict that the British have come to expect. This is not an orderly dispute of ranks and files, it is *most* unsportsmanlike, as the British discover a most peculiar Boer tactic – irregular soldiers roving and wreaking havoc throughout the land. *Commandos* are what they call themselves, tight bands of volunteer fighters brilliantly led by Commandant-General Piet Joubert.

The Boers are tough, straight shooters and at *home* on the veldt – while, in many ways, the British *Rooi Baatjes*, Redcoats, marching about in serried ranks are little more than target practice, with the white cross in the middle of their uniforms forming a convenient bullseye. Some British troops wearing the new-fangled khaki-coloured uniforms seem to survive marginally longer, but that cannot alter the final result.

By March 1881 the British government of William Gladstone has lost all appetite for the fight, and agrees to the establishment of the Second Republic of the Transvaal.

All seems calm, the conflict resolved and the politics stable, until . . . one day in 1884, Transvaal Vice-President Paul Kruger and Commandant-General Piet Joubert are having a meeting when a joyous burgher arrives burbling with the news that a new gold-reef has been discovered around the burgeoning settlement of Johannesburg.

'Instead of rejoicing,' Joubert says, with extraordinary prescience, 'you would do better to weep; for this gold will cause our country to be soaked in blood.'[10]

Paul Kruger entirely agrees.

'Gold!' he growls. 'Do you know what gold is? For every ounce of that gold you will pay with tears of blood.'[11]

Those tears began with thousands of prospectors from across the British Empire, including those from the colonies of Australia, flooding in – so many that Britain demands that the *Uitlanders*, as the Dutch refer to them, be given voting rights. They are, after all, providing the huge majority of the South African Republic's tax revenues, but have no political power.

This is not right! The American War of Independence had been fought and won on the principle of 'no taxation, without representation', and Britain now conveniently believes in it too.

Say, what?

Your thousands of *Jan-come-latelies* want to come into our republic, dig up our gold, AND have voting rights? There are so many of them that it is clear to Kruger et al that, if they were to grant it, the Transvaal would effectively be little more than a subjugated British colony, because the Boers would be in a democratic minority in their own republic. After all, of the 100,000 residents of the republic, about 60,000 are whites, of whom 34,000 are British subjects. It would be a democratic takeover!

And so the Boers resist, and prepare to take arms against a sea of troubles.

By 1895, the situation teeters on open war as from Rhodesia, the British-controlled territory to the north of the Transvaal, the founding father, Cecil Rhodes, organises and funds 'the Jameson raid' – some 600 British men, mostly from the Matabeleland Mounted Police, invade Transvaal in the hope that the British Uitlanders will take up arms and rise to join them.

The leader of the raid is Leander Jameson, a man so admired in Britain that the great Rudyard Kipling sees fit to write a poem immortalising his pluck:

> ... *If you can make one heap of all your winnings*
> *And risk it on one turn of pitch-and-toss*
> *And lose, and start again at your beginnings*
> *And never breathe a word about your loss;*
> *If you can force your heart and nerve and sinew*
> *To serve your turn long after they are gone,*
> *And so hold on when there is nothing in you*
> *Except the Will which says to them: 'Hold on!'*[12]

For hold on Jameson does, long past the point of sanity. Yet finally there is no way around it: the raid bears no fruit, as the Uitlander uprising does not eventuate as Jameson had hoped – with one of the groups that failed to rise being the 500-man 'Australian Corps' of Uitlanders. After first being thrown into prison by the Boers, Jameson is handed over to the very British he had been fighting for and he is imprisoned in Holloway prison in England for 15 months on the charge of 'organising an illegal expedition into a friendly state'.[13]

Still, the Boers are left without doubt: war is coming once more, one way or another, sooner or later. That much is confirmed by the British Colonial Secretary, Joseph Chamberlain, shortly after the Jameson Raid publicly agitating for 'Home Rule for the Rand', insisting that there are enough British prospectors on 'the Rand', the area around Johannesburg where most of the goldmines are, that they could form a self-governing British protectorate!

Bedankt, thanks, but there is already a self-governing country in place, called the *Zuid-Afrikaansche Republiek* of Transvaal. The British don't quite seem to understand, and are unlikely to understand any time in the near future.

What is needed to resist the British is arms, and Paul Kruger – now President of Transvaal – is prudent in spending a good deal of his nation's wealth on providing them, buying state-of-the-art weaponry from the finest arms manufacturers in Europe, including heavy artillery and 50,000 Mauser rifles from Germany – superior to the British .303s, for the fact they can still be accurate at a distance of 2000 yards, as opposed to just 1500 yards. But as the British must not know of the arms the Boers will soon take against their future foes, many of those rifles are packed tightly into pianos, and make their way to the Transvaal by way of China first, and then to the port of Delagoa Bay in Portuguese-held East Africa, the Boers' sole sea outlet to the world.

Not that the Boers don't have some respect for English weaponry, and as a matter of fact they are quick to buy an enormous shipment of Maxim-Nordenfelt Pom-Pom guns – a cross between a small cannon and a machine gun, capable of firing as many as 25 one-pound shells fed through a belt, in five seconds, at a range up to 3000 yards, making the sound of *pom-pom-pom-pom* as they explode on impact. The British Army had rejected this gun, but the Boers buy them in bulk.

It is not that such weaponry will ensure they win the war – but it does mean that for England to subjugate them this time it will take more than 25 Troopers and a stroppy Sergeant . . .

CHAPTER ONE

BREAKER MORANT ET AL

They mustered us up with a royal din,
In wearisome weeks of drought.
'Ere ever half of the crops were in,
Or the half of the sheds cut out.

'Twas down with the saddle and spurs and whip
The swagman dropped his swag.
And we hurried us off to the outbound ship
To fight for the English flag.

The English flag, it is ours in sooth
We stand by it wrong or right.
But deep in our hearts is the honest truth
We fought for the sake of a fight . . .[1]

Banjo Paterson, 'Our Own Flag'

In any part of Australia if you mention Morant's name you will
be asked, 'What did he take you down for . . . ?' No sum was too
small for him to borrow, no person (male or female) too poor for
him to bleed – for under a superficial politeness he was utterly
selfish. It is true he was careless with money when he had it; he
is reported to have shared a considerable sum with a comrade;
but when he was short of cash then someone else must pay, no
matter whom. Free and easy back-block Australia stood such a
creature for many years . . .[2]

Windsor and Richmond Gazette, March 1904

Hot-headed. Violent at times, he was a great horseman.[3]

The World's News, April 1902

Christmas Day 1896, outside Walgett's Barwon Inn, Christmas
cheer, free beer, if a colt clears . . .

Betcha, Harry!

  Betcha, what?

That you can't jump your blindfolded horse over these two six-wire fences that line both sides of the road.

A bet, you say, to test my mettle?

You have got the right man.

For they don't call Harry Morant 'The Breaker' for nothing. Over the years he has broken more horses than he has made love to beautiful women . . . though it is perhaps a close-run thing, down the home straight, as the crowd cheers.

Born in England and coming to these sandy shores before he was yet twenty – disembarking at Townsville in June 1883 – the Breaker is a bold bastard of a man. He has roamed the countryside breaking horses, bedding women and borrowing money, occasionally even paying it back.

So, yes, Breaker Morant will take all of your bets. His mighty mount – for the Breaker only rides beauties – has a long rag securely tied around its head so it is certain that it cannot see a thing. And now, as the well-lubricated crowd gathers around, the Breaker backs the horse up before the first fence, leans down, and even appears to be whispering to it, if you can believe it. It is the pause the mob needs to look at him even more closely. A strange cove, this'un. The son of a Duke, or an Earl I think, or maybe an Admiral – I can never get it straight – but he is always almost aggressively dishevelled. No airs or graces with him, it's as if because he knows and we know he's a much higher class than us, he simply doesn't have to bother with grooming, with new clothes, with doing buttons up. Just his accent, his superior breeding and his *riding* ability will get him through.

And what's he doing now?

The Breaker rubs the lucky penny he always wears around his neck, and leans down once more, for a few last whispers to his horse.

Now he is still. His horse is stiller still.

Tension mounts as the Breaker straightens up.

And now as the Breaker's heels drive into its sides, the mount bounds forward and gallops straight towards the first fence at full cry! A seeming instant before it is about to crash head-long into the solid beams – some turn away, for fear of what they are about to see – the Breaker lifts his hands from the reins to demonstrate his complete mastery of the horse in an adult version of 'Look, Ma, no hands!' before yelling 'OVER!'[4]

And indeed, before their very eyes, the beast leaps high to clear the fence by a good foot before surging once more straight on to the next fence.

As before, the Breaker lifts his hands, yells 'OVER!'[5] and . . . over she goes!

'The colt made a wonderful leap and cleared the fence' according to one old bushie 'by a full twenty feet!'

Well, at least that's how the old bushie will tell it ever afterwards, not to mention the Breaker himself, with every tale of the Breaker growing taller in the telling. But his legend grows: no feat is beyond Harry Morant, no lair dare too outrageous, no dame he cannot tame. And such panache!

The jump well cleared, Morant bows to the crowd with a rugged elegance that only he can pull off. His horse is his stage, and his audience will remember that performance as long as they live.

Morant gets free drinks, precious cash, and is saluted with '*Merry Christmas, Harry!*' by all in the bar.

It is just one more story to go with his growing legend up and down the east coast of Australia, but most particularly in the backblocks of New South Wales and Queensland.

A contradictory man of demonstrable charm and harm, verve and swerve, poise and noise, he is prone to attracting more mixed reviews than a touring troupe of Shakespeare thespians north of Townsville. Such had been his way, all his life. In England, he had been born to very humble circumstances, the son of Edwin and Catherine Murrant, one-time Master and Matron of a workhouse in Somerset. Edwin Murrant had died before his son was born, making things difficult for his mother, but still she had made sacrifices and used every contact she had to see him educated at the local Royal Masonic Institute for Boys – accepted on his fourth application – where on the one hand he had received prizes for French, Classics, German, Dictation and Elocution, and on the other hand . . . had been constantly in trouble with the headmaster for misbehaviour that included thieving from the larder and probably being 'the boy who robbed the Donation Box'.[6]

He was also notable for his capacity to lead the other boys astray, a pied piper with a wolfish grin, the heart of the devil and the guile of a conjuror. It seemed to amuse him.

Still, that education among the lads of a higher social stratum had come into play in the Australian colonies, allowing him to tell stories about being the wayward son of a famous English Admiral. It seems to please the people, and gives him leeway in which he can work his charm, and spin his believable fantasies, often working in stories of his friendship with famous people on far distant shores. Works a charm! Not only does he extensively study the works of George Whyte-Melville – filled with dashing aristocrats setting the hounds loose as they charge out on jolly hunts – he even lets slip that Whyte-Melville is a family friend, and when the Breaker was a wee lad, he was given his first riding lessons bouncing on the novelist's knee, as the novelist told him jolly stories!

Why yes, it is true!

Whyte-Melville would put a little hunting cap on Breaker's infant head, put a hunting crop in his chubby fist and with a 'Tally Ho!'[7] take him in great swinging bursts of his leg, over imaginary fences.

Such entrancing yarns!

(Another favourite of Morant's from the world of fiction is the character Tony Lumpkin from the famed eighteenth-century play *She Stoops to Conquer*, a hard-drinking, hard-gambling fellow who effortlessly switches between an upper-class and lower-class persona as the occasion suits, who lies as easily as he breathes, and gets through an endless variety of colourful scrapes.)

Changing his name occasionally, from Morant to Murrant to Harbord back to Morant, proves useful for evading creditors of legal bent.

'A shortish man,' a contemporary will note of him, 'large features, small eyes (too close together), clean shaven, his skin red with alcohol, a horsey look about his dress, the manners and speech of a gentleman, of surprising physical courage (particularly on horseback), quite destitute of moral courage or moral principle; fond of exercise in the way of sport, he would never willingly exert himself to earn an honest shilling if he could borrow it off no matter whom; a confirmed dipsomaniac.'

All up, Morant shamelessly takes his habit of milking generosity and bilking bills from a hobby to a full-time pursuit . . . and finally all the way to a fine art.

'Probably no man this side of the world ever owed so many unpaid accounts – most of them paltry. From North Queensland to South Australia there appears to be hardly a town that he did not bleed.'[8]

But still, so garrulous, such a magnet for so many people wanting some colour in their lives!

'One of his common tricks for exciting charity was to say he had been robbed. The writer has known him to have been robbed – according to his own account – three times within a week of sums varying in amount from twenty to forty pounds. If they would take him in he always put up at the best hotel in a town. As he never meant to pay, price was no object.'[9]

Breaker's charm is long and lasting to many women, though his first wife of just a few months, Daisy May O'Dwyer, an immigrant from

Tipperary come to Queensland as a governess on the same Fanning Downs Station on the Burdekin River 12 miles east of Charters Towers where the Breaker was a stockman, is a likely exception . . .

Theirs had not been a match made in heaven. Having met in Far North Queensland, they'd had a whirlwind romance. For young Daisy the first clue as to what she could expect came when her groom promised the presiding Reverend at their ceremony in Charters Towers £5 against the money that was *just* about to arrive from his aristocratic family in England, only to never pay up. (This was not the worst thing the Breaker did to a Reverend, but we'll get to that.)

Yes, pigs might fly when the Breaker actually paid his debts. But, as it happens, even then they will likely be stolen ones, as witness the 32 pigs he is charged with stealing just four weeks after stealing Daisy's heart at the altar, at much the same time as he is charged with stealing a saddle. There is some confusion because, upon his arrest, Breaker had assumed it was for yet another matter of writing false cheques and so had started denying that first – but he may be forgiven for the mistake, if not the rest of it, as to keep track of all his crimes he would have had to put another man on, and simply couldn't afford it.

With his cheques bouncing all around her, his creditors lining up at the door and Daisy always unsure of his whereabouts on those nights when he was not in the local lockup, she soon decides that she wants no part of such a marriage after all – and quickly separates from him. (She will never finalise the divorce, and soon takes up with another man, by the name of Bates, to become Daisy Bates, a name she will make renowned for her work with the Aboriginal people.) It is no matter to the Breaker. There will be other women, and other towns where his reputation is not yet trashed, and in his admittedly charming, nay, *disarming* manner, he is quick to move on. He is, after all, such a colourful character, so gregarious, so brilliant with horses, so good to spend time with, that he is usually able to sail on, leaving chaos in his wake with no more thoughts about it than a horse has about leaving droppings. He is, after all – did he mention? – the son of Admiral Sir George Digby Morant and had himself studied the art of naval seafaring at the Royal Naval College.

Helping him in his travels and notoriety is a developing capacity for writing compelling bush-verse, the first of which, written on a Warrego sand ridge, is published in *The Bulletin* in 1891:

> *The camp-fire sparks are flying*
> *Up from the pine-log's glow,*

The wandering wind is sighing
That ballad sweet and low;
The drooping branches gleaming
In the firelight, sway and stir;
And the bushman's brain is dreaming
Of the song she sang, and her.
And the murmurs of the forest
Ring home to heart and brain,
As in the pine is chorused
'Will he no come back again?'[10]

Many other women are smitten, one later noting that, amid all the bad reviews, 'it has occurred to me that a few lines from a woman's point of view might be of interest . . . My personal acquaintance with "The Breaker" was but of short duration on two separate occasions when he was droving through Queensland. The first time he spent ten days in a certain district, during a race and show week, and, happening to be hostess to a large party, chiefly of young people, I pressed Harry Morant into my service as right-hand man, or, as he called himself, "Cook's mate," and during that time I both saw and heard a good deal of him. He was a capital man in a house party, but, alas, he made love indiscriminately to all the girls and the younger married women, insisting to me that that was the very best way to entertain them and keep them happy; while in the wee small hours he corrupted the young men with stories of his own reckless doings to the rattling and excitement of dice or cards. Harry Morant was a man no two women ever agreed about, for while one would call him, "so handsome," another would vote him "downright ugly"; at the same time, all loved him, either openly or in secret . . . He was essentially of the order of men "who love and ride away".'

Other characteristics also stand out.

'He could be brutally cruel when his temper was roused or he had been drinking. I never, but once, saw him the worse for liquor, and then he made an exhibition of himself, for which he was most abjectly sorry next day, and apologised all round. He was a most reckless rider, no feat was too daring for him . . .'[11]

A supreme self-promoter, it is not just that he talks about his feats, he continues to record many of them in verse, managing to capture the essence of bush-life. On the subject of breaking horses, for example, he is published in the pages of *The Queenslander*, in a poem entitled 'Old Harlequin', and signed by the Breaker:

Oh do you remember the first time I rode you,
The same day I roped you in Dufferem's yard?
One foot in the stirrup, I'd hardly bestrode you,
When down went your head bucking uncommon hard,

Old fashioned buck-jumping, no 'pig jump' nor rooting,
Your tail was jammed tight 'tween your muscular thighs,
Your back is an arch. Lord how you went shooting,
Snorting and squealing up to the skies!

. . .

Hard and often you bucked, before you grew steady,
Or suffered your rider his stockwhip to crack;
And now after a spell you're uncommon ready
To shift any new chum who gets on your back.

There easy old man! Let me slip on your bridle
And stroke your slim neck, so glossy and brown,
Three whole month's spell, it's too long to be idle,
You may carry me quietly into the town.[12]

Quite where the Breaker comes from *specifically*, and what he is about seems to depend on his company. Put him on the other end of a seesaw with a chameleon and he would be the perfect counterweight – as rather than changing his colours to hide, he changes to stand out.

According to him he is, variously, the son of an English Admiral, the black sheep of a distinguished family in Devon, in India, in Cognito or wherever the Breaker's fancy and imagination takes his past next. Romance always trumps truth, and truth soon becomes fiction in the Breaker's hands.

And, as if the talk of the folk about him wasn't enough, on occasion Morant would add to it by writing about himself in the third person, writing bush stories for *The Bulletin* and *Windsor and Richmond Gazette*, including one notable yarn of driving 1000 head of bullocks from Pitchery's Creek to Muswellbrook, via ol' Coonabarabran. In the middle of them, 'fifty old warriors – as hard-hided, long horned pikers as ever chewed mulga-leaves'.

Well, the stockmen had their hands full, no doubt about that.

Those warriors?

'They uster flash out like wild pigs out of a Culjoa lygnum bush! – and send all the rest of the cattle to blazes. And when them Pitchery

Creek pikers got fair going, all Hell's population with a stockwhip in each hand wouldn't stop 'em. Well, that trip we had a bloke with us who had come on the roads for experience. He was a quiet, decent little chap, who could ride above a bit – and he was a cousin of the station bosses.

'We uster call him "the Honorable Harry" – part because he was the son of a Dook or a Major General, or something of the sort, at home in England; and part because he was very honorable in the matter of his liquor, for he'd never take a nip without asking everyone there "what his poison was?" No, we never passed a shanty but what the Honorable Harry acted honorable.'[13]

Ah, but still that wasn't the Honourable's strong suit!

I am telling you – and Harry himself, don't forget, is telling you – what happened one night when the bullocks stampeded, with 'an old white-backed brindle bullock – a notorious rogue – in the lead, and a couple of "ballys" close up behind him'.[14]

The stockmen go out after them, and one is doing his best to get in front of the rogue to turn them when, as that stockman will recount, 'all of a sudden, like a condensed bit of lightning, up slides the "Honorable" on old Yanalong, and whips by me like a swallow. Then I sees him lean over his horses off side, and – galloping all the time – he strikes a match on that old white-backed brindle bullock's near horn, and lights the cigarette which he had in his (the Honorable Harry's) mouth!'[15]

Of course that rogue bullock realises he has met his master and slows to a halt, bringing the entire mob to heel . . .

'Ah, the Honorable Harry was a fine horseman!' Morant finishes his own account of his derring-do. 'He had a good nerve, and a wonderful pretty seat on a horse.'[16]

If there are any rules – unspoken or otherwise – that say one shouldn't tell wonderful stories about oneself, Breaker Morant has never heard of them.

Of course, from time to time there are less savoury stories, too, some of which make it into the public domain though, luckily for him, they're often in remote areas where bad news doesn't travel far.

The *Western Champion*, up Blackall way in central western Queensland, is a case in point, recording in 1889:

> Harry Morant was brought up under arrest, for obtaining money under false pretences having sold a horse to Mr. J. Samuels, Forest Grove, which he had already sold and given receipt for same to

J. H. Grimshaw of Ambo. Morant was found guilty, and was given three months with hard labour in Rockhampton gaol.[17]

The warrant for his arrest for this charge actually captures a little of the man himself, 'being about 26, 5 feet 8 inches tall, stout build, brown hair and moustache, slight stammer in speech and boasts of aristocratic friends in England'.[18]

The Rockhampton *Morning Bulletin* reports of the same affair:

> The Bench had before them this week a man named Harry Morant, to all appearances a well educated, refined young fellow, who was charged on a warrant with obtaining money by false pretences from Mr. Samuels, of Muttaburra. The accused complained that it was a trumped-up case.[19]

Morant fails to talk his way out of this one. Very well then. After all, what is a small stint in gaol to the likes of the Breaker?

It at least provides a regular meal and lodging for a good period of time and he is not long out before his roguish charm sees him inveigle his way back into an entirely new set of chums.

As a matter of fact, one day in the mid-1890s, the most beloved bush poet, Andrew 'Banjo' Paterson, is working as a journalist for *The Bulletin*, sitting in his dingy little office . . . in the dusty, dirty city . . . when a letter comes direct, in a writing unexpected, from Paterson's uncle, Arthur Barton:

> There is a man going down from here to Sydney and he says he is going to call on you. His name is Morant. He says he is the son of an English Admiral and he has good manners and education. He can do anything better than most people, can break horses, trap dingoes, yard scrub cattle, dance, run, fight, drink and borrow money, anything except work. I don't know what the matter with the chap is. He seems brimming with flashness. He will do any dare devil things as long as there is a crowd to watch him. He jumped a horse over a stiff three-rail fence one night by the light of two matches which he placed on the posts.[20]

Banjo files the letter, as he always does, even as . . . through the open window floating . . . the *language uninviting* of the gutter children fighting, comes fitfully and faintly through the ceaseless tramp of feet.[21]

He is fascinated by characters from the country and this'un sounds interesting.

Ah, yes, and let us not forget the most famous equine episode of all regarding the Breaker – Dargin's Grey, the great buck-jumper.

And yes, I do mean great.

This horse is a cross between a storm, a kangaroo, and the Devil himself, capable of throwing the very best, and in recent times has even slung the legendary 'Dandaloo rough-rider from the Bogan, and 32 other crack riders at the various Shows in the colony', from his back. They've brought him up to the Hawkesbury Show to take on the local bucks and he has already sent several of the local valiants soaring very high and now low as the crowd roars.

'The animal is an 8-year old,' the *Windsor and Richmond Gazette* will describe him, 'a rough-looking grey, but very muscular.'

And ain't that the truth?

Dargin's Grey takes on board the only two riders brave enough to have a go, only to be just as quickly bucked off, with the latest one knocked out as he falls, and carried from the arena.

But what now?

Why it is this fellow recently arrived, Mr H. H. Morant – the man they call 'The Breaker' for reasons unknown to many of the locals – who has been penning poems and stories for the *Gazette*, who steps forward, resplendent in relatively new threads.

The crowd is incredulous.

'*Him* ride?'

'A newspaper Johnny – him sit a buck!'[22]

'There'll be an inquest, sure as eggs.'[23]

Only a few Queenslanders down for the show, who know who this man is, dare to demur.

'He'll ride him all right,' one old drover is heard to say.

With Dargin's Grey now back in his chute and blindfolded to keep him calm, the Breaker climbs atop him, put his boots in the stirrups, and firmly grips the front of the saddle with his left hand, before placing his right hand in the air, the signal to show one is nearly ready.

The stockman grips the lever that will open the gate to the chute and waits.

'Outside!' the Breaker roars, and in an instant, as the crowd roars in excitement, the chute opens, the blindfold is ripped off and he is indeed outside, and atop this bucking bronco from hell. And look at him go!

When, after five seconds, the Breaker is still atop Dargin's Grey, the roar goes up another pitch – this is a real contest – but when the stirrup leathers break as the snorting, bucking beast goes completely wild, there is not a person there who is not shouting at the top of their voice!

For, unbelievably, the Breaker, is *still* going!

No, his boots are no longer in the stirrups, but far more significantly his spurs are driving into Dargin Grey's sides, lashing him, *piercing* him, making him understand who is boss!

Of course the pain sends the beast into a jumping, bucking, snorting, twisting, pitching cyclone of horseflesh but the Breaker doesn't blink. Still he rides him high, one hand skyward, as he demonstrates his mastery. After 20 seconds it starts to happen. The jumping lessens a little, the bucking buckles a bit. Dargin's Grey might have met his match.

For still another 20 seconds the nag does its best, with jumps that would have sent a lesser man flying, but are no trouble for this man.

For he *is* the man.

'Ere a minute has passed, Dargin's Grey is beaten, and stops, with the Breaker still atop him, allowing this recent arrival to Windsor to lift both hands in the air in triumph.

First the crowd is stunned, a momentary calm *after* the storm.

But now they are on their feet, stamping them and cheering him wildly as he takes Dargin's Grey on a lap of victory, the nag doing everything at his tiniest command.

'It was a popular victory,' the newspaper records, 'and the "Breaker" was carried shoulder high all over the ground.'[24]

So stunning is the feat that a collection is taken up, bringing together a considerable amount of money, but the great man rises to the occasion. 'Give it to the hospital,' he says smilingly. After all, the two badly injured riders before him will likely be needing some help.

It is a very popular move.

But then, again, comes that startling cruel streak amidst all the bonhomie.

His manner of leaving Windsor will long be recalled.

For he is just heading off one evening, riding his horse Cavalier to places unknown across the Blue Mountains – hopefully filled with people who haven't heard of his reputation yet, who might be happy to lend him money – when his way is blocked by the Salvation Army band, which is playing hymns in the street.

The Breaker asks them to move out of the way.

They decline, amid a flurry of trombones and trumpets.

The Breaker asks them again to move out of the way.

They decline once more.

What's a man to do?

'The "Breaker",' the *Windsor and Richmond Gazette* will chronicle, 'jammed in the spurs, and took 'em flying.'[25]

The Breaker is soon on his way to the Blue Mountains, while the Salvation Army band's next hymn is distinctly on the wobbly side of things.

It is all part of a consistent wave of trouble that the Breaker leaves in his wake.

'At the Penrith Police Court on Friday,' the *Nepean Times* records on 5 November 1898, Alfred York, 'charged with being drunk and disorderly at Springwood, pleaded guilty, and was fined 5s and 7s 4d costs; fine paid. Henry Morant was similarly charged, but in this case the summons had not been served.'[26]

Why not?

He had already bolted to Gunnedah to avoid the summons, and a month later the *Windsor and Richmond Gazette* reports, courtesy of one of the notes the man himself is constantly sending to journalists to keep his name fresh in the public domain: 'Mr. H. H. Morant ("Breaker") has got as far as Gunnedah, and writes wishing old Windsor friends a Merry Christmas.'[27]

As well as trouble, there is sometimes more than a hint of violence about him. One of his larks was to encourage Aboriginal stockmen to box a few rounds with him by first hiding his genuine expertise in pugilism, before unveiling it to beat them to a pulp.

''Arry M'ran,' one old stockman would recall many decades later, while ruefully rubbing his jaw, 'Oh, he hitter hard.'[28]

On another occasion, the Breaker entered in the Sydney Hunt Club Steeplechase at Randwick, riding Bay Lady while a friend, John Fitzpatrick, rode a big, hard-pulling chestnut, in a race which was started by the well-known Sydney solicitor Robert Lenehan waving the starting flag.

'Going down to the sod wall,' Fitzpatrick would recount, '[I] was riding rather wide, so "screwed in" to get straight go at the wall, [and] crossed "The Breaker." A string of choice words followed from the hard riding, devil'm'care "Breaker"; he could never forgive a man for infringing the etiquette of the "gentleman rider".'[29]

Courtesy of this move, Fitzpatrick won, whereupon after they have all dismounted, the Breaker heartily takes him by the hand and exults 'A good win, old chap, I congratulate you!'[30] before a strange thing happens.

Within an instant, his face darkens, and he explodes: 'By the way, you crossed me at the sod wall! I've half a mind to straighten your bally hide!'[31]

In the end he doesn't, but like the race itself, it is a close-run thing.

•

Mr Paterson?

Someone to see you.

One fine day at the offices of *The Bulletin* in the Scandinavian Hall at 107 Castlereagh Street, the periodical's most beloved writer and poet, 'Banjo' Paterson looks up to see a visitor being ushered towards him – and clearly not just any visitor.

Most people who come to these offices are wide-eyed with wonder at just being here. They betray humility, reservation and deference.

But not this fellow.

Big, bold and blustery, he has walked into this place as if he not only owns it, but single-handedly *built* it.

'Banjo,' he says, with hand outstretched, 'my name is Breaker Morant, and I know your uncle, Arthur Barton.'[32]

Banjo looks him up and down and will ever after recall his first impressions.

For his visitor is 'a bronzed, clean-shaven man of about thirty, well set up, with the quick walk of a man used to getting on young horses, clear, confident eyes, radiating health and vitality'.[33]

While the Breaker before him seems a far cry from the 'son of an English Admiral [with] good manners and education' his uncle had described, Banjo finds himself instantly warming to the animated and articulate fellow nonetheless.

'I've been stopping with your uncle, Arthur Barton,' the Breaker goes on to say, 'and when he heard I was coming to Sydney he told me to be sure and call on you. Fine man isn't he? He knows me well. He said if anybody could show me round Sydney you could.'[34]

Thus, splendidly installed, Morant does what he does best – spinning fabulous yarns, entirely unshackled from the chains of tedious truth. It is sufficient that they be true enough to be credible, with at least a tenuous link to real experiences and, as Banjo listens, the Breaker talks of stag-hunting in Exmoor up Queensland way, of slaughtering wild cattle with a knife alone out beyond Dubbo.

Time drifts along as the visitor chatters away, seemingly without a care in the bally world. The Banjo and the Breaker discover they have much in common, starting with a passion for verse, only matched by their passion for the Australian bush, its characters and yarns. Clearly, the Breaker is one of those great characters himself, and when it comes to colourful yarns it turns out he has dozens of them where he is the lead character!

Who could forget when he outran fire itself, galloping through a roaring bushfire as the flames licked at his back? Such mastery had he of his mare that he blindfolded the beast to keep it steady while sprinting through the last of the blazing brush.

Not to mention the legend of Dargin's Grey, it hardly bears repeating – and yet of course Breaker Morant delights to regale the tale to Paterson once more.

Banjo – himself an enthusiastic if amateur steeplechase rider – is transfixed, pleased to meet such a colourful chap, most particularly one from his beloved Australian bush.

The afternoon sails swiftly away . . . until nearing three bells on the Town Hall clock, the Breaker suddenly looks at his watch.

'By Jove,' says he, 'I've enjoyed myself so much talking to you that I forgot I had to cash a cheque. And now the banks will be shut. Perhaps you could cash a cheque for me for a fiver? I've got to pay some bills and I've run myself clean out of money.'[35]

Strangely, Banjo near hates himself for saying it – almost as if he is letting down an old friend, despite the fact he has known the Breaker for only a couple of hours – and expresses his regret that he just does not have the funds upon him at this time. But . . . a suggestion?

'Perhaps you can let your creditors wait till the banks open in the morning?'[36]

But of course!

With a laugh and a dismissive wave of the hand, the Breaker signals that he takes no offence whatsoever. He has tried it on, Banjo has flicked him away with an elegant deflection over the slips cordon for four runs, and the visitor is even full of admiration for the way he has done it.

In any case, the burgeoning friendship between the two – the Breaker's trips to Sydney become more frequent, and he never fails to see Banjo – provides Paterson with ever more material for his poetry, some of which are directly based on Morant.

> *Born of a thoroughbred English race,*
> *Well proportioned and closely knit,*
> *Neat, slim figure and handsome face,*
> *Always ready and always fit,*
> *Hardy and wiry of limb and thew,*
> *That was the ne'er-do-well Jim Carew.*
>
> *One of the sons of the good old land –*
> *Many a year since his like was known;*

Never a game but he took command . . .

Good as they make them was Jim Carew.
Came to grief – was it card or horse?
Nobody asked and nobody cared;
Ship him away to the bush of course,
Ne'er-do-well fellows are easily spared;
Only of women a sorrowing few
Wept at parting from Jim Carew.[37]

Far from take offence at this characterisation of his life, and prediction of his future, Morant – always on the lookout in any case for new names to run up debts under – takes to occasionally using the name 'Jim Carew' as he signs himself in to hotels and the like.

And Banjo is not the only one to draw inspiration from the Breaker, with other bush poets taking up their own thumbnails dipped in tar to add to his lustre with their own verse. When, for example, in December 1896 the Breaker turns out on a patch of ground cleared by the Bogan Gate Hotel near Parkes for a scratch 'England' team to play polo against 'Australia', which includes his great friend the poet Will Ogilvie and a few other novices, it is Ogilvie who captures the Breaker's part in the winning side:

And the sharp bright spurs were crimson,
and the ponies wet with foam,
When the lads who played for Britain waded
in to fight for 'Home.'
Then somehow, in a scrimmage, a face and
stick got linked,
And the timber, broke in pieces, though
'The Breaker' never winked;
The mallet went to hospital, whilst 'The
Breaker' bathed in gore,
Went sailing through the scrimmages more
fiercely than before.[38]

As to the Breaker's own poetry, it continues to flourish to the point he is occasionally mentioned in the same breath, or at least the same articles, as Banjo. Such is the case when one journalist writes about the painter Tom Roberts' studio at Vickery's Chambers, 76 Pitt Street, where something of a 'salon' of interesting people is held on Thursday afternoons, to carouse and talk all matters to do with the creative arts.

'There are usually one or two poets to be found here, A. B. ("Banjo") Paterson and H. Morant, alias "The Breaker",' notes the *Windsor and Richmond Gazette*, in 1898. 'H. Morant looks like a man who has been used to horses all his life, has a sunburnt face and a non-society air, but "Barty" Paterson, as he is familiarly called, although the singer of bush delights, is a thorough town man in appearance, thin faced and clean shaven, always to be seen at Government House balls, Town Hall concerts and fashionable first nights, with a great hobby for polo.'[39]

And while Morant's verse gives him even greater notoriety, it is still the case that few who actually know him predict anything other than a sorry end.

'"The Breaker" is one of the few jinglers of rhymes whose [work] finds a ready acceptance by *The Bulletin*,' runs another contemporary account. 'The writers of that unique production are truly a mad and melancholy crowd; one half of them are driven at a maddening gallop down the great incline of life by love of liquor, or steeple-chasing, or cattle-droving . . . while the other half get there just as rapidly by sitting down in a quiet corner and brooding over this weary, wicked, and sin-stained universe.

'"The Breaker" belongs to the first-named crowd, and will doubtless go on verse-making and fence-topping until some day his horse misjudges the height, and then – well, most likely they'll carry his mangled remains on a shutter to the nearest cemetery . . .'[40]

And maybe they will. But in the meantime, the Breaker continues on his maddening gallop, up the country, down in the Big Smoke, and back again, always on the move, usually a step ahead of his creditors, and mostly just beyond the clutches of the law. Every now and then, when the law gets too close, he toys with the idea of heading back to England because, he tells Banjo Paterson, he wants to go 'home to the land of my forefathers and feed on fatted calf',[41] but the problem is getting there. If you can't get a job as a deckhand – and he has no maritime experience per se – the only alternative is to pay £25 for the fare, which for a man like Breaker Morant might as well be £25,000 for all the chance he has of paying it.

And so he must stay for the moment, scratching and scrounging a living the best he can, a relentlessly ragged rascal, breaking horses and separating fools from their money, hoping something will turn up.

•

In Southern Africa the tension between the Uitlanders and the Boers continues to rise.

'By July 1899 the situation had become so serious,' Deneys Reitz, the 17-year-old son of Francis Reitz, the Secretary of State for the Transvaal, records, 'that my father ordered us up to Pretoria, as war with England seemed inevitable. We said good-bye to Bloemfontein, the town where we had been born and bred and where we had spent such happy days, and journeyed north, leaving behind us the peace of boyhood, to face years of hardship, danger, and ultimate exile.'[42]

The response of the Australian colonies to the news that a war between the Motherland and the Boers is looming is heartening to those in London. For those Wild Colonial Boys don't take it as England's problem alone, but rather an affront to the British Empire, the very Empire they are a part of. And their view is that of the Motherland: the outright refusal of the upstart Transvaalers to grant the vote to their English-speaking subjects must be answered with force! So strong is this view in Queensland that on 11 July a cable is sent from the Governor of that fine colony to Westminster offering a contingent of 260 Troopers from the Queensland Mounted Infantry together with a machine-gun section to head to the Transvaal, in the event that hostilities break out.

The British Colonial Secretary, Mr Joseph Chamberlain, replies immediately with a grateful cable:

> Her Majesty's Government highly appreciates the loyal and patri-otic offer of Queensland, and hopes occasion will not arise to take advantage of it, but if it should, they will gladly avail themselves of the offer.[43]

Queensland's offer of troops to the Mother Country is quickly matched by similar offers from all of New South Wales, South Australia, Victoria, Tasmania, Western Australia and New Zealand. Reserve units around the colonies answer the call, and quickly advise how many men are willing to serve. The Tenterfield Mounted Rifles, for example, commanded by Major James Thomas, advise that they have 20 Troopers ready to go, and are readily accepted.

•

Around the Boer republics, the chain of events, the waltz towards war, is viewed with growing alarm.

In the northern Transvaal, a giant of a man by the name of Tom Kelly is watching events closely. Of joint Boer and Irish blood – his father had deserted from the British Army, after witnessing British cruelty to the Boers after the Battle of Boomplaats in the Cape Colony in 1848, to take up with a Boer woman – Tom now realises, like everyone, the vibrant life he leads here with his wife, Maria, four sons and three daughters is under threat.

They have worked hard to build their life here on their *plaas*, farm – *Boschkopje* – some 20 miles north of Pietersburg. Their days are filled with seeding and harvesting their wheat, barley and maize crops, feeding their cattle and poultry, occasionally fixing their machinery – including the sophisticated air-meter windmills, which draw the water from far below the surface – and being with their families. On Saturday afternoons they play tennis with neighbours, before sometimes attending community dances on the Saturday night, while on Sunday mornings they attend church. On special occasions they will have as many as 16 people around the mahogany table, for a three-course meal of *bobotie*, spicy minced meat with egg, and for dessert, milk tart with cinnamon, all of it with the finest Dutch crockery and shining silverware, waited on by as many as three of the house-servants who have been trained for the role. In winters Tom Kelly and his neighbours often head north on wild hunting trips, crossing the Limpopo River into Rhodesia, returning with valuable ivory and pelts.

Occasionally, their collective skills in hunting elephants and the like are required to put down Native uprisings, with Kelly the Acting Commandant of the local Spelonken sector of the Zoutpansberg Commando – Commandos are now the rough citizen militia formed in every Boer community to defend themselves against the Natives, with every able-bodied man required to serve when needed. There are some 30,000 farms just like theirs, across the Transvaal, including in that thinly populated northern region of the Spelonken, where a strong-willed kind of man, Barend Viljoen, is living an honest life, making a solid living on the farm he shares with his family. And just outside Bloemfontein, Hermanus and Elizabeth van Zyl are scratching out a much more humble living on their own few acres.

Over in nearby Zululand, Louis Botha is busy with the machinations of the Transvaal Parliament while he watches over his own farm. Likewise, Jacobus 'Koos' de la Rey is content with *Elandsfontein*, his farm in the Lichtenburg district near the Transvaal town of Mafeking, while Christiaan de Wet's farm, *Rooipoort*, is one of 20,000 such farms in the Orange Free State.

And, of course, they have all followed the growing tensions between the Transvaal Republic and the British Empire with great interest and ever more trepidation. None of them wants war, but nor do they want to be pushed around, to have what they own – and their forefathers had taken from the Africans, *helemaal eerlijk*, fair and square – to be taken from them in turn.

There is no real question. The Boers in the Orange Free State will stand in solidarity with the Transvaal Parliament. They may have no particular quarrel with the British, but these Boers are nothing if not loyal. Yes, they will stand, come hell or high water.

But what will come of this stand? Brinkmanship that takes them to the brink or right over it into battle?

'I don't think there will be war,' Tom Kelly says at this time to an acquaintance, 'but if there is, I shall be in it.'[44]

•

The charismatic Welsh backbencher in the House of Commons, David Lloyd George, is quite sure that there will be a war, and he is even more sure that he wants nothing to do with it. Just 36 years old, and currently on a trip to America, he devours the daily news reports and is more certain than ever that it will happen.

'The prospect oppresses me with a deep sense of horror,' he writes to his younger brother, William. 'If I have the courage, I shall protest with all the vehemence at my command against the outrage which is perpetrated in the name of human freedom.'[45]

And he knows only too well who is behind it.

In the vacuum of leadership created by having a weak and distracted Prime Minister, Lord Salisbury, it is that Imperialist to beat them all, Joseph Chamberlain, the Secretary of State for the Colonies – who believes there can be no better fate for all the peoples of the world than to be drawn into the British Empire, whether they like it or not – who is driving the whole thing. Not for nothing is Chamberlain known as the 'Birmingham Judas' because of a particularly brutal political manoeuvre he had pulled many years earlier, whereby he had got his way with no regard for who was damaged by it.

If possible, he must be stopped and Lloyd George intends to do what he can, by returning to Britain immediately.

'It is wicked',[46] he writes to his wife, Margaret.

God give him strength.

•

President Paul Kruger is a very simple man of simple tastes, and enduring ancient beliefs, up to and including genuinely believing the earth is flat,[47] something which has proven to be a political virtue as he has risen to the top job in the Transvaal by virtue of that very approachable simplicity, and is now a beloved figure.

Affectionately known to his people as *Oom Paul*, Uncle Paul, Kruger is more than just a head of state, he is closer to the head of the family, deeply cherished for his humility, despite his eminence.

'The President of the Republic lives in what we could call a whitewashed cottage,' an American journalist will chronicle of these times, 'like that of a pastor. The church in which he preaches to his people faces him across the street. On the porch of his cottage, with a cup of coffee at his elbow and a long pipe between his lips, he transacts the affairs of state. The children from the school house on the corner come to visit him at recess and hang over his fence . . . they talk to the President and he talks to them.'[48]

Nearby, his second wife, Gezina – the mother of 15 of his 17 children – walks by with full pails of milk she has just squeezed from the Krugers' dairy cows, ready to sell to the neighbours. Yes, she is proud enough of the statue of her husband that is being shaped in the middle of Church Square, but she is firmly of the view his top hat should be hollowed out at the top as to catch the rain, to provide a kind of birdbath for the passing warblers, bee-eaters and striped swallows – and says so.

These are simple folk. And it is for very good reason that, right now, the sculptor should be inclined to etch, even deeper, the worry lines on Kruger's noble visage.

For war with the British Empire now seems inevitable and the President is all too aware what that will mean for the Transvaal Republic – widespread death and destruction. They will be a small country in Africa, up against the combined might of the British Empire. But what choice do they have? To succumb to the British demands would mean their destruction in any case. *Honour* demands they resist.

And given war's inevitability, it might be that military sagacity demands they attack first? It is with this in mind that President Kruger gives the orders to gather their forces, to equip them, to prepare them. In these last days of July 1899 those forces do indeed converge on the Transvaal capital, Pretoria, as the streets rattle and clatter to the mass of mounted troops in ragged columns followed by artillery units all making their way to their gathering points, across the cobblestones laid just this year. Most of them are on their way to the Natal border, with the idea being to attack the British where they are weakest.

One young man determined to be in it is Deneys Reitz, son of Transvaal's State Secretary. On this particular morning in early September, he is with his father at the *Ou Raadsaal*, the Old Council Hall, an imposing sandstone building in the main square of Pretoria, when they run into the President himself.

Deneys can't resist, and tells the nation's leader that the office of the Field Cornet – the organiser, and 2IC of the Pretoria Commando – had outright refused to enrol him for active service because he was a year younger than the desired age.

Oh, really?

Looking him up and down carefully – there is no doubt he is a fine figure of a lad – the old man pauses for a moment and then growls: '[General] Piet Joubert says the English are three to one – *Sal jij mij drie rooi-nekke lever?* Will you stand me good for three of them?'

'President, if I get close enough I'm good for three with one shot.'

It is the kind of response the President delights in hearing. The youthful conceit notwithstanding, the war effort needs young men with this confidence, this love of country. Turning to his colleague, Deneys' father, he asks how old the lad is.

'He is seventeen, Mr. President.'[49]

'Well then, Mr. State Secretary, the boy must go – I started fighting earlier than that.'[50]

Two minutes later Piet Joubert himself – nudging 70, the craggy Commandant-General of all the military forces of the Transvaal, who had achieved distinction in the Boer War of 20 years earlier – is handing the young man a new Mauser rifle, together with a bandolier of ammunition. Deneys is thrilled, though also very quietly wonders if the old man before him is going to be up to the monumental task ahead.

'He was a kindly, well-meaning old man who had done useful service in the smaller campaigns of the past, but he gave me the impression of being bewildered at the heavy responsibility now resting upon him, and I felt that he was unequal to the burden.'[51]

Nevertheless, for the moment, all that counts is that Deneys is on his way, and after farewelling his family joins the nearly 15,000 horsemen gathering on the border of Natal, and finds his place in the unique Boer command structure.

'Our military organization was a rough one,' he would recount. 'Each commando was divided into two or more field-cornetcies, and these again were subdivided into corporalships. A field-cornetcy was supposed to contain 150 to 200 men, and a corporalship nominally consisted of 25, but there was no fixed rule . . .'[52]

•

Across the Australian colonies, the slide to war against the Boer is watched closely. As the *Bendigo Independent* reports to its readers on 21 September 1899:

> There is a general understanding that in the event of war breaking out and the British Government accepting their services, an Australian Contingent is to be dispatched to the Transvaal. In Queensland and New South Wales the movement is much further afoot than in Victoria. Queensland practically has its contingent ready to sail whenever the Imperial authorities say the word, and in New South Wales there are the names of about 2000 volunteers on the list. In New Zealand it is much the same.[53]

The only real question is, when will the Boers make their move?

•

On 26 August 1899, the British Colonial Secretary Joseph Chamberlain had spoken plainly in public, knowing his views would be reported in the Transvaal. If agreement is not reached, Chamberlain said, then 'having taken the matter in hand, we will not let it go until we have secured conditions which once and for all shall establish which is the paramount power in South Africa'.[54]

Translation?

Aside from motivations of gold and political power the British are appalled with the Boer treatment of the Native peoples. While Blighty had done away with slavery and denounced forced bondage as an affront to the human spirit, the Boers remained well and truly in its thrall. The means by which the British intend to convince the Boers of the evils of slavery is, of course, the British Army. There is no better way than boots and bullets to 'establish which is the paramount power' in the region. In July of 1899 there are 6000 British Troopers in Cape Colony and Natal, a paltry figure compared to the 60,000 Boers. Yet by August that number has doubled to 12,000, and by September it grows to 22,000.

On 21 September the *Raad* of the Orange Free State meet and decide that, despite the fact that they have no Uitlander issue in their own republic, and therefore no quarrel with Britain, they have no choice but to honour an alliance previously signed between them and Transvaal and to stand with their brother Boers to the north.

By 9 October, President Kruger judges all is in readiness, and at 5 pm on that day his government issues an ultimatum to Britain demanding that: 'The troops upon the borders of the republic should be instantly withdrawn, that all reinforcements which had arrived within the last year should leave South Africa, and that those who were now upon the sea should be sent back without being landed. Failing a satisfactory answer within forty-eight hours, "the Transvaal Government will with great regret be compelled to regard the action of Her Majesty's Government as a formal declaration of war, for the consequences of which it will not hold itself responsible".'[55]

Britain's stern response is sent the next day by telegram, by the British High Commissioner for Southern Africa, Sir Alfred Milner: '. . . The conditions demanded by the Government of the South African Republic are such as Her Majesty's Government deem it impossible to discuss.'[56]

The stage is set, with a clear question posed, as later elucidated by one close observer at the time, Sir Arthur Conan Doyle: 'Should Dutch ideas or English ideas of government prevail throughout that huge country? The one means freedom for a single race, the other means equal rights to all white men beneath one common law. What each means to the coloured races let history declare. This was the main issue to be determined from the instant that the clock struck five upon the afternoon of Wednesday, October the eleventh, eighteen hundred and ninety-nine.'[57]

The middle of October?

Perfect.

President Kruger had been steering for that very thing, stalling the opening of hostilities until now, when the grass on the veldt will be at its most verdant, and able to support the horse-mounted army he is about to unleash. It had not been easy . . .

CHAPTER TWO

BOUND FOR THE BOERS

*Was it possible to find an irregular soldiery with the same power
of initiative and resource [as the Boers], the same freedom from
the bias of the drill-book and barrack-square within our own territory . . . ? The answer of Australia was the Bushmen. They were
all men who could ride and shoot . . . 'These men,' [squatters] said
in their letters to the newspapers, 'have bushcraft – they can drive
a mob of cattle for hundreds of miles across mountain, plain, or
river to a given point. They are used to roughing it in the open.
They can get their own food, and cook it; and, if need be, they
can live on the smell of an oily rag for a time. They would excel
in capturing horses and cattle.' In short, said they, 'the Bushmen
will play the Boers at their own game'.*[1]

The Reverend James Green,
The Story of the Australian Bushmen

*Certainly there was nothing in Harry Morant's life or character
worth recounting – and notwithstanding a lot of gush that was
written about him by a few who like to be considered 'Bohemians'
– which, in their case, means a life led very much after the manner
of the man they slobbered over – birds of a feather, in fact – this
bashi-bazouk horse-breaking, horse-BORROWING, flippant
rhymster who posed as a blue-blooded aristocrat was not worth
a second thought.*[2]

Letter to the *Windsor and Richmond Gazette*, 1904

11 October 1899, the Natal border, Pom-Pom for the Poms

As it happens, Deneys Reitz is just in time, for on the evening of the day
in which the deadline passes, President Kruger gives the orders and at
dawn the following day 15,000 Boers cross the Transvaal border into
Natal, even as another 14,000 Boers cross the border from Orange Free
State attacking towards the main British garrison in Natal at Ladysmith,
from the west.

In short order, Ladysmith is under siege, just as are the towns of Mafeking, which serves as the capital of the Bechuanaland Protectorate to the west of Transvaal, and Kimberley, situated to the north of Cape Colony. Yet another Boer force will soon invade Cape Colony, heading for the town of Colesberg, strategically significant for the fact it is filled with a large Boer population that might join the invader.

Still more Boers surge forth from the Orange Free State, and there are soon no fewer than 40,000 Boers in hostilities – most of them on horseback – against just 22,000 British troops, and most of them are mere infantry.

Most galling to the English in the face of this general disaster? There is an embarrassment of options. But the most appalling of the galling is the Boer use of English-made Maxim-Nordenfeldt Pom-Pom guns, which are now unleashing *hell* on the English defences.

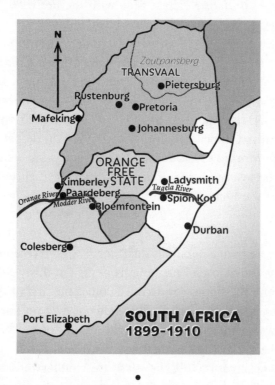

•

When the news of war breaks in the Australian colonies, it is greeted with great exultation, bordering on hysteria. Oh how the people cheer, as they gather round the bulletin boards outside the major newspapers, where the glad tidings are posted. Men set their jaws and declare they will join immediately. Women feel proud.

'Boers behaving like frenzied savages'[3] reads one headline, soon matched by a series of them.

Outrageous Conduct.

Brutal Boers.

Acting Like Savages.

Bullying Women and Children.

'The refugees from the Transvaal report that the Boers are behaving in a frenzied manner towards those leaving the country,' reports one paper. 'They enter trains with a ferocious and semi-savage air, and point rifles at the passengers.'[4]

The headlines set the tone of just what it is that the noble sons of the British Empire will be up against, as they head off to repel them, and teach the brutes a lesson.

The South Australian Register runs with the headline: 'War Begun. Boers Advancing. Natal Invaded. Brave Uitlanders.'[5]

In the South Australian Assembly that very afternoon a motion is carried 18 to 10 to send the First South Australian Contingent on its way to Southern Africa immediately, with the only opposition coming from members of the Labour Party while some German-born members of the House left the chamber, so as not to record their votes.

'The Legislative Council has already authorised the despatch of troops,' the *Newcastle Morning Herald and Miners' Advocate* reports, 'so that no time will be lost, and it is understood that the men will sail by the same vessel as the Victorians'.[6]

•

Yes, it is no more than a nebulous dust storm at first, creeping across the veldt. But now look closer. Emerging from the flat dusty veldt, and now starting to climb the slopes towards us, comes the first of the Transvaal forces, intent on invading Natal. Hundreds of men on horseback, nay, neigh, *thousands*. An army, yes, but with no uniform. These strapping Boers have their coats across their saddles, their sleeves rolled up and their rifles slung across their backs, ready to bring forward at a moment's notice. In their rolled-up kit on the horses' rumps are their swags, and hanging from their saddles is everything else they need to live off the land, from blankets, to pots, to freshly slaughtered pigs.

For Deneys Reitz and his weary but still exuberant comrades it has been a long and difficult ride to get to the border of Natal, as they have had to wind their way through difficult passes and over rugged mountains. And yet here is the shining moment to make the hearts of the warriors soar, as they come out into open country on high, and can suddenly see the vista splendid before them: a beautiful plain through which runs the mighty Buffalo River and all the green hills and pleasant valleys of Natal stretching beyond. Over yonder horizon, they know, just a little further still, lies the English town of Ladysmith, which they hope to occupy as a first blow on the British.

Without a word now, all the horsemen rein in and gather around their grizzled commanding officer – 'clad in [a] black claw-hammer coat, and semi-top hat trimmed with crêpe, a style of dress and headgear affected by so many Boer officers as virtually to amount to insignia of rank'[7] – General Daniel 'Maroola' Erasmus, who sits easily on his horse, gazing 'silently on the land of promise'. Just a short way ahead is the stream that marks the actual border.

And now General Erasmus turns his horse to face his men to say a few portentous words.

'Natal,' the craggy old warrior says, 'was a heritage filched from our forefathers by the English, which must now be recovered from the usurper.'

It will be up to them to reclaim it for the Boer people.

'Amid enthusiastic cries,' Reitz will recount, 'we began to ford the stream. It took nearly an hour for all to cross, and during this time the cheering and singing of the "Volkslied" anthem were continuous . . .'[8]

Oh, sing one, sing all!

> *Four coloured waves o'er our dear land,*
> *The Transvaal flag on high,*
> *And woe betide the imperious hand*
> *To haul it down should try*
> *Wave now aloft in our bright sky*
> *Flag of the Transvaal free;*
> *Our enemies before thee fly*
> *And happier days shall be.*
>
> *. . . And with God's help we then the might*
> *Of England overthrew,*
> *And free once more our banner bright*
> *Waves fair in spotless blue.*
> *It cost us heroes' blood to gain,*
> *More sore was England's fall.*

The good Lord did our cause sustain
We give Him praise for all.[9]

The Boers ride on, as Reitz puts it, 'into the smiling land of Natal full of hope and courage'.[10]

Unsure of where the British resistance will come from, but determined not to present a bunched target when they encounter it, the Boers spread out laterally, with Reitz's group spanning several miles.

'Far away, on either side we could see the other forces moving abreast of us. There was not a man who did not believe that we were heading straight for the coast . . .'[11] One of the columns Reitz sees is that of Ben Viljoen, leading the Johannesburg Commando.

Yes, once they have destroyed the British garrison at Ladysmith they can then capture the ports – preventing British reinforcements immediately arriving that way – and Natal will be for the Boers once more!

On this same day, of course, other Commandos of Boers are crossing borders at other key places. From Harrismith in the Orange Free State, 10,000 Boers are also pushing to Ladysmith from the west via Van Reenen's Pass, while almost as large a force under the legendary General Piet Cronje – a legendary lion of a man, 64 years old, who had been taken on the Great Trek as a baby, and covered himself in glory in the First Boer War – is already on the outskirts of Mafeking, just as another 5000 Boers from Bloemfontein have surrounded the mining town of Kimberley. In Cape Town every report coming in beckons British disaster.

•

In response to all of the Boer machinations, declarations and abominations, England moves quickly, but still not so quickly as the *Daily Mail* and *Morning Post* journalist, a Mr Winston Churchill.

The Harrow and Sandhurst graduate has been born to a famous family, and has a notably illustrious forebear in General John Churchill, who, among other triumphs such as defeating those rapscallions in the Monmouth Rebellion of 1685 to secure the crown for James II, had defeated the French at Blenheim in 1704, naming his palace after the battle.

His statue atop a column at the family's Blenheim Palace estate had been the beacon of young Winston's childhood; a reminder that he, too, must achieve something great.

No, Winston is not content to rest on the laurels of his forefathers.

For one thing, he is far too busy trying to outdo and so lay to rest the restless ghost of his perpetually disapproving and distantly caustic father, the famous Lord Randolph Churchill, who had promised so much only to deliver so little and who was dead at 45. Whatever else happens, Churchill is determined to be a whole lot more than 'the son of Randolph' and to escape his father's fate, a man blessed with everything but the will to see it through. Winston has already seen action of his own as an officer of the British Army, moonlighting as a war correspondent all the while. The Boers are just another in a long line of uppity subordinates needing to be crushed, as Winston has already witnessed the Cubans revolt against the Spanish before himself fighting the Pathans in Afghanistan and serving under Kitchener in the Sudan.

On all occasions he has been in dangerous situations with bullets whistling nearby, but had not been worried.

'I do not believe the Gods would create so potent a being as myself,' he had written to his mother, 'for so prosaic an ending.'[12]

Now resigned from the army, going to a war in Africa as a correspondent will likely be a lot more thrilling and on a much grander scale than his previous two wars, and he simply *must* be there!

As fast as he is in making plans to get there, however, his friend Oliver Borthwick – now the fast-rising 26-year-old editor of the *Morning Post* – is faster, and the Boer ultimatum had not ticked out on the tape machines for an hour before he is looming over Winston with an offer for him to be the *Morning Post*'s principal war correspondent for the war which is surely to come.

Winston Churchill accepts on the spot, later noting that the offer of '250 pounds a month, all expenses paid . . . [was] higher I think, than any previously paid in British journalism to a war correspondent, and certainly attractive to a young man of twenty-four with no responsibilities'.[13]

It is indeed a measure of the regard in which young Churchill's writing is held – not to mention his pluck and ability to get into the thick of the action – that his salary is certainly more than two of the most noted literary lions of the day, Rudyard Kipling and Arthur Conan Doyle, who are also in South Africa and writing. (The fact that Kipling is on holiday and Conan Doyle is there in his capacity as a military doctor does not dissuade Churchill from his claim; he is the highest-paid observer in the land! Detail will not detract from his feat or his gall.)

Churchill makes his arrangements and swiftly books passage – together with his own cache of 18 bottles of Scotch – on the earliest possible steamer heading to Southern African, the *Dunnottar Castle*, setting off on 11 October 1899. It is the same vessel that will be bearing Sir Redvers Buller, who's been appointed to command all the British forces in Southern Africa. Buller, a British bulldog of a man if ever there was one – all jowly aggression, who can bark with the best of them – is a brave man, a previous recipient of the Victoria Cross for his heroism during the Zulu War of 1879. Yes, there is some question as to whether he is capable of commanding large combined forces, but it is thought that the value of his previous experience in Africa might make up for the queries about his command abilities.

•

In the ordinary course of things Mafeking would be no more than a dusty speck of a town just below the Kalahari Desert, an outpost of Empire consisting of little more than a railway station, a hospital, a Masonic hall, a few government buildings like a courthouse, library and prison together with half-a-dozen stores dotted around the central market square and a few hundred rather dilapidated houses containing perhaps a thousand or so equally dusty residents.

In peacetime the town is of minimal importance. But in wartime the fact that it stands on the Cape Town to Bulawayo railway line and is just on the Cape Colony side of the border with Transvaal makes it an attractive target for the massed Boers of the Transvaal to attempt to subdue. So attractive, in fact, that just the day after war is declared they begin their attempt to do exactly that. First General Cronje has his troops who have slipped over the border cut both the town's railway and telegraph lines, to totally isolate it. Then an emissary is sent forth to demand the town's surrender. And finally, after that demand is rejected by the British commander, Colonel Robert Baden-Powell, at 9 am on 14 October the Siege of Mafeking begins. First there is the sound of an explosion in the distance, then, just an instant later, a whistling, and now, before their very eyes, a shell bursts through the roof of Colonel Walford's stable and kills a horse while, remarkably, no other horse or man in the stable is touched. But it proves to be just an opening salvo as soon shells start exploding all over the town, even as sniper bullets start taking their toll, and a railway truck filled with dynamite and a long fuse is sent rolling down the hill. (Mercifully, the fuse proves to be not long *enough*, as the whole carriage explodes well before it hits the station.)[14]

What will do most damage from now will be General Cronje's nine field guns, including a prized Creusot 'Long Tom' big gun – capable of firing 10,000 yards, double the distance of the longest-range British guns – which the defenders will nickname 'Old Creechy',[15] for the distinctive sound it makes when it fires the 94-pound shells that cause such extraordinary devastation when they land. Still there are ways of coping. As the Old Creechy is positioned atop a visible hill a couple of miles to the south-west, it is earnestly watched. When her barrel goes up, ready to fire, a bell rings . . . followed by another bell when the puff of smoke from the muzzle indicates the shell is on its way. At this point there is mayhem for some 12 seconds while everyone scrambles to whatever trench they can get to, until such time as the shell has exploded.[16]

Fortunately in the weeks leading up to the war, Baden-Powell had put together reinforcements to go with the 500 strong soldiers of the Protectorate Regiment – including some 300 Troopers from the Bechuanaland Rifles and as many from both the Cape Police and the town itself. There are also 300 Africans armed with rifles whose job it is to defend the actual perimeter, referred to, perhaps inevitably, as the 'Black Watch'. Unfortunately there are no trenches dug for them, and the trenches in the town are for the British soldiers only, so they will just have to do the best they can.

Now, to run messages between them all, together with ammunition, Baden-Powell can call on the services of the Mafeking Cadet Corps, which is no more than junior soldiers aged between 11 and 15, all of them led by the 13-year-old Sergeant Major Warner Goodyear. They all prove to be good scouts.

For artillery, the defenders have just two muzzle-loading, 7-pounder guns and a cannon so old it fires a small projectile 'exactly like a cricket ball'.[17]

•

At Elandslaagte on 21 October, just a week after the war had begun – 300 Troopers of the Imperial Light Horse, of whom half had been Australians living in Cape Colony when the war broke out – go all out to stop the advance of the Transvaalers on Ladysmith.

'It was,' Boer leader Ben Viljoen would recount, 'the baptismal fire of the Imperial Light Horse, a corps principally composed of Johannesburg [Uitlanders] who were politically and racially our bitter enemies.'[18]

Moving swiftly around the Boer left flank, the Light Horse dismount and, by virtue of short rushes between the rocks, soon get into position to launch a full-blown charge, which sends the Boers fleeing.

General Ben Viljoen is shocked.

'It was at sunrise that the first shot I heard in this war was fired,' he would recount. 'Presently the men we dreaded were visible on the ridges of hills south of the little red railway station at Elandslaagte.

'Some of my men hailed the coming fight with delight; others, more experienced in the art of war, turned deadly pale. That is how the Boers felt in their first battle.'[19]

The Boers are defeated that day – and one of those, a fighter from a corps of Dutch volunteers, the 'Hollanderkorps', is Cornelis van Gogh, the younger brother of an obscure dead Dutch artist, Vincent van Gogh – but the only outcome of the Battle of Elandslaagte is just a small delay in the Boer advance.

Colonel Henry Rawlinson – on the staff of General Sir George White, who commands in Ladysmith – writes in his diary:

> 22 October. Hamilton and Haig came in [to Ladysmith] at 11.30am and gave me a detailed account of Elandslaagte. The Boers seem to have fought like men, particularly the Johannesburg Commando. We have no soft job here.[20]

But beyond that, all the news is grim. They can do little but wait until superior forces – ideally both numerically, and in terms of quality – arrive from around the British Empire.

•

In Cape Town, when he arrives on 30 October 1899, General Sir Redvers Buller is greeted with mixed news – varying between extremely bad and catastrophic. The Boers have advanced on all fronts, and practically before his orderly has put his bags down, Ladysmith is under full siege, while the Boers have also come across the border of Cape Colony and are now beleaguering another railway town in Colesberg.

High up in the northern Transvaal, the Zoutpansberg and Rustenburg Commandos – the former under the command of Tom Kelly, who used to pass this way hunting elephants for ivory – have crossed the Limpopo and successfully attacked two British outposts in Rhodesia before withdrawing. Kelly's 400 Boers had attacked at Pont Drift right on the Limpopo, and one of the men killed, serving with the Rhodesian Regiment, was Trooper George Nethercott, from Beechworth in Victoria – newly married, with a two-year-old child – the first Australian to be killed in action in the Boer War. Tom Kelly returns to the northern Transvaal as an even more respected figure and is soon put in charge of raising another 150 volunteers for his Commando, using one of three portable steel forts near Sweetwaters Farm as their base. Not only must they continue to attack the British, but also push back on any potential Native uprising.

Everywhere General Buller looks meantime, the Boers are breaking out of their own territories and attacking British positions, even as the imagination of the British Empire is captured by tiny Mafeking still holding out against such overwhelming odds.

For the first time, people are interested in this: the most unheard of place they've *never heard of*! Now with 8000 Boers attacking the key outpost, it means the British supply line between Cape Colony and Rhodesia is no more.

The Boers are also laying siege to the mining town of Kimberley some 200 miles to the south.

Yes, it is a humiliation for the British, but it is not as if the Boers are laying siege to the likes of Durban, Port Elizabeth and Cape Town – for if ever the British in Southern Africa lost their ports and the means to easily bring tens of thousands of reinforcements from all over the British Empire, they really would be in grave peril. Those inland towns will have to be relieved, but the fact the British still have the ports means that they have the means to do it. The only question is, when can the expected mass of fresh soldiers from the British Empire get here?

30 October 1899, aboard the *Kent*, leaving Sydney Harbour[21]

A little over a century earlier, Governor Arthur Phillip had sailed triumphantly up what would be Sydney Harbour, expanding the footprint of the British Empire.

Now the strengthened British Empire is calling her loyal sons home – or at least to her aid – and those sons are leaving with great pride and no little fanfare. On this day of inclement skies, as the newly fitted out *Kent* raises both anchor and steam and starts gently pulling away from Pyrmont wharf, the crowds cheer, the band plays 'Rule Britannia' and the departing brave troops wave merrily back. They are the first raft of the first draft of officers and men of the NSW Lancers – together with their mounts in their hastily constructed stalls below deck – who in Cape Colony will be joining their brethren of A Squadron, who have been training in England.[22]

Also aboard, as proudly reported by the *Sydney Morning Herald*, is none other than their newly minted war correspondent Banjo Paterson – who 'takes over letters of introduction to Cecil Rhodes and others in authority, so that he expects to be enabled to see whatever is to be seen'.[23]

Though, as reported by the worthy *Truth*, 'lots of ladies present complained that "Banjo," in his broad wide-awake hat and oilskin, did not look romantic . . . he did look eminently practical', and that is the main thing.

And hark now, as the ship picks up steam, and moves out into the harbour proper.

'Then the cheers from those who had braved the rain commenced to ring out. They were hearty cheers, spontaneous and genuine. They signified a peculiar trait in the Australian character. One of the easiest things to do is to espouse Australian enthusiasm on any subject which does not immediately concern them.'[24]

As it happens, however, it all does concern Banjo Paterson most intimately and he could hardly be more enthusiastic. There is no doubt that the Motherland has right on her side, and it is right and proper that those of us in the colonies fight to protect her interests. Besides, everyone knows that Boers are only a step or two, if that, above animals. Uncouth, unwashed, uneducated, they are a venal breed who would as soon shoot you as shake your hand. They have defied Great Britain and must be disciplined for their trouble, and the trouble they have caused. Outrageously, the Boers have invaded Cape Colony, Natal, Rhodesia and Bechuanaland; and the Transvaal Secretary of State, Francis Reitz, has declared the aim of the war is to bring about 'a free United South Africa, an ambitious Afrikander Republic stretching from the Zambezi to Table Bay'.[25]

Disgraceful! Such aggression, such presumption by the uppity and savage Boers must be resisted and punished, and Banjo knows he is just the man to document it for Sydney readers. At 35 years old he is at the height of his powers – and with no wife or children, like his friend the Breaker, he has no reason not to embark on such an adventure.

Most of the troops with him feel the same, as they blow kisses to their families and friends, now just tiny figures back on the docks. They shift to the stern, straining for last looks. They are on their way.

●

It is *the* question that much of the English-speaking world is wondering. How is Ladysmith holding out, as it remains under siege by the Boers?

Since it began, two weeks ago, no-one has been able to get into or out of the besieged town, and there is no solid information available. Today the task of trying to get through falls to Major John Cayzer of 7th Dragoon Guards, now head of the signals section, Natal Field Force. Can he get close enough to Ladysmith to try and communicate via heliograph – a system of opening and closing a small shutter above a mirror to direct flashes of sunlight in Morse Code across distances as far as 20 miles?

Today, as he has done on previous days – albeit with no success – Major Cayzer climbs to the top of the highest hill in the area and starts flashing queries in the direction of Ladysmith only to get absolutely noth . . .

No, wait!

There is a flash back! And another one! And still another one.

Excitedly, he writes down the letters as they come, which he can review once completed.

'H . . . O . . . W space D . . . O space . . .'

Completed, he puts all the letters together to look at the full sentence.

'HOW DO YOU LIKE OUR POM-POM GUNS?'[26]

Oh.

Bloody Boers. Some of them speak English, and clearly one of them is on a hill between them and Ladysmith. Nevertheless, Major Cayzer and his men keep pushing ahead and climbing hills until one day they are close enough that the heliograph messages coming back seem to be genuine! But how can he be sure?

Cayzer asks his heliograph correspondent to go and find Captain Brooks of the Gordons and ask him what town Cayzer owns a house in. The heliographist does exactly that, and finds Brooks, whose response is so pithy the heliographist repeats it, word for word: 'Well, I always thought Cayzer was an ass, now he proves it by forgetting where he lives.'[27]

Thereafter, the name of Cayzer's town, Gartmore in Perthshire, becomes the code word so both sides can be sure they are not talking to a Boer.

15 November 1899, Estcourt, he shall never surrender . . . well, hardly ever

They don't call Winston Churchill 'Pushful the Younger' for nothing. By November he is at Estcourt, in Natal, 41 miles south of Ladysmith. As Churchill will chronicle, 'it occurred to the General in command on the spot to send his armoured train along the sixteen miles of intact railway line to supplement the efforts of the cavalry'.[28] Which is why the young war correspondent had, in turn, finagled his way aboard this armoured train filled with soldiers, a telegraphist and a single naval gun. All together they are nudging across the dramatic countryside on this fine morning, 'tween the rolling hills and enormous flats that lie north of the small town of Estcourt, reconnoitring that stretch of the line heading towards Colenso, which lies some miles further on. By going up and back and keeping their eyes open they should be able to see if there are any signs of the Boers moving on from Ladysmith and even advancing on Estcourt.

As pleased as he is to be approaching the front lines, young Churchill feels far from safe, noting that, 'Nothing looks more formidable and impressive than an armoured train; but nothing is in fact more vulnerable and helpless. It was only necessary to blow up a bridge or culvert to leave the monster stranded, far from home and help, at the mercy of the enemy.'[29]

Still, with no fewer than 150 soldiers on board, and a naval gun, it is not as if they are without arguments of their own, should it come to it.[30]

Are they all nervous?

Yes. Beside themselves. For they are travelling through country known to be infested with Boers. And yes, this so-called 'armoured train' has been configured so that heavily armoured carriages and the carriages bearing the men are in front, with the engine behind – in theory protecting it – but no-one is fooled.

That much was demonstrable by the fact that the train, daily taking men and supplies forward from Estcourt to the troops trying to get through to Ladysmith, had already been ambushed twice, and it is bound to happen again sometime soon. Though this is regrettable, Churchill is not unduly worried. He is convinced he has great things awaiting him, and the notoriety he will gain by being the first journalist into Ladysmith is simply a step on the way to putting himself into a position to achieve it.

•

Normally, the train would have stopped at Frere, but so keen is Churchill to keep going that he manages to convince the man in charge of the expedition, Captain Aylmer Haldane – an old friend, who he had bumped into just the night before – to go even further into enemy territory.

'Had I been alone and not had my impetuous young friend Churchill with me,' Haldane will later write, 'I might have thought twice before throwing myself into the lion's jaws. But I was carried away by his ardour and departed from an attitude of prudence.'[31]

•

As it happens, from hidden spots in the distance, the Boers are indeed watching this train – 'a long brown rattling serpent with the rifles bristling from its spotted sides' as Churchill describes it – with more than usual interest, and none more than one of the most charismatic figures in the Boer Army, and their youngest general to boot, Louis Botha.

Just 37 years old with – like most Boers – a background in farming, the strapping six-foot blue-eyed Botha is the son of *Voortrekker* parents and a celebrated veteran of the Zulu wars. He knows there is little point in attacking the train now, filled with bristling soldiers with guns and ammunition. No, much better to wait for its return journey when it will only be bringing back the wounded and exhausted.

As soon as the train is out of sight, thus, Botha gives his men their orders and they swing into action. At the base of a steep hill, where the tracks take a sudden curve, they begin to amass enough stones that the train will be derailed when it hits them. This accomplished, they return to the top of the hill to secrete themselves to wait for the train's return and . . .

And here it comes now!

From their high position they first see the puffs of steam rising in the north and before long can hear it. The English train is heading back to them. Well, they are ready . . .

•

For Winston Churchill, it is all a tad alarming. After passing the outpost of Chieveley they had seen men *behind* them on horseback.

'Certainly they were Boers,' Churchill would recount. 'Certainly they were behind us. What would they be doing with the railway line? There was not an instant to lose. We started immediately on our return journey.'[32]

Ever restless, Churchill stands on a box and pokes his head above the top of the armoured truck he is in at the rear, just in time to see a very strange thing. Just up ahead there is a hill that the tracks must rise over, and right near the top he can see a bunch of roughly attired men – looking suspiciously like Boers – clustered around something, seemingly setting up . . .

Guns. Three of them. Mobile guns all primed and looking for targets, targets with much the same contours and constructs as . . . the truck Winston is sitting in right now.

'A huge white ball of smoke sprang into being and tore out into a cone, only as it seemed a few feet above my head. It was shrapnel – the first I had ever seen in war.'[33]

A vicious spray of metal peppers the armoured train, the sound of bullets ricocheting off the steel like some hellishly discordant orchestra with gargoyles on cymbals and the Devil himself on drums. Not for nothing does 'the devil's tattoo' refer to a drumming sound exactly like this beating of the bullets on the armoured side of the train. The damage is noticeable, great dents pockmarking the plating of the train, though not enough to bring her to a halt. The engine picks up speed, belching black sooty smoke from its stack as it rounds a curve and begins to descend a steep incline.

Winston, meanwhile, finds himself with a troubling thought. Surely that *couldn't* be the extent of the Boers' efforts. They can't have thought their guns would prove enough to pierce the train's armour; they'd need to derail it somehow . . .

And *somehow* is transformed from speculation to reality in an instant.

With a hideous shriek of metal twisting against metal, the train lurches sharply as a section comes free from the tracks beneath. Winston and the troops go flying, bouncing around like small pellets in an iron barrel.

Detangling themselves from themselves, the troops rise from the heap they have fallen into only to discover that . . . whatever knocked the section from the rail was not enough to knock the engine itself. Well, that's one good thing.

Rising to the occasion, and creating a position for himself, Winston Churchill takes charge, inflated by the power vested in him by . . . absolutely no one.

Right. Men, I want you on the tracks. Whatever debris derailed us, I want it gone. Move it. Turning to the dazed and delirious driver, Churchill shouts over the 'repeated explosions of shells and the ceaseless hammering of bullets',[34] and orders the man to use the engine as a makeshift battering ram. Yes, they might have derailed part of the train, but all we need do is clear the tracks and we'll be back on our way. You'll see.

Once the rail is clear and the worst of the wounded have been seen to, Churchill continues to call the shots.

Driver! Continue on to Blue Krantz River and wait for us.

However, as there are still soldiers further back on the line, someone must see to them. Churchill himself promptly disembarks and begins following the rail back down the line. Now free of this upstart journalist who thinks he has the authority to give orders, the driver releases the brake and the train begins to move. Despite what it has gone through, it has no trouble picking up speed as it continues on to Blue Krantz River, though the driver sees no need to engage the brake. In fact, the train speeds right over the river, and the brake remains untouched until Estcourt. Winston is on his own.

As ever, it is like Churchill is protected by a magic spell. While shells burst and bullets continue to ping all around him – ricocheting off the sides of the derailed carriages – the young correspondent takes command and organises the soldiers to fight back.

In the end, however, it is no use.

The Boer numbers are too overwhelming, their aim too deadly, the toll they are taking too devastating. Even Churchill can see there is no use in fighting to the bitter end when they would all be wiped out, and so while other soldiers surrender, he decides to make a run for it, charging across the rails towards what he hopes will be continued freedom.

And now he sees him. On the other side of the railway is a tall, dark Boer on horseback with a rifle in his right hand.

Now reining the horse in, the Boer points the rifle at Churchill, staring down the sights, and shouts something in Afrikaans.

They are 40 yards apart, and this is the moment.

Should Churchill go for the Mauser pistol he has secreted – despite his official status as correspondent meaning he must not be armed – and try to bring the Boer down, or even for such as him would this be the equivalent of committing suicide when up against a Boer with a rifle, this close?

Churchill cannot help himself – 'I thought I could kill this man [and] I earnestly desired to do so' – and swiftly brings his right hand to the pistol in his belt . . . only to find it is not there.

'The Boer continued to look at me along his sights, if he fired he would surely hit me, so I held up my hands and surrendered myself a prisoner of war.'[35]

While the wounded are tended to by Boer doctors, Churchill joins the rest of the British soldiers who have been captured and they begin the long march towards the train that will take them to the newly established prisoner-of-war camp in the Boer capital of Pretoria.

En route for Pretoria, this time on a Boer train, Churchill finds himself with little else to do but fall into polite conversation with his guard, a 'polite, meek-mannered little man very anxious in all the discussion to say nothing that could hurt the feelings of his prisoners'. A farmer from the Ermelo district, this Mr Spaarwater is a tremendously likeable fellow and Winston finds himself enthralled.

The conversation ambles along amicably enough until it takes a sudden strange turn.

'No, no, old chappie, we don't want your flag,' says the Boer, 'we want to be left alone. We are free, you are not free.'

'How do you mean "not free"?'

'Well, is it right that a dirty Kaffir should walk on the pavement – without a pass too? That's what they do in your British Colonies. Brother! Equal! Ugh! Free! Not a bit. We know how to treat Kaffirs . . . in this country. Fancy letting the black filth walk on the pavement! Treat 'em with humanity and consideration – I like that. They were put here by the God Almighty to work for us. We'll stand no damned nonsense from them. We'll keep them in their proper places. What do you think? Insist on their proper treatment will you? Ah, that's what we're going to see about now. We'll settle whether you English are to interfere with us before this war is over.'[36]

Late November 1899, Cape Town, the roos ruffle

For Banjo Paterson and the men of the NSW Lancers there is good news and there is bad news.

After 30 days of rather tedious steaming across the Indian Ocean, they spy the African coast and, shortly afterwards, two British ships pass, coming from that coast.

The good news comes after the Captain has signalled they are friends, from Sydney, and asks the question by semaphore for news of the war.

'Constant fighting going on,' the answer comes back, which sees great cheering from all the men! There will be enough of this war still left for them to fight in, hurrah, *hurrah*, HURRAH!

The rather less positive news comes when they arrive in Port Elizabeth, full of vim and vigour and ready to fight . . . only to find that . . . well, none of the British mob seems to particularly care.

'We went to the club at Port Elizabeth and said we were Australian troops. The English officers were politely indifferent. We explained who we were, and where we came from, and conveyed no impression.'[37]

Only one thing saves them. It so happens that, on this very day, thrilling news has come through about the 'fighting 29', that is, the squadron of mighty NSW Lancers who'd just arrived from Britain, having registered a great success the previous day at a place called Graspan.

Yes! Didn't you know? Just 29 lancers on horseback, up against a force of Boers several times the size, *chaaarged*, and routed the brutes.

'When we said that we were the same regiment that had been in action the day before,' Banjo Paterson tells the *Herald* readers, 'that made all the difference. We were no longer outsiders, no longer a handful of Australian refugees crawling along the coast in a disconsolate tramp steamer; we were of the brotherhood, and could hold up our heads with the best. The kangaroo was himself again . . . ! This morning we were nobodies; now we are full-blown soldiers, and can ruffle it with the best of them.'[38]

Now if one of the knacks of good journalism is being in the right place at the right time with notebook in hand, then this is the very occasion when the *Sydney Morning Herald*'s Banjo Paterson is an exemplar of the art.

For not long after arriving in Cape Town with that first draft of the NSW Lancers, he just happens to be in the innermost room, the sanctum of 'the castle' – the Dutch-built stone fort completed in 1679, in which the British now make their war HQ – when an interesting scene takes place. At the centre of the room 'a much-decorated military veteran with a bald head, a grizzled moustache and an eye-glass', is giving dictation to three underlings at once, even as clerks run about in ever-diminishing circles bearing cablegrams, letters, and notes from people wanting just a moment of his attention. Before him on the table is the detritus of previous communication, each and every one marked 'URGENT'. And now, a clerk rushes in . . .

'Cablegram from Australia offering [more] troops, sir!'

Military Veteran: 'No! Can't have 'em. It has been decided not to use blacks, except as a last resource.'

Clerk: 'But these are *white* troops, sir – the local forces. It is officially desired that they be taken if possible.'

Military Veteran: 'Who is the Australian Commander-in-Chief? I didn't know they had an army at all. I knew they had police, of course!'

Clerk: 'There are seven distinct cablegrams, sir; seven distinct Commanders-in-Chief all offering troops.'

M.V. (*roused to excitement*): 'Great Heavens! Are they going to take the war off our hands? Seven Commanders-in-Chief! They must have been quietly breeding armies all these years in Australia. Let's have a look at the cables. Where's this from?'

C: 'Tasmania, sir. They offer to send a Commander-in-Chief and –'
pauses, aghast '– and *eighty-five* men!'

M.V. (*jumping to his feet*): 'What! Have I wasted all this time talking about eighty-five men! You must be making a mistake!'

C: 'No, sir. It says eighty-five men!'

M.V.: 'Well I am damned! Eighty-five men! You cable back and say that I've seen bigger armies on the stage at Drury Lane Theatre. Just wire and say this isn't a pantomime. They haven't got to march round and round a piece of scenery. Tell 'em to stop at home and breed!' (*Resumes dictation.*) 'At least five thousand extra men should be sent from India in addition to . . .'

C: 'Cabinet instructions are to take these troops, whether they're any good or not, sir. Political reasons!'

M.V. (*with a sigh*): 'Well, let 'em come. Let 'em all come – the whole eighty-five! But don't let it leak out, or the Boers will say we're not playing 'em fair.'[39]

25 November 1899, Pretoria, Transvaal, model prisoner

Have you heard, Deneys?

On a rare visit back to Pretoria to visit his father, the young man hears that we, his fellow Boers, have an interesting prisoner at the State Model School – none other than 'Winston Churchill, a son of Lord Randolph Churchill, of whom I had often heard'.

Not only that, but he is demanding an interview with Deneys' father Francis, the Transvaal Secretary of State, who suggests that Deneys accompany him to find out what he wants.

The young man is not long in finding out.

After passing through the sentries they are confronted – the right word – by young Churchill.

'I am not a combatant, but a war correspondent,' he says, 'and I must be released.'[40]

The annoyed Francis Reitz has no interest in the argument.

Finally accepting his fate, Churchill at least presses on the Secretary of State to take with him some of the articles he has written for his newspaper in England and, if he has no objection to them, see them sent in the mail via the one Boer outlet to Europe – the shipping service still running from Marseilles to Delagoa Bay and back.

That evening, Francis Reitz reads out portions of the articles to his family and declares that 'Churchill is a clever young man.'[41]

30 November 1899, Cape Town, Banjo waltzes about

Banjo Paterson has imagined the Boers as 'long and wild and hairy',[42] rough approximations of humans, but no more than that. And now he hears that a Boer soldier who had been wounded in the process of being captured is being held at one of the Cape Town hotels. Most fortuitously a mutual friend has arranged to introduce them.

Banjo Paterson can't get there quick enough, eager to see a Boer fighter up close.

But who would have thought it?

'He was not long and wild and hairy.'[43]

Rather he looks 'refined and educated',[44] and is a highly sophisticated doctor, with not just a degree in medicine but also in English. He even plays a mean game of billiards, able to compile a break of 50!

'Apparently,' Banjo concedes, 'these Boers are at any rate partially civilized.'[45]

Not that this fellow makes any bones about how hard the Boers will fight them, when it comes to it, even going so far as to say, as Banjo will recount it, 'if the Boers catch our hospital orderlies with rifles in the ambulances, they will be entitled to shoot them. He evidently looks on us as less civilized than his own people – the poor fish.'[46]

Perish the thought. Whatever else you might say about the British war effort, there is no way they ever have armed hospital orderlies, just as they would never shoot unarmed prisoners.

All up?

There is no way around it.

'All the talk about the Boers being savages is nonsense.'[47]

Still, for Banjo, his education in the ways of this war continues apace. As well as getting to know something of the Boers themselves, he is also half bemused, half appalled, at the way the English class system works, when it comes to both officers *and* war correspondents.

While on a long railway journey in the company of two ladies of Cape Town, the subject of a spectacularly incompetent English officer arises, and the English ladies are frank to the inquisitive Australian.

'They should never have sent him out, my dear. Goodness knows how old he is, and he rouges and wears stays. No wonder he walked his men right straight into a Boer camp, instead of going where he was told. But, of course, he's a great friend of the Prince of Wales.'[48]

He's *what*?

A great friend of the Prince of Wales, and that is enough to explain his position as an eminent English officer in the Boer War.

'From these and similar remarks,' Banjo will chronicle, 'one gathered that . . . [British] military appointments were like the Order of the Garter – there was no damned merit about them. It was hard for an Australian to understand how the machinery worked; but brother correspondents, including Prior and Hands of the *Daily Mail*, told me that everything in England was run by aristocratic cliques, each clique being headed by some duchess or other.'

Do tell?

'They fight like cats over the big jobs,' the correspondents told him, 'and the man whose duchess can put in the best work, gets the job.'[49]

As Paterson will soon learn, even the correspondents themselves are ridden with class consciousness.

Correspondents for *The Times* are regarded as the top of the pile and not only expect special consideration from all and sundry, but receive it!

'With the English passion for regimentation,' Banjo notes with wonder, 'they all wore a tooth-brush stuck in the band of their hats, as a sort of caste mark. If you were a *Times* man you wore a tooth-brush; if you were not a *Times* man you didn't dare do it. No, sir!'[50]

Needless to say, not only does Banjo Paterson have no toothbrush in his hat, he does not aspire to have one. What he does want, however, is to see some action for himself like a real war correspondent and a week later, on 8 December, that honour is his when he is present at the Battle of Arundel.

The thrill is indescribable, but describe the battle itself – his first – he must, together with its context. The forces of General John French, some 2000 strong – the Carabineers, 10th Hussars, Inniskilling Dragoons, O and R Batteries, Royal Horse Artillery, the Berkshires and Suffolks, the NSW Lancers and New Zealanders – have been engaged in pushing the Boer forces ever further back in the north of Cape Colony. On this occasion the Boers had taken a stand on the kopjes around Arundel, a small railway station some 350 miles north-east of Cape Town. If the Boers break through to the sea here, they will cut off Natal from the Cape Colony. General John French – a man with a body like a coiled spring and a chin like a clenched fist – has decided to clear them out. As this will be the first major action in which Troopers from Banjo Paterson's homeland will be involved, the *Sydney Morning Herald* correspondent has been given permission to cover it.

What most interests him is the actions of the NSW Lancers, named for the fact they actually bear lances, descendants of the lances used by knights in shining armour in days of old, and now 9-foot-long bamboo and ash poles, with a narrow spear point on one end. They had been training in England when war had broken out and they'd immediately volunteered for duty.

Action, at last!

'It was only a small skirmish that was going on, but quite exciting enough for beginners such as ourselves,' Banjo tells his readers of the *Sydney Morning Herald*. 'The battleground was a great big plain (called *veldt* in this country) with a circle of irregular hills round it. These hills are very rugged and stony, and are called *kops* if of a great size and *kopje* (pronounced coppy) if small. All Africa so far as we have seen it is either veldt or kopje . . . No better fighting ground for cavalry could be found than the veldt, and no worse ground for them could be found than the kopje.'[51]

Initially Banjo ventures forth with the 10th Hussars and the Royal Horse Artillery, going at some Boers moving across their right flank. While the Lancers are kept back for the moment, ready to assist where needed, the Hussars push forward into the kopjes, seeking contact, and, sure enough, 'these kopjes proved to be alive with Boers, and a brisk rifle fire was started. Horses began to drop, and the regiment retreated as fast as it could, but still keeping together and in good order. It was a wildly exciting thing to watch the steady gallop of horsemen and to hear the crackle of musketry.'[52]

But what now?

Suddenly from a kopje about a mile and a half away comes the boom of a big gun, and Banjo realises they are under artillery attack.

'We waited in suspense while a shell screamed its way through the air and burst with a great roar about one hundred yards past our guns. At once our two small guns wheeled like angry wasps to face this new foe, and then we saw to what accuracy artillery fire is brought nowadays.'

For now . . .

'Our right-hand gun roared answer, and we watched in suspense to see where the shell would light. *Bang!* It lit right on the spot where the Boer gun's smoke had come from, and we heard no more of the big fellow that day. Our guns were vigorously plied, and shell after shell was pitched right into the gap where the Boers had fired from. The accuracy of fire was wonderful.'

Now, at last, the NSW Lancers are called forth to assist a party of infantry who are under attack and they respond without hesitation, only to find – to their evident disappointment – that the Boers recede at their sight and the attention of the big guns.

Never mind. Banjo is satisfied.

'This country is an ideal place to see fighting. The entire absence of trees makes it possible to see for miles, and if one gets up on a good big kopje one can see away over the plain the guns shelling a hill; on another flank a mounted infantry force dismounting to pour rifle fire into a Boer stronghold . . .'[53]

12 December 1899, Pretoria, Winnie in the Poo

In the quadrangle of his Pretoria gaol, Winston Churchill is lurking with intent, prowling with purpose, waiting his moment.

Oh, recite it, William Shakespeare . . .

> Nor stony tower, nor walls of beaten brass,
> Nor airless dungeon, nor strong links of iron,
> Can be retentive to the strength of spirit . . .[54]

Some 50 yards away the warden is clanging the dinner bell summoning all prisoners from their dormitories for whatever slop is being served tonight. Now is the time . . .

Moving with the other prisoners across the quadrangle towards the mess, at the last instant the 24-year-old aristocrat ducks away to secrete himself in what he calls 'the circular office', otherwise known as the toilet. There will be no roll call until just before lights out, meaning he has at least 90 minutes to go through with his plan. His every sense tingling, Churchill half expects a shout to go up to the effect that a prisoner is missing, at which point a frantic search will begin but . . . there is nothing. Through a chink in the metal casing, he watches the two guards on sentry duty very carefully, each man in his designated position.

But after 30 minutes, the moment comes. One goes to talk to the other, with both their backs turned to him. Leaving the office, Churchill moves silently in the now deep twilight towards that part of the unguarded wall that is still more sheltered by a tree and, with an uncharacteristically athletic leap for the deeply untalented rugby prop he once was, manages to get his hands to the top of the wall and slowly try to haul himself up . . . only to find he has insufficient strength. Again he tries, and again he fails. On his third attempt, powered by the horrid realisation that if he doesn't do it this time he will definitively fail, he . . . just manages to get one leg to the top of the wall, which allows him to swing his whole body up.

'The top was flat. Lying on it I had one passing glimpse of the sentries, still talking, still with their backs turned . . . fifteen yards away. Then I lowered myself silently down into . . . the adjoining garden and crouched among the shrubs. I was free. The first step had been taken and it was irrevocable.'[55]

As quickly as he can without attracting attention, the escapee walks through the streets, averting his eyes from the many burghers who are all around, always fearing he will be challenged but managing to blend in, until he successfully makes his way to the Delagoa railroad, where he manages to jump aboard the 11.10 goods train from Pretoria, and get a spot in the corner of a carriage! For supplies he has 'four slabs of melting chocolate and a crumbling biscuit', hopefully enough to sustain him until he can work out how to make his way through the 300 miles of enemy territory to get back behind his own lines. It will be all the more challenging for the fact that it is little exaggeration to say the only words he speaks of Afrikaans are 'Pretoria' and 'Bloemfontein', but he intends to manage it somehow.

Back in the prison, they find a letter that Churchill has left on the bed.

> To Mr. de Souza,
> Secretary of War, South African Republic
>
> Sir,
> I have the honour to inform you that as I do not consider that your Government have any right to detain me as a military prisoner, I have decided to escape from your custody . . .
>
> I therefore take this occasion to observe that I consider your treatment of prisoners is correct and humane, and that I see no grounds for complaint. When I return to the British lines I will make a public statement to this effect. I have also to thank you personally for your civility to me, and to express the hope that we may meet again at Pretoria before very long, and under different circumstances. Regretting that I am unable to bid you a more ceremonious or a personal farewell,
>
> I have the honour, to be, Sir,
> Your most obedient servant,
> WINSTON CHURCHILL.[56]

Once the alarm is properly raised, posters are pasted up all over Pretoria with the photo of Churchill, above an offer of £25 reward for his capture, '*dood of levend,* dead or alive'.

In Great Britain – already shocked by the constant headlines of bitter defeats and massive loss of life – the fact that young Churchill has escaped is seized upon by the press. A humiliation for the uppity Boers. This son of Lord Randolph has done it! Just where he is, no-one knows, least of all the Boers, but with every day that passes and he is not captured hope grows that he has made good his escape.

15 December 1899, Pretoria, a strange train of events

Raising his head from an impromptu bed smelling of coal residue and old hessian in a dark corner of the train carriage, Churchill finds himself without the adrenaline that had electrified him last night. He is cold, calculating, and conscious that he must flee his post before the sun rises. Darkness will be his ally. But the time for idle contemplation has passed. He must act. Now.

'The train was running at a fair speed, but I felt it was time to leave it. I took hold of the iron handle at the back of the truck, pulled strongly with my left hand, and sprang. My feet struck the ground in two gigantic strides, and the next instant I was sprawling in the ditch considerably shaken but unhurt.'[57]

Miserable, morose and meandering through the veldt, Churchill is struggling. Dusty and desperate, it has been a dreadful four days since leaving the prison. Exhausted beyond all redemption, he is as unhappy as he has ever been in his life, thinking of all of his friends at home, no doubt in their comfortable evening dress, content after dining in Piccadilly and returning from the theatre while here he is, near fainting with hunger, so thirsty that his tongue feels like it is swelling larger than his mouth. Finally he realises. He must take the most desperate action of his escapade so far . . . or simply collapse.

Ideally, he will be able to find a 'Kaffir kraal' – an African village of simple huts, surrounded by a fence to contain their animals – where his white skin, mixed with their kindness, might help him to get a dry and warm place in which to sleep and, even more importantly, something to eat and drink.

And now he sees it.

A lantern! A small light in the night.

It is just a mile off and . . . past caring . . . stumbling in his eager weakness . . . Churchill keeps pushing towards it only to find it is at least four miles off . . . and it is not a 'Kaffir kraal' at all.

Instead, the light is coming from the window of a small hut by a coalmine. Whoever is in there will be a European, and most likely a Boer.

What can he do?

He must throw himself on their mercy, because to stay out here any longer will be to collapse.

His heart in his mouth – there is some chance he will be shot on sight – he bunches his fist and now knocks on the door.

There is a stirring within. Someone is coming!

The door is opened by 'a tall man hastily attired, with a pale face and a dark moustache',[58] peering at this young good-looking fellow who has knocked on his door.

Ignoring the absurdity of his own story, Churchill, in his Harrow-goes-to-Sandhurst accent, starts babbling how he is a Boer who has fallen off a train whilst skylarking.

The fellow looks at him, smiles, and bursts out, in perfect English: 'Thank God you have come here! It is the only house for twenty miles where you would not have been handed over.'[59]

The man is English!

John Howard. And I am jolly pleased to meet you, Mr Churchill. Do come inside and have a whisky.

'I felt like a drowning man pulled out of the water, and informed he has won the Derby,'[60] Churchill will recall.

And yet, as Howard advises while the young correspondent quaffs whisky and a leg of mutton, he is still not safe.

There will be so many Boers about in the morning it is important that Mr Howard has young Churchill well hidden before they return at dawn. You must follow me.

With haste, Howard leads him across a small yard into the mine itself. In an old and abandoned tunnel, Churchill must stay, sleeping on a pile of dirty litter – overrun with white rats with pink eyes.

You must wait here while I organise the next part of your journey.

And wait Churchill does for the next seven days, with the only high points being when Howard visits to bring him food, water and – *oh, the joy* – some of the Pretoria papers with accounts of his escape and the desperate attempts to recapture him. For the first time he realises just how big the news of his escape likely is in Britain. That is, if he really can get away.

As it happens, however, through a stroke of remarkable good fortune, this mine is not only attached to a railway with Delagoa Bay in Portuguese East Africa at the other end, but his host knows a fellow who is about to send a consignment of wool on it, a fellow who owes him a favour.

'These trucks were to be loaded at the mine's siding,' Churchill will recount. 'The bales could be so packed as to leave a small place in the centre of the truck in which I could be concealed.'[61]

Finally, the night comes when Howard leads him back to the cage, up into the fresh night air and away to a nearby railway siding where, in a carriage filled with wool bales, a small nook has been left, a space wide enough to lie in, high enough to sit up in.

'In this I took up my abode. Three or four hours later, when gleams of daylight had reached me through the interstices of my shelter and through chinks in the boards of the flooring of the truck, the noise of an approaching engine was heard. Then came the bumping and banging of coupling-up. And again, after a further pause, we started rumbling off on our journey into the unknown.'[62]

Two horribly uncomfortable days later, the train arrives at a station called Lourenço Marques, 30 miles across the Transvaal border in nominally neutral Portuguese East Africa.

The time has come. No sooner have the African workers begun unloading the wool bales, than Churchill steps forth, startling a couple of them. Whatever inclination they might have to raise the alarm is immediately quelled by his haughty glare – he is a white man and don't you forget it – and in short order he is in the yard and moving towards the gates where, just as planned, an Afrikander by the name of Burgener who is secretly supportive of the British cause, is waiting. Wordlessly, the two exchange glances and when Burgener heads off into town, the young correspondent follows him far enough behind that he is always comfortably in sight – until he stops before a particular residence, and gazes intently at the roof. And now Churchill sees it too!

'Blest vision! . . . I saw floating the gay colours of the Union Jack. It was the British Consulate.'[63]

Ah, if only the Consul's secretary could be as remotely excited.

'Be off,' says he dismissively. 'The Consul cannot see you to-day. Come to his office at nine to-morrow, if you want anything.'[64]

Churchill's response would shame Vesuvius after being denied entry to the Volcano Club. Indeed, he is so loud that within 30 seconds the Consul himself appears and asks the intruder his name.

Winston Churchill . . .

'From that moment every resource of hospitality and welcome was at my disposal. A hot bath, clean clothing, an excellent dinner, means of telegraphing – all I could want.'[65]

Now *that* is a little bit more like it.

That very evening he is on his way to Durban where, four days later upon arrival, he finds himself received as nothing less than a great hero of the British Empire, 'as if I had won a great victory. The harbour was decorated with flags. Bands and crowds thronged the quays. The Admiral, the General, the Mayor pressed on board to grasp my hand. I was nearly torn to pieces by enthusiastic kindness. Whirled along on the shoulders of the crowd, I was carried to the steps of the town hall, where nothing would content them but a speech, which after a becoming reluctance I was induced to deliver. Sheaves of telegrams from all parts of the world poured in upon me.'[66]

Before long Churchill is even ushered to the HQ of Sir Redvers Buller, where the notably downcast Commander-in-Chief questions him at length over what he had seen in the Transvaal, his impression of the strength of the Boers, their willingness to go on with the fight. Churchill tells all, at which point Buller congratulates.

'You have done very well. Is there anything we can do for you?'

Yes!

'I should like a commission in one of the irregular corps which were being improvised on all sides.'[67]

Well, then. As Churchill well knows it is not an easy request. In recent times so many military officers had been moonlighting as war correspondents – with Churchill in both India and Egypt the prime example – that the whole practice had been banned by the War Office. And yet . . . under these circumstances . . . given what young Churchill has accomplished, it is not altogether unreasonable that he be given a rank to move more freely through the army, to be able to order a recalcitrant Lieutenant to let him through to the front lines, rather than merely ask him. Could an exception be made? Buller stands, takes a couple of tours around the room before making his decision.

'All right,' he tells Churchill. 'You can have a commission in Bungo's regiment. You will have to do as much as you can for both jobs. But, you will get no pay for ours.'[68]

An added dimension to the celebrations for the escape of Churchill, as he soon finds out – and the reason Sir Redvers had looked a little like a beaten dog – is because it is the one bit of good news amid what has been an all but unmitigated disaster for the British forces. For Churchill's feat has come right in the middle of what will ever after be known as 'Black Week' for Britain, suffering three solid defeats starting with the Battle of Stormberg where the forces of General Gatacre had made no headway at all in recapturing Stormberg railway junction – crucial for the supply of his army – and had further suffered 135 casualties, with two big cannons lost to the Boers and no fewer than 700 British soldiers captured. The next day at Magersfontein the British suffered an even greater calamity, with no fewer than 1000 men killed and wounded. Just two days after that, at the Battle of Colenso, General Buller himself tries to break through to Ladysmith with a massive 17,000 British troops, only to be beaten back by a mere 5000 Transvaal Boers under the charismatic if ruthless leadership of General Louis Botha. Commandant Tom Kelly is among those at the battle, 'fighting with distinction' alongside another 600 from the Zoutpansberg Commando.

In all, for Black Week, Britain had suffered 2300 men killed or wounded by the Boers in just three battles.

Taking on the hard-riding, sharpshooting Boers in Boer territory with regular forces advancing in serried ranks is proving disastrous.

What Britain needs, urgently, is new leadership and more manpower.

After all, General Redvers Buller has become known as 'Reverse Buller', for his many defeats and retreats, and even the 'Ferryman of the Tugela'[69] for the number of times his army crossed the Tugela River to attack, only to have to cross back again in abject defeat.

In England, the War Cabinet decides to immediately dispatch England's hero, veteran of many a colonial war, Field Marshal Frederick Roberts VC, to take overall command of the war, while General Buller can be retained to oversee the operation in Natal.

Happily, tens of thousands more of their own soldiers – together with colonial troops who can shoot and ride every bit as well as the Boers – are on their way, and will surely be able to overwhelm the brutes.

CHAPTER THREE

BOBBING AND WEAVING

*That this meeting recognises ... that Australian troops have proved
themselves worthy equals of the heroic soldiers of the British
Empire, who are so sublimely fighting the battles of civil and religious liberty and devoutly prays that their lives may be spared and
that they may return with joy and victory to their native shores to
receive the blessings and thanks of their country. It is also resolved
that a copy of this resolution be forwarded to his excellency Field-
Marshal Lord Roberts, the Commander in Chief, South Africa.*[1]

Resolution passed by citizens of Queanbeyan, 26 February 1900

11 January 1900, Cape Town, Lord Roberts arrives

The great day has come.

After the setbacks of Mafeking, Kimberley and Ladysmith, after the
triple disasters of Black Week, the fact is that this rather dapper little
man in spick and span strides and glinting chest is nothing less than
a Godsend for Britain. For today is the day that Field Marshal Lord
Frederick Sleigh Roberts VC – known far and wide to the troops as
'Bobs' – arrives in Cape Town, aboard the steamer *Dunnottar Castle*.

Positions everyone.

When a man of this kind of military grandeur arrives – he had effectively started his military career by earning a Victoria Cross for his
bravery during the Indian Mutiny and risen from there to run the entire
British Army – one does not walk, one marches. One is never at ease,
one stands to attention. And if you must scratch your brow, do it while
snapping off a salute, just in case.

As it happens, the Field Marshal comes with a flood of 40,000 fresh
British Troopers – many of them mounted, ready to sort the Boers out
– and a distinct sense of purpose, of fulfilling a higher duty.

With the red complexion of one who is either a drinker or burned
that way by the sun – maybe both – the intelligence of his pale blue eyes
shines even a little brighter than it otherwise would. He is impressive on

first meeting and has such a fierce focus on whatever matter is at hand he tends to take those around with him. (And this, notwithstanding the fact that just weeks before arriving he had been given the news that his only son, the 27-year-old Freddy Roberts, had been killed at Colenso trying to recover guns lost to the Boers – the only solace being he had displayed such heroism he was to be awarded a posthumous VC to match the one held by his father.)

Typical of Lord Roberts, when only the best will do, his Chief-of-Staff is another British legend, Lord Herbert Kitchener, the hero of the recapture of Khartoum in 1898. Already the two have formulated a strong plan, which will start with taking the baton of leadership from General Buller.

'I shall handle Buller with all possible tenderness,'[2] Lord Roberts assures his staff, and will be as good as his word. But it is precisely because Buller has made such a hash of things that Roberts and Kitchener have so much to do.

Bolstered by the forces that have arrived with them, they intend to make judicious use of the swelling ranks to capture the twin Boer capitals of Bloemfontein and Pretoria. There are now an imposing 100,000 men, a number that almost doubles that of the Boers.

General Lord Kitchener intends to be much more hands-on in the general prosecution of the war. His administrative load as Chief-of-Staff notwithstanding, he intends to get out and about, doing what he does best, striking the enemy wherever he finds him, ruthlessly, brilliantly and with nary a thought for mercy. Ever and always, his own calculus for how good or bad a week his forces have had turns on the weekly 'bag' – in hunting parlance how many animals shot, but in Kitchener's context how many of the enemy have been, ideally, killed or wounded, and failing that, captured. This is a *war*, and he intends for Britain to be on the winning side, no matter what it takes.

For the moment, however, he has a great deal to do at HQ in Cape Town. The most important thing is to get things properly organised in order to have as many Troopers in the field as possible, well supplied enough to keep overwhelming the Boers for as long as possible.

13 January 1900, Adelaide, the Breaker at his best

With one flourish of his pen, it is done.

Breaker Morant has come a long way, first from England, down many dusty tracks of New South Wales, Queensland and lately South Australia, propping up many a bar in the same, and . . . it has to be said, filling out nearly as many prison bunks as marital beds of other men's wives. But now, so high are his debts, so pressing his creditors, so menacing the legal authorities, it seems the end of the road is nigh unless he signs this document.

A small parenthesis here. Seriously, the last two years, particularly, would have completely broken a man of less robust spirit. Pursued from pillar to post, scratching a living in the hot-as-blazes bush, he has still been dropping lines to all and sundry, and occasionally gets a mention in the local paper, 'Mr H Morant (The Breaker), is on his road home to Windsor',[3] but when he did turn up back in Sydney nothing could hide his shabby appearance, gaunt look and sheer . . . poverty. His poem of the time, 'A Departing Dirge', had captured his mood:

> *Saddle-gear and horses sold*
> *Fetched but scanty stock of gold*
> *Scanty!! Yet the whole damned lot*
> *Publicans and Flossies got.*
> *Since I in this country landed*
> *Ne'er before was I so 'stranded'.*[4]

Others, too, could see the walls were at last closing in on him.

'Free and easy back-block Australia stood such a creature for many years,' a long-time acquaintance would later note. 'It is a mark of his genius that the Hawkesbury, being had by him once, and knowing his character quite well, allowed itself to be had again in exactly the same way. But latterly he was getting old, his beery face and red nose were not so attractive; and going south his luck deserted him. Melbourne was too hot for him in a month; and Adelaide was his Waterloo. They did not appreciate him in the city of the churches.'[5]

Beating a retreat to a cattle station just outside Renmark, on the Murray River, he had stayed only long enough to rally a few locals to come with him back to Adelaide, this time to enlist. And so here he is with four fellow members of the Renmark Defence Rifle Club.

All of them are *still* a bit dusty from their wild all-night send off at Renmark, as it takes a week to fully recover from something like that, but now through their weary eyes so bleary, the relevant document is placed before them, and a pen proffered. The Breaker scans the document briefly.

> We the undersigned, do hereby solemnly, sincerely and truly swear
> that we will be faithful and bear true allegiance to Queen Victoria,

her heirs and successors according to law, and that we will faithfully and severally serve as members of the South Australian Volunteer Contingent enrolled for service in South Africa, and we hereby severally bind ourselves . . . until discharged to be subject to the provisions of the Army Act in force for the time being in Her Majesty's Army . . .[6]

You bloody beauty.

By so committing himself, he can hopefully start a new adventure free from those who would do him down, before getting a free trip back to England. Beyond everything else, he really has no choice. This is the one door left open to him.

He takes the pen and signs.

From now, Breaker Morant is part of the Second Contingent of the South Australian Mounted Rifles, and it does not take him long to get into the swing of things, as witness his swinging polo mallet, a week after joining, in the venerable grounds of the Adelaide Polo Club, at Victoria Park.

The whole scene is reminiscent of the famous Banjo Paterson poem . . .

> It was somewhere up the country in a land of rock and scrub,
> That they formed an institution called the Geebung Polo Club.
> They were long and wiry natives of the rugged mountainside,
> And the horse was never saddled that the Geebungs couldn't ride;
> But their style of playing polo was irregular and rash –
> They had mighty little science, but a mighty lot of dash:

For on this day, at the Adelaide Polo Club, Breaker Morant is at his very best – astride a polo pony, wheeling, dealing, breaking, cutting, swinging his mallet and . . . *scoring goals*. He is playing for a scratch team formed from Troopers of the Second Contingent, and of course they have called themselves the 'Geebungs' on the Breaker's completely false assurance that Banjo Paterson himself had based his famous poem on their, ahem, star player, pleased to meet you.

And as it happens, their opponents on this day, the mighty Adelaide polo team, really are dead ringers for the Cuff and Collar team of Banjo's conception:

> As a social institution 'twas a marvellous success,
> For the members were distinguished by exclusiveness and dress.

They had natty little ponies that were nice, and smooth,
  and sleek,
For their cultivated owners only rode 'em once a week.

And never have they seen anyone like the Breaker. For he really does have a way of moving on a horse that is poetry in motion on the ocean; less a man on a nag than a single unit, a streak of equine lightning across the turf, albeit capable of turning on a sixpence, picking the gap and getting into perfect position for the Breaker to swing again and . . . GOAL!

The Cuff and Collar team are shocked. Against a rough scratch team like this, they are struggling? Surely not a team of *their* pedigree?

Largely due to the Breaker's extraordinary pluck and luck, the Second Contingent's polo team is able to go blow for blow with their highly fancied opponents to make it 8–8, nearly four chukkas done, with just a minute to go, as the crowd roars in appreciation.

Ah, say it, Banjo, one more time for the road, what happened in the poem when there were so many dead and injured that 'the game was called a tie'?

Then the captain of the Geebungs raised him slowly from the
  ground,
Though his wounds were mostly mortal, yet he fiercely gazed
  around;
There was no one to oppose him – all the rest were in a trance,
So he scrambled on his pony for his last expiring chance,
For he meant to make an effort to get victory to his side;
So he struck at goal – and missed it – then he tumbled off
  and died.[7]

Not on this occasion, however.

For on this occasion, the Breaker swings, scores, and Adelaide's *Evening Journal* records a win for 'the Geebung boys' – 9–8! – while adding 'their style of playing polo was irregular and rash, They had mighty little science but a mighty lot of dash . . .'[8]

And none more dashing than the Breaker!

Did ya see him?

Did ya SEE him?

Never seen anything like it, I tell you!

The Breaker is the toast of the unit, and thereafter could also have likely won a gold medal for drinking, carousing and storytelling as off into the wild night they go.

It is the Breaker at his best.

Before departure, of course, the men must put on their uniforms, groom their horses till they shine, polish every tiny piece of brass on man and horse, and ride in columns of fours – oh, how grand they look, as they clip-clop through the streets, and the people cheer – to visit the South Australian Governor, Hallam, Lord Tennyson, at his summer residence of Marble Hill. Some of the Troopers are overawed at being in the Vice-Regal presence – and the son of Alfred, Lord Tennyson – but not the Breaker. No matter that he bears only the stripe of a Lance Corporal, he still keeps His Excellency entranced with his stories, and even more particularly the Governor's wife, Audrey, Lady Tennyson, who hangs on every word.

Did you know, Hallam, that Corporal Morant is the son of Admiral Sir George Digby Morant, and grew up at Brockenhurst Park! His Excellency did not know that, but is very pleased, and impressed, to hear it. It makes the Breaker something very close to his social equal, which is not easy to find in the colonies. Please, do go on, Lance Corporal Morant.

One of his comrades will remember the scene ever afterwards.

'No matter where you put Morant, he was always easy, natural, interesting, and amusing.'[9]

But hark now, as His Excellency addresses this fine body of men.

'My men,' he begins in his high clipped English accent, 'I am sure that you are feeling proud of going to fight alongside our British troops in South Africa, among the best in the world ... You are leaving your homes and all that is dearest to you, in order to join in a great work, that of freeing your kinsfolk from the tyranny of the Boer, of winning for them their civil, political, and religious liberties, and of overthrowing those mad Boers who have remorselessly broken their solemn pledges and treaties, and who have ruthlessly invaded our territories. Great Britain has called upon you to help her, and you have answered the call magnificently.'[10]

However resounding the three cheers for His Excellency, they are as nothing to the cheering of the South Australian people, a fortnight later, as the Second South Australian Contingent makes its way through the streets of Adelaide. For again those streets are packed with *roaring* crowds on both sides, as the men march down Lipson Street to board the *Surrey*, which awaits them at McLaren Wharf on the Port Adelaide River.

On this glorious summer's day, just like mother used to make, the clip-clop of the horses is completely drowned out by the cheering, the applause, the shouts of exultation . . . and that's just for the Breaker. For yes, though the South Australians turn out in force to farewell their mighty men, and do indeed express their adoration, there is no-one there more vigorously enthusiastic about the whole affair than the Breaker himself. For of course it really feels as if he knows half the people there – and *all* the pretty women – and he is laughing, cheering, carrying on with the best of them. So close does the crowd press that in places the mounted men must move in single file only, allowing the Breaker – who has given himself a slightly new name, Lance Corporal 'Henry Horland Morrant', to mark the occasion – to use both his left and right hands to furiously press the flesh with all those reaching out to him.

Of course when they arrive at McLaren Wharf on the Port Adelaide River, things get serious once more as they must load the horses, by use of cranes lifting slings placed under the protesting nags and swinging them over, which takes some doing given there are 120 of them, followed by their seven officers and 112 Troopers with all their kit.

Among them the reporters of *The South Australian Register* note down the particulars of all, and lap up every lie that the Breaker tells them, without question, all of which will be faithfully reported the next day:

> Morant, Harry Harbord, journalist, Renmark, son of Vice-Admiral Morant, of U.S. Club. London, S.W. Served in West Somerset Yeomanry and Cavalry. Born at Devon. England, December 9, 1870. Known as 'The Breaker,' of the Sydney 'Bulletin', for which paper he has written verse for ten years. He is a member of the Sydney Hunt Club. Single.[11]

No matter that in that brief passage there are six lies – his actual name is Edwin Henry Murrant; he is not a journalist, nor an Admiral's son; has not served with the West Somerset Yeomanry and Cavalry; was not born in 1870 and never a paid-up member of the Sydney Hunt Club – that is just the Breaker.

But finally all is completed and by late morning on 26 January 1900, with a couple of blasts on her whistle, the *Surrey* is on her way, bound for the Boer War.

Though just one of 119 officers and men on board, the Breaker's departure on the *Surrey* is remarked upon, for all that, with an old comrade, Will Ogilvie, a bush poet, who sends a poem to *The Bulletin* which is published soon afterwards.

> *Whatever they may say*
> *You're a fighter all the way*
> *(Goodbye Breaker)*
> *Let us put your faults behind*
> *Let us put your better qualities before*
> *For we're glad to hear you've signed*
> *And we'll drink the red night blind*
> *To another Bulldog fighter for the war!*

Not to be outdone, when *he* is the subject of the moment, the Breaker jots down his own bit of verse.

> *Here's the burden of my song;*
> *'Goodbye, old girl! Old chap, so long!'*
> *Hardest loss of all I find . . .*
> *To leave the good old horse behind.*
> *So-long, Cavalier!*[12]

Breaker Morant is not quite sure where he's going, what he can expect, but he sure knows what he is leaving behind – debts, disasters and too many destroyed relationships to count.

Beyond mere adventure – he is always up for that – the Boer War represents a chance to start again.

Across the Indian Ocean, now heading west, Morant, as he is always wont to do, continues to make friends quickly, inserting himself at the centre of every riotous storytelling session, reciting poetry he has penned and learned, bits of Byron and shots of Shelley. He is extremely popular with nearly all, while getting close to a few, and none more than a fellow by the rank and name of Trooper John Morrow, whose passion for, and knowledge of, horses rivals Morant's own. The two take their deck exercise together, walk their horses together, mess together, and talk late into the evening. Morrow believes all of the Breaker's fantastical tales without question, which is always a good start for the Englishman when forming bonds.

The stature of the Breaker continues to rise.

As there is a shipboard publication, *The Vedette*, there is even an outlet for the Breaker's literary talents as he contributes some verse. True, there is a major stink when *The Reveille*, which is the rival publication put out by the West Australians they have picked up on the way, makes some defamatory comments about . . . well, about the Breaker actually.

Strangely, Morant himself does not seem too troubled by it, perhaps due to the fact that he has generated such comments about himself for most of his adult life. But the Second South Australians are outraged on his behalf, and even threaten legal action against the publishers of *The Reveille*.[13] Yes, it all settles down, and the ship sails on regardless, leaving much the same churning waters in its wake as the Breaker always does.

Morant is, of course, just one of some 4000 soldiers from continental Australia now heading towards the Boer War, many of them still chafing in their new khaki tweed uniform complete with field service jacket, cord pants, field service hat, the leather leggings known as puttees, and black leather boots that they must shine to a mirror finish.

Aboard the *Euryalus*, there is Fred Booth, a 19-year-old grazier from Harkaway in Victoria, with the 2nd Victorian Mounted Rifles, who had served as a private soldier in the Victorian Mounted Rifles in the pre-war militia. A fellow with a quiet intensity, raised with the firm idea that England is 'the Motherland', he is heading to the Boer War with an enormous sense of duty, and privilege, to serve. As ever, he is never more than a cat's miaow away from his mate, Wally Clark, a plumber from Shepparton, and for both of them this feels like the beginning of an enormous adventure. They are young, they are free, they have fast horses and are good shots. So what better thing to do than take on the Boers in the service of Her Majesty?

Aboard the *Atlantian* there is a Tenterfield solicitor and local newspaper proprietor, Captain James Thomas, sticking close to his life-long friend and fellow Tenterfield man, Sergeant Major James Mitchell, and their unit, the NSW Bushmen. The Reverend James Green is from England – but migrated to New South Wales in 1889 – and is sailing as Wesleyan chaplain to the NSW Citizens' Bushmen. Lieutenant James Annat is something of a soldier of fortune, having already fought Boers, Zulus and Indians, and is shortly to board the *Duke of Portland* in Brisbane with his fellows of the 3rd Queensland Mounted Infantry. The distinguished lawyer Captain Robert William Lenehan – 14 stone of well-bred bonhomie, topped by a magnificent moustache – is already well on his way on the *Southern Cross* with the 1st NSW Mounted Rifles, whose numbers include Corporal Peter Joseph Handcock, a singularly undistinguished shoeing-smith from Bathurst, who is somewhere between a simple man, and a bit simple.

Individually and collectively, they all must engage in the rhythms and sometimes rigours of shipboard life for the three-to-four week passage.

Each morning from reveille at 6 am, the 30 or so men designated for this day must begin by mucking out the ship stables, taking two horses at a time out of their stalls before shovelling out their manure and throwing down lime, before feeding and watering each horse and walking them around on deck. Rinse and repeat three times a day.

The Troopers in turn are fed and watered in their own 'messes' for breakfast, lunch and dinner – with at least one meal washed down by a good portion of lime juice to prevent scurvy. (True, all too often whatever is eaten or drunk is soon thrown up over the side, as many men are desperately sea-sick, but this usually dissipates after a few days.)

The time between is filled with everything from sick parades, to physical instruction to drills for 'man overboard' and 'abandon ship' to stretcher and signalling drills – learning Morse code and how to both send it and read it, via cable, heliograph or flag.

The hardest thing though? Learning how to wash their own clothes.

'A good many of the men,' Fred Booth notes, 'never saw a wash-tub before.'[14]

Every Sunday morning there are religious services.

Now with God on their side more than ever before, they must get back to the decidedly ungodly work of getting better at killing their fellow man. To keep their battle readiness up, every day the men are given five rounds for their rifles and, after a biscuit box or the like is thrown off the stern, 12 men at a time are ordered by the Sergeant Major to fire at it in volleys until it moves out of easy range at about 700 yards. This is frequently followed by bayonet exercise where, again in groups of 12, they must compete against each other, thrusting and parrying as if fighting for their lives, albeit with bayonets sheathed in scabbards.

'We haven't much chance,' Fred Booth will report to his mother, 'as our division is all mounted men – the infantrymen have the best chance. They have learnt it previously.'[15] The idea is to learn how to wield your bayonet to do the maximum amount of slashing on the largest number of enemies, all while protecting yourself and your comrades, as the drill instructor's orders bark out: 'Fix bayonets!' 'Shoulder bayonets!' 'Port bayonets!' 'Charge bayonets!'

This then is shipboard life aboard the vigorous vessels carrying Australian troops across the Indian Ocean.

Carried on the waves of the Indian Ocean, thousands of Australians and New Zealanders are being lectured and drilled, prepared for the protocols and practices of the fights to come. These are the powers that the Army Act will have over each and every one of you men. Clean your rifles every day, men. Never salute a Sergeant, men, only officers.

The all but universal hope is that there will be enough war left by the time they arrive – if only they could go *faster* than the current 12 knots! – so they could take on real Boers, and prove themselves as *Soldiers of the Queen*, just as the song goes.

To do so they will need to be fit, meaning that every day includes mass 'extension exercises' up on deck and consisting of push-ups, star jumps, physical jerks and the like, before heading back downstairs to attend lectures on everything from the importance of personal hygiene to how to keep your rifle clean and how to shoulder arms. There are also lectures based on the principles of the British 'Red Book', the *Manual of Military Law*, covering such things as how to treat enemy combatants who have surrendered:

> The first principle of war is that armed forces, so long as they resist, may be destroyed by all legitimate means. The right of killing an armed man exists only so long as he resists; as soon as he submits he is entitled to be treated as a prisoner of war.[16]

The ships sail on, their occupants ideally getting ever better prepared for whatever challenges lie ahead.

On the joyous side, they sometimes see whales, and sometimes pass other troopships out there in the vast eternal blue of the Indian Ocean, always occasioning much cheering from both decks, and sometimes shouts of recognition.

On Fred Booth's ship they haul a grand piano up onto the deck to hold grand sing-alongs, helped along by the ship's band, composed of all those Troopers who have brought instruments with them and know how to play. At dinner, a note is passed from the Captain giving their current co-ordinates of latitude and longitude; how far they have travelled in the previous 24 hours, and how far they have to go to get to Cape Town.

Great excitement comes for all when they sight Africa for the first time, usually Natal.

'The coast is very mountainous,' Fred chronicles, 'and we noticed some very steep passes through the mountains. It looks just like an immense slice cut out of the mountain.'[17]

His eyes shine. He cannot wait to do his duty for Britain, the Mother Country he often refers to as 'home' in letters to Victoria, even though he has never been to England.

Breaker Morant feels the same. This war is a golden opportunity to rebuild his reputation, make some real money, get back to England and become a crucial cog in the military machine that both defends and expands the British Empire.

23 January 1900, Battle of Spion Kop, Buller tries to reverse the reverses

Yes, the incoming Commander-in-Chief Lord Roberts is starting to make his weight felt across the board by reorganising the army flowing into South Africa. The main line of advance will be towards the Boer capitals, and he will command it. Buller in Natal will play a subordinate role.

But still General Redvers Buller has a chance to redeem his reputation if he can just successfully lead the force to relieve Ladysmith – a siege that has captured the imagination of much of the English-speaking world, just as has the siege of Mafeking.

Despite the fact that General Buller and his forces have twice failed in this venture – being forced to . . . reverse – this time he tries a different tack, by deviating past the main Boer forces blocking them, and swinging left up the Tugela River, before approaching Ladysmith from the west.

It works, to a point, until the Boer forces regroup and dig in on the largest hill in the area, Spion Kop – which rises some 1400 feet above the surrounding plain, just 12 miles from the besieged town. Buller is confident that if they can storm its heights and take it from the Boers, they will be able to use its summit and their own superior artillery to devastate the surrounding enemy positions.

General Warren and the 11,000 men of his 5th Division are assigned the task: take Spion Kop. The plan is for the infantry to capture it first, at which point they can get the artillery on top too, and start blasting the Boer positions.

Late on the night of 23 January, Reverse Buller personally reverses a little to get to his HQ atop Mount Alice, some three miles away on the south side of the very Tugela River he has earned his nickname from. Meanwhile the Commanding Officer of 9th Brigade, Major General Edward Woodgate, moves forward 1700 of his men, with the lead element of 360 dismounted Mounted Infantry – many of them Australians – under the command of accomplished British officer, Lieutenant Colonel Alexander Thorneycroft. In the case of who goes there, all know tonight's password – 'Waterloo'.

So it is that in the wee hours, under the cover of both darkness and a heavy fog, two battalions of Lancasters and Thorneycroft's men push up to the higher reaches of the hill – overcoming a fleeing Boer picket with a bayonet charge as they do so.

Though the Boers leave behind one dead comrade, they are able to get away and warn their *broers*, '*Die Engelse is op die kop!*'[18]

And, good God!

They are indeed upon the summit. In the darkness and the fog, the English have reached the far crest of the flat hilltop, *die kop*, and in the morning will be looking down on the Boers. About a thousand Troopers strong now, though with only 20 picks and 20 shovels between them with which to dig in. They do their best, though the lack of picks is a problem that soon pales into insignificance, as they begin to realise this position isn't all it's cracked up to be.

From here, they can see that the plateau slopes gently, then *surprisingly* drops abruptly away, revealing that the summit is not the ideal defensive position. There is, however, a ledge further down which offers a more commanding location. Men are instantly sent scurrying towards this vantage point, only to come immediately under fire.[19]

SKETCH PLAN OF SPION KOP

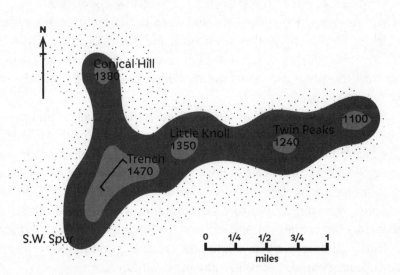

But it is just after 8 am, as the fog clears with the early morning sun, that the full horror of their situation is starkly revealed. In sum, the

British now find themselves to be sitting ducks, rather than the vengeful eagles they had hoped to be.

'From the right,' runs one contemporary account, 'the men in the trench and lower crest were enfiladed by the Little Knoll and the Twin Peaks; on their front and left they were rained on by bullet and shrapnel from Conical Hill, Green Hill.'[20]

•

'Die Engelse is op die kop!'[21]

As it happens, Deneys Reitz, with fellow Boer volunteers, is among those who hear the call. They are just having breakfast this morning some four miles away, when the message gets through.

Op die kop?

On the hill?

If that kopje falls, the whole Boer position, which extends for 20 miles upon the range of kopjes along the north bank of the Tugela River, will be compromised and they'd likely have to give up the siege of Ladysmith.

Quickly now! A Boer force is being assembled at the base of the hill to retake it, and their help is needed. Reitz and his companions are on their way within two minutes. Breakfast can wait. They are soon galloping towards Spion Kop arriving in time to see nearly a thousand Boer riflemen climbing the steep hill . . . and now under fire!

Oh, how courageous they are. For despite the fact that some drop under the English fire, all the rest push on. No man falters from his duty, and though many English soldiers are now rising to meet the final rush, still the Boers are up to the challenge and charge upwards ever upwards to the crest.

There are a few seconds of vicious hand-to-hand fighting and then it is the Boers who push over the crest, and out of view of those below!

Reitz and his men tether their horses and race up the hill in support, passing the dead and dying – both Afrikander and English – as they go. Shouting encouragement, a strange accent stands out. A Scotsman speaking Afrikaans, 27-year-old Jack Hindon, who deserted the British Army a decade before and settled in the Transvaal, waves the *Vierkleur*, the Transvaal flag, when he reaches the crest, and continues forth, with Reitz not far behind, frequently passing dead Boers.

Some are his life-long friends, but there is no time to grieve the dead, let alone stop and help the wounded. As he reaches the crest himself – gasping for breath with their rapid climb – it is clear that those heroes who had already cleared the summit had not got much further, because only 20 yards on, the British are dug in and pouring fire upon all the fresh arrivals! Most of them, like Hindon, have gone to ground to return the furious fusillade, though Reitz and several others follow the orders of the Boer officer in command and work their way around the crest of the hill to try and take the English from the flank, only to be forced back as the bullets fly and Boers fall like flies.

'During my absence about fifty [English] soldiers had run forward to surrender, but otherwise things were going none too well. We were sustaining heavy casualties from the English . . . immediately in front of us, and the men grew restive under the galling point-blank fire, a thing not to be wondered at, for the demoralising effect of Lee-Metford volleys at twenty yards must be experienced to be appreciated.'[22]

Whole heads explode, flesh fleeing from bone, ripped into ribbons by .303 bullets that need only travel inches before reaching their quarry.

•

In the thick of the action, as ever, is the now widely celebrated 'Lieutenant' Winston Churchill. On this day, still believing that he has a rendezvous with destiny rather than an appointment with disappointment, he keeps pushing towards the top of the hill in the mid-afternoon, where he realises just how grave the situation is.

'The severity of the action was evident,' he will recount. 'Streams of wounded, some carried . . . trickled, even flowed down the hill, at the foot of which two [British] hospital villages of tents and wagons were rapidly growing.'[23]

Atop the hill, Private Frank Barnes from Ballarat, a member of Thorneycroft's Mounted Infantry – which is one third made up of Australians – watches closely, and will recount: 'It was a horrid sight to see our poor fellows trying to crawl out of the firing line after being shot, only to be wounded again, or else shot dead. One had his face blown away by a shell. Another was shot in the neck and when he called for a drink he could not swallow it as the water ran out of the wound. I hope I shall not see the like again.'[24]

Standing sentinel, still and silent as a statue, General Edward Woodgate is observing one of the key markers of the true British military man – entirely ignoring whizzing bullets and scything shrapnel, to the despair of his senior staff who beg him to take cover – only to take a bullet to the head. The 54-year-old with the best walrus moustache in the British Army cries out and slumps to the ground bleeding badly, as medics rush forward. He seems to be dead, and Colonel Alexander Thorneycroft, the 41-year-old former High Sheriff of Staffordshire, takes command. So intense is the fire upon them now, and so demoralising has been the fall of General Woodgate, that some of the English now raise their hands in surrender, and begin to walk across the flat-topped hill towards the Boers, who know they have this battle won, only . . .

Only to see a man as enormous as he is apoplectic run out and start shouting in English.

It is Colonel Thorneycroft himself and he roars at the Boer commander, even as bullets whistle by and shells land.

'I'm in command here! Take your men back to hell, sir, I allow no surrender!'[25]

Somehow or other, Colonel Thorneycroft is even more terrifying than the Boers, and they turn.

'Follow me!' Thorneycroft commands his own men who'd been about to surrender – he will deal with them later – and leads them back to the trenches.

An hour later, the flood of British stretchers coming down the hill is stronger than ever, as the Boers have only intensified their fire. One of those stretchers coming down, brushing by Churchill, bears the still bleeding form of General Woodgate. It will be touch and go whether he can survive.

The stretcher-bearer taking the lead as ever, is the very man who has set up the Natal Indian Ambulance Corps, with the sole aim of saving as many human lives as possible.

He, too, in his own way, believes in his own star, in his own destiny, so that his fellows have long remarked at his total lack of fear of being bit by bullets as he heads out onto raging battlefields to drag the wounded to safety.

Mahatma Gandhi heads on down the hill, Winston Churchill pushes on up to the top, passing the Gujarati man somewhere along the track, and stays on that battlefield – measuring about 200 yards by 300 yards – for the better part of the day.[26]

'Corpses lay here and there,' the Englishman will recount. 'Many of the wounds were of a horrible nature. The splinters and fragments of the shells had torn and mutilated them. The shallow trenches were choked with dead and wounded.'[27]

For while the bullets continue to miss Churchill – apart from neatly slicing the jaunty feather he keeps in his cap – they miss few of the other Troopers and the men continue to be cut down. At one point Churchill finds Colonel Thorneycroft sitting on the ground 'surrounded by the remnants of the regiment he had raised, who had fought for him like lions and followed him like dogs'.[28]

•

And so the battle atop Spion Kop continues to rage with a bitter and bloody stalemate ensuing, as both sides refuse to cede despite suffering terrible losses.

'The sun became hotter and hotter,' Reitz will ruefully recount, 'and we had neither food nor water. Around us lay scores of dead and wounded men . . . We were hungry, thirsty and tired; around us were the dead men covered with swarms of flies attracted by the smell of blood . . . When at last the sun set, I do not think there were sixty men left on the ledge.'[29]

It is only in the silent watch of the night that the Boer commanding officer allows his men to withdraw, on the reckoning that with just two dozen of them holding the summit, they could not possibly hold on when the British renewed their assault. In all likelihood there will be a company of English on their way to attack them right now in the night, and they will be too weakened to hold on.

'We fully believed,' Reitz will recount, 'that the morning would see them streaming through the breach to the relief of Ladysmith, and the rolling up of all our Tugela line.'[30]

•

It is a tough decision, but Colonel Thorneycroft believes he has no choice. They have fought the good fight throughout the day, and held on against all odds. But having exhausted their rations and water while running out of ammunition, surrounded by the dead and dying, and keenly aware that if dawn the next day still finds them here they will only face another day's barrage of shattering shells – and they still don't have any tools to dig themselves in deeper – he gives the orders. Withdraw.

Yes, technically he does not have the authority to give such an order. But when the note he had sent back requesting that authority had received no reply, it is clear the life-and-death decision for himself and his men must be taken on the facts he knows. *Withdraw.*

And so they do, slipping away in the night, dragging their wounded with them.

•

As Reitz and his companions reach the bottom of the hill, all is in chaos, as wagons are being packed with the entire Carolina Commando getting ready to retire. The strong view is that Spion Kop has been lost, and there is no alternative but to abandon it, and get out – *quickly*. There is a real mood of panic. *Die Engelse* must be near!

And yet, just as the first of the wagons are starting to leave, a man on a horse gallops among them, and forcefully shouts at them to *hou op!* – stop! He is well dressed for a formal occasion, less so for a war. Collared shirt, clean jacket, crisp tie, this man is not your ordinary burgher. His voice mimics his dress as he speaks with an angry authority unusual to the breed of burgher raised on the virtues of the Bible.

It is the new Commandant-General Louis Botha, who has just taken over from the seriously ill Piet Joubert, who fell from his horse in Natal and still hasn't recovered fully.

The words pour out of Botha, his eyes flashing his anger: 'The shame will be on you if you desert your posts in this hour of danger!'[31]

You must stay. We must make our stand here and *skiet die Engelse*, shoot the English!

A rough kind of calm returns in the manner of a storm suddenly losing its fury.

Morale is lifted.

The wagons are unloaded, and the men of the Carolina Commando return to their positions on either side of Spion Kop. It might be lost, but they will just have to dig in and hold their positions regardless.

Louis Botha rides off, and spends the rest of the night, as Deneys Reitz will recount, 'riding from commando to commando exhorting and threatening, until he persuaded the men to return to the line'.[32]

What the morning will bring, no-one is sure. But they are going to make a stand.

•

God has surely smiled upon them.

While the Boers have been bracing themselves for the fire from on high that will shortly burst upon them – they have been digging in through what remained of the night – in fact, things turn out quite differently! For now, on the summit, they suddenly see two Boers, waving their distinctive broad-brimmed hats!

The British have gone! The summit of Spion Kop is all ours if you come quickly! And so the Boers do, charging up once more, and digging in once more. The two Boers had been searching for a missing brother, and had continued climbing in the night looking for him, only to get to the summit and find it abandoned.

'The English were gone,' Deneys Reitz would recount, 'and the hill was still ours.'[33]

•

The full ramifications of the British disaster become apparent. Not only have they failed to take Spion Kop, or advance their position in any way, but they have suffered no fewer than 243 fatalities with just over a thousand more wounded – and many more of the latter would have died had it not been for the extraordinary selfless work of Gandhi and his fellow Indians of the Natal Ambulance Corps. (The Boers casualties are about a quarter as many.)

The day after the battle is over, Reuters reporter Vere Stent visits Spion Kop. The previous day he had been stunned to see the grace and courage of the Natal Indian Ambulance Corps in action, how they moved in mule trains carrying waterbags up the slopes to provide succour to the wounded and nary blinked under fire, and he would later reminisce:

> The galling rifle-fire, which heralded their arrival on the top, did not deter the strange looking cavalcade, which moved slowly forward, and as an Indian fell, another quietly stepped forward to fill the vacant place. It was on such occasions the Indians proved their fortitude, and the one with the greatest fortitude was the subject of this sketch, Mahatma Gandhi. After a night's work, which had shattered men with much bigger frames I came across Gandhi in the early morning sitting by the roadside – eating a regulation Army biscuit. Every man in Buller's force was dull and depressed, and damnation was heartily invoked on everything. But Gandhi was stoical in his bearing, cheerful, and confident in his conversation, and had a kindly eye.[34]

The result, however, remains unchanged. Not just a British defeat, and not merely a bitter one. Most of all, such an overwhelming result for the enemy has left them *humiliated*.

The whole episode confirms Churchill's view in a letter sent to his family a fortnight earlier, 'Buller started out full of determination to do or die but his courage soon ebbed and we stood still and watched while one poor wretched brigade was pounded and hammered and we were not allowed to help them. I cannot begin to criticise for I would never stop. If there was anyone to take Buller's place I would cut and slash – but there is no well-known General who is as big a man as he is and we must back him for all he is worth – which at this moment is very little . . .' He went on, '. . . the horrible part of it all is that Ladysmith will probably fall and all our brave friends be led off to captivity and shame.'[35]

What is urgently needed, the British High Command knows, is more colonials, men who know how to take on the Boers at their own game, men who can live in the saddle, off the land, and by the seat of their pants when necessary – men who can ride through the night, shoot through the day and show no mercy.

As the British war correspondents must sorrowfully record, Spion Kop is one of the most cataclysmic defeats inflicted on British troops since the Crimean War, nearly half a century earlier. It is made all the worse by the fact that, the morning after the battle, Boers go to the effort of taking photographs of the massed British dead on the battlefield – photos which will shortly be published all over the world.

•

It is less a formal policy than an unofficial practice but from now, four months into the war, whenever British forces determine that local Boer Commandos who attack them have benefited from local Boer homesteads, or homesteads have concealed Boer train wreckers, quick action is taken. Those homesteads are burned down, as are their stables, while their crops are destroyed and their animals seized to feed the British Army. It is done as revenge, as ensuring that the same Boer farmers can't cause the loss of British lives again, and as a spectre to others – you co-operate with the Commandos at your peril.

For a few days around the turn of the year, the Boer farmer Andries Lubbe allows the local Commando to use his farm in the western half of Orange Free State for training purposes. On 9 January the British forces quickly slip across the border to burn his house and stables to the ground, before burning his brother-in-law's homestead for good measure and then just as quickly returning to Cape Colony.

Let this be a warning to you all.

In these first weeks of 1900 it is not, *ipso facto*, an automatic response, but it certainly occurs frequently enough that by 3 February 1900, Transvaal's President Kruger and President Martinus Steyn of Orange Free State formally write to Lord Roberts, calling his attention to 'the burning and blowing up of farmhouses and of the devastation to farms and of goods therein, whereby unprotected women and children are deprived of food and cover'.[36]

Lord Roberts replies and denies, insisting this has not occurred and that, furthermore, it is his intention to prosecute the war with 'as little injury as possible to peaceable inhabitants and private property'.[37]

The burning happens regardless.

And yet the Boers take the same approach – albeit with even *less* mercy. 'If you don't join the Republicans,' one disaffected Boer will record the common experience, 'you are made prisoner, your wife and children turned out homeless, your farm destroyed . . . [so] before you see your wife and family left starving and God knows what else, you join them.'[38]

You are with us, or you are agin us. Either way, you risk your farm burning before your eyes.

9 February 1900, Slingersfontein, the Boers close in

It has taken some doing over the last 10 weeks but, at least for the moment, the British forces have managed to stop the Boer incursion around Colesberg, by placing 5000 Troopers in an arc to contain them – on the southern-most tip of which lies the British camp of Slingersfontein.

In an effort to ascertain the enemy's strength and activity to the east of this position, on this morning 37 men of the West Australian Mounted Infantry, together with a similar number of Inniskilling Dragoons, are sent out on patrol to report back what they see.

Moving out at 4 am on this Friday, 9 February, the men under Major Hatherley Moor spread out from each other a little, linearly. It is not necessarily that they expect to be shot at, but against the possibility of an ambush it is as well not to present a concentrated target. Within an hour or so they are approaching a typical Boer white-stone farmhouse – 'five or six rooms, a small orchard, surrounded by rough stone walls from three feet six to four feet in height, and about two feet thick, a small cluster of Native huts, and a kraal for cattle, made of rough, heavy stones, topped by cakes of sun-baked manure, stored by the farmers for fuel'[39] – when it happens.

On the right flank, Major George Hatherley Moor of the West Australian Mounted Infantry is with three officers. It is just on 6 am, when one of the Troopers suddenly sees a white horse on the hills to the right – a creature from a fairy tale that shall soon turn grim – with, he thinks, a Boer astride?

Bringing the glasses to bear, they can now see them clearly: 'a large line of the enemy moving in a direction towards the camp'.[40]

The shock is rapid. For if they can see the Boers, there is no doubt that the Boers will soon see them . . .

'Retire to camp!'[41] comes the order from the English commanding officer, Captain Haig. This is a threat. That many Boers, hundreds of them, moving towards the camp at Colesberg clearly presages an attack, and their comrades will need to be warned. It is urgent, thus, that they get away and, if at all possible, hold the Boers up. Barely is the order to retire to camp out of his mouth, however, before they all come under a very brisk fire from the hilltops.

Ambush! Suddenly, these mounted forces of the British Army find themselves under attack from all sides, as the Boers close in.

Volleys of shots ring out, again and again and again, as some of the Inniskilling Dragoons tumble to their deaths. Among the West Australian Mounted Infantry, two horses go down. Trooper James Ansell gallops up to one man and calls out, 'Hop on the back, mate!'[42] reaching down to pull him up in one smooth action, just as happens with the other horse-less Trooper, and they are soon on their way, as a mad retreat begins.

No matter, in his notably rounded vowels, the Commanding Officer of the Inniskilling Dragoons, Captain Haig, orders Major Moor and his West Australians to hold yonder kopje against the flood of Boers now coming on, to allow the rest of the force to get back to camp some five miles away and save themselves.

So heavy and loud is the fire now, with the crack of rifles followed by spurts of dust on the veldt, and the West Australians spread so far apart – as they have all been trained to spread to 'open formation' once under fire, so as to make a more difficult target – that Major Moor cannot make his orders heard.

All Moor can do, thus, is make straight for the top of the designated kopje, while signalling for his men to follow him, which is no easy thing, but they manage.

'Whenever an Australian found himself in a tight place he simply dug his spurs into his horse's flanks,' one admiring South Australian war correspondent will note, 'lifted his rifle, and blazed into the ranks of the foe. If his horse was shot dead under him he coo-eed to his mates, and kept his rifle busy, and every time the coo-ee rang out over the whispering veldt the Australians turned in their saddles, and riding as the men from the South-land can ride, they dashed to the rescue.'[43]

One of those with his horse shot from under him is Major Moor himself, and he starts to run for the kopje, presenting an easy target for the Boers to shoot down, only to have the West Australian Lieutenant Darling swoop in, and allow him to jump up behind. Together, as the bullets ping all around, they drive their heels into their valiant steed and continue to make for the kopje with all the others, their bodies slung as low as they can manage on their horse's neck, trying to shield themselves as much as possible from the Boer fire. To a man, all the troops are experienced horsemen and ride as if born in the saddle. The end result is that the valiant group of West Australians do 'not leave a single man in the hands of the enemy'.[44]

By the time the West Australians get to the top of the hill, they are a force 27 strong, and Major Moor instantly barks out orders.

'Lieutenant Darling, take four men, and hold that small rise to the left to prevent the enemy outflanking our position. You men, gather up our horses and take them to the back of the hill, to ensure our means of escape. The rest of you, all hands, build stone heaps.'[45]

They get to grips.

As it happens this particular kopje is superbly situated on the floor of this narrow valley that, if they can hold it, they really will be able to provide great covering fire and allow the Inniskillings to get away, get back to camp, and warn the men there of the 400 Boers heading their way.

If, that is, the bloody Boers can get past the Australians.

•

Coming hard after the fleeing forces of the English, the pursuing Boers can barely believe their luck. The English are clearly beaten and the Boer Commandant has no hesitation in giving the order: 'Press on and cut them to pieces.'[46]

Given that there appears to be nothing between them and victory, they try to do exactly that, having the satisfaction of seeing the English scurry before them, at least those who the Boers have not already cut down with shots at full flight – which is many.

But . . . what now? Just up ahead, some of the retreating forces are making for a notably high kopje, and are now firing back at them? Are they mad? We Boers are 400 strong, and these are how many? Two or three dozen at most?

What can they be thinking? Nevertheless the fire now coming from the landmark is troublesome, starting to cut into the Boer ranks, as this particular kopje is so big and so central to this narrow valley that it is the key to the position.

Who are these men starting to pick them off?

'Our spies told us it was held by Australians . . .' one of the Boers will recount. 'If we got that kopje there was nothing on earth to stop us. We laughed when we saw that only about twenty Australians remained. There were about 400 of us, all picked men . . . we sprang up eagerly and dashed forward.'[47]

•

Here they come!

Like a bunch of demonic Jack-in-the-boxes, the West Australians rise above their rock walls for just the instant necessary to bring their .303s to their shoulders, take aim at the rising Boers, and fire off a round – often to be rewarded by a groan and the barest sense of a thump in the distance as a body hits the ground. Again and again and again! Up, aim, fire! And they are careful to do it at irregular intervals, and at different spots behind the wall of rocks, so the Boers below will be able to make no predictions as to which of the many dangerous Jack-in-the-boxes before them will rise when. To the stunned amazement of the attackers they are not faced by the mad panic and retreat they had expected – the panic they had benefited from when chasing English soldiers.

'We did not know the Australians then,' the Boer will recount. 'We do now.'[48]

•

Atop the kopje, the Australians are all too aware they are fighting for their lives, the point made graphically when in the mid-morning Lieutenant Geoff Hensman lifts his head at the wrong moment and is badly hit. With enormous bravery, Corporal Michael Conway crawls forward to try to drag the respected officer back to cover, only to be shockingly hit himself, with a good part of his head blown off by a Boer bullet. He slumps, dead. In such a situation it would be madness for anyone else to go out there, but that is exactly what Private Alexander Krygger does!

Even though bullets are bringing up spurts of dust all around him, and chipping fragments off rocks which cut the skin, he is able to grab one rock, and then another, and then still another, and place them in a wall to provide the tiniest measure of protection for the grievously wounded men and himself. Seeing what he is doing, the other West Australians throw rocks his way so he can build it up further and he soon has a very low wall built, against which the Boer bullets bounce uselessly. Tragically, such courage as he has displayed cannot save Conway, who dies very quickly, but as Krygger binds another's wounds with a pair of puttees, Lieutenant Hensman is holding on! The young man's bravado alone lifts the others as they continue to pour fire down on the bloody Boers – who still can't believe what they are up against.

•

Desperate now, following the orders of the Commandant, the Boers ready themselves to make a concerted rush on the Australian positions, on the reckoning that they can't all be shot at once and just the vision of so many charging men will make the *verdoem* Australians waver and break. And they will further be helped by the fact that this time they have brought their Boer artillery forward and are raining down shells on the Australian positions. On the Commandant's signal, the shelling will stop, and the men will charge.

On my count . . . *een* . . . *twee* . . . *drie* . . . NOW.

As one, the brave Boers charge up the hill. And indeed, it really is not possible for the West Australians to get them all. But they do get . . . enough.

'We could not face their fire,' the Boer survivor will recount. 'To move upright to cross a dozen yards meant certain death and many a Boer wife was widowed and many a child left fatherless by those silent men who held the heights above us. They did not cheer as we came onward. They did not play wild music: they only clung close as climbing weeds to the rocks and shot as we never saw men shoot before, and never hope to see men shoot again.'[49]

Still, there have been so many Boers rushing forward that they have indeed succeeded in getting a pod of men within 10 yards of both the Australians on top, and those defending the small rise on the left flank. Might one last rush do it?

It is at this point that both Major Moor and Lieutenant Darling give their orders: 'Fix bayonets.'[50]

Just below, the Boer defenders can see the bayonets gleaming in the sunshine above the rocky parapets, waving, *beckoning* them to keep coming.

Now, do you want to rush us, take us on? Who wants it first?

The short answer is: none of them.

'I consider,' Major Moor will chronicle, 'that our fixing bayonets kept [the Boers within ten yards of us], in check.'[51]

(For one thing, the Boers do not use bayonets themselves. Tight physical confrontations of this nature are not their way of fighting.)

What *now* for the Boers? Well, if they must bring yet more big guns forward and simply blast the top of the hill apart, then so be it. The order is given for yet more guns to come forward, with shells. And yet . . . such brave men! Before raining down hell upon them, the Boer Commandant 'admiring those brave few who would not budge before us in spite of our numbers, sent an officer to them to ask them to surrender promising them all the honours of war'.[52]

Now mid-afternoon, it is a West Australian Sergeant who calls back, making reply for them all: 'Aye, we will hold up our hands, but when we do, by God, you'll find bayonets in 'em. Go back and tell your commandant that *Australia's* here to stay.'[53]

And stay they do. Yes, they continue to take heat with all of Privates France, Ansell and Baird suffering wounds of various seriousness, but they are holding on.

So be it.

Can they withstand the big guns?

Let the serious shelling commence. In short order, the top of the hill becomes the top of hell, an inferno of exploding shells, dust, smoke, flying dirt and shattered rocks. Again, however, it is the big rocks that provide the shelter the Australians need and it is really only direct hits that do real damage – and there are few of them.

The West Australians simply will not move.

'We shelled them all along their scattered line,' the Boer will recount, 'and tried to rush them under cover of the artillery fire but they only held their nests with stouter hearts, and shot the straighter when the fire was hottest and we could do not anything but lie there and swear at them, though we admired them for their stubborn pluck. They were but twenty men and we were four hundred.'[54]

And their spirits seem remarkably high.

'Come and take us if you can!'[55] one Australian voice roars at them.

Not that the Australians don't have some serious problems. In the late afternoon, Lieutenant Darling – who, with horse-holders and the wounded, has in fact 32 men – is running short of ammunition and has to send runners to get more rounds from the men holding the horses. It is done quickly and their careful, devastating fire continues.

It is only when night falls that Moor even *thinks* of retreat. Even now, it goes against the grain, but as they have succeeded in allowing the English soldiers to get away, and with six wounded men needing medical attention, Moor knows it is the right thing to do as he and his men slip away. They proceed on the one route determined by the scouts that the Boers have not blocked.

'We all rushed down the hill,' he will recount, 'and after seeing every man mount we all galloped off as hard as we could. I consider, that we were able to hold our own against such odds owing to that splendid way in which Lieut. Darling and our men held our left flank, [Lieutenant] Hensman, until put out of action, and Private A. Krygger both doing splendid work, the latter especially. We fixed bayonets twice – and I know no single man of us would have surrendered, as we thought we were to hold that hill to the last.'[56]

Under the circumstances, the shattered, battered Boers might be forgiven for letting them go – who wants to face that for another day? It is only at dawn when the Boers finally gain the summit to see the uniforms of the three dead left behind – there had been no opportunity to bury them, and they trusted the Boers to do the right thing – that they see the mortal proof they had been up against *Australians.*

There is nothing for the Boers to do but indeed bury their own and the enemy's dead, and get their own wounded soldiers the medical attention they need.

•

A few days after the battle, an Australian prisoner, war correspondent Alfred Hales, who had been taken to a Boer hospital to help with his recovery, is sitting miserably in the garden when approached by a cheery Boer nurse, accompanied by three newly wounded Boers.

'I have brought some Boers who know something of your countrymen, Mr. Australian,' she says, clearly in an effort to cheer him up. 'I thought you would be glad to hear all about them.'

'By Jove! Yes, nurse. If I were not a married man, I should try to thank you gracefully.'

'Oh, yees, oh, yees,' she answers, with a laugh, 'that is all right. You say those pretty things; then, when you go away from here, you tell your wife, and you write in your papers we Boer girls are fat old things, who never use soap and water. All the *Rooi Baatjes* do that.'

And off she goes, leaving behind the wounded Boers and – soon enough – half-a-dozen wounded 'Tommies', English soldiers, who gather round as the Boers tell their story. It is about a recent action up near Slingersfontein.

'There was one big kopje that was the very key of the position.'

This, as it turned out, was the one occupied by the Australians.

'If we once got that kopje there was nothing on earth could stop us. We could pass on and sweep around the retiring foe, and wipe them off the earth, as a child wipes dirt from its hands, and we laughed when we saw that only about twenty Australians had been left to guard the kopje.'

But now the shock!

'Scarcely had we risen to our feet when they loosed their rifles on us, and not a shot was wasted. They did not fire, as regular soldiers nearly always do, volley after volley, straight in front of them, but every one picked his man, and shot to kill. They fired like lightning, too, never dwelling on the trigger, yet never wildly wasting lead, and all around us our best and boldest dropped, until we dared not face them. We dropped to cover, and tried to pick them off, but they were cool and watchful, throwing no chance away. We tried to crawl from rock to rock to hem them in, but they, holding their fire until our burghers moved, plugged us with lead, until we dared not stir a step ahead; and all the time the British troops, with all their convoy, were slowly, but safely, falling back through the kopjes, where we had hoped to hem them in. We gnawed our beards and cursed those fellows who had played our game as we thought no living men could play it.'[57]

Hales listens, completely transfixed.

'I felt my face flush with pride ...' he will recount, 'for the story concerned men ... who grew from childhood to manhood where the silver sentinel stars form the cross in the rich blue midnight sky ... At that moment, with British "Tommies" sprawling on the grass at my feet, and the Boer farmers grouped amongst them, I would sooner have called myself an Australian commoner than the son of any peer in any other land under high heaven.'[58]

And he is far from the only one deeply impressed.

The British High Command is particularly admiring; they have confirmation that these are just the kind of men they need to bring the Boers to heel.

These fellows from the Australian colonies are simply outstanding, and the best thing for the moment will be to split them up among the British units as they continue to arrive, so they can help teach the traditional British soldiers how better to live off the land, fire from the saddle, and keep going!

And the best news is that plenty of reinforcements are on the way, coming from all six colonies.

•

The sons of the British Empire continue to answer the call. Every day brings ever more ships to Cape Town. The place is now a hive of activity which might have turned into chaos, if not for the extraordinary organisational capacity of the British race.

'The very first impression you get,' the Reverend James Green notes when his own ship arrives from Sydney, 'is an enlarged conception of the power of Britain. Here are gathered fleets of great four-masted ocean tramps and mail liners side by side. You see at one wharf our old friend the *Austral*. Look around! There is an Atlantic White Star liner, twice as big. The Clan line, the Castle line, the Dominion line, the Royal Mail line, the P. and O. line, the "saints" – *St. Dunstan* and *St. Andrew*, ride at anchor with the "mores" – *Prinsmore* and *Maplemore*, and so on, rank upon rank, all round the bay and every dock full. The cry is "still they come," for three or four times each day another huge transport steams quietly into the bay lined with troops and loaded with guns, stores and deck upon deck of horses or mules. No other power in the world could do it.'[59]

And once ashore things are even more impressive, as you see engines on the dock rails pulling nine wagons at a time, all of them fully loaded with war matériel, even as teams of horses and mules at work driven by Cape 'boys' haul lesser loads to supply depots, directed by quietly efficient transport officers who can call on *centuries* of experience in harnessing local populations for the greater glory and power of the British Empire.

'You can see naval officers trotting round the docks on polo ponies managing things in vigorous style,' Green documents. 'At every dock and wharf there are armed sentries, and things are managed in a strict military way, no one passing unless he wears the Queen's uniform or is on business. Then you see the ability of the Briton born to rule.'[60]

It is also true, mind, that some of the British soldiers sniff with disdain at the very sight of the 'Orrrr'stralians', but that is just the way of these things. For the colonials, of course – everyone knows – are uncouth, unwashed and uneducated. And there is no-one worse in these regards than the Australians. Give them New Zealanders, Canadians or even *Indians*, any day.

For their part, most of the said colonial Australians don't care and are just excited to be there.

'It is the most wonderful sight I ever saw to see the bay full of shipping,' Fred Booth writes to his mother. 'The bay is full of transports – about 50 large steamers and as many more sailors.'[61]

And the best thing of all?

'We have just heard that Ladysmith and Kimberley have not yet been relieved. We are going to camp tonight and then on to Kimberley.'[62]

In short, there is still enough of this war left for them to fight in!

CHAPTER FOUR

BESIEGED

Eat, drink, and be merry, because to-morrow we die.

George Whyte-Melville, Breaker Morant's favourite
writer, 'The Object of a Life', 1876

Mid-February 1900, Battle of Paardeberg, Modder River, Orange Free State

We don't want to fight but by Jingo if we do, the beloved song penned 20 years earlier runs, *we've got the ships, we've got the men, we've got the money too . . .*

All of which describes, as it happens, the situation for Lord Roberts as the ships have brought the men he wants – no fewer than 80,000 soldiers – together with a staggering £20 million worth of munitions. The difference is, with 'Reverse' Buller now demoted to commanding only in Natal, he and his Chief-of-Staff General Lord Kitchener do want to fight as soon as possible. It all means that on 11 February 1900 his prime troops, now five divisions strong and massed at Hopetown on the Orange River, prepare to push north along the railway line. After the besieged town of Kimberley is relieved, they will then turn east to move on the belligerent Boers' Orange Free State capital of Bloemfontein, before turning north again to the Transvaal's capital, Pretoria. At that point, with the two Boer capitals secured, the war will hopefully be over.

It will be a two-pronged attack on Bloemfontein, with this prong alone – coming from the west – boasting no fewer than 40,000 Soldiers of the Queen, of whom 8000 are mounted, all of them supported by 2000 wagons and 25,000 horses, mule and oxen.

With a wave of Roberts' hand, the cavalcade begins, trampling the barbed-wire fence which marks the border of Orange Free State, and then continuing over the dusty veldt from there.

'Here at long last was the Imperial steamroller,' one historian will describe it, 'a whole army corps in motion across the sand, under the canopies of dust and amid the yells of the African drivers, the wheep of long whips, the squealing of the mules. Here too was . . . Kitchener, chief of staff to the Field Marshal, Lord Roberts. There might be less glamour about this great army than its predecessors in imperial history. There were no flags or drums as the men pushed their way through the strands of barbed wire that marked the Free State frontier.'[1]

At the pointy end of this throng – leading the charge – are the men of General John French's 'flying column' of 5000 Troopers who will be detached from the main thrust on Bloemfontein to relieve Kimberley, and among them are 500 Troopers of the Queensland Mounted Infantry and the NSW Lancers, together with the intrepid war correspondent, Banjo Paterson, who is stunned at the sheer *size* of the operation. In the company of another correspondent, it takes no less than two hours as – eager to get somewhere near the front, where the action is likely to be – they go from one bullock train to the next. Nearing the front at last they are hailed by a heavily decorated Staff Captain of a certain brigade, with the ribbon of a Victoria Cross sewn into his uniform.

Say, fellows, you haven't seen hundreds of supply-wagons for a certain brigade, have you?

'How many wagons are there?'[2]

'There ought to be a few miles of it,' he replies blithely. 'There are three thousand five hundred mules, besides a lot of bullock-wagons.'

Yes, Field Marshal Roberts' column is *that* big.

'This trifling item,' Banjo recounts, 'was absolutely lost and swallowed up in the mass of mounted men, wagons and guns.'[3]

How could the Boers possibly hold out against such a force, particularly when their fighting force is hampered by a large number of women and children travelling with them? Banjo Paterson simply cannot see how it could be done. It is true this will be no rapid advance as they can go no faster than the 12 miles a day of their slowest component – the oxen whose regular slaughtering will feed this army – but no matter. It is not their speed that counts, particularly, it is its inexorable nature of their progress. The only issue will be if they can continue to feed it by gathering food along the way, particularly once they leave the railway line on which most of their supplies flow.

Besides all that, at least when French's mounted force detaches to move on Kimberley, they really will be able to move quickly, covering as much as 30 miles a day.

'It was a weary, dispiriting four days' toil – first eastward over the veldt, across the Riet River,' Banjo Paterson will recount, 'and thence northward to the Modder [which marks part of the border with Orange Free State]. Sixty thousand troops were on the move, and there was to be no turning back.'⁴

The second prong of Field Marshal Roberts' thrust, meanwhile, will be a much smaller force of just 5000 Troopers under General Ralph Clements, pushing north from the border town of Colesberg – the only place the Boers had actually penetrated the Cape Colony.

Among this force, the just arrived Trooper Fred Booth of the 2nd Victorian Mounted Rifles is stunned at how quickly everything is happening. He and his fellow Troopers had only arrived at Cape Town a little less than a week earlier – 'It was a beautiful day and clear sky and the cloud on the Table Mountain was simply glorious . . . the table cloth was pure white and moves slowly up and down the side and top of the mountain'⁵ – to be greeted on deck by Field Marshal Lord Roberts himself, clearly eager to determine whether the freshly arrived Australians and their horses would be fit enough for what he has in mind. And clearly they had passed muster, for they had barely a chance to get their land legs back before they had been hustled onto a train heading north to Colesberg, to get ready for the big push. Yes, an enormous adventure, but a desperate one. Like all of the men, Fred has eyed warily the ambulance wagons coming back from the front line, often filled with half-dead men missing limbs. Is that to be their fate in just a few days' time?

Mercifully, there is not too much time to think about that.

All of them have been issued with new Lee Enfield .303 rifles together with 100 rounds of ammunition, of which half are carried in their bandoliers, and half in their saddlebags, as 5000 of them set off to the north.

A final spear to the heart of the Boer War effort will be 2000 men under Colonel Herbert Plumer – an accomplished officer, despite being later described as 'the spitting image of Colonel Blimp'⁶ – who will push down from Rhodesia to, hopefully, finally relieve Mafeking.

And this then is the British answer to the Boers. If you, as two small and inconsequential republics lost in the wilds of Africa, wish to thwart the will of the British Empire, you will have to take on the British Empire's loyal sons drawn from all over the world. And now, no fewer than 80,000 of them are on the move, coming at you!

In the case of Fred Booth and his comrades the key part of these first few days will be just getting across the Orange River, which marks the southern border with Orange Free State, and it will be no easy task as the Boers have taken the extreme step of dynamiting away the middle two spans of the one bridge in the area, and are now dug in on the other side of the river, sniping at all who come close.

Very well then.

General Clements calls for the artillery and, over the next few days, blasts all the Boer positions to shift them, even as Booth et al use their .303s to fire across the river at every fleeing Boer they see. Again, it is an extraordinary thing to aim a rifle at another human being and pull the trigger, but the fact the Boers are firing back at them – and hitting more than a few – helps quell whatever initial reluctance they feel. This really is *war*, and never more so than when the Boers' Maxim guns are brought forward.

'I was on an observation post and saw the whole affair beautifully. They turned their guns on to us but did no damage. When they retired our engineers set to work to throw a pontoon over the river. The river is 750 feet wide where they put the pontoon. Nearly 10,000 troops with wagons crossed that day so that was quick work. There was great rejoicing amongst us on crossing into the Free State.'[7]

Those 40,000 marching on Bloemfontein from the west, in the convoy which has Banjo Paterson in its midst, are equally thrilled when they cross, as is Paterson himself. And he remains amazed at just how vast the whole operation is, how unstoppable they are. Noting the similarities of the Orange Free State with the centre of Queensland – 'excellent grazing land, but with no surface water' – it is that topography which allows them to take it all in.

'Over these open plains one can see for many miles, and when we crossed a place of high ground we could see the long stretch of wagons reaching out into the dim distance front and behind us. Every wagon had its 12 oxen and its two negro drivers, and its load of stores and supplies. There were upwards of 4000 bullocks in that line of wagons.'[8]

Sometimes there is resistance from the Boers.

'The roar of the guns on our right showed where somebody was fighting somebody, but we paid no heed to that . . .'[9]

Far more troubling is the exhaustion of the horses, particularly the Argentine ones – shipped in bulk by the British Army, at a cost of £8 each and with a very good reason to be so cheap – they wilt, wobble and wither in the heat and dust of the hurly-burly advance. The farms they are passing have windmills and water supplies, certainly, but not remotely enough to sustain 40,000 men and 20,000 animals.

'As for the gun horses, they were dropping in their harness, and every here and there along the line a pistol shot told where some good horse was being dispatched to put him out of misery.'[10]

Every few hours the Boers do indeed put up some serious resistance, usually digging in upon a kopje and firing upon the lead elements of the cavalcade, at which point the cavalry and lancers take over.

'And here it occurs to me to say,' a Staff Captain will note, 'that a cavalry charge in a picture and a cavalry charge in reality are vastly different. In pictures the horses are all sleek and well groomed, and charge at top speed, pulling hard, and dash in among the foe, who conveniently mass themselves together to be speared at. As a matter of fact, in all the charges I have seen the horses are starved and worn out dead tired before they start from want of feed and want of rest. They are carrying about 18 st. weight, and giving a long start to a light enemy. Our cavalry will never catch the Boers as long as they live.'[11]

What moves the Boers, thus, is less the cavalry actually riding among them, so much as the *threat* of a horseman using cold steel against them. With no tradition of the bayonet, sword or lance in their martial history, the naked blade is close to the only thing for which the brave Boers show real fear.

Finally, two days after departure, Kimberley is sighted on the far horizons. Everyone wants to know: 'Are they still besieged?' 'Are they in distress?' 'Can they help us if we attack?' 'Are there many Boers around?'[12]

Banjo is right there as the Brigade Signaller, Lieutenant Hume, climbs to the top of a hill and, with hands shaking with excitement, sets up his helio. General French and his staff are also there, anxious for answers.

'This is the relief column coming to Kimberley,' Hume flashes.

Shortly, some flashes come back, and Hume jots them down.

'What regiment are you?'

It is an underwhelming response. We have braved shot and shell to come to your aid, we tell you we are here, and you come back with something as bland as that?

'This is the relief column coming to Kimberley,' Hume repeats. 'Under the command of General French.'[13]

'What?'

It is an enormous anti-climax, born of the fact that those in Kimberley have been fooled by the Boers before, and cannot believe that this is really a relief column, at last come to their aid.

There is nothing for it but to push on, getting ever closer to the town, expecting to be attacked at any moment. And, sure enough –

'Suddenly a shot or two from a [Pom-Pom] came from a kopje on the right, and fell among the New Zealanders. Our guns at once commenced to pound the kopje, while the main body went on towards the town.'

The Boer resistance does not last long, and near the outskirts of the town, French's men come across the abandoned Boer camp.

'They left their coffee half-drunk, their meals half-eaten, and their tents standing, and fled.'[14]

Yes, as extraordinary as it seems, the famed Boer leader, General Piet Cronje and his 7000 Boers seem to have decided that, in this case, discretion is the better part of valour, and they have slipped away, to fight another day.

The road into Kimberley is open, for the first time in four months.

As ever, the intrepid correspondent for the *Sydney Morning Herald* is right there as General French makes his triumphant entrance. This time, there is no need, or chance, to be underwhelmed.

'The people had been half starved and limited to a quarter pound of horse flesh each day; they had been hiding in holes in the ground. Poor wretches, no wonder they cheered. They rushed at the general's horse to caress him, they cried, they waved their hands, and ran alongside up the line. When they heard there were three Australians they gave us a great cheer all to ourselves.'[15]

Now, despite General French wanting his men and horses to get some much-needed rest, a heliographed message from Lord Roberts insists that they turn around and pursue General Cronje and his men immediately!

Well, it is always said that General French 'can think at a gallop,'[16] and on occasions like this he can give orders at the same rate, barking at his exhausted men in a furious flurry. Within hours French and his men set out in ragged pursuit. 'Compelled to abandon many guns . . . the continuous "*crack, crack, crack,*" of the rifle told that horses were being put out of misery'[17] but they finally corner Cronje and his men 40 miles from Kimberley at a difficult crossing of the Modder River outside of Paardeberg.

Or are they cornered? Many of Cronje's senior men insist they should cut their losses, abandon their wagons and fight their way through the weakest point of those who surround them and get away – but General Cronje refuses. He is heir to the Boer belief from the *Voortrekkers* onwards that a Boer without his wagon is an axe head without a handle, a compass without a needle, and insists that, in any case, even if his army escaped without that which is in the wagons, they would be incapable of fighting anyway. Nevertheless, General Christiaan de Wet now approaches with his own column, and is more than willing to fight their way through to Cronje's, if he will only agree to move fast.

'Our arrival had made a way of escape for General Cronje,' General Christiaan de Wet will recount. 'It is true that he would have had to abandon everything, including his wagons, but he and his burghers would have got away in safety . . . But General Cronje would not move.'[18]

And neither will his wife, Hester Susanna Cronje, who unfailingly accompanies him on his campaigns – staying close to their wagon and providing every home comfort she can to him. General Cronje is an old-fashioned Boer like they don't make them anymore, short and chunky, ever and always with a wide-brimmed round hat, often stroking his thick beard with one hand, while brandishing the whip he uses to control his wagon oxen with the other.

He will not be running from the British.

Which is his choice. But hundreds of Cronje's men refuse to obey their leader and indeed get away, while the rest – *Grawe in!* – dig in, and prepare to fight for their lives.

The result is a dispute among the leadership of the British forces as to just how Cronje and his men should be taken on. General Lord Kitchener insists on a full-on frontal assault on the 6000 heavily dug-in Boers armed with Mauser rifles. The Divisional Commander given the task, General Thomas Kelly-Kenny, however, is equally insistent that such a move would be too costly in casualties for his men of the 6th Division and the better plan is to simply surround the Boers and starve them out. Kelly-Kenny is ultimately responsible for the lives of 15,000 men and has enough clout that he is able to insist that Lord Roberts himself be consulted.

When a message from the Commander-in-Chief comes back via heliograph that Kitchener's orders are to be obeyed, Kelly-Kenny has no choice.

Upon Kitchener's plan, the first company of infantrymen advance in extended order on the morning of Sunday, 18 February, going straight towards the Boer sharpshooters. Banjo Paterson watches closely as the first company approaches the Boer trenches, spreading out laterally as they do so. As they near, the correspondent expects to see them launch a charge, but something else entirely happens. After a fearful fusillade of fire from the Boers, practically the entire company is shot down!

Even more extraordinary?

'There was no flinching. Up came another company, and down they went, being completely swept away. Company after company went up, but were swept away, till at last Kitchener found that, with a frontal attack, the trenches could not be taken.'[19]

And my Lord is still not done.

For even as General Lord Kitchener rides by he brings his glasses up and spies several hundred Boers dug in on another kopje. Who can he get to remove them?

Well, at this very moment, as Paterson documents, around a hundred 'dirty, hungry, tattered soldiers, leading their tired horses,' come by.

'Who are you?' Kitchener asks.

'New South Wales Rifles, Sir,' replies Captain John Antill, with a mixture of deep fatigue and terrible foreboding.

'Well,' says Kitchener, 'there are some Boers on that kopje, will you go and drive them out?'

'Well, Sir,' Antill replies, 'neither my men nor my horses have had anything to eat for two days. Does it matter if we get some rations, first?'

'Go now,' says Kitchener, 'and get some rations when you come back.'

Yes, Sir.

Antill and his men do their best and, against all odds, manage to get a foothold on the kopje, and over the next few hours even manage to do some damage to the heavily entrenched Boers until, in the words of Banjo Paterson, Kitchener sends '3000 men to help them in a task which he had asked 100 men to do before breakfast'.[20]

In the end, however, no number of men can shift all the Boers dug in at Paardeberg, and when Lord Roberts arrives the day after 'Bloody Sunday' as it will be dubbed – with a thousand British Troopers killed or wounded – Kitchener is finally obliged to do what he should have done in the first place, what he had been urged to do, bring the big guns forward to blast the blasted Boers into oblivion.

'Poor old Cronje's laager,' Banjo Paterson tells his readers, referring to the Boer term for his circle-of-wagons encampment, 'was easy to be seen stuck on the bank of the river, a jumble of bullock wagons, tents, and gear of all sorts, quite unprotected, and played upon by our shells from all sides. He and his forces were hidden in the river bed, and there he lay at bay like a scorpion ringed round with fire. All round his camp is open country, quite level, with a chain of hills about two miles from the river. On these hills we had our guns, and at the least sign of movement in his camp shell after shell went at him.'[21]

Days of heavy shelling proceed, the ground shaking from dawn to dusk and the air filling with acrid smoke and distant screams. The fact that Cronje and his men *still* resist, will see Banjo later laud 'the remarkable stubbornness and wonderful fighting qualities of that handful of men, accomplishing one of the most magnificent things done in the history of the war'.[22]

Finally, however, after a week, General Cronje must bow to reality and surrender with his surviving 4000 men – a major Boer disaster. On the morning of 27 February 1900, the Boer leader, with an air of crushing sadness, rides along behind the lines of his men and gives orders that white flags are to be placed a hundred yards apart, along all the trenches.

The surrendered Boers, including Cronje and his wife, are disarmed and marched away, Cronje still holding his oxen whip. Most of these, and subsequent Boer prisoners, will be sent to camps in far-flung parts of the British Empire like India, Ceylon and St Helena to sit out the rest of the war.

It is a short time after their departure that Banjo Paterson lays eyes on the great English General for the first time, when – typically – 'Bobs' visits one of the hospitals where the freshly wounded lie.

'A very small, grizzled old man – they say he is seventy – but he sits his horse like a youngster. Though he is studiously polite to everybody, he has broken several generals already, so the brass hats and the red-collared popinjays of staff officers are wondering, when they go to bed at night, whether their jobs will be gone in the morning.'[23]

Tragically, after this particular Battle of Paardeberg, the field hospitals groan with grievously wounded British and colonial soldiers.

For while it is true that General Cronje is now in Kitchener's 'bag', as are 4000 of his Boer Army, the cost of the victory is appalling.

No fewer than 348 of General Thomas Kelly-Kenny's men have been killed outright. And the wounded are so numerous that, as they are gathering up to be put in bullock wagons and taken to the nearest established hospital with actual doctors and nurses, 50 miles away, the convoy of bullock wagons extends no less than six miles.

'On Lord Roberts arriving,' Banjo Paterson chronicles, 'he openly expressed his displeasure at what Kitchener had done, and Kitchener soon after left with a bodyguard, putting one in mind of Napoleon in his retreat from Moscow.'[24]

Paterson is appalled.

And he is not alone.

Winston Churchill is another who has extremely strong reservations about Kitchener's sheer bloodiness when it comes to warfare, his seeming lack of care for deaths on both sides.

For he has seen it before, only 18 months ago after the Battle of Omdurman in the Sudan, there had been no fewer than 10,000 Sudanese left wounded in the field, and they had all been butchered by the Anglo–Egyptian army on the express orders of their commander, Kitchener himself.

'I shall merely say that the victory at Omdurman was disgraced by the inhuman slaughter of the wounded,' Churchill had written to his mother, 'and that Kitchener was responsible for this.'[25]

And he really had been, with Lieutenant Fison of the 5th Fusiliers recording that, before this same battle, Kitchener 'issued orders that all wounded passed over [as the troops advanced during or after the battle] had to be bayoneted'.[26] In the words of war correspondent George Steevens, who was at Omdurman, 'It was not a battle, but an execution.'[27]

This was not a one-off moment of barbarity from Kitchener, but his *modus operandi*, with another war correspondent, Ernest Bennett, noting the slaying of the wounded had become customary since the Battle of Atbara five months before, where Kitchener also commanded, invoking for his troops before the final slaughter the memory of General Charles Gordon and his men who had been wiped out in the Battle of Khartoum 14 years earlier: 'Remember Gordon. The enemy in front of you are Gordon's murderers.'[28]

His troops had responded accordingly, without mercy, slaughtering all before them.

And yet, in the here and now, even after such wanton sacrifice of his *own* men at the Battle of Paardeberg, Kitchener remains in place. Quietly, for it will not do to say it out loud now as a war correspondent, Banjo Paterson is not an admirer. Again, he sees the mark of the man up close, in his visits to hospitals.

'Lord Kitchener, the next soldier to the commander-in-chief, was a different man altogether [from Bobs],' he will later note. 'He was a great strategist, a harsh, relentless fighter, and at the same time a man who considered the men as so many pawns in the game. He often had occasion to go into the hospitals, but was never known to speak to the wounded, or even enquire about their treatment, and while the troops loved and trusted Lord Roberts they feared Kitchener.'[29]

Right now it is still Kitchener at Lord Roberts' right hand as they prepare to launch the biggest action of the Boer War to date . . . the push to capture the Orange Free State capital of Bloemfontein. First, however, 'Bobs' knows it is imperative to tell the Boer population of the futility of more resistance. It is with this in mind that he now issues a proclamation to all those in the Orange Free State:

> I . . . warn all Burghers to desist from any further hostility towards Her Majesty's Government and the troops under my command, and I undertake that any of them who may so desist, and who are found staying in their homes and quietly pursuing their ordinary occupations, will not be made to suffer in their persons or property on account of their having taken up arms in obedience to the order of their Government.
>
> Those, however, who oppose the forces under my command, or furnish the enemy with supplies or information, will be dealt with according to the customs of war . . .
>
> Orders have been issued by me, prohibiting soldiers from entering private houses, or molesting the civil population on any pretext whatever, and every precaution has been taken against injury to property on the part of any person belonging to, or connected with, the Army.[30]

That is the general idea, anyway. Whether his troops will obey it is another matter.

•

In Bloemfontein, the news of General Cronje's capture is devastating. All President Steyn can do is to replace him quickly and to appoint General Christiaan de Wet as the Commandant-General of all Orange Free State forces, completing a meteoric rise for one who had begun the war as an ordinary burgher, before becoming a Field Cornet and then, in December 1899, a General in command of several Commandos.

•

It is not pretty for the new men to see, but . . .

But, these things happen pretty often.

For in the ongoing clashes with the Boers, local homesteads are . . . well . . . they are burned to the ground. Sometimes it happens when British officers are sure that the said homesteads have been used as Commando camps. Other times it is when it is known that a particular Boer homestead has been supplying a particular Commando with food, and so must be punished. Such burnings are, as it is put on one occasion,

'a warning to the Boers that such depredations as they had carried out
... could not pass with impunity'.[31]

It is not systemic, mind, only happening a little over a couple of dozen
times in the first few months of the war, but the rate is increasing, and
the Boers are appalled. This is not 'warfare', as they had imagined it.

As to what happens to the families of the destroyed homesteads, the
view of the British is that this is not their problem. The Boers can work
it out. Some move in with other families. Some drift to the towns where
they become part of a growing group of refugees.

Mid-February 1900, Cape Town, conversing with a contrarian

It is quite the occasion.

After his first real taste of a grand-scale battle, Banjo Paterson has
returned to the capital of the Cape Colony with a specific interview in
mind. For he has become interested in the fact that, despite the Cape
Colony being at war, not everyone wishes to join the war effort, and
some even wish to – if you can believe it – publicly speak out against it!

One of these, he had been fascinated to learn, is no less than the famed
author Olive Schreiner, the sister of William Philip Schreiner, the Prime
Minister of the Cape Colony – and today is the day he has arranged
to interview her. And oh, what a contrast to the war zone he has come
from – all dust storms, bush, angst, grime, blood and dead men – to
now be in a carriage behind gaily trotting horses as they take him along
the blossomed boulevards of the swanky suburb of Newlands, with its
grand mansions, manicured lawns and . . .

And, Sir?

Olive Schreiner will see you now. She proves to be a 'little woman,
small in stature, but of very strong physique, broad and powerful; her
face olive-complexioned, with bright, restless eyes, and a quick mobile
mouth. She spoke fluently and with tremendous energy, her thoughts
emphasised by a sharp, uplifted finger'.

There are, she says, far more people in South Africa *against* the war
than for it, and that includes many of the English Cape Colonists she
knows. But they are not the issue at hand. She wants to bring it closer
to home for this visiting Australian journalist.

'You Australians and New Zealanders and Canadians,' she says
emphatically, 'I cannot understand it at all, why you come here light
heartedly to shoot down other colonists of whom you know nothing
– it is terrible. Such fine men too – fine fellows. I . . . saw your men in

camp; oh, they were fine men – and to think that they are going out to kill and be killed, just to please the capitalists!'[32]

Oh yes, Mr Paterson, make no mistake. This is all about gold and land, and nothing to do with liberty, democracy and justice, the things actually worth fighting a war for.

'It is terrible – such men to come and fight against those fighting for their liberty and their country. You people – you are all volunteers! Why have you come? . . . You say that England was at war, and you wished to show the world that when the mother country got into a war the colonies were prepared to take their place beside her! Yes, but you ought to ask, you ought to make inquiries before you come over. You Australians do not understand. This is a capitalists' war . . !'[33]

Yes, a capitalists' war, all put together by wealthy men to make more wealth at the expense of the poor men who have to fight, most of them duped into thinking they are doing their patriotic duty. But they have been fooled, don't you see, Mr Paterson?

Banjo Paterson thanks her for the interview and says his goodbye, having much to think about as he makes his way back to his lodgings. The more he learns about this war, its rights and wrongs, its balance of power, the more it becomes clear that it is not as straightforward as it first appears. But he must be careful. On the one hand he resolves to put her views, in full, before his readers – they deserve to be fully informed.

On the other hand, however, he also decides he must distance himself a little from them, making it clear that while she is *sincere*, she is also *misguided* and, in the way of these things, he starts mentally composing the words he will soon cable back to Australia for publication.

> It seems a pity that this woman, who is no doubt a great literary genius, should be wasting her time and wearing out her energies over this Boer War question, instead of giving us another book as good as her first one; but after an interview with her one comes away with a much more lively and human interest in 'our friends the enemy'. If things are as she says, if the Boers are going to make it a war to the bitter end, then England has a sorry task before her. If the Boer scatter and break to the mountains they will be practically unreachable, and the English people are too humane to care about levying reprisals by destroying their homesteads and leaving their wives and children without shelter . . .[34]

Late February 1900, Orange Free State, the push goes on

The fighting is as bitter as it is brutal and bloody.

Harassed by Boer sharpshooters and artillery all the way, Field Marshal Roberts and his men continue to push on Bloemfontein from the west, while General Clements and his men push from the south. To try and block them, the Boers scrap and snipe at them all the way, positioning themselves on kopjes to fire down upon them, launching ambushes before quickly disappearing, focusing their fire upon every narrow river crossing where the British forces must be tightly bunched.

The further the British forces get from their supply lines, the more desperate for food and water they become, and so too do their reprisals at Boer resistance.

And now the rarity becomes familiar. For when they lose men to Boer ambushes, sometimes the soldiers take their revenge by burning to the ground the nearest Boer homestead they can find. The women and children are ushered out first, and then they burn it, after helping themselves to whatever stores of feed and water the farm possesses.

How else can they keep moving? With 40,000 men and 20,000 animals, eating 160 tons of food and forage a day, or 80 wagon loads, most of the supplies they had initially brought with them in the wagons are gone and so they must live off the land.

Yes, the *Manual of Military Law* had insisted that all else being equal inhabitants 'may be required to provide supplies at a moderate cost',[35] but there is no time or – more importantly – disposition for this. Looting is also a big part of it.

'Within 800 yards of the farm we halted,' one soldier would recount, 'and the infantry blazed a volley into the house. Then we marched up to it, and on arrival found it locked up and not a soul to be seen, so we broke open the place and went in. It was beautifully furnished, and the officers got several things they could make use of, such as bedding, etc. There was a lovely library – books of all descriptions printed in Dutch and English. I secured a Bible, also a Mauser rifle . . . After getting all we wanted out of it, our men put a charge under the house and blew it up. It seemed such a pity. It was a lovely house with a nice garden round it.'[36]

The forces keep moving towards Bloemfontein, with the good news also coming through on 28 February that, to the far east in Natal, the forces of General Redvers Buller have liberated Ladysmith. That leaves just one town still besieged by the Boers . . .

Late February 1900, Mafeking, hunger pangs

'I am so hungry, I could eat a horse and chase the rider,' is an expression many of those defending Mafeking have grown up with. These days, they, too – just like those who had been besieged in Kimberley – must content themselves with simply eating the horse to survive. It is a desperate measure – as it removes their last remaining capacity to break out and get away – but Colonel Robert Baden-Powell feels he has no choice.

He will not *surrender*.

For all the grimness of the situation, however, there remains curiously gentlemanly interaction between the besieged and the besiegers. In an effort to keep morale up, Baden-Powell has allowed various games of polo organised by his rather roly-poly Chief-of-Staff Colonel Charles Hore. But what truly makes things interesting is when he allows his men to play cricket on Sundays – which draws a stiff note of scandalised protest from the officer commanding the Boers outside Mafeking, General Jacobus Snyman.

Does Colonel Baden-Powell not know that Sunday is the Day of the Lord, the day of rest, a day when it is just not *right* to play cricket?

Still, not all the Boer officers feel like that, with one of General Snyman's younger subordinates, Commandant Sarel Eloff – one of the 35 grandsons of President Kruger – also writing to Colonel Baden-Powell:

> I see in *The Bulawayo Chronicle* that your men in Mafeking play cricket on Sundays and give concerts and balls on Sunday evening. In case you will allow my men to join in, it would be very agreeable to me as here, outside Mafeking, there are seldom any of the fair sex . . . If you accept my proposition I shall, with my men, be on the cricket field and at the ball room at a time so appointed by you.
> I remain
> Your obedient friend
> Sarel Eloff, Commandant.

Baden-Powell is quick with his reply: 'I should like nothing better – after the match in which we are at present engaged is over.'[37]

He adds a further flourish.

'Perhaps the return match should be postponed until we have finished the present one and that as we are now two hundred not out, and Snyman, Cronje, &c., have not been successful he would suggest a further change of bowling.'[38]

And the fact remains: every extra day they hold out is another day they keep the estimated 8000 Boers besieging them, and their guns, away from other fronts.

So, take the punishment, soak it up, and be proud. The good news is now, with Kimberley relieved, a relief column should start soon from there, and perhaps one also from the north, from Rhodesia . . .

13 March 1900, Bloemfontein falls, Banjo rises

At last, a month after setting off, the word is passed.

Bloemfontein is now on the horizon!

Not only that but, just as had happened in Kimberley, the Boer defenders have suddenly melted away – disappeared in the night, so as to live to fight another day. Bloemfontein is completely at the mercy of the British.

What a story! Banjo Paterson moves with unusual speed. In the company of two other war correspondents – admittedly taking their life into their hands – they gallop forward ahead of the troops, unsure of what kind of reception they will receive in this one-time Boer stronghold.

And there appears to be no problem at all, as within minutes Banjo and his two fellow correspondents gallop over the open veldt in a rough race to see who will have the honour of being first into Bloemfontein. On his Australian-bred colt, Banjo channels the Man From Snowy River – *He sent the flint stones flying, but the pony kept his feet,/ He cleared the fallen timber in his stride,/ And the man from Snowy River never shifted in his seat,/ It was grand to see that mountain horseman ride –* and leaves the other two behind.

The odd thing? Once in the town proper they are all warmly welcomed by the townsfolk, who pump their hands, clap them on the back, offer three cheers and behave as if they could not be more thrilled at having their town captured.

'It was,' he would recount, once again struck by the similarity of the Boers' world to Australia, 'little different from riding into Yass.'[39]

For once they enter the town – wide streets, brick buildings, electricity lines, and a population that looks to be 5000 or so – the truly rustic nature of the place becomes ever more apparent.

And now, everywhere Banjo goes, people are coming up with all kinds of questions, but one in particular: 'When will we see Lord Roberts?'[40]

As it happens, Banjo's particular task right now is exactly that, to chronicle the General's reaction to the glad tidings. It is for this reason he now leaves Bloemfontein, riding through the 'cavalry closing in round the town like a huge net', until he is guided to the kopje where Lord Roberts is stationed.

'I then rode up to the kopje and had the honour of announcing to Lord Roberts that Bloemfontein surrendered.'[41]

Sticking tightly to 'Bobs' as the conquering General enters Bloemfontein two hours later, Paterson is soon composing the words that will shortly appear in the *Sydney Morning Herald* reporting the capture of Bloemfontein, under the banner of

WITH LORD ROBERTS
ENTRY INTO BLOEMFONTEIN
'BANJO' PATERSON FIRST IN
SCENES OF INTENSE ENTHUSIASM
IRRESISTIBLE WAVE OF INFANTRY

> ... As the procession, headed by Lord Roberts and his staff, approached the town a giant commotion was observable ... Instead of sullen, scowling faces we saw only bright looks and fluttering handkerchiefs, while our ears were greeted with wild cheers. Amidst such rejoicings, Lord Roberts reached the Market-square, whence he proceeded to the Parliament House, and thence to the Presidency. There was there a fresh and yet more impressive outburst ...[42]

The capture of this town – the capital of Orange Free State – is clearly a major breakthrough, a sign that the Boer is nearly now defeated, and all that truly remains is to also capture Pretoria.

Given that the army of Lord Roberts is truly exhausted, and has moved well beyond its supply lines, it will need to stay in this area for at least a month to await replacements for the thousands of horses which have died of exhaustion, and to build up their stock of supplies and war matériel, before moving north once more. For the most part, thus, Lord Roberts' forces make their enormous camp on the edge of the town, and are allowed to stand down. Occasionally his troops are given leave to enter Bloemfontein itself, meaning the streets soon fill with soldiers from around the British Empire, including the Canadians, New Zealanders, Irish, Australians and of course the spectacularly garbed Highlanders and members of the Black Watch – both of the latter remarkable for the fact that their tartan kilts now have an apron of khaki in front. (The Scots Greys cavalry regiment believe in the virtues of khaki so much that they have even dyed their horses that colour.)

Watching them all warily are any number of Boer refugees, 'mostly men who have fought against us and have laid down their arms, and are now afraid of the Boers',[43] together with black-garbed women – local residents mourning the deaths of their husbands, brothers and fathers. There are so many of them it is rare to see a Boer woman in the normal garb, displaying any colour whatsoever.

For his part, Banjo Paterson soon takes lodgings with one of those Boer widows, who in many ways seems typical of this crazy mixed-up war where both sides boast members of the nominal enemy in their ranks. In her case, while her husband was killed fighting on the side of the Free State, her brothers are fighting for the English near Kimberley.

As to the four refugees in the house, once again Banjo is afforded the opportunity of talking to the 'enemy' up close, and once again comes away stunned. Local farmers, for the most part, they can chat knowledgeably about Tasmanian merinos and the merits of Vermont rams. They are thinking of introducing Wolseley sheep-shearing machines into their sheds, because they seem to be the most sophisticated.

'These people,' he writes for his readers at home, 'are the semi-savage, ignorant Boers of whom we heard so much.'[44]

But then there are their stories of how they had lost their farms – including simply having them torched, and their families turned out, for no good reason beyond an administrative error; the British burned the wrong farm.

Again, it makes Banjo wonder about this war. His education in the ways of the Boer, and the whys and wherefores of this war, continues over the next few days as he begins to venture out of Bloemfontein and finds that they are much as Olive Schreiner had described them: fundamentally decent people. They seem to be a lot like . . . well, to be frank about it, a lot like Australians, people who have forged strong lives in a remote country, courtesy of their courage, honesty, hard work and resilience.

'The owners of these farms, and their farmhands,' he will chronicle, 'have the latest air-meter windmills, they use the springs of water to the best advantage in irrigation, and in their towns we can get anything that could be got in an Australian town of similar size. If one goes to these outlying farms, the man of the house is always away on commando, but the Afrikander woman is as a rule the exact counterpart of the girl of any Australian country town. They are great on tennis – nearly every farm has its tennis-court.'[45]

And the similarities don't stop there.

'They have their little assembly balls; and one clique does not mix with the other clique, just as in Australia. In peace time they go to Johannesburg for balls and races and so forth.'[46]

The difference now, of course, is that those fine women are no longer going to balls and races, but are heading off to military hospitals to act as nurses. They, too, are impossible not to like, and admire. A good part of it, he must admit, is their sheer *humanity*. Why, he has seen with his own eyes how, even as the English Army has continued on its relentless push to the north, many of the Boer women in the newly occupied territories have turned up at their military hospitals, and 'started nursing the sick Tommies with just as much interest as their own men'.[47]

The fact that he is a non-combatant war correspondent even allows him to see some of the Boer Commandos up close. On one occasion at this time, when heading north beneath the flag of the Red Cross in the company of two surgeons with an ambulance to pick up a wounded soldier, they come around a kopje to suddenly find themselves right in the middle of a Boer Commando troop.

Yes, it had been quite a shock, but there is no danger. The Boers recognise the sanctity of the Red Cross and, once it is established that the visitors are medical men and a war correspondent, are happy to talk.

Banjo looks very closely, trying to get a feel for these men, the much-vilified enemy. He is struck, once again, by their resemblance to a breed he knows particularly well.

'We saw,' he will recount, 'a lot of rough, dirty, bearded men, just like a crowd of shearers or farm-hands, as no doubt most of them were. Each man was leading a pony and carrying a rifle. The rifle was the only thing neat and workmanlike about them. Their clothes were poor, ready-made slops; their hats every kind of battered old felt; their saddles were wretched things, worn out of shape. No two men were dressed alike; they were all ages, all sizes and all classes; all were dirty, with rough, unshaven faces.'

They are not travelling with Cape carts, for this close to the English they have to be able to move quickly, and they have no quartermasters nor stores of supplies to draw on. No, each man is just living off the land the best he can, in this case leading their horses to the barn, where they get whatever forage they can.

'Each man,' Banjo writes admiringly, 'was his own ordnance, supply, and remount department.'[48]

Once the Boers have established that their visitors are trying to find a wounded English soldier so he can be brought back to their own lines, they send two of their own men in the company of a young English-speaking lad, just 15 years old, to accompany Banjo and the surgeons and ease their passage. Banjo likes the lad, and is fascinated to hear his views on the war as they make their way towards the wounded Tommy. Clearly, the equation for the land is very simple. Their homeland had been about to be invaded by the English, so they had been quite within their rights to strike first and resist them thereafter. What honourable people would not do exactly as they had done?

Yes . . . well. That is certainly what Australians would do under the same circumstances and there is really no getting around that. Still . . .

'How long will the Boers go on fighting?'[49] Banjo asks.

'Till the last Afrikaaner is killed,' the lad replies firmly, before touching one of the two Boers who have come with him. 'If there is only he and I left, we will fight till we are both killed and then you will have the land. Till then, no.'[50]

He means it and it seems that so do the two Boer men with him. For the first time Banjo Paterson starts to appreciate just how much fight the Boers still have in them.

'I am a wonderful fellow,' the lad goes on brightly. 'I cannot miss a man up to eight hundred yards. The English are brave enough, but they cannot shoot.'

The biggest problems the Boers have had so far, he says, are that, 'we suffered too much from hair and guts . . .'.

Perhaps you could explain?

'All our generals were old men, fat men with big beards. They had fought Zulus, and we thought they could fight a war, but they could not handle big numbers of men. A hunting-party, yes; but a war, no. Now we have trained men, like Botha, and we will do better. Cronje was one of the old generals, and we have better fighting generals than Cronje.'[51]

Later that day Banjo Paterson returns to English lines with much more to think about. The conversation with the Boer lad had been revelatory. And his own experience had been similar to that of other war correspondents, with one of the Americans, Richard Davis, telling his own readers: 'There are many boys in the Boer army. Four of them are sons of Reitz, the Secretary of State of Transvaal. The father told me proudly of how the youngest, 15 years old, covered a British Tommy and called on him to hold up his hands. The Tommy threw down his gun and said to the boy, "I don't care. I'm blooming well sick of the war, anyway. Ain't you?" "Oh no," protested young Reitz, "for father says that when the war is over he's going to send me back to school."'[52]

16–20 March 1900, Kroonstad, Council of War

Yes, back in the day, all roads led to Rome.

But for the on-field Boer leadership now, all roads lead to Kroonstad, some 135 miles north of Bloemfontein, where the government of Orange Free State has removed itself to.

And so it is no particular coincidence that, nearing dusk on this early evening of 16 March, the greatest of the youngest Orange Free State Generals, Christiaan de Wet – a man with a notably fiery personality, with remarkable service against the Sotho as a teenager, and at the great victory against the British at Majuba in 1881 – falls in astride his ubiquitous white Arab mare Fleur beside the most famous of the old Transvaal Generals, Piet Joubert. They are both bound for the same Council of War beginning in Kroonstad on the morrow to decide the crucial issue – where to from here?

De Wet is a little wary from the first, knowing that the 69-year-old Joubert is as 'Old School' as they come. At one point a few months earlier, Joubert had called off a particularly promising attack, simply because two Boers had been struck by lightning – which he had interpreted as an infallible sign from the Almighty to retreat.

'It seems incredible,' one of the younger generals, Ben Viljoen, had noted, 'that in these enlightened days we should find such a man in command of an army.'[53]

Still, on this occasion, hail fellow well met, though hale and hearty General Joubert most certainly isn't. Though the old man remains the Commandant-General of all Transvaal forces, it is obvious he still has not recovered from his fall the previous November and seems to be continuing by force of will alone. He looks, frankly, like a man whose last gasp cannot be far off, but equally as one who is committed to fighting the British to that very last gasp. The two Generals are able to compare notes for the first time in many months.

Indeed, things are grim across the board as, despite their many victories in separate battles, nothing is stopping the British from winning the war – by simple dint of the number of men and amount of munitions they are putting in the field.

In the course of the conversation, General de Wet mentions that he has given his own men leave to return to their homes, until 25 March.

'Do you mean to tell me,' General Joubert rasps, 'that you are going to give the English a free hand, whilst your men take their holidays?'

De Wet is untroubled by the charge, sure of his ground.

'I cannot catch a hare with unwilling dogs,' de Wet replies. 'You know Afrikanders as well as I do, General. It is not our fault that they don't know what discipline means. Whatever I had said, the burghers would have gone home; but I'll give you my word that those who come back will fight with renewed courage.'[54]

And General de Wet means it too, later noting, 'I preferred to command ten men who were willing to fight, rather than 100 who shirked their duties.'[55]

The next day the Council of War is held in the Kroonstad Town Hall on Cross Street. Most of the Cabinet Ministers of the two republics and as many of the Generals who can be spared from the field are present – alongside Joubert and de Wet are such important Generals as Koos de la Rey, Louis Botha, Christoffel Froneman, and J.B. Wessels – together with some 40 of their senior officers. At the head of the room, President Martinus Steyn of Orange Free State sits side by side with 'the simple statesman, grown grey in his country's service, President Kruger'.[56]

And now begins the war of words, the battlefield of negotiation where reason fights with pride for victory, or at least honour in defeat or withdrawal.

'We knew, I scarcely need say,' General de Wet will recall, 'that humanly speaking ultimate victory was out of the question. That had been clear from the very beginning. For how could our diminutive army hope to stand against the overwhelming number at the enemy's command?'[57]

No, this is not about beating the entire British Empire with the armies of their two small republics. But perhaps what could be done would be to exact such a price from the British that they would settle for a negotiated peace on terms much more favourable to the Boers than if they simply surrendered now. Yes, that is it.

But how?

It takes a great deal of discussion over the next three days, and occasionally fierce debate. But by meeting's end the plan is clear.

'Besides deciding to continue the war more energetically than ever,' de Wet will recount, 'we agreed unanimously that the great wagon-camps should be done away with, and that henceforth only horse-Commandos should be employed.'[58]

There will be no more grand armies supported by lumbering wagon trains heading off to fight enormous set-piece battles with their British counterparts. The Boers could never win such battles, and congregating in that manner made them perfect targets for the British to crush with their superior artillery and overwhelming numbers.

No, the Boers decide, much better if we break into smaller bands, return to our home districts, live off the land, from the network of Boer farms who could still keep us fed, and instead of trying to stem the British advance by defending across a broad front, we will *attack* the enemy through guerrilla warfare from all sides, break up their supply lines, hitting them in the flanks and in the rear, disrupting their communications and using our mobility to advantage against their slow-moving columns. Keep it up for a year or two and the khakis will tire of the blood and money expended and *beg* us for a peace.

The new plan, as defined by the leader of the Johannesburg Commando, Ben Viljoen, is 'to fight whenever we can, and to retire when we cannot hold on any longer'.[59] It is not, however, a simple matter of being a band of fugitives, Louis Botha's secretary, J.R. van Stuwe, will note.

'We retreated or we advanced according to a plan, teasing, enticing and tiring out the enemy.'[60]

From now, the Boer republics are to be divided into separate regions, with each one assigned a Commando commander charged with raising a guerrilla army, sustaining it, and using it to strike the enemy at every turn, cutting the British supply lines and weakening them.

Koos de la Rey is appointed to command the western Transvaal region, with Jan Smuts under him; Christiaan de Wet gets the Eastern Orange Free State; Louis Botha takes over eastern Transvaal.

They are, by and large, the younger men of the military leadership who embrace the new tactics, to strike hard and get out, again and again and again.

•

Back in Bloemfontein near the end of the month, a rare pleasure awaits Banjo Paterson.

It is to be the night of the correspondents' dinner, where the couple of dozen correspondents covering the war host the Governor of the Cape Colony and High Commissioner of Southern Africa, Sir Alfred Milner, together with the Lords Roberts and Kitchener, to a grand soiree at the largest room in Bloemfontein, which lies at the railway station and famously comes complete with the best cook in the colony.

From the moment of entering the room the great Australian poet is transfixed. Everywhere he looks, there are great figures, most of whom he deeply admires.

Rudyard Kipling!

'He is a little, square-built, sturdy man of about forty. His face is well enough known to everybody from his numerous portraits; but no portrait gives any hint of the quick, nervous energy of the man. His talk is a gabble, a chatter, a constant jumping from one point to another.'[61]

And of course, here are the two principal guests of honour, my Lords Roberts and Kitchener.

Paterson looks on one with great favour, the other with equal disfavour. He has recently seen Roberts up close when the Field Marshal had visited the newly set up military hospital at Bloemfontein, bustling only because he was eager to visit as many of the wounded as possible – asking them all how they are, lifting their spirits and asking all the medical officers if they have everything they need, can he do anything for them.

But Lord Kitchener?

Paterson stiffens at his sight. He had not been an admirer since witnessing the wanton slaughter of good men at the Battle of Paardeberg, all on Kitchener's absurd insistence that his men, including Australians, charge at the Boers' entrenched positions. Some clue as to how he could have ordered that without blinking, and express no remorse afterwards, is provided right now just by looking at him.

'As far as mobility of expression goes, you could put Kitchener's face on the body of the Sphinx, and nobody would know the difference. He has the aloof air and the fixed expression of a golf champion.'[62]

Gentlemen, to the table!

Banjo is thrilled to find himself seated right by Kipling.

The two talk easily, while not always agreeing.

'I'm off back to London,' Kipling says, 'booked to sail on the eleventh. I'm not going to wait for the fighting, here. I can trust the army to do all the fighting here. It's in London I'll have to do my fighting. I want to fight the people who will say "the Boers fought for freedom – give them back their country". I want to fight all that sort of nonsense.'[63]

Banjo Paterson is quietly not so sure it is all nonsense. For one thing he is far from convinced that all the fight has gone out of the Boers and that it will soon be over. And for another, he is not quite sure that freedom wasn't *precisely* what the Boers are fighting for.

Still, when you are dealing with a man who had penned the words for 'The White Man's Burden', exhorting America to join Britain in doing its duty to savages . . .

> Take up the White Man's burden –
> Send forth the best ye breed –

Go send your sons to exile
To serve your captives' need
To wait in heavy harness
On fluttered folk and wild –
Your new-caught, sullen peoples,
Half devil and half child
Take up the White Man's burden
In patience to abide
To veil the threat of terror
And check the show of pride . . .[64]

. . . it is perhaps best to keep your own counsel.

But hark . . .

For now it is time for some speeches, beginning with a witty address from Lord Roberts, thanking the correspondents for their hospitality and noting that he regarded them as nothing less than his 'comrades in arms' and in thanking them insists that if 'I have to submit my work to any tribunal, I know no body of men more fitted to give an accurate, skilled, and impartial decision than the body of correspondents who have accompanied my army to Bloemfontein'.[65]

His tribunal sips their wine and sagely withholds judgement for the moment. Never heckle the hand that feeds you.

'The army,' Lord Roberts proudly proclaims, 'has behaved in a manner which has no parallel. Although they were marching through a hostile country, there had been no robbing, no pillage, nor any kind of crime.'[66]

Yes, well. This is far from true of course, but this is not quite the time to say so. Moving on . . .

For now, after the applause for Lord Roberts falls away and some light table conversation resumes, Lord Kitchener stands, a sparkling crystal glass in his right hand, and needn't even pause half a beat before the room falls entirely silent.

'Gentlemen,' he says, 'I propose a toast to the health of . . . Paul Kruger.'

Ignoring the gasps, Kitchener goes on with a small glint in his eye that in another man would have been a twinkle.

'For Paul Kruger has done more to knit the British Empire together than any man that has ever lived. He has been consistent throughout in his refusal to budge an inch from his position, and he has enabled us to make a white man's country of South Africa.'[67]

Guffaws. Wild applause. Light cheers.

Kitchener will go on to toast the health of the press censor, Lord Stanley, which is a little less well received, as censors and war correspondents are natural enemies, but no matter, Kitchener's toast has been the moment of the night, and they all recognise the truth of it. Irrespective of the rights or wrongs of the Boer War, the fact that men from all the nations and colonies of the British Empire have fought together and died together really does bind them together – their sacrifice providing the raw material for thousands of speeches, paeans, sermons and political exhortations in dozens of parliaments for generations to come.

•

One of those men is Trooper Fred Booth, still pushing north to Bloemfontein from Colesberg with General Clements' column. Booth has not changed clothes for six weeks. Every day, it seems, they have faced what feels like slow starvation and gone to sleep hungry. Sometimes the hunger can only be satisfied by carving off whatever non-rancid bits of meat they find on carcasses of beef *coated with tar* that have been brought from the coast in an effort to keep them fed. Other times they go hungry. Equally problematic is keeping their horses fed, and it is a measure of the congenitally honest Fred's desperation that more than once he crawls several hundred yards in the darkness to steal cobs of corn for his nag from a farmer's field that has been placed under British guard to prevent exactly that from happening.

Either way, still hungry or not, the dawn brings the call – onwards. On this day at least, he is able to pause just long enough to write to his mother.

> It is a grand sight to see the procession of troops, battery after battery of artillery ammunition columns; regiment after regiment of infantry. The Maxim guns, stretcher-bearers, water carts, ambulance wagons. Then the lancers and mounted infantry. Then the engineers and then follow the wagons, mule wagons and bullock wagons. There are 7000 troops in the column which is several miles in length. If we get to camp about 11 am the last wagon would arrive about 7 pm. What was once a deserted plain soon turns into a regular town and all is hustle and bustle at night with all the lights and fires about combined with the noise, you would imagine you were in Melbourne. We move off every morning before daybreak . . .

I heard today that Lord Roberts intends or hopes to be in Pretoria by June 1st. We will be there for a month then leave for home.[68]

Good. For like most of his comrades, Fred has just about had enough.

Emotionally, the whole experience has been wearing enough, even beyond all the killing and losing your brethren to Boer bullets.

'It would break anybody's heart,' he tells his mother, 'to see the destruction of deserted farms in Cape Colony. They burn tables, chairs and pianos for firewood.'[69]

31 March 1900, Sanna's Post, 20 miles north-east of Bloemfontein, Modder most foul

It all happens so quickly, the British forces defending Bloemfontein's waterworks on the Modder River are completely taken by surprise. With no warning, no fewer than 2000 Boer guerrillas – later found to be under the command of General Christiaan de Wet, descend from the hills and with dynamite destroy the pumps, the water tanks and the filtration plants, without which clean water cannot flow to Bloemfontein, and are gone again as quickly. Just hours later the same guerrilla army devastates a small British convoy, killing or wounding 155 British soldiers and capturing seven guns and 117 wagons.

From now, Lord Roberts' army camped outside Bloemfontein will have to rely on unsafe water.

Of course the British commanders send out a column to go after de Wet's force but the Boers seem to have . . . disappeared, melted into the veldt.

There will be more, much more of de Wet and his men to come in the area. Three weeks later Banjo Paterson is out on patrol with some of General French's cavalry some 46 miles south-east of Bloemfontein, around Dewetsdorp, when he comes across the aftermath of one action after de Wet's men had launched an ambush on the patrol.

'We soon . . . came upon a couple of blazing farmhouses,' Paterson will recount. 'There had been a fight there that day, and the Boers had fired from the farmhouses, though they were flying a white flag, and a Major of Roberts' Horse had been fatally shot. In revenge our people had ignited the two houses . . .'[70]

This Boer War is a highly ugly affair, and ever more troubling for the *Sydney Morning Herald* correspondent, who can't help wondering, to begin with, if the women and children of those farmhouses – now homeless – deserve this.

And here now, not long after his return to Bloemfontein, Banjo meets this young English war correspondent they've all been talking about, Winston Churchill. His escape from the Boers had been close to the most joyous story of the war so far and, beyond that, the Sydney man has long admired the beautiful way he writes, his evocative way of bringing the war alive for his readers, so he is more than pleased that the two get on well from the first.

'[He has] such a strong personality,' Banjo will note, 'that the army were prepared to bet that he would either get into jail or become Prime Minister.'

Churchill has no doubt which one it will be, and as a matter of fact it is why he is covering this war in the first place.

'This correspondent job is nothing to me,' he tells Banjo, 'but I mean to get into parliament through it . . . I am going to plaster the *Morning Post* with cables about our correspondent, Mr Winston Churchill, driving an armoured train, or pointing out to Lord Roberts where the enemy is. When I go up for parliament again, I'll fly in.'[71]

In the meantime, he is hugely enjoying this war.

'I thought it quite sporting of the Boers,' he will later note, 'to take on the whole British Empire . . .'[72]

CHAPTER FIVE

THE PUSH TO PRETORIA[1]

The foe was brave, original in method and untrammelled by pre-
cedent of officialdom. Moreover, the strength of the Boers in men
and armament was beyond our expectation, and the knowledge of
the country and native races which they possessed was an advan-
tage which well-nigh doubled their strength, considering the long
line of communications which the British advance necessitated.
How to face the situation was a problem which was felt throughout
the whole empire.[2]

Reverend James Green,
The Story of the Australian Bushmen

Cry 'Havoc!' and let slip the dogs of war,
That this foul deed shall smell above the earth
With carrion men, groaning for burial.[3]

William Shakespeare,
Julius Caesar, Act 3, Scene 1

3 May 1900, Karee Siding, 10 miles north of Bloemfontein, pony pong

The stench of dead horses would curl your hair, turn your stomach and make an outdoor dunny at the height of summer . . . gag. A combination of African horse sickness, malnutrition, exhaustion and glanders has killed so many that one of the 40,000 Troopers gathered by Lord Roberts on the veldt just north of Bloemfontein will write to his family in Victoria, 'I have never seen so many dead horses anywhere as I have seen here . . . They make the air very thick. We can almost cut it with a knife.'[4]

In fact, the disease and death among the mounts *and* their men is much of a muchness with no fewer than 8000 men having passed through the military hospitals set up at Bloemfontein, of whom around 1000 have died, with the major culprit being the waterborne disease of typhoid – brought on by the destruction of the town's waterworks.

Nevertheless, Lord Roberts has determined it is time to push north once more with the surviving horses and men.

111

Having massed his forces on this flat veldt over the last fortnight of April, on this day Lord Roberts gives the order and the push to Pretoria, just 290 miles away, begins.

'It is grey dawn,' Banjo Paterson encapsulates the feel of it all. 'The stars are growing pale in the cold frosty sky, and away to the east a faint cheerless white light begins to spread over the plain. Away on all sides spread the dimly seen stretch of veldt, in some places reaching to the limit of human sight, in others terminating abruptly in some towering rocky mound called a kopje . . . With a rush and a clatter and a swing, the guns fly past behind the madly straining horses, while the drivers ply their whips, and the men on the limbers with clenched teeth hold to their seats as the guns rock and sway with the pace they are making. "Action Front," and round come the trained horses like machinery, and like lightning the men uncouple the limber and place the gun in position. The range is calculated and the order goes: "At three thousand. Fuse fourteen. Ready. Fire number one gun!" And with an exulting scream, like a cockatoo freed from a cage, away goes the shell across to the little knot of galloping men. An absolute silence prevails as the shell whizzes away out of hearing, and then "bang" it has burst right over the little dust cloud that is travelling across the plain. It is a splendid shot, and a buzz of congratulation arises, and a wild feeling of exultation wakes in every man's breast. This is something like sport, this shooting at the enemy with cannon at a range of over three thousand yards of country – close enough that you can see whether you hit or miss, but not so close you must see the grisly results of a hit.

'"Hooray! Give 'em another."'[5]

From the first, both Fred Booth of the 2nd Victorian Mounted Rifles and Breaker Morant of the Second South Australian Contingent are in the thick of it as both their units are now integral parts of Colonel St George Henry's 4th Mounted Infantry Corps – a thousand soldiers on horseback charged with making first contact with the enemy, identifying their position and ideally pinning them down before the guns can come forward to destroy them.

Typically, the Breaker captures the experience with just a few tight lines of verse, in this case, 'Drawing Fire'.

> *In the cool fresh, fragrant morning come the troopers riding by,*
> *With their profiles silhouetted 'gainst the Dawn's faint orange sky,*
> *As silently and slowly Night's sombre shadows drift and melt.*
> *And 'tis 'Sections! Open order!' to our work upon the veldt.*

But the loveliness of Morning there's small leisure to admire
When the Mounted Rifles' mission is to find and 'Draw the fire!'[6]

Equally typically, the Breaker still finds time to get a letter to his journalist friends in Australia, to keep his notoriety alive, with the *Hawkesbury Advocate* soon able to assure readers, 'The existing doubt as to whether Harry Morant (the Breaker) had really gone to South Africa, we can now set at rest on the best of evidence, a post card from the "Fighting Line".'[7] And of course the Breaker, with carefully contrived casualness, manages to set just the right cavalier tone, noting for his friends in Australia that 'over here one has the consolation of a speedy exit to paradise'.[8]

And so it goes.

'We are now right on the fighting line,' Fred Booth writes proudly to his sister, 'and are further north than any other troops ... Every time we go out we are fired on, and any sheep or cattle we see between our lines and theirs we commandeer. We are trying to run them short of supplies. I have not yet been hit, but have been under very heavy fire.'[9]

Now that they are on their way, the action across the wide veldt – 'the country is very open, one immense plain with slight undulations'[10] – is fast, furious and unrelenting.

'Our first greeting was their big gun opened on us and dropped their shells right amongst. They dropped a dozen before our artillery stopped their gun. Shrapnel shell bursts in the air and sends down a perfect hail of bullets within a radius of thirty yards. We then advanced and drove them out of the kopjes.'[11]

But, of course, the Boers have only retreated so they can regroup and return, fiercer than ever.

With the next concentration of Boers sighted up ahead, the guns are again turned on them, 'and they soon scattered. We galloped after them and dismounted and went on a ridge and poured volley after volley into them. We were under a very hot fire while advancing. Some Boers that we couldn't see were peppering us terribly.'[12]

Time for defensive action.

'Stand to your horses!'[13] the Colonel himself roars, and the men rush to their steeds, holding hard on the reins and awaiting the order to mount. The orders have been given just in time, for only a minute later the Boers bring one of their own dreaded Pom-Pom guns to bear and, with near perfect range, wreak havoc. Five horses are killed with the first shot – though not cleanly, some of them having a leg or two blown away first, which sees them agonisingly trying to crawl away trailing their bloody stumps. Many of them stampede and it is hell's own work to gather them in once more and go again, but that is what they must do. It is perhaps in such activities that Breaker Morant is at his best, for, while being every bit as good a shot as most of his fellow Troopers, and braver than most, there is not *one* of them who gets near to his ability to grab the reins of a horse galloping by, leap a'saddle, round up the other steeds at full tilt, and restore them to their original Troopers.

'We mounted at once and scattered,' Booth recounts of such episodes. 'The shells were bursting all round us and just then 2000 Boers came galloping over the ridge and opened a heavy fire on us.'

Right beside Booth, 'Poor Lilley, our Adjutant, was shot in the head just near me and fell down in a pool of blood.'[14]

The Troopers fall back, the guns are brought forward, the range determined, the cannon loaded. Fingers in your ears as the artilleryman shouts his orders, and now the explosion.

The puff of dust goes up and we cheer, just as the rolling thunder of the explosion reaches us. Not a direct hit, but close.

Another puff, this time right among them, even as they are scrambling to get away. 'We killed a lot that day,' Booth records, 'and drove them back 20 miles. We also captured Brandfort.'[15]

Capturing that town is good news. The bad news is when Fred Booth's 2nd Victorian Mounted Rifles are invited to lead the victory parade, their Commanding Officer must reply: 'But my men have no trousers.'[16] Usually, men are caught with their pants down. Have these Victorians really *caught a town* while wearing no pants at all? More or less. At least no 'trousers' that are anything more than rags. The victory parade will have to go to the better-attired, those not on the pointy end of the spear. On that subject, they are very quickly back on point in any case heading out after the retreating Boers, and pushing hard.

Somewhere up ahead the Boers will set themselves once more, dug in atop a kopje, perhaps on our flanks, and it will be a question of how many of us they kill in the first few shots and salvoes before we can use our superior firepower and numbers to get some of them in return. But even if they kill more of us than we do of them it doesn't matter. We now have 120,000 soldiers on the ground in South Africa – 40,000 in this column – with more on the way, and so have men to lose. And the Boers don't . . . So desperate are they for even an approximation of manpower, they are accepting boy-power, in a few cases even having 11-year-olds in their ranks.

And yet, though *nothing* alters the fact that we are advancing at the steady rate of eight miles a day – the speed of their slowest oxen – still the Boers manage to do damage, making it intense for those on the prow.

'We were under a very hot fire while advancing,' Fred Booth notes. But the fire upon the Boers is hotter still.

It is for good reason, Fred proudly notes to his mother, that their unit has become known to 'the English Tommies as "the Devil's Own" because we get into the hottest fire and come out with the least loss'.[17]

The next key obstacle to present itself is the Vet River, the first of three major rivers to cross before they get to Johannesburg and then Pretoria.

•

For Deneys Reitz, it has been a darkly dispiriting day, riding towards the oncoming British forces, only to be confronted by a flood of Boers coming the other way.

Hundreds of them!

Yes, they claim they are moving to 'fresh positions', but Reitz has the distinct impression that most of them are 'on their way home for good. They said that great swarms of British troops were on the move, and that it was useless to think of fighting them in the open.'[18]

Undaunted, Reitz and his dozen fellow Commandos keep moving forward until, after dark, they arrive at the Vet River where they intend to make a stand, and so ready themselves to make camp for the night. But what's this?

A Boer they come across tells them that the great Boer General Koos de la Rey is in a camp nearby. Young Reitz has known the General, and most of the Boer leadership – both political and military – since childhood, and with his men makes his way towards him, settling down the sentries as they go. A tight community, many of the Boer guerrillas either know each other directly, or know someone who knows the other.

Finally, nearing midnight, they come to the General himself – a venerated veteran of the First Boer War – his craggy, bushy features lit by the campfire, sitting by his brother who is nursing an arm that had been shattered by a bullet that very afternoon.

Is that you, young Deneys?

Dit is Generaal, en good om jou to sien. It is, General, and how good to see you.

Welcomed to the fire, the young fellow sits by this 'splendid looking old man with a hawk-like nose',[19] as they compare notes. The situation, the General makes clear, is very black. The town of Brandfort has fallen and Kroonstad is threatened. For the advance of the British Army, after capturing General Cronje and 4000 of his men at Paardeberg, had been relentless. After taking Bloemfontein, they are 'now advancing on the Transvaal'. With most of the Boer forces scattered and demoralised, and with the lack of defensive cover between here and Pretoria, the General sees 'little hope of stopping them'.[20]

Of the many problems they face, one is a lack of fresh manpower – a lot of the men from the Commando units have returned to their farms.

'The Free State commandos,' the old man reports, 'have disappeared altogether, although I believe that President Steyn and [General] Christiaan de Wet are trying to reorganize them somewhere in the mountain country to the east, but for the time being they are out of action.'[21]

And beyond manpower, they also lack food for themselves and their horses, together with guns and ammunition.

Despite it all, however, the General has plans and, as Reitz will recount, the old man 'had been busy in the western Transvaal raising fresh commandos, and infusing new spirit in the fighting men by his ceaseless activity and by the great affection they had for this wonderful old man'.[22]

They will fight for him, and even die for him, and de la Rey returns their ardour in kind. The next day, while young Reitz is with him, they must bury some of their dead and, standing at the grave, 'de la Rey addressed us in eloquent words that moved many to tears, for besides being a fighter he had a fine gift of simple speech'.[23]

And that is de la Rey all over.

'I was surprised,' Reitz records, 'that he managed to keep so many with him, considering the way in which things were going to pieces, but he had more control over men than any officer that I had seen thus far.'

As for what to do now, de la Rey is clear.

Continue to fight. Specifically, *tonight*, he orders Reitz and his companions to head south for half an hour and there wait until dawn, at which point they must find the Boer defensive line and thicken it up for the British who will be not far away.

Ja, Generaal. Yes, General.

A warm handshake.

Tot ons weer ontmoet. Until we meet again.

To his men, Reitz is clear: *Opzaal.* Saddle up.

Taking their leave, Reitz and his men ride south for four miles where, normally, they might have made camp, so exhausted are they. But it is so cold – below freezing – there is simply no point in setting up tents as they know that sleep is out of the question. All they can do is wrap their blankets around themselves sit tightly together against the freezing night breeze, and await the dawn.

•

The looting and then burning of Boer homesteads continues apace now as the British forces move deeper into enemy territory, becoming progressively more desperate for food . . . and still more hard-hearted about the horrors of what they are doing.

'The first sight which met my gaze,' one war correspondent would recount, 'was that of a score of men, some with their feet on the necks of turkeys, ducks, and fowls. Quicker than it takes me to tell the story, the women and children had been discovered in an outhouse; several troopers were occupied pouring paraffin about the flooring and walls of the house. Within five minutes the dwelling was ablaze. Still the womenfolk rushed in and out, trying to save what they could.'[24]

And the truth is, the Troopers are following the direct orders of 'Lord Roberts "to render untenable" the farms of such men who, having surrendered, were found to be still in league with the enemy, or were but making use of British magnanimity as a means to save their property, while they still actively favoured the enemy'.[25]

As recounted by the correspondent of the *London Morning Leader*:

'General French and General Pole-Carew, at the head of the Guards and 18th Brigade, are marching in, burning practically everything on the road. The brigade is followed by about 3500 head of loot, cattle and sheep. Hundreds of tons of corn and forage have been destroyed. The troops engaged in the work are Roberts' Horse, the Canadians and Australians.'[26]

Dawn, 4 May 1900, Vet River, 60 miles north of Bloemfontein, the British are coming

It is a strange thing to live a life where you are distinctly aware that every sunrise may be your last . . . and rarely has Deneys Reitz felt more distinctly like that than at this moment.

Atop the ridge that runs some 40 miles north of Bloemfontein, the Boer defenders of Orange Free State look out and see a mass of brown and pink, the muted colours of the British uniform blending in with the countryside. Here they come . . .

'We . . . soon made out dense masses of English infantry on the plain.'[27]

The advance guard of mounted Troopers they had seen advancing the night before has swelled unbelievably overnight.

'First came a screen of horsemen, and behind a multitude of infantry, guns and wagons throwing up huge clouds of dust. We looked in dismay at the advancing host, for there were thirty thousand men approaching, whilst on our meagre front there may have been between three and four thousand Boer horsemen, strung out in a ragged line on the rising ground to right and left of us.'[28]

It is obvious by the jittery way his fellow Boers sit on their horses there is no common feeling to make a stand here, and rightly so. In previous weeks, preparing for this push, they have been massing their forces, blowing up bridges, positioning artillery and caching shells and ammunition. But nothing can quite prepare them for seeing the sheer *numbers* of enemy arrayed against them.

'Against such heavy odds, the task was manifestly beyond them.'[29]

What they can do is at least damage the leading fringe and so they prepare, having their horses led back down the ridge a way, while they load their Mausers, take to their bellies and take aim.

Laat elke skoot tel! Let every shot count!

Kill the *verdomde rooi nekke*. Kill the damn red necks!

And so they do. But nothing can stop the flood.

'The enemy forces came steadily on until their scouts were close to us. When we fired at these they fell back upon their regiments; the batteries unlimbered and in a few seconds shrapnel was bursting over us.'[30]

Terugtrek. Pull back.

Beweeg vining! Move quickly.

Back to the horses, and away, 'galloping back with field-gun and pom-pom shells besprinkling us as we rode. We had no casualties, but a number of men from other Commandos were killed and wounded before we got clear, and after a hard ride we slowed down at a deserted farmhouse to breathe our winded animals.'[31]

And so it goes.

As most of the English troops are infantry they can move no faster than marching pace as a body, meaning most of the battles of the day are fought between the forward horse-borne elements of Lord Roberts' forces – including Fred Booth and Breaker Morant – and the retreating Boers, who overall suffer very little loss. In a stuttering manner they fall back until the English scouts come up and fire upon them before falling back as the enemy cannon are brought forward and Boer shell-fire sweeps them like the gusts of a terrible storm.

'We had to exercise ceaseless vigilance to keep the English horse from [our] wagons that were struggling to get away,' Reitz chronicles. 'There must have been over a thousand of these, for, in addition to General de la Rey's transport, there were a great many vehicles belonging to the civilian population fleeing before the oncoming invasion. By dark the English had pushed us right back to the Vet River, a distance of twenty miles or more, and next morning we had scarcely time to prepare a hasty breakfast before we could see the columns again advancing towards us.'[32]

(And yes, this congregation of 1000 wagons is in contravention of the Kroonstad resolutions insisting that the Boers should no longer use their cumbersome carts, but the typical good burgher so loves the comfort of his own wagon – a mattress, a tent, his own 'boy' to cook, cutlery, a personal supply of whisky – it is hard to separate him from them.)

As they cross the river at a particularly shallow drift, which allows both the wagons and horses to make their way through, they note a tall distinguished-looking man on horseback observing them. Right beside him is a man with a long flowing beard and piercing wild eyes, rather ostentatiously carrying a Bible.

For now, in consultation with this man, General Koos de la Rey and his Boer Commandants position their forces in a four-mile front along the Vet River, on both sides, to make sure the British pay as heavy a price as possible at the crossing. Sure enough, they can see now British infantry 'feeling their way over the plain that ran down to the river, and before long were volleying at us from tall grass in which we could only just see where they lay'.[33]

Soon enough the great black mouths of the British guns turn their appetite elsewhere, their barrels primed to shell the Boer positions, while the Boers fire back at whatever gun crews they can get a bead on.

'Our horses were safe in the riverbed behind, but owing to the thorn trees fringing the bank our view was impeded, and we had to crawl to the outside edge of the bush to see the enemy, with the result that we had practically no cover and had casualties almost at once. Several men were killed and wounded close to me, and altogether it was a beastly day.'[34]

At 3 pm the British forces are close enough that their infantry can charge, bayonets to the fore.

'The shell-fire and the casualties had shaken us, and when the British rose to their feet, and from their rear some three hundred cavalry came riding, sword in hand, we rose to fire a few wavering shots, and then broke for the river behind, tumbling down pell-mell to get our horses.

Leaving our dead, we rode up the opposite bank and went racing across the open to the hills a mile to rearward.'[35]

By sundown most of the British forces have crossed the Vet, and some have moved far enough north that they are starting to outflank Deneys Reitz and his comrades, who have been holding the extreme western end of the Boer defensive position.

It is time to withdraw completely.

'We trekked on till after midnight, our only crumb of comfort being our Native boy awaiting us beside the road, his voice quavering with emotion at seeing all four of us, still alive. The withdrawal was continued next morning without waiting for the enemy, and by midday we were across the Sand River, thirty miles and more from the scene of yesterday's encounter.'[36]

At least the Boer defence has allowed most of the wagons to get clear, but the pattern is now set with the British surging forward until they are hit, falling back to let their artillery dislodge the Boers, at which point they move forward once more ... their galloping silhouettes appearing on the southern horizon, more often than not against the backdrop of a billowing dust-cloud generated by tens of thousands of men coming behind ...

In this instance, as recounted by Deneys Reitz, 'it was towards evening of the next day that they came – a small advance guard of two hundred horsemen with a gun, riding so fast that before we could stand to arms they were on the south bank of the Sand River, and had killed one of the [men] preparing to dynamite the bridge'.[37]

The only thing capable of stopping the mass of the British juggernaut would be another massive juggernaut, and the Boers don't have one. In this encounter Reitz and his comrades at least bring down two enemy scouts and get close enough to talk to the wounded men.

'They were both Canadians, badly wounded, one of whom told me that many thousands of their people, as well as Australians and other colonial forces, had volunteered for the war, as if the odds against us were not heavy enough already.'[38]

There is no time for further reflection, and they leave the wounded to be collected and cared for by their own men. Reitz and his companions must get away, move back, pausing only to gather in the careering horses who have had their riders atop shot from their saddles, and put them together with those of the Boer brethren who have had their horses shot out from under them.

•

Fred Booth, Breaker Morant and their comrades of Colonel Henry's 4th Mounted Infantry Corps are exhausted, now having been at the pointy end of the British push for weeks on end without relief. They are half-starving, always thirsty, always shelled and shot at – the lead elements of the push suffer casualties every day, mostly from Boer snipers – and even at night there is precious little respite.

'What sleep you do get,' Fred writes, 'is lying down in your clothes with all accoutrements on – 150 rounds strapped on your back – but we have to put up with it for the Boers are in front of us in great force. Last night we heard that an Australian patrol was fired on, two were shot dead, some wounded and the rest captured . . . There is some talk of sending us home to England when the war is over.'[39]

For yes, that's it. Despite their many struggles, nothing changes the fact that the great British beast of war can be irritated, it can be harassed, it can even be temporarily delayed. But it cannot be *stopped*.

With every passing moment it draws nearer precious Pretoria.

After the Vet River is crossed, the Sand River is equally conquered by all forces by 10 May and Kroonstad captured on 11 May. Still, as the Boers move closer to their base of Pretoria so too do their defences stiffen, together with the firepower they can bring.

'The Boers have some very good guns and they make good use of them,' Fred Booth records. 'It was a terrible strain when the shells are screaming amongst you and burst. Bullets seem a nothing compared with shells.'[40]

Still Booth and his comrades push forward, which sees the shells continuing to fall 'with a swish all round me. It is marvellous how I escaped. As we trot away to cover we look down the line to watch the other fellows. Then we see a shell burst and cover a fellow with dust we eagerly watch till the dust clears away.

'Even amongst all the fire we keep a fairly good line with our proper interval. We ride company behind company and if we bunched up at all there would be terrible slaughter . . . everyone admits how terrible artillery fire is, yet no one attempts to move till he is told and no matter how good your horse you never move to get cover any quicker than the regiment such is British discipline.'[41]

(By God it comes at cost though. The next morning Fred Booth visits the Inniskilling Dragoons, to find them burying their dead. There were no fewer than 14 in one grave, with another 40 wounded.)

Such is the cost of the advances they have made.

And yet, while the forces of Lord Roberts really are making huge advances in the Orange Free State so are his forces under Lieutenant Colonel Herbert Plumer about to make a major breakthrough in Bechuanaland . . .

17 May 1900, Mafeking, rejoice, rejoice!

It is the way of the Boers. They will fight like a caracal in a corner to slow and blow away all British strays they can isolate. But when a large enough British force does fight its way through towards a besieged town – and it is clear they can't be stopped – then the Boers are just as inclined to suddenly melt away in the night, preserving their ability to fight another day. As a guerrilla force with no manpower to spare in trying to stop the unstoppable, there is to be no useless sacrifice of their own lives.

So it proves on this evening when Major Walter 'Karri' Davies of the Imperial Light Horse – a prominent Australian, who'd been a Johannesburg Uitlander for 15 years before the war – cautiously pushes forward with the advance guard, when one of his men suddenly says with wonder:

'There's Mafeking . . .'[42]

Almost as one, each man brings his glass up and peers across the veldt. And sure enough . . .

'There it lay,' the war correspondent Filson Young of the *Manchester Guardian* records, 'the little town that we had come so far to see, a tiny cluster of white near the eastward horizon, glistening amid the yellowish-brown of the flats. We looked at it for a few moments in silence . . .'[43]

And now they push on.

When, on the edge of the town, they stop to tell the first man they see that they are the advance guard of the relieving force, the answer is amazingly laconic.

'Oh, yes,' says the fellow, 'I heard you were knocking about outside somewhere!'

Either way, after 217 days, the siege of Mafeking is over, and real celebrations break out soon enough when Colonel Bryan Mahon himself rides into town at the head of his troops and the survivors realise that it really is all over and the Boers have gone!

In all, 101 British Troopers have been killed, and 123 wounded. Most devastated have been the 300 men of the 'Black Watch', the Africans forced to defend the perimeter of the town. It will much later be alleged that some of them had died of hunger, as Baden-Powell had 'systematically reduced their rations in order to feed the white minority'.[44] There had been a similarly cruel calculus in operation among the town's civilians, with it being estimated that no fewer than 700 of the African residents had died of starvation.

As High Commissioner of Southern Africa Alfred Milner had previously noted of affairs in this part of the world, 'You have only to sacrifice "the n . . . r" absolutely, and the game is easy.'[45]

In Britain there is nothing at all laconic in the reaction when the news gets through, with the jubilation on the streets of London so hysterical that a whole new word is invented to describe it: 'mafficking'.

•

This is the way of it for now: the British push and the Boers fall – down or back.

One of the Boer defenders, Hendrik van Themaat, finds himself firing at the advancing British between a young man and an old man. When the young man's rifle jams, he explodes with frustration, roaring, *God Verdomp!* Goddamn!

'Our lives are in God's hands,' the old man gently admonishes him, 'and he could summon us to eternity at any moment.'[46]

Now, of all times, is not the time to be blaspheming.

'Now began anew the long-drawn humiliation of retreat,' Reitz records. 'All day we were driven relentlessly; the British herded us like sheep to the incessant shriek of shells and the whizz of bullets, and by evening we were a demoralized rabble fleeing blindly across the veldt.'[47]

The way is clear . . .

For this, friends, is not merely hundreds of horsemen splashing through the ford over a river. It is who those horsemen *are* that counts, and what that river represents!

For yes, on this 24th day of May 1900, the advance guard of Lord Roberts' British forces cross the Vaal River – trans the Vaal, if you will – and, digging their spurs into the sides of their dripping mounts as they come out of the river, are now *galloping* into Transvaal. The rich goldfields of the Rand in Johannesburg are now only 40 miles to the north, and Pretoria another 40 miles beyond that.

Given that today is the Queen's Birthday, the British Army is particularly enthusiastic to cross the Vaal into Transvaal on such an auspicious day – what a gift for Her Majesty! – and now the main body of the troops are rushed forward.

'So down the steep bank they went,' Banjo Paterson records, 'guns, carts, wagons, and all, and set to bumping and splashing their stores across the river. The guns got across all right, but numbers of the carts capsized or broke down, or for a while there were no less than four carts at once upside down in the middle of the river, while the half-drowned horses splashed and floundered like grampuses.'[48]

By the evening, the entire column is safely over the river and gathered on a green flat of the Transvaal, surrounded by once proud kopjes that now must bow to the British majesty.

Rum is issued to the troops to mark the occasion, to toast Her Majesty and to sing their favourite songs. No fewer than 20,000 voices strong, their words soar into the sparkling night sky . . .

> *It's the soldiers of the Queen, my lads*
> *Who've been my lads, who've seen my lads*
> *In the fight for England's glory, lads*
> *When we have to show them what we mean*
> *And when we say we've always won*
> *And when they ask us how it's done*
> *We'll proudly point to every one*
> *Of England's soldiers of the Queen.*[49]

A good time is had by all, bar the Boers.

The next morning as the British forces set off once more, the invaders behold a strange sight.

'At daylight,' Banjo records, 'we saw the Boers sitting in dozens, like little wooden figures, in the distant mountains, looking disconsolately at our approach. They had come up to oppose our landing, but were luckily a day late. They did not attack, and we toiled over the high hills [towards Pretoria . . .]'[50]

As to the Boers fleeing before them, the Boer leader of the Johannesburg Commando, Ben Viljoen, sorrowfully chronicles, 'The roads to Pretoria were crowded with men, guns and vehicles of every description and despondency and despair were plainly visible on every human face . . . We asked ourselves "What is to be the end of all this and what is to become of our poor people?" . . . The greatest confusion naturally prevailed, and as all the generals gave different orders, no one knew what was to be done. General Botha intended to offer resistance . . .'[51]

So they do, at least a little, with the remaining forces available. But with 35,000 British troops now pushing north, and just 5000 Boer defenders trying to stop them, the parallels with Thermopylae become unavoidable.

King Leonidas may have been bold, brave and brash – a spirit worthy of a Boer – but at the end of the day, King Leonidas lost.

In the case of Ben Viljoen, history risks repeating itself . . . repeating itself.

30 May 1900, outside Johannesburg, French letters for the night

This time it is less a case of merely happening to be in the right place at the right time, for Banjo Paterson is going to an enormous effort to be there, as he accompanies a dispatch rider taking communications from General French, who is pushing north from a position west of Johannesburg, to Lord Roberts and his forces east of Johannesburg.

At 3 am the riders arrive, Lord Roberts is roused, and he emerges from a back room where he has been sleeping on a small stretcher, dressed in his night-shirt.

Paterson observes carefully as the old man, looking every bit his 70 years and more, methodically goes through each dispatch, marking it to the attention of particular officers, who will have them before dawn. When finally completed, it is as if Roberts notices Paterson's accent for the first time and asks how the Australian troops with French are getting on.

Banjo replies with quiet pride that they have been fighting very successfully indeed, which prompts Roberts to remark.

'When I first saw the Australians, I thought they were too untrained to be of much use. But the work I have given them to do is the best proof of what I think of them now.'

'The only thing the Australians need,' Banjo replies, taking the opportunity to pass on the plea he has heard from all quarters, 'is more horses.'[52]

'That's what everybody wants, more horses,' Bobs replies, before turning to the staff officer and crisply ordering him: 'Make a note of that. Stir up the remount people and let me know what they are doing.'[53]

Banjo Paterson says his goodbyes and not long afterwards runs into Winston Churchill who has – *of course you have, Winston, because only you could get away with it* – ridden through the heart of Johannesburg on his *bicycle*, to ensure that his latest death-defying prose can be delivered to his newspaper in time for the next editions.

'The town,' Banjo will recount, 'was full of Boers drowning the sorrows of their retreat in drink. If they had recognised him, they would most likely have shot him, as they were a bit out of hand, and he had written some things that they bitterly resented. One must hand it to this Churchill that he has pluck.'[54]

But to the business at hand.

With the fall of Johannesburg – where Lord Roberts arrives in triumphal procession the next morning, looking as crisp and as fresh as ever – it is obvious to most that Pretoria, just 40 miles to the north, will also quickly fall and this war will soon be over.

And so Lord Roberts now issues a proclamation to be read out and posted in public places:

> To the
> Inhabitants of the South African Republic
>
> ... I, Frederick Sleigh, Baron Roberts of Kandahar and Waterford, KP, GCB, GCSI, GCIE, VC, Commanding-in-Chief Her Majesties Forces South Africa, am authorized by the Government of Her Majesty to make known and do hereby make known as follows:
>
> All burghers ... who are willing to lay down their arms at once, to bind themselves by an oath to abstain from further participation in the war, will be given passes to allow them to return to their homes and will not be made prisoners of war ...
>
> Given under my hand and seal, at Johannesburg, this 31st Day of May 1900
> Roberts
> Field-Marshal
> Commanding-in-Chief, South Africa.[55]

The response is fairly swift as, even from that very day, many Boers bow to the inevitable, come forward with their arms and hand them in at the many offices set up in the towns for this very purpose, before signing a declaration that they will no longer participate in hostilities against the British. They walk away relieved.

Yes, this war has been terrible. And devastating for their country, which now truly still exists in name only. But at least they have their lives and their livelihoods, with their homes and barns still standing, their animals in their corrals, and their crops in the ground. With their details recorded, this should give them protection.

With Johannesburg secured, it means the precious goldfields of the Transvaal are now occupied by the forces of the British Empire, and it seems there remains just one last city to capture, before the war is surely over.

The fall of Pretoria, the final sovereign jewel in the Transvaal crown, seems little more than a formality. Many of the Boers think the same.

On 1 June, an exhausted Deneys Reitz is with his equally shattered Boer column falling back from Johannesburg to Pretoria when, out to their east and in a roughly parallel course, they can see a British mounted column heading to the same place. And yet far from firing at each other, neither column blinks.

'Indeed,' Reitz records, 'I believe the English could have ridden among us that day, without firing a shot, so strong was the conviction that our army was disbanded and the war at an end.'[56]

It is only when the English come within sight of the two old forts on the ridge that lies on the south side of Pretoria that they must take pause, as those forts start to belch fire upon them with every cannon they have.

Still in the prow of the British push, Fred Booth and the men of the 2nd Victorian Mounted Rifles are all too aware of those cannon when suddenly shells start bursting among them, taking down horses and men.

As they get still closer, it is obvious the cannon on those forts must be neutralised. The mounted forces momentarily retreat behind a small kopje therefore, as the biggest of all their big guns are brought forward.

'We call them Weary Willies,' Fred Booth will explain to his family. 'It takes a span of forty bullocks to draw one. They are manned by the Naval Brigade.'[57]

(And therein lies a story. While at the beginning of the war the superior range of the Boers' 'Long Toms' had been a real problem, Captain Percy Scott of the Royal Navy had come up with a solution – designing and building gun carriages strong enough that the fort guns defending Cape Town could be used in the field. A group of sailors had become the gun crews and two of those guns had been on the whole push to Pretoria, and . . . here they are now!)

Classified as 4.7-inch quick-fire naval guns, they have a range of 10,000 yards and are capable of firing no fewer than five 45-pound shells every minute. Yes, the weight of each gun is a massive seven tons, which is why the oxen must strain so to bring them forward, but it is worth it.

While the Weary Willies start blasting the forts and manage to destroy the Boer guns one by one, Lord Roberts' Troopers – 12,000 of them, including Fred Booth and Breaker Morant – set themselves up on the long line of kopjes just south of the town and fire upon the few remaining defending Boers.

'I had some very narrow escapes,' Booth tells his family. 'Several bullets landed within an inch or two while we were lying in the grass and the next shot hit the next man to me in the shoulder . . . We were behind rocks but when we fired we had to raise our head and shoulders above and then the bullets would hum about us.'[58]

The Boers are brave, but Lord Roberts' firepower – both in terms of rifle-wielding Troopers and Weary Willies – is simply overwhelming.

•

Gentlemen? Assemble if you would.

An urgent meeting of the leading Boer officers is called outside Irene Estate near Pretoria and it is while there they hear the news: '*Oom Paul*', President Kruger, has left Pretoria on a train and in a rush, closely followed by his Cabinet, intending to re-establish themselves in Machadodorp, a town in the eastern Transvaal.

Soon enough another telegram arrives, informing them that 'a crowd has broken into the Commissariat buildings in Pretoria and is looting them'.[59]

That evening at ten o'clock, two strapping brothers on horseback hurry along the suddenly deserted streets of Pretoria, eager to get to the family home of their parents in the suburb of Sunnyside, which they have not been able to reach for many months. It is Deneys and Hjalmar Reitz, hoping against hope that their mother and father might still be there only to find . . .

All is in darkness. Their parents had departed with some pace, several days before, with their father in particular danger, given his senior position in the Kruger government.

They would report that neighbours told them, 'President Kruger and your father had run away and that Pretoria was to be surrendered to the British in the morning after which the door was slammed in our faces . . . The next morning the streets were full of leaderless men, knowing even less of the situation than ourselves. All was confusing, with looting of shops and supply depots and a great deal of criticism of our leaders.'[60]

4 June 1900, Pretoria, strange dental work

Well, this is an odd situation for a 25-year-old Sydney dentist to find himself in. Out of dentistry school, William Walker had been in practice in Balmain for just three years when the Boer War began.

He had joined the NSW Mounted Rifles, risen to the rank of Lieutenant and done well, seeing action in the capture of Bloemfontein and the advance to Johannesburg across such fierce battles as those at Karee Siding, and the Vet and Sand rivers.

That very morning, as it happens, he had done so well in chasing
and capturing a Boer gun – demonstrating his usual pluck and initiative – that he had again come to the attention of his seniors, at the
very time they had been given a particular task. For also that morning
General Ian Hamilton had sent word to the Imperial Mounted Infantry's
Colonel Henry de Lisle to send one of his officers into Pretoria to seek
the Boers' surrender.

And Colonel de Lisle had known just the man – that quiet Sydney
Lieutenant, you know the chappie . . . young Walker. De Lisle had come
to know him a little and considered that 'he could be depended upon to
carry out a game of bluff without being detected'.[61]

Yes, just the chappie.

'Now, lad,' Colonel de Lisle had said to him, beaming, just an hour
before, 'you've done so well, are you fit to take the white flag into
the city and demand they surrender in the name of Lord Roberts and the
British Army?'

'Rather!'[62] Walker instantly replied, meaning . . .

Meaning that now here he is, slowly walking down the wide and dusty
boulevards of Pretoria, holding high de Lisle's riding crop to which is
tied Walker's white handkerchief.

It had seemed like a good idea at the time . . .

But is it?

Is this even sane, to be the sole representative of the British Empire
walking unarmed into the lair of the lion they have just humiliated,
asking them to sign their own surrender? He can feel many eyes upon
him as he keeps striding forth, sometimes past the smoking ruins of
houses that the British artillery has just destroyed, past wounded Boer
soldiers in bloody and tattered clothes who stare at him with glazed
eyes, past caring. But all he can do is keep walking to the town centre.
It is his duty.

He keeps going until he arrives at the Town Hall where he meets the
mayor and his council.

Mr Mayor?

There is an emissary here under a white flag, saying that he has come
in the name of Lord Roberts, the Commander-in-Chief of the British
Army, demanding our surrender. Not sure if he is bluffing, in indicating
the entire British Army is right behind him, but I don't think so.

Show him in.

And so, in a story he will tell ever afterwards, that is how an unarmed
Sydney dentist effectively received the surrender of Pretoria, which seems

tantamount to the surrender of the South African Republic and the end of the war! And what a story indeed for young Walker, the most excitement he had ever expected to see were chipped teeth and root canals, not the total collapse and surrender of *empires*. It is agreed that Walker will escort the Mayor back to see General Hamilton where the surrender can be made formal. But, one thing before we go.

Would you, Lieutenant Walker asks, sign my white handkerchief? With extraordinary good grace under the circumstances, the Mayor does so, as do Generals Hamilton, Hutton and de Lisle when they arrive to complete the formalities. So too does Lord Roberts when he arrives.

It is just another day in the life of a Sydney dentist, on the loose in the Boer War.

Well done, young Walker.

Ah, but there is still *some* unfinished business, and Winston Churchill is the man to finish it, only minutes after he comes galloping into the Boers' fallen capital. His escape from the prison had seen its closure for lack of security, with the inmates transferred to a new one just a few blocks away and . . .

And there it is!

On the other side of a dense wire entanglement stands a long tin building.

Churchill, being Churchill, cannot resist the dramatic and theatrical gesture, and so raises his hat and cries out.

Great Britain is here!

The cry is instantly taken up inside the building, as the men who had been his fellow prisoners recognise his voice. No matter that Churchill is accompanied only by his cousin Charles, 9th Duke of Marlborough, Military Secretary to Lord Roberts, while they are now confronted by armed Boer guards, some of whom recognise the infernal Englishman who had escaped all those months ago. Their lack of numbers and weaponry is more than made up for by the grandeur of Marlborough's dress, 'resplendent in the red tabs of the staff', and he now rather magnificently calls for the Commandant. In the chilled pause that follows – it seems clear to the guards that anyone who shoots at this extraordinary figure would himself soon be shot – the prisoners rush forth from their quarters, cheering, yelling.

It is the sentries who break first, throwing down their rifles. With this, the gates are flung open, the last of the uncertain guards have their weapons seized by the long penned-up British officers who surround them, and from seemingly nowhere a Union Jack is magically produced!

'The Transvaal emblem was torn down,' Churchill chronicles, 'and amidst wild cheers from our captive friends the first British flag was hoisted over Pretoria. Time; 8.47, June 5. Tableau!'[63]

Oh, the sheer joy of it for those who have been advancing to Pretoria all these months.

'We were marching on our way to fight,' Fred Booth records, 'and just in sight of their fort, we heard the news that Pretoria had surrendered. Then you should have heard the cheering, cheer after cheer went up and as the news spread from regiment to regiment we could hear them still cheering in the distance.'[64]

They enter Pretoria thus, as triumphant troops. Although this capital does not seem to be really a capital place?

'There is no paper published in Pretoria,' one Trooper will later note of the place, 'which is a half-finished sort of town with real good buildings and tumble down shanties side by side. No footpaths to speak of, and you may at a street corner find a drop of two feet from the so-called pavement to the street, while verandah posts are in the middle of the path and an open water-race in the middle of what is left of the pathway.'[65]

It is, and no mistake, a rather unprepossessing kind of place to have been at the centre of so much trouble for the British Empire.

In any case, the main thing is that Lord Roberts' proclamation is having a rapid effect.

'The Boers,' Banjo Paterson reports to the readers of the *Sydney Morning Herald*, 'are giving up their arms in hundreds at the Government buildings. Big sturdy bearded men riding in on their marvellous African ponies, and solemnly depositing their well-beloved rifles at the door, and solemnly riding away again.'[66]

It is possible, just possible, mind, that there will still be a little resistance from the die-hards as 'a few drifting commandos look like making things unsettled for a while. [But] Lord Roberts will, no doubt, deal with them and we Australians all devoutly believe that this is practically the end of the war . . .'[67]

Conan Doyle, among many, agrees, later telling his readers: 'Pretoria was in our hands. It seemed to all of us that the campaign was over and that only cleaning-up remained to be done . . .'[68]

For his part, Winston Churchill is not so sure, noting, 'there were still many thousands of wild fierce, dauntless men, Botha, Smuts, de la Rey and Hertzog, who now fought on not for victory, but for honour . . . The roving enemy wore no uniform of their own, they mingled with the population, lodged and were succoured in farmhouses whose owners had taken the oath of neutrality and sprang into being, now here, now there, to make some formidable and bloody attack upon an unwary column or isolated post.'[69]

The point of continued Boer resistance is further made with some passion by President Martinus Steyn himself, who soon issues a proclamation of his own that – despite what has happened and Britain proclaiming the former republic is now 'The Orange River Colony' – in fact, *Die Oranje-Vrystaat*, 'the Orange Free State is not extinguished but is still fighting unconquered . . .'.[70]

CHAPTER SIX

REJOICE!

*In carrying on these 'moveable' fights ... the greatest qualities
needed for the troops were mobility, dash and intelligence, and
in all these qualities the Australian and New Zealand regiments
without exception proved their excellence. It must never be
forgotten that the Australians were accustomed all their lives to
finding their way in the open, to noticing what was taking place
around them, and to relying on themselves at a pinch; the English
'Tommies' were drilled and trained to obey orders, and there their
ideas stopped. It was not that the Australians were any braver
than the English, but that the latter were less intelligent and had
less practical outdoor experience ...*[1]

Banjo Paterson

11 June 1900, Diamond Hill, V for Victory, but no VC

'Another great green plain, with dotted farms and the huge khaki column
slowly spreading across it,' Conan Doyle will begin his account of the
Battle of Diamond Hill, just 12 miles to the east of Pretoria. 'The day
was hot, and 10 miles out the Grenadier Guards had about enough.
Stragglers lay thick among the grass, but the companies kept their double
line formation, and plodded steadily along. Ten miles sounds very little,
but try it in the dust of a column on a hot day, with a rifle over your
shoulder, a hundred rounds of ammunition, a blanket, a canteen, an
empty water-bottle, and a dry tongue.'[2]

Worse, try it when 6000 aggrieved Boer fighters are intent on making
a serious stand. For yes, though much of the British leadership has
assumed that the Boers must give up, now that both their capitals are
occupied, the Boer Generals Louis Botha and Koos de la Rey did not
get the memo.

Between them they have assembled their forces atop the rocky peak
known as Diamond Hill, both in preparation for retaking Pretoria, and to
protect their link with the outside world, the crucial railway to Portuguese

East Africa, which lies beyond. No matter that Lord Roberts' forces are so exhausted after the push from Bloemfontein that not one of his units can get much beyond half strength. Those Boers must be moved, and on 11 June, the British General – amazed that the Boers have not sued for peace, but determined to finish them this time – unleashes 16,000 Troopers against them, including Colonel Henry's Mounted Brigade.

Fred Booth and Breaker Morant are two of many, thus, who on this hot, dry and dusty afternoon approaching Diamond Hill suddenly see something entirely unexpected. It is two groves of gum-trees, both clearly flourishing more than most Australians in these climes!

After camping for the night just beyond the second of these, the Australians are able to sleep with that glorious smell of eucalyptus in the breeze and – reinvigorated – the following morning approach the range of kopjes just four miles ahead.

Their advance hits that half of the Boers commanded by General Koos de la Rey, whose men manage to stop the British advance guard in its tracks.

For most of the rest of the day, the .303s and Mausers exchange distinctly unfriendly greetings before, late in the afternoon, the soldiers of the Queen launch a full-blown charge which, though initially successful, is soon hit by a full-bottle counter-attack.

'Walking over the field afterwards,' the *Adelaide Observer*'s special correspondent chronicles, 'it was curious to notice how Mauser and Lee-Metford cartridge shells lay mingled together, showing how the same spots had been seized as points of vantage by either side.'[3]

'It was the closest thing to a reverse we have yet had,'[4] Lieutenant Percy Vaughan of the 1st Australian Horse will note. Still, the overall British numbers are such that, despite their heavy casualties, they are able to keep pushing up Diamond Hill and exchange close-range fire with the Boers among the rocks.

Typically, Winston Churchill is right on the front lines near the top of the hill – and under heavy fire – when he suddenly sees the Boer defenders falling back. It is obvious to him that *now* is the time to storm the crest of the hill and win the day before the Boers can bring forward their own reinforcements, but to his amazement the officers on the ground give no such orders.

Well, the hell with that.

Taking his own life in his hands, Churchill runs back from the front line, bullets giving up spurts of dirt all around his flying feet, and now mounts the first horse he can find, still charging across open ground, until he gets to General Hamilton to apprise him of the situation.

Now, General, *now*, the battle is won if you only can give the orders to storm the summit immediately.

Now, it is not the usual way of things for war correspondents to be telling Generals what they should and shouldn't do, but this is no usual war correspondent. For one thing, young Churchill is still the toast of Britain for his daring escape, for another he has the largest readership of any war correspondent in South Africa, including those at Whitehall . . . and for another, Hamilton has come to appreciate that the aristocratic young man is astute in his assessments. And the gasping correspondent really has come from the front lines and seen this with his own eyes.

Hamilton gives the order. Runners are dispatched, the British troops just below the crest soon storm forward and, just as Churchill had predicted, the day is won. Diamond Hill is secured, and the Boers' last chance to retake Pretoria is gone.

For Churchill's bravery in risking shot and shell, Hamilton goes so far as to recommend him for the Victoria Cross, but both Roberts and Kitchener decline on the grounds that Churchill is 'only a Press Correspondent'.[5]

So be it.

Churchill, among many, has had enough.

'I decided to return home,' he will note. 'Our operations were at an end. The war had become a guerrilla and promised to be shapeless and indefinite. A general election could not long be delayed. With the consent of the authorities I resumed my full civilian status and took the train for Cape Town.'[6]

Conan Doyle certainly agrees and books the next passage home, eager to get his book on the just finished Boer War out before Christmas. Rudyard Kipling is also on the first British-bound ship leaving from Cape Town.

For their part, many of the soldiers like Fred Booth who have been in the thick of the action for months, seem to feel two primary emotions – amazement to still be alive, and relief that it is nearly over.

'Sickness has played terrible havoc amongst our regiment,' Fred writes to his sister. 'Out of five hundred [of my original regiment] only two hundred are left. Heard today another private and two officers are dead. I am as well as ever and have never yet been sick.'

But the main thing?

This battle has surely finished the Boers.

'We are expecting the end of the war at any moment,'[7] Booth writes home.

Such views do not please many of the most recently landed Australians, many from the Queensland and Western Australian contingents. The problem is, it doesn't look like there will be much need for them, bar a little garrison duty along supply routes like that from Mafeking to Pretoria. There will be staging posts every 30 or 40 miles or so between the two towns. Colonel Robert Baden-Powell establishes one at Zeerust in early June; Colonel Herbert Plumer with the Rhodesians establishes his own at Elands River some 28 miles to the east; and on 13 June, A Squadron of the NSW Citizens' Bushmen, under the command of Major James Thomas, the Tenterfield lawyer, captures the town of Rustenburg, the last link in the line of posts from Mafeking to Pretoria. Pretoria is a further 40 miles on from there. With those posts established, all large bodies of soldiers moving from Mafeking to Pretoria, or the other way, can now be assured of food and shelter after a day's hard march.

It is all very dull stuff, 'a sort of peaceful triumphal march', with Boers surrendering everywhere they go, and the only troubling thing being, as Major Thomas notes to the *Tenterfield Star*, 'I fear that nothing like the proper number of Mauser rifles are handed in.'[8]

It is a worry. The gap between the number of Boers and the number of rifles on the surrender list can only make one doubt the sincerity of the Boers, who have perhaps only nominally surrendered?

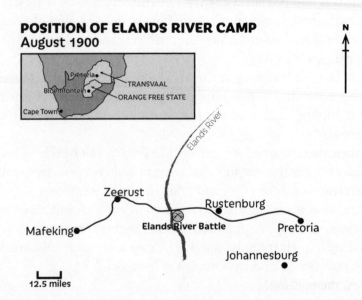

POSITION OF ELANDS RIVER CAMP
August 1900

N

Pretoria
Bloemfontein
TRANSVAAL
ORANGE FREE STATE
Cape Town

Elands River

Zeerust
Rustenburg
Mafeking
Elands River Battle
Pretoria
Johannesburg

12.5 miles

Well, many of Major Thomas' men actively hope so. If only they could get a *little* action in, before heading home. Hopefully, something will turn up.

•

And something just might turn up for Major Thomas and his men, for a minority of Boers, the *bittereinders*, bitter-enders, have decided the war is NOT over. Under Generals Koos de la Rey, Christiaan de Wet and Louis Botha they've unleashed a series of damaging raids. Their prey is small, vulnerable British columns and outposts.

In furious reaction, Lord Roberts issues another proclamation:

> Whereas by Proclamation dated the 16th day of June 1900 of Lord Roberts, Field-Marshal, Commanding in Chief Her Majesty's Forces in South Africa, it was notified to, and the inhabitants and principal civil residents of the Orange River Colony and the South African Republic were warned, that whatever wanton damage to public property, such as Railways, Bridges, Culverts, Telegraph Wires, etc., took place, the houses of persons living in the neighbourhood would be burned, inasmuch as such destruction could not take place without their knowledge and connivance . . .[9]

This level of Boer commitment, manpower and firepower, a week after Pretoria has been taken, is quite shocking. The marauding Boers are still out there.

'The capture of Pretoria,' the surprised Banjo Paterson reports to his readers, 'does not appear to have ended the war.'[10]

It appears this snake can operate independently of its head.

All it has truly ended is the Boer government, as Lord Roberts announces the formal annexation of the *Zuid-Afrikaansche Republiek*, and the establishment of the new official name of 'The Transvaal'.

Late June 1900, Pretoria, Breaker snaps some Burleigh

It is one of those things.

A chance glance in a single direction at a random moment, and the consequences – as a dynamic domino falls in a particular direction, which hits another and then another and then another – are extraordinary.

But already we are ahead of ourselves.

On this day Colonel Jose Gordon is walking across Pretoria's main square, late for a lunch at the Pretoria Club with his friend Bennet Burleigh, the well-known war correspondent, when he happens to spy at a distance Breaker Morant. That slightly bow-legged strut of the champion horseman, that demeanour, that sheer *swagger*, he would know it anywhere – not to mention the unshaven look, the frayed jacket, the scruffy boots. There is no time to say hello to his former shipmate coming across from Adelaide, but when, a short time later, Burleigh asks him to recommend 'a good daring rider and first-class bushman', who could be counted on to dash his reports from the front lines to the nearest telegraphist so as to get back to the *Daily Telegraph*, everything quickly falls into place. For of course Gordon immediately thinks of Morant, telling the correspondent the Breaker is 'a gentleman, a good rider and bushman, and I don't think he personally fears anything',[11] and as soon as the following morning it is done!

So well connected is Burleigh he is able to have Morant brought to him, make the offer, have it gratefully accepted, and secure his transfer from the 2nd South Australian Mounted Rifles by late morning on the next day!

•

In the corner of the Pretoria bar, the two Englishmen – one in his late thirties, the other at least 60 – take a seat and get to it, sipping whisky and telling stories until late into the night, even as they blow plumes of grey smoke and let out uproarious guffaws in equal measure. Breaker Morant and Bennet Burleigh go well together from the first. Personally, they are both supremely colourful men and as fond of telling a good tale as listening to one.

The burly Burleigh has quite a tale to tell. Born in Glasgow, his first work has been as a shipping clerk but a thirst for adventure had seen him travel to North America to join the Confederates' side during the American Civil War, where he had been captured, escaped, taken part in raids, only to be captured and escape again, evading a sentence of death – before turning his hand to journalism, where he had prospered as a war correspondent ever since, covering everything from the war in the Sudan to the First Boer War.

'The call of the bugle and the whiff of powder has lured him to the battlefield,' it will be written of him, 'and he has invariably sent vivid, often brilliant, messages to his Journal.'[12]

If the Breaker's stories can't quite match him in reality, they at least get close in the realms of fantasy and did I tell you, Bennet, how as the son of the great English Admiral George Digby Morant, I once . . .

Burleigh is enthralled, though his taste runs more to stories from the Australian bush, which the Breaker has in plenty, and some of them – a few – are even true!

Professionally, the two work well, with Burleigh providing unfailingly brilliant copy, and the Breaker getting it to the dispatch office come what may.

As a matter of fact, the Breaker also impresses many of those in the esteemed circles in which Bennet Burleigh moves, with most of them completely taken in by his fabulous lies. And there is no effort he will not go to in order to keep those lies going! One contemporary will later swear that the Breaker really is the son of Admiral Sir George Digby Morant of Brockenhurst Park because, as a matter of fact, he had personally seen letters to him from the Breaker's mother and sister – the Admiral's wife and daughter – written to him from Naples and Marseilles! Why, he can see those cities written clearly in the addresses listed in the top right-hand corner of the first page, together with the date.

(For as long as 20 years the Breaker has been using the same ruse, understanding the power of a forged letter left lying about to convince people of his bona fides.)

And there was still more proof beyond that!

'In the letter family matters were touched upon, and left no doubt in my mind as to his identity.'[13]

Oh yes, he knew there was tension between the Breaker and the Admiral, for the Breaker had never hidden that! Why, he personally had accompanied the dashing dispatch rider as he went to visit a lawyer in Pretoria, 'prevailing upon him to write to the irreconcilable Admiral, and intercede for him'.[14] It was an unfortunate matter, to be sure, that the old lion of the Royal Navy should be so suddenly declining to pay the Breaker's bills, but in good faith this fine fellow was trying to put things to rights, don't you worry about that. (Oh, by the way, as he is a *bit* short, you couldn't *perhaps* lend . . . But of course! Say no more.) And so the Breaker's legal visit makes him a tidy profit, as ever.

Early July, Major Thomas arrives at Elands River

Major James Francis Thomas from Tenterfield is most displeased. Ten months gone in this war and not only have he and his men of the A Squadron of the NSW Bushmen seen no action but there is *still* little prospect of any. They have now lobbed up at this out-of-the-way outpost of Elands River, some 80 miles west of Pretoria, on the supply line between Mafeking and the former Transvaal capital. And while their brother B and C Squadrons of the Bushmen have already been lucky enough to have had some scrapes with the Boers, A Squadron is ordered to do garrison duty here for a spell.

Major Thomas is not the only one who is disgusted.

'We often wonder,' the A Squadron's Lieutenant Richard Zouch writes home, 'what our numerous friends in New South Wales would say if they could only see our present plight, and how we are treated. We came here to fight, but instead of that we are "dumped", down by the wayside, and, I regret to say, are sorely neglected.'[15]

And what a place to be stuck!

One of the problems is there is simply no shelter to speak of, with the outpost consisting of little more than the memory of a farm, scattered ruins and overgrown walls, and the rest of it like an enormous rugby field, about 400 yards in length and 350 yards wide, with the main camp like 'an upturned saucer', tilted on an angle down to the river itself.

There is space for a hundred wagons, corrals for 1500 horses, mules and cattle. As the supply line between Mafeking and Pretoria had become ever more stretched, this outpost had been furnished with resources to keep 3000 men going for a month, enough to sustain a large army moving in either direction for a week.

The whole position has two mid-sized kopjes just beyond its borders to the south and many high kopjes further away surround it. The ground of the post itself is a boulder-strewn slope, a little over half a mile from the spot where the Rustenburg road and the telegraph line ford the Elands River, with a mill on the slope. On either side of the rise, the small Brakspruit and Doornspruit creeks empty into the Elands.

In a little less than a fortnight after Major Thomas' arrival, Captain David Ham's Victorian Bushmen arrive after escorting a supply convoy from Zeerust – one that includes hundreds of oxen and horses – and after those wagons have been unloaded they, too, make camp. The oxen and horses are free to graze in a corralled section on the ground gently sloping away to the west of the camp. Some 200 of the men here are Australians, while there are also some 200 Rhodesians, with a small smattering of British and Canadian soldiers . . . which is unlikely to be enough to defend it against a major attack, should one eventuate, for if you put out the men needed to defend the surrounding kopjes you would not have enough to hold the post itself.

Still, that is unlikely to happen.

For the most part it goes well, but there are some concerns, led by the fact there are *still* very few Mausers being handed in. Could there possibly be some kind of Boer resistance forming up once more, out on the veldt?

Hopefully not, because, as noted by the Reverend James Green, while passing through the nearby outpost of Zeerust – also on the supply line route from Mafeking to Pretoria – many of the British regiments have a certain hollow-eyed exhaustion about them.

•

It is just one of those things soldiers say, that no-one thinks anything of at the time.

Fred Booth is with his close mate Wally Clark, on patrol passing by near Pienaarspoort just 15 miles out of Pretoria, when Clark mentions in passing, 'It'd be hard luck to get clipped now after getting so far through the campaign . . .'[16]

Oh so true.

They are tired.

They have come far, and survived many battles.

The war is surely nearly over.

But still they must be careful.

When they spy a Boer homestead up ahead, six of them are sent forward some 300 yards, to act as scouts. If there is going to be any trouble, it is for the scouts to draw it to their scattered form and so spare the broad mass of them. Still, it looks all right and as the scouts are right by the homestead with no problem, Fred, Wally and their dozen companions head towards it, eager to get water and, possibly, feed for their horses when . . . when seemingly from out of nowhere, no fewer than a hundred Boers bearing rifles jump out from the house, and from the top of a nearby ridge, shouting, 'Hands up!'[17]

The four scouts nearest the homestead are cut off and throw down their weapons and put their hands up with equal alacrity to save their lives, while Fred and Wally wheel their horses and gallop away as if their lives depend upon it, because they do.

And yet the Boers are too quick and open a withering fire upon them, using 'explosive bullets' – ones they have carved a notch in the top of so they will expand on contact with the flesh, rather than drill cleanly through.

Right beside Fred, Wally Clark suddenly takes a bullet through the thigh and slumps forward and now off his horse. Fred wheels, even as Wally tries to crawl to the cover of an ant-heap just a few yards away . . . only for . . . the next explosive bullet to near take his head off.

'The rest of us had great luck to get away,' the grieving Fred records. 'We could get no cover and had to ride right out of range.'[18]

Such is the way of this war, however, that when the Second Victorian Contingent's chaplain and doctor jointly go out in the afternoon waving a white flag, they are well received by the Boers and, after an exchange of whisky and tobacco between the two sets of enemies, the locals allow the invaders to treat the wounded prisoners, while refusing to liberate them. They will, however, hand over . . . the body of poor Clark.

The next day, thus, sees 12 sombre Troopers – a couple of them openly weeping – marching in lock-step across a quiet spot of the veldt, bearing the hastily constructed coffin in which their dead comrade lies. And now, as he is softly and sorrowfully lowered into his eternal resting place, the Last Post is played, there is a minute's silence and reveille is sounded. Three volleys are fired into the air, a passage is read from the Bible by the Second Contingent's Commanding Officer, Colonel Tom Price, and without a single word being spoken thereafter, they depart, wondering which one of them will be next.

As Fred writes to his family, 'A military funeral on the veldt is not the most cheering thing in the world.'[19]

Poor, poor Wally . . . and his poor family.

11 July 1900, Nitral's Nek, 18 miles west of Pretoria, underarm deliveries

It all happens so quickly the 300 men of the Lincolnshire Regiment never quite know what hits them. They can hear it though, for a horrible few seconds that distant thunder turns into a faint whistle, then a high-pitched whistle that grows so loud so fast it sounds like a scream approaching, a scream faster than the one that will soon explode from the mouths of your comrades who stand and fall in tatters and remnants all about it. How did it happen? Well, as the official reports will frame the horror, the carnage and the chaos proceeded in an orderly manner. On the Mafeking to Pretoria road, they are heading to Rustenberg and are just 20 miles west of the former Transvaal capital, passing through some high kopjes around the small outpost of Nitral's Nek when the silence is shattered by the blasts of shells landing all around.

Troopers sprout angry red splotches all over their torsos and fall like polka-dotted dominos, each one a human life snuffed out. From those kopjes, the men of General de la Rey's Commandos continue to pour in fire for the rest of the day until the Lincolnshire Regiment surrenders, together with their precious supplies and two guns. General de la Rey's men, now heavily laden with the loot, are gone just as quickly. On the same day, the 7th Dragoons are defeated in a small fight just north of Pretoria; while 20 miles south of Nitral's Nek, at Dolverkrantz, the Gordons run into an ambush and have 36 men killed. (A miraculous survivor is Captain Arthur Turner, the well-known Essex batsman who is also one of the last remaining underarm bowlers. As all his men fell about the gun battery he was commanding, Captain Turner kept laboriously loading and firing it himself despite being wounded three times as he did so.)

•

General Koos de la Rey is both pleased and worried. It has been a great thing to have had their band so reinforced by new recruits, and they can now put no fewer than 3000 men under arms, on horseback, into the line. It is an extraordinary number composed of seven Commandos, including 'the Lichtenburg men . . . reputed the best fighting men in the Transvaal',[20] all united under his leadership. They have been put together into an unusually large army, at a time when remaining dispersed is the tactic most vigorously pursued by Commando units engaging in guerrilla tactics, for a very specific purpose. As a body the Boers are ever more desperate for supplies. Yes, many of the remaining Boer farms will take the risk of resupplying them what they can, and are quick to hand over sheep and cattle to be slaughtered but such desperate measures cannot be sustained or remain sustaining. As de la Rey writes in a letter to his beloved wife, Jacoba Elizabeth, who he addresses as 'Nonnie', some of his men don't have shoes, while others are in rags. All of them are desperate for 'a nice new khaki suit',[21] not because they want to look like Englishmen, but because they want to be *warm* like one. Though initially in two minds as to whether it is the right thing to strip the clothes off British soldiers they have captured – as it is like looting, which he opposes – in the end he has come to agree with the dictum of fellow Boer commander Ben Viljoen '*Necessitas non habet legem*' – necessity has no law.

But what they *truly* need now are military supplies, and nothing more than rifles and bullets. While the British .303s are not as good as their own Mausers, they're a whole lot better than the 30-year-old Martini-Henry rifles that most of de la Rey's men have been using since a lot of them had handed in their Mausers before returning to the fold. Yes, those .303s, with their ammunition, would make an enormous difference.

Though de la Rey has succeeded in getting many armed recruits to join him in the last two weeks, there are many more Boer burghers who would join if they could just be armed. Most of them, after signing the neutrality deal that Lord Roberts had proposed, had handed in their rifles and gone home.

For every rifle they can now get, they will get another commando!

And with their own Boer warehouses in the cities now under lock, key and a round-the-clock British guard that leaves only one place where rifles can be obtained.

Yes, they must attack one of the British staging posts, overwhelm their men, and then take their guns, their ammunition and their food. And Elands River is the obvious choice. It is the most isolated one, surrounded by high kopjes, defended by only a few hundred men.

General de la Rey just needs to bring his own artillery forward from admittedly distant parts, continue with gathering his forces – in mid-July he writes to President Kruger that he has 1200 men in his laager waiting to be armed – get his men into position, and they can begin.

Happily, they continue to be supported by ever more Boer Commandos coming their way, equally desperate for supplies and eager to pick this plum.

14 July 1900, Elands River, 70 miles west of Pretoria, Major action

This is rough country, filled with rugged kopjes, ragged bush and scattered anthills, almost as if, on the sixth day, God had used up the last bits of odd landscape He possessed and made some terrain perfect for ambushes, and even better for full-blown open attacks. It means that on this cool evening, Major Thomas' A Squadron of the NSW Citizens' Bushmen, some 100 horsemen strong – on patrol a dozen or so miles away from their camp at Elands River – are wary as they make camp for the night. There are, they know, Boers about.

Major Thomas gives his orders to set up three Cossack posts – each one a four-man pod, set up several hundred yards from the camp to provide warning of any attack – which is as well. For they are settling in for their evening meal when they hear thundering hooves coming their way . . .

It is from one of the men from one of the Cossack posts, with troubling news: 'There are some men galloping towards the wagons.'[22]

Danger!

Saddle up once more.

They have only just accomplished it, when shots ring out all around, and bullets fly – coming from atop a kopje over to their right, about 400 yards away – with one of the first hit being Major Thomas' horse, Gragin, which goes down hard with a shattered leg. Fortunately Thomas is able to roll away and even escape the hail of bullets now pinging from rocks all around them. They have found the Boers all right – some 50 or 60 strong – and all of the Troopers take whatever cover they can behind the anthills and fire back the best they can. The ensuing battle goes for an hour, with some of the Troopers managing to use the anthills and the enveloping darkness to move forward on the flanks to bring the attackers under serious fire – at which point the Boers abandon their position to melt off in the night. The Australians have been very lucky. Despite coming under a full-blown attack, with hundreds of bullets fired at them, the only human casualty is one slightly pinged and lightly winged wounded Sergeant. The following morning they are able to make their way back to Elands River without problem.

Beyond everything else, the attack confirms that the Boers are still out there, still dangerous, still . . . getting ready to strike?

20 July 1900, Elands River, give us our orders

Another day, another contingent of Troopers arriving at the Elands River outpost . . .

For Major Thomas the best news of all is that among the fresh arrivals on this day is his dear friend, Sergeant Major James Mitchell, who had been delayed due to falling ill while in Bulawayo. The two embrace like brothers, a couple of men from Tenterfield on the adventure of a lifetime and now reunited once more. Yet another to arrive on this day is the NSW Bushmen's chaplain, Reverend James Green.

It is as well to have gained such reinforcements, for only two days after they arrive, the Boers *again* demonstrate their danger in this territory, and just how powerful they are becoming.

On the morning of 22 July, Colonel Henry Airey of the NSW Citizens' Bushmen is following the orders of General Baden-Powell and leading 400 Troopers on horseback from Rustenburg to Elands River, where they will then escort the precious stores and Troopers at Elands back towards Rustenburg – when it happens, at 8.15 in the morning.

They have just forged Koster River, halfway between the two, and are still some 20 miles from Elands River – when, as they are crossing a flat, four abreast, volleys of shots ring out and, an instant later, Troopers slump forward and horses go down.

The cry goes up from the English-born Colonel issuing only two orders: 'Fours, left!' and 'Dismount!'[23]

'The air about us seemed alive with angry loud-noted bees,' war correspondent Bert Toy, for Perth's *Inquirer and Commercial News*, notes, 'and perplexing little reports, exactly like the sharp crack of a stockwhip, came from close, above, below, and around us . . . The men slid from their snorting, shivering horses, and dropped in a long, ragged line in the grass facing the hills. They could see ringing the crests those lines of sangars, from behind which the enemy were discharging their magazines in feverish haste; they could hear the vicious little cat-spits as the bullets struck the grass around them, and the blood showed red on the khaki of a comrade here or there.'[24]

So massed are the enemy snipers of the Boer General, Hermanus 'Manie' Lemmer – prominent at the siege of Ladysmith, and from the Lichtenburg Commando – and so sustained is the Boer fire, that within only a very short time the defending troops have sustained many casualties. Their number includes Bugler James Keogh who, even as he was dismounting, has taken a bullet through the cheek that has exited through his neck, leaving two grievous wounds, both of which bleed like tapped kegs. His wounds are bound, but it is plain to all that they are dreadful injuries that he may not survive.

Amid all the carnage, the Troopers look to Colonel Henry Airey for leadership. For nearly four hours they are pinned down and all they can do is fire at what few Boers they can see, always on an individual basis and cognisant of the fact that each man only has 100 rounds. But there is no concerted action, and 'the little *"psst! psst!"* still sounded in the grass at every point; the stockwhips still cracked promiscuously on the flat, and half-a-dozen poor devils now sprawled groaning, blood-stained and helpless on their rifle-stocks'.[25]

As the hours pass, frustration arises at the lack of orders.

'The men had grown angry at this damnably one-sided tragedy – this being killed and not killing. "Give us orders, sir! Tell us to do something – anything, we don't care what it is, we'll do it,"[26] was the cry. Their immediate officers, as angry as themselves, could only tell them to "sit tight": orders had to come from above them.'[27]

Despite message after message being passed for Colonel Airey to take command and give some orders, so they can make a concerted and organised effort with the firepower they have left, the men are left wanting. Wherever he is, he has his head down – and not in a good way.

In the meantime, the Boers keep picking off the soldiers, while continuing to slaughter the easy targets of the horses, and by midday some 200 of the 300 horses have been badly wounded or killed, the whole of them an extremely messy maelstrom of agony and death.

'Then high above the din came an agonised "My God! They've got me!" and Trooper Scott dipped to the ground among the thumping hoofs. "Poor Scott – through the groin, too. Get the horses off him. Mind there, mind . . . you fellows." Ah! There's the doctor!'[28]

It is around this time that Colonel Airey decides the best option is to give up, and some in his vicinity even begin to wave white handkerchiefs. But sometimes help can come from the strangest places. Nearby to the whole conflagration a farmer's 19-year-old daughter, Emily Back – of British background, born in the Cape Colony, but with ancestry on both sides of the battle – has emerged from her kitchen to realise she is right by a mid-sized battle. Of course, the obvious thing is to go back inside and hide under the bed, but she does no such thing. No sooner has she seen a Victorian Bushman near to her shot than she rushes forth and, though bullets ping all around, she is able to wrap bandages around the worst of his wounds and get him back to her farmhouse. Now, to stay safely inside?

Not her.

There are still many more wounded, and so she now busies herself tending them, dressing their wounds and bringing them water, while the battle goes on all around her. Yes, she is very brave, though she does have one advantage over the men in that, as she knows, the Boers would never fire directly on a woman.

Meanwhile, though it takes many hours, finally – due most particularly to the leadership of Captain Charles FitzClarence, who rallies the men to fight back – the Australian Bushmen are able to drive the Boers off, before burying their nine dead. This including their Bugler James Keogh, who had held on for over five hours before succumbing. As they still have dozens of wounded, it is out of the question to push on to Elands River and so instead they retire to the larger camp at Rustenburg, where they can get the most medical help, in the more secure corral.

Those at Elands River will have to manage on their own. Advised by a dispatch rider what has occurred, Major Thomas is reminded just how vulnerable their position is, and it is not simply for their lack of firepower, with just 500 men against the rumoured 3000 Boers that General de la Rey has under his command.

More than ever, Thomas becomes aware of the vulnerability of their physical position. Surrounded by the higher kopjes, it seems to him, as he will record, that they are 'so placed as to almost invite an attack; a large quantity of valuable stores which we were in charge of, offering a tempting bait'.[29]

To make matters more complicated, as the Reverend Green documents, 'day by day Dutch refugees came to our camp with their wagons, stock and families, escorted by patrols, until we had thirty-eight camped together'.[30] They are, as one Australian NCO, Sergeant Syd Austen, records, kept in a 'small laager formed in the middle of the camp for the protection of such of the loyal Dutch as had sought refuge with us, and there they lived in a stone enclosure about ten feet square'.[31] The garrison makes sure that they have plenty of food and water, with many a man getting a little misty-eyed contemplating the children and thinking of his own children, and their mother, so far away.

For his part, Captain David Ham, a judicious kind of man from Ballarat, is not sure of them, writing, 'I believe some of them are spies, but we have to trust them.'[32]

To complete the cosmopolitan nature of those in the camp, there are also no fewer than 50 Africans, most of them labourers and drivers, together with a sprinkling of runners and servants – following the usual practice in these parts to get the Natives to do the most menial and dangerous work.

With his men positioned on the eastern side of the outpost, it prompts Major Thomas to take a close look at their defences, and just how they can be strengthened. To this point his men are in charge of six small 'forts', or *sconces* as they are called, 'made of stones and earth, biscuit boxes and flour bags',[33] with a Lieutenant and NCO for each.

In fact, the sconces are small semicircular walls, the earth and piled slate ramparts indeed bolstered by everything from boxes of biscuits and mutton to bags of flour – *anything* that might stop a bullet or a piece of shrapnel. The sconces will offer positions between the forts from which they can shoot, while protecting themselves – and allow them to get from one sconce to another with the least time exposed. Major Thomas is so insistent that they concentrate on building a line of defence against the most likely angle of attack that, over the next few days, 'This sconce or breastwork [became] about 60 ft long, 4 ft high and 3 ft 6 in through.'[34]

Keep going!

Get it even higher and build up the walls with whatever you can find. And from now on, every man at Elands River must be ready to 'stand to arms' – go to the spot you have been assigned to defend from, and face the most likely direction of an enemy attack, with loaded rifle and wait until you get the order to 'stand down' – against the possibility that the Boers will choose to attack at that most propitious time of dawn, when alertness is low and attackers invisible from a distance.

25 July 1900, House of Commons, Westminster, Welsh wizard makes a blizzard

Order! Order!

The Member for Carnarvon Boroughs, David Lloyd George, has the floor, has something to say about this Boer War and does not intend to hold back.

'A war of annexation,' he thunders, 'against a proud people must be a war of extermination, and that is unfortunately what it seems we are now committing ourselves to – burning homesteads and turning women and children out of their homes . . . the savagery which must necessarily follow will stain the name of this country.'[35]

And even now he is only warming up.

'If I were to despair for the future of this country,' he continues to exclaim, 'it would not be because of trade competition from either America or Germany. Or the effectiveness of its army, or anything that might happen to its ships; but rather because it used its great, hulking strength to torture the little child.'[36]

Make no mistake!

The hands of the British government are 'stained with the blood' of Boer children.

The response is predictably vitriolic, with the Welshman soon accused of being an '"anti-Briton" who was in fact a traitor to Britain',[37] and he is no less than burned in effigy in three boroughs in his Welsh electorate, before again being besieged by a mob at a public meeting and being heavily struck on the head with a mallet.

Does Lloyd George back off?

He does not.

He continues to speak out – ignoring the constant heckle in the public domain of 'do you wish the Boers to win?'[38] – and, after making a speech in his home constituency of North Wales, he is again bludgeoned in the head for his trouble. Still Lloyd George keeps going and shortly thereafter gives a speech in Birmingham against the Boer War, which attracts a crowd of 30,000 supporters of Joseph Chamberlain protesting the Welshman's very presence. They surround the hall with, as Lloyd George will tell the story, an 'intent to kill me'.[39]

That much is evident from the fact that the angry mob throws anything that comes to hand to shatter every window in the building, before breaking down the door and rushing the speaker's platform, bearing sticks, bricks, hammers and knives. Hustled away from the podium by the police, the only way he manages to survive is by donning a constable's uniform and helmet, and slipping away out a back exit. He is fortunate. Behind him, 40 people are injured, and two are killed. Joseph Chamberlain takes a grim pleasure in the riot and openly laments Lloyd George's escape. Lloyd George's hair turns white practically overnight, though he is still in his thirties.

The British Prime Minister, Lord Salisbury, for the most part stays clear of the fray, privately referring to the Boer War as 'Joe's war'.[40]

•

At Elands River, the fact that the Boers are near and in an aggressive mood becomes ever more apparent.

In the last days of July, the Boers take measures to eliminate the very grass that the stock have been grazing on day by day, before being returned to their corrals in the evening.

'The Boers,' Captain Ham notes on the first day of August, 'have been setting fire to the veldt all round us, and we are continually belting this enemy. All the kopjes are brilliantly lighted of an evening, the dry grass burns like tinder, fanned by the evening breeze it takes some stopping.'[41]

Reports come in that the Boers have been commandeering yet more men from surrounding farms, as their force grows for an attack.

How to stop that attack?

It seems clear that they will not be able to.

But what they can do is to do all possible to survive it, to hold off the Boers, and live off the supplies they have until the Boers themselves give up and go away. Mercifully, their food and ammunition supplies are beyond plentiful. What they lack, however, is water for themselves and their animals. That can only come by trekking to the nearest water supply, a small creek, the Doornspruit, that runs down to the river and between the two closest kopjes to the outpost. It is with that in mind that

Lieutenant Richard Zouch, a tough-as-teak grazier from Bungendore, is assigned to dig in with his men on his kopje, and make sure they control that key watering point.

This hill soon becomes known as 'Zouch's Kopje' – overlooking the Doornspruit, that creek about 400 yards south of the main camp – while another will be 'Butters' Kopje' – rising from the opposite bank, just south of the creek, from Zouch's – after Captain Sandy Butters, an equally tough Rhodesian officer, though he was born and raised in Scotland and retains a Scottish brogue as thick as Edinburgh Castle, took up its defence. Between their two kopjes runs a *kloof*, a deep ravine, right down to the river itself, which could only be taken by the Boers by exposing themselves to withering fire from the men with Butters and Zouch on their kopjes. If those two officers and their men – in Butters' case, 'with 100 men, 25 of whom were New South Wales Bushmen'[42] – can hold those two hills, the spot they can get their water-carters to is secure, and the camp can be safe on that count at least if the worst comes to the worst.

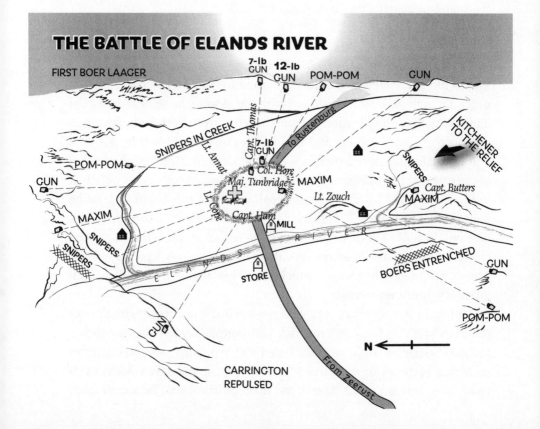

THE BATTLE OF ELANDS RIVER

Still, on the western fringe of the Elands River Camp, Captain Ham does not believe an attack will be any time in the next few days but to keep his men occupied more than anything else asks them to begin building a trench.

Alas, there is immediate resistance to the very idea. This is *not* what we signed up for! Heading to South Africa, they had envisioned charging across the veldt, with pistols in hand and rifles at the ready – not engaging in the rather unmanly exercise of digging ditches. They are *Troopers* not labourers.

Captain Ham, for one, does not care for their reluctance and simply *orders* his men to get on with digging.

'We may be attacked at any time,' he says with some force, before heading off on other matters.

His mistake? He has neglected to tell them how *deep* to dig the trench.

For when he returns at dusk it is to find, to his astonishment, 'a trench, a little over six inches deep, all of it being made by the shovel'.[43]

At the end of this ludicrous excuse for a 'trench' the men have used flat stones to spell out a rough inscription:

> Erected to the memory of the Victorians who were compelled to dig this trench. Fort Funk, August 3, 1900.[44]

•

These are tough times for Colonel Hore, in command of all troops at Elands but barely able to command himself to rise of a morning. In good times, the fine-looking Englishman with the moustache so heavily waxed and pointed you could suspend empty teacups from both ends, had been an effective enough officer. But now? Recently brought low by malaria, and generally exhausted by this war – the siege of Mafeking had spent his reserves of physical energy and emotional resilience – he is only just holding on. What he most wants is calm, and on this count at least he is momentarily satisfied. The regular patrols sent out to look for signs of a build-up of Boers – perhaps building for an attack – have returned to report that, on this afternoon at least, there is no sign anywhere. This is not to say they won't attack soon, just that it is clear that such an attack is not *imminent*.

And, wonderfully, that very afternoon word had come through over the telegraph that General Frederick Carrington had left Zeerust with a force consisting of '1000 men, Bushmen and Yeomanry, and 500 infantry with two batteries or 12 guns, four pom-poms, and seven Maxims'.[45] Once they arrive in two days' time their position will be secure and, in all likelihood, Carrington and his men will be able to escort all of Hore's men, and all of their precious supplies, all the way to Zeerust.

It means they just have to hold on for another day to be safe, and that shouldn't be too hard.

So confident is Hore that on this, the night of 3 August 1900, a concert is held to entertain the Troopers – many of whom sing along – and the collective tones of nigh on 500 men, officers and Troopers all, soon float over the veldt, singing one of the Troopers' favourites, 'The Man Who Broke the Bank at Monte Carlo'.

All together sing . . .

> As I walk along the Bois de Boulogne
> With an independent air
> You can hear the girls declare
> 'He must be a Millionaire.'
> You can hear them sigh and wish to die,
> You can see them wink the other eye
> At the man who broke the bank at Monte Carlo.[46]

And with 301 of the Troopers being Australians, why not sing that song that is rapidly becoming an Australian classic?

The dulcet tones of 300 voices ring out across the veldt . . .

> Click goes his shears; click, click, click.
> Wide are the blows, and his hand is moving quick . . .

It is all so catchy that even some of the 200 Troopers from Rhodesia and the small handful of Canadians and Brits hum along. Though pleasing to the men, and a morale booster, it is perhaps less pleasing to the gathered 1500 cattle, horses and mules, who occasionally moo, whinny and grunt in rough protest.

The singing is so loud that it carries all the way to the tops of surrounding kopjes, where grunting and groaning Boers continue to push their guns into position . . .

> The ringer looks round for he lost it by a blow
> And he curses that old shearer with the bare-belled ewe
>
> . . .
>
> Click goes his shears; click, click, click.[47]

Yes, a proud thing they are doing, which gives their singing extra gusto if not necessarily added tune. Major James Thomas' friend from Tenterfield,

Sergeant Major James Mitchell, is a particularly lusty devotee of the song and does something between belting it out and bellowing it out.

They are two men, a long way from home, in rough and perhaps dangerous circumstances, but the fact they have each other's back through thick and thin is something.

With the concert finally over, there is some discussion among officers within earshot of Reverend Green expressing the robust view that 'the Boers would never attack Elands River'.[48]

Look, it's not certain.

'If they *did* come with a few guns they would shake us up all right,'[49] is another refrain, but it seems very unlikely.

One soldier with the Victorians, Corporal Charles Norton, even complains to his Captain that he has seen no actual fighting since he came to South Africa, and feels it highly unlikely that he will find any at this outpost.

'Never mind,' Ham jokes in reply, 'several fellows who've been looking for a fight have got more than they wanted!'[50]

In any case, it is time to turn in for the night. There remains just one more thing to do for these officers and those close.

They stand around the campfire to sing 'God Save the Queen', before the rather pale Colonel Hore warbles out, 'Three cheers for the Australians!' – heartily responded to by all those from the other countries.

And yet, even before the echoes of those cheers have died away, as Reverend Green chronicles, 'the heliographist [who has waited until the safety of the darkness to walk from Cossack Hill, some distance away], came over to the commandant with a message which informed us that from 2800 to 3000 Boers were gathering to attack us under Generals de la Rey and Lemmer'.[51] They reportedly have with them 'three pom-poms, one 5lb. gun, one 7lb. gun, and a 12lb. Elswick Q.F gun, with an unknown number of Maxims'.[52]

Hore does not believe any of it, or at least does not believe such an attack is imminent – as there would have been many more signs – and does nothing. In any case, General Carrington and his men will be here just the day after next, so the plans of Generals de la Rey and Lemmer will come to nothing.

•

Around a small campfire by a sheltered kopje a few miles east of Elands River, General Koos de la Rey and his Field Cornets discuss their position. All is in readiness. They now have no fewer than 3000 combatants ready to throw at Elands River. They have 60 empty wagons, ready to carry away the haul of supplies once the defenders surrender, which shouldn't take long. All that remains is to move our artillery – a single 15-pounder cannon, three 12-pounders, a 7-pounder, three Pom-Poms, together with a Maxim gun – into position onto the kopjes that surround the outpost, ensure that such weaponry has plenty of ammunition stockpiled beside it, and that we have as many snipers as possible in position when dawn breaks, using the river banks for cover. Yes, the moon is just six days off being full, so you will have to be careful not to be seen by any sentries they might have posted, but it shouldn't be too difficult.

Around him now, the General has his Field Cornets, each in charge of various parts of the operation, waiting only for his order to begin. And now, as the light from the fire flickers over his handsome and craggy features he gives it with a simple nod of the head.

Begin. We attack at dawn.

CHAPTER SEVEN

THE BATTLE OF ELANDS RIVER

The Elands River fight seems to have slipped from the memory of a people who made much of lesser performances; but to soldiers it is easily the Thermopylae of the war . . . More shells were fired into that little place than into Mafeking, and . . . the Colonials will long remember Elands River. It was their own show: without generalship or orders, against all the easy traditions of civilised warfare, the small band . . . vindicated the ancient dignity of arms.[1]

John Buchan, author of *The Thirty-Nine Steps*,
in his book *The African Colony*, 1903

When the ballad makers of Australia seek for a subject, let them turn to Elands River, for there was no finer resistance in the war.[2]

Sir Arthur Conan Doyle, *The Great Boer War*

It was on the fourth of August, as five hundred of us lay
In the camp at Elands River, came a shell from de la Rey.
We were dreaming of home faces, of the old familiar places,
And the gum trees and the sunny plains five thousand miles away.
But the challenge woke and found us
With four thousand rifles round us;
And Death stood laughing at us at the breaking of the day.[3]

George Essex Evans

4 August 1900, Elands River, attack!

It comes with the first glow of the new day. There is just enough light for the freshly risen soldiers to grab their boots, and begin their breakfast of boiled porridge, even as griddling steak is being prepared to go with their hard biscuits and bully beef. If the morning's piercing call to reveille is not enough to wake up every man, the smells of those simmering oats and sizzling meats certainly are. A full belly awaits. The night sentries have just been dismissed, and all others observing orders to stand to arms from 5 am to 6.15 am are just standing down, when, in the morning stillness, the crack of dawn is just that and more as . . .

CRACK!

CRACK!

CRACK!

A flurry of rifle shots shatters the morn.

Major Thomas charges from his tent, instantly joined by the still half-dressed Reverend Green, who is greeted with a cry from his African servant, Jim, who has been stirring the porridge on the fire: '*Bass! Bass! De Dootcheman.*'[4]

'Nonsense,' the very Reverend verily replies, 'the butchers.'

Yes, that's it. You must be mistaken. It is merely the squadron's butchers, slaughtering some of the cattle to keep the camp fed.

Major Thomas, however – recognising the three shots in quick succession as the agreed signal of alarm from one of the Rhodesian sentries on Butters' Kopje – knows otherwise and roars orders for A Squadron to follow him to their sconces, as he races across the open ground, darting left and right in a zig-zagging course as now *real* BULLETS pick up spurts of dust all around. If *these* are the camp butchers, they have a case to answer.

Not that Jimmy is fooled for a moment.

'Plenty *Dootcheman*, Bass,' he says. '*Icona brekifus* – no breakfast.'[5]

For of course, as both Jimmy and Major Thomas now know – even as the panicked riderless horse of one of the sentries gallops into the camp – it really is the Boers attacking, as they now appear firing their rifles, coming from the riverbed they had been crawling along all night to get into position. Their initial point of attack is on one of the guard-posts that has been placed by the water supply point, and such is the layout of the camp that they have been able to get within 900 yards without being detected. Now driving forward at a jog-trot, with partial protection provided by the British horses stampeding up from the river where they were being watered, the Boers are sniping as they come.

'All this was easily understood,' James Green chronicles, 'for the volleys were heard louder and louder, and the bullets began to whistle over our heads.'[6]

In the extremity of the situation, a catastrophe perhaps about to descend upon them, it is strange how the most innocuous thoughts occur to some of them.

'This is the real thing; now,' Green says to himself, 'what must I do? Well! If I am to do anything at all I must put these puttees on securely.'

The alternative – 'rushing about during the impending fight with my puttees dangling loose in the air – is unthinkable'.[7]

Puttees on thus, with a hitch knot to hold them secure, the reverend charges forth, just as is happening all over camp, with Troopers and officers running hither and thither, some still half-dressed, 'others with one puttee on, and the other off', as they race to their trenches.

Major Thomas and all his Lieutenants, NCOs and Troopers of the NSW Bushmen make it to their *schantzes* on the eastern side of the perimeter only just in time, for within seconds they see random flashes in the distance. The more experienced soldiers among them know what those flashes are. They are punishing promises that hell is now to come bearing down from the heavens above.

Everyone down!

And, sure enough . . .

Now comes a dull whistling getter ever louder,[8] and suddenly there is an explosion as the shell lands, with flying shrapnel, smoke and dust, as Major Thomas will record, 'shells and long-range volleys of musketry were pouring into the main camp from all sides'.[9]

Mercifully, the Boers don't have it all their own way. For, sure enough, the besieged Australians and Rhodesians can now hear, from Butters' Kopje, their Martini-Maxim open up – *thump-thump-thump*, very vigorous 'knocking on the door', the men call the distinctive sound, as it spits forth 550 bullets a minute in short vicious bursts – right at whatever Boers the gunners can see.

A ragged cheer goes up, for good ol' Corporal Crawford and his men.

Within seconds though, the Boers' own 12-pounder gun comes into play right back at them, those shells 'bursting as . . . hundreds of shells fan-wise shot forward with every explosion'.[10]

For yes, these particular shells are timed to explode some 20 feet above the ground, releasing myriad shrapnel balls – each one the size of a small marble – that hit a devastatingly wide area. Practically every living thing within this circle of destruction is hit.

(The Boers are hammering this kopje for good reason, as de la Rey is certain that the spot Butters and his men hold is '*de sleutel van de geheele positie*', the key to the whole position.)

Pom-Pom shells are another matter altogether.

Each shell is a full pound of lethal power ready to burst with twisted metal and blackened shards, every sliver of scrap a razor that will slice through anything unfortunate enough to be nearby when it explodes. It matters not if the Pom-Poms hit a man dead on or merely collide with the ground. The effect will be much the same.

'It sends ten shells at a time on their deadly errand,' Private Robert Hallett records, 'and they are all round you before you know where you are.'[11]

Within seconds of these first shells hitting, a signal had been sent down the telegraph line to Zeerust to warn they are under attack at Elands River. There is just time for a return cable to reconfirm that General Carrington and his force, 1000 strong, had left the day before and will get to them soon – and all the quicker, as Zeerust will send out a cyclist to hurry him on – but before a second cable can be sent to Zeerust with more detail, a second round of shells shatters that very line.

•

On the western side of the encampment, the Victorians under Captain Ham are also under fire, with all of the men scrambling to get into what cover they can – including the bare scratch in the earth some of them had so reluctantly dug the day before.

'Rushing hurriedly from our resting places,' Captain Ham chronicles, 'the men instinctively took advantage of the cover previously prepared, as a perfect hail of lead splashed around them, while the contents of nine guns were concentrated on a space of only 150 yards square. Shells were bursting into fragments everywhere, and we stood in the midst of one little spot in a zone of hellish fire from the circling kopjes. We were a mere handful of less than 400 strong.'[12]

Personally, finding the back trench full up, Ham jumps into the next one along which is no bigger than a foot deep by two feet wide, and finds that Colonel Hore had got there even quicker, having actually been conducting a trench inspection on the western section of the camp when the barrage had begun. It is an odd thing to, even momentarily, be lying on top of your Commanding Officer but the grunting and graceless Hore makes no complaint, perhaps in part because any piece of flying shrapnel or the like would undoubtedly hit Captain Ham first.

And indeed, a short time later, a shell bursts and two men lying to the right of Captain Ham take the full force of the charge.

Corporal Charles Norton becomes an amputee in an instant as a shell passes through him, cutting cleanly through his arm. But the shell is not finished yet, and continues through the woodwork of Trooper Walter Smith's rifle before reaching Trooper Frank Bird's leg, lopping it free and sending it flying, only to crash into the dirt beside Captain Ham.

Norton, meantime, begs Ham to shoot him, but mercifully dies before Ham can even consider it.

Trooper Bird feels strangely numb . . . like he is floating somewhere between the roaring of his body and the ringing in his ears . . . the slowness of his arms and the lack of his . . . leg? When he feels down for where his leg should be, all he senses is a ragged wetness.

Close by, when Trooper Walter Smith at last lifts his head, all he can see are two of his best mates, including Birdie, writhing in agony, even as they utter feeble cries. Rushing to Birdie, his first thought is to carry his mate to the hospital wagon, only to find himself covered in blood as Boer bullets start to ping and sting all around. Smith cannot do it, and lays Birdie down. Mercifully, another Trooper manages to get through to the hospital and a stretcher party comes running to carry the grievously wounded man to the doctors who frantically work to save his life.

Dig, men, dig!

Just yesterday afternoon it had gone against the grain to be digging trenches like this – almost beneath their dignity – but now there is no argument, as the lot of them turn into 'Three-Clods-Harrys'! That is, they dig so furiously that there seem to be three clods in the air at any time, even as billowing clouds of dust from the many exploding shells engulf them all and make breathing difficult.

Dig FASTER, men!

And still, the hard rain falls.

'The Boers had taken up positions for their guns on three sides of us,' Lieutenant Charles Abercrombie of the 3rd Queensland Mounted Infantry will recount, 'and by the reports and the direction of the shells it became evident that they had a 12-pounder, 7-pounder, and pom-pom on our east side or front, while on the sides, or north and south of us, the Boers had mounted both a 7-pounder and pom-poms.'[13]

All that, and the fact that swarming snipers from on high are firing down on them at the tiniest sign of movement anywhere, means that their situation is, in sum, appalling.

Reverend Green quickly mobilises some assistance. As the hospital is currently accommodating two wounded men, Lovatt and another, in one of the wagons, which is very exposed, they are just shifting them to a lower and safer place, when one of the shells explodes in a manner to cause grievous wounds to another couple of Troopers, and they quickly must dump the previously wounded in as safe a spot as they can find, so that – as the cry goes up, 'Stretcher-bearers!' – they can use the stretchers for the newly wounded.

'One has to be in an engagement to see what "the glorious death of the soldier" really is in these times of modern artillery,' Reverend Green chronicles. 'One man was lying with one arm blown away, and a great hole in his side such as is made in the earth with a shovel. As I lay by his side, the shells flying over us, he rocked from side to side in his agony.'[14]

Just next to him, Trooper Bird is lying, screaming in agony, with a completely shattered leg, the shards of bone mixed with the gristle of tendons and bloody flesh.

'Stretcher-bearers, now!'

They arrive and, knowing the last thing this stretcher needs for stability is hands shaking with fear, run across open ground with the bullets pinging all around to get him back to the hospital, such as it is.

They are just in time for now, as Reverend Green chronicles, 'the three pom-poms began to play upon us. What a horrid noise they make! It is something like a locomotive struggling up hill and emitting great gusts of steam to the accompaniment of a steam-hammer.'[15]

And as the shells fall, man and beast alike are torn asunder, soon to be no more than blackened blood and bone.

•

On the south-western corner of the camp in Captain Ham's position, there now emerges yet more horror as shell after shell lands among the hundreds of oxen, horses and mules tethered right by them – sometimes killing or maiming a couple of dozen at a time as blood, gore and intestines flow across the veldt. One particular blast blows 12 mules, tied closely together, apart. Extraordinarily, while 11 of them are killed – with one having its backbone torn out so neatly by a piece of shrapnel that its coat falls to the ground 'like a rug'[16] – the mule in the middle is entirely untouched. Nearby, of seven horses tied to a wagon, five are killed or near killed by another shell.

Why so many, in this spot particularly?

Colonel Hore comes to the conclusion that it is the '20 oxen teams tied up on each side' making an obvious target for the Boer artillery spotters on high.

Once they have sorted themselves out in the trench, Hore moves quickly, shouting at the 'Kaffirs' and ordering some of the lower ranks to leave the relative safety of the trenches and 'cut them loose!'.[17]

Trooper John Fortune does as asked in a mad dash and certainly, once the surviving oxen are untied – because many of the initial 40 are already dead – it doesn't take long for them to disperse, so maddened are they by panic, as they charge wildly all over the camp, some trailing their bloody entrails behind them.

The African 'boy' sent to assist him, only manages to get a few yards before a 12-pound shell bursts nearby and takes his legs off. Ham's troops can only watch as the poor fellow crawls his way pitifully towards the Captain's tent.

Everywhere can be heard the groans of the wounded and dying. 'Some were cursing, some praying, and still the carnage went on . . .'[18]

Trooper Walter Smith, having recently witnessed the agonies of Troopers Norton and Bird, is keeping his head down, lying in his trench with his legs crossed, when a 12-pound shell bursts nearby. A piece of shrapnel flies his way, striking him fairly on the knee. He jumps what he estimates is 'four feet in the air', sure that his leg is off. But, upon his making what he terms is a 'post mortem examination',[19] he finds – wonder of wonders – that he is fully intact with only a knee wound to show for his near-death experience.

Through all this, the poor horses continue to be slaughtered, their pitiful screams almost as shocking as their gushing blood and trailing entrails.

Perhaps there is some slight diminution of fire around them once the oxen are gone. And yet, as Captain Ham still regrets to report:

> The shells and pom-poms came thick and fast . . . especially round our trench, as we were on the west side and right in the cross fire of all the guns, of which there were 9 in all, some 15-, 12- and 7-pounders and 3 pom-poms. At the fort we had only one Maxim (which used to choke occasionally) and a 7-pounder muzzle loader, for which there were only 120 rounds of ammunition.[20]
>
> . . .The horses were stacked on each other, nearly all killed by pom-pom and shrapnel, others were left standing on three legs, others again had their jaws shot clean away, while others would be staggering round and round nearly cut in two.[21]

•

On the kopje commanded by Lieutenant Zouch, just outside the main camp, the shells are falling thick and fast, sending up either geysers of sand and stone, or . . . blood and flesh. Zouch himself just narrowly escapes being killed when he rushes from his tent just before a shell hits it, while his beloved 'Burrowong' horse, tethered nearby, is not so fortunate and takes a direct hit, instantly turning it into flying bloody chunks.

'The only wonder,' Zouch will later note, 'is that we were not *all* killed.'[22]

As the shells continue to fall and the bullets to fly, what had been a relatively orderly encampment becomes a maelstrom of dead and wounded animals, dead and wounded Troopers and shattered wagons.

From his trenches east of the main camp, where he commands 60 NSW Citizens' Bushmen, Lieutenant Zouch can now see the tiny flashes of flame that mark the Boer guns atop the distant hillsides, and counts the time it takes for the shells to land. *One* monkey, *two* monkeys . . . *five* monkeys, *six* monkeys, EXPLOSION!

By quick calculations, it means their guns are just a bit over 2000 yards away. While obviously well out of range of their .303s, they can at least be reached by their 7-pounder cannon – the old-fashioned muzzle-loading type from 30 years before, requiring the laborious shoving of powder and shot down the length of the barrel of the round to be fired, as opposed to the modern breech-loaders as features in *all* of the Boer artillery. It can still fire a fearful round, but accurately hitting something at over 2000 yards is another matter.

Still, even getting close is good, for while killing the gunners is great, just bringing the Boers under fire is good enough, as everyone fires less accurately when they themselves are being shot at.

Not that the Australians aren't deeply annoyed for all that.

'We have only one 7-pounder gun,' Lieutenant Robert Gartside notes in his diary, 'and [in that one], the cartridges will not go home well in. They only fire it now and again. Fairly hundreds of tons of provisions here and only this pop gun to help us against the Boers. More blundering. Someone has done it.'[23]

Still, there are some successes, and never more than when the 7-pounder crew are able to bring a shell down on the nearby farmhouse where some Boer snipers have congregated – a direct hit – raising a raucous cheer from the men.

We are fighting back!

We are not lambs to the slaughter, we are the lions of the veldt and you'll meet with the fury of our jaws if you test us! While nearly all of the men are impressive under fire – many of them experiencing it for the first time – none is more impressive than Major Walter Tunbridge and Lieutenant James Whamond Annat, situated in the north-east perimeter of the camp. Neither man blinks, no matter how many close calls they have and both are a blur of activity encouraging all of their men to not only protect themselves but also fight back.

•

Trooper Bird, as with the other wounded, is now being transported to the hospital. So desperate is the situation that the doctor knows there is only one chance to save him – he must operate on him *now*, in the open, with the only cover provided by the surrounding ambulance wagons.

Taking a bottle of chloroform, Dr Duka of the Queensland Mounted Infantry pours some on a cloth and holds it to the groaning Trooper Bird's nose. That at least should deaden some of the pain as, after tightly applying a tourniquet above the severed end, he saws through the bone and sutures the remaining skin shut over the stump. As the operation progresses, his assistants, including Reverend Green, are forced to crouch and crawl to deliver each swab and instrument.

•

No sooner has Captain Ham followed through on his decision to move himself and his men a short distance to a position that had been slightly banked-up the previous day than Colonel Hore, suddenly relieved of his protective layer of fellow soldiers, moves in tightly behind them.

'From this small cover we went over to the rear of our horse line,' Captain Ham recounts, 'and behind 700 oxen that were tied up the night before. Through the hail of lead we took up our place there, and lying only behind six inches of cover, heard the whistle of bullets just like a hive of bees, swarming, splattering, and splintering the rocks. The shells screeched in broken fragments above our bodies.'[24]

Still, Ham and his men lie with their rifles at the ready, expecting a swarm of Boers to appear at any second. For the moment, however, there are none to be seen. But the fire upon them remains dreadful, and the sniper fire extraordinarily accurate.

'We have been told that the Boers cannot shoot,' Captain Ham chronicles, 'but that is all nonsense. If a head appeared above ground, four or five bullets whistled in close proximity, and several men were wounded in this manner, and this from long ranges.'[25]

It begets the most extraordinary scenes. One man, just a few along from Ham, and not sufficiently low in the trench, takes a bullet through his shoulder at an odd angle. But unlike most bullets, content to pass cleanly through and maim their target, this one chooses a rather remarkable trajectory.

'It passed through the arm,' Captain Ham records, 'out of the shoulder, through the top of the shoulder, and through his jaw, and he spat it out of his mouth, uttering the exclamation, "Oh! Lord!"'[26]

Good . . . GOD!

Captain Ham has some doubts if there will be anyone left alive by dusk, but is relieved to be still alive this long, with one piece of shrapnel having already cut his face, while another has taken a little from the back of his hand.

'I had often wondered how I would feel under fire,' he would recount. 'Well, all through the day I never felt the least anxiety for myself, and I felt I would come out of it perfectly safe. I listened to the shells shrieking and the bullets humming and singing with a certain amount of indifference. One of my men ACTUALLY WENT TO SLEEP.'[27]

Around him, others are chatting between explosions.

Yes, says one, it's 'Very hot,' in these parts.

On the other hand, his mate replies with a laugh, 'We have not come this far to hear pianos playing.'[28]

When shells explode in particular proximity still another will call out, 'Hullo, Bill, are you alive yet?'

Ideally, Bill will reply.

'At the same time I heard the groans of dying and wounded men. Some were cursing, some praying, and still the carnage went on . . .'[29]

•

Major Thomas and his Troopers of the NSW Bushmen are holding on, concentrating on making their trenches ever more secure against shells and bullets – while also looking out for any Boers who might dare to approach within shooting range, when the explosions of landing shells suddenly move closer to them. And now there is a whistling sound that builds into something very like a shriek, before there is an explosion, followed by actual *human* shrieking. Right beside Major Thomas, Trooper Jack Waddell – a 'fine, strong young fellow from Burrawang, and a jocular kind of bloke' – has been hit in the chest by the 'screw of a pom-pom'[30] and both his hands together are incapable of staunching the blood flow. The terror in his eyes says he is aware that he will likely die and . . .

Sure enough, the beloved Jack – beloved son of Scots immigrants David and Elizabeth – 'A crack bush rider and perfect master of bushcraft, a man of happy temperament,'[31] is dead within minutes. Killed with him is his horse Jackpot. Only six months earlier, when he had left Hedley Edols' property at Burrawang, the boss had said he could pick any horse to take to South Africa, so he had picked Edols' own horse, that beauty called Jackpot.

All but precisely the same thing happens just a few minutes later again to Trooper James Duff in the sconce to the right, though he is killed instantaneously. Both bodies are laid out, and covered with a blanket, while their comrades fight on. They are in the fight of their lives, *for* their lives, and can only even contemplate burying their comrades once the shelling has eased, which doesn't appear will be any time soon.

Next to be hit is the sconce to Major Thomas' left.

Just after it explodes, several of the NSW Bushmen run out wounded, one of whom is Major Thomas' dear friend from Tenterfield, Sergeant Major James Mitchell.

'Don't bring all those men into this sconce!' Major Thomas shouts to Mitchell. 'There are too many in it already, and there is plenty of room in the one on your left.'

'I can't go,' Mitchell rasps in reply, while showing a bloody leg. 'I am hit.'

With this, Mitchell struggles to get what cover he can, lying under a wagon at the back of the sconce, the dark blood now spurting from the mangled wound on his right leg.

'Are you badly hurt?' Thomas asks in a much softer tone, shocked at what he sees.

'I think my leg is broken,' Mitchell replies, over the ongoing roar of the shells and the continuing squeals from the dying animals.

'No, it can't be broken or you would not have gone so far.'[32]

The main thing for now is to get him better cover, and what medical treatment they can. Once they are inside their own sconce, Major Thomas looks more closely at the wound and is a little heartened, as it appears to be only a flesh wound, and he is able to staunch most of the blood flow by tightly tying his handkerchief around it.

'You must stay in here for the moment,' he advises his friend, 'as the field hospital is in an exposed position, and getting to it means risking getting hit.'[33]

Mitchell, gasping and pale, readily agrees, and so lies, resting not far from where poor Waddell and Duff lie dead.

Looking at them all, Major Thomas has one thought: 'My poor Boys. There will be a lot more of us join you before the day is over.'[34]

Elsewhere around the perimeter, similar scenes have taken place, as the Boers continue to pour in shells, and push forward on the defenders where they can – scoring some direct hits as they go.

The only upside of the shells is that many of them hit 'cases that: held the tucker, such as biscuits, jam, tinned dog [cans of bully-beef], and other luxuries . . . all packed up in the middle of the camp, and scattering tucker all over the place and we used to buck up and help ourselves; in fact, we were told to do so.'[35]

Even better, as the Catholic Chaplain with the NSW Citizens' Bushmen, Father Francis Timoney, records, the shells would 'open up boxes of champagne, whisky, brandy, and cigars. Moreover, it was better that our men should enjoy these luxuries rather than the Boers, and unless relief came, all the stores would assuredly fall into the hands of the enemy.'[36]

Don't mind if they do.

It is not uncommon thus, for many of the defenders to be smoking cigars and have a dram of rum handy, as they keep their fire up on those who wish to obliterate them.

Death, destruction and severed limbs aside, there are worse ways of fighting a war.

•

For those on Zouch's Kopje, some 400 yards from the main camp, the situation is bitter. In the early bombardment, as one Trooper, Fred Bates, would chronicle, 'Every time a man is hit we can hear the groans. One would think the heavens were falling in when the cannons are firing.'[37] Of course, the Troopers in this forward position try to get something of their own back, by firing at the Boer positions, only to find that the Boers see their .303 bullets and raise them half-a-dozen shells exploding right on their position!

•

Finally the job is done, and Trooper Bird is left to rest, with heavy biscuit boxes placed all around him for some protection from the ongoing barrage, while Dr Duka immediately turns his attention to another man who had been brought in with a bullet through his spine, only to receive no fewer than another seven pieces of shrapnel in his body when a shell had hit the hospital. All Dr Duka can do is keep working amidst all the growing gore.

In the meantime, as one newspaper report will recount, the 'Kaffirs were ordered to improvise a hospital tent, 20ft. by 9ft., by placing full biscuit and meat boxes on each other, forming a wall 4ft. thick and 8ft. high, with tarpaulin thrown over the top for a roof.'[38]

What can they do with the severed leg?

Well, clearly it can't just be left lying around, like the various bits of cattle and sheep that are everywhere. This is a *human* leg. It must be treated with a certain level of respect, if not the reverence with which one would bury a whole body. One of Duka's soldierly orderlies is assigned the task, and the leg is soon buried in a shallow grave. He does not say a prayer, of course, but at least breathes thanks when it is done, and the ghastly protuberance is fully covered and he can head back to the hospital, knowing he will never have to see it again.

There, he finds the bullets flying around worse than ever, so bad that the always brave Reverend James Green is frantically crawling from one patient to another, trying to get them better protection, out of the line of fire, as Mauser bullets smash into and through whatever little protection they have.

Even as the Reverend crawls, ducks and winces, however, he can't help but notice the worthy Dr Duka calmly continuing his operations out in the open, saving the lives of whatever men he can. And the wounded continue to flood in, with one soldier from Wagga Wagga, near cut to pieces from shrapnel, carried in and still able to proudly say, 'I played the man anyhow . . .'[39]

Yes, he did, and is still doing precisely thus. A short time later a groaning, dying Kiwi is brought in, so far gone, and he knows it, that the Reverend does the only decent thing and gently asks him what he would like his people at home to be told.

'Tell them . . . I trusted in God,'[40] the Kiwi gurgles out.

'Yes,' the Reverend Green says, before offering something else he will tell them. 'And died game.'[41]

The New Zealander groans his agreement, and does exactly that.

And now here is a grizzled Queensland soldier who has taken the bullet from a Mauser through his chest.

'Old Mulga's hit at last,'[42] he cries, seemingly rather proud of the fact. Nevertheless, one of Dr Duka's orderlies is quick to apply a clean compress to the wound to stop the gushing, whereupon Green asks, 'Now, what else can we do for you?'

'Give me a smoke,'[43] replies Old Mulga, laughing, happy as a pig in mud.

And who now?

Why it is Farrier Sergeant Major Hampden Livesey, a Townsville plumber and a Freemason of the Queensland Mounted Infantry, also bleeding badly, with a bad wound from a flying splinter. Now, famously within his unit at least, Livesey is the nephew of Joseph Livesey, the founder of the British temperance movement. Again the orderly presses a fresh compress to the wound, before blithely pressing him to drink a brandy, adding, 'The chaplain says, you are to take it, it'll do you good.'

'I don't care if twenty chaplains say I can take it,' Sergeant Major Livesey roars. 'I've vowed I never will, and won't break my vow to save my life.'[44]

What he does want to do, is go back out and fight the Boers *immediately*, and it takes some finesse for Dr Duka to have him agree to wait till after lunch, at which point some of his strength should have returned. (In fact, as Dr Duka well knows, by that time his loss of blood has made him much weaker, and he no longer feels inclined to uselessly risk his life more than he is by just staying in this hospital, with bullets continuing to fly – so badly that a Rhodesian soldier goes from being a volunteer helping Dr Duka to becoming his patient when one of the flying bullets brings him down. Dr Duka barely blinks, and simply adds him to the list of those who need his urgent attention.)

•

In the meantime, the dreadful shelling goes on, putting the wind up more than a few Troopers.

'Well, Jack, old man,' one of them will later write a letter describing the experience, 'the best writer in the world cannot describe heavy shell fire to give one who has never been under fire, the slightest idea of what it is like, and I will not attempt. From a big gun there is a terrible roar, and a moment after a screaming sound coming closer and closer to the ground until it strikes and bursts with a tremendous bang, pieces flying in all directions – any one sufficient to kill or maim a man for life. I have seen one burst and kill six horses.'[45]

On and on it goes as the sky rains death and the ground shakes and trembles beneath it.

All that most of the defenders can do, as the shells continue to fall, is use their bayonets and whatever implements come to hand to make their trenches deeper, scratching out whatever earth they can – with the bare minimum being enough of a pouch to get their body into – and once the dirt and stones are loose enough, throwing it up to create something of a growing rampart between them and the Boer guns.

Meanwhile those mighty men on the artillery keep firing the best they can, until finally full darkness descends and, for the first time in over 12 hours, relative calm descends on Elands River.

•

Up by the No.1 sconce, a relatively heated confrontation is taking place between two of the most senior officers at Elands River.

In the wake of the pounding they have taken from the beginning, Colonel Hore, who has lately taken up residence in this grotty grotto, is clearly shaken and says out loud, 'If the fire on us tomorrow is as hot as it was today, I will surrender,' something to which Major Tunbridge takes great exception. In front of their fellow officers he tells Colonel Hore that while the Englishman personally might surrender with whoever will join him, he and his fellow Queenslanders will not.

Rather, he says, 'I will draw all my Queensland troops out and take up a different position and fight it out to the last.'

Listening, Corporal Bruce Skelton· is impressed. Hore really is on his own when it comes to surrender.

'Every man in the camp, Rhodesians [under Butters] and all,' he chronicles, 'would have followed Tunbridge or Annat to the end.'[46]

•

Still surrounded by the biscuit boxes in the makeshift hospital, Trooper Bird now fully comes to, beginning to foggily remember it all, the explosion, my pain, my *pain*, my leg, my . . . where is it?

Where is my leg?

As gently as possible, it is explained to Bird that Dr Duka had no choice. It had to be amputated to save his life.

Yes, yes, yes, but where *exactly* is my leg now?

It has been buried, out by the storeroom, why?

Because I had £4 still in the trouser pocket!

Once again, a Trooper is dispatched with a shovel in hand. The leg is exhumed, the money retrieved, and this time the leg hopefully buried for good.

•

After this first fury of their full-blown attack is spent, de la Rey's artillery men estimate they must have poured at least 1700 of their oh so precious shells – for they have ceased manufacturing them, and can only fire the ones they get in raids – into the Elands River Post. Surely all that remains now are pillars of smoke rising from the ashes?

•

There is barely a horse, mule or cow left standing.

As shells continue to fall right among the panicked beasts, the horror is nigh on indescribable, but David Ham will do his best.

'I shall never forget,' he will recount, 'and the scene of horses swinging their legs, some of them with them off altogether, some crawling about on their stumps, or with their entrails dragging on the ground, can only be seen to be realised. I never want to see such carnage again. It was a sad sight.'[47]

Some of those worst hit are put out of their misery with a bullet to the head, while the rest must be left to suffer at least a little. It is the dead humans that are of most concern, of course. Around the post, some five men have been killed – 'not counting several Kaffirs', Major Thomas notes – though the hospital is filled with wounded.

•

The night, the night, the blessed *night*!

Never has the darkness come so slowly, nor been more appreciated. What sweet relief it is, the bombardment mostly ceases and with creaking limbs the men unbend themselves from their cramped positions and for the first time in well over 12 hours stretch their limbs, move about and work out who is still all right and who has been hurt. But there is little time for too much, as now they must get to work! What is obvious already is that if they are going to survive this siege what they most need is more protection and as the only true shelter that can be found will be underground caverns, which right now are solid dirt, it falls to them to start digging!

Yes, tools for such an undertaking are scarce, but this does not deter the effort. Anything that can assist with the chore is brought into service. Bayonets, iron bars and penknives are deployed as well as shovels and picks.

'There were only forty picks,' Catholic chaplain Father Francis Timoney notes. 'The ground was adamantine. Men freely offered one, two, and even £3 for the loan of a pick for one hour. Silence hung heavily over the kopje that night. No words were spoken, except an occasional whisper. Only the jingle of spades, shovels, and picks proclaimed the presence of human beings.'[48]

Yes, for both the Australians and the Rhodesians this really is as far from being out on the open veldt – where they had excelled – as it is possible to get. Instead of charging forth on horseback with the wind in their hair, they must dig in like mad things. It is a shock.

'They had expected to come in on the action as glamorous outriders,' one contemporary account will note, 'saviours of the empire, just as the fighting was ending. Instead they found themselves garrisoning a pestilential pirates' fiefdom, and plunged into a hunt on unfamiliar ground for deadly bandits who had all the advantages of local knowledge, battle experience, and sheer desperation.'[49]

But on this occasion there is no way around it, and there is no complaint. They all understand. Dig in, digger, or die.

At least one officer, however, really does give his men a choice.

Lieutenant Robert Gartside brings his own 25 Troopers together and asks them straight whether they are prepared to hold their assigned post against all comers.

'If there is a man among you who is not prepared to sell his life dearly,' he says, 'you can go to another part of the fort.'[50]

Not a single hand goes up. Not a man approaches him later.

'I am proud to say,' Gartside will note, 'that all said they would stick to me through thick and thin. These men were composed of Victorians and West Australians.'[51]

And so the digging goes through the night, with the only break from the grunting, groaning and cursing that goes with the sheer effort of it being the pitiful moaning of wounded oxen and goats, 'so with our revolvers we put them out of pain. The moonlight only added effect to the ghastly scene, and to those who had not previously seen the horrors of warfare, it was a terrible baptism.'[52]

Upon their own kopje, Lieutenant Zouch's men are equally digging furiously. There can be no question of abandoning this position for, without it, the camp would be denied water, but they must be able to make their position more tenable to hold, and the deeper they go, the better it is. The dirt is used to make something of a breastwork in front of them, and in short order they have a trench some feet deep. To disguise their position behind the breastwork, they 'covered it over with limbs of trees and earth, put a lot of green leaves in front to hide the stone and we feel pretty safe'.[53]

Careful though. They still must have enough men on duty to guard those struggling down the hill to the river to fill their water carts – without which the defence of their outpost must fail.

'As soon as the Boers heard the water carts,' one of the Troopers will recount, 'they generally opened fire.'[54] At this point Zouch's men unleash hell on the Boer sniper points, firing at the flashes and obliging them to keep their bleeding heads down. Soon enough they actually send out raiding parties of 50 soldiers to attack the Boer gun crews directly.

It is not just that the 500 men need half as many gallons a day, but their surviving collective animals need ten times that amount! The animals can be led down to the water, which helps give cover from the snipers when you walk bent over, but it will take at least two filled water carts to ensure the men get through another day – with each load poured into suspended waterproof tarpaulins, which serve as the camp reservoir.

Even then, however, the Boers don't give up on their plan.

'Every night,' Captain Ham will recall, 'the Boers used to train their seven guns on us, and let them off at all hours up to 1 a.m., so that we were not safe night or day, and a hail of rifle bullets also accompanied the salvo from the guns.'[55]

Over on the eastern side of the main camp, a dozen Queensland miners are going at it hard, splitting slabs of slate from their initial small trench and methodically turning it into a large underground cavern measuring twelve feet by four feet, by four feet high as the night wears on. In the pre-dawn they use those slabs of slate as extra fortification on the shell side of the upstairs *schantzes*, before covering them with saplings and sandbags.

No such solution is possible for the 'hospital' near the centre of camp as it is no more than three ambulance wagons covered by a tarpaulin, and the only protection that can be organised in the short term is a foot high wall of stones in front of one wagon and – far more importantly – a big red cross sewed into the tarpaulin. The red cross may stay the hand of a more virtuous Boer, but it will do nothing against the screaming metal that arcs down from above.

In the meantime, as opportunity allows, the *schantzes* are deepened and the underground caverns enlarged, with wagons overturned above to give further protection. They even stack boxes of 'meal' – the South African staple of ground maize flour – overhead, on the reckoning that they, too, can absorb the cruel shards of shells. And they are right! Many times a shell lands and there is an enormous puff of billowing flour dust, but no-one hurt!

Though it does not come easily to some of the defenders to so dig in – there seems something unmanly about it? – even they do their rough and ready best.

And finally, at the conclusion of this terrible day, there is the matter of burying the dead. By the ethereal glow of the midnight moon, the bodies of the five Troopers killed by bullets and shrapnel are carried to a spot just outside the camp, and buried together in one large pit that has been prepared. There is no time, or energy, to hold a service. Once the siege is over, that can be attended to. For now, they must put all their energy to simply surviving.

•

But now, something else odd. What is going on? In the mid-morning of the second day of the siege, the guns suddenly fall silent and an eerie silence settles on Elands River, punctuated only by still more screams of wounded animals . . . followed by shots coming from the Troopers who take advantage of this lull to put the poor brutes out of their misery. It is a sound no soldier can get used to, the recurring slaughter an irony too potent to ignore, each bullet and shriek reminding them of what may come for any and what must come for some. No-one is sure what the Boers are up to, only that the uncertainty brings a pause that is welcome.

But clearly, they are up to *something*. For now we can see in the distance the Boers have moved some of their guns from the kopjes surrounding Elands River and have horses pulling them along the Zeerust Road. Are they retreating? Could it be?

Or have they, perhaps, received word that something is coming along the Zeerust Road that will be of even more interest to their guns?

That might be it! For now, around noon, some of the officers with field glasses see something . . .

Yes! About four miles off, to the west, it looks to be the advance party of General Carrington's relieving force coming along the road in extended order.

If the Boers, perchance, give up in the face of it, Carrington's mob will be here within the hour, and the siege will be over – rejoice, rejoice!

And cheer they do as they see the vanguard of General Carrington's advance guard – magnificent mounted men 'open out in beautiful order as they came'.[56]

And yet, of course, they are not the only ones who have seen them. For now, before the very eyes of the defenders, the Boers start shifting both the direction and position of their guns on surrounding kopjes to face this new threat. So too, it is apparent that Boer snipers are moving forward on the big kopje overlooking the road from Zeerust.[57]

•

Gereed!
 Mik!
 Vuur!
 Ready ... aim ... fire!

In an instant there is the crack of thunder and a burst of flame and smoke emitting from the Boer cannon as the shells streak away, aimed at the precise part of the road where the kopjes on either side ensure that there will be no easy escape for Carrington's men, that the shrapnel will have full impact.

The Boers watch with grim satisfaction as the shells land, explode and cause carnage as the Troopers – most of whom have no battle experience – fall from rearing horses, some shot, some torn apart by shrapnel. Some of them, bleeding, crawl away.

•

What is going *on?*

Having left Mafeking on 1 August with orders to bolster the force at Elands River Post, General Sir Frederick Carrington has with him some 500 men of the Rhodesian Field Force, and as many from the NSW 6th Imperial Bushmen. They had been getting near to their destination, when they heard cannon and rifle fire up ahead. Scouts had been sent forward, only to return with the deeply troubling news – the men of the Elands River Post are under siege by an enormous force of Boers.

Cautiously, many will say too cautiously, Sir Frederick then ordered his men forward into the Reit Valley that leads to the post, perhaps cognisant of the famous poem by Lord Tennyson about the 'Charge of the Light Brigade', in 1854.

> *Half a league, half a league,*
> *Half a league onward,*
> *All in the valley of Death*
>   *Rode the six hundred ...*
>
> *Cannon to right of them,*
> *Cannon to left of them,*
> *Cannon in front of them*
>   *Volleyed and thundered;*

And sure enough there they were!

First they'd seen the glint of guns on the kopjes up ahead – both cannon and rifles – and then the advance guard had come under fire.

Yes, for the moment the guns of the Boers are too distant to do much damage but it is a shock nevertheless.

There must be 100 riflemen now firing at them, together with dozens of cannon. And every step forward Carrington and his men take brings them ever more into range. Already some of the forward men are starting to sprout red shrouds on their shoulders, chest and torso, before groaning and slumping forward or back.

Carrington decides to proceed with even more care. Leaving the wagons at the western end of the valley under the guard of some 200 of his Troopers, while continuing to push advance patrols of Bushmen and Imperial Yeomanry in extended order to the fore. Let us advance, and see if the Boers might bow to just our threat? Yes that . . . *might* . . . work?

Carrington is unsure as this is his first encounter with the Boers this war, just as it is for many of his men.

Such is not the case for the vastly experienced General de la Rey, who is close to bemused at the naïvety of the British tactics. He looks at Carrington's hesitant deployment, clearly raw troops who have not done this before and 'recognised the raw column as a target, not a threat'.[58] De la Rey calls for General Hermanus Lemmer to come to him, and quickly gives his orders. Take your men and outflank them. Move forward, get yourselves into position and then shoot them down.

Yes, he could allow this newly arrived force to enter the post and then surround them, *too*, but, on consideration, by destroying this new force before the very eyes of the force under siege, it should provide a maximum return for a minimal loss of his own men.

•

Urgently, Carrington brings such artillery as he has forward to try to blast the Boers from their hilltop positions – all under the watchful eyes of the Boer General, Manie Lemmer.

Lemmer, born on a farm nearby, knows the ground on both sides of the British thrust as well as the back of *both* his hands, and slides his men – including the Lichtenburg Commandos, 'the best fighting men in the Transvaal'[59] and the Marico Commando, 900 in all – into position.

And now they wait, for Lemmer to give the word, via a flashed heliograph signal.

Steady, steady, steady . . . a little further still . . . just a tiny bit further until you are entirely in the trap and . . . NOW.

The signal flashes, and the Boers open a torrent of fire and lead from both flanks.

'The bullets commenced to whistle around our ears,' Lieutenant Granville Ryrie, from New South Wales, will write to his wife, before adding the good news. 'Anyhow they did miss me and I could hear the bullets go whizz, ping just past my ears.'[60]

But they don't miss many, as a dozen of Carrington's men go down in the first volley.

•

Watching through his field glasses from the hospital in the early afternoon, the Reverend Green had followed the whole thing, first spying what he knew must be Carrington's relief column, arriving at last.

'We could see them in the distance,' he would chronicle of the first blessed vision of them, 'and what a sight they were! We saw the vanguard open out in lines of squadron and advance, whilst we cheered.'[61]

'How many? "Three! Four! Five!" Yes, we agreed on five [squadrons]. Still the line was steady.'[62]

There had been rejoicing around the hospital, and none more than from the grievously wounded Troopers. Perhaps they might live, after all, if they can just be relieved and so evacuated back to the real hospitals in Pretoria.

Green chronicles the events which follow, starting with the British attack.

'. . . the extended line closed in and galloped to the rear, and the guns advanced and planted shell after shell beautifully over the kloof by the river from which the Boer marksmen had fired'.[63]

And so it proves as they get closer, once the Boers from on high see them coming and turn their guns upon the relief column. Carrington's men engage in turn, bringing their own artillery forward to start firing.

Around Green those in the hospital even raise a ragged cheer at the distinctive sound of the British guns opening up on Boer positions.

And for two hours the boom of the British guns rolls over them with scattered pauses that are . . . *what?*

Clearly . . .

getting longer . . . .

with the artillery sounding ever more . . . . . .

. . . . distant.

Like counting the time between seeing the lightning and hearing the thunder, the men begin to wonder if the storm truly *has* passed. What is the meaning of this? the wounded in the hospital plaintively ask.

Green and his fellow doctors suspect only too well what it means – Carrington and his men are in full retreat. But, for the moment, they tell their patients that it just shows that 'Carrington will *come in another way*.'[64]

No, *really*.

'Indeed,' Green will recall, 'we almost persuaded ourselves that his retreat was a masterly movement whereby he would *verneuk*, fool, the Boers, take a lot of prisoners and, appearing dramatically at an unexpected time and place, enter the camp amidst wild rejoicing.'[65]

But even though the presumed relieving force get to within half a mile of the Boers, it is a supremely difficult exercise, given that with the effective firing of artillery, height and vision is all, and while the Boers can clearly see them and direct their shells accordingly, there is no broad mass of Boers that Carrington's men can see to fire at. Still they keep firing, hoping for the best, even as they are ordered to fall back. In war, sometimes, men have to be abandoned, sacrificed on the altar of military expediency. It is as simple as that.

Ride on. Ride away.

•

Not long before the sun goes down on this, the second day of the siege, a few scattered shells and Pom-Poms start to land on the Elands River Post once more – which the defenders take as less an attack than 'our friends [letting] us know that they had still some guns here'.[66]

It has been a long and dispiriting day, and there is relief as it comes to an end. As soon as the sun goes down the Troopers gratefully crawl out of their sconces and get to their surviving horses, to feed and water them. It is clearly something the Boers had been expecting, for right when the Troopers are in the thick of the horses a whole new volley of shells roar in once more, and once more there is chaos, with rearing, bleeding horses and roaring men. How long can they endure this hell on earth?

Mercifully it does not last long, for even the Boers realise that those first shells will immediately disperse the surviving men and horses and there is no further point. In total, the defenders calculate – for each shot is carefully tabulated – the Boers had poured in '116 shells and 356 pom-poms, making a total of 472', a rough third of what they endured the day before.

Extraordinarily, for all that, they have only had one Trooper killed and one wounded.

•

Back at Zeerust, Carrington is quick to cable his carefully crafted report to Lord Roberts, which makes his panicky and shambolic retreat sound like a calibrated and reasoned affair that all competent commanders would have done.

> Any further advance in face of the fire that was met with could only have resulted in disaster and I had to give the order for a retirement. The withdrawal was very carefully and well carried out.[67]

6 August 1900, Elands River, Ammo amass Annat

Just like yesterday and the day before, the shroud of valley vapours of the night nestle in the folds of the land until the red rays of the rising sun seek them out to disperse them ... only minutes before snipers' bullets and 12-pound shells alike start smashing into the defences of the defenders of Elands River.

In fact, perhaps today is the one where the snipers, particularly, come to the fore? That at least is the early impression as this dawn brings a much heavier *ping, ping, ping* than usual, interspersed only by a few shells and Pom-Poms as it seems likely the guns they had used the previous day against Carrington are not yet fully back in position.

And now Queenslander Lieutenant Annat – a very popular if quietly spoken officer in his mid-thirties, commanding the Queensland Mounted Infantry's D Company – has another idea, which he puts to the nearest officer who might approve, Major Tunbridge.

While some of my men keep the Boers pinned down and away from their guns, why don't I take 30 of my best men forward and see if we can steal those very guns?

Corporal Bruce Skelton recounts, 'About ten o'clock they placed a pom-pom and one twelve-pounder on a small hill fifteen hundred yards off. We saw them putting them there, and Major Tunbridge sent Lieut. Annat with his troops (4th Division), to try and silence them. We went out a little way, and took shelter where we could, and one man started to find the range. The Boers then started to play havoc on the camp with these two guns. When they least expected it, we (thirty of us) poured in a volley and knocked two over. We kept up volley after volley, which drove them away from their guns, and we kept them away till dark.'[68]

Captain Ham will recount that Annat 'took his men out from the camp some 200 yards nearer to the Boer trenches, and by cool and deadly rifle fire fairly drove the gun off to a more distant position'.[69]

Another will recall, 'He put two shells from the 7-pounder fair on top of the enemy's 12-pounder killing half a dozen horses and as many men.'[70]

Captain Ham, however – for one – is distressed to see the manner in which the enemy get themselves and their gun out of danger.

'The Boers moved their gun with characteristic craft and duplicity,' he will recount. 'They put it in an ambulance wagon, and so escaped fire during the transit . . . The removal was plainly visible from my trench, but the ambulance wagon prevented what would have been a deadly fire being opened on the gun.'[71]

The retaliatory attack is so successful that Annat is keen to go and capture the two Boer guns.

This time, though admiring Annat's pluck, Colonel Hore orders him to abandon the plan as just too risky. No matter, his men already could not admire him more, with Private R.J. Hallett exulting to his family that Lieutenant Annat is 'as game a man as ever lived. All the time of the siege he was foremost in everything – always cheering his men and speaking a kind word to everyone'.[72]

(Hallett also cannot help but compare the pluck of Annat and many of his fellow officers with the lack of it displayed by the man meant to be commanding them.

'If our Colonel had been as game as our officers, [the Boers] would have gone long ago: but all he thinks about is hanging on to his dugout. Colonel Hore is in charge, but we never get a sight of him. He was alive through the Mafeking siege, and it is a bad job he was not kept there.'[73])

Undaunted by Hore's refusal, Annat and his squad continue throughout this long day to counter the onslaught from the Boers.

•

Despite their own losses, however, up atop the surrounding kopjes the ebullient Boers continue to belch their fire, as do the Boer snipers lower down. Surely the defenders of Elands River will not be able to take much more of this? Surely, sometime soon a white flag will be displayed as they bow to overwhelming firepower and numbers?

For now, however, there is no such flag apparent and they continue to pour the shell-fire in, even as their snipers fire off volleys at everything that moves.

One of the British soldiers records the most frustrating thing of all, which he notes from the odd shell that doesn't explode on impact.

'Most of them are captured shells, bearing the British broad-arrow. It's a bit of hard luck when you get shelled with your own shells.'[74]

Those . . . *bastards*!

•

So accurate is the fire from Annat's artillery that, as the long day progresses, some of the houses they can see on the other side of the river start to wave the white flag in the hope they will be spared. Annat and his men might be so inclined if not for the fact they can still see the regular puffs of smoke coming from their windows, which indicate that there are snipers at work there.

Annat and his men start pounding them, too, and the popular officer is as busy as usual, ducking quickly from one sconce to another across open ground, ensuring that all of his men are doing all possible to protect themselves and defend against the Boers, when a particularly sharp sharpshooter wings him. In fact the bullet just glances his head enough to neatly remove his right eyebrow, bringing forth a gush of blood down his face which makes everything appear a lot worse than it actually is.[75]

Though badly shaken – how close he had come! – the Lieutenant's most profound emotion is a mixture of relief and resolution.

First comes the relief.

I will live! I will return home to Charters Towers once more. See my parents again. Fall into the arms of my fair Isabella again, who has promised she will be waiting for me at the docks.

And then the resolution. I will be fine! Just bind me up, and I can keep going!

He is bandaged up, the white cotton around his skull soon sprouting a bright red flower as the blood seeps through, and he keeps going, one of the most respected and admired men at Elands River. Still, such extraordinary *luck* he has had. To have come that close to instant death, to have escaped with only a minor wound, is quite extraordinary.

6 August 1900, approaching Elands River from the east, Butters bred

Now it is the turn of General Robert Baden-Powell and his force of 2000 Troopers to come out from their Mafeking garrison to try and relieve the besieged outpost. Just as they are setting off a dispatch rider comes through with a message from Lord Roberts:

Carrington reports he was unable to get to Hore. Enemy in force with artillery and pom poms. He fears that Hore must therefore surrender. This will be a very bad blow to us both in prestige and materially.[76]

A follow-up cable confirms Lord Roberts' fear that Elands River has surrendered, and Baden-Powell is ordered to retire his column to Pretoria.

•

Of all the poundings taken, none is more fierce than those on Butters' Kopje, and never more than on this late afternoon when it seems like four in every five shells fall upon them – as the Boers have clearly decided, correctly, that if they destroy the resistance there, all of Elands River must fall.

'The idea of the Boers,' Reverend Green will note, 'was evidently to get on this kopje, from which they could easily get Zouch's, as they overlooked it; then we should no longer be able to get our water at the river.'[77]

The shells fall, the plumes of smoke and dust billow forth, and to the men in the main camp it seems impossible that any living thing on Butters' Kopje could possibly survive.

'But ever and anon,' the Reverend Green will recount, 'when we feared for them, their volleys rang out and their Maxim rapped away, at which our men used to say: "Good old Butters. Listen to him knocking at their door".'[78]

The following evening, a new tactic is tried. Butters and his men, atop their kopje, see them coming.

A mob of sheep and goats heading their way!

Old African hands recognise the tactic. It had been developed by the Matabele warriors, with the idea being that the animals provide cover for the warriors crawling quickly behind.

Very well then.

Men, hold your fire.

Let them keep coming. It suits us for them to keep coming.

The result is a slaughter, and not just of the animals.

For Butters allows them to get within 50 yards, before the first shots are fired. The leading animals fall, the rest run shrieking, leaving . . . the Boers!

There they are!

It is a turkey shoot, and the Boers are gunned down by witheringly accurate fire.

It is not so much a fight as it is a firing party, and not even so much a firing party as an abattoir. It is all over in 20 minutes.

Regular soldiers – trained to advance even while their fellows fall all around – might have managed it. But not these Boer Commandos. They are brave men, but they are too few to build an advance on huge numbers of casualties and so must pull back whenever the fire is too fierce.

•

Back at the main garrison, as the sun starts to fade on the third day of the siege, things are quieter. The Boers have dispatched a few desultory shells. Like the day before, they are sent less in hope than with warning – we are still here, and not going anywhere, so don't go trying anything.

As it happens, however, the shells come down just as Lieutenant Annat – who has been in high spirits all afternoon, still marvelling at his luck of the morning, and occasionally putting his right hand to the bandaged spot on his face where the bullet had glanced him – is waving a cheery adieu to the neighbouring sconce he has been visiting, and makes his way back to his own.

One moment he is just ducking from one spot to the next, having left Major Tunbridge's HQ in the middle of the camp, right after making his daily report and has only gone a few yards when . . .

When the next moment, there is a shot in the distance from the Boer big gun the men know as 'Mr Krupp', followed by a sudden whistling getting ever louder and more shrill, and . . .

And the 12-pound shell lands directly behind him with a fearsome roar to sever both his legs nearly clean off and blast a gaping bloody cavern into his side.

Captain Ham, just coming out of HQ himself, is so close the flying human debris 'scattered blood and fragments over me'.[79]

Remarkably, Lieutenant Annat is still alive.

'Stretcher-bearers, now!'

The cry rings out across the camp.

With enormous bravery, for the snipers now have their measure too, his men frantically carry him to the camp hospital as the bullets ping all around. Alas, it is futile, for he lasts but a few minutes.

Though they don't know it yet, in Queensland a fine woman is suddenly a widow and her five children – aged from seven down to the three-month-old he has not yet met – are without a father.

Here at Elands River the appalling news spreads quickly and his men are overcome by grief. He is the only significant casualty on this day – hit by the last shell fired of the afternoon. His body, carefully wrapped in a Union Jack, is buried that night in a location just outside the trenches, together with two other men who have succumbed to their wounds from the first day.

'The deceased,' Sergeant Austen will chronicle, 'was admired by the whole of the garrison for his energy, sound soldierly qualities, and absolute fearlessness, and his sudden and untimely demise cast a deep gloom over all.'[80]

Trooper Arthur Corfe of Toowoomba agrees, writing, 'Ever since the commencement of the bombardment, Annat had been running from sconce to sconce cheering and encouraging us all, regardless of danger. None of us hesitate in saying he was the best and bravest officer at Elands River.'[81]

And so say all of them.

'His death cast quite a gloom over us,' another notes. 'We had already lost a lot of men, but they were only wounded.'[82]

And he is not the only one to die.

When Captain Ham finally makes it back to his original tent after this terrible day to retrieve the rugs he will need for the cold night ahead, it is to find 'that the poor black fellow [who had also lost his legs on the first day of the siege] had crept into the tent and laid himself on my bed. There he had bled to death, saturating rugs and bedclothes with blood.'[83]

Will there be respite in the night?

The brave defenders can only hope so but, not long after dark, just as everyone is getting up and about again, the Boers send down some more salvos, expecting to catch them out – and succeeding.

The fiends had even lit four fires in key spots around the outpost to enable them to be more accurate, and continue to fire by firelight.

Those *fiends*!

CHAPTER EIGHT

THE BEAT GOES ON

For the first time in the war, we are fighting men who used our own tactics against us. They were Australian volunteers and though small in number we could not take their position. They were the only troops who could scout our lines at night and kill our sentries while killing or capturing our scouts. Our men admitted that the Australians were more formidable opponents and far more dangerous than any other British troops.[1]

A Boer historian on the Siege of Elands River

7 August 1900, Rustenburg, bad news travels fast

Major Thomas Machattie, the Commanding Officer of the Australian Bushmen's C Squadron, is devastated, having just heard the news. The whole lot of them, gone!

'We have heard that de la Rey attacked Elands River and General Carrington endeavoured to relieve them from Zeerust, but finding them too strong was compelled to leave the poor wretches to their fate, and this after three days' bombardment. We heard there were many killed and wounded, besides the loss of a large convoy of over 100 wagons, containing our mails, clothing, boots, food, &c., and the surrender of those not killed, amongst whom was A Squadron of Australian Bushmen under Major Thomas.'[2]

Of course, the word spreads far and wide. Higher up the ranks, that word is a little better informed, but only a little.

Lord Roberts is not told that they have surrendered, only that – via Carrington – the situation with the colonials at Elands River is hopeless, and that in any case it would take more men than he can spare to go to their relief. Much more important at the moment is hunting down the 2500-strong force of General de Wet. It is so important, General Lord Kitchener has just departed with 10,000 men – a carefully chosen fast-moving force composed of a mix of mounted infantry, regular British cavalry, a small amount of infantry, artillery and machine-gun crew – on that very exercise.

So, yes, when it comes to the colonials at Elands River, Field Marshal Roberts is clear.

'We must, I deeply regret to say,' he writes to his subordinate, General Hamilton, 'leave Hore's garrison to their fate.'[3]

8 August 1900, Elands River, fourth day of siege, it was the worst of times, it was the best of times

Back in Australia, for many of them the day might have begun with the *cock-a-doodle-dooooooo* ... of the rooster. Not here. No sooner have the first red rays of the sun begun to glint and tint the higher reaches of the kopjes above Elands River than – good morning! – the shells from a 12-pounder begin exploding all around the camp. Most problematic, however, is the one that lands right in the very *middle* of their brave outpost.

How much more can they take?

In the makeshift hospital beneath the Red Cross flag – where Sergeant Major Mitchell and all the other wounded have been taken to – the first thing they know is a flash in the gloomy dawn from on high, then an ominous pause, then a shriek getting louder – coming our way! – and finally a shattering blast – *right among us!* – followed by more bellowing from those few animals that remain.

Only for ...

What is that shriek, louder than every other one we've heard?
EVERYONE DOWN!

The 12-pound shell is a direct hit on the hospital itself, sending splinters and shrapnel flying, all in the billowing dust-cloud. It is like an earthquake arriving in a shattering shell, the blast itself causing once solid things to splinter in turn and smack, smash, thrash and slice the patients and doctors, even as their whole world turns upside down and the cruel calculus of death works its way through the laws of physics. Screams and curses abound all around. When the smoke has cleared it is apparent that Mitchell has been hit *again*, and four other patients are also freshly wounded.

Mitchell's injury is the most concerning, however, as he's been wounded badly, particularly on his left leg. Reverend James Green only has to have one look at the shattered and shredded remains of Sergeant Major Mitchell's leg – all bone shards, hanging ligaments and pulverised red flesh – before he knows how serious it is.

After an examination, Dr Duka advises that there is nothing for it but an amputation above the knee.

Now comes the hard part.

'It was my duty,' Reverend Green will recount, 'to persuade him to submit to the operation.'[4]

Mitchell groggily agrees, but sends for Major Thomas.

The two old friends talk into the early evening – not as Major and Sergeant Major, but indeed as old friends. Mitchell advises he is happy to have his leg amputated, and Major Thomas admires his fortitude.

'He was very plucky, and seemed quite cheerful . . .' Thomas will recall. 'He told me that he felt very little pain, and that while he was under chloroform he fancied he was in the midst of a big battle.'[5]

Dr Duka wastes no time.

After an orderly presses a rag soaked with chloroform down over Mitchell's nose, they do not have to wait long for some sign that it is having an effect.

'Now then, men, get out on parade,' Mitchell begins, seemingly convinced that he is out there once more – *Company, presennnnnt, arms!* – getting the men in order.

With this, Dr Duka reaches for his tourniquet and, after so tightly binding Mitchell's leg just above the shattered calf that the part below it immediately turns white, he reaches for his amputation saw and begins to work the metal teeth into the flesh.

Still Mitchell is at least partly elsewhere as, with the chloroform taking further hold, he continues to bark more commands on the parade ground.

No more than one minute later it is done and if the patient is not quite 'resting comfortably', he is at least more comfortable than he had been and a better chance of surviving this calamity.

Reverend Green himself has been luckier. Though a vicious splinter has penetrated all of his steel trunk and its contents, a volume of *Tales from Blackwood* and the Bible, he is unhurt physically – even if his remarks about the Boers tended away from strict Christianity. For this is not a case of 'turn the other cheek', this is for the Boers to observe the most basic tenet of civilised warfare, by sparing all things beneath the Red Cross, and . . .

And what is *this*?

Cease fire!

It is a Boer on horseback bearing a white flag, resplendent in the sun. He has come with a message. As he passes through the perimeter and right to the heart of the suddenly quiet Elands River Camp – for the Boers, too, have stopped firing for fear of hitting their own man – the defenders cannot help but notice that the insignia on the Boer's saddle shows that it was originally the property of the NSW Bushmen.

The fellow, a smart-looking Lieutenant of the *Zuid-Afrikaansche Republiek*, in turn looks at the filthy men emerging from their hovels with wonder. For, of course, all of them have preferred to use their quart of water for drinking rather than shaving, washing themselves or, God forbid, their clothes, and most are blackened. Very oddly, some of them are smoking cigars, as if they wouldn't call the King their uncle!

This, despite the sheer *stench* of this place, that vomitous smell that arises from hundreds of dead and bloated animals decomposing, lying all around in the midst of their own lifeblood and excrement. It is all the well-heeled visitor can do not to throw up, but many of the locals, puffing on their cigars, barely blink.

And your business, sir?

The Boer has come with a message for Colonel Hore. In the battle two days before with General Carrington's relieving force, they had badly wounded and captured a leading scout by the name of Lieutenant Collins, of the South Australian Bushmen, who is being attended by Dr Francis Douglas of the same regiment. The Lieutenant had taken a bullet through the back that had gone right through him and he is in a bad way. The Boers are eager to send both the wounded man and his medic back, so they can be cared for by actual doctors.

This *is*, and no doubt about it, very decent of them. Colonel Hore quickly gives orders for a Cape cart to go out and bring the men in – an extra pair of healing hands for the hospital is a bonus, together with getting better care for one of their men – but sends with it a note of bitter protest, insisting the Boers stop *targeting* that hospital, as they had this very morning!

With the formalities completed, and Lieutenant Collins and Dr Douglas safely arrived, the barrage and sniping commences once more, and continues throughout the day. The biggest victory for the defenders in fact comes that night when, in the wee hours, Lieutenant Zouch leads ten of his best men on a night-raid to one of the nearby farmhouses where a particularly troubling sniper has been raising hell. Not only do they capture the presumed sniper and take him prisoner but they also capture no fewer than 14 large loaves of freshly baked bread, prepared for the Boer Commandos but now in the defenders' possession. A good night's work!

In fact, such a good night's work that, from this point on, regular sorties of the defenders out into Boer lines to attack whatever camps they can find, before stealing away just as quickly, become standard. It adds a whole new dimension to their defence.

'The bullets are flying around all day and now and then at night,' one Trooper will recount. 'It is hardly safe to stick up one's head above the bags, as we are completely surrounded by Boer snipers, who are only 900 yards away. We caught one sitting in a tree the other night, a couple of men having taken off their boots and put on four pairs of socks, got right under the tree, and brought him down before he knew they were there.'[6]

That same night, as on all the previous nights, the digging goes on.

'I fancy an underground plan of Elands River Camp would make anyone laugh,' one digger records, 'such workings were never before seen, every man his own architect in burrowing a hole, and by jove they are necessary, the shells can do such fearful damage.'[7]

In any case, if the worst does come to the worst, they will, the Australians decide – as chronicled by one soldier – 'lie low, and when the Boers got near enough, to charge with fixed bayonets. The men swore they would never surrender, nor be taken prisoners.'[8]

9 August 1900, Elands River, surrender unrendered

'Cease fire!'

Again the cry rings out on the morning of 9 August.

Again the guns from both sides fall silent as the same Boer emissary from the day before – if anything looking even smarter, this time on saddle of the Imperial Yeomanry, clearly taken from General Carrington's forces – comes forth under the same white flag, clearly wanting to parley.

He has come with a written explanation from General de la Rey for the shelling of the hospital the day before, and an offer to them, all penned on the back of three telegraph forms.

9/8/00

Assistant-Commandant General de la Rey to Lieut. Colonel Hore
Commanding Officer
British Camp, Elands River
I regret that some patients and wounded in the hospital were fired at from our cannons. I am obliged to tell you that it was your Honour's fault, as your hospital ambulance is in a very small camp

in the vicinity of your cannon, as placed by your Honour, so that cannon-fire would most likely strike the hospital . . .

I wish your Honour to earnestly consider that the time has come to have no further bloodshed. Your resistance, which has kept up so bravely, must now come to an end.

If your Honour surrenders the camp, with everything in it (without hiding or ruining anything in it) then I am prepared to give a security to your Honour, that I will send you and your troops to the nearest British force to which you choose to go. Your commissioned officers, in such case, will retain their arms in recognition of your courage in defence of your camp.

Please be so kind as to give me your reply as soon as possible. If necessary, I am ready at any time to hold a conference with your Honour on the subject to arrange details,

> J. H. DE LA REY
> Assistant-Commandant General
> Z.A.R.[9]

It is, and no doubt about it, a handsome – if desperate – offer.

If the defenders surrender their supplies and the camp's position, they will be granted their lives and can fight again. Surely, under the circumstances, no-one could blame them for surrendering? They are totally outnumbered, being constantly shelled by guns on three sides, with only a tenuous supply line to water. They have several dead and many wounded needing better medical help than can currently be provided, and they have been abandoned by the two British forces sent to relieve them.

The emissary also gives them a verbal warning from General de la Rey. If they don't give up, by the following day the Boers will have a 94-pounder gun, a Creusot Long Tom, capable of 'blowing them off the face of the earth'.[10]

For once Colonel Hore reacts quickly, calling what amounts to a Council of War – his senior officers gathered in his headquarters bunker, including Butters, Zouch, Tunbridge and Thomas – to talk it through. Alas, the Colonel's need for speed soon emerges. For he is eager to surrender from the first and says so, urging his officers to accept the reality of the situation. They are outnumbered, surrounded, hounded and pounded. They clearly will not be able to hold on much longer in any case. Why lose more good men killed when they will have to give up in any case?

His senior officers beg to differ, and do so perilously loudly.

The first man to speak is Queensland's Major Walter Tunbridge, who rejects the very idea of surrender. He asks how on earth he could return to the men who had fought so courageously over the last five days, repelling the Boers, withstanding the barrage, burying their dead, binding their wounded and . . . tell them it had all been for *nothing*, that they are going to *surrender*?

You, Colonel Hore, can surrender if you must, and I cannot stop you. But we are Queenslanders and we don't surrender. If necessary, though we only be a hundred, we will withdraw from your surrender, and fight our way through the Boer lines.[11]

'We never came over to South Africa to surrender to the Boers,' he says with a volume that betrays his emotion. 'We came to FIGHT, and fight we will.'[12]

One of his men, born and bred north of the Tweed, will record his admiration.

'The Queenslanders would have all followed him, and I believe we would have got through.'[13]

And Tunbridge is strongly supported by Major Kelly, the Captains Thomas, Cope and Ham – and the Lieutenants Cornwall and Zouch.

'It was a moment of intense excitement,' Father Timoney will recount. 'Colonel Hore, the nominal leader, would have handed over his rifle at once. The Australians said "*No, never,*" in one voice.'[14]

Understood?

'The Australians said, to one man . . . they would rather die than give in, and if the white flag was put up over the laager they would go on shooting just the same.'[15]

They mean it.

There is no reason to surrender, Colonel, when we can continue to fight on. We have plenty of supplies, in fact so much that we are duty-bound to fight to the last to keep them from the Boers. Every day we hold on saps them further of their own resources. We will not be surrendering.

And, perhaps, there is another fact at play. The *men*, Colonel. What will they do if we announce we are surrendering? There is even a story abroad that 'the men would shoot any officer who urged surrender'.[16]

And there really is a great deal of angst-cum-anger among the men at how long this meeting is taking. What is there to discuss? Isn't the answer obvious? *No.* We are not surrendering. Why not just say so, NO, and be done with it?

Captain Ham is one who has been amazed at the enduring morale of his Troopers, despite the grimness of their circumstances, and is convinced that Colonel Hore has got it wrong.

'All this time our men were in good heart,' he would chronicle, 'and there would have been no surrender until the last bullet had been fired, and the bayonet had found a resting place in the heart of the foe.'[17]

But, outside in the trenches, they want to know: if the officers are taking this long, perhaps they are discussing terms?

'Some of the men,' the Reverend Green will note, 'were afraid that the time taken to consider the Boer proposal was a sign that we were going to surrender . . .'[18]

But no.

In the end, in the face of the united opposition to his proposal, Colonel Hore really has no choice. To surrender without the support of his officers would see him risk a court martial (even if the Troopers didn't shoot him first).

Very well then, gentlemen, we will fight on, and I shall so advise the emissary.

It does not take long for the decision to get out, whereupon . . .

'The suppressed cheers of the men echoed the decision all over the camp. There was no time to think of rations or sleep. Every man was at work in a minute, some building stone walls, others burrowing in the ground to make bomb-proof shelter.'[19]

As to Colonel Hore, he carefully composes his written response to General de la Rey.

> I beg to acknowledge the receipt of your letter of August 9, 1900, containing your demand for the surrender of the British troops at Elands River camp, and in reply must inform you that, as this post is held by Her Majesty's forces I decline to surrender.[20]

With heavy heart – he is not well, and simply no longer has the constitution to maintain his warrior heart of old – he now makes his way through the stares and glares of his men to deliver the note to the emissary.

And here he is now.

Colonel Hore hands over the note, and a few words of explanation.

'Even if I wished to surrender to you,' he says, 'and I don't, I am commanding Australians who would cut my throat if I accepted your terms.'[21]

So be it.

The Boer emissary must return to General de la Rey with the note he's been given, together with a scrawled note some of the Australian soldiers had already given him to pass on to his bloody Boer mates:

> If de la Rey wants our camp, why does he not come and take it?
> We will be pleased to meet him and his men, and promise them
> a great reception at the end of a toasting fork. Australians will
> never surrender. Australia forever![22]

Colonel Hore returns to his trench, though that evening he does emerge briefly to find an African runner and give him the princely sum of £10 to find Carrington and beg him to return and rescue the garrison.

And now, as ever, he goes back to his trench – a general absence that will be noted.

'Colonel Hore remained underground from the first day,' Father Timoney – widely regarded as the worst horseman in the contingent – will note, 'and a team of mules would not drag him into the light.'[23]

True, notes a Queenslander, Sergeant Austen. 'Lieutenant-Colonel Hore . . . was a senior officer here, with Major Hopper in command of the garrison. It is very much to be regretted, however, that from within half-an-hour of the firing of the first shell neither of these officers were seen . . . unless it was after dark, when the firing from both guns and rifles was over for the day for all intents and purposes, and the actual work of carrying out the defence of Elands River devolved practically on Major W. Howard Tunbridge . . . and a few other colonial officers [particularly Sandy Butters], who, like himself, were not afraid to see personally that effective measures were taken to defend this little camp . . .'[24]

Farrier Sergeant Major Hampden Livesey is a little more oblique in his disparagement: 'We were a lot of little convoys got together under Colonel Hore (I ought to spell his name differently) . . .'[25]

Really!

Ah, Captain Butters!

For, as it happens, de la Rey's emissary, before making his way back to his own lines, decides to try a ruse. Making his way to Butters and his men atop their kopje on the south side, he conjures a lie.

'The main camp has surrendered,'[26] he says. Surely Captain Butters and his men will do the right and obvious thing, and lay down their arms and come with him now?

Actually, no.

Butters, a proud Scot with an accent thicker than haggis, declines in his own fashion. When Father Timoney asks him a short time later precisely what he had said, the response of Butters wouldn't melt in his mouth: 'I taud them that I widna gie them or surrender an empty tin kettle, and if the main camp had been daft enough to give in, I wod kick the Boers oot o't and tak it back again.'[27]

The messenger, as another Trooper notes, had been given 'five minutes to clear out or you are as good as dead'.[28]

Father Timoney loves it, noting 'Captain Butters is deservedly one of the most popular men in our army.'[29]

•

What now!

Gryp hom! Grab him!

In the moonlight, one of the Boer sentries in position all around Elands River has seen a flitting figure and, after alerting the others, the man is soon brought to ground.

It proves to be a 'Kaffir' runner, bearing a message from Colonel Hore to General Carrington, begging for him to return to save them. The message, of course, is passed to General de la Rey, who takes heart from it. For all their opponent's bravado in refusing to surrender, they clearly cannot hold on for much longer.

•

Captain Ham is struggling with his men.

It is not that they are losing the will to fight. It is that they want to fight *too* much, want to get out and shoot at the snipers, manoeuvre forward across open ground, take the bastards *on*, and take them *down*.

'They would not believe,' Ham would recount, 'that it was an order not to do so, and I heard them even accusing me of cowardice because I would not let them go out.'[30]

The whole dreadful thing is enough to break the spirit of any man, though it must be said some of those who call on the Holy Spirit seem to manage a little better. Their numbers include the 38 Dutch refugees in the camp – those who do not wish to fight with the Boers, but will be punished for that by de la Rey's men if they leave. They just want to survive.

On this day, 12 August, when there is less shelling and sniping than the day before, the Dutch manage to hold something of a Sunday service, replete with psalm-singing and the old men reading from the scriptures as they all pray. In the afternoon Reverend Green even joins them to conduct another service, attended by some of the more pious of the Troopers.

In the meantime, every day Major Thomas has been visiting James Mitchell in the hospital, to find him descending rapidly. He has fever, only small bursts of lucidity and is wasting away before their very eyes. On this day the doctor tells Thomas that Mitchell cannot possibly live, and is proved right within hours, as the Tenterfield man breathes his last, shuffling off this mortal coil with barely a sound as Thomas stands over him.

That night, in the moonlight, once the shelling has stopped, Major Thomas and three fellow Tenterfield men sorrowfully dig his grave – though they do have to throw themselves down several times when it seems the Boers have seen their silhouettes and fire off some volleys. The grave dug, they place some grass on the bottom for Mitchell's eternal rest and comfort, wrap the dead man in a blanket and are about to carefully lower him down, when it happens . . .

Great eruptions in the distance are followed by a piercing whistle, growing louder . . . louder . . . *closer*. They do the obvious: Sergeant Major Mitchell's body is momentarily abandoned as they jump into the very grave that they have prepared for him. (No disrespect, it is just that further wounds to Sergeant Major Mitchell would be rather beside the point.)

Only after the shell lands nearby and the smoke has cleared do they swap positions with the unfortunate Tenterfield man, before throwing the earth back upon him.

'It was a sad duty for us,' Thomas will report back to his readers in Tenterfield, 'the saddest I have seen in South Africa, Sergeant-Major Mitchell was always a keen soldier. He was for fifteen years attached to the Tenterfield corps . . . Now he has filled a soldier's grave, and I think there is none better – far better than to die, perhaps, of some lingering disease.

'This war is a sad, cruel business – but it is an unavoidable evil. I think we all wish it was over – it is getting wearisome.'[31]

14 August 1900, Elands River, rabbit habit

The siege grinds on, a veritable meat-grinder.

'We are a dirty-looking lot now,' Trooper Samuel McCurdy from the Victorian Bushmen notes, 'nearly everyone has grown a beard and we have not been able to have a wash since this fight began. Officers, doctors, parsons and men, we are all alike living underground and like the rabbits pop out when it is dark.'[32]

Needs must, they spend their night-times adding to their fortifications.

'We are determined to fight like Trojans. Now that we are broken in to it, the hum or fizz of a bullet does not send such a nasty feeling through us.'[33]

It *is* disquieting for all that.

McCurdy now pauses, before taking up his pen once more, explaining, 'I have to stop writing every few minutes, as the shells come so close to me to find out whether I am still alive.'[34]

He and his companions are, but only just . . .

16 August 1900, Elands River, here comes the cavalry

The idea of Lord Kitchener personally pursuing a master of the open veldt like General Christiaan de Wet does not sit well with everyone.

'The Piccadilly generals,' Banjo Paterson will note, 'say that Kitchener is only a n . . . r-fighter, well enough when the enemy will rush at him and try to stab him with a spear, but not exactly the man that they – the Piccadilly generals – would have selected for the job of catching de Wet.'[35]

For one thing, while de Wet travels light on the veldt, and essentially lives off the land, Kitchener travels grand, and heavy.

Banjo puts it rather well: 'The fact is, that there are now 12 British Generals and about 30,000 men cruising round the Orange River Colony in chase of de Wet, who has got about 4000 men, and who is as hard to put one's finger on as a flea.'[36]

Kitchener's own language, as expressed in a cable to Secretary of State for War, William St John Brodrick, is every bit as bleak: 'It is a most difficult problem, an enemy that always escapes, a country so vast that there is always room to escape, supplies such as they want abound almost everywhere . . . I wish I could give you better news.'[37]

On this particular occasion Kitchener, with his strong force of 10,000 Troopers, is heading on his way to hunt down the troublesome General Christiaan de Wet and his army when it happens, not far from the outpost of Bethlehem.

A galloping horseman approaches.

Kitchener's men are wary, ready to shoot him at the first sign that he is foe not friend, but it proves to be one of Kitchener's own scouts, who had caught a 'Kaffir' runner taking a message from de la Rey to de Wet, which is believed to be important. Kitchener does not gasp to read the translation of it, for he is not the gasping kind. But it *is* extraordinary.

I have the British in a corner [at Elands River]. They have a valu-able convoy, but am unable to take it without more men and more guns; send them along at once, and the prize is ours, I am unable to get it with the guns and men I have at present.[38]

And so, de la Rey's question to de Wet: *What shall I do now?*[39]

And the dispatch is dated just a few days earlier!

Carrington's report had it that Elands River had surrendered, that they were all gone. But here is seeming proof that that is not the case, that they are *still holding on.*

Stunned – how could such a mistake have been made, with brave men abandoned? – the dour Englishman is at least grateful that he is in a good position to move to the rescue. As one who did not arrive at this position of pre-eminence by tarrying when it came time to making decisions, he makes this one on the spot.

'We must help those fellows at any cost,' he says to his senior officers, 'and not lose, a moment . . .'[40] 'Let us go and see if they are alive.'[41]

A cable is also sent to his Chief of Staff, General Ian Hamilton, to divert his own column:

> Information received from Hore at Elands River dated the 10th shows that he was still holding out. He had had 27 casualties and had refused De la Rey's demand to surrender. Carrington has been ordered today from Mafeking to Zeerust . . . it is essential that you should reach Elands River post in sufficient strength and as speedily as possible.[42]

The fully focused pursuit of General Christiaan de Wet will have to wait. Portions of the column will be sent to other commanders. With 2000 men we turn to the west and head for Elands River. And, Broadwood, get the finest men from your Mounted Brigade and have them ride hard in advance of us. If they can get through, they must tell the men of Elands River to hold on, for we are on our way.

Cue the bugles. Here comes the cavalry.

•

Out on the high veldt with his men, General de Wet is pleased to find out that the British have stopped their pursuit. Once again he has out-foxed them.

'I must have misled the English . . .'[43]

And yet if de Wet is relieved by the news, General Carrington, now back in Mafeking, is nothing less than devastated to hear that the men of Elands River are still holding on.

For he has staked his reputation on the fact that Elands River was somewhere between lost already, or at least not worth saving . . . only to find they have successfully fought on!

So panicked had he been by his experience that, after retreating from Elands River at all pace, he and his men had paused at Zeerust only long enough to burn all the supplies there, before high-tailing it, *wee-wee-wee all the home way home* to Mafeking.

In sum, the survival of those at Elands River has shown his leadership as panic unbecoming of a British officer. The consequences have been so dire, it will not be long before he is relieved of his command and ordered back to Rhodesia.

•

At Elands River itself, they are holding on. Only at night do they get up and about, while the rest of their time is spent lying in the trenches from five in the morning until seven o'clock at night.

'I can tell you it is no joke,' Trooper Fred Bates chronicles in a letter to a friend. 'We go up to the camp every second night for tucker, and it is moonlight and the Boers can see us crawling up, and sometimes the bullets come a bit too close for my liking. We are completely surrounded. This makes the eleventh day and no relief has come yet.'[44]

Some men, perhaps not surprisingly, are starting to break under the strain. It is possible some are hallucinating, and their hallucinations are becoming infectious.

For on the very late afternoon of 15 August – a surprisingly quiet day, with almost no shelling and only scattered sniping – some even insist that, to the far south, they can see an enormous column coming their way. By bringing field glasses to bear and straining their eyes, even a couple of officers go further and conjure up visions of 'a mass moving with flanking parties and advance guards out'.[45]

Extraordinary, how the mind can play tricks on some blokes. Even officers!

But at least the still sane ones put them right: 'They are trees, and you will see them again in the morning.'[46]

Of course, bets are laid about who is right, and who is wrong.

Not long after it gets dark, three rockets explode in the eastern sky – clearly a Boer signal for something, but no-one is sure what.

Still, on this very night two officers are in their usual position, forward of the weakest flank, just down from Butters' Kopje, when the one with the keenest eyes is sure he sees something.

Movement in the moonlight.

With one hand he grips his rifle, with the other he alerts his companion and points, whispering, 'There's a man crawling up to us through the long grass, cover him with your rifle and I'll challenge.'

Once sorted, the call goes out.

Who is that?

'What place is this?' a broad voice comes back.

'Elands River garrison.'

'I have a message from Lord Kitchener. If you hold out till tomorrow morning he'll relieve you.'

There is more movement, and soon enough the man emerges from the long grass, to come up and shake their hands.

'Any Australians here?'

'Any number of 'em.'

'Good enough,' says he. 'I'm a "Sandgroper" myself.'[47]

•

What's that?

What?

That!

It is those on the highest point of the Elands River outpost – those on Butters' Kopje – who see it first, the next morning. From the south, mingling with the red tinges of the rising sun illuminating the veldt, and right on the hundredth of the hundred horizons that stretched before them, a small brown puff of something appears, something that is not part of nature, and is gradually, ever so gradually, getting bigger.

Could it be . . . ?

Is it?

They stand up, and lean forward, in the instinctive if curious manner of humans towards things of great interest seen at an even great distance . . .

It is! And this time there are ever fewer doubters, as '380 anxious pairs of eyes watched the movements of this party',[48] and swiftly come to the conclusion: a vast regular army, an enormous body of men on horseback, is coming towards them. They are now 15 miles off, and closing fast.

Here comes the cavalry!

The Boer scouts soon confirm exactly that – a convoy of mounted British soldiers, no less than ten miles long – and the obvious decision is taken. Those few Boers who remain also pull out, and the siege is over, after 12 days, as the pointy end of the convoy arrives.

First come the 17th Lancers, followed by the 9th and 16th Lancers with the 10th Hussars and the 5th Mounted Infantry close in behind. Now come the Imperial Yeomanry, the 6th Dragoons and the Natal Rifles as the bearded brutes of Elands River emerge from their dugouts in their tattered clothes, their roughly bound wounds, their thousand-yard stares with bloodshot eyes. The newly arrived soldiers – some holding their noses against the unbelievable STENCH when arriving in a place where dead carcasses have been rotting for nearly a fortnight in the sun, and not all of the dead soldiers have been buried yet – are stunned at what they see.

Still, each side cheer the other – the horsemen for the heroic defence of these extraordinary fighters; the defenders for the horsemen who have at last come to their relief.

At 8.30 am, just behind the leading squadron, one particularly spar-kling, swish group of 150 lancers, pennants waving from their lances, enters the camp and, right behind them it is . . . him! I am sure of it!

Kitchener *himself*! He's here! That one, over there, the slight figure sitting high in the saddle who looks like he has a steel poker for a spine, so straight up does he sit, so red is his face as he glares balefully at all around with those glittering diamond eyes, that bristling moustache which always signals extreme disapproval.

I don't think he's particularly pissed off right now, I think that is just the way he looks?

The defenders come from everywhere to see Kitchener in the flesh, and to greet their rescuers, to have it confirmed with their own eyes – it is true – they are saved, by Kitchener and his men!

Yes, the Lord is their saviour, they shall not want. He has travelled 27 miles on the first day, 25 on the second, and now here he is.

Looking around with wonder, Kitchener himself notes: 'Only colonials could have held out and survived in such impossible circumstances.'[49]

Kitchener's officers are equally stunned, some of them so impressed with what will clearly ever after be remembered as an iconic defence that they pocket shell fragments as souvenirs.

But say, cobber, if you like a mere bit of shell so much, you'd love this unexploded pom-pom shell I have. I was going to take it home for my kids, but for as little as £5 it's yours! All right, all right, £4.

Most interesting to the new arrivals is just how the defenders had managed to dig their trenches so deep, their tunnels so long, and make their fortification so strong. They are stunned – stunned, do you hear me? – to learn much of the burrowing had been done with a bayonet.

'What beggars these colonials are for fighting,' one of the British officers is heard to say to another companion. 'If it had been our Tommies they would have surrendered.'[50]

The Australians simply do not have the good sense to consider surrender, which leaves *winning* as their only option.

And yet, as shocked as many of Kitchener's men are to see these mole-men of Elands River emerge, some of *them* are, frankly, also a little shocked at the condition of their *rescuers*.

'Lord Kitchener's troops looked different from what one would expect from seeing pictures of soldiers,' one would write home. 'They had been on the war path for ten months, and they were in rags – and most of them had their toes sticking out of their boots.'[51]

Seriously, as Lieutenant Zouch notes, most of the boots are 'more string than leather'.[52]

Truly, it is quite shocking, with the Reverend Green noting 'officers and men alike in rags and tatters'.[53]

The troops who have just arrived, while pleased to have saved the defenders, are even more pleased to get their hands on the available stores, as they begin to load them all in the carts available.

'It was almost pathetic to see how the starving Tommies helped themselves when opportunities occurred,' Green recounts. 'Here there would be a group of them picking up tins of beef scattered from a broken box ... Men filled their helmets, the horse's nosebags, old haversacks and mud-coloured handkerchiefs with flour, and even officers were glad to have "good places" pointed out to them where they could supplement their commissariat by the addition of odd boxes of things.'[54]

Yes, sentries are placed by the most precious of the stores, but it does little. For every sentry has a friend and sooner or later, 'some hungry Tommy would come along and say, "I say, matey, do you know where I could get some 'scoff'?"'

And the sentry would reply: 'There's some bully beef round the corner there, but you ain't supposed to take it, but I can't say anything if I don't see you.

'And the sentry would march away in the opposite direction whilst the Tommy helped himself.'[55]

Most of the remaining supplies, of course, find their way into carts and are soon on their way, under heavy escort, to Zeerust.

•

Around and about the camp now, newly arrived officers of Kitchener's convoy walk and talk, making admiring conversation with the defenders, trying to work out exactly how they had done it.

Some of their remarks are duly recorded, to be sent home in letters to Australia.

'Most interesting thing of the campaign.'

'Cannot understand how they make such fortifications during the night.'

'Just shows what determined men can do . . .'[56]

Much later, the most famed Boer military leader of all, General Jan Smuts, will record his own thoughts on the achievements of the Australians and their fellow defenders.

'There can only be one opinion about the fine determination and pluck of these stalwart Colonials, to many this terrific siege must have been their first experience of serious warfare. Deserted by their friends and then, owing to unreasonable obstinacy, abandoned by their disappointed enemies, they simply sat tight until Kitchener's column, which was in pursuit of General de Wet, finally disinterred them from the carcass-covered Kopje, into which they had burrowed so effectually that it seemed unlikely they would ever come out of it.'[57]

•

For his part, General Koos de la Rey rides away, gutted. 'The Lion of the West', as he is known in the western Transvaal, a man whose famous hawk nose is synonymous with his ruthless nature, had been counting on the rifles, ammunition and food at Elands River. Now, not only have they failed to get anything, they have uselessly wasted further resources, including 7000 precious artillery shells, trying to get it. Their situation is now more desperate than ever, and they will be relying on remaining Boer farms to keep them going.

•

At Elands River it is time to take stock and, as well as everything else, work out just how much stock they have lost. Before the siege began, the Elands River camp had 487 horses, 269 mules and 356 transport oxen. Now, there are just 56 horses, 29 mules and 106 oxen left. They had started with a total of 505 men, of whom there have been 73 casualties, including 17 fatalities.

On that terrible subject, there is something that must be done before they leave this Godforsaken spot. For over the next day, all of the graves are cleaned up. White stones are gathered from surrounding hills and placed both around them, and to form a cross in the middle. Some even have headstones, with the names of those who will lie there for eternity chiselled upon them. Particular care is taken with the grave of the revered Lieutenant Annat, for whom his men still actively grieve.

For him, a large slab of slate is taken from the river itself, and laboriously hauled to the spot before Trooper Waltisbuhl and Sergeant Major Glass carefully manoeuvre it into place at the head of his grave, with the words standing out clearly:

> In memory of Lieutenant Annat, 3rd QMI, who was killed here
> in action on the 6th August, 1900.[58]

As a final touch, a barbed wire fence is constructed around the sacred ground to ensure that no animals will unwittingly desecrate the graves.

And now, to farewell them properly, late on the afternoon of 17 August, all of the survivors of Elands River, bolstered by hundreds of Kitchener's men, form up in a square around the graves as a service is held, presided over by Reverend Green and Chaplain Patrick, who has lately arrived with the relief column. A bugle call begins the ceremony, followed by prayers and a hymn; the voices of a thousand men, including Lord Kitchener, softly take up the beloved words.

> *Abide with me; fast falls the eventide;*
> *The darkness deepens; Lord, with me abide;*
> *When other helpers fail, and comforts flee,*
> *Help of the helpless, O abide with me.*[59]

Their voices soar as 'yonder on the crest of the hill the Union Jack still flies, and not far away our Red Cross flag is flying. These flags bear testimony to the spirit of the men sent from Australia, Rhodesia, and Canada, who by the sacrifice symbolised by the one flag, have sustained the prestige indicated by the other.'[60]

Ah, that flag. Every time it has been knocked over by the blast of exploding shells it had been carefully resurrected once more and though it is battered, shattered and tattered, still she flies! And still they sing, a thousand strong, a thousand made stronger by each verse that passes their lips.

> *Swift to its close ebbs out life's little day;*
> *Earth's joys grow dim, its glories pass away;*

Change and decay in all around I see;
  O Thou Who changest not, abide with me.

And now the firing party of the Queensland Mounted Infantry, the men of Lieutenant Annat, point their rifles in the air and, on the Sergeant Major's call, fire volleys.

Between each one, different bugle calls are played, and after the last one the Last Post is played.

The twilight deepens, fast falls the eventide . . . and the men quietly recede, some of them weeping, some of them breathing the words for comfort more:

Change and decay in all around I see;
  O Thou Who changest not, abide with me.

In his tent, Captain Ham dashes off a letter home, before packing up.

'Though our casualties amounted to about 70, we still KEPT THE UNION JACK FLYING in the centre of our camp. I have been promised this flag as a memento, and needless to say I shall prize it very much, although it has been riddled with shot and shell.'[61]

•

With the morning's first light, Kitchener and his grand army ride out, bar one division under General Paul Methuen, whose job it will be to escort the survivors of the Battle of Elands River to Zeerust then Mafeking. For those survivors it will be no small thing to make the 70-mile distance, given that, in the absence of their now dead horses, they must make their way on 'Shanks' pony' only – walking.

'It was . . . very hot,' the Reverend Green chronicles, 'and we all realised how unpleasant it was to be footsloggers, trudging along in the heat. But the thick cloud of dust rising from a column ten miles long was even worse than the heat.'[62]

Yes, it is a rather down-trodden and dusty ending for this extraordinary saga, but what a reputation they have now established to both precede them, and follow them for the rest of their lives!

'It is impossible to give you anything like an idea of what they must have gone through,' one British officer with the relief force will write to the London *Times*. 'I do hope Great Britain will show its gratitude to these Australians for the brightest page in the history of the war. Let it be known far and wide. Come out and see the place, and if your heart doesn't tingle with pride, or a lump get in your throat, and if a prayer doesn't fly to heaven at the sight, you must be harder and colder than an iceberg. I tell you, these men deserve anything the Old Country can give them.'[63]

Even the Boers will be moved to record their valour.

'Never in the course of this war,' General Jan Smuts, who served alongside de la Rey, will note, 'did a besieged force endure worse sufferings, but they stood their ground with magnificent courage.'[64]

The war correspondents agree.

'This stand at Brakfontein on the Elands River appears to have been one of the very finest deeds of arms of the war,' Conan Doyle will note. 'The Australians have been so split up during the campaign, that though their valour and efficiency were universally recognised, they had no single exploit which they could call their own. But now they can point to Elands River ... When the ballad-makers of Australia seek for a subject, let them turn to Elands River, for there was no finer resistance in the war.'[65]

CHAPTER NINE

THE BREAKER BREAKS AWAY

We've drunk our wine, we've kissed our girls, and funds are
    sinking low,
The horses must be thinking it's a fair thing now to go.[1]

'West by North, Again', by Breaker Morant, 1895

He was a jolly sort of a chap.[2]

Trooper Muir Churton on Breaker Morant

Unlike Milner, Kitchener developed a deep respect for the Boer
generals and particularly for General Botha ... At the Middelburg
Conference, he sent out a large military escort to greet the Boer
generals with full military honours, as they entered the town ...
At Headquarters, Kitchener came out to meet them and Botha
recorded: '... offering me his arm, he led me into the room'.[3]

Jane Meiring

14 August 1900, Pietersburg, razer cuts

It is time for Lord Roberts to remove his velvet glove and reveal the cold iron fist beneath.

To this point, the proclamations of Lord Roberts have simply encouraged the Boers to give up, promising rewards if they do so.

By Proclamation No. 1 of 1900, for example, burghers who had not taken a prominent part in the hostilities were allowed, upon taking an oath, to return to their homes, and were not dealt with as prisoners of war. And Proclamation No. 2 of 1900 had ensured that burghers to whom passes and permits had been granted might retain their stock, or take them to the winter veldt.

But with the broad failure of those proclamations, Kitchener convinces Roberts that 'it is manifest that the leniency which has been extended to the Burghers of the South African Republic is not appreciated by them, [and] is being used as a cloak to continue the resistance against the Forces of Her Majesty the Queen'[4] and so Lord

Roberts now formally withdraws those proclamations and replaces them with a new one.

From this 14th day of August 1900 onwards, all those who have taken the oath of neutrality, 'and who have in any way broken such oath, will be punished with either death, imprisonment, or fine, [and] all Burghers in the districts occupied by Her Majesty's Forces, except such as have already taken the said oath, shall be regarded as Prisoners of War, and shall be transported or otherwise dealt with as I may determine'.

Oh. And one more thing.

'All buildings and structures on farms on which the scouts or other forces of the enemy are harboured will be liable to be razed to the ground.'[5]

From now on, you're either with us, or agin us – and will face the consequences.

As a matter of fact, broadly concurrent with the proclamation being issued, 'Reverse' Buller issues an order of his own and, in short order, not only is the homestead near Standerton that General Louis Botha had built with his own hands burned to the ground – just as his animals are slaughtered, and his crops burned to a stubble – but a photographer is dispatched to record the destruction, so the photos can be sent directly to Botha himself.

Roberts follows up with a warning to General Botha: 'In order to put these views into practice, I have issued instructions that the Boer farmhouses near the spot where an effort has been made to destroy the railroad or to wreck the trains shall be burnt, and that from all farmhouses for a distance of ten miles around such a spot all provisions, cattle, etc., shall be removed.'[6]

•

Through it all, Breaker Morant is doing exceedingly well, using his masterful skills as a horseman and his exceptional bravery to take Bennet Burleigh's dispatches through shot and shell, through battles hot as hell, and get them to the telegraphist in the nearest town to get the news out to the world. But as to what happens when it is over and Burleigh departs? Well, that is a question for tomorrow, a day the Breaker never deals with until it comes.

•

Having defeated the Boers at Belfast, in what would be the last set-piece battle of the war, in these last days of August, the British forces make it all the way to Machadodorp in the far eastern Transvaal in the knowledge they are closing in on capturing *both* Boer Presidents. Most of the interest is on *Oom* Paul Kruger, as it is an article of faith with the British troops that the President of Transvaal travels with the very last of the republic's wealth. And not just the dull wealth of banknotes and dirty pennies. The railway carriage is filled to the brim with *gold*, that deep, glowing yellow brought up from the black mines of Johannesburg.

Oh yes, for both escaped prisoners and spies attest to its existence, and as reported by Banjo Paterson, 'They had seen the bar gold stacked in the truck like slabs of timber and many an Australian trooper pictured himself charging on to that truck when no Provost Marshal was near enough to interfere with his operations. The question will not be "Where is *Oom* Paul?" but "Where is that truck full of bar-gold?"'[7]

The latter is anyone's guess. But at dawn on 20 October 1900, the former becomes apparent. A fine Dutch warship, the *Gelderland*, has pulled into the docks at Delagoa Bay overnight to find now hundreds of foreign volunteers who had fought for the Boers milling about, asking the newly arrived crew to throw them food, cigars and clothing. They are Americans, Irish, Germans, French and even a couple of Australians, who have accepted the British offer of £10 and a free passage home if they will simply agree to stop fighting for the Boers and leave the war. While they wait for their own ships to come in, they are trying to keep body and soul together, and the *Gelderland* looks like the place to start.

But now, who is this, in the dark indigo of the pre-dawn?

It is an old and distinguished-looking man in a stovepipe hat, surrounded by a tight entourage. It is, of course, President Paul Kruger, come to board the *Gelderland* as it has been sent by Holland's 20-year-old Queen Wilhelmina to Portuguese East Africa specifically to rescue him. Yes, there is a British naval blockade, but the Dutch sovereign has negotiated with the British to allow President Kruger to leave, as it is judged that once it is known he has fled, to Europe, it will be devastating to Boer morale. And he has arrived so early, sneaking from his previous accommodation, because he does not trust the British to fulfil their side of the deal. He finds the Captain still in his pyjamas.

In the early afternoon of the next day, the *Gelderland* sails out of Delagoa Harbour, with the glasses of dozens of Captains of Royal Navy ships tightly upon her. Their funnels are blowing no black smoke. The ships are still. The agreement is being observed. President Kruger gets away.[8]

•

Another on the high seas at this time, albeit in entirely different circumstances – the SS *Wilcannia* is a much more modest vessel, and no-one upon it is quite escaping for their very life – is Banjo Paterson, as convinced as everyone else that the war is, mercifully, all but over. Just days before leaving, at Brandwater Basin in the eastern quarter of Orange Free State, he had chronicled the surrender of 4000 Boers under General Hendrik Prinsloo. 'We saw carts – miles and miles of carts – driven by fat old Rip Van Winkles, with white hair streaming down their backs, driven by dandified young Boers with peaked caps and tailor-made clothes [or] driven by grinning Kaffirs . . . Many women and children came in with the prisoners, the women almost black with sun and wind and exposure. They had all been crying, and they formed a pitiful procession as they filed off into the prisoners' camping ground.'[9]

Those poor wretches.

1 September 1900, Occupied Republics, annexation vexation
The war is over. They hope.

Certainly, there is continued Boer resistance, but Field Marshal Roberts has a plan to mop up the last of that, and on this day yet another proclamation is issued and posted up on walls and published in papers in all Boer population centres.

PROCLAMATION
Annexation of the South African Republic.
Whereas CERTAIN TERRITORIES in South Africa hitherto known as the SOUTH AFRICAN REPUBLIC have been conquered by Her Majesty's forces, and it has seemed expedient to Her Majesty that the said Territories should be ANNEXED TO, and should henceforth form part of HER MAJESTY'S DOMINIONS . . .
. . . Her Majesty is pleased to direct that the new Territories shall henceforth be known as THE TRANSVAAL.[10]

Yes, there will be ongoing resistance, but, as ever, Field Marshal Roberts has a plan for this. The key must be to deny those Boer Commandos who continue to fight any chance of sustenance from Boer sympathisers, while also protecting those Boers, the '*hensoppers*', hands-uppers, who have taken the oath of neutrality.

In short, Roberts gives orders for camps to be established – on a basic model of tents on spare ground near to population centres and railways for supply, as had been done outside Mafeking on an ad hoc basis in July – where the Boer population can be contained.

At Bloemfontein the place selected is some two miles out of town, with some rough tents 'dumped down on the southern slope of a kopje right out on the bare brown veldt'.[11]

With these camps now being established all over South Africa it is ever more the job of the British forces – many of them Australians – to 'sweep' the countryside, looking for Boer guerrillas to capture or kill, before squiring their families back to the refugee camps. Still, as ever more are herded in, the wired enclosures become known as 'concentration camps', a corral for the families who have absolutely no desire to be there. They are part protection, part prison, and the Boers inside are unsure whether they are being saved or damned.

Their African servants and farm-workers, meanwhile, are secured separately in nearby concentration camps where the conditions are even worse.

Such activities of course bring in ever greater numbers of Boer families, among them Mrs Elizabeth van Zyl and her seven children – including the notably delicate seven-year-old Lizzie – all of them taken under armed guard into the Bloemfontein camp. From the first, because the father and husband of the household, Hermanus van Zyl, is off fighting with the Bloemfontein Commando, the members of the family are marked down as 'Undesirables' – the designation for those where the father of the family is still part of a Commando – meaning they will be receiving less rations than those families where the male has laid down his arms and is no longer fighting. Some 'undesirable' families are able to cope with such privations by paying extra money to get better food and more of it, but the van Zyls have been financially ruined, and there is nothing. What few valuable things they had still possessed had been looted when the soldiers came to take them to this camp, and so they must simply live in the appalling conditions they are given: a tent, with no bed or even mattress, no table and at no charge.

Lizzie starts to ail from the first, which occasions Mrs van Zyl to earn cash by taking on work for the more well-off families, doing washing for them. Under normal circumstances that might have not been too hard, but as the only water for washing is a stagnant pool a little over half a mile away, it is an exhausting process as she spends her day traipsing back and forth, always carrying a heavy load – particularly on the way back when the clothes and linen are wet. Lizzie, meantime, is left in the care of her eldest sister, Heiltje. They cope the best they can but Lizzie seems to lose weight every week, just as the weight of this nightmare grows upon her mother.

Late September 1900, Pretoria, time to go

This South African sojourn has been a lark for Morant, and he has done well. But this war had only ever truly been a means of getting away from the colonies, and getting a free ticket back to England, and now that he has served his time here, and the war seems practically over in any case, there seems no more reason to stay. After all, Bennet Burleigh has joined those concluding that the war is practically over, and will return to England himself, meaning there are not many more dispatches for a dispatch rider to dispatch. The Breaker has performed admirably riding for the London *Daily Telegraph*'s war correspondent, so the time is right for him to ride back to England via boat, the prodigal son, the pilgrim progressed at last.

Once he has seen his sister Annie, a music teacher in Devon, he may likely return here for another well-paid stint, serving with Baden-Powell's police force, to keep the peace in the occupied republics. To make sure of a place with these police, the Breaker pursues any bureaucrat who might be of help, one of whom is particularly promising. Lieutenant Percy Hunt is a genuine blue-blood English officer with a great passion for all things to do with horses and polo, who is in turn stunned at the Breaker's deep knowledge of one and the same. As deep knowledge of horses is a universal currency – a measure by which Harry Morant is truly a wealthy man – the two begin to spend their evenings together, drinking and talking.

The fact that both Englishmen have lived experiences that the other deeply covets helps them form a strong bond. Though nearly a decade younger than the 37-year-old Morant, the thing about Lieutenant Hunt for the Breaker is that the English officer really *is* everything that the Breaker has pretended to be over the last couple of decades. Born to a good family at Pau, France, on the northern edge of the Pyrenees, and educated at the 350-year-old Bromsgrove school in Worcestershire, the blue-eyed boy Hunt is a handsome professional army officer of great elan – wearing impeccably presented tailor-cut uniforms and smoking tailor-made cigarettes – who for much of the war so far has been with General French's Scouts, albeit rarely in the front lines. Right now, true, he is working as a mere marriage registrar in the newly established British administration, which now oversees all civil matters in the Transvaal, but he is desperate to see action in the front lines and is sure the best of the war has now passed him by. But, oh, how he listens, entranced, as the Breaker tells him of his many experiences. For the Breaker, in turn, is closer to what Hunt has pretended to be – a man of action.

The battles! The near-misses! The scrapes! The *action*!

Each man soaks up the detail of the other's life. But Morant takes a study of Hunt, each detail, each mannerism, another arrow added to his quiver of aristocratic impersonation. Oh yes, Hunt even gives Morant contacts to look up while in London, and the Breaker heads to Cape Town, where his ship awaits. He and Bennet Burleigh arrive in the most southern African city in late October, and stay at the famously flash Mount Nelson Hotel, where for several days they are able to wine, dine, and outdo each other with storytelling.

A young British officer who was with them on one occasion will leave an account.

'Morant was one of the most amusing fellows I ever met, and a gifted *raconteur*. I remember one night at the Mount Nelson, when Bennet Burleigh and I sat up all night in his room and I listened to these two telling stories. Laugh! I don't think I ever laughed so much in my life before or since, and it was broad daylight when we realised the time, and cleared off to have a tub and breakfast.'[12]

The bill for Morant's libations, when it comes, is enormous, but the Breaker barely blinks. As the son of Admiral George Digby Morant of Devon, of course he can pay without blinking. It is just he doesn't have the money with him right now. Tell you what, let us add a generous tip, send the bill direct to my pater and I can assure you it will be paid immediately.

The charmed publican agrees, and the Breaker takes his leave, aboard the *Dunvegan Castle*, still with Bennet Burleigh and, as it happens, General Redvers 'Reverse' Buller, who is returning to England on the same ship.

Now, not all those who have served their time in South Africa are so lucky as to be allowed to leave, and one of them is the highly disgruntled Fred Booth.

If he could, Fred would take his hat, his coat and his umbrage to head immediately home, but the authorities will not allow it.

I mean, can you believe, the Victorian government has insisted that while *most* of the Victorian Contingent can return home having served their agreed time, those like me who had been in the Victorian militia before the war must remain until the government decides otherwise?

Never has Fred felt more like an Australian, and less like a British subject than now. This war has opened his eyes to the failures of the

Harry Morant's young wife, formerly Daisy May O'Dwyer, c. 1884. The marriage did not last. Later, Daisy became Daisy Bates, renowned for her work with Aboriginal people. From the *North Queensland Register*, 21 April 1902. (Trove, NLA)

MRS. EDMUND HARRY MURRANT.
MARRIED AT CHARTERS TOWERS, MARCH 13.

From the *Sydney Mail*, 12 April 1902. Part of a feature on the exploits of Breaker Morant.
(Trove, NLA)

LIEUTENANT MORANT AND A FRIEND
BOXING SOMEWHERE BACK OF BOURKE.

£ 25.—.—

(wijf en twintig pond stg.)
belooning uitgeloofs door
de Sub-Commissie van Wijk V
voor den Specialen Constabel.
dezen wijk, die den ontvluchte
Krijgsgevangens
            Churchill
levens of dood te dezen kantore
aflevert. —

            Namens de Sub-Commi.
                    Wijk V
            LODK de Haas
                    Sec.

Translation.

£ 25

(Twenty-five Pounds stg.) REWARD is offered by the
Sub-Commission of the fifth division, on behalf of the Special Constable
of the said division, to anyone who brings the escaped prisoner of war

CHURCHILL,

dead or alive to this office.

            For the Sub-Commission of the fifth division,
                    (Signed) LODK. de HAAS, Sec.

Captured by the Boers even though at the time he was a war correspondent not a combatant, Winston Churchill staged a daring escape from Pretoria gaol – prompting reward posters for his recapture 'dead or alive'. (Alamy)

Boer troops in the field. They often formed tight-knit groups of irregular soldiers – volunteer fighters who were at home in the harsh environment of the South African veldt. (AWM 129017)

British artillery firing on the Boers across the Modder River. (AWM P00413.003)

General Cronje's men waiting to be assigned tents in their prison camp. The battle of Paardeberg was hard-fought with heavy casualties on both sides. (AWM P00413.043)

Members of the 1st NSW Mounted Rifles stand beside a 1-pound Pom-Pom gun. A cross between a small cannon and a machine gun, Pom-Poms were used extensively by both British and Boer forces. (AWM P00422.012)

Boer 'rebels' being moved, under heavy guard in railway trucks, to be interned in Cape Town. (AWM P00653.105)

Three generations of armed Boer soldiers, 1900. Left to right: P.J. Lemmer (65 years), J.D.L. Botha (15 years), S.J. Pretorius (43 years). The Boers' strong family bonds and love of country were intangible but powerful assets. (AWM P01537.026)

Colonel Robert S. Baden-Powell, British commander at the siege of Mafeking (and future founder of the Scouting Movement). After Mafeking, Baden-Powell set up a police force to keep the peace in the occupied republics; Breaker Morant claimed to have been given a commission in this force. (AWM A04930)

Lieutenant James W. Annat of the 3rd Queensland Mounted Infantry, a hero of the Battle of Elands River. His fame was such that Queen Victoria requested his photo from Annat's widow. (SLQ, John Oxley Library)

Graves of Australians killed in the Battle of Elands River. Conan Doyle wrote of the battle, 'When the ballad-makers of Australia seek for a subject, let them turn to Elands River, for there was no finer resistance in the war.' (AWM C280342)

2nd South Australian (Mounted Rifles) Contingent, non-commissioned officers, prior to embarkation for South Africa. Harry Morant is front row, right. (AWM P00220.003)

Aerial view of the enormous concentration camp for Boer prisoners of war at Cape Town. Prisoners were housed in both the smaller enclosure and the much larger one behind it. (AWM P01115.009)

A COMBINED ASSAULT ON THE PLATFORM.

Artist's impression of the deadly riot that ensued on 18 December 1901 when MP and future prime minister David Lloyd George, described by newspapers as a 'notorious Boer sympathiser', took the podium at Birmingham Town Hall to denounce Britain's part in the war. Lloyd George, in fear of his life, had to escape the building disguised as a policeman. From *The World's News*, 1 February 1902. (Trove, NLA)

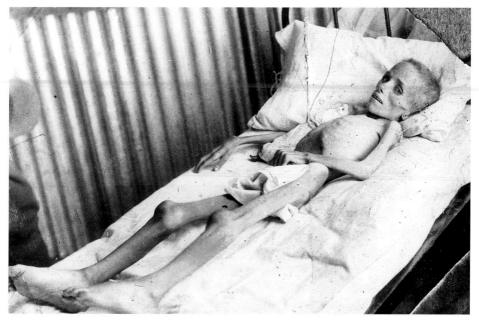

Lizzie van Zyl, a Boer child whose plight was highlighted by English welfare campaigner Emily Hobhouse, but who nevertheless died from malnutrition in the Bloemfontein concentration camp. Thousands of Boer families deemed 'undesirable' by the British were held in the camps in conditions of extreme privation. (Alamy)

British government, the sense that they are happy to use colonials as second-class subjects.

'Since the others left,' Fred writes to his mother in high dudgeon, 'we have been remounted and have been on the warpath again. They mount us on Argentine broncos while the English society pets get beautiful English and Australian horses. These Argentine broncos have no heart, absolutely no brains, and are knocked up after a couple of days' march. A man practically throws his life away to go into action on a bronco and the Imperial Government ought to be ashamed of themselves.'[13]

And yes, sometimes you can get Boer horses, but most of them – particularly those near the goldfields, where they provide power for some of the machinery – have been near worked to death.

Fred is equally appalled when he and his comrades ask for new uniforms only to be told they will have to pay for them. Oh, *really*?

'We are volunteers,' Fred speaks on behalf of them all. 'So if you want us to buy our *own* uniforms, because *you* won't pay for them, we are going *home*.'[14]

They receive new uniforms, paid for by the British Army.

•

It is typical of the Breaker on three counts. Firstly, he has no sooner arrived in London in late November than he has called upon the Agent General for South Australia in London, Sir John Cockburn, to let him know that the famous Breaker is in town. Secondly, he tells comprehensive lies about both his current rank and having *already* received a commission with the prestigious police force being set up in South Africa by Robert Baden-Powell to keep law and order in the occupied territories. And, finally, he sends an account of his meeting and claim to friendly journalists in Australia, knowing it will get him a few lines to keep his name alive.

The *Adelaide Observer* is one of the papers that carries the fresh deceptions a month later: 'Lieut. Morant, son of Col. Morant of Renmark, who has been fighting in South Africa after receiving a commission in Gen. Baden-Powell's police force, has been granted six months leave of absence. He is now in England and today called on the Agent General for South Australia. He will shortly return to the Cape to take up his duties.'[15]

Yes, while in Australia he had claimed to be the son of Admiral Morant of Bideford, Devon, here in London he claims his father is Colonel Morant of Renmark . . . perhaps you've heard of him?

•

Come December, at last Lizzie van Zyl has been moved into the 'hospital' at the Bloemfontein camp, such as it is – essentially just a larger tent with bunks and an overworked English doctor and nurse. On the one hand there is the problem that neither the doctor nor nurse speaks Afrikaans, but on the other hand what ails Lizzie is all too apparent – she is an already delicate child who, for too long, has been denied sufficient sustenance. They do a little, though so lifeless is the child they come to believe she is mentally deficient. Only shortly after arriving, the child arouses herself from her torpor to start weakly calling, 'Mother, mother, I want to go to mother,'[16] whereupon another Boer woman, Mrs Botha, comes over to console her, to tell her that her mother has gone washing.

'Do not interfere with that child,' Mrs Botha is told sharply by the nurse, 'for she is a nuisance.'[17]

•

For months now those in Zoutpansberg, that large area of the northern Transvaal which has the outpost town of Pietersburg at its centre, have watched events to the south with horror and amazement. As the only part of the *Zuid-Afrikaansche Republiek* still under Boer control, it means they must now continue the fight alone, despite the fact they are running short of both provisions and ammunition. They will continue to harass whatever British patrols they find, launch ambushes, and fly the flag in the only part of the Transvaal still under its rightful government.

At least one passionate leader arises, appointed by Acting President Schalk Burger, standing in for Kruger. He is a 32-year-old lawyer of notably religious bent by the name of Christiaan Frederik Beyers, who in September arrives from the eastern Transvaal with the aim of uniting the remaining Commandos of the north under his command. Through charm, guile and demonstrable fearlessness – as well as an extraordinary ability to sense British weakness and strength alike, and to steer his forces accordingly – he proceeds to do exactly that.

All too aware that they should have invaded Zoutpansberg much earlier, my Lords Roberts and Kitchener keep a watching brief, knowing that sooner or later they will have to send their armies north to mop up the last of the Boer resistance.

October 1900, Banjo changes his tune

Banjo Paterson has had enough. Yes, while writing stories for his Sydney readership, he has had to be careful to hide his true views on the Boer War, and to only intimate what he truly wanted to say. For one thing, no correspondent writing heavy criticism of the war would be long allowed by the British Army to continue reporting from the front lines. And for another, to feed the quite jingoistic mood of the newspaper readership had meant that trenchant criticism of the whole war would not necessarily have been well received by his editors.

Too bad. Even before leaving South Africa he had broken cover enough, in his last missive before departure, to get a couple of pertinent things into the august pages of the *Sydney Morning Herald*:

> The Boers are certainly bearing out the prediction of Olive Schreiner who stated to the writer at Capetown quite early in the war, that after we got to Pretoria they would begin to give trouble. One cannot help admiring [Boer] pluck and determination. All the stories about the Boer savagery are nonsense. To the eye of an English globe-trotter they, no doubt, seem very rough and uncouth, and so would a lot of Australian back-block settlers, but, as matter of fact, the Boers are a very commonplace lot of farmers and settlers. The local grocer, and feed merchant, and commission agent, and blacksmith have shouldered their Mausers and gone out into the laagers; the parsons have remained behind, and, as a rule, they preach defiance to the last.[18]

And now that he is back on home soil, embarking on a lecture tour, there is no reason to hold back. But will the audience feel they are getting their money's worth if he doesn't deliver up jingoism, and instead gives the real situation?

'Those anxious for the truth,' *Truth* observes of his lecture, 'were in a great minority.'[19]

Certainly, he is welcomed cordially enough by the small crowd, but the fact that he is 'painfully nervous',[20] presages something of that which is to come. For, from the moment he launches into his lecture, it is obvious that he is *not* here to simply bury the Boers.

As a matter of fact, despite what you might have heard, many of the enemy have distinguished themselves by their sheer humanity in dealing with the British wounded. Why, he saw with his own eyes what happened when a severely wounded British soldier fell to the ground in a battle outside Heidelberg, his lifeblood pouring out of him. Abandoned by his own men, he obviously only had minutes to live, if that.

'But a Boer saw him, and walked down to him; and the British force, deciding that his only object could be to rob the wounded man, straight way opened a hot fire on the Boer. But the Boer waited long enough to bind up the man's hurt, and save his life. Then he stood erect, and walked back from the hot fire, scatheless.'[21]

It is a polarising account, and for good reason.

'He had the most fatal faculty of telling the truth,' the correspondent for *Truth* will report. 'Though this was warmly welcomed by many, it was resented by most, and "a frost," began to be writ large over the enterprise. Fancy a man, in this jingo-cursed age, being found honest enough and brave enough to say that he had a poor opinion of the English Tommy, and believed him very much inferior . . . He described Kitchener as a bully, A BRUTE, AND A BLUNDERER . . .

'We take this opportunity of congratulating him upon his work, and of telling that section of the public which loves the truth that they cannot do better than patronise the few remaining lectures which Mr. Paterson is to deliver. "Banjo," here's to you!'[22]

Ah, but Banjo Paterson has even a lot more than this to come and is already working on a poem which he will soon get published – in England of all places. It is a complete refutation of the war, and a finely aimed slap to all those who have supported it from the start.

> And next let us join in the bloodthirsty shriek, Hooray for Lord
>   Kitchener's 'bag'!
> For the fireman's torch and the hangman's cord – they are hung
>   on the English Flag!
> In the front of our brave old army! Whoop! The farmhouse blazes
>   bright.
> And the women weep and their children die – how dare they
>   presume to fight!
> For none of them dress in a uniform, the same as by rights they
>   ought.
> They're fighting in rags and in naked feet, like Wallace's Scotchmen
>   fought![23]

In Britain itself, news is also getting out of what is going on, as reports of wanton destruction carried out by British troops begin to filter into the press by way of letters from soldiers in the field. Captain March Philips gives a quite shocking account of the agonies endured by the

Boers, 'The various columns that are now marching about the country are carrying on the work of destruction pretty indiscriminately, and we have burnt and destroyed by now many scores of farms. Ruin, with great hardships and want, which may ultimately border on starvation, must be the result to many families . . .'[24]

One interested reader is a British anti-war campaigner by the name of Emily Hobhouse – who is Secretary of the Women's Branch of the South African Conciliation Committee, a group recently formed to oppose the war and specifically devoted to the 'dissemination of accurate information', about it. Once she reads about 'the hundreds of Boer women who became impoverished and were left ragged by our military operations . . . the poor women who were being driven from pillar to post',[25] she moves quickly. First she establishes the Distress Fund for South African Women and Children, and then quickly books her passage for the Cape Colony, intent on seeing for herself what the situation is.

'I came quite naturally, in obedience to the feeling of unity or oneness of womanhood . . .' she will note of her feelings at the time. 'It is when the community is shaken to its foundations, that abysmal depths of privation call to each other and that a deeper unity of humanity evinces itself.'[26]

A bee in her bonnet?

No, an entire *swarm* of them.

11 November 1900, Pretoria's Melrose House, Kitchener Cabinet

It is done in the HQ at Pretoria, with little more than a warm handshake, one salute proffered and one salute returned – as on this morning Lord Roberts hands over command of the British forces in South Africa to Lord Kitchener. The relevant writs have already been issued and signed. It is done.

Field Marshal Lord Roberts has accomplished in South Africa exactly what he came to do: dispersing the Boer armies before capturing the Boer capitals, Pretoria and Bloemfontein. Just gone 70 years old, it is time to retire and enjoy his reputation as Britain's finest living general. It will be for his Chief-of-Staff, Lord Kitchener – shortly to be promoted to the rank of Lieutenant General – to assume command and tidy up the loose ends; hunting down the small bands of junior burghers who still roam the veldt.

Lord Roberts, your carriage awaits . . .

Bobs departs, now able to do what he has been wanting to do for many months – visit the grave in Natal of his beloved son, Freddy, who had been killed in the Battle of Colenso, while bravely serving with the

King's Rifles. From there, he will head home to his still-grieving wife, Nora, so they may mourn together. Never has he felt so completely, so shatteringly exhausted.

And for his part, Lord Kitchener is also able to do what he has been aching to do for months: take this wretched war by the scruff of the neck and shake it hard, as ruthlessly and mercilessly as a rabid dog with a sick rabbit.

After moving into Melrose House, perhaps Pretoria's grandest residence – all grandfather clocks, mahogany furniture, turrets and ballrooms, positioned in the middle of manicured grounds[27] – Kitchener issues the orders that will harden the entire British approach, a furious formality that will turn his will into law at once.

To this point it has been frustrating to have had only influence on events, rather than command of them, and now he moves swiftly, promoting his own coterie of favourite officers, moving on the dead wood, activating his own plans.

The first thing is to come up with a response to the new Boer strategy of living off the land in smaller groups, using guerrilla tactics. First they must destroy the farms of all the Boer sympathisers, burning their crops, killing or capturing their livestock, putting the women and children of those farms in the 'concentration camps' on the edge of the major Boer towns.

They also need to consolidate their hold on the Boer territory they have conquered by building 'blockhouses' – a variety of pillboxes, some of stone with three levels, others simple little forts for half-a-dozen men – along the railway lines to protect them from attack, by putting up guarded barbed wire fences across the usual thoroughfares of the Boer Commandos.

From now on, there need not be a connection made between a particular attack and a nearby Boer homestead. *Burn them anyway. Deny the Boers any chance of sustenance. Get it done. Destroy all Boer dwellings and farms where renegade Boer fighters might take shelter.*

And so it begins, all across the territories of the occupied republics . . .

Galloping hooves in the distance. Getting closer. Snorting horses just outside. Shouts, in that strange English tongue. The sound of the garden gate opening. Scuffling, shuffling boots getting closer still, and now a pounding on the door, even as your dogs bark.

'We did not leave many crops standing,' Trooper Walter Oakes of the NSW Mounted Rifles would recount '. . . and burned down dozens of houses . . . The worst of it is when the women go down on their knees and pray to us not to burn them out; but it must be done, and it's a job I detest.'

At least, there are some acts of decency, with Trooper Oakes also recording, 'Many of our fellows have given their day's ration of biscuit to women and children burned out in this way.'[28]

But the bottom line remains: Trooper Oakes and his fellows have been ordered to wipe out the means by which an entire people support themselves.

Private Fred Booth is another obliged to follow orders.

'There are many things that occur in this war that I can't tell you except by word of mouth,' he writes to his mother carefully. 'We are bringing all the women and children in from the farms. We only let them bring their bedding and clothing. We give them no warning just ride up to the house, with a wagon and then tell them to pack up. They lock up their house and leave all their goods behind sometimes they have a beautiful home these places being some distance out they are left at the mercy of the Kaffirs who loot everything of value. Then the burning of farms causes often a heartrending scene but we are quite justified in doing it. We burn all crops and food-stuffs. It seems hard but it will take hard measures to subdue the Boer. Not until all Boers are either killed or taken prisoners will hostilities cease. Kitchener is the only man who will finish the war.'[29]

The Boer side of the experience is appalling.

'I instinctively felt when I saw the horsemen coming nearer that our turn has come at last,' one Boer woman would recount. 'About half an hour later a number of horsemen, accompanied by a small wagon drawn by mules, came up to the house. Their corporal came to the front door, while the troops stormed in at every door, I went to the corporal, but oh how cruelly his words pierced my heart. His greeting was, "I've come for you. Be ready to start in fifteen minutes".'

The Boer woman pleads with the Corporal, begging to be left alone.

'You can take everything you like, and burn the house, but leave us here.'[30]

'If you don't come, I'll let the men put you on the wagon.'[31]

And now the barn and all its stored grain is set alight, to ensure there is *nothing* left for the Boer Commandos to live off, even when the weeping families are gone.

At least such cruelty is sometimes tempered by decent officers.

'When the house was burning,' one Boer woman will recall, 'one of the troops took my little baby of twenty days old and threatened to throw it into the fire, despite my pleading. As he stood on the verge of throwing my child into the fire, one of the officers came and took the child out of his hands and returned it to me.'[32]

Others are not troubled at all.

'We sat down and had a nice song round the piano,' a Private Bowers will recall many years later. 'Then we just piled up the furniture and set fire to the farm. All columns were doing it . . . The idea was to starve the Boers out.'[33]

13 December 1900, Nooitgedacht, the Reitz stuff

This time, General Ralph Clements, whose camp at Slingersfontein had been substantially saved by the actions of Major Moor's Australians atop the kopje, simply doesn't know what hits him and his men. One moment he and his troops are asleep in their camp at Nooitgedacht in the western Transvaal, and the next they are engulfed by about the same number of marauding Boers, galloping through tents, firing at everything they see, clubbing down anyone who comes within range.

Some of Clements' men manage to resist, but most see it as their duty to get away to fight another day. Of his 1500 men, some 650 are killed, wounded or captured. In any case, the most important thing is the attackers have secured precisely the kind of supplies – horses, rifles and ammunition – they have been hungering after for months.

Among the victors is none other than Deneys Reitz, who has continued to grow in stature as a fighter. As he approaches two wounded English officers – one with a bubbling red fountain where a thumb should have been, and the other with a broken arm, he overhears the remark of one.

'Here comes a typical young Boer for you,' he says, *sotto voce*, before addressing the new arrival in a louder voice.

'Do you understand English?'[34]

'Yes,' young Reitz replies.

'Then will you tell me why you fellows are continuing the war, because you are bound to lose?'

'Oh well,' Deneys Reitz replies, 'you see, we are like Mr Micawber, we are waiting for something to turn up.'

Stunned as they are, the two have the grace to burst out laughing with the thumbless one finishing, 'Didn't I tell you this is a funny country, and now there is your typical young Boer quoting Dickens.'[35]

Reitz would love to stay and chat, but there is too much to do, starting with joining all the others in smashing open cases and ransacking all the tents and wagons.

It is while they are so engaged that General Beyers, their commander, rides up, raging, and orders them to pursue the fleeing British soldiers. But Reitz and his fellows decline.

'We considered that the object of the attack was to capture supplies and not soldiers, as soldiers would have to be released for want of somewhere to keep them.'[36]

After all, the only alternative would be to shoot them and that is *unthinkable*. And so they continue, with Reitz and his youngest brother helping themselves to fresh horses, now having three each.

'Searching out saddles and wallets to match,' Reitz chronicles, 'we loaded our caravan with spoil in the shape of tea, coffee, salt, sugar, food, clothing, books and other luxuries of which we had long been deprived.'[37]

December 1900, Pretoria, block, stock and barrel

Kitchener wastes no time putting plans into action to form up what will become no fewer than 90 mounted columns – up to a thousand Troopers on horseback, backed by a couple of artillery pieces and Maxim guns – who are given the task of 'sweeping' the remaining Boer territory, looking to wipe them out. Ideally, the Troopers will be men who can ride and shoot as well as they can live off the land – capable of moving as fast as the Boers, cornering them, and calling in other columns to assist in finishing them off.

Now to further restrict the movement of the Boers and to protect his own supply line, Kitchener also gives orders to begin construction of what will amount to an extraordinary industrial-level building effort of no fewer than 8000 blockhouses along all the railway lines, separated by no more than 1000 yards to remain in sight of each other and joined by both barbed and telegraph wire.

With remarkable rapidity the chain of blockhouses continues to snake across the veldt, strangling Boer movement, and the only places spared are those in truly remote areas such as the northern Transvaal in the region above Pietersburg, where there is no railway line to protect.

That area, as it happens, is so remote, so sparsely populated and unimportant with its poor roads, not to mention lack of gold or diamond mines, that the British do not bother with it and it continues to roughly function as a Boer republic. (Beyond everything else, it is fever country in those parts, with many among the population suffering from typhoid, a condition that brings with it fevers, weakness, abdominal pain, vomiting,

quite often a skin rash with telltale rose-coloured spots, and too often
. . . death.)

All up, the British are happy to steer clear of it.

'We found Pietersburg to be quite republican,' the leader of the
Johannesburg Commando, Ben Viljoen, records of the last months of
1900. 'All the officials, from high to low, are in their proper place in
the offices, and the *Vierkleur* flying from the government buildings.
The railway to Warmbaths was also in Boer hands. The Pietersburghers
had also kept up telegraphic communication, and we were delighted to
hear that clothes and boots could be got in the town [and] we got one
hundred fine horses.'[38]

21 December 1900, Melrose House, Pretoria, a fatal concentration

With a flourish of Kitchener's pen, it is done. 'AG Circular No. 29',
a confidential memorandum going out from the Adjutant-General, the
Commander-in-Chief's Chief-of-Staff, to the most senior officer in each
district, is designed to deny the Boer guerrillas all sustenance and support
from remaining Boer sympathisers. To do this, Kitchener asks for nothing
less than the forced removal of all men, women, children and Natives
from the district which the enemy's bands persistently occupy.

It has already been tried on a small scale, but now is the time to start
turning it into a major operation. Civilian kraals, tent cities surrounded
by a fence of barbed wire, should be established near railway lines to
help with their supply.

As for the Natives? We won't bother with the ones in kraals on
the veldt, they aren't worth our time. But the ones who are already
on the Boer farms, they may prove useful. They will be the first port of
call should any work need doing, and they will even be paid for their
work, albeit, of course, at Native rates.

It is nothing less than a scorched-earth policy. By shutting down the
Boer farms, the British will deny the Boer fighters all succour while they
send out their own flying cavalry to mop up remaining bitter-enders,
most of them found in the areas north, west and east of Pietersburg.

Kitchener's approach is as simple as it is brutal: 'I look more to
the numbers I kill and capture than anything else,'[39] he had written
to the man he had succeeded, Lord Roberts. And those actual numbers
are important to him, a measure of just how well the war effort is going,
as he notes to the British Secretary of State for War, William St John

Brodrick. Kitchener reports, as ever, that 'the real criterion of the war is my weekly bag'.[40]

All of his senior officers are aware of the 'bag' tally, and know that their job is to keep it full. The problem now is how to counter the Boer's guerrilla tactics to get their own forces out there on the veldt, to find the Boer guerrillas and kill them. The only way to do that now is to have a guerrilla campaign of your own to form up 'irregular' regiments filled with merciless horsemen as capable as the Boers of living off the land, riding through the night, shooting through the day . . .

And yes, just before returning to England one of the last memorandums issued by Lord Roberts had sought to limit the burning of Boer homesteads – 'No farm is to be burnt except for an act of treachery, or when troops have been fired on from the premises, or as punishment for breaking of railway or telegraph line, or when they have been used as bases of operations for raids, and then only with the direct consent of the general officer commanding'[41] – but Lord Kitchener takes a far more implacable approach. While not declaring open season on all Boer homesteads, Kitchener will turn a blind eye towards arson, even arson committed without the appropriate paperwork being completed. He does not formally rescind the Roberts' order, but everyone understands, and the billowing smoke of burning farmhouses soon spreads across the veldt as never before.

December 1900, Pretoria, a proclamation

It is the military equivalent of the town crier in days of yore, gathering people in the village square before crying out 'Hear ye! Hear ye!' and delivering whatever news my Lord in yonder castle wishes to make known. In this case however, the Lord in question is Kitchener, it comes from his HQ in Pretoria and the proclamation he wishes to make known is stark.

> It is hereby notified to all burghers, that if after this date they voluntarily surrender they will be allowed to live with their families in Government laagers until such time as the guerrilla warfare now being carried on will admit of their returning safely to their homes. All stock and property brought in at the time of the surrender of such burghers will be respected and paid for if requisitioned by the military authorities.
> Signed
> *Kitchener.*[42]

Surely, they would be silly burghers to reject such an offer, most particularly after his forces are unleashed as never before to make sure that his weekly 'bag' over-floweth?

Quietly, however, and entirely contrary to the announced intention, the next day Kitchener issues a memorandum to general officers pointing out the advantages of interning *all* 'men, women, children and Natives from the districts which the enemy's bands persistently occupy. This [is] the most effective method of limiting the endurance of the guerrillas, as men and women left on the farms, if disloyal, willingly supply the burghers, and if loyal dare not to refuse to do so.'[43]

Of course, to accommodate the orders – if not remotely the influx to come – many more camps are 'constructed', if building a few open latrines and throwing up a few tents can be so called.

•

Coming up Sydney's George Street on this fine morning of 1 January 1901, the day of Federation, the day the nation is to be *born*, band after band form part of a grand procession on their way to Centennial Park where the precious founding document will be signed!

The pageant proceeds, the crowd cheers – an estimated half a million have turned out for the occasion – and the many Union Jacks wave gaily in the morning breeze.

There is a delirious aspect to it, though not everyone is swept away. A writer for *The Bulletin* magazine, whose mood is clearly out of kilter with those around him, is quick to note just who makes up most of the procession.

'Instead of the battling "men and women who really make Australia" there were soldiers and soldiers and soldiers, emphasising the sadness that Australia, the land of peace, has become for British ends a land of war . . .'[44]

In Southern Africa those men from the colonies who are now officially 'Australians' continue to shed blood – both their own, and that of the Boers – with the only real change to the former colonial units being that, across the veldt, hat-changing ceremonies take place whereby the former colonial badges are removed, and replaced by the newly formed symbol of the Australian Army, the 'Rising Sun' badges formed by bayonets taking the shape of the sun's ascension.

17 January 1901, Pretoria–Delagoa Bay line, Murder on the Disoriented Express

The men are guided only by the moonlight as they flit from shadow to shadow, getting closer and closer to the two long ribbons of steel just ahead, only barely illuminated.

They are a handful of Boers under the command of a canny Scot, Captain Jack Hindon, who is General Ben Viljoen's specialist in the field of blowing up railways. After deserting the British Army in Zululand 13 years before, Hindon had fought for the Boers thereafter, becoming a full citizen of Transvaal, and in this war has wreaked havoc. Tonight he and his men carry with them a specially manufactured mine. A Martini-Henry rifle has been 'sawn off four inches before and behind the magazine, and then the trigger guard filed so that the trigger . . . [is] left exposed'. This will be the detonator, to let off the bucket of tightly packed dynamite they also have with them.

Here?

Yes, here, just over the rise so that succeeding trains coming from the west won't see the carnage until they are right upon it.

Carefully now, they remove enough ballast under the rail so the bucket of dynamite can fit snugly beneath it, and take all the removed stones to put in the bucket they will take with them. Now for the sawn-off rifle, which is loaded. It is placed underneath the track with the trigger touching the underside of the track. The weight of the train will push down the track slightly, pressing the trigger. The rifle will fire into the detonators that will explode the dynamite.

Carefully now – oh so carefully, for with just one mistake it will blow them up – everything is set, and they steal away in the night, just in time.

For, far from the west, they can now hear it, the faint *chugga-chugga* of the engine mixed with the distant *clickety-clack . . . clickety-clack* rasp of circular steel rolling along divided steel, the sounds of the train coming from Pretoria.[45]

Captain Hindon is more than usually excited as this might be a more than usually big prize. His intelligence is that there will be no fewer than *three* trains coming along the Pretoria–Delagoa Bay line on this night, and if they can derail the first one, the second and third might be sitting ducks, enabling them to get the food, shoes and clothing the Boer forces so desperately need.

Closer now, closer . . . closer. Hindon and his men can see the train in the moonlight, the steam particularly billowing as it instantly condenses on this cold night, its searchlight scanning the tracks ahead for obstacles, now approaching the spot where the mine has been placed.

Clickety-clack . . . clickety-clack . . . clickety-clack . . . clickety-BANG! The dynamite goes off, the train is derailed and before the bleeding driver can gather himself, he is confronted by Hindon with his dozens of Boer brethren on horseback, pointing their rifles at him. Unfortunately, it is no more than an empty coal train, but no matter. The fact that it is blocking the line is what truly counts, and the next train is already approaching. This time, the second driver is confronted by both the vision of the derailed train ahead and the galloping Captain Hindon riding alongside yelling at him to 'Stop the train if you wish to remain alive!'[46] Alas, this train, too, is an empty coal train, leaving the third train as their last chance for a good haul.

Mercifully, the final train proves to provide exactly that, a good haul of British troops who surrender after a brief fight – *and* a bulk supply of ammunition, clothes and shoes. The Boer wagons are brought forward, loaded with the booty and sent on their way.

It has been a good night's work and they soon gallop away into the night.

The British troops who have surrendered watch them go. As the Boers generally have no capacity to imprison a large number of soldiers, the usual practice is to strip the British down to their undergarments and point them in the direction of the nearest British outpost – in this case, Balmoral Station.

It is a bitterly cold night, and it is a humiliating thing to walk through the veldt in your smallclothes, but what choice do they have? The main thing is, they are *alive*.

On the Boer side there is jubilation. The new tactics are working better than ever. They have disrupted the British, stolen their supplies, enhanced their own, humiliated the British, lifted the morale of their own people – and all without losing a man!

Late January 1901, laagered at Tafel-Kop, a prophet prepped

A strangely old-fashioned kind of man is Koos de la Rey, a man who insists on fighting the war *his* way, and a strange way it is. No, not just because wherever he goes in the field his wife, Nonnie, is right behind him, complete with a heavily laden wagon *and* a buggy, both drawn by the one sturdy horse, together with their children, three servants and sundry chickens and cows.

That insistence on family being close by has many adherents. No, the true strangeness comes from his insistence on the presence of another in his retinue, a kind of mystic 'holy man', Nicolaas van Rensberg. Through visions that come in his dreams from no-one less than God, this 'prophet' is apparently able to guide de la Rey and his men away from disasters that haven't happened yet, and towards triumphs once they follow his pronouncements.

The 36-year-old van Rensberg, known to one and all as 'Siener', Afrikaans for 'seer', and complete with the long flowing beard and piercing wild eyes required of such men, hails from Palmietfontein in the eastern Transvaal.

De la Rey not only listens to his counsel – convinced he has saved the Boers on many occasions – but has no doubt van Rensberg has been sent to the Boers' aid by God. President Steyn feels the same.

On this particular day in January 1901, Deneys Reitz is present while General de la Rey holds his daily chat by his cart, where many of his men gather to hear his views and news. Now giving way to 'Siener', de la Rey listens as the prophet talks of his latest vision and the heavily bearded Boers lean in close to catch his every sacred word.

The vision is extraordinary, my friends!

Siener's eyes glaze over as he details what he saw – the fight between a black bull and a red bull goring each other in shocking manner, with blood gushing forth, until finally with a deathly groan the red bull sinks defeated to its knees.

. . .

. . .

Do you not see?

. . .

. . .

The red bull is of course Britain, and *we* are the black bull! Yes, the news of late has been grim, but *we are going to win this war*!

The men listen, entranced, as the wild-eyed holy man finishes his account, his arms outstretched as though awaiting the crucifix.

Suddenly, he comes back to them from his communion with God.

'See who comes!' he says, pointing now to a distant horseman galloping furiously towards them from the east. Shortly thereafter, in a cloud of dust and speckled lather, the horseman arrives, and hands to General de la Rey a letter which has come direct from General Botha hundreds of miles away.

General de la Rey opens the letter, reads it, and his face lights up before, in a voice heavy with emotion, he says, 'Men, believe me, *die trotse vijand se nek is gebuig*, the proud enemy is humbled.'[47]

A stirring among the men. A tremor of excitement. Of wonder. Siener had just predicted this!

De la Rey goes on.

'The English propose a peace conference.'[48]

Another stirring!

'Coming immediately upon the prophecy,' Reitz will recall, 'it was a dramatic moment and I was impressed, even though I suspected that van Rensberg had stage managed the scene.'[49]

26 January 1901, Bloemfontein, concentrated horror

It has been a long journey, across the oceans, through Africa, and most exhaustingly through the maze of British military and civil officialdom – Lord Kitchener himself placing severe restrictions on where she can go – but at last on this day Emily Hobhouse arrives at Bloemfontein concentration camp to see for herself the conditions. From the first she is truly . . . *appalled*.

> Imagine the heat outside the tents and the suffocation inside! . . .
> the sun blazed through the single canvas, and the flies lay thick
> and black on everything; no chair, no table, nor any room for such;
> only a deal box, standing on its end, served as a wee pantry.[50]

The squalor and disease – measles, typhoid and dysentery!

The desolate Boer women and children!

And though the last of the Boer Commandos persist with daring raids on the British supply lines, the horror of their struggle is that they doom their own families, unwittingly robbing them of food and medicine. Everywhere Miss Hobhouse looks she sees the most disgraceful conditions, for the most part brought on by lack of British will to do anything about it.

This, *this* is the result of the new Empire policy to house women and children in refugee camps?

'I call this camp system a wholesale cruelty. It can never be wiped out of the memories of the people.'[51]

Most shocking of all is what she sees when she visits the 'hospital' and notices wee Lizzie van Zyl, just seven years old. The sheer emaciation of the girl takes her breath away. All skin and bones and heaving like a sick puppy on a hot afternoon, it is a wonder that she is alive at all, let alone still able to communicate. Ah, but she does have some spirit, despite it all.

'She was a curiously winsome little thing,' Mrs Hobhouse will recount, 'and she was able to sit up and play with the doll I brought her.'[52]

What is the cause of her terrible condition?

The English nurse – who is doing her best to care for her – has no doubt.

'Her mother starved her,' she says firmly.

'Do you have proof of so serious an accusation?' Miss Hobhouse asks.

'The neighbours said so . . .'[53]

More likely, it seems to Emily Hobhouse, is that it is the British policy of giving little food to the 'Undesirable' families. What the ailing child truly needs is good food and serious medical care – of which neither is available for Undesirables.

Mostly Miss Hobhouse is just profoundly shocked at the abysmal nature of the entire camp. She had been told it was for the benefit of the Boer women and children, but how can that be true, when all she can see are half-starved Boer women with their too often emaciated children, exposed rib cages and bloated stomachs all, broiling in tents that are too hot by day and too cold by night? Most of them sleep on the ground. It is as if the evil serpent from the Garden of Eden has been let loose on earth, *by the British* – which is the most shocking thing of all – a thought that might well crystallise on her second day there. For that morning she is talking to a family in their tent, when one of the women suddenly screams and points.

It is a deadly puff adder, slithering from under the tent folds towards them!

Everyone flees, except for Hobhouse herself, who simply takes up her parasol and beats the snake senseless.

'I could not bear the thing could be at large in a community mostly sleeping on the ground,' she would recount. 'After a struggle I wounded it, and then a man came with a mallet to finish it off.'[54]

Emily Hobhouse is a formidable woman, and she is *not* to be trifled with.

Sir? I should like a dray to the railway station, if you please, as I move on to the next concentration camp.

Not far away, and not long afterwards at the Bloemfontein Residency – now effectively an officers' mess for the occupying British – a good time has been had by all. Such a good time, as a matter of fact, that after 'several months of the Gay Gordons and [the boisterous Scottish dance] *Strip the Willow*', a problem emerges as the floorboards of the ballroom floor start to show wear, which threatens to make the officers' wives trip mid-dance.

'Happily for the accounts of the officers' mess, a use was found for the old ones. They were sold to Boer women to make coffins for their children, at the price of 1s 6d a plank.'[55]

•

The arrival of that energetic busybody Emily Hobhouse is only one of Lord Kitchener's problems at the moment. Another one that keeps popping up is absurd rumours that he personally has given an order that all those Boers who surrender be shot anyway.

The very *idea* of it!

And it is not just that the rumour circles among the soldiers, it is that it has made it into the press in Britain!

'They seem to be telling curious stories in England about killing prisoners,'[56] Lord Kitchener writes to Lord Roberts, now Commander-in-Chief at the War Office in London, in late January.

And it doesn't stop there.

'The report that all prisoners are killed has reached Cape Town where the Attorney General is prosecuting the paper for libel. It is most absurd as [the reporters] see our reports of taking prisoners most days and they see the prisoners passing through to Ceylon, but people will believe anything.'[57]

It is not just a matter of his own reputation being damaged, though that is bad enough. It is that if the Boers themselves start to believe it then they won't surrender, and this wretched war will drag on and on!

•

Annie Botha has had quite enough of this war, thank you very much. She has told her husband, General Louis Botha, that the killing on both sides must stop, and that he must pull back from his implacable opposition to negotiating a peace. And if he won't listen to her, perhaps Lord Kitchener will. A strong woman, she packs her valise, tells her husband what she is doing and heads off to see what terms the English General might be prepared to offer.

It is the beginning of a major role for her, shuttling between the two sides with messages, which is not always easy. On this particular occasion, she has to travel for three days in wild country to even get close to Kitchener.

Returning to her husband, still leading his men in the field in the western Transvaal, she bears a verbal message from Lord Kitchener to General Botha, and a letter, with a new suggestion from the British headquarters. Asking to be taken to her husband, she finds him pacing up and down in an agitated manner.

'You must leave me,' he says urgently. 'You must get back as soon as you can. I am blowing up the line!'

Very well then. After imparting her message from the British she is on her way, only to be gathered in by nearby British forces and taken to the British General.

He tells her to get back on the train back to Pretoria.

'But my husband is going to blow up the railway,'[58] she says matter-of-factly.

'He won't blow it up if you are on it,'[59] replies the British General.

And he is right.

January 1901, Rustenburg, razer burns

In this Boer War, the age of proclamations, of giving warnings of what will be done if the Boers don't behave, is over.

For the truth is the Boers don't seem to want to behave, no matter what the penalty, and so there seems to be only one way forward and it lies by way of moving over scorched earth. Raze the lot of them – homesteads, and even whole towns.

In Kitchener's words just the month before, 'Every Boer farm is an intelligence agency and a supply depot,'[60] and if that means the only way to remove that threat is to burn the Boers out – all 30,000 homesteads across the two former republics – then so be it. Ever more Boer homesteads are put to the torch, *as a matter of course*, just as their crops are destroyed – again to deny the Commandos sustenance – a policy that the driving force of the program, General Ian Hamilton, calls 'acting the locust'.[61]

Early February 1901, Portsmouth, not known at this address

And what's this now?

It is a letter delivered to the grand home at Brockenhurst Park, just a short way from the English port of Portsmouth, addressed to Admiral G. D. Morant, and originating from the Mount Nelson Hotel in Cape Town:

> We shall be obliged if you will give us particulars as to the where-
> abouts of Mr H. H. Morant. This gentleman, whom we understand

is your son, stayed at this hotel in November last, representing himself to be a correspondent attached to the staff of the *Daily Telegraph*. As he left without discharging his liability amounting to £16.13.00 we shall esteem it a favour if you will let us know what course we had better adopt. We are averse to taking the matter to court till we have heard from you.[62]

Unfortunately for the hotel, Admiral Morant does not live at this address. The letter is instead received by Flora Morant, whose late husband, John, was a cousin of the admiral's father.

Flora's solicitor is consulted and a stiff note sent in reply, advising that the Admiral does *not* know this man, and would *not* be held liable for his debts – and so good day to you, I *said* good day to you.

•

Where *is* Breaker Morant?

As it happens, he is right at the heart of the most talked about event on the planet as we speak. When she shuffled off this mortal coil and crown in late January, Queen Victoria had the ring of her late husband Prince Albert on one hand, and the ring of the servant thought to have been her later lover, John Brown, on the other, such was her love for both the men in her life. But the love of the people for her personally was not so divided, and she is mourned in all parts of the British Empire, including South Africa.

'The death of the Queen seems terribly sudden,' Lord Kitchener writes to Lord Roberts in London, 'we can hardly realise it. She took such an intense interest in all that went on out here that I greatly fear the strain of this war may have shortened her life.'[63]

Her funeral, after reigning for nigh on 64 years, is the grandest in the history of the British Empire, and on this morning from everywhere they come, ready to take part in the grand procession down the Pall Mall, before the sombre crowds, as she makes her way to her final resting place beside her beloved Albert in the mausoleum in the grounds of Frogmore House.

In the courtyard of the Colonial Office in London at 9 am, ready for the final procession in the late morning, which will have none other than Lord Roberts himself at its head, 'are men from every corner of the Empire, no fewer than 42 different colonial corps being represented. There were men from every Australasian state, from the Roughriders of New Zealand to the Bushmen from Queensland. With the Canadians were cowboys of Strathcona's Horse from the West, and Royal Canadian Infantrymen from the East. From South Africa were troopers of the Rhodesian Horse in the north, to the Natal Carbineers in the south, while tea-planters from Ceylon, and Lumsden's troopers from the very slopes of the Himalayas, mingled with gold-diggers from the scorching plains of Western Australia, and the snowy vastness of North-Western Canada.'[64]

Among them all, in the midst of the generally subdued atmosphere, one figure is enough of a standout for his garrulousness, his sheer *presence* that one Australian journalist records it, based on what the Breaker tells him.

> Lieutenant Morant, of B.P.P., who went out with the Second Contingent as corporal, is now in England, and is visiting friends in Devonshire.[65]

In fact, of course, he is not a Lieutenant; despite wearing the uniform, he has no position in the army at all, and has no rank. But, that is just the Breaker. As if he were ever going to miss out on something so grand as this!

Truly, however?

His time in England has been ... underwhelming. Impoverished, among the impoverished people whence he had sprung – living in a tight tenement with his sister Annie, in the midst of a dank, cold English winter – it was not an experience to lift a man's spirits. After all, here he was back again, 20 years after leaving England for the colonies, as poor as he was when he started, aging and with few prospects. His mother had died the year before, and his sister Annie – unmarried and with no means to speak of – had no little resentment at his long absence, much of it without contact from him.

And here in England he has no reputation at all, no renown. He is not 'the Breaker', and not even 'Harry Morant'. No, he is just Edwin Murrant, the name he was born with, the one raised in the nearby workhouse – a place for those poor souls with nowhere else to go, composed of mostly orphans, unemployed, the elderly, the ill and the mentally unstable – and any claims to be the son of Admiral Morant would have seen people laughing in his face!

Yes, a couple of quick trips to London to mix with the few people there who knew something of his cavalier capers, less the legal troubles, had helped, but in the end it had only highlighted his poverty once returned to Devon – pass the penury butter, Eddie.

What to do?
Where to head?

There is, truly, only one course available to a man when he is a nobody from nowhere that no-one cares about. To be a somebody he must go somewhere where he counts for something.

He cannot stay in England to slowly wither on the vine. He cannot return to Australia where he would face the same angry creditors and stern magistrates as when he left. That leaves . . . South Africa and a return to the Boer War. He has been claiming for months to anyone who would listen that he had a commission with Baden-Powell's police force and, though that is not true, if he returns he must be a chance of picking up a commission with either them or another unit? And beyond everything else, England is so damn dull! The war had been his kind of life: on the frontier, in the open, with danger never far away.

Yes, he will return, and books his passage forthwith. Something will hopefully turn up, some unit in need of a man with the Breaker's skills.

•

The endgame of this war, Kitchener knows, is going to have to be even more brutal than the last 18 months.

'The men are getting indifferent,' he writes to the Secretary of State for War, William Brodrick, on 1 February 1901, 'the Boers treat them very well as prisoners and I believe they are not always very pleased when they are released . . .'[66]

To begin with thus, he needs harder men at the coalface. But that is far from his only problem.

'The Boers show no signs of any wish for peace without their independence. I cannot say how long it will go on. Not counting voluntary surrenders we reduce their forces at the rate of about 1000 a month – that was my bag for Dec. and Jan. maybe a little more. It is a most difficult problem, an enemy that always escapes, a country so vast that there is always room to escape, supplies such as they want abound almost everywhere . . .'[67]

In sum, blockhouses, newly appointed brutal District Commissioners and myriad concentration camps will not be enough. They will still need boots on the ground and in the stirrups to hunt down and kill the last of the Boers, and it is with that in mind that on 8 February he sends for Provost Marshal Robert Montagu Poore to come and see him at Melrose House.

Yes, General?

Provost Marshal Poore, I desire you to create a unit, a kind of Commando of our own, made up of some 500 Boers who have already come over to us, or surrendered but now willing to fight for us, with the specific objective of 'looting cattle from the enemy'.[68]

Of course, General.

In fact, the origins of the idea had been recorded in a letter Kitchener had written to Roberts in London, a couple of months earlier.

'Nothing upsets the Boers in the field as much as seeing their men surrendered fighting with us. I am somewhat increasing our burgher corps. This has a twofold advantage as it gives employment to the young men who have surrendered and have nothing to do in the burgher camps and also it greatly depresses the Boers in the field seeing their own people fighting against them. Some of these burghers are excellent men and very good at chasing their brother Boer.'[69]

As to looting the Boers' cattle, it made sense – taking a crucial food supply from the enemy, and giving it to their own men.

Eleven days after the meeting with the Provost Marshal things are so on foot, the boots are practically ordered – and the new corps even has a name, the Bushveldt Carbineers, or 'BVC' for short.

But there is a real problem.

Yes, notices have been put up all over Pretoria, Bloemfontein, Cape Town, Durban, at ports, train stations, bars, anywhere and everywhere idle or relieved soldiers might be enticed, making the offer clear:

RECRUITS WANTED
who can ride and shoot
To Proceed to Pretoria At Once
Special inducements to men joining the above Corps.
**Every facility given to those desirous of leaving before the
termination of the war.**[70]

And yet there is a distinct lack of Boer volunteers – just eight officers and nine men after the first day and no more than three dozen in total after a fortnight. It might be that taking money to fight against their own is simply not an attractive option but, whatever the reason is, the rather chubby man nudging towards 40 who has been appointed to command this new unit, the newly promoted Major Robert Lenehan – a graduate of Sydney's famed St Ignatius College, he is a blue-blood Australian lawyer, who is tipped as a future Supreme Court justice – knows he has no options. To fill out his unit, he must cast the net much wider and bring in British Empire soldiers, most particularly those who have finished their term of enlistment with their own units, but who can be persuaded to stay on with this new unit.

The rather scrappy-looking form they sign is in keeping with the rather scrappy outfit they are intended to be.

> I ... agree to serve in the Bushveldt Mounted Carbineers for a period of six months, or until the cessation of hostilities and I hereby promise to obey the order of my superior officers and to be loyal to his Majesty King Edward VII his heirs and successors; and I declare that I can both ride and shoot.[71]

The terms offered to them are attractive: no less than seven shillings a day, the same as a Warrant Officer and more than double the usual pay of a Private. Now if the nature of the offer, this far into the war, means that the more grounded of potential recruits – those with families and jobs waiting at home – are reluctant to join, while those of more devil-may-care lives are happy to let the devil take the hindmost or even ride shotgun if he will ... then so be it.

For now what Major Lenehan needs are men who can ride, shoot and survive in sparse scrub. He can worry about character later. The truth is that most of the regular troops regard irregular troops as 'scallywags', the kind of soldiers who just don't fit in anywhere else, and this kind of military work is well beneath them, which becomes a self-fulfilling prophecy. In the absence of those regular troops being available, it is the irregular scallywags the Army must turn to.

Now if ever there was a man who could be classified as an irregular scallywag, it is Breaker Morant. He is a man with a reputation recently roughly redeemed by war who has now returned from a stint in England.

As one who can ride like the wind, live off the land, and lead men, he'll do. A bonus for Morant is that he knows Major Lenehan quite well, having kicked around with him a little in Sydney when they had come across each other in polo circles.

True, there had been some initial reluctance from the Major, but the Breaker's charm goes a long way.

'My Australian impressions of Morant,' Lenehan would later recount, 'would not have led me to entrust him with a commission. But the man I saw in South Africa was a much changed Morant. He had seen service, and had earned high praise, and had won a commission in Baden-Powell's Constabulary.'[72]

(For Morant, it remained positively *miraculous* how persuasive the well-placed lie could be. Merely invoking the name of Baden-Powell's

Constabulary, and saying they wanted him, gave his application a sheen that did not properly belong to it.)

Like all of them, Morant is put on no less than seven shillings a day, 'the extra two shillings, being on account of the dangerous and precarious nature of the work'.[73]

You . . . bloody beauty!

Another who finds the salary of the BVC of great interest is James Robertson, who has started the war as a humble Corporal in the 2nd West Australian Mounted Infantry and steadily risen from there to the point that he is even offered the rank of Captain in this new outfit, if he will just agree to join.

Recruiting agents are sent out to sweep the ports, looking for soldiers about to return home to an uncertain future, who might be tempted to join the BVC and the chance to have regular, well-paid work in their immediate future. And then return home with money in your pocket, yes?

Major Lenehan is also not above promising promotion to lure potential candidates. This includes contacting a particular Australian by the name of Sergeant George Witton, at this time with the Victorian Imperial Bushmen. Major Lenehan advises him of his intent to form an artillery section as part of the BVC and if Witton can achieve discharge from the VIB and personally raise the 30 men needed, then he will see Witton raised to the rank of Lieutenant. Witton promises to try. Another recruit is Peter Joseph Handcock, attached as 'Veterinary and Transport Officer',[74] the former blacksmith and current shoesmith now promoted to the rank of Lieutenant in return for joining the BVC, and able to aid any horse in need of new shoes and any unit in need of a crack shot who will do any duty, no questions asked. (A strange cove, Handcock. On the one hand he has the ability to achieve the rank of Lieutenant from a starting point of being a Farrier Sergeant at the beginning of his service in this war. On the other hand, he brings to mind the insult that if his brains were made of dynamite, they wouldn't blow his hat off. That is too strong for Handcock, but certainly his hat wouldn't go far.)

Also joining are such sundry characters as Trooper Robert Cochrane, a newspaper editor in Queensland's Charters Towers before the war. Cochrane is a born crusader, more with the pen than with the sword, and has a strong desire for justice and progressive social change – desires which this war has failed to satisfy so far.

Lieutenant Charles Hannam, 24, from Brisbane joins as does the 22-year-old John Silke from Sydney, whose convict father had taught him enough about working with horses to get him employment working on 'nag ships' bringing the animals to South Africa from Australia. Like so many of them in the BVC, despite the fact he has never been an actual soldier . . . he'll do.

A very few turncoat Boers still come in, including Trooper Johannes van Buuren, a 25-year-old wagon driver, with a mother in Kimberley and a gutful of what his fellow Boers have done to bring this terrible war on in the first place.

And now, who is this fellow who carries himself so well, the one speaking with the Kiwi accent who has the strange combination of having an air of strength about him, mixed with the saddest eyes you've ever seen?

His name is James Christie, a 32-year-old farmer with piercing blue eyes hailing from the district of Clutha in the far south of the South Island of New Zealand and he has the most tragic of all tales to tell, if ever he decides to tell it, which is unlikely. It had happened only a year before, on 4 March 1900, on the very Saturday night he and his wife had left their beautiful property *Keithmore* – on a gracious bend of the Clutha River – to spend their first night in town away from their six children. They had slipped away after bedtime . . . only to receive the shattering news on the Sunday morning, the day of the Lord.

There had been a . . . fire in the wee hours of the night. The servant girl, Lonie Walker, had done her best, and even got the three-year-old Helen into her arms, to charge out through the burning house . . . only for little Helen, terrified, to wriggle free. She had perished, as had three more of their children, James, nine; Douglas, seven; and Fowler, five.

And that was that. The Christies' lives had been destroyed. Within six months they had sold the property, every animal on it, and every stick of furniture. His marriage to the pregnant Florence is in the balance. And he has come to South Africa now, 'through no intense patriotic feeling burning within me, but the need for change after the dark days, when all that I treasured was lost to me forever'.[75]

'So I had a go at the Bush Veldt Carbineers,' he would recount, 'seven bob a day to oversee colonials, and signed on, and was examined the same afternoon, so you may be sure I was hustling round.'[76]

Bit by bit the BVC comes together, albeit with still very few Boers. Australian recruits are numerous, attracted by the fact that an Australian is in command and their own skills match the ones that are required. Also, there is the fact that the BVC is not picky, and proves happy to take on recruits even when they have track records of drunkenness or violence, of being too old or too young and inexperienced for other units, or of being downright hopeless, with one recruit signed on despite having been dismissed from Roberts' Horse as 'useless and undesirable and not up to standard'.[77] It's all right, cobber, the BVC will give you another chance. Just sign here.

Australians make up no fewer than 40 per cent of the roster of 320 Troopers, with the rest coming in much smaller contingents from Britain and the Cape Colony, together with a handful of Americans, New Zealanders, Canadians and one German. There are also several local settlers, one of whom is a former member of the Natal Carbineers, Frank Eland, who has no sooner joined the BVC than he is posted to Pietersburg, not far from where he had been born and raised.

In sum, the BVC are a motley crew – a mix of the old and the bold, the young and the desperate and, most particularly, those with no better options than joining an outfit destined to be operating in such dangerous realms. No fewer than a third of the new recruits have no military experience whatsoever, and some have never even ridden a horse.

Lord Kitchener, nonetheless, is confident in their potential. After all, he had recently written to the Secretary of State for War, William Brodrick, on that very subject:

> I should recommend [we get] as many colonials as possible. They only
> cost the same as [English] Yeomanry and are better for our work.[78]

A later assessment from Kitchener to the same man will be equally acclamatory:

> The colonial contingents from Australia and New Zealand are
> really a very fine lot of men and as keen as possible. It is a great
> pleasure to see such troops.[79]

Late February 1901, Middelburg peace conference, bridge too far

It is, if not a meeting of the minds, at least a meeting of military muscle as General Lord Kitchener and General Louis Botha sit down opposite each other in a room at Headquarters.

There are many issues at hand, the foremost of which is the possibility of peace.

Kitchener's terms are clear. If Botha's forces 'immediately cease all hostilities and surrender all rifles, ammunition, cannon, and other munitions of war in the hands of the burghers . . . His Majesty's Government is prepared to:

'Grant an amnesty in the Transvaal and Orange River Colony for all *bona fide* acts of war committed during the recent hostilities.'

They will also immediately repatriate 'all prisoners of war now in St Helena, Ceylon, or elsewhere . . . and ultimately to concede to the new Colonies the privilege of self-government . . .

'Both the English and Dutch languages will be used and taught in public schools when the parents of the children desire it, and allowed in Courts of Law.

'As regards the debts of the late Republican Governments, His Majesty's Government cannot undertake any liability . . .'

However . . .

'The new Government will take into immediate consideration the possibility of assisting by loan the occupants of farms, who will take the oath of allegiance, to repair any injuries sustained by destruction of buildings or loss of stock during the war . . .'

But on this point let General Lord Kitchener be particularly clear:

'As regards the extension of the franchise to Kaffirs in the Transvaal and Orange River Colony, it is not the intention of His Majesty's Government to give such franchise before representative Government is granted to those Colonies, and if then given it will be so limited as to secure the just predominance of the white race.'[80]

In response, Botha makes clear from the first the Boers are not prepared to cede sovereignty to the British and therefore intend to fight on, no matter the inducements that are offered to lay down their arms. Naturally enough, the subject soon moves to the manner of fighting this war.

Very well then . . .

On the singularly sensitive subject of the burning of farms, Lord Kitchener says even if they can't reach agreement on an armistice for the moment, he will agree to have his troops stop the destruction on two conditions.

Firstly, Botha's guerrillas must stop using those homesteads as bases and supply depots. And secondly, the Boers themselves must stop burning the farms of those Boers who have taken the oath of allegiance!

'If you continue such acts,' Kitchener says as they sit opposite each other,[81] 'I will be forced to bring in *all* women and children and as much property as possible to protect them from the acts of the burghers. Now, will you be willing to spare the farms of neutral or surrendered burghers? If so, I am willing to leave undisturbed the farms and families of burghers who are on commando, provided they do not actively assist their relatives.'[82]

Botha can make no such commitment to a foe so merciless, so barbaric as to continue with its policy of concentration camps. There are now no fewer than 45 of them scattered throughout the former Boer republic holding some 70,000 women and children, while no fewer than 25,000 male Boer prisoners they have taken have been sent to camps in places like India, Ceylon, the Bermudas, Portugal, Madagascar and the island of St Helena. Louis Botha thinks such incarceration of women and children and the splitting up of Boer families by sending the men to far-flung camps unconscionable – and says so forcefully.

But Lord Kitchener does not apologise.

'Owing to the irregular manner in which you have conducted and continue to conduct hostilities, by forcing unwilling and peaceful inhabitants to join your commandos, a proceeding totally unauthorised by the recognised customs of war, I have no other course open to me, and am forced to take the very unpleasant and repugnant step of bringing in the women and children.'[83]

Botha in turn does not apologise at all for forcing reluctant Boers to join the cause. He is quite simply, *not sorry*, and sees no reason why he should be.

'I am entitled by law to force every man to join and if they do not do so, to confiscate their property and leave their families on the veldt.'[84]

'How then,' Kitchener asks, 'can I protect surrendered burghers and their families?'

Botha is implacable.

'The only thing you can do is to send them out of the country as if I catch them, they must suffer.'[85]

Such is the tenor of their discussions, which go on for four days, always reaching the same impasse, leavened only by the fact that in the evenings Kitchener and his associates teach Botha to play the very English card game of bridge, for money. The end result is that Botha must write Kitchener an IOU for £15, and Kitchener makes a gift to Botha of 50 card packs before the peace talks end.

Until we meet again.

The upshot of the meeting, and the Boers' final rejection of the British peace process, is that Lord Kitchener hardens his tactics even further, as do the Boers.

If this really is to be a battle to the death, then there can be no more mercy on either side. Kitchener's forces burn ever more Boer farmhouses. And the Boer Commandos are ever more implacable to the same Boer families: you are either with us, or against us. And if you are against us, you may expect the worst.

'If you don't join the Republic [Transvaal],' one Boer ruefully notes, 'you are made prisoner, your wife and children turned out homeless, your farm destroyed.'[86]

In this Boer war on Boers it is enough to have signed the oath of neutrality with the British to be at risk. And if your farm is near the British and has somehow been left unmolested by them, the strong suspicion is that you have likely signed.

Though there is no hope for peace, Kitchener at least feels he now knows the enemy better and their weak points.

'They evidently do not like their women being brought in,' he writes to Lord Roberts, 'and I think it has made them more anxious for peace.'[87]

Louis Botha returns, first to his wife and then to his men in the field, issuing a famously rousing appeal.

'Let us,' he thunders, 'as Daniel in the lions' den, place our trust in God alone, for in His time and in His way He will certainly give us deliverance.'[88]

•

For those Boer soldiers still in the field the new British program is more than merely confronting, though still their stoicism remains remarkable.

'The soldiers made for the farm we had just vacated,' Deneys Reitz will recount one particular experience, 'and soon smoke and flames were issuing from door and windows. As we looked on, two old fellows rode up and joined us on the hill. With a curt greeting they dismounted and sat among the rocks, silently watching the work of destruction below. For a long time neither of them spoke. It was only when the roof fell in amid a shower of sparks, that the elder of the two sighed and turning to the other said, "Brother John, there go those teak-wood beams I brought from Pretoria after the Jameson Raid".'[89]

Their resolve is unshaken, their will does not falter. They will fight on.

Moving from their hilltop, they head down to the valley floor where a particular women's laager is situated – essentially women and children who have left their own destroyed homesteads, but who wish to remain free of the concentration camps.

And there they are, about 30 wagons, with about 100 women and children, all under the rough care and command of these two brothers.

'Now that the British are capturing the civil population,' Reitz will recount, 'it had become the practise for the women on farms, when hostile forces approach, to load what they could on wagons and join hands with others similarly situated.'[90]

•

The blockhouses have sprung forth in the veldt like desert flowers after spring rain – within six months there will be 8000 in all, each one garrisoned in eight-man pods by 50,000 British soldiers – mini-forts that now stretch along the key railway lines.

'As we glided slowly out of a station,' one correspondent records, 'away ahead of us would stretch the long vista of the line, dotted here and there with the little fortresses. We would gather speed, and the sun glinted on steel as the garrison of the nearest blockhouse began to fix bayonets and fall in. Then as we swept swiftly forward the little squad of men came abreast of us, and the bayonets rose and fell symmetrically amid the solemn solitude. Then the blockhouse was whirled away behind us and lost to sight. So it went on for mile after mile.'[91]

One officer will later recall his experience while manning a blockhouse by a railway line on the Orange River. He had been playing a game of chess with a fellow officer when a Sergeant put his head through the door.

'Rocket just gone up, Sir. No. 509 report through the telephone that they are surrounded.'[92]

Both men jump up, one of them with clear relief, 'accidentally' kicking over the chessboard, as he had been on the point of being check-mated. Seizing their rifles and bandoliers, they dash outside ordering everyone to man their positions defending the fort.

The phone rings, and the Lieutenant snatches it up. It is Blockhouse 509, just down the line.

'Yes, what is it?'

'Boers driven out,' comes the scratchy reply. 'Hit two, [and they've] gone towards 510.'

The Lieutenant then tries to get hold of Blockhouse 510, only to find that the line to them has been cut or broken.

At least, however, he is able to get the HQ at Spitfontein on the line and is able to send for an armoured train bristling with soldiers and a cannon, before, against the evening sky, another rocket goes up, signalling another Boer attack is underway. It seems the Boers are attempting to cross the line, cut the wire and move through, but are themselves being attacked by the blockhouse one down. The Lieutenant must dispatch his own force to help, and does so. Ideally, they can hold them up till the armoured train gets here, and then destroy them.

Sure enough . . .

'A *bang* from the approaching train is answered by a whirl of smoke, and a spitting crack on the Boer position, and the enemy are scouring off through the night.'[93]

Kitchener's men have won the day against the Boers, using overwhelming manpower, backed by industrial and technical grunt that the Boers simply cannot match. The blockhouses are working, strangling the life out of the Boers, just as the concentration camps are sapping the will of the Boer population to resist. It is for good reason the British Commander-in-Chief soon attracts the sobriquet of 'Stonewall' Kitchener[94] as his blockhouses continue to proliferate.

In the meantime, Kitchener continues to push for peace, liaising with Mrs Botha on frequent occasions.

One sticking point is the 300 Boers of the Cape Colony who, technically, had committed treason against Queen Victoria by taking up arms against her troops. Kitchener is happy to accede to Botha's insistence that they be pardoned, to end the war – *anything* to end the war – but the British High Commissioner, Lord Milner, wants them given six-year prison sentences.

Kitchener writes to the Secretary of State for War, Sir William Brodrick.

> Milner's views may be strictly just but to my mind they are vindictive and I do not know of a case in history where, under similar circumstances, an amnesty has not been granted. We are now carrying on a war to be able to put 200 or 300 Dutchmen in prison at the end of it. It seems to me absurd and wrong . . .
>
> Mrs Botha has written to her husband to ask if the amnesty question is now the only one they are now fighting for . . .
>
> Yours very truly
>
> Kitchener[95]

Late March 1901, Pretoria, train-ing for the Boers

All up, it has been a remarkably rapid raising of a force. Less than seven weeks after Lord Kitchener's order to Provost Marshal Robert Poore, the Bushveldt Carbineers are mustered to take part in their first action. At long last, the time has come to move on northern Transvaal, and the BVC is assigned the task of assisting Colonel Herbert Plumer's column of 1300 men, which is even now moving out of Pretoria and pushing north to Pietersburg, some 140 miles north-east of the Transvaal capital.

For yes, ten months after the capture of Pretoria, now with the failure to reach an agreement at Middelburg with Louis Botha, Lord Kitchener has realised that with the war enduring they must move on the last place in remaining Boer territory where Commandos still roam unmolested.

The route of Plumer's column lies along the Pietersburg–Pretoria railway track and the task of the BVC is to make sure that all the supply trains that must move along the line – to keep the Troopers watered and with plenty of ammunition – are secure from the attention of Boers who might like to blow them up.

The BVC soon develop their own way of stopping such attacks.

Taking as prisoners some of the Boers in the area where the attack occurred – and not caring that they had nothing to do with the actual ambush – they put them in the second carriage, and tell them that if they don't reveal where the next mine is set up, they will be blown up with the train.

And it is true that they still won't reveal it. But when, sure enough, they proceed and the first wagon is blown off the track, it means the Boer prisoners are now in the first carriage themselves. *Now* they talk, and with some enthusiasm at that. Just a little over a fortnight after leaving Pretoria, Plumer's force has covered most of the distance, and Pietersburg lies at their mercy, just ahead, over yonder ranges . . .

CHAPTER TEN

PIETERSBURG

*Two wounded Boers that we have here reckon that the Boers have
a terrible set on Australians. They said that they are not nearly
so frightened of the British. They say that the Australians murder
them when they get near them. Pity help the Australians if any
of them get taken prisoner; they will shoot them straight away.*[1]

Edward McKinley, NSW Medical Corps, writing to a friend,
26 December 1900

8 April 1901, Pietersburg, grass fire

Now with a trickle, now with a river, now with a flood . . .

The scouts of the Yeomanry and Australian Bushmen are the first of
Plumer's column to near the outskirts of the northern Transvaal Boer
town of Pietersburg. Behind them, at a safe distance, come the bulk of
the 2000-strong force – among whom are no fewer than 800 Australians
and New Zealanders, including Major Robert Lenehan and a detachment of the Bushveldt Carbineers – the whole lot under the command
of a triumphant Colonel Herbert Plumer.

Overall, the advance, as they had pushed through the small towns that
line the railway north, has been so rapid – their force so overwhelming
– there had been only minimal resistance and that had been quickly
overcome by one group in particular.

'Great bravery was shown by eight Australian Bushmen,' the Australian
papers will proudly note, 'who expelled 40 burghers from Iron Pass,
capturing the pass, which is key to Pietersburg. Two Bushmen were
wounded in the fight. Colonel Plumer commended the Australians for
their gallantry.'[2]

As they are moving on to the town itself, they find the Zoutpansberg
Commando based in Pietersburg has only just got out before them, grabbing whatever weaponry, ammunition and supplies they can get their
hands on at short notice and galloping away.

It is a great thing to take a town without a shot being fired and among the vanguard, and not far behind Colonel Plumer, are two officers of the Tasmanian Bushmen, Lieutenants Walter Cresswell and Arnold Sale. Both are relieved to have taken the town so easily and are just ambling along Vorster *Straat*, entirely unaware that cruel happenstance sees the village schoolmaster Gerard Kooijker – a member of the local Commando who has remained behind, and determined to defend his town and school to the last – hiding in the long grass with a Mauser to his shoulder and lining them up.

Steady, steady . . . now!

Two rifle shots ring out, and two bodies collapse in a heap. The sniper is a crack shot, and the officers are dead before they hit the ground.

Gerard Kooijker now jumps to his feet waving a white flag – only to suddenly take up his rifle once more, once the troops approach him, and fire off *more* shots.[3] Another soldier goes down, as do several horses.

Treacherous bastard!

And now – as the troops run towards him – he throws down his rifle and puts his hands in the air, shouting, 'I surrender! I surrender! I surrender!'[4]

Too late, cobber.

'The men walked up to him,' one Trooper recounts, 'and without hesitation ran a bayonet through his body, and in the heat and stress of the battlefield this action of the soldiers was applauded.'[5]

In terms of an introduction to Pietersburg, it is emblematic. The town is the end of the line for the railway and also close to the end of the line figuratively. It marks the border of the badlands where men are the most desperate and life is cheaper. In these parts, for the rough and raw, the law is a luxury they can no longer afford.

For now, for Lord Kitchener's 'bag', Colonel Plumer's men take 60 Boer prisoners, who are soon sent on their way in the cattle cars to end up in a camp in Ceylon or St Helena or the Bermudas, while the haul also includes the capture of 'one artillery piece, destroyed 210,000 rounds of rifle ammunition and 1000 rounds of artillery ammunition'.[6]

Pietersburg is ours for as long as we can defend it, against the vicious Boers who lie just beyond the perimeters like hungry wolves waiting to pounce. Only men like those of the BVC – rangers and rogues and renegades – could hope to survive in such territory, and subdue the last vestiges of Boer resistance in the area. Colonel Francis Hall of the Royal Artillery – a rather grizzled old-time British Army man, who operates by the book, insists on no nonsense and polished brass buckles in equal measure – is appointed as the Area Commandant, to be in overall command of both Major Robert Lenehan's BVC and Colonel Scott's 2nd Gordon Highlanders as well as Colonel Carter's 2nd Wiltshire Regiment, who are to be the garrison force of Pietersburg itself.

Now, for an Intelligence Officer and District Commissioner for the whole area, Lord Kitchener has already personally appointed a man well known to him, Captain Alfred 'Bulala' Taylor, while also hiring informants to reveal the whereabouts of the Boers, and about which civilians are loyal, and which are not.

Taylor's appointment by Kitchener is controversial but considered. For yes, there are some within the British Army who worry about Taylor and his methods, but few who can argue that such methods get results one way or another, and that is what is needed right now. He is the living embodiment of the ends justifying means. Lord Kitchener has always been of the view that the only way to control tough and bloody areas is to send in tough and bloody men – and few men in the British Army have a more bloodily earned reputation for ruthless violence than Taylor.

After all, Taylor's nickname came from the Natives.

'Bulala' means 'Killer', a title that Alfred Taylor has earned many times over in his bloody command. A few years earlier, as a British officer devoted to suppressing any possible Native uprisings in Rhodesia, Taylor had been having trouble with one of the Native chiefs, 'Dallamon'.

This fellow, as charismatic as he was rotund, was also believed to be the incarnation of an ancient Karanga God, 'Mlimo' – therefore revered by both the Matabele and Mashona peoples. Dallamon had been agitating his fellow Natives. He had been saying such outrageous things as the English had no right to take the land, to dispossess the local population, to impose their laws on people who never agreed to it. Taylor's solution had been simple. Protected by a corps of soldiers, he gathered a crowd of Natives, and had this holy man brought to him. Taking Dallamon before a large granite rock, he pulled out his pistol, aimed it at the Native leader's back, and pulled the trigger seven times until he was indubitably dead. Yes, God is dead when Alfred Taylor wishes it. That was the Dallamon problem solved, and 'Bulala' Taylor's reputation for vicious violent cruelty consolidated.

For his part, Taylor is pleased. Though his is a civil, not military, appointment, he knows himself to be at his best in areas a little beyond the law, and in this position he will have full scope for his sometimes Machiavellian, sometimes vicious, talents to command the area through the force of his will and the power of the guns he commands.

The main thing for now is to keep adding to Kitchener's bag, and the men of the BVC are soon busy mopping up whatever resistance they find in these badlands around Pietersburg, following Kitchener's two broad decrees. These are to capture or kill whatever Boer guerrillas they find, while burning down the farms of those who support them; and to round up their families and put them in the concentration camps.

The flow of those who surrender or are captured is so great that yet one more concentration camp is established on the edges of Pietersburg, with 1000 inmates on the day it opens, rising to 2000 within a month.

Alas, there is no sign of the Boer in the area that they most want – the former farmer now turned Commando, Tom Kelly, the leader of the Zoutpansberg Commando, who speaks Bantu, the language of the Tsivenda people, as fluently as he speaks English and Dutch.

'He is a rampant Boer agitator,' one of the war correspondents will describe him, 'and as fond of fighting as a Matabele warrior . . . All the present leaders are up to the old standard of the fighting Boer. They care nothing for life – their own or that of their enemy; in fact, they go into a fight with the determination to die sooner than accept defeat.'[7]

And he's confident of his powers, too.

While fully aware that the English forces are out looking for him and his Commando, Kelly doesn't hesitate to send a message via an intermediary to Captain Taylor that, 'The first Englishman who comes near my wagon will be shot.'[8]

Oh, and one more thing.

If I catch you, Taylor, you will be given 'four days to die'.[9]

•

Ah, if his friends in England could only see him now.

No doubt they fondly imagine their chum, Lieutenant Percy Hunt, charging across the veldt, his reins between his teeth, firing at Boers with both hands instead . . . of the reality . . . *stuck here* in this wretched office, doing endlessly routine paperwork, overseeing army clerks and being the one held responsible if they make any egregious errors.

As the army now runs the civil administration of the Transvaal, one of the bureaucratic chores is to register marriages, check that the clerk has copied the names correctly – *Adolf Jappe and Anne Vileboer on 27 March 1901, both of Sunnyside, Pretoria* – give each marriage a number; sign the marriage certificate; enter the details in a huge leather-bound register; look up at the clock to see how long until knock-off time.

Under such circumstances any visitor is welcome but when this one proves to be that ragged, red-faced charmer, the ever-garrulous Breaker Morant – passing through Pretoria on an affair for the Bushveldt Carbineers – it is a delight.

The hours pass quickly, and before they know it, their time is at an end. Morant takes his leave with a twinkle in his eye and a warm adieu, and departs for his next adventure.

With a heavy sigh, Hunt returns to the tedious bureaucracy of Boer nuptials, not at all sure he wants any part in helping the bastards to breed, but knowing he has little choice.

•

As it is now just over a year since the first soldiers arrived from New South Wales, Queensland, Victoria et al for the Boer War, Cape Town is awash with suddenly liberated Australian soldiers who've served their 12-month term and, after drinking the town dry, are intent on getting home. There are a few, though, who cannot yet contemplate returning to their old lives, and so are looking for opportunities to stay on; however, Major James Francis Thomas of Tenterfield fame is not one of them. He has had his adventures, including the Battle of Elands River, earned his medals and now sets sail back to Australia, back to Civvy Street, back to a land where the *bush hath friends to meet him, and their kindly voices greet him in the murmur of the breezes and the river on its bars*, but no 'veldt', no Boers, no Commandos. Give him gum-trees, kookaburras and the good people of Tenterfield any day, and twice on Sundays. He will be happy to take off his uniform and fling off his title and become a country lawyer once more.

Home, James, and don't spare the horses.

1 May 1901, Pretoria, a candlelit letter for one

A gentle and notably rounded man is Sergeant Frank Eland, albeit one with a sharp intellect. Born, raised and educated in England, he has grown to powerful manhood in South Africa – establishing himself on his mother's farm, *Ravenshill*, in the northern Transvaal, and coming to love this land and *all* of its peoples, not just the white ones. For yes, Eland is one of that rare breed of Englishman who does not just dismiss with a tired wave of the hand the 'Natives' as an amorphous mass, right before barking out orders at the nearest ones. Rather, he notes and navigates with respect the differences between the tribes, their languages, their customs and their land.

For his own part he is settled as never before, having recently married the beautiful young love of his life, Dora, who he affectionately nicknames 'Doggie' just as she refers to him as 'Old Man' (a jest as she is more than ten years older than him), while they both refer to their cherished newborn baby girl as 'our Babs'. What he most wants for them all is peace, and after calculating that the best chance of that is a quick British victory, that is with whom he has thrown in his lot, rather than his many Boer neighbours.

Joining the BVC had been a Godsend as it allows him to patrol the areas surrounding *Ravenshill* where his mother still lives, while writing as often as possible to Dora at Pietersburg.

Tonight, as his fellows are lost in revelry – read drinking, as a 'concert' is taking place in their camp in Pretoria – Frank does exactly that, stealing away to put pen to paper.

> My darling,
> . . . I am writing by candle light stuck in a bucket while an impromptu concert is going on outside. There are a good many troops here and it's a lovely moonlight night.

A cry in the near distance.

Come on, Frank, the lads want a song from you!

Coming . . . coming! Reluctantly, Frank puts the letter to his darling away for now, before dashing to join the lads and adding his fine voice to the Carbineer chorus. The following morning, only mildly hungover, he finds himself squashed and squeezed into a train carriage designed for half the number, with the rest of B Squad. Squatting in a corner, Frank resumes his letter to Dora, trying to take his mind off the fact that, passing through strongly held Boer territory, they could be derailed by dynamite at any time. To try and forestall this, the BVC has continued their practice of carrying Boer prisoners in the front carriage of every train and, though it hasn't always worked, it has at least allowed the multilingual Frank to talk to them, to assess the local situation.

> The prisoners I spoke to say the Low Country Boers have still a lot of fight in them. They cursed the Boers with us; as traitors etc, etc. My darling – it feels so strange to be near home again. Every station here along the line, as on the Natal line, is converted into a blockhouse and entrenched and earthworks thrown up and barbed wire entanglements put all around . . .

Yes, thank goodness Dora cannot see this land as it is now, meaning she must picture it as it was. Time to finish up.

> Heaps of love to you both,
>> Ever your loving,
>> Old Man
> Excuse writing. I've not been [drinking] but the train is shaky.[10]

And so are a few of the men, truth be told, as they slowly roll ever closer to the badlands. While Major Lenehan and his most senior officers will remain at their established HQ at Pietersburg, the 120 Troopers of this BVC detachment are on their way to Strydpoort, 30 miles to the south-west of Pietersburg, to set up a base there from which they can start mopping up local Boer resistance – just as the BVC's A Squadron will shortly be heading to Sweetwaters Farm, 70 miles to the north of Pietersburg.

To pass the time as the train pushes south-west, this fine fellow, Breaker Morant – a lieutenant with a loose hold over the lads and larrikins in B Squadron – is reciting ribald poetry and riotous stories from his life in Australia. The Breaker is the toast of the train, the cream of the carriage, as merry laughter rises above the *clickety-clack*.

A charming fellow is the Breaker, with a particular soft spot for young Frank. He has even promised to ride the mail through himself as he gets the next supplies; he knows how the Sergeant longs for news of wife and bairn and will do his best to oblige.

For his part, the Breaker is prospering – as has ever been his wont, when back in the saddle again.

After his depressingly dull time back in England it had been a relief to get back to Southern Africa to not only join the Bushveldt Carbineers, but also, to be quickly posted here. His main activity now is going out after stray Boers, even if they must do so, as he writes to a friend 'on DAMNED awful bits of horseflesh. But, with judicious nursing, I've got the horses a lot fitter and better than they were.'[11]

That notwithstanding, by the time they have left the railway line and continued the last long 30-mile haul overland to Strydpoort with their horses, both men and beasts are completely done in.

'A sick and sorrier crowd of men who arrived at camp would be hard to picture,' Trooper James Christie will recount. 'Some had left their horses on the road and put their saddles on the wagon, others towed wearily at their horses.'[12]

But wait, what now? Despite the collective exhaustion, only *minutes* after arriving at the Strydpoort camp, Breaker Morant is in action. Having got wind of five armed Boers in the area while on their way to the camp, he grabs fresh horses, leaves camp at 3 am, and hits the Boers at daybreak, whereupon they quickly surrender.

'Got 'em without any loss,' the Breaker will boast to Major Lenehan in his report. 'Five Mausers and whips of ammunition. There are two other Boers reportedly about. With luck, we'll secure their scalps . . . The men I've got here are VERY satisfactory. Eland is an excellent Sergeant, and the Afrikander troopers – especially Botha – are invaluable owing to their thorough knowledge of Dutch and Kaffir.'[13]

The other standouts include that rather brooding chap from New Zealand, Trooper James Christie, and a younger fellow, Trooper John Silke from New South Wales. In the same mess together, these two enjoy each other's company and have that most crucial thing soldiers in the field can have – trust, the belief that the man next to you can protect your flank, just as you will protect his.

'We are armed with .303 Lee Enfield rifles,' James Christie records, 'and carry 50 rounds in our bandoliers and another 100 in our holsters.'[14]

And things are not all bad.

'The free open-air life agrees with me, the spice of danger just the thing I liked.'[15]

Sergeant Frank Eland would like a little more himself of that very spice of danger, but on that last raid had been desperately disappointed, telling his wife, 'I did my best to go but Morant . . . would not spare me . . .'[16]

That is typical of the Breaker, he is a devil-may-care chap, but he won't see his men harmed if he can help it, and while he cherishes Eland for many things – starting with his ability with the local languages, and generally sunny nature – his view is that Eland should not be risked in a likely gun battle, when any soldier with a gun might do it as well, and a young father like Frank should be preserved.

A small parenthesis here. Just like Morant's friendship with Captain Hunt, the Breaker's bond with Frank Eland is a surprisingly sudden and, in this case, very strong one. There is something in Eland's wide-eyed innocence, his love of his wife and baby, his devotion to duty, that the Breaker less wants to emulate, for all those things have long ago passed him by . . . more than he wants to protect.

The Breaker has lied his way through life, and left a string of outrage in his wake. Young Frank is as honest as the day is long.

Close parenthesis.

For now, the time is to settle into their new digs, as these 22 members of the BVC find themselves bivouacked in the open, no tents and living rough – only Morant and Eland have the relative comfort of bunking down in a covered wagon – with two companies of the Wiltshire Regiment.

Their base is on a small patch of open ground, surrounded firstly by thick brush and a little further away many kopjes, upon which they must place lookouts in sangars and rifle pits to make sure there are no Boers about – at least none that can't be easily picked off. Their horses, meanwhile, are tethered in a nearby 'mealy patch' – a field of corn – by a small stream, shockingly pathetic brutes that they are.

'The horses are a miserable lot,' one reports, 'weedy, half thorough-bred, ponies – about 13 hands high and very low in condition ... It is no stretch of imagination when I say it would be no great effort to carry [mine].'[17]

Still, they will have to do.

Perhaps the only thing more miserable than their horses are the people they have come to subdue.

'Most of the Boers who surrender are in a miserable state,' Trooper McInnes records, 'rotten with fever and crippled with rheumatism, and they are greatly surprised that they are treated well when they come in.'[18]

In the course of their work Sergeant Eland becomes popular with all of the BVC's B Squadron for his hands-on approach – never asking the Troopers to do anything he would not do himself – and the Breaker, too, soon has his admirers.

'Our Lieutenant,' James Christie writes home, 'is a short, squat, rubicund-hued English Colonial, who has not, so far, troubled us with drill or unnecessary work.'[19]

Indeed, never a man for drill or parade at the best of times, out here Lieutenant Morant judges there to be no need, and doesn't even care what his men wear, which is as well, because it is not much.

'I have only had my boots off once a week to change socks since I donned khaki and ammunition belts,' Christie says, 'and I can sleep on rocks with only a waterproof sheet under me as comfortably as on a spring mattress, while the bed on the mealy patch I have just now is pure luxury.'[20]

Another who is particularly impressed with Morant is Lieutenant Claude Jarvis, a young British officer, who is struck by the glamour and erudition of this elegant fellow, who seems the 'beau-ideal of a cavalier'.[21] For you see, while at first blush the Breaker looks to be 'a typical roistering hard case who took no heed of the morrow',[22] Jarvis soon sees that Harry Morant carries the poetry of Byron and Browning in his saddlebags and loves nothing more than to give them all a burst of Byron before riding off to capture Boers! Say it, Breaker:

> Here's a sigh for those that love me
> Here's a smile for those that hate;
> And whatever sky's above me,
> Here's a heart for every fate . . .[23]

And with those words still ringing out across the veldt, Morant – the drover with the argot of an aristocrat, the poet who looks like a peasant but possesses the bearing of a blue blood – bids a fond farewell. As he rides off to the hazy horizons of yonder, Jarvis is left to ponder the fact that the warrior poet is not just some romantic ideal, but a reality in this very man.

'He was a brilliant fellow, and a very good sort,' another Trooper who served with him will comment. 'He used to write poems as we jogged along on horseback, and he didn't know what fear was.'[24]

The work at hand is nothing if not dangerous, as each patrol takes the men through, as Christie describes it, 'so much scrub that one cannot see any distance ahead or on either side, so one never knows the moment a bullet may send him to kingdom come, and with all that we get careless'.

May 1901, Bloemfontein concentration camp, blank ruin

Mrs van Zyl can no longer bear being away from Lizzie and, fearful for her life, brings her back from the hospital to the family's tent where, day by day, and into the night she sits beside her daughter – now lying on the tiny filthy mattress someone had given them – mopping her brow and murmuring maternal comforts to her. And there Lizzie lies, as one camp resident will chronicle, 'trying to get air from beneath the raised flap, gasping her life out in the heated tent'.[25]

The camp doctor does not come to visit, and that same fellow camp resident is trying to get a little wooden cart made up so that Lizzie might be drawn out into the open air in the cooler May evening when the tragically inevitable thing happens – Lizzie dies in the night, her mother sobbing beside her.

For her part, Emily Hobhouse is already on her way back to Britain, spending her time aboard the ship writing up her diary and reports, which she hopes to publish in some form, exposing the hell on earth that is the British concentration camps. Again, and again, she reviews her notes, what she has learnt . . .

Thousands, physically unfit, are placed in conditions of life which they have not strength to endure. In front of them is blank ruin ... If only the English people would try to exercise a little imagination – picture the whole miserable scene. Entire villages and districts rooted up and dumped in a strange, bare place.[26]

... Some people in town still assert that the camp is a haven of bliss. I was at the camp today, and just in one little corner this is the sort of thing I found – The nurse, underfed and overworked, just sinking on to her bed, hardly able to hold herself up, after coping with some thirty typhoid and other patients, with only the untrained help of two Boer girls – cooking as well as nursing to do herself. Next tent, a six months' baby gasping its life out on its mother's knee.[27]

... Another child had died in the night, and I found all three little corpses being photographed for the absent fathers to see some day. Two little wee white coffins at the gate waiting, and a third wanted.[28]

... In most cases there is no pretence that there was treachery, or ammunition concealed, or food given or anything. It was just that an order was given to empty the country.[29]

•

Captain Frederick Ramon de Bertodano is an unlikely name for a red-blooded blue-blood Australian aristocrat, but there it is. Schooled at New England Grammar School, he had attended St Paul's College at the University of Sydney to study Arts Law. Educated, refined, well connected, he journeyed to England then, in 1896, he left for Rhodesia intending to work as a solicitor ... only to end up fighting in the Matabele War. In 1900 he had enlisted in the Manchester Regiment, rapidly gaining his commission as Captain.

Now he is the Chief Intelligence Officer for the northern Transvaal. As he is also the grandson of the Marquis de Moral of Spain, Ramon de Bertodano is regal and refined, an elegant aristocrat to his very core. He is tasked with listening to words and whispers from Middelburg to Mafeking, each one collated into a daily report by agents official and otherwise, each one a minuscule piece in a massive puzzle.

His purpose on this day is to complete a journey to the far north, to the newly conquered outpost of Pietersburg, where he intends to visit an old friend from Sydney, Major Robert Lenehan, now in charge of the BVC.

De Bertodano beams as he walks to outpost headquarters, eager to see his man Lenehan, only for the smile to die a second after reaching the front desk. For alas, it is not Lenehan who awaits but instead a snake of a 'commander' of ill repute, a villain with an impeccable moustache so delicate it is a wonder he can't help but twirl it in his fingers. He is a spy, a fixer, a cheat and a charlatan – and all that before breakfast. De Bertodano sees him as neither soldier nor civilian, more as a criminal for hire, an entirely corrupted officer, a lackey for the likes of Lord Kitchener and Cecil Rhodes when there is dirty work to be devastatingly done. The man that de Bertodano glowers down at has been known to him for over five years.

'Bulala' they call him. *Bulala* Taylor. *Killer* Taylor.

Oh yes, de Bertodano knows him of old.

'I had met him in Bulawayo during the Matabele Rebellion in 1896,' he will later recount. 'Neither his face nor his eyes prepossessed me and his reputation stank to Heaven.'[30]

That reputation?

'He was notorious and distrusted by most white men he came into contact with.'[31] De Bertodano is one of them, and a single story shall suffice to illustrate why. In the Matabele War of 1896, a soldier had been talking to the infamous Taylor and found him a most charming fellow, right up until Taylor noticed a Native standing nearby. Quick as the flash from Taylor's gun, the Native lay dead. The soldier was stunned, but Taylor was as calm and cold as a sliver of ice.

'The Captain then replaced his revolver, and went on talking as if nothing had happened.'[32]

There are hard men in war. Tough men. And then there are the men who are so hardened to killing that they barely blink at committing *murder*. 'Bulala' Taylor is one such man. 'Capable of anything' is not a descriptive phrase when it comes to Captain Alfred Taylor, it is a résumé.

Captain Taylor greets Captain de Bertodano with polite formality and is sorry that his visit to the BVC Pietersburg HQ appears to have been wasted. But it is not a wasted visit for de Bertodano, it is a red flag. That such a man as Taylor is in some sort of command over British soldiers is dangerous at the best of times. In a remote region, with no official eyes upon him, well, maybe it is simply asking for trouble – serious trouble and plenty of it. What do you think is going to happen, sooner rather than later?

De Bertodano wastes no time in going to Lord Kitchener's Director of Military Intelligence, Colonel David Henderson, in Pretoria, to warn him of the situation and to request that Taylor be removed from his position. Colonel Henderson raises the question with Lord Kitchener, but action is not taken. After all, the good Lord has hand-picked Taylor to fill that specific post and to remove him would be to acknowledge an error. Beyond that, Captain Taylor has no official military position within the BVC. He is a District Commissioner who happens to share territory with the BVC at the present time. But it is not the formalities that worry de Bertodano; the realities are what concern him. Taylor seemed to him to be in control, a far more dangerous thing than 'command'.

15 May 1901, Strydpoort, praise from the Lord

Frank Eland is delighted as he gazes at a picture of the prettiest girl in the world; she is chubby, bald and nine months old. The Babs. *Isn't she lovely?* Every Trooper must agree, nodding and grinning at the proud insistence of her fervent father, Frank. He shakes hands with the bearer of good tidings, the well-known mailman Breaker Morant, and sits in the shade of his tent to compose a reply to Dora, whose freshly arrived letter tells him that she has just moved to a safer haven, a small farm named *Fernhill*.

He has news of his own.

'I paraded the men at 2.30 pm and Morant read out an army order from Kitchener praising the BVCs for the good work they had done.'[33]

Yes, Lord Kitchener smiles upon those unconventional chaps in the BVC, fighting Commando fire with fire. And there will be more action to come.

29 May 1901, Vlakfontein, 20 miles south-west of Johannesburg, reporter of slaughter

The significance of what happens on this day is less the actual event than the report that emanates from it. A patrol of the Imperial Yeomanry is proceeding south from Rustenburg on a farm-clearing assignment, when, in a typical Boer ambush – with no warning, and lightning speed – they are attacked from all sides.

The battle does not last long and one of the British Non-Commissioned Officers, Acting Sergeant Donald Chambers, manages to secrete himself in a ditch, in perfect position to observe what happens next.

One of their own soldiers, only slightly wounded, is going from man to man among his more severely wounded comrades to offer them water when it happens. Some Boers arrive, and one of them, 'a short man with a dark beard . . . carrying his rifle under his arm as one would carry a sporting rifle',[34] approaches two of the wounded.

Lieutenant Arthur Spring and Sergeant James Findlay are quickly binding each other's lacerations to stop the blood flow when the Boer, 'wearing a pink puggaree, round his hat',[35] walks up to them, points the muzzle of his rifle at their heads and with two quick shots kills both men! Another British officer is even shot through the head with his own revolver.

Once the war correspondent Mr Edgar Wallace apprises himself of the details supplied by various witnesses and makes his outraged report, a version of the whole devastating episode will make it into the *Daily Mail* in London. Under the headline of 'The Battle of Vlakfontein', he relates an eyewitness account of the outrage.[36]

> He declares that he saw two Boers belonging to Commandant Kemp's commando deliberately shooting the British wounded, four of whom they killed in this cowardly manner. Among those who have lost their lives were a sergeant who was only slightly wounded and an officer who had sustained a more serious injury. The former was offering a drink to the latter when they were both shot down by their dastardly enemies.[37]

Even stronger than the outrage of the British public, however, is the reaction of General Lord Kitchener at this story leaking to the press. For he knows the truth: the more set the British public are against the Boers, the less inclined they will be to accept the negotiated peace terms he wishes to put before them at the first opportunity. Kitchener wants this war to be over as soon as possible, but with the British public now wanting Boer blood more than ever before, it has suddenly become even more difficult.

Early June 1901, northern Transvaal, like flies for his sport

The Sweetwaters Farm and Hotel? Some 70 miles north of Pietersburg, owned and run by the hard-working Charlie and Olivia Bristow, it is nothing if not a rustic establishment – composed of the original homestead, accommodation block, canteen, dining room, piano room, trading store, several bedrooms and coach shed.

Old Charlie is an Englishman, born in Kent, while his rather more boisterous wife, Olivia, is from these parts and is the real driving force – both of their marriage, and this well-established country hotel. This feminine force of nature sorts the servants, sets the menu, rouses on the cooks, welcomes the guests and is, in her manner, the Master Matriarch of all she surveys – which in recent times, admittedly, has not been much in the way of casual travellers providing custom. Still, they have one notably faithful patron: none other than Commandant General Christiaan Frederik Beyers, who is commander of all northern Transvaal forces.

But . . .

But when it becomes known that A Squadron of the Bushveldt Carbineers will be arriving late in the first week of June, in the company of Captain Alfred Taylor of the British Army Intelligence Department, Commandant Beyers decides that discretion is the better part of valour, and so decamps with his men. For, whatever else, Beyers does not wish to make trouble for mine hosts, Charlie and Olivia Bristow, and nor does he wish to have a pitched battle with the BVC, as that is not the way of things in these dark days. General Beyers and his Commandos break camp just days before the BVC's A Squadron arrives.

June 1901, Wandsworth, Wales, publish and be damning!

The time is propitious. Just days after Emily Hobhouse had completed her account of the appalling situation of the concentration camps in South Africa, Lloyd George himself invites her to visit him so she can tell him directly the lie of the land, to expose the lies of the British government on the subject. Which is why, on this hot summer's afternoon, she is sitting in his back garden reading from her diary, while the Welsh wizard smokes and gazes pensively into the distance, though clearly soaking up every shocking word as he regularly winces. The extracts extract pity and sorrow in equal measure from her listener, and how could they not? *Do go on, Miss Hobhouse.*

'. . . a girl of twenty-one lay dying on a stretcher. The father, a big gentle Boer, kneeling beside her; while, next tent, his wife was with a child of six, also dying, and one about five also drooping. Already this couple has lost three children in the hospital . . . for the most part you must stand and look on, helpless to do anything, because there is nothing to do anything with.'[38]

As she finishes this particularly moving section, she gets to the nub of the question she has come to ask of this extremely influential politician, the one with the loudest voice so far against the horrors of the Boer War.

Should she work these diary entries into a book?

Lloyd George, as is ever his wont, gives an instant opinion.

'No,' he pronounces, 'publish it as it stands!'[39]

First presented to the parliament within days, Emily Hobhouse's report on the concentration camps in South Africa hits Great Britain like a sudden thunderclap on a sunny day. Just when it had started to seem like the long and wretched war in South Africa might be coming to an end, Miss Hobhouse comes out with these extraordinary allegations – probably nonsense, mind – about systemic British brutality to Boer women and children, causing tens of thousands of deaths.

Appearing under the title of, *To the S.A. Distress Fund, Report of a visit to the camps of women and children in the Cape and Orange River Colonies*, it is not long in getting to the nub of the reasons for this extraordinary number of fatalities:

> Numbers crowded into small tents: some sick, some dying, occasionally a dead one among them; scanty rations dealt out raw; lack of fuel to cook them; lack of water for drinking, for cooking, for washing; lack of soap, brushes and other instruments of personal cleanliness; lack of bedding or of beds to keep the body off the bare earth; lack of clothing for warmth and in many cases for decency . . .[40]

There is only one way forward, she says. The camps must be abolished.

The outcry, not surprisingly – both in support, and condemnation of her personally – is immediate and strong.

The very next day David Lloyd George thunders in Westminster that, unless the camps are abolished, 'a barrier of dead children's bodies will rise between the British and Boer races in South Africa'.[41]

Against that, Mrs Millicent G. Fawcett, the English political leader, activist and writer, is emblematic of the response of many when she criticises Emily Hobhouse in the *Westminster Gazette*, writing that the camps are 'necessary from a military point of view'.[42]

But Hobhouse has her supporters too . . . At the Holborn Restaurant in London, the Leader of the Liberals, Sir Henry Campbell-Bannerman, has the floor, with something to say about the policy of Foreign Minister Joseph Chamberlain.

'What is that policy . . . ?' Sir Henry asks rhetorically, concerning Chamberlain's latest. 'Devastate their country, burn their homes, break up their very instruments of agriculture. It is that we should sweep – as the Spaniards did in Cuba; and how we denounced the Spaniards! – the women and children into camps . . . in some of which the death-rate has risen so high as 430 in the thousand . . . When is a war not a war? When it is carried on by methods of barbarism in South Africa.'[43]

For his part, General Lord Kitchener is entirely unmoved. Not only does he not want the camps closed, he actually wants to embrace an even more hard-line policy, sending a cable to Alfred Milner:

> I fear there is little doubt the war will now go on for considerable time unless stronger measures are taken ... Under the circumstances I strongly urge sending away wives and families and settling them somewhere else [like St Helena, the Bermudas, India, etc, where we have sent the Boer men]. Some such unexpected measure on our part is in my opinion essential to bring war to a rapid end.[44]

The British Secretary of State for War, William Brodrick, rejects this suggestion out of hand as unworkable, and so nothing substantial changes. Within a month it will be officially tabulated that there are 105,437 residents of the Boer camps, after suffering 1878 fatalities in those camps in the previous month. The next month it has grown to 109,418, with the month's fatalities at 2411.

7 June 1901, Pietersburg, sweet waters run deep

The orders have come from Lord Kitchener himself. A Squadron of the Bushveldt Carbineers, under the command of Captain James Huntley Robertson, are to trek from Pietersburg to establish a forward base camp some 70 miles to the north, to a spot near the outpost of Louis Trichardt, where their task will be to hunt the Boers causing havoc in the region.

Captain Robertson will be accompanied in this remote region by Captain Alfred Taylor, in the role of Acting Native Commissioner – and he will in turn be accompanied by men from the nascent Intelligence Department, charged with assessing the strength of the enemy, spotting weakness, and working to get co-operation of the local population by whatever means necessary.

Their base will be at Sweetwaters Farm. As a sign of who is truly running things, it is Captain Taylor who takes over General Beyers' former room, with his men of the Intelligence Department occupying a whole suite of rooms at the hotel, while Captain Robertson and his men of A Squadron set up camp on the open ground some 300 yards to the south-west.

As is his way, within days, Taylor recruits a number of spies, including Anthony and Adolf Schiel – the sons of a man who had led the German Commando, fighting side-by-side with the Boers – and another Boer turncoat by the name of Leonard Ledeboer. In return for some money on the side, their job will be to keep their eyes and ears open to all things to do with ... everything, and report back to him.

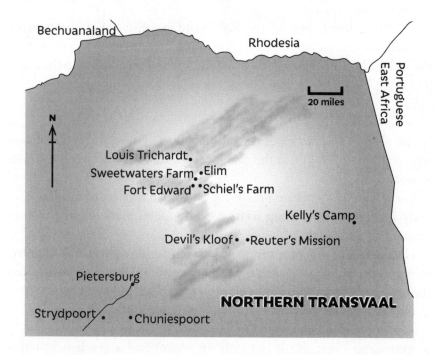

Now, although it is Robertson who is nominally the one in charge, responsible for hunting down the Boers in this region wherever he finds them, there are . . . issues.

For one thing, leading men in such rough country, in such a brutal war, is suited to a rougher and more brutal man than him. Robertson, born in Mexico, the son of a Scotsman who has dragged his fortunes up from textile mills and cotton mills, is a hard-scrabble fellow who now seems to be playing at something else entirely, getting about with a clean handkerchief tucked into the cuff of his jacket, standing on a plank at parade to keep his polished boots out of the mud, while his 'boy' stands beside him holding his magnificently groomed horse. He is like a man *playing* at what he thinks a Captain should be.

While the scallywags in the BVC are amused by it – and even like him for his permissive attitude to anything and everything – for the regular Troopers, the honest soldiers, Robertson is a mockery of what is right and proper. Look at him now, a 'swazzer' and a poser, marching on parade while . . . *smoking a cigarette?*

For the common soldier, it is too much. This is not a man they can respect, let alone follow, and in any case he does not appear to even want to lead, being far more interested in the Afrikander women in the area than chasing down and killing their husbands.

Underwhelmed, one of the BVC soldiers notes that the men of A Squadron 'treated their officers with impunity. Robertson so distrusted them that for his personal protection he kept a loaded pistol handy day and night.'[45]

•

In the absence of Duchesses organising ruling cliques and working out who is to get which job, in this war, once again, the Pretoria Club comes into its own.

For it is in this gathering place for all British officers of influence, in early June, that Percy Hunt hastens with a particular course of action in mind.

Having lately been informed that his services will no longer be required in marriage affairs with the civil administration, he is well aware that this exclusive venue is just the place to broadcast the news.

He needs a new position, ideally a battle position.

Leave it with us.

You know Hunt. He is not only an officer and a gentleman, but a regular officer of the British Army, and a fellow of no little standing who plays a cracker game of polo. If he wants a new position on the front line against the Boers, it is up to us to find him one.

As ever, there is a lot to be said for knowing the right people, for within days, and notwithstanding the fact that he has precisely *no experience* in managing a squadron of mounted infantry, Hunt is offered a captaincy in the Bushveldt Carbineers.

He is not only available, but eager.

Perfect. His bureaucratic position formally ends on 15 June, and he is free to take up his new position on 16 June!

This is the outfit to which his rough friend, the fascinating Harry Morant, is attached and his first request to Major Lenehan is that the Breaker be transferred to join his own squadron. As a more than capable horseman and soldier, and one of the most entertaining men he has ever met, Morant will be a great boon to his work – and the request is quickly agreed to.

The die is cast.

Sundown, 12 June 1901, Wilmansrust Farm, near Middelburg

All is starting to fall quiet in the fading twilight as the men of the 5th Victorian Mounted Rifles begin to settle in for the night. Under the overall command of British officer Major General Stuart Beatson, they have been fighting their way from Middelburg to raid a laager under the control of General Ben Viljoen, suffering a few casualties *every day*, and are exhausted – but at least this area seems a little safer. So yes, it is possible that their sentries are a little late in getting to their posts, caught as they are between fatigue and relief to be nearing their base.

Still, as most of the Australian Troopers are by the fire eating their evening meals or laying out their swags, *someone* should have challenged those flitting figures making their way into the camp as night closes in, even if those figures are clothed in the usual khaki uniforms of the British themselves.

Everything is very relaxed and the first thing anyone knows is when the newly arrived ones shout, 'Hands up, you Australian bastards!'[46] bringing their rifles to bear.

But even throwing their hands skywards does not save most of those who comply. For within seconds all is firing at close quarters, flashes from the muzzles at close range, thundering death.

'Thank God our horses were between us and them,' one Trooper will recount, 'because the first volley mowed down our mounts like a gust of wind.'[47]

Several hours later, a messenger brings the news to Major General Beatson at his own camp some 11 miles away and, though the Australians in his corps are eager to ride immediately to their countrymen's assistance, the British officer insists they 'stand to their horses until daylight',[48] for safety's sake. It means when they arrive the following morning, the Boers have got clean away, losing five men, while taking with them fresh horses and artillery – and leaving in their wake 18 dead and 42 wounded Australians. The dead are mournfully buried in the one grave, the wounded carefully but quickly taken to Middelburg Hospital, some 40 miles away.

Does Major General Beatson grieve for the dead?

Not that the survivors can see. Instead, this harsh disciplinarian displays nothing more than outrage at the laxness which has allowed it to happen and clearly holds *all* the survivors responsible for what he sees as a humiliating defeat rather than a company catastrophe.

'I tell you what I think,' he roars within earshot of Australian officers, 'the Australians are a fat, round-shouldered, useless lot of wasters . . . In my opinion, they are a lot of white-livered curs.'[49]

The words soon make their way to the men themselves, where they are very poorly received.

The *outrage* of it!

We are burying 18 dead mates, and this Pommy prick – who had never led troops into battle before us – is slurring our entire *nation*, like what happened was a national character flaw and not simply because there was a stuff-up with exhausted sentries who were on the lookout for Boers, not blokes in khaki!

They further hear that Major General Beatson had remarked that he 'wished *all* the Australians were shot'.[50]

DISGRACEFUL.

So strong is the feeling that it comes to a head.

When, a week later, word is passed that Major General Beatson wants the Australians to move out at 7 o'clock that night, what starts a light grumbling among the men, soon builds into an edgy rumbling.

'There were a lot of men standing about in the lines talking about piling arms', as in, throwing their weapons in a pile and refusing to obey the order to move out, at least not under that Pommy prick.

When Corporal Shields overhears the remarks, he tells the Australians in his thick English accent, 'That would be very foolish, as half of you would be shot.'[51]

But Private James Steele, an outspoken man from Gippsland with the Victorian Fifth Contingent, has had enough.

Whirling on the corporal, he says, 'Better to be shot than to go out with a man who has called us "white-livered curs". Our country would think far more of us if we refused to go out under such a man.'[52]

Oh yes, make no mistake.

'We'll be fools if we go out with him again,'[53] he declares loudly.

Within 30 minutes, Steele is placed under arrest in the company of Privates Herbert Parry and Arthur Richards, 'it being believed that they were trying to cause a mutiny amongst the men.'[54]

Are the British, perhaps, facing a *mutiny*?

Not without punitive action they're not, and all three are promptly court-martialled for inciting mutiny and – after never being given their own legal representation to seriously contest the charges – sentenced to *death by firing squad*.

The British government does not even bother to inform the Australian government of their intent to shoot three of its soldiers, even if Lord Kitchener commutes the sentences to '10 years in jail for Steele and one year of jail with hard labour for the other two soldiers, to be served in British prisons'.[55] Mercifully however, 21 influential Australians living in England present to King Edward VII a petition humbly beseeching for the soldiers to be released, and in the end Lord Roberts will be not long in releasing them and quashing the decision of the court martial, 'his decision . . . generally applauded by the British press'.[56]

•

Home is the sailor, home from the sea,
And the hunter home from the hill.[57]

As it happens the heroics of the NSW Bushmen's Contingent on the rise at Elands River is the single event of the Boer War to date that has most captured the Australian imagination and on this coldest day in years – with the whole area covered in a blanket of snow – we at Tenterfield are beside ourselves with pride that one of our own, Major James Thomas, has led them so well!

The Mayor, local dignitaries and the town's leading citizens practically elbow each other out of the way in their eagerness to pump his hand as he steps onto the station platform, even as the band strikes up 'Soldiers of the Queen' and the entire procession heads off to the Town Hall for a more formal welcome ceremony. On their way there the procession passes Tenterfield Superior Public School, where, as chronicled by *The Star*, 'the boys, drawn up under the Union Jack, cheered the returning soldiers, and generally, Tenterfield streets have not been so animated since the local Show'.[58]

While gratified with his reception, Thomas is soon so overwhelmed by men contacting him – wanting their own part of the South African glories – that he is not long in writing to both the NSW and Commonwealth governments offering a hundred new Bushmen that he is willing to lead back to the Boer War! The offer is soon accepted.

CHAPTER ELEVEN

PALE RIDERS

As a horse soldier under strict discipline [Morant] might have been a success; as an officer in independent command he was bound to be a failure; for he could not command himself . . . With unlimited drink under his hand for months, everything was possible; and the man was a moral coward who having committed one crime when drunk would not have hesitated at other crimes for self-protection. A crooked mind, not perhaps wholly responsible; heroic on the physical plane, a dastard on the moral plane . . .[1]

Letter to *Windsor and Richmond Gazette*,
2 March 1904

Late June 1901, northern Transvaal, a rush, a push and the shot is ours

In the wake of a mercifully uneventful scrap with some attacking Boers – only a few shots fired, for not a single casualty – Captain Alfred Taylor leads his patrol towards a kraal to gather information on their attackers.

The Natives watching their approach freeze at the very sight of Taylor. 'Bulala' is here.

While Taylor begins his aggressive line of questioning in his fluent Afrikaans, Corporal Michael McMahon leads some of the party on a little trek to see if there might be any Boer stragglers nearby, or perhaps their trail.

One of the Natives has attracted the particular interest of Taylor. It is the way his eyes dart back and forth, clearly desperate not to be questioned. He must know something.

Jy! You, Taylor calls him forth. *Waar is die boere? Where are the Boers?* Well?

'*I konna*,'[2] replies the Native, in his own language, which Taylor also understands. I will not tell you.

Wrong answer.

At least Captain Taylor thinks so.

With one fluid motion the English officer takes out his pistol, brings its muzzle up to the Native's head, and pulls the trigger. There is an almighty crack, and the Native falls dead, half his head splattered on the veldt.

Completely shocked, one of Taylor's men, Trooper George Lucas, races on horseback the short distance to Corporal McMahon's party.

'Taylor's shot a n . . . r!'[3]

McMahon and his Troopers race back to find a very calm Taylor still standing over the dead Native like nothing has happened, though surrounded by Troopers drained of all colour. The Natives, each one sprinting for the hills, are not nearly so shocked. This is just another in an eternal line of white men with guns who have come to murder and maim them.

How does the Englishman himself justify such an atrocity? Well, this is a civilian matter, you see. Taylor is the local Native Commissioner, and by the power vested in him he will do whatever he damn pleases when it comes to his role in commissioning the Natives. Yes, there might be problems in killing a white man like that, but rarely will you need to face British justice for killing a black man in cold blood.

Corporal McMahon does not take so cavalier an attitude. Military or civilian, black or white, that was a human being, with a mother and father and quite likely a wife and children of his own.

What in the *hell* just happened, Captain Taylor?

Oh, the shot? A casual Captain Taylor shrugs as he glances at the still-warm body beneath him.

'I fired to frighten him. Unfortunately I fired too low.'[4]

There are few lower than Captain Taylor.

2 July 1901, Sweetwaters Farm, Taylor-made murder

A few days later, the messenger gives the news to Captain Taylor.

Six Boers in two covered wagons are on their way to Sweetwaters Farm, ready to surrender.

Corporal Ernest Browne is one of the patrol that prepares to leave the outpost, under the command of Captain James Robertson. But . . . just a moment.

Before they leave, Captain Alfred Taylor wants to have a word, on a subject unknown. The men sit astride their horses, waiting for Captain Robertson to return so he can give the word in turn, and it doesn't take long. Robertson soon calls Squadron Sergeant Major Kenneth Morrison to him, and gives his orders.

Captain Taylor, he says, wants him to take men out to shoot dead the surrendering Boers. No prisoners.

'Should I take [such] orders from Captain Taylor?'[5] Morrison asks.

'Certainly,' Robertson replies crisply, 'as he is commanding officer at Spelonken.'[6]

(Taylor is not any such thing, actually. A civil appointment, he has no *actual* authority over the military men, a distinction lost on most, as his magnetically dark personality sees him in control regardless, obeyed by men who lesser ranks now must obey in turn, and so the poison spreads.)

Morrison finds himself repeating the orders to a disbelieving Sergeant Dudley Oldham. In civilian life Dudley is a mild-mannered accountant from a close family in Gawler, South Australia. And now he is being ordered to shoot unarmed men who have laid down those arms in the belief that the British would be honourable and simply imprison them?

Well, he will not have it.

'I refuse to shoot them,'[7] he tells Morrison. And so now Morrison finds himself enforcing the orders that he just questioned himself.

'It is an absolute *order*,'[8] he tells Oldham.

As the Troopers wait outside it is only clear to them that there is an absolute barney going on inside, before a furious yet pale Sergeant Oldham goes out ahead at a flat gallop, while Morrison comes back to the rest of the patrol. He calls out Troopers Eden, Arnold Brown, Heath and Dale and speaks to them for a few minutes, before they, too, gallop out after Sergeant Oldham in the direction that the surrendering Boers are said to be coming from.

And now, at last, Sergeant Major Morrison makes his way back to Corporal Ernest Browne who, with Sergeant Stevens, is at the head of the next troop.

'I have told Sergeant Oldham and his party to shoot the six Boers . . .'[9] he says.

'You are not to take notice of the white flag,' Sergeant Major Morrison continues firmly, 'and the Boers *are* to be shot. These are Captain Taylor's orders.'[10]

And who gave those orders originally? some of the men ask.

'They are *Captain Taylor's* orders,'[11] Morrison repeats.

And there are the Boers!

Up ahead they can see the two wagons, presumably filled with the Boers approaching, and so fire a few shots in their direction – the bullets blasting off nearby rocks – to see if there is any fight coming back from them, or if they have truly just come in to surrender.

The answer is soon apparent. There is no returning volley, no crack of gunfire, and waving white flags soon emerge from both wagons, at which point the patrol rushes forward to surround the wagons, their rifles at the ready.

After some barked orders to come out, the wary Boers – who look like they are starving – emerge. All of them are relieved of their rifles, bandoliers and all ammunition, and are searched to make sure they carry no pistols or knives. They now stand uneasily, blinking in the direct sunlight, defenceless, unsure of what will happen next. Their numbers include a 12-year-old boy, Petrus Geyser, and a sick man in one wagon.

As the Australians scan the landscape all around it seems that there are no witnesses . . .

Has the wind changed?

No. But a certain silence settles heavily on the soldiers as they wait for what they know is coming. And here it is . . .

'You know your *orders*,' Sergeant Oldham says to his Troopers with heavy emphasis, nodding to the newly surrendered Boers, 'and they must be carried out.'[12]

The Troopers look at each other.

Yes, they know their *orders*.

Are they going to do this?

They are going to do this.

One among them, Trooper Barend J. van Buuren, shifts uncomfortably. A Boer himself, he had joined the BVC just months ago, one of the three dozen or so 'joiners' in the outfit, men who had seen that the writing on the wall was daubed in their own blood, and decided they wanted no part of it. But a man who could turn once could always turn again and van Buuren had always been kept at arm's length. He has never quite fitted in. At least, however, as he speaks to the Boers in their mother tongue – barking at them to line up, 10 yards away, and turn to face the armed Troopers – the prisoners are reluctantly doing just that.

As they turn and face, however, and the Troopers unsling their rifles, the eyes of the prisoners widen with growing horror as the thought occurs . . .

Surely they're not . . . ?

They couldn't be about to . . . ?

Ready!

Dear God! *Lieve God!*

Aim!

Please, no! *Alsjeblieft niet!*

FIRE!

The volleys burst forth and each Boer falls dead. Wisps of smoke rise listlessly above the scene, the stink of cordite, and that curiously moist smell of freshly spilled blood wafting away with the wind. Now for the sixth Boer, who is lying sick in the wagon. Trooper Eden goes into it and dispatches him with a bullet to the breast.

'The Boers,' Trooper George Heath will note, 'never made the slightest resistance.'[13]

With the shocking act now done, the wagons themselves are thoroughly searched, led by Lieutenant Handcock. One of the Boer prisoners, in an effort to save himself before he was executed, had said to Handcock, within earshot of Trooper Solomon King, that there was a cashbox in the wagon with gold and £1000 in cash in it, and there was more where that came from if they could just be allowed to live. So Trooper King is watching and listening with more than usual interest as Lieutenant Handcock walks past carrying the cashbox, to say in his slow-speaking, lugubrious way, 'There is over one hundred pounds here in paper money.'

'I thought there was over one thousand pounds,' Trooper King says. 'Can't you divide it amongst us?'

'No,' Lieutenant Handcock says quite primly, almost offended at the suggestion. 'I can't do nothing like that.'[14]

Perish the thought.

Ironically, much later, at least the notes of money are distributed among the men as curios, if nothing else. (In the here and now, their oxen are herded forward to be handed over to Captain Taylor, who, with the help of Sergeant Major Kenneth Morrison, will soon have them on their way to his farm just over the border in Rhodesia, no more than 30 miles away, where they can be sold for a windfall profit.)

Inevitably though, the sheer brutality of what they have done soon turns some of the men quiet, as they make their way back to Sweetwaters. Passing the spot an hour after the shooting, BVC Trooper Edward Powell is appalled to come across the bodies.

They were, he will recount, 'lying in the road each with a wound right in the forehead. One . . . also had a wound in the neck. At once the feeling came over me that this had not been a fight but a slaughter . . . I saw Captain Robertson on the spot gazing at the bodies.'[15]

Trooper Sidney Staton, who is with Powell and equally appalled, has no doubts once he looks at them.

'They had no [rifles] and from the position in which the bodies were lying it was evident they had not died fighting.'[16]

The distress felt by some of the men is not shared by Captain Taylor who slyly smiles with satisfaction.

Corporal Ernest Browne watches now as once more Captain Taylor swings into deadly action, and rides alone to the 'Kaffir kraal', where he gives the Natives strict instruction about what evidence they are to give if anyone asks.

Some of them agree instantly. Some resist which is . . . inconvenient. 'Three inconvenient ones,' Browne chronicles, 'were chased and shot.'[17]

Dead.

Such an atrocity should, of course, be reported to the Zoutpansberg Native Commissioner, with the problem being that . . . Captain Taylor himself holds that office. And the matter is of so little moment to him, he doesn't even feel the need to mention their deaths in any official report, as they are only Natives, no more than flies for 'Bulala' to brush away, just as he has always done.

Trooper Barend van Buuren cannot take the same approach, and is haunted by the events of the morning.

What has he done?

What has he done?

In the hours after the shootings of the unarmed Boers, van Buuren – an introspective kind of man – barely speaks, and is clearly enormously disturbed, his haunted eyes gazing into the campfire as he recalls the horror that he has wrought. The next day, the only way he can get through is to drink heavily, which sees him that evening talking to some of the Boer women – even if they are captives – about what had happened.

Oh, how Lieutenant Handcock roars at him. How dare he talk of operational matters to anyone outside of their corps? How *dare* he talk to Boer prisoners in the first place? Just whose side are you on? We thought we could trust you. But now, we really wonder. Chastened, suddenly quite sober, van Buuren heads to his swag. And yet, by the following morning the horror of what he had seen and done is still with him and, over breakfast by the fire, he confides to fellow Trooper Edward Powell his thoughts.

'I do not care what the officers say,' he rasps in his thick Dutch accent, 'I will not see murder passed by and nothing said about it.'[18]

So be it.

It is time to get on with the tasks of the day – the key one of which is given by the Captains Taylor and Robertson to the usually and usefully obedient Lieutenant Handcock. We want you to resolve the van Buuren issue, on the grounds that the turncoat might turn once more. Yes, there have been mutterings overheard. They say the Boer has had the hide to accuse them of 'murder' when it comes to 'surrendering' *Boers*!

Who knows who he might tell? The real danger, of course, is that he will tell his former fellows, the Boer Commandos who surround them even now, somewhere in the scrub.

Captain Robertson builds to the point.

'We have thirty prisoners and Boers are near. And the man might give us the slip and give us away.'[19]

How to resolve the problem?

Captain Robertson cannot be clearer: 'We will have to shoot him.'[20]

We?

We, Handcock knows, means *you*.

'It is *right* to shoot traitors,'[21] Robertson adds, on the reckoning that Handcock might have a working moral compass in need of some adjusting to point to the polar opposite. But, no need. After he has finished his brief chat to the Captains, Handcock – as a man closer to a moral vacuum, an automaton that just follows orders – simply comes back and calls for Troopers, including van Buuren, to accompany him on a patrol to scout for some Boers apparently in the area, and they are all soon on their way.

The deeper they move into this whole country of rolling hills and wild gullies covered in little more than short brown grass and stunted, half-hearted trees the more assured Lieutenant Handcock seems to become. Strangely, despite his previous warning, he doesn't seem particularly concerned about Boers – they pass obvious ambush points without hesitation – and still he guides them ever deeper into the gullies.

There is an eerie silence in parts like these.

'Unlike the silence of the Australian bush,' one man notes, 'it is an absolute silence – there is not the hum and whirr of insect life in it, nor the ceaseless movement of foliage, or lowing creek.'[22]

What is more, it is a silence that brings a curious effect.

Whereas in Australia the very vastness of its 'apparently boundless undulations of gum-trees, or plains stretching out in never-ending perspective, produces in the mind a profound melancholy', here on the veldt it is different.

'As you look across its vast distances, and note the blue-capped kopjes – all lying within your vision in a deep silence, which is only accentuated by the infrequent barking of the jackals – a terrible feeling of isolation comes over you. You feel as if you were the last man in the world.'[23]

Quite.

Perhaps even the last man in the world, at the very end of the world.

And now Lieutenant Handcock splits his patrol once more, taking four men with him to the left, while sending the other five out to the right.

'Fan out . . .' Handcock orders his men and the parties split from each other, the rhythm of their hooves remaining as constant as the beat of the men's hearts.

The idea is to proceed laterally, with some 500 yards between them left to right, so they can check a very wide expanse of the bush, not the narrow corridor surveyed if they remain in single file. There will inevitably be snipers here somewhere, or at least some Boers up ahead, so you can expect a shot or two to ring out from them or us, but don't break formation for anything less than a major gunfight.

Yes, sir.

•

Out in this scrubby, gully-strewn country, the Boer turncoat Trooper van Buuren is riding along in a particularly rough patch where he is obscured from the vision of the others when he turns a little, hearing another horseman coming close. Ah, it is Lieutenant Handcock, suddenly riding up right beside him, perhaps to give some new orders.

But no.

Only a couple of seconds after pulling up alongside on his horse, Lieutenant Handcock pulls out his revolver, brings it up to point at van Buuren's breast and pulls the trigger. Van Buuren immediately tumbles off his horse, whereupon Handcock puts two more shots in him, just to be sure, before riding off quickly.

•

Trooper Muir Churton, out to the right – who had van Buuren in his eye-line only a minute before, hears the shots – then he hears thundering hooves and looks up to see Lieutenant Handcock coming his way.

'Keep a sharp lookout,' Lieutenant Handcock says simply and calmly, 'we have just lost a man back there.'[24]

Churton agrees to do exactly that.

Only a short time later, Lieutenant Handcock gallops up to Trooper Edward Powell, who is keeping watch at an observation post closer to the fort.

Handcock is alone. Which is more than passing strange.

'I see you came in with a led horse and an empty saddle?' Trooper Powell asks quizzically.

'Yes,' Lieutenant Handcock replies, 'we had a brush with the Boers. They ambushed and killed [van Buuren].'[25]

Good . . . *God*. Powell, too, feels certain that Handcock has just murdered van Buuren!

Despite being, yes, a cross between a simple man and a bit simple, Lieutenant Handcock is also as cold-blooded as a snake on the southern tip of Tassie in June. Yes, leadership requires a level of detachment, but to brush off the death of a man under you as though it were nothing completely chills the blood of Troopers Edward Powell and Muir Churton. Perhaps it would behoove them to just keep their eyes peeled for Peter Handcock and a rifle.

Usually, on such a tragic occasion, a party of Troopers would be sent out to retrieve the body so the fallen comrade could be given a decent Christian burial.

But no such thing happens, which makes Churton, for one, even more suspicious. He does not leap to conclusions; he has already made his conclusions and now has them confirmed by inaction.

'I saw no Boers that day,' he will later note, '[and] neither did anyone else on patrol. And I am convinced that there were none in the neighbourhood. I agreed with the opinion expressed by others that there had been foul play.'[26]

This is further confirmed by the fact that Handcock frequently threatens to shoot any man who voices dissent on the dubious turn of events.

That evening, around the fire, conversations are muted. Eyes are averted. There is not a man among them who does not know what has happened to van Buuren. *This* is what happens to those who don't co-operate, who Captain Taylor feels he can't count on. You are liable to take a bullet from one of your own officers at any moment.

Beyond the silencing of van Buuren himself, the clear hope is that it will help silence all other potential dissenters.

And yet . . . ?

And yet, beyond the firelight, there are hushed conversations that grow stronger and longer as the night darkens.

The men are not happy, as witness the whispers in the night.

That was murder, any way you want to dress it.

Something must be done. The authorities must be told.

Which ones?

Who can we trust?

Lenehan?

No, higher still.

Colonel Hall is our man. Surely, as a Colonel he will be free of this callous corruption that has infected our Lieutenants, Captains and Majors?

This is not the time to talk on it, but let us quietly meet later.

A restless night is passed in the bleak wilderness of the northern Transvaal.

Restless for all, but Peter Handcock. The Lieutenant sleeps safe and sound. The Bushveldt Carbineers near him do not, nor will they ever again.

Early July 1901, Pietersburg, trouble at the Inn

Now what?

Lieutenant Colonel Francis Henry Hall, the Officer Commanding the army garrison at Pietersburg – along with all military matters from that city to Pienaars River to the south – only has to read the first few paragraphs of the report in front of him before allowing himself an inward groan. It's all about the BVC, that ramshackle regiment up in the far north that have been generating a good trickle of prisoners for transportation overseas. Written by one of the many secretive Intelligence agents scattered in the northern Transvaal, it alleges that things are out of control up the way of Sweetwaters Farm, that there is 'poor discipline, unconfirmed murders, drunkenness, and general lawlessness in the Spelonken'.[27]

Well, it is always a risk. The further you move military units from regular barracks the more you risk precisely this kind of thing happening – and all the more so when it is a hastily raised irregular force, with no iron-clad tradition to guide them, and more often than not populated by the rough and ready, the wild and woolly, and sometimes the demonic and dangerous. What makes this report particularly troubling, however, is that a Boer woman has accused the man in nominal charge, Captain James Robertson, of molesting her. Murders, drunkenness and general lawlessness are not good. But an English officer sexually molesting someone is a serious slur on the good name of the British Army. It is not what an officer and a gentleman should ever be accused of, let alone engage in.

With little hesitation, Colonel Hall issues his orders.

Captain Robertson – accompanied by the worst of A Squadron – is to return to Pietersburg forthwith to face an inquiry on four grave charges: murder, molestation, cowardice and robbery.

(At the conclusion of this inquiry, which in fact will only go tentatively into the first charge, Robertson will be given the choice: resign immediately and return to England, or face a possible court martial. He shall choose the former, and go quickly. But this is all to come.)

Who to replace Robertson, now?

The obvious. We will get that fellow who has just joined us, the polo fellow, the newly promoted *Captain* Percy Hunt if you please. He shall take over.

5 July 1901, Pietersburg, best endeavours

Fall in!

On this fine but freezing July morning, the men of the BVC B Squadron stand beside their mounts for 'stable parade', where both they and their horses are closely inspected – though for battle-readiness only, rather than some absurd need for polish and *Blanco*, which counts for nothing when the bullets start to fly.

And the bullets were flying last night, 4 July, at Naboom Spruit, a tiny outpost halfway between Pretoria and Pietersburg, where 150 Boers led by the ubiquitous canny Scot, Jack Hindon, had with uncanny timing attacked a British train bearing a platoon of Gordon Highlanders placed upon it as an escort. Nine soldiers and a subaltern had been killed as a result, while 11 others had been wounded in the 20-minute engagement.

It is news profoundly shocking to the British military hierarchy in Pretoria, which had dare hoped that the Boer threat in the area was receding – and now this!

Some heroic details at least emerge.

The last four men left standing had continued to fire despite having no cover, until three of them were killed and the last man badly wounded. Once that sole survivor had been captured, he was asked by the Boer Commandant De Villiers why they had not surrendered sooner.

'Why, man,' the heavily bleeding Trooper had replied, 'we are the Gordon Highlanders.'[28] Like all those captured, the man is given immediate medical care and treated well.

One of those killed, Lieutenant Alexander Archie Dunlop Best, only 22 years old, had been a friend of both Captain Hunt and Breaker Morant.[29]

•

A day later, at sunset, Morant and his returning patrol roll up to cheers from the rest of the BVC.

This time though, the usually garrulous Lieutenant barely seems to acknowledge the welcome. Something is up.

At 9.30 pm he comes to see Frank Eland and, without preamble, orders him to 'Get ten men saddled up for a patrol. We are going out after ten Boers and a Cape cart who have been seen by the cattle guards in the afternoon.'[30]

There is a hardness to Morant right now that Eland doesn't quite recognise, the sparkle in his eye replaced by a glint of steely determination to wreak revenge on Boers in general, even if he can't get to the specific ones that killed Lieutenant Best. For yes, he has heard the dreadful news and is, as Eland will later write to his wife, 'very cut up',[31] about it.

The way Morant tells it to him, the Boers outnumbered those on the train by twenty to one and seem to have 'shot men down in cold blood'.

Perhaps further moved along by Hunt's own grief and rage, Morant wants some kind of revenge and does not particularly care who has to pay the price, so long as they are Boers. The mate of Captain Hunt and the Breaker has died – no, more than that, *has been murdered* – and Morant will not rest, don't you worry, Captain Hunt, till he has seen justice exacted with his own bloody hands.

'If we had come up with that party of Boers that night,' Eland tells his wife, 'we would not have taken any prisoners.'[32]

As it happens, they do not take any Boers that night, nor the following day, returning to Pietersburg exhausted in the wee hours of the morning to a good tot of whisky and sleep. The Boers' day will come, and a day of reckoning Morant clearly intends it to be. At least they can soon get to grips as, on the day of the funeral for Lieutenant Best, the men are told by their new Commanding Officer, Captain Percy Hunt – who they find is a rather pukka Pom, himself desperately eager to get into action – that the move of the BVC B Squadron to Sweetwaters Farm some 60 miles to the north, starts, tonight!

We will be heading off just before midnight as a matter of safety. Two nights and two days of hurried travel follow, before they arrive at Sweetwaters Farm where A Squadron is residing under the supreme guidance of Captain Alfred Taylor.

Not surprisingly, as Frank Eland writes to his darling wife, 'A. Squad were not very pleased to see us; discipline was very lax with them and there are several very ugly rumours with regard to the conduct of several of them. I believe a court martial will be held and if they do their duty, a verdict of murder ought to be returned.'

Oh yes. Not to put too fine a point on it, but it has to be said, if only to his wife.

'Don't mention this to anyone out there. There are several fellows in this crowd who would stop at nothing; they'd shoot and rob their own mother!'

Well, that ends from now.

With Captain Hunt and Morant in charge, backed by the good men of B Squad, things will soon be put to rights, have no fear, darling. As soon as the morrow, Captain Robertson will be on his way south with 'some of the worst of A Squad'.[33]

Left behind will be six Troopers and a couple of officers to bolster the numbers of B Squadron, their numbers surprisingly including Lieutenant Handcock, who only a fortnight earlier had been one of the principal perpetrators of the murder of six Boers. Despite that, or perhaps in fact because of that, Captain Taylor had been particularly eager that Lieutenant Handcock stay on.

A photo, a Kodak special, is taken to mark the moment. They are a motley crew: Handcock, grim and glaring at the lens, broods with menace; the resplendent Breaker to his left is bold and proud with a smile and a smoke. Beside him sits Dr Thomas Johnston, civil surgeon and friend to all BVC officers, but particularly close to Morant. Captain Hunt is the most proper among them, somehow refined and elegant despite the circumstances, centre stage and the lynchpin of the scene. To his side is Captain Taylor, staring straight ahead with piercing eyes and a faint smirk, smarter than them all and he knows it. Lastly lies a Lieutenant, the nervous Henry Picton, dwarfed by his confident comrades. *Smile please, would you, gentlemen?*

They don't know it at the time, but this photo will be the only physical proof to ever exist of Captain Hunt in command.

Mid-July 1901, leaving East London en route for Pietersburg

After a week of hard train travel from East London the 30 Australian Troopers that Lieutenant George Witton has recruited, sworn in and equipped to be the gun detachment of the BVC, are now getting closer to their destination, noted by ever fewer houses and a strange sense that they are being . . . watched? Does every kopje hide a pack of Boers about to descend upon them?

The banter between the 30 Australian Troopers with Witton is long gone now, as a certain grimness settles upon them, an awareness . . . a quiet *alarm* . . . at just what it is they might be facing on this mission.

The mood darkens further when, coming into Warm Baths station, Witton gets a close look at the bullet-peppered carriage in which

Lieutenant Best and the Gordon Highlanders had been ambushed by the merciless Boers.

'The iron walls,' Witton would recount, 'had been about as much protection from Mauser bullets as a sheet of paper; the truck was riddled like a sieve.'[34]

More troubling is what happens a few hours later on the way to Pietersburg, when they pass a tiny outpost called Naboom Spruit.

Here, *right by the line*, are 10 fresh graves of Troopers, just like them, from the train they had just seen, who only a few days before had been, just like them, on their way to Pietersburg when . . . their train had been ambushed, gone off the rails and the Boers had then been all over them, killing survivors.

The Australians look on, aghast.

Are they to finish up in graves like that . . . just like them?

Fer Chrissakes, you blokes on the guns, keep a lookout for them bloody Boers!

Finally, they pull into Pietersburg, that town some 160 miles north of Pretoria that is the literal end of the line. For a soldier of the British forces, it is not quite hell, but you can likely see it from here on a clear day. Everything to the north, east and west of here are the Boer badlands.

Jesus . . . *Christ*.

Witton and his men grab their kit and march in desultory manner to their barracks, such as they are. A fitful round of routine in this Godforsaken place follows – essentially caring for their horses – and though it is noted that Major Lenehan seems to be taking an awful lot of time in Pretoria, no-one can truly blame him. If any of them had been Commanding Officer of the BVC, they, too, would have taken a couple of weeks to see about the guns. And Pretoria, which had seemed like the worst shithole in the world as they had been passing through, now looks as glamorous as the St Kilda boulevard on a Saturday night.

•

The Captain is gone, long live the Captain.

Yes, Captain Robertson has departed this realm, but there will be no rest for the wicked. Captain Hunt is a man in a hurry – at long last given the operational command he has long aspired to, he is eager to make his mark – and in the first days in command is a blur of movement and orders. Most of those orders, true, are guided by Captain Taylor as he knows the country and has the local intelligence of enemy movements and local Natives.

One of the Captain's first orders is to move from their current camp by Sweetwaters Farm to another spot, just two miles to the south-east, to a 'fort'. This proves to be not the kind of fort of popular conception so much as a portable and collapsible set of steel walls designed to safely house as many as 25 men in whatever part of the badlands they found themselves.[35] The good Captain regards it as a better place to hold out should they ever find themselves under a serious Boer attack.

'Our troop was first into fort and picked our place to camp,' James Christie recounts to the *Clutha Leader*, 'and generally tidied things up – or rather the Natives we commandeered did so under our supervision, as no one does any work he can commandeer a n . . . r to do.'[36]

By 18 July things are in good enough shape that they raise the Union Jack over the newly christened 'Fort Edward', named of course for their new gracious monarch, and after a parade and a salute of the flag with bayonets fixed – all arrayed in full dress to honour the occasion – each man is allocated 'a liberal libation of whisky to celebrate the occasion',[37] and of course to toast His Majesty.

'A salute was fired,' Trooper McInnes records, 'the National Anthem sung by the troops and a bottle of whisky broken (carefully, into a bucket!) to christen the flag, and the troops treated to whisky, and our photos taken by one of the ladies present – for even in this out of the way place we have ladies.'[38]

(Olivia Bristow is of course one of them, as is Marie Reuter, the wife of the Reverend at the local mission, but there are also some Boer women like Magdalena Schiel, whose husband is a prisoner of war in St Helena.)

Heavy drinking remains a staple of life among the BVC. Normally one would look to the officers to put a stop to it, but when Lieutenant Morant, with his red hue, his bravado and his penchant for one-upmanship, prides himself on being able to drink any of them under the table, it would be a little beside the point, not to mention absurd.

And so to work! Their job, as they know only too well, is to round up and subdue the remaining Boers in the whole area. Luckily, in learning the local ropes, Captain Hunt has great support from Lieutenant Peter Handcock just as Handcock has always supported all his Commanding Officers. Captain Hunt is the new leader, Lieutenant Morant his key support and whatever they want is fine with him. His own father had died when he had been little more than a toddler, and one way or another Handcock has always gravitated to authoritative men thereafter, eager to do their bidding. He is here to follow orders, as simple as that, and if those orders give better vent to vice and viciousness, he is more enthusiastic than ever.

For his part, Hunt is starting to realise just how much drinking is a part of the daily and nightly life of his Troopers. Their favourite drinking song, 'Little Brown Jug', has turned into a synchronised filling and raising of little brown jugs. With this corps, every day is a bloody rum rebellion, sometimes in the morning, sometimes in the night, and more often than not twice a day.

One evening when James Christie arrives back at Fort Edward from patrol, it is to find that, while Captain Hunt has gone out on a patrol of his own with Lieutenants Morant and Handcock, the men had got into the stores of rum and are roaring drunk!

And even when they try and restore order by placing some men under arrest the madness goes on, as not only does one drunken Trooper narrowly miss a sentry when he fires upon him, but both the Sergeant Major and the Quartermaster have to be arrested for drunkenness. When the outraged Sergeant Major decides to scarper to Pietersburg, six Troopers are sent out after him, and *none* of them returns.

At least while in camp the men have fairly light duties, courtesy of the local Natives they have hired for little above nominal fees.

'We have a lazy time,' Trooper Ronald McInnes notes for the folks at home, 'plenty of Kaffir boys to cook our scoff, fetch wood and water, wash our clothes, groom, feed and water our horses, and fetch coffee to us in bed – and all this on active service . . . The corps is nothing more than police . . . there are as many Boers in the area as there are BVC, so there will not be much fighting . . .'[39]

That, at least, is the way it seems.

And yet just two days after the flag is raised over Fort Edward, and with just half an hour's notice – for that is the way Captain Hunt operates, making snap decisions – Frank Eland is one of the handful of men selected to go with the Captain and Lieutenant Handcock to the Ellerton goldmine some 50 miles to the east.

But careful now!

They all know that one of the particularly dangerous Boer leaders, Barend Viljoen, in charge of the 300-strong Letaba Commando, is in the area, and so they must keep a strong lookout. Quite what it is all about, Captain Hunt does not share with his men, only that he expected to meet someone at Fonseca's store, deep in the Spelonken. That person, when they arrive on the Saturday evening, proves not to be there, so they return to the fort on Sunday morning . . . to find there has been trouble at the camp in their absence.

When Lieutenant Picton – one of the BVC's more hot-blooded officers – had discovered that some of the Troopers had looted some of the rum from a supply convoy heading from Pietersburg to Fort Edward, he had promised holy hell on their arrival, in language that would make a sailor blush. The Troopers, in turn, considering rum the smallest of recompenses for being in this hellhole in the first place, had threatened to shoot Picton for his trouble.

This had proved to be merely their opening remarks . . .

The ringleaders had been arrested only to get away, riding hard back to Pietersburg, but after Captain Hunt gets a message through to Major Lenehan, they are detained, and will soon be discharged from the regiment in disgrace.

Good riddance. On the lookout for further misbehaviour, Lieutenants Morant and Handcock are soon hauling English Corporal Herbert Sharp up before Captain Hunt for a tongue-lashing before dismissal. And rightly so.

Sharp, the cur, had been caught red-handed trying to *sell* a British uniform! This wasn't the innocuous hocking of a mere piece of cloth. This was the attempted sale of a *weapon*, to the enemy no less. Had those Boers got a hold of it, they could have got the drop on us before we knew what hit us. Sharp – one part humiliated to two parts infuriated – is on his way back to Pretoria in disgrace before he knows quite what hit him.

Captain Hunt remains a man in a hurry, and his concern is less with the ones who are gone than the quality of the ones who remain, as he is eager to get his best men into the field.

As a matter of fact, Sergeant Eland is thrilled to be able to write to his beloved wife upon his return, 'Captain Hunt told me he was much pleased with my work and report and had given it to Captain Taylor, the Head of Intelligence and acting Native Commissioner here. I arranged to go to see him in the afternoon; he is at Bristow's [Sweetwaters Farm] where we first camped a mile from here.'[40]

Yes, of course he has heard stories of 'Bulala' Taylor being a cold-blooded killer but, in person, he must say the Englishman proves to be charm itself. And as a corps, the BVC actually is accomplishing some things in terms of bringing in Boers and their cattle, to send the former on their way to the camp at Pietersburg and the latter to . . .

Well, most of the latter to the British Army, with an inevitable tithe being taken for the interests of Captain Taylor.

'The corps did good work,' one Trooper would recall, 'and . . . we captured more prisoners and cattle than any other corps that was out.'[41]

Part of this is due to the energy of their officers.

'Handcock was a man of no education,' another Trooper will recall, 'and Morant was smart all round. They were good to their men, and were always there when fighting was going on. They were no cowards in action, that was certain.'[42]

The only thing . . . ?

Sometimes, the generally affable and garrulous Morant, particularly, displays a streak of savagery that takes everyone by surprise. One time, while out on patrol, they have all made camp and settled down in their swags for the night when, near midnight, Morant and Handcock return from a reconnoitring expedition. They have found no Boers, but do have a monkey with a long tail and tie it by its own tail to a stake in the ground.

And now, despite everyone trying to sleep, and despite the staggering cruelty of what they are about, they take turns trying to shoot the squealing monkey with their revolvers as it jumps around. The aim of their hideous game is not to kill, as that would stop their fun stone-dead, but just to wing it initially. Just enough so they can record a hit, but it can keep jumping.

Some of the Troopers protest, only to get short shrift from both men.

'If you don't like the work, you can go over and join the Boers,' they are told.[43]

What can they do about it? Nothing.

And yet this same cove, back at Fort Edward, was sometimes known to have such a streak of kindness in him, he would bring 'milk and comfort to the kiddies',[44] in the small holding pen they had for surrendered Boers, before transporting them to the concentration camp at Pietersburg. He is an exceedingly strange bloke, a man as capable of kindness as cruelty, without a single straight line in his whole character.

And the grog is a real issue – not just with Morant, but other senior officers too.

'The quantity of drink most of the officers consumed was simply marvellous,' one of the BVC Troopers would recall. 'Night after night they had carouses. In the morning they would hold a mock court martial over the man who succumbed first on the previous night, and he would have to "shout" a case of whisky or champagne, as the case might be. Many of the officers were always more or less mad with drink.'[45]

In this field, there is one clear stand-out.

'Morant,' one Trooper will recall, 'could stand liquor so well that all the whisky in Spelonken wouldn't have given him one drunk week.'[46]

CHAPTER TWELVE

HUNT

*I think they killed for the love of killing. Yes, that was it. It wasn't
loot they wanted, for when they shot Boers who came in with
loaded wagons they never took a thing. It seemed to me they
liked killing.*[1]

Former member of the Bushveldt Carbineers in
an account to the *Ballarat Courier*, 1902

I am in blood
Stepped in so far that, should I wade no more,
Returning were as tedious as go o'er.

William Shakespeare, *Macbeth*, Act 3, Scene 4

July 1901, the Camps, bagged, tagged and buried

In no fewer than 45 concentration camps across the occupied territories,
things are tighter than a rusted nut on an abandoned Cape cart. Camps
designed to hold 20,000 Boer women and children are now overwhelmed
with 60,000 of them – and *still* wave after wave of yet more Boer refugees keep crashing on their shores and washing over them. Yes, British
medical men do what they can but it is all too little against all too much
and as the sickly sweet smell of decomposing bodies hangs like a heavy
pall over every camp, the priests chant the last rites so often that even
the British can recite them by heart. Needs must, even their stiff upper
lips must tremble in the face of the unintended consequences of what
had started out as a humanitarian policy, only to descend into this hell
on earth. It is a full-on fiasco which sees women and children dying in
their thousands, and they will continue to do so if things do not improve
soon – which they won't, for the war is going too well for that! So, there
we are, caught in the vice-like grip of a fatal success.

The more that Lord Kitchener's brutal tactics work, the more his 'bag'
bulges, the worse the situation becomes.

Even those camps overseas – in other parts of the British Empire like
India, Ceylon and St Helena – advise they can no longer fit an errant

sardine, let alone any more shiploads of Boer prisoners. The only thing that is certain is that this cannot go on. Something must break, for the camps cannot absorb the flow. It is all so much more trouble when you take them alive.

•

There is no doubt about it.

The wretched Hobhouse woman is causing such a stir that in Westminster the Secretary of State for War, William Brodrick, knows he must first take some of the action she is insisting on, and also inform her of that fact by letter, in order to settle her down a little:

> War Office
> Dear Miss Hobhouse,
> The Recommendations contained in your letter of June 4 on the subject of the Concentration Camps have been most carefully considered, and I am now in a position to give you the opinions which have been formed on them by the Government, and which, I think you will agree, generally speaking meet with your wishes . . .
>
> I have every hope that within the necessary limitations imposed by camp life all reasonable provision will be found to have been already made in the Concentration Camps, for adequate food and the necessaries of life, with proper medical treatment, schools of instruction, religious ministration . . .
>
> Yours faithfully
> St. John Brodrick.[2]

29 July 1901, Fort Edward, a mystery for Christie

Captain Hunt's martial spirit and drive needs an outlet, a target, and that is precisely what Christie has been sent out to find. It has taken a lot of careful inquiry and manoeuvring but, from atop this kopje, and directing his glass in the direction he had been told, Christie can now see it!

It is a small Boer laager, a corral of carts.

The hard part will be to find out, without getting killed for their trouble, just how many Boers dwell within, but Christie is up for it. That night they leave their horses tethered at a good distance, and slowly venture forth on foot by the tepid moonlight.

The clouds part now and there is a moon to see by 'but we could not count the men or horses, as we were in the light and they in the shade, but judged from the wagons and horses what was likely to be a fair thing'.

Their guide, who has better sight than they, gives them a more precise estimate.

'There are about twenty,' he whispers to Christie, 'with more horses than men. Sixteen oxen in big wagons, six oxen in one Scotch cart and six horses in spring wagon.'

Hurrah! Christie cannot wait to crawl out of here safely and get word back to Captain Hunt: they have found a sizable Boer depot.

'This laager was being used as a collection depot, etc, for conveyance to the larger laager, further over in the Modjadji mountains at Barend Viljoen's – a commandant, Native Commissioner, and veldt cornet, a sort of Lord High Everything in the Locality, who had some 80 to 100 men always with him.'[3]

But no, despite his high emotions, Christie's cool head prevails.

'I felt inclined to do the bluff act and rush the place firing wildly and quickly; but as our mission was to get information, not to attack, after consultation we decided that we should send in word.'[4]

A man departs at first light with a message for Captain Hunt, allowing Christie to fall into a very rough doze.

'Speaking for myself, I had no sleep at all since leaving Camp, so fell dozing; while some scoff was being prepared at a kraal, only to wake with a start to think a Boer was asking me to kindly hand over my rifle.'[5]

•

Good news, Captain Hunt! One of Christie's scouts has come with word of the discovery of a Boer laager, just waiting for some bold BVC men to take it unawares. Captain Hunt moves swiftly, barking orders as he goes.

He will take 17 men with him. Get your saddles on your horses, your rations in your kit, your rifles loaded and your dander up.

We move out before this hour shall pass.

Lieutenant Morant, you will stay here and, literally, mind the fort. And you, Sergeant Eland, will come with me.

Frank Eland's eyes shine at the news. When he is able to write to his wife that Captain Hunt personally selected him to go on a mission, he knows her pride will match his own.

But Lieutenant Morant is *not* pleased. It is one thing for young Frank to go out when he personally can keep an eye on him, cover his back, and his flanks, but he is too green to go on a mission like this without that care.

I need Sergeant Eland back here with me. I would really rather he not go, if you don't mind, Captain.

Despite Morant continuing to demur, in the end, as Sergeant S. G. Robinson will recount, 'it was not till the men were absolutely in the saddle that the Lieutenant consented to Captain Hunt's importunity . . .'.[6]

For yes, with a nod to young Frank, Lieutenant Morant agrees that he can go after all, and he is in the saddle within moments.

•

On the evening of 2 August, Lieutenant George Witton is minding his own business in the mess at Pietersburg, and the very next morning he is on his way to Fort Edward, in command of Sergeant Major Hammett and 20 reinforcements to help out Captain Hunt. They are apparently doing fine work up there, but are under such pressure extra manpower is needed. It is a long ride through some wild country and Witton and his men must constantly be on the lookout for Boers. After 80 miles and two days they know they are getting close and this is confirmed when a lone horseman suddenly appears ahead, who proves to be Lieutenant Charles Hannam, who has come out to guide them in.

Once they arrive, Lieutenant Witton is being introduced for the first time to Lieutenants Morant and Handcock, and advised that Captain Hunt himself is away on patrol in the Modjadji district.

•

For the Bushveldt Carbineers, this is not so much war as it is a *hunt*. They are not charging to battle, so much as riding to a capture. For Frank Eland, particularly, it is thrilling, his spirits soaring as he, and the clatter and clutter of men, move closer to their quarry, now in a deep valley with ravines off to either side. The shadows lengthen, but they keep moving. Captain Hunt is even more cock-a-hoop – the laager larger than any spotted recently, it will be a plum prize for an officer with pluck. Might it be that of an important Boer Commandant? And what a triumph, if so, for one so recently trapped overseeing a blooming marriage registry . . . The plan for the moment is to press on as fast as possible, to cover the 40 miles to Buffelsberg, where they can rendezvous with Christie, and there, through stealth and steel, steal their way forward in the night to capture the Boer laager. To feed the men and water the horses there is time for a stop at the farm of Mrs Magdalena Schiel, with one other purpose in mind. For despite her husband currently being a guest of Her Majesty, in detention on St Helena after being captured with a Commando, she has always been remarkably co-operative with British forces, as have her sons, both of whom now work as enthusiastic Intelligence agents for Captain Taylor. At Captain Hunt's behest one of those sons, Anthony, agrees to come with them, to act as a guide and provide extra firepower.

But now comes the wonderful news. Only shortly after setting off, they hear word from some Natives. The most notorious Commando leader of the whole Zoutpansberg – Barend Viljoen – is even now holed up in his farmhouse in the folds of the Modjadji[7] mountains, with just a few of his men.

Captain Hunt can barely breathe for the excitement of it.

This, *this* is precisely what the ambitious English officer has been waiting for. It is, Mother, a chance to make one's mark, a chance to be mentioned in dispatches rather than just delivering them, a chance to snatch some flame of gory glory from these dying embers of a war. In short, it is a Godsend chance to prove himself, to his men and himself.

The laager found by Christie and his men can wait, as they go after this much more important target. Where can they get at short notice the larger manpower they might need? The ever-reliable Sergeant Frank Eland has the answer. By virtue of his deep ties with the local tribe, he is sure he can convince them to provide some warriors to accompany them, armed with their assegais, the cruel iron-tipped hardwood spear that is their weapon of choice. No, they cannot be relied upon to be in the front line of the attack, but could be useful as backup.

While Frank heads off to talk to them, Captain Hunt addresses the men, his voice still crackling with the excitement of it. The original objective of this mission has changed. We are now going after none other than Field Cornet Barend Viljoen himself!

The men stir – the younger ones, who are as inexperienced as Hunt, mostly enthusiastic at the prospect of a real fight; the more grizzled ones realising that, up against the legendary Viljoen, that is likely what they will get.

And so it is that Hunt and his men ride through the night to Reuter's Mission Station, conveniently located only a short ride from their target. Their Captain at this point in proceedings is feeling invincible. This is what he's been waiting for.

Reverend Reuter and his wife are friendly to the British and greet them warmly, but their smiles quickly disappear when Hunt tells them what he plans to do this night. Yes, they confirm, Barend Viljoen's farm is 'only about six miles away'.[8] But it is not the getting there that is difficult, it is the getting out.

Trooper Silke listens with some alarm as Captain Hunt blithely receives and refuses to heed a lengthy warning.

'I warn you, be careful!'[9] says Reverend Reuter.

'The house is unassailable!' echoes his wife.

'It is in a rocky kloof,' says Reverend Reuter. And do not think your enemy will be slight. 'Although fifteen Boers are at the main homestead there are forty at Botha's farm four miles away on the other side, and there are only two ways out of the kloof once you get in.'[10]

Don't you see? Even if you successfully attack Viljoen and his men, Botha and his men will cut you down before you can get out. It is MADNESS to make such an attack.

But Captain Hunt will not be dissuaded. He thanks the Reuters for their hospitality and their advice, and his party make ready to leave around 11.30 pm. Saddle up, men.

Trooper Silke watches carefully as Captain Hunt approaches each of his four Sergeants – Eland, Gray, Oldham and Robinson – in turn and tells them the same thing: 'If I am shot, get out of the kloof before daylight.'[11]

Wee hours, 5/6 August 1901, Devil's Kloof, 40 miles south-east of Fort Edward

About a mile off, they can now see the house itself in the moonlight, illuminated by the dappled light coming through the golden shower trees that surround it, together with the stables on either end.

Time to leave the horses, and do the final mile on foot. Carefully now, Captain Hunt and his men move to the house. Yes, he has only 17 Troopers in number – plus Anthony Schiel – all backed by 50 armed Natives, but that should be enough as he has been told by the Natives of the Modjadji tribe that Field Cornet Barend Viljoen has no more than 20 Boers of his Letaba Commando with him.

The men of the Modjadji, believing the promises of the British that once the Boers are beaten some of their land will be restored to them, are prone, it is noted, to 'follow a patrol like a flock of vultures, armed with all kinds of weapons, from a cowhide shield and bundle of assegais to the latest pattern of rifle'.[12]

And yet, while *en masse* they might appear like an impressive force, some of Hunt's men have concerns about the Natives, noting, 'they were worse than useless in action. They might fire one shot, but would then clear out and hide in the long grass until the fighting was over, appearing again on the scene to loot and plunder everything they could lay their hands on.'[13]

Now they are much closer, Viljoen's house reveals itself clearly at last, a squat, rustic, ramshackle building with a chimney at one end, from which the odd spark now flickers into the night sky.

Captain Hunt gathers his Troopers to him.

We are going in. Sergeant Eland, I want you to stick close to me. I am going to get close, tell them they are surrounded and then call upon them to surrender.

'Silke, you take your fifty n . . . rs along the road and stop within fifty yards of the house. If they don't surrender, wait until you hear a shot and then rush the house with the n . . . rs.'[14]

Silke is bewildered at such orders.

Really?

Just walk up, and call on them to surrender, and the Boers are going to throw out their weapons and come out with their hands up? When has such a thing *ever* happened?

Perhaps he should say something?

Captain Hunt, after all, has never led such a venture in his life, and seems to be making decisions on the run, but . . .

But he is the superior officer and has given his orders. Silke has too much experience to want any part of this madness, and is more than happy to stay well back.

Hunt and Sergeant Eland – beside himself with nervous excitement at the honour done to him, to have Captain Hunt's back for such a venture – are already moving off.

Captain Hunt feels like a cross between a wolf in the night, going in for the kill as he pads across the moonlit landscape and . . . something a little less bold. For the truth is, despite his rank, and the fact that he is a professional British Army officer, the truth is . . . he has never actually fired a shot in anger before, and certainly not at another human. That is why he has insisted on giving them a chance to surrender. It is the gentlemanly thing to do, and will avoid bloodshed.

Either way, to capture or kill this many Boers will be a real feather in his cap, and worth the risk. Schiel is quietly dispatched to a hill at the rear of the farmhouse, accompanied by a party of Natives.

Captain Hunt and Sergeant Eland are close enough now to see it all clearly.

Silke is still peering after them, shaking his head.

The Viljoen farmhouse is on sloping ground, with about 30 yards up to the front four steps, where a stone path proceeds for another six paces, where there is another four steps, then flat for another six paces, and two more lots of four steps before finally arriving on to the wide verandah, where the front door awaits. All of the steps have low walls on either side.

It is not, in sum, an easy place to charge without making noise. Moving forward, their rifles at the ready, no-one speaks a word for fear of alerting the Boers, which could well prove fatal to the attackers.

•

Inside the house, Barend Viljoen has been carefully watching Captain Hunt and his men approaching. They have known of this coming attack for a few hours, having been forewarned by one of their scouts, who had been watching their approach from a high hill for most of the day. And so everything has been made ready to receive them in the time-honoured Boer fashion in war-time. His men are placed in sheltered positions around the house with strict instructions to keep themselves secreted and silent until Viljoen himself fires the first shot. The key will be to allow the attackers to get as close as possible before launching.

Closer . . .

Come closer . . .

Still closer and . . .

•

Blithely unaware of what awaits, Captain Hunt is now in position, his men ready behind him.

It is time to take the plunge.

Viljoen! We have you surrounded! I call on you to surrender!

A shot rings out – fired by one of the secreted Boers in the broad direction of a flitting figure in the darkness he has spotted – and in a split instant the evening's silence has exploded into a crashing fusillade of gunfire. The Boer firepower is overwhelming in the darkness. Quickly realising the situation, Troopers all around Captain Hunt duck for cover.

But not Captain Hunt. This is his moment. Bravely, or perhaps insanely, he charges forward, firing at the flashes as he goes. He is closely followed by the ever-faithful Sergeant Frank Eland – husband of Dora, father of Babs – who also fires as he goes.

Through the window they see silhouetted figures and fire their shots accordingly. Precisely who shoots who and when will never be quite clear. But if the mark of the principals in any battle is that they are closest to the action, let the record show:

Inside the house, both Barend Viljoen and his brother Johannes – the two silhouetted figures in the window – go down hard, mortally wounded, followed quickly by another Boer, Gerhardus Hartzenberg.

Hunt and Eland are running now, their feet flying over fraught footing, trying to bring their rifles to bear, to get in shots of their own. Angry flashes ahead, the shattering roar of guns and . . .

HIT . . .

Am I hit . . . ?

I am hit . . .

I am hit . . .

Captain Hunt has got to within 20 paces of the door before the questing question becomes very clear carnage, the first bullet *has* taken him, hitting him in the breast, and he staggers some few yards more before collapsing. *Still* Frank Eland does not falter. A few paces behind his Captain, he charges forward into a blizzard of Boer bullets. But now, with just a small cry in the night, he too goes down, shot through the hips and lower stomach.

Trooper Silke tries to send his Natives forward to the rescue but it is to no avail. They merely retreat in the opposite direction – except for one old man who stays by his side, only to be shot through the head for his trouble.

'I could not see any of our chaps going to the house,' Silke will recount, 'and I was too well "educated" to go myself so I went back into the ditch and waited . . .'[15]

As to the Natives with him, for the moment they are *not* a force to be reckoned with, having no more desire than he has to charge armed Boers in the darkness.

Eventually, when the blaze of fire dies down, Silke ventures forward, seeking contact with his own men, and soon enough finds Sergeant Samuel Robinson, 'nearly dead with fright'.[16]

'Hunt is dead,'[17] Robinson whispers.

Refusing to believe it, Silke keeps moving, going from man to man, until it is established that all are accounted for bar Hunt and Eland. Most of them agree that the two missing men are very likely dead, as they had been right at the forefront of the attack. With great reluctance, Sergeant Dudley Oldham, now the man of highest rank left alive, feels they have no choice but to return to Reuter's Mission and they do so, Silke will record, 'with heavy hearts, for Hunt and Eland were well liked, especially Eland'.[18]

Sadly, they move off in the night, gather their horses, and head back towards Reuter's Mission.

•

The shattered group of Troopers under Sergeant Oldham arrives back at Reuter's Mission Station with the dawn, and soon wakes the Reverend with the appalling news. Reverend Reuter listens to the garbled story of the firefight for as long as he can, before bursting forth with what must be said.

'How could you leave your captain like that?'[19] he bellows.

Silence . . .

No simple answer emerges that can satisfy someone who wasn't there. *But we were! And you had to be there to understand just how strong the Boers were, how many there were, how it was simply out of the question to stay there and fight on.*

The Reverend Reuter accepts no such reasoning, but does at least accept that nothing at all can be done for now. After the women of the mission rustle up some corn meal, Oldham and his men gratefully avail themselves of the bunks that are offered and collapse until it is time to head back . . .

However, after a few hours, they are alerted by a messenger who informs them that young Schiel has the Viljoen farmhouse surrounded – and he needs help!

The men rouse themselves as best they can and head once more towards the farmhouse. The plan is to back up Schiel, and hopefully recover the bodies of their fallen Captain and Sergeant.

•

Christie's party now makes its way to Reuter's Mission. There they are aggrieved to learn from Reverend Reuter that there had been a fight at Viljoen's farm, and that Captain Hunt and Sergeant Eland are missing.

'The men are all around the house,' Reverend Reuter tells them. 'The Boers cannot get away.'

With that news, urgency is paramount.

'We got some dynamite and fuse from him,' Christie will recount, 'and we went helter skelter down the mountain, feeling now that Hunt and Eland were missing, that revenge was the only thing that we were looking for.'[20]

•

Horsemen, ahead!

Among James Christie and his men, hands fly to rifles, and they immediately dismount and take cover, to present a less obvious target if shooting breaks out.

In fact, mercifully, it proves to be Captain Hunt's party of their own BVC, but . . .

But there is no Captain Hunt.

'We thought you were all around the [Viljoen] house,' Christie says, quizzically.

The sorry tale emerges, from Sergeant Oldham.[21] They had ridden out once more this day in the hope of retrieving the bodies of their Captain and Sergeant, only to find themselves the target of Boer snipers as they neared their destination. They had retreated once more, without locating Hunt or Eland.

Distressed to hear it all, Christie reluctantly decides he and his men must accompany them back to the mission station and so passes the next few hours listening 'to tales of valour and bravery from sundry troopers, which led us to the conclusion that the home of Barend Viljoen must be full of nothing but dead Boers'.[22]

Back at the mission, Sergeant Oldham is quick to dispatch a rider to Fort Edward, with a report of what has happened, and urgently requesting reinforcements be sent forth.

There is little to do but wait until the following day to undertake a salvage operation.

7 August 1901, Fort Edward, galloping bad news

Someone is coming!

It proves to be one of the Carbineers who'd gone out with Captain Hunt. He is on his own, and looks shattered. Get Lieutenant Morant.

Sir, I regret to report we were ambushed. Captain Hunt and Sergeant Eland both killed.

The Breaker stands, shocked, the blood draining from his face.

'I swear,' he says with sudden Shakespearean gravitas, 'the bitterest vengeance on anything in the shape of a Boer.'[23]

Lieutenant Morant may still speak like a poet, but gone is all love and laughter, all bravura and banter, and all that is left is a cold-eyed bleak fury in search of . . .

Revenge. It is all Morant can speak of, it is all that he can think about. It *consumes* him.

Revenge for the death of Captain Hunt and Sergeant Eland, and by God or by the Devil, he no longer cares, the Breaker will get it. Notwithstanding the tragic news, the sudden transformation strikes Trooper Frank Hall as very odd. Morant knows nothing of the details of their death, just that they have been killed – and yet he is convinced from the first that they died in something other than a fair fight. It will be death for death, whether they fell foul or fair. It is an oath sworn in grief and in heat, but Frank Hall cannot see the Breaker cooling soon, and his grief seems to consume him.

Charles Hannam, too, is puzzled at Morant's reaction, 'Hunt's death seemed to put him off his head. It is hard to understand how the captain had been worshipped by Morant.'[24]

But Morant is as deadly serious as he is – and he means it – seriously deadly.

'They have murdered my best pal, and there shall be no more mercy,'[25] Morant says to Hannam, in the slow and slightly slurred manner that perhaps indicates he has been drinking heavily.

The first man to receive a direct order from new commander Lieutenant Morant – now the highest-ranking officer of the BVC thanks to the bullet of a Boer – is Lieutenant George Witton.

'Get every available man out.'[26]

Yes, sir.

In short order, all BVC Troopers in camp at the time are standing to attention in front of Lieutenant Morant – with a bristling Captain Taylor beside him – only to watch the Breaker have what amounts to a nervous breakdown. For so awash is Morant in heavy emotion that it is all he can do to stand, let alone speak. Yes, he is a good composer of verse for *The Bulletin* and other publications, but now that the time has come to compose himself it is beyond him, and the lightly sobbing silence hangs heavy as the men shift uncomfortably.

'Men . . .' Morant begins, before faltering badly, and trying one more time. 'Men . . .'[27]

But it is no good. He is too deeply grief-stricken and angered to put words together, so Captain Taylor must take over.

'Men,' he says, 'we must avenge the death of your captain, and give no quarter.'[28]

Within the hour 60 men are on their way under the command of Lieutenant Morant, riding grim-faced in their lead, heading straight to Reuter's Mission. Captain Taylor has given them a German guide who claims to know the country, so they can get there all the *quicker*. And for Morant, that speed is clearly vital.

He is at home on a horse, in control once more and ready to lose control as soon as a Boer is sighted. They are more posse than patrol now, more seething lynch party than Soldiers of the Queen, as they ride hard through the shimmering heat to find and to kill.

Or at least that is the way Morant would have them be – it is just that the state of his mind is still the cause of speculation among the men. Is he quite right in the head? His very troubled state is evident from the unbalanced way that Morant treats the guide, who has the dual misfortune of not only being a German with little grasp of the English language, but also having even less clue about where they are at any time, constantly confessing to being completely lost.

'I think you are doing it on purpose!'[29] barks Morant with such violence in his voice – *Bloody Germans all support the bloody Boers!* – that the guide's knees wobble. George Witton watches as the Breaker rages, curses and threatens *his own guide*!

'I am becoming afraid for my life!'[30] the guide whispers in his thick accent to Witton. Becoming? He should have started paying attention earlier! As it happens, Witton's fear is less for the guide than for Morant himself. For while the guide may be lost geographically, Morant is lost to all reason, whipping his own horse like a red-headed stepson to get more distance out of it. *Onwards, onwards! Right course or wrong – further, faster!* Forty miles of hard riding will be gone, and the horses in a sickly lather of muddy dust, before Morant concedes to a halt – both nags and Troopers panting like beaten dogs, even as night at last mercifully descends. But even now, stopped, Witton can see that the fire they are gathered around to cook their evening meal is not close to the intensity of the fire in Morant's eyes, as he paces about, never at rest, at the mercy of a fury within that will only be quenched with more killing.

'Its effect upon Morant was terrible,' Witton will chronicle. 'Instead of being the usual gay, light-hearted comrade whom I had known for three days, he became like a man demented.'[31]

•

Lost. Nigh everything is lost. Much of Breaker Morant's future plans had rested on Captain Hunt providing an entrée to the well-heeled world after the war had finished. And now, in one brutal action, that has all been taken from him. It is devastating, infuriating and emotionally wrenching all in one. Yes, Hunt is dead, which is tragic. But what future does Morant *himself* now have, as an aging horse breaker who is still pursued by the law in Australia, and is a nobody's nobody in England?

There are few options left. The only one with any real chance comes via Captain Taylor who, like Hunt, seems very well connected – appointed to his position by Kitchener, no less! – and who has all kinds of plans to claim the Boer farms after the war, particularly those whose owners had been killed. Taylor and Sergeant Major Morrison have openly discussed exactly that and there has to be at least some chance that Morant could get in on it too. At the very least it makes him more disposed to do exactly what Taylor orders, and those orders right now are to sweep the district clean of Boers – one way or another.

7 August 1901, Viljoen Farmhouse, gather by the river

Having come from Reuter's Mission at dawn, Christie and his men now approach Viljoen's house in the mid-morning with great care, not knowing what to expect . . . only to find . . . 'Kaffirs in hundreds coming away with whatever they could carry in the way of furniture'.[32]

In their own version of 'acting the locust', the Natives have looted the house of everything not bolted down. Yes, they report there are no Boers at all in the area, but still James Christie and his men approach as warily as they do wearily, creeping from rock to rock until they are right upon it, and . . .

And oh, dear God.

Here is the body of Captain Hunt just 20 paces from the verandah.

It is a body stripped of all possessions, all dignity – naked to the world, bare bar a pair of filthy socks.

'I examined the body,' Christie will recount, 'and found he had been shot through the heart from the front, and out below the right arm, as it were sideways when he had been crouching down.'[33]

It looks like he has died very quickly and the only other even slightly untoward thing he notices is a small bruise on his forehead.

Frank Eland's equally naked corpse is nearby, lying in a drain. Again, his body is examined closely, and it is clear that the bullet that killed him has gone from side to side through his lower stomach. No other wounds are apparent bar a tiny incision on the instep of one foot, likely caused by the flick of a knife cutting away his bootlaces while his body was being stripped by the Natives.

At least there is proof that perhaps they did not die in vain.

'On entering the house,' Silke recounts, 'we found Viljoen and another Boer stripped also.'[34] A pool of dried blood is found in another room.

The Natives have been very thorough indeed.

After the two dead Boers are hastily buried out the back, the Troopers commandeer a buggy and after Christie, Silke and the still-shaking Sergeant Robinson place the bodies of Captain Hunt and Sergeant Eland with some ceremony upon it, they all begin wearily heading back to Reuter's Mission.

They arrive to the sight of a woman in her mid-fifties standing, waiting for them, her head bowed, her hands clasped. She has grace, she has dignity, she can only just stay standing, so great is her grief.

It is Sarah, the mother of Frank Eland. While completely broken inside, still she keeps her composure as her son's body, his face and torso covered by a coat, is carried inside with Captain Hunt's corpse, where the ladies of the mission wash and dress the bodies. Troopers John Silke and Andrew Petrie, meanwhile, are assigned to make two coffins.

•

The wintry sunshine just manages to make it through the clouds but has nothing left to warm the veldt with as Morant and his men continue to ride down the narrow rough tracks. The land around is covered with boulders and prickly bush, and their eyes are now forever scanning back and forth for any signs of a Boer ambush.

But what's this?

They are still a long haul away – 20 miles out from Fort Edward – when they come across Lieutenant Picton with several Troopers escorting Boer prisoners. In the space of a few minutes Morant dispatches a couple of his Troopers to escort the prisoners back to Fort Edward while Lieutenant Picton and the rest of his men are added to his patrol. For what Morant has in mind, he needs as many men with rifles as possible.

And he is determined to get there as quickly as possible, come what may.

'We hurried on, and made a forced march,' George Witton will chronicle, 'off-saddling every four hours or so to give the horses a rest, and then on again.'[35]

•

At the mission, the coffins have received their final nails.

'We finished one in which the body of our sergeant was placed,' Silke sadly chronicles, 'and four bullocks were hooked into a buggy and his remains brought up to his own farm.'[36]

Sergeant Eland's coffin is across the front seat, as slowly, carefully, mournfully, as evening falls, they make their way the four miles towards *Ravenshill*, where Frank Eland's mother still lives. Sarah Eland is helped down from the wagon. She has been crying but now composes herself once more as dear Frank Eland's coffin is lowered and placed before her. Again, with great care, the top plank is prised loose so she may gaze down upon her beloved's blessed form, one last time. Taking the photo of Frank wife's Dora that she has with her, she kneels, kisses his cold forehead, and places the photo on his breast.

'My only son . . .' she says softly. 'You never gave your mother a moment's anxiety in your life. You were a good lad.'[37]

Now dressed in black, Mrs Sarah Eland accompanies them as they return to Reuter's Mission Station for the burial of Captain Hunt.

As the coffin of Captain Hunt is being lowered into the freshly dug grave, just behind the Reuter's Mission Station, the young girls of the mission – all newly converted to Christ – sing with fervour.

> *Soon we'll reach the silver river,*
> *Soon our pilgrimage will cease;*
> *Soon our happy hearts will quiver*
> *With the melody of peace.*[38]

Standing over the open grave, the Reverend Reuter conducts a service before Sergeant Oldham takes over once more, ordering a rifle salute – with a difference.

Because it is thought the enemy might be close, the Sergeant orders them to do a 'dumb salute',[39] mock firing without even a blank – the only sound to be the metal click of the hammer as it moves forward into the empty chamber.

'Saluting party . . .'

'Present . . .'

'Fire!'[40]

At this point there is the expectation of a unified click.

Instead there is the shattering roar of a rifle, and the Troopers instinctively duck and go for their pistols, sure they are being ambushed. Mercifully, they are mistaken, as it is not the opening shot from a crack group of Commandos, but a shot from one of their own.

Unthinkingly, one of the Troopers, by force of long repetition over many months . . . accidentally loaded a bullet into the rifle breech.

The subsequent shot practically puts a new part in the hair of Marie Reuter – meaning they are narrowly spared a perhaps even more tragic second funeral.

The scene is reminiscent of the poem by Charles Wolfe, 'The Burial of Sir John Moore after Corunna'.

> Not a drum was heard, not a funeral note,
> As his corse to the rampart we hurried;
> Not a soldier discharged his farewell shot
> O'er the grave where our hero we buried . . .
>
> Slowly and sadly we laid him down,
> From the field of his fame fresh and gory;
> We carved not a line, and we raised not a stone,
> But left him alone with his glory.

•

As night falls, Morant and his patrol are still some 40 miles away from Viljoen's house, where the tragedy took place, and finding themselves by a Native kraal – a small village, surrounded by a rough fence – Morant reluctantly orders a halt so the horses can rest and be fed and watered until such time as the moon rises and they can move off again. In the meantime, he dispatches one of his men, an Intelligence agent, to gather up an army of Natives to accompany them on the promise of a few British pence and the chance to raid a Boer house. (No need to tell them it has already been looted.)

At one o'clock in the morning, just as the waning moon rises, throwing a haunting and ghostly light, they move off once more. Alas, their German guide is now more flustered than ever as, not surprisingly, he continues to lose his way, which makes Lieutenant Morant more furious than previously – which is really saying something.

Things are at their worst when, convinced that the ford for a particular swim is right in front of them, because the guide tells them so, the men trot forth only to find themselves 'floundering about in a deep muddy bog'.[41]

Still they keep going, and the sun rises on them still struggling forth. By midday they have reached the Letaba Valley in the Modjadji mountains – a realm of the mythical and treacherous, an atmosphere that makes them feel like they've wandered into the faraway land of an adventure novel, or perhaps another book, with an even more ominous feel?

Yea, though I walk through the valley of the shadow of death . . .
Morant's men are uneasy as they go further into the valley.

They pass from path to path, every which way swamped in fecund foliage, battling nature with every step. It is beautiful, but it isn't easy. By four in the afternoon they spy Reuter's Mission Station in the distance, just as the sun begins to dip. The light radiates around them as it makes a warm silhouette of the three-storeyed Victorian house on the horizon. How out of place it is, like something torn from the fabric of a fashionable London street and sewn back in the heart of the Transvaal.

Yes, greeting them, at least the best they are able, are the survivors of Captain Hunt's patrol, who advise they have just buried their tragic Captain the day before.

First things first, Morant immediately goes to visit the grave to stand silently before it, with his head bowed, before abruptly turning on his heel. With jaw set and eyes blazing, he returns to the mission homestead where he fires questions at survivors, focusing on the state of Hunt's body when found and seizing upon any scrap of evidence that might indicate that Hunt and Eland had been mutilated – anything to take his fury to yet new levels. It is one thing for Captain Hunt to have been killed in battle. But for his body to be desecrated like this, disrespected, treated worse than a slaughtered pig? It is *inhuman*, and now he vows to the others, in a voice that will brook no opposition, that once they catch up with the Boers, 'I will give no quarter and take no prisoners.'[42]

James Christie, having lately been a member of Hunt's burial party, finds himself summoned by the newly installed Commanding Officer, Lieutenant Morant.

'He was holding audience with some sergeants about Captain Hunt's death, and as they had such long-winded reports to give in, and, after listening to a lot of twaddle, I begged to be excused.'[43]

Witton expands on the said twaddle being discussed.

'He had met with foul play . . . his neck had been broken, as his head was rolling limply in the cart when he was brought in. His face had been stamped upon with hob-nailed boots, his eyes gouged out, and his legs had been slashed with a knife . . .'[44]

Christie's blue eyes widen. He knows the truth. He has seen both corpses with his own eyes, and has no interest in disseminating lies. There is something very odd going on – and though Christie doesn't know it yet, it doesn't stop with spreading lies about mutilation.

Overcome with grief and rage at the sudden loss of the two men he was closest to in the unit, even as he takes over the first military command of his life, something inside the Breaker breaks, as he crosses a line and embarks on a path that heads only ever lower, starting with the usual complete fabrications. For while the men make preparations at Reuter's, Morant decides now is the time to *unburden* himself.

You all do realise that Captain Hunt was my most intimate friend in South Africa . . . we were at school together.

This is surprising, given the nine-year age gap between them, but no-one wants to query a grieving, angry man, and he goes on.

We travelled to England together last November, and while in Devon became engaged to two sisters. Fantasy overtakes reality, and the Breaker convinces himself as he speaks, building a bond that cries for vengeance.

To the men, it's a little odd, true, that they were engaged to *sisters* and it has never come up, but so be it. Again, in the face of real grief one's instinct is not to weigh up whether the grief-stricken is telling lies. But those lies are completely benign compared to what comes now, on the spot.

'I have direct orders from headquarters at Pretoria,' he tells George Witton, 'not to take prisoners.'[45]

Yes, if they find the Boers who have done this, then, even if they surrender, he intends to slaughter them.

With that in mind, Morant has already sent his Intelligence agents forth to make their inquiries among the Natives and settlers, and ideally send runners back. The first of those runners arrives at daybreak, breathless with the exertion and the news: the Boers who had been in a farmhouse at Devil's Kloof are now trekking north-west towards the Waterberg region. No matter that they have a day's start. Lieutenant Morant is insistent that the sooner his men start, the sooner they can catch the Boers. With his posse now grown to four dozen or so, he leaves behind a handful of soldiers to protect the mission station, and they head off.

Morant rides at the head of the column, 'gloomy and sullen, and eager to overtake the retreating enemy'.[46]

A hard day's riding ensues, as they drive their horses well beyond exhaustion, but manage to make fast progress. Just as the sun is setting, the scouts well up front of the column come back with the news: they have sighted the Boers!

Yes, the Boers have stopped for the night – 'laagered', as they set up camp in the middle of an encircling barricade of wagons – at the base of a chain of kopjes.

Beside himself with impatience, Morant wishes to attack immediately and gives his orders on the fly. Lieutenant Picton you take half-a-dozen men and come at them from the right flank. We will carefully move forward to make a direct attack.

Alas, even before Picton can get his men into position, Morant and his own forces have opened fire on the laager. From the top of the kopje, Witton arrives just in time to see the attack go in and looks down to see the Boers around the campfires reaching for their guns, and crying out, 'Allamachta! Allamachta!' 'God Almighty! God Almighty!'[47]

Below, there is a mad scramble of horses, and flying clods of dirt from thundering hooves as the Boers essay to make their escape. It seems likely that Lieutenant Morant has been too hasty in his attack, as all his men are not yet in position. By the time the Carbineers have rushed the laager it is to find that those who could flee have fled, abandoning their wagons, their wounded horses and men. Groaning underneath one wagon they find a badly bleeding Boer with a bullet through his heel. He is wearing parts of a British uniform. That is enough for the Breaker.

Grim-faced, implacable, Lieutenant Morant gives his order: 'Shoot him.'[48]

It is quite shocking.

The Boer presents no threat. He is unarmed and wounded. It takes convincing from the officers but, for the moment at least, Morant agrees not to have a summary execution. But it is not decency that persuades him to not engage in such drastic action so much as the point being made that 'the firing might attract the Boers'.

Respectfully, Lieutenant, it is more prudent to withdraw to a safe position for the night.

Reluctantly, Morant agrees and, taking the hobbling young Boer with them – he says his name is Floris Visser, and he is about 20 years old – they make their way to the top of a nearby kopje, set up a bivouac and post sentries against a surprise attack. No, of course they cannot sleep, but after taking such precautions at least they are fairly confident of making sunrise.

'The night was intensely cold,' Witton will recall, 'and we had had nothing to eat since leaving the mission station. We had travelled with stripped saddles to make it as light as possible for the horses.'[49]

Ideally, they will renew their pursuit on the morrow at first light but, as it happens, those first streaks of dawn bring with them a Native runner bearing an urgent message from Captain Taylor, ordering Morant to return immediately. There is only a skeleton crew left behind at Fort Edward and reports are coming in of a party of Boers in the area who just might be heading their way!

Very well then, they must abandon the chase.

Sure enough, after setting fire to the captured Boer wagons and gathering up the oxen to drive back to Fort Edward, the BVC are soon on their way, and make good progress until they stop in the late morning to slaughter a beast for lunch, which is where the opportunity presents itself.

No sooner does Witton arrive with the rearguard than Morant – smelling of stale alcohol, a little glazed in the eyes – approaches.

'This man,' he tells Witton pointing to Visser, 'has been concerned in the murder of Captain Hunt; he has been captured wearing a British uniform, and I have got orders direct from headquarters not to take prisoners, while only the other day Lord Kitchener sent out a proclamation to the effect that all Boers captured wearing khaki were to be summarily shot.'[50]

Witton, by his account, is appalled. It had been one thing for Morant to float the idea the previous evening when the heat of battle was still upon them. But now, in the cold light of day, he still wants to shoot a man in cold blood? He has only known Morant for a short period, a time that also spans how long he has been on the front lines of this frontier war. He wants no part of gunning down an unarmed man who has effectively already surrendered.[51]

'Leave me out of it,'[52] Witton says to Morant, with brave force under the circumstances.

As Witton looks on, he realises that Morant is more intoxicated with power than any man could be on hard drink. God help the man who stands between him and his vengeance.

But Breaker Morant will not have it, and glows even more red than usual. The officers are not to be given a choice about whether or not they wish to be left out of it. For the Breaker wants to convene a court right now, a drum-head court martial, with the judges to be himself and his fellow officers, as they ape on the battlefield a rough and ready stab at British justice, Morant having added a single word to the traditional 'justice is blind'.

Drunk.

No, not that he is rip-roaring gone at this minute. But his heavy drinking of the night before is certainly not helping now, as decisions, vows and wild oaths made in the wee hours have survived both the light of day and vague sobriety to be entirely intact. If it please the court – a small gaggle of goggle-eyed Lieutenants gathered at the behest of their Commanding Officer – M'Lud Breaker Morant, who has pulled a double shift today as Chief Prosecutor and President of the Court, if you prefer, now presents the sum total of his evidence.

This man, Visser, was found wearing a British uniform. I say we shoot him. Case closed.

With no time or capacity for the defence to make his own case, M'Lud Lieutenant Handcock does what he always does and agrees with the Breaker. Lieutenant Picton hesitates and then votes no, while Lieutenant Witton abstains – all of which is far from the unanimous verdict the Lord Breaker is seeking.

Morant's ruddy face is now flushed with fury at finding disgraceful dissent placed in the path of his righteous rage.

So that is how it is?

It is.

Well, it is a majority and that will do. Case closed. Verdict – Visser *will* be shot. Court martial over.

As robin-chats sing brightly in the near-distance, Morant turns on his heel and barks at Sergeant Major Clarke: 'Fall-in ten men for a firing party.'[53]

Clarke does not have his heart in following the order, and in any case, there is immediate resistance, not least from Lieutenant Picton, who is suddenly told he is to command the party that Clarke forms up.

The bloody cheek of Morant! How can he order the only officer and member of the court who voted *against* the shooting to now *conduct* the shooting? It is obviously Morant's way of telling him that, while he may try to wash his hands of this verdict, they will soon be coated in blood regardless.

As for the men, well, most of them feel like Witton.

They are fundamentally decent men, and shooting an unarmed prisoner outrages that very sense of decency. So strongly do they feel that before long Clarke takes Witton aside: 'Some of the men don't like this cold-blooded job. Will you speak to Morant?'[54]

Witton does as requested, but Morant is insistent.

'I have my orders,' he hisses at Witton. 'What I am doing I am perfectly justified in.'[55]

Both men are aware that a Rubicon of death is about to be crossed – shooting an unarmed man – but the key man simply doesn't care.

'You didn't know Captain Hunt,' Morant continues sharply, '[but] he was my best friend. If the men make any fuss, I will shoot the prisoner myself.'[56]

Witton stands his ground regardless, and scrambles away from the fray, hoping the effort it will need to assemble the men will take enough time for Morant to cool down.

After all, as his eyes drift to the man condemned to die, Witton is filled with pity. Visser sits alone in a cart, his back to the officers who are deciding his fate, completely oblivious of the decision. Even this infuriates Morant, who wants him more engaged before he is shot, an active participant, not this passive, pitiable figure. Why won't the bastard put up a *fight*? A strange thought occurs to the rough warrior poet.

Why not make the man write?

'Tell him to write a letter to his wife, or mother, or anyone he wishes,'[57] Morant orders. Still Visser shows little interest until he is informed that he is to die within minutes, at which point he does indeed start to put down on paper his love for his mother. (Sadly, though the letter will be completed, it will never be delivered – as it is nothing more than a dispensable prop in Morant's theatre of death and can be quickly discarded.)

Meanwhile, Morant is approached by Trooper James Christie who, unaware of the whole drum-head court martial, questions an order the Lieutenant has given to burn the Boers' Cape cart.

'Then what about the wounded man?'[58] Christie reminds his commander.

'They should have taken my advice last night and shot him.'[59]

Christie walks away, a little stunned, thinking this must be just more wild talk from the Breaker, which has been happening more and more since Captain Hunt was shot. But no, now Lieutenant Picton approaches him to say that he has been chosen to be a member of the firing party that is to shoot the Boer.

WHAT?

'The Boer has been tried by court martial and sentenced to death,'[60] Picton states plainly.

Sentenced to death?

'What for?' asks Christie pointedly.

'Oh, don't know, but I've warned you,'[61] replies the blushing Picton. (It will hardly do to tell Christie he entirely agrees with his reluctance and even admires it. Better to profess ignorance.)

Don't know? What in heaven's name is going on?

'Well I'm not going to do it,' Christie says flatly.

With a sigh, Picton carefully nods to the distant figures of Morant and Handcock, now in deep consultation, and says, *sotto voce*: 'They can make you a prisoner.'

'Then I'll go prisoner,' Christie says in a very loud, outraged voice, which attracts the attention of the others, 'but I'll not shoot a wounded man.'[62]

There is a rumbling of agreement from many others, while still more decide to make themselves scarce. They don't want to take on Morant, still less do they want to disobey a direct order. But what they want to do least of all is shoot an unarmed prisoner, and so they melt away.

Still Christie goes on with it, saying, 'If you are dead on for shooting, you should have followed up the Boers! Come what may, I will not make up one of the firing party.'[63]

As for the Breaker, he is making a final attempt to gather intelligence from the condemned man, in the brutal manner that Captain Taylor has taught him, and now instructs Trooper Botha to translate his words: 'You might tell me something about the Boers for as your doom is sealed anyhow you needn't tell any lies.'[64]

It is not much of a bargaining chip and while Visser's doom may be sealed so are his lips.

And so Morant tries again: 'If you tell the truth your life will be spared, if you tell lies you will be shot.'[65]

Botha translates and follows up with Morant's questions.

'How was Captain Hunt killed?'[66] asks Morant.

'He was killed in a fair fight, shot through the chest,'[67] replies Visser.

'His neck was broken?'[68] Morant asks and answers.

Visser vehemently denies it, furiously shaking his head in a manner that requires no translation. That is simply *not* the way it happened.

'What are the plans of the Boers?'[69] Morant asks.

'They do not intend to stay around here,' replies Visser, as Botha translates. 'They are trekking to the Woodbush to join Beyers' Commando.'[70]

There is little more to be said. Still, Taylor's Intelligence man, the Boer turncoat, Leonard Ledeboer, does feel obliged to tell Visser that, despite answering, he should *still* prepare himself to be shot, which prompts the alarmed and aggrieved Boer to have Ledeboer translate his remarks to Morant:

'You promised to spare my life if I answered truthfully!'[71]

'That was idle talk,' replies Morant, bemused. 'We are going to shoot you.'[72]

Tragically for Visser, and unaccustomed as he is, Breaker Morant is now telling him an absolute truth.

Still the rumbling about the shooting goes on, to the point that Lieutenant Picton half *pleads* for volunteers: 'It is no crime to shoot him as he is outlawed!'[73]

An ugly impasse threatens when Sergeant Major George Clarke comes up to Christie and says, 'It's all right, we have got another man. You will not be asked to do it.'[74]

Even now, however, Christie is not placated. It is not just that he does not want to do the shooting himself, he *does not want it done*. Christie has support in his loud outrage, with Sergeant Euston Wardell Wilson – who had himself been a prisoner of the Boers and well treated – being particularly vocal against it, his role as a Non-Commissioned Officer notwithstanding.

It is all getting so out of hand that Lieutenant Handcock roars in support of Lieutenant Morant, 'If you're so chicken hearted I'll shoot him myself.'[75]

Morant proves so ferocious on the subject – almost as if Visser is not the only one who will be shot – that the Sergeant Major has no choice but to push the men to co-operate and, bit by bit, a few do indeed come forward, with one remarking it was a chance 'to get a bit of our own back'.[76]

Botha has been told to take part, but is very unhappy about it.

'I know him good,' he tells Christie. 'I went to school with him. I don't like to do it, but they will shoot me if I don't.'[77]

But now what?

With the Breaker's encouragement, the Natives form a circle around Visser and begin some kind of dance of death, whooping, chanting, stomping in rhythm, as the terrified Boer looks back at them, all as the men of the BVC watch uneasily. Whatever is happening is primal, primitive, brutal, and so far removed from justice it is blood-curdling. Only Morant and Handcock seem to enjoy it as they are observed, 'looking on approvingly'.[78] So pleased is the Breaker that he arranges a gift and 'Two oxen were killed for the Kaffirs to celebrate the occasions.'[79]

It is too much for many Troopers watching.

'There was a lot of discontent among the men,' Trooper Muir Churton would recall, 'who let the officers see that they were intently disgusted at the whole proceedings.'[80]

So much so that when Lieutenant Picton approaches Churton to join the firing party he, too, refuses 'point blank',[81] with such vehemence that ·it attracts the attention of the always menacing Lieutenant Handcock, who comes over.

What is the trouble?

A lot of the Troopers don't want to shoot the prisoner.

Handcock is appalled, and says so to those who are refusing.

'You can go to hell,' he barks, 'and I will do it myself!'[82]

James Christie considers his position. Obviously, short of drawing his own gun, he cannot stop this now. Perhaps he should walk away from the whole thing, spare himself the horror of this cold-blooded murder, for that is what it is.

No. On reflection Christie decides to try and comfort Visser the best he can, and then stand *witness* to the horror.

'I deliberately walked over to the cart wherein the youth sat,' he will recount, 'intending to muster up what Dutch courage he had and to speak to him.'[83]

In response, the lad takes from his pocket and writes another note that he asks be given to his family. Beyond that, though?

'A slight twitching of the face,' Christie chronicles, 'was all the concern he displayed.'[84]

But now it is time.

Upon Lieutenant Picton's reluctant command, some of the young African men put a blanket beneath Visser and carry him in the direction of the firing party that has now formed up, placing him with his back turned to them some 20 yards in front. Visser is facing a small river, and he watches the water flow as the men behind him line up.

As they do so, Lieutenant Morant addresses the firing party telling them they must not forget that this was a man being held in part responsible for the death of Captain Hunt. He then moves off and says to James Christie, watching grimly nearby, 'Christie, I know it's hard lines for him, but it's got to be done.'

It's more than hard lines frankly – it's a death sentence. But this is just how Breaker Morant is, always the grown-up schoolboy, repeating the adolescent argot and calling the other lads by their last names. It's as though he is stuck back in school perpetually pretending to be a Prefect in a Sixth Form he never actually attended. *Hard lines?* This is murder, Morant.

'See how the Boers knocked Captain Hunt about,' he leads.

But Christie won't have it.

'Captain Hunt,' he said, 'died a soldier's death. He was killed in a fair go, and beyond being stripped there was no maltreatment of him; and anyhow the Kaffirs might have stripped him.'

'No,' Morant insists, 'Captain Hunt's tunic and trousers had been found in the Cape cart.'

'But, the boy was not wearing them.'

Morant hardens at this confronting fact being presented, and makes clear the conversation is over.

'Anyhow, it's got to be done. It's unfortunate he should be the first to suffer.'[85]

'It is not right to shoot him,' Christie persists.

Enough. Morant turns on his heel, and nods to Lieutenant Picton to get on with it.

There is a deadly pause, before Lieutenant Picton barks his first command.

'Firing party, ready.'

The soldiers raise their rifles.

'Aim!'

They bring the butts of their rifles to their shoulders, and peer down the sights – many of them praying that the rifle they bear is loaded with a blank, as they have been promised that five of their rifles are.[86]

Now the Boer utters not a word, but simply clasps his hands to the heavens above. *Here, vat my hand* . . . Lord, take me . . .

'*Fire!*'

The volley of shots echoes around the valley and, Visser, with angry red splotches all over his shirt, falls back – oddly – *towards* his executioners.

Perhaps, with the last bit of life-force in him, Visser wants to be as confronting as possible to his executioners? Because his body, bloody as it is, still twitches. All eyes of the Troopers now go to Lieutenant Picton, the highly reluctant commander of this whole disgrace, who now grimly steps forward with his revolver in hand.

He's not, is he?

He is.

Slowly, purposefully Picton walks towards the writhing Boer, praying that the man's body will go still and silent before he reaches him.

But no.

Oh, God.

'The idea of blowing the brains out of a corpse,' Trooper Churton will recount, 'so turned my stomach that I could not look.'[87]

But the others do and see Picton slowly lower his arm, point the muzzle of the gun at Visser's shaking head and . . . and . . .

And what is this nonsense?

Tiring of it all, Lieutenant Handcock steps forward, snatches the revolver from Picton's hesitating hand and, without any further ceremony, as Trooper Sidney Staton will note, fires the pistol, 'blowing out Visser's brains'.[88]

Breaker Morant watches on implacably. The Rubicon is crossed. An unarmed prisoner has been shot on a trumped-up charge, after a trumped-up court martial.

In outraged protest, on the spot, Christie tears off his BVC badge, and openly curses what has happened. And he is not the only one outraged.

'Shooting an innocent man that cannot [even] stand to take his death,' Trooper Frank Hall will note, 'awakes big feelings in most hearts, and more than one lanky Australian swore with a gulp that justice should peep into this.'[89]

Witton hears the shots in the distance and winces. It is a very distasteful affair, which he will struggle to rationalise, managing only to note: 'War is calculated to make men's natures both callous and vengeful, and when civilised rules and customs are departed from on one side, reprisals are sure to follow on the other, and the shocking side of warfare in the shape of guerrilla tactics is then seen. At such a time it is not fair to judge the participants by the hard and fast rules of citizen life or the strict moral codes of peace.'[90]

There are many who still cannot believe what they have just seen, and still more who wish to see the corpse itself. Trooper Sidney Staton is one who wishes to bear witness. And yet when he moves forward to survey the body, his way is blocked by Lieutenant Picton, who says quite primly, for all the world as if the murdered man were a fairground ride and Staton has not paid his fare: 'As *you* would not help to shoot him *you* cannot go to see him.'[91]

CHAPTER THIRTEEN

MURDERS MOST FOUL

The first principle of war is that armed forces, so long as they resist, may be destroyed by all legitimate means. The right of killing an armed man exists only so long as he resists; as soon as he submits he is entitled to be treated as a prisoner of war.[1]

Manual of Military Law, 1899

11 August 1901, Fort Edward, clothes maketh the man

The sentry at Fort Edward picks pieces of biltong from his teeth and gums as his eyes turn lazily to the returning patrol.

Who is that in the lead? One could almost swear it is Captain Hunt. But look closer. Why it is Lieutenant Breaker Morant, riding at the front of his men, but he is cloaked in ... Captain Hunt's old uniform!

As outrageously ghoulish as it might seem, it is true – Morant himself is now wearing the very jacket taken from Captain Hunt that was found in the Cape cart. Certainly, it is no crime for Morant to do so in the way it was for any enemy combatant to do so, but still. It is more than passing strange, jarring, discordant, but in the current dangerous mood abroad among this troop, most particularly at the top level, it is not something on which anyone dares comment. Right now, Morant is a man to keep clear of, to avert your eyes from, to avoid conversation with. Don't draw attention to yourself and you might be all right. He seems a man possessed by a strange and savage mourning that is growing *by the day*, rather than diminishing.

Now Morant must file his report of their activities to Major Lenehan, and chooses a cheery and conversational tone.

> My Dear Major,
>
> A runner goes to Pietersburg this morning, so just a hasty note, as I happen to be in camp. You know how cut up we must have been over poor Hunt's death. I'll never get such a good pal as he proved to be. I wish to the Lord that I'd been out with him that night – he might have got wiped out all the same – but the

damned Dutchmen who did it would never have left the house. ~~We've killed 13 of them up to date now, and that crowd haven't~~ a blanket left to wrap themselves in. It was a damned hard job to write to Hunt's girl, which same I did after we returned. Poor old Hunt! God rest his soul! But he 'died decent'. I've lost my best mate, and you've lost your best officer.

By God, there must have been some wastrels there that night when poor old Hunt went under. I suppose Mortimer has told you that his body was stripped, neck broken, etc, etc, by the Boers.

I fancy you've heard some fairy tales to the detriment of Taylor! You must remember the source they come from. Hunt got on with him famously right from the first, and I, Handcock, and the rest of us couldn't wish for a better fellow to work with. We work ourselves, men and horses damned hard, but Taylor lends us every assistance, and his 'intelligence' is the most reliable I've struck in South Africa. Handcock you know! And I find him worth the other two in himself . . .

By the way, if there are any scattered things of Hunt's about Pietersburg camp, will you look after them personally? Poor old chap – he left his ponies and all his gear to me . . . If you could only come up here for a week, I think it would do a power of good in many ways, and I hope, if you do come up, you will not be dissatisfied with our work.

Good-bye Major!
Yours obediently,
HARRY H. MORANT[2]

Good old Breaker! Chin still up despite his 'best pal' Captain Hunt being murdered and mutilated. This is not quite the way some, Trooper Christie for instance, recall things, but like all of Breaker's tales it will grow in the telling. And grow. Until one could get the idea that the Breaker and Hunt had been bosom friends from youth instead of rather recent acquaintances. As for Captain Hunt's body – the way that corpse was mutilated, Breaker could barely arrange the pieces in the grave he dug all by himself. As ever, reality and fantasy mix with Morant; a dull truth becomes a sparkling lie, until the facts drown under his relentless rhetoric. Strangely, they never hear him speak of Frank Eland, his young friend who also died. The Breaker has an eye to the story that will sell, the fable that fascinates, and so the fallen commander, his bloodied body beaten by bastard Boers, takes centre stage. Sergeant Frank Eland retreats to the wings of Morant's subconscious; never to be mentioned by Morant again. Why, Morant does not even meet his mother or write to his widow! A strange fellow, the Breaker, he prefers to live in the tragedy of his own stories rather than face any pain that might be all too real. *Farewell, Frank.*

•

In Pretoria, in the face of this extraordinary ongoing resistance by the Boers – despite the blockhouses, the concentration camps, the destruction of their farmhouses, the network of spies and roving bands of irregular troops hunting them down – General Lord Kitchener decides to up the ante one more notch, sending out emissaries with a grim warning for the enemy Generals.

General Christiaan de Wet is on a farm at Blijdschap, between Harrismith and Bethlehem, when he receives Lord Kitchener's latest proclamation:

> All Commandants, Veldtcornets and leaders of armed bands – being burghers of the late Republics – still resisting His Majesty's forces in the Orange River Colony and the Transvaal, or in any part of His Majesty's South African possessions, and all members of the Government of the late Orange Free State and of the late South African Republic, shall, unless they surrender before the 15th September of this year, be banished forever from South Africa;[3]

President Martinus Steyn of the Orange Free State, who is travelling with de Wet and his army, is a little more lyrical in his rejection of the proclamation, which he has also received:

> Now, as regards the Proclamation itself, I can give your Excellency the assurance as far as I am myself concerned, that it will make no difference to my fulfilling my duty faithfully to the end, for I shall be guided by my conscience and not by the enemy. Our country is ruined; our hearths and homes are wrecked; our cattle are looted, or killed by the thousand; our women and children are made prisoners, insulted, and carried away by the troops and armed Kaffirs; and many hundreds have already given their lives for the freedom of their fatherland. Can we now – when it is merely a question of banishment – shrink from our duty?

Yes, he would be happy to meet with Kitchener to discuss peace.

But in order that I may not mislead your Excellency, I have to say that no peace will be accepted by us which imperils the independence of the two Republics . . .

In the meantime, make no mistake, they will fight on and with no apology.

If it is a crime to fight in one's self-defence, and if such a crime is to be punished, then I am of opinion that His Majesty's Government should be satisfied with the annihilation of the country, the misery of women and children and the general desolation which this war has already caused.

M.T. STEYN,
State-President of the Orange Free State.[4]

In the meantime, one of those taken to the concentration camps at this very time is none other than the mother of General de la Rey, Adriana Wilhelmina de la Rey.

'She is 84 years old,' one of the sorrowful British soldiers notes in his diary. 'I gave her some milk, jam, soup, etc. as she cannot eat hard tack and they have nothing else. We do not treat them as we ought to.'[5]

•

Unlikely as it seems, Boers in the vicinity of Fort Edward keep surrendering.

'We went N.E. about some 50 miles and captured the Boers,' Trooper McInnes records on 16 August, 'who had a wagon and cart and a lot of cattle. Sending these in with a small escort . . . the next morning 20 of us set out and made another haul of seven wagons, with ox and donkey teams, a lot of cattle, rifles, ammunition, and 14 Boers . . . when these were on their way to the fort, a dozen of us made up our minds to go after a notorious character named Klopper . . . We dropped on them about daylight and surprised them, catching them without a single shot, and got them safely to fort . . .'[6]

For a unit whose orders, by Morant's account, are to take no prisoners, they are remarkably inconsistent.

19 August 1901, Fort Edward, Taylor's tempest

To the likes of Captain Alfred Taylor, Morant is more than merely useful. He is not just a tool, he is a *machine* – wind him up and send him off, and he just keeps going, harvesting all Boers before him. For Taylor to work his malicious manoeuvres he needs pliable officers who understand the thrust of his words unspoken, his raised eyebrow at the right moment, his *indications* of what must be done without necessarily needing a written command.

Captain Hunt had been useful in this regard, so inexperienced was he in leading a squadron of mounted infantry that he constantly relied on Taylor's guidance.

But Morant?

He is perfect. A capable enough leader of men, with no problems with making money on the side, he also now has such a white-hot grievance against Boers that Taylor can mould him into a missile to be fired wherever he wills.

Which means the information that the rider coming their way on this morning will deliver is of more than usual interest.

For it is Trooper Petrie advising that eight Boer prisoners are being brought in. Ledeboer – one of Captain Taylor's key Intelligence men – is currently with them. Very well, then.

Captain Taylor goes to Breaker Morant, and the two begin to hatch a plan. It will require a strong stomach, as we must deal with deception and overcome one of the hallmarks of weaker men – a debilitating sense of morality. But Taylor and Morant are as one on this. They have no such weakness and agree: *Very well, if it is to be done, 'tis well it were done quickly.*

And it must be done.

'Sergeant Wrench, go out and meet them,'[7] Morant orders sharply. You will be accompanied by six Troopers, including the Dutch turnabout, Trooper van der Westhuizen. Get going.

Before their departure, Morant offers a joke.

'If you bring the Boers in as prisoners you will have to find them food out of your own rations and *I* will give none!'[8]

Well, *maybe* it is a joke.

The Boers are two days' ride out. Sergeant Wrench is to find them and escort them back to Fort Edward. *I will meet you on your way back in.*

Shortly thereafter, 20 men upsaddle – throw their saddles on to their horses' backs and secure them – and head out on patrol under Lieutenant Hannam, with their destination . . . a secret. Yes, it has come to this. So paranoid is the whole BVC, so convinced are the 'Intelligence' Johnnies that informants, spies and Dutch Double Agents – perhaps even Double-Dutch Agents – are everywhere that not even its own Troopers are told where they are going until such time as they are well clear of Fort Edward. All they are told is it is to be a 'three weeks patrol: no one could tell where, no kits, ride light'.[9]

Lieutenant Hannam waits until they are within eight miles of their own fort before informing the men: 'we found we were going to hold the post at Reuter's Mission Station'.[10]

The Reverend Reuter has been threatened by the Boers before, they've warned him that they won't tolerate his harbouring of British soldiers. They've assured him of a house in flames and a fiery end if he keeps it up. But to a man of God, what is the heat of a burning home to the terrible inferno that waits for those who are not pious in their time on this earth? He is not afraid. The Boers will not deter him.

19 August 1901, Potgietersrus, Daniel into the lion's den

The worry lines on Captain Frederick de Bertodano's rather noble visage are on this day etched deeper than ever. Having been called to the British garrison of this regional outpost to see a sick Australian, John Craig – a clerk in the British Army Intelligence Office – he now realises just how sick his patient is. For Craig, as is readily apparent by his horribly swollen neck, is 'suffering from goitre'.[11] It is now urgent that he be transported to Elim Hospital, some 110 miles away, as soon as possible.

'The difficulty is to get you there,'[12] he tells Craig. After all, getting a sick British officer safely across territory swarming with Boer Commandos is no small thing.

'I can let you have a Cape cart,' a voice with a Germanic accent says, 'a pair of mules and a driver.'[13]

De Bertodano turns to see a beloved local identity, the Reverend Daniel Heese, who has himself come to visit the sick Craig this morning and now follows up: 'May I offer to accompany him? He is not in a fit state to be left to a native driver only.'[14]

De Bertodano hesitates. The bearded Heese, a gentle and considerate man of God, is, he knows, one of the fellows from the Berlin Mission who have come to this Godforsaken land to give the locals a little God, for all the good that will do. A little over 30 years old and married to the fine Johanna, he is based in Makaanspoort, some 15 miles south-west of Pietersburg, and is one of the few members of this entire community who is trusted by Boers, English and Natives alike for the fact that he has only ever worked for the welfare of all, regardless of race, religion or regiment.

De Bertodano considers. Few people would be a better chance of getting the young Australian to desperately needed medical help than the Reverend Heese, as the Boers – deeply religious themselves – would never hurt a man of God.

And so yes, Reverend Heese, I accept your offer.

While the Native helpers strap in two fresh mules, one on either side of the pole at the front of the two-wheeled four-seater carriage, de Bertodano and Heese just manage to get the groaning Craig into the carriage and as comfortable as possible, before the Reverend Heese offers a hand of farewell.

A grateful de Bertodano takes the brave Heese's hand and shakes it warmly.

Godspeed, padre. It is men such as you who can restore one's faith in *humanity*, let alone the good Lord.

Heese and the Native driver depart, bearing the groaning John Craig.

19 August 1901, outside Fort Edward, thank you, Mr Ledeboer, we will take it from here

For the most part, Sergeant Wrench and his Troopers look over the eight shambling Boers who have just been handed to their care with something even approaching sympathy. For they look like what they are: defeated men who have given up on their country, their cause and their dignity. There is still, however, just enough left in them to look back at one of Wrench's men with disdain. Yes, they can still glare at Trooper van der Westhuizen, a turncoat Boer now fighting with the British.

Yes, we are defeated, but at least we fought to the end for our own side, at least we never betrayed our country, our family.

And van der Westhuizen indeed struggles to meet their gaze. For he knows some of these men, by last name at least.

Is that Voedkom? Yes, that's him. My God, here is De Press, looking at him like a piece of shit on his shoe. And there is Carl Smit, surely? Yes, it is, the very burgher he used to know when he had a nice farm just out of Pietersburg. Not anymore, of course. God and the British know what remains of it now.

Ledeboer also notes the presence of Smit and sneers. Their last interaction, before the war had taken hold, had been a shouting match over Smit claiming that Ledeboer's father-in-law owed him a lot of money. Well, look at him now.

Ledeboer turns away and chats merrily to Sergeant Wrench. Eight Boers! Quite a bag. And beyond this fresh slew of prisoners they have also got a wagon with a span of donkeys, together with a fine herd of cattle. But the best of all?

Sergeant Wrench is as stunned to see 'they had in the wagon a sack of valuable specimens of gold and each had money'.[15]

They begin the slow trek back towards Fort Edward, all the while awaiting the appearance of Lieutenant Morant.

23 August 1901, Elim Hospital, dust to dust

A sensitive, emotional man is the Reverend Daniel Heese. A man of God with an enormous spiritual life, it is part of his calling to have empathy for all living creatures, and his tears are frequent.

On this occasion, however, he tries to hold himself back, to regain control, to gather himself, despite the fact he is standing over a dead body. In fact, he is taking pause. After 24 hours, his mad mission of mercy has ... failed. The ailing Australian, John Craig, had been such a very brave man, never complaining in his rare moments of lucidity, and even finding the strength to thank the missionary for his unstinting efforts to save him. But nothing had worked.

Craig had died within two hours of arrival at Elim Hospital and now lies before the Reverend Heese, merely the earthly remains of a spirit that is now hopefully with the Good Lord in *Himmel* above.

In any case the Reverend is now anxious to be off. For one thing it will be his beloved daughter Hilda's first birthday in just three days' time, and he has just enough time to get back home. But as his wife, Johanna, is heavily pregnant with their second child, it is important that he gets back to her as quickly as possible anyway.

And with that, Heese's driver arrives with his wagon and Dr Liengme bids farewell to the Reverend as he climbs aboard.

Godspeed to you!

23 August 1901, Fort Edward, the rule of Rule 303

Lieutenant Morant soon makes his way to George Witton to tell him he is required to accompany him on a patrol to go and meet Sergeant Wrench and the prisoners.

Yes, sir. Witton agrees and upsaddles to soon be heading out from Fort Edward in the company of Lieutenants Morant and Handcock and Sergeant Major Ernest Hammett, together with two Troopers.

First, however, Morant must briefly stop at Captain Taylor's office, while the others wait outside. Quite what is discussed is not clear, but not long after he emerges and they are on their way, Lieutenant Morant calls George Witton forward to ride alongside him and Sergeant Major

Hammett for a short time and divulges the news: 'I intend to have the prisoners shot.'[16]

Both Sergeant Major Hammett and Witton are shocked, and try to talk him out of it.

The Breaker takes umbrage.

'I am quite justified in shooting the Boers,' he says stiffly. 'I have my orders. I will rely upon you to obey me.'[17]

'I have *my* orders?' Strange words from a commander who should give orders! Oh yes, those orders clearly come from Taylor, who has no military authority over Morant and the BVC at all, but in this place at this time that is a mere technicality if it is even raised at all. Morant is in command for the first time and Taylor is the old hand, with vast experience in murderous manipulation.

For now, George Witton ventures a question of his own.

'Harry, how can you have prisoners brought in and shot . . . so close to the fort?'[18] he finishes lamely.

Morant looks at him with a malicious, thin-lipped smile.

'It is a matter of indifference,' says he, '*where* they are shot.'

Precisely as had happened after Hunt and Eland had been killed, Morant, overcome with impulses that he seems incapable of reining in, had no sooner consulted with Captain Taylor than the BVC had been awash in the blood of surrendered Boers.

But while killing Visser – amidst the pursuit, battle and capture – had been one thing, this is quite another.

Witton still does not think the Breaker means it; but one thing gives him pause – Morant's lack of obvious emotion. He is as fixed, cold and certain as a freshly inserted bullet.

Witton feels an entirely different kind of chill. It is the freezing fear that *alea iacta est*, the die is cast, and that surrendered soldiers are about to be shot. For Morant now looks capable of anything as he snaps the reins, drives his heels into his horse's flanks and takes off at breathtaking pace – Morant's impulses and the horse are now clearly as one, galloping forth with no restraint.

The Breaker rides swiftly under the South African sun today, and George Witton strains to keep pace.

Just six miles from the fort they see them.

There are eight Boers and a matching set of BVC captors. Instantly in charge, Morant relieves Wrench; the bedraggled prisoners – thin, sad, exhausted, beaten – are sharply ordered to stay tightly together and trek on to the fort. Morant speaks quickly to Ledeboer, and in a moment he is riding off along with Trooper Schwartz in one direction, while a confused Sergeant Wrench is sent . . . in the *very same direction*? He has been instructed to patrol slowly but surely, keeping his eye out for Boers. Pardon? For Boers? For just *any Boer*?

Yes indeed, Sergeant Wrench, and go with him, van der Westhuizen, for 'a large number of Boers are close at hand'[19] says the Breaker. One is no different from another.

It seems that their instructions are but a distraction, a task for the sake of a task, and Wrench and van der Westhuizen roll their eyes. They cannot shake the feeling.

This isn't right . . .

'Go about a mile ahead,'[20] says Morant impatiently, seeing their scepticism and adding another odd instruction: 'If you hear shots in front of you, gallop back to the wagon.'[21]

Yes, sir, we'll scout for the Boers, at once, sir, thank you, sir. The Troopers ride off into the distance, eagerly awaiting the moment they are out of sight. Having gone far enough, they slow to a trot, and soon they simply 'ride leisurely'.[22]

After passing the Mission Hospital without pause, Morant and the remaining men are just three miles from the fort when Morant stops the wagon and calls the Boer prisoners off the road, ordering them to line up side by side in front of him. They reluctantly do so, sensing danger, and find themselves confronted by this suddenly angry officer, flanked by his armed Troopers.

Morant barks questions at them that sound more like accusations.

Where are your other men?

How many of you are out today?

Where can we find Commandant Tom Kelly?

What were you planning to raid today?

The prisoners give one or two desultory answers, to at least be seeming to co-operate, but offer nothing of any value. In any case it does not seem as if this officer truly wants information, as he is asking them collectively – the least likely manner in which one of them would betray their Boer comrades. No, he has some other intent. They just don't know what it is yet – though their widening eyes, darting every which way, are some indication that they suspect it is not good. Why have they been pulled off the road like this? Why are these questions all being put to them so suddenly, with no real interest in the answers?

Schoolmaster William Daniel Varmeyer is particularly worried.

He does not like the way this is turning. There is a coldness to their captors, an aversion of their glances, almost like they don't dare look at them, almost like they wish to have no human connection with them whatsoever, perhaps because . . .

Because they intend to do something entirely inhuman?

But surely not. These men are not savages, and by and large the Boers have treated their own prisoners well. Surely these men from Australia, a civilised country, could not be intending to commit an atrocity and . . .

And suddenly, a familiar figure hoves into view on the horizon. It is his friend, the Reverend Daniel Heese, with his 'boy' driving.

It is a relief to see a familiar face.

For his part, Reverend Heese is confused and no little alarmed by what he sees. On the one hand there is a flock of BVC soldiers lying down in the grass, with their gaze averted from him, while just beside them a group of Boers are standing.

Something is . . . amiss.

Ordering his driver to pull up, Heese climbs down and greets the man among the Boers he knows best, the local schoolmaster, Varmeyer, whose wife is a very good friend of his own wife, Johanna.

Varmeyer speaks frantically, if quietly.

'Daniel,' he whispers, 'I and the other prisoners are very uneasy as to our ultimate fate, although we have surrendered voluntarily.'[23]

Well, what is to worry about then? They are not fighting – they have surrendered.

'Nothing can happen to you,' Heese says comfortingly. The same might not be said for Reverend Heese himself as he looks up to see an enraged Breaker Morant approaching. What the HELL is he doing, talking to prisoners? Yes, he is a padre, and not even a Boer, but in the Breaker's view padres are more often than not Boer sympathisers and he will not have it.

Stop speaking to these prisoners! As a matter of fact:

'Get up into the wagon and consider yourself also a prisoner!'[24] roars Morant.

'No,' replies Heese stoutly. The Lieutenant is furious that he, a Reverend, spoke to the prisoners? It is all so very odd, so very disquieting. And why are Morant's soldiers still all lying around, almost like they are waiting for him to be on his way, knowing nothing will happen while he is here?

His bluff called, his bluster blocked, the Breaker reverts to calm and charm.

My apologies, Reverend. These days one can't be too careful. Go ahead, padre, but please be careful and watch out for the blasted Boers. We have these surrendered Boers, certainly, but their cunning comrades might be just up ahead, lying in wait and ready to attack.

Somewhat perplexed, the Reverend and his driver continue on their way.

•

With the Reverend Heese now departed, the road is empty, the coast is clear and the time is right to blot out some Boers. The order is given by Breaker Morant. A firing party must be formed.

All in favour? Not quite, for Morant is informed that three Troopers are having second thoughts about this order. Troopers Thompson, Duckett and Lucas. Morant paces in front of the three men now, staring at them, daring them to speak. Then the Breaker speaks, in full flight, overflowing with a swell of verse and vengeance.

'Were you friends of the late Frank Eland? Did you know the late Captain Hunt?'[25]

Yes, they did.

Very well. The Breaker continues to these tentative Troopers: 'Have you seen Lord Kitchener's proclamation to the effect that "those who take up the sword shall perish by the sword"? The Lord has delivered eight Boers into *our* hands and *we* are going to shoot them!'

'I . . .' Trooper Lucas begins to object, but Morant finishes for him. '*I* have *orders* and must obey them, and *you* are making a mistake if you think *you* are going to run the show.'[26]

The Troopers are silent; mutely obedient now.

Lieutenant Morant turns his attention back to their eight Boer prisoners, who stand, watching him ever more warily.

Three shots are heard in the distance. Morant does not even turn in their direction. He has clearly been waiting for these very shots.

'Have you any more information to give?' Morant asks with a curious finality, as his men stiffen at the pre-arranged signal.

For when the prisoners shake their heads, no, no further information, Morant suddenly steps back, his place taken by a soldier with a rifle being brought to bear, just as all the soldiers are bringing their rifles to their shoulders, and . . .

Why are the soldiers opposite them lined up, almost like a . . . *oh, dear God, no, it couldn't be could it* . . . firing party? They're not really going to SHOOT us . . . ?

Morant gives the signal.

'That's for Captain Hunt.'[27]

The volley of shots thunders out, and seven of the Boers go down. One, however, is only wounded and dashes straight at the man who shot him, George Witton. Bleeding, roaring, the Boer – 'a big, powerful Dutchman'[28] by the name of Carl Smit – grabs the end of the rifle 'with the intention of taking it and shooting me, but I simplified matters by pulling the trigger and shooting him'.[29, 30]

For another instant all is a volley of shots, and screams, but when the last echo has rolled away – including a couple of pistol shots from Lieutenant Handcock to extinguish the last signs of life – the eight Boer prisoners lie dead, grotesque in their shattered bodies and agonised grimaces.[31]

Witton, the sole actual combatant among a field of executioners, stares at the corpse he has just created, the dead eyes somehow managing to stare accusingly. But Trooper Ledeboer is quick to offer a reassuring word. He had known the dead fellow well, and his death is nothing to trouble yourself over. Why, in recent times, Ledeboer's own father-in-law had been harassed by this fellow over a debt. Well, now, no more.

'He was a most notorious scoundrel!' exclaims Ledeboer. 'He had previously threatened to shoot me, and was the head of a band of marauders!'[32]

•

Sergeant Wrench and Trooper van der Westhuizen, who have been sent on a faux fool's errand by Morant, are puzzled. They do indeed hear three shots coming from the Bristows' place at Sweetwaters Farm, and ride *towards* it, when suddenly a volley of shots – well over a dozen – ring out in the distance *behind them*. *What the hell is going on?* They can see a distant figure at Sweetwaters Farm, is this the villain who fired at them?

Now, Lieutenant Morant had specifically ordered Sergeant Wrench to ride back if he heard any shots, and they have heard many. But again, unwilling to play a part in a play he didn't write, Wrench takes van der Westhuizen with him and they do not ride back, they ride *on*. Wrench wants to know *who* that figure is at Sweetwaters Farm.

Good Lord. As they get closer, they can see an agitated man pacing back and forth in 'an excited manner',[33] and it is . . . *Captain Alfred Taylor*, now staring at them in astonishment!

'Sergeant Wrench, did you hear any shots?'[34] asks Taylor, as if he hadn't just fired some himself.

Trooper van der Westhuizen is most surprised by the answer his companion gives.

'No,'[35] replies and lies Wrench simply.

No? Captain Taylor is also surprised, as it is obvious that Wrench is mad, deaf or . . . devilishly clever, in which case he is very dangerous.

'All right,' says Taylor softly, through narrowed eyes. 'Go on to the fort and off saddle.'[36]

And so the duo departs, towards Fort Edward, Wrench feeling the eyes of Taylor boring into him from behind. Just what that bevy of bullets – a burst of three, followed by a flurry of fifteen – had been all about, Wrench is still not sure. But he would put his left nut on the fact that Captain Taylor not only knows, but was right behind it – just as he is behind everything that happens in this man's army. The weight of the day presses. There is evil in the air. Is it time to keep your head down, or to lift it, and speak up? To take arms against a sea of troubles, or simply row away? For some minutes both Sergeant Wrench and Trooper van der Westhuizen are quiet, until the latter comes out with it, asking his Sergeant *why* he lied to Taylor about hearing the shots?

'For private reasons,' Wrench rasps in reply. 'I did not know what Captain Taylor would do if I said I *had* heard them!'[37]

Something is going on here, and it is dangerous. Wrench is still not sure just what it is. But at least he feels certain where the danger is coming from – Captain Taylor.

•

The grin of the ghoul creeps across Morant's face. He is positively gleeful as he looks at the fallen before him, the limp frames and still chests with gaping bloody holes.

All that counts is that the Boers are indeed dead. They have been shot on his orders, and he makes no apology for it. Not now, not ever. If necessary, he will give the same orders again, and he expects them to be obeyed without question, just as he obeys orders.

Don't you know these bastard Boers are the same bastard Boers who mutilated Hunt and then murdered him?

Quietly – very quietly under the circumstances – George Witton thinks this is most unlikely but Lieutenant Handcock blithely agrees with Morant. No doubt about it, cobber. They *were* the same Boers that so ruthlessly mutilated Captain Hunt and Frank Eland before killing them like wounded dogs. And these bloody Boers will at least get the benefit of a decent burial – once the Native scouts finish digging a grave – and will neither be mutilated nor left out for the bloody blacks to scavenge over like the Boers did for our fellows. They should count themselves lucky to have been killed so cleanly!

Witton's reply comes only inadvertently, in his facial expression, but it is enough for Morant to sharply order him to depart; to take some of the men and Boer belongings back to Fort Edward with the wagon.

Thompson, Duckett and Lucas stand, stunned, dumbstruck by the gravity of what has happened. This isn't a mission, it's mass *murder*. But Morant has a sharp eye out for precisely the kind of debilitating sense of morality he can see signs of now. Wasting no time in setting them straight, he marches up to them with a simmering fury that makes his red face glow redder still as he spits it out.

'I would advise you men to play into my hands,' he menaces, 'or else you know what to expect.'[38]

Yes, they now do. With no other words being needed, Morant turns on his heel and stalks back to the scene of the bloody carnage, where Handcock is now overseeing the burial of the Boer bodies.

Resolutely, Morant makes his way back to Fort Edward. No sooner has he removed the saddle from his horse than he spies a vehicle in the distance . . .

But now what?

A cart being drawn by a pair of mules is approaching, rumbling forth at a fair clip and bearing . . . who?

Breaker Morant looks closer.

Christ! It is Reverend Heese, with an aghast look on his face. What does he know? What has he perhaps heard on the 'bush telegraph'?

What might he tell others?

Instantly, Morant leaps onto his horse bareback and with practised ease – his back ramrod straight, his legs so tight on the nag it knows the Breaker is in charge – gallops to cut off the missionary, who he is fast considering to be a troublesome loose thread in this otherwise tightly woven scenario.

Once overtaken, the Reverend hastily presents his pass to Morant for perusal.

'I am in possession of a pass allowing me to travel freely.'[39]

Oh, I see. Signed by *Captain Taylor*?

Why, yes.

Very well then, Reverend.

We wish you well. The best thing is to tie this white cloth to your cart so that it will be clear that you are a neutral, non-hostile party, a non-combatant – to make sure you are readily identifiable to any distant observer.

Relieved that there will be no trouble after all, the Reverend and his driver depart, the man of God still unsure why the Lieutenant with the red hue had such a thin-lipped smile as he farewelled them. Something does not feel quite right . . .

For his part, Morant simply stays there, stock-still, carefully watching the path taken by the missionary, before turning away and riding back. A pity the Reverend had seen what he had seen. Still, so be it. This is a war, not suited for gentlemen of faith, and it is all very well for them to be shocked by it. But the men of the BVC have been charged with winning this war, one way or another. Those who go beyond the strict rules of warfare, mostly made by those who have never heard a shot fired in anger, can seek contrition from the men of faith when it is over. At least from those who are still around.

•

Morant wastes no time in heading to Taylor's quarters at Sweetwaters Farm, to tell him of what has happened.

Usually unflappable, Taylor's face turns to thunder as it sinks in. He knows Heese to be that most dangerous of men – courageous and righteous in equal measure – and there is a real chance he might soon be on his way to the authorities in Pietersburg. This is a threat to them all. And he need say no more. Morant is instantly on his way, looking for Handcock, who he finds in the horse lines.

'Upsaddle your horse,'[40] he orders, before leaning in close to whisper for a short time.

'Are you game to follow the missionary . . . ?'[41] he continues.

Finally he stops, at which point Handcock climbs on his horse and, within earshot of Trooper van der Westhuizen, Morant calls out, 'Mr Handcock, do your best.'

'All right,' Handcock replies grimly, 'I know what to do.'[42]

Corporal Herbert Sharp watches the unfolding scene closely. This has been the most extraordinary morning, starting with the eight Boers being gunned down by the side of a road. But what now? Morant is happy to execute eight prisoners in the public light of day, but now has something so secret he must whisper it to Handcock? What on earth must *that* be about?

Whatever it is, Handcock is quick to get his rifle and ride off, a lone horseman with a gun, in the direction Heese took. But no, now that he looks even more closely – always advisable, when it comes to an armed Handcock – he can see that the Lieutenant is taking a slightly different road to the missionary . . .

•

For Silas Sono, a Native youth in his late teens, it is just another late morning in his native land. The sun is shining brightly, the birds are singing, and after running an errand he is now on his way back down the track to his home at the Kreuzburg Mission Station, near Fort Klipdan. As the sun climbs to near its peak, he is just singing softly to himself, looking forward to walking through the outpost of Mailaskop just a few miles up ahead when he hears the familiar rattle of a cart approaching from behind.

Ah, it is a Cape cart, a slim carriage pulled by a couple of mules, and as it passes he recognises the Reverend Heese, his head buried in a book, which is very likely the Bible. Silas nods to his driver, who he also knows a little, and it is only when the carriage, with a white rag tied on the back, is about to disappear over yonder hill that a thought occurs: 'I could after all ask whether *Mynheer* would permit me to sit with him on his wagon in order to get home more quickly.'[43]

If he is quick, he just might be able to catch him and . . .

And what now?

There is another traveller coming from behind. This is slightly surprising because the road is usually empty. Two travellers in the space of as many minutes! Silas steps off the road as the grim-faced lone rider on a panting bay horse, with a rifle slung across his back, gallops by.

'He wore khaki clothing such as the soldiers wear, a light-coloured hat with a cloth of motley colours, red, blue, white and black, and had stripes . . . He was a young, stocky man, his face was shaved except for the moustache that he wore. He wore two cartridge-belts crossways over his shoulders and his breast pockets were filled with cartridges.'[44]

Silas waves at the rider and yells a greeting, but there is no reply at all, not even an acknowledging nod. This looks to be a man on a mission, and his grim countenance suggests it is not necessarily a good one.

Still Silas runs on, until he reaches the top of the rise, affording a panoramic view all the way to the next rise.

And there they are, down in the hollow! He can see Reverend Heese riding on in the distance – the whole scene taking place on the road about six miles west of Sweetwaters Farm – and, strangely, notes the fresh tracks of the horse which just passed him, and the fresh footprints of its rider!

Odd. Very odd. But with just a glance Silas can see from the tracks how the rider had dismounted to lead the horse off into the bush – strange behaviour from someone who had been in such a hurry.

And now a shot in the distance.

Good. Perhaps the Reverend has spied some game, and must stop to gather it in after shooting it?

BANG! BANG! BANG!

There are four shots in all, encouraging Silas to run even faster, for the Reverend surely must have hit something, meaning he can certainly catch them now and . . . now something really strange.

For, as he gets closer, he sees the cart off to the side of the road, poking out from the top of thick grass, empty, with not even any mules in sight. But wait, look closer, there is *one* animal remaining, but it is not one of the Reverend's mules.

Rather, it is the bay, the horse of the mysterious lone rider, the soldier in khaki. The horse stands alone, with no rider . . .

Walking warily through the long grass, unsure what he will find but for some reason afraid – suddenly the day weighs heavily – Silas makes his way through the grass towards the Cape cart. About 50 yards away, the lone horse stays eerily still 'bridled and saddled, with the reins lying on it'. But there is no sign of the rider, nor of the Reverend Heese, nor his driver. His mules? Silas tries to stay calm 'but the inkling rose up in me that the shots, the empty wagon and the saddled horse had to have a sinister connection; and fear crept into my soul'.[45]

Still, bravely, he presses forward, his eyes flicking from side to side, his ears straining for a sound, a clue. Alas, what he finds right beside the buggy neither stirs, nor makes a sound. It is a fresh corpse, missing the top of its head, as a bullet has clearly been fired point-blank into the forehead, almost certainly with a dum-dum bullet designed to expand on contact.

'I recognised his face and recognised his clothing I had seen him at Elim and seen him near Mailaskop when the spider [wagon] drove past – it was Mr. Heese's driver.'

And now silence vanishes along with caution and Silas finds himself screaming to the veldt: 'WHAT IS THAT? HERE A PERSON HAS BEEN MURDERED! WHO MURDERED HIM?'[46]

Hands trembling, teeth gritted, Silas stills himself just long enough to perform a most unpleasant task.

'I laid my hand on the body and felt that it was quite warm.'

Which explains *one* of the shots he had heard.

What of the other three?

What in *God's name* just happened? And for that matter, where is the Reverend, where is the one man who could make sense of what the fates have visited on them?

The questions whirl and swirl in Silas' brain with one result:

'Such a terror came over me that I could think of nothing else than to run home and report.'[47]

And run he does, more swiftly than ever before, running all the way to Kreuzburg Mission Station with fear making him fleet of foot as never before. And he would have run even faster, if not for the fact that he was regularly looking back over his shoulder, praying not to see a lone horseman coming after him – for yes, he has no doubt that was the man who shot the driver.

Run! Murder is stalking the Transvaal today, *run*, Silas, *RUN!*

•

Over and over, the same dream. Men are about to be shot down in cold blood. One of them, the bravest of the lot, charges at him, and he, George Witton – the fifth son of David and Rebecca Witton, from Longwarry, Gippsland – pulls the trigger of his .303 *for the second time*, only to see that brave man fall back with a bloody hole in his chest. He is dead, dead, DEAD! And he, George Witton, is the one who *killed* him.

Always he wakes with a start, hoping it is all just a bad dream, only to realise the crushing truth – it really has happened, and he really has shot down a brave man in cold blood. It has come to this.

Roused by a Native servant for lunch, he eats alone and miserable. Oddly, but in keeping with the eerie feel in the air, the fort seems strangely deserted of dining companions today. Still, as evening falls, both Breaker Morant and Peter Handcock return separately before dining together in a rather loud manner, watched by the miserable men under their command. For everyone knows it. A line has been crossed today. Shooting Visser after a drum-head court martial had been one thing. But gunning down *eight* surrendered prisoners is quite another.

And yes, of course, Morant had assured them that these were the same Boers who had killed Captain Hunt and so it was only rough justice, but nothing can change the fact – they had been shot in cold blood and that chill is now with all of the BVC and will not be dissipated no matter how much bloody Morant forces his laughter, storytelling and poetry. And now that they have crossed that line, what the hell comes next? What new atrocity will this fiend try to force them into?

August 1901, Fort Edward, a stitch in time

Fast falls the eventide.

Typically, at this time when in camp, Lieutenant Morant is lying on his bunk in his tent, sipping rum and jotting down things in the notebook on his lap, while Lieutenant Handcock smokes on his own cot just across from him, staring vacantly at the canvas above. (Sometimes Handcock lies and thinks, mostly he just lies. The Breaker just lies naturally.)

If there is a difference on this evening it is that the Breaker is neither penning some verse, nor dropping notes to journalists in Australia to keep his name alive. No, this time he is actually writing a request for a *real* court martial!

And he is ready now.

A few minutes later, while in his own quarters, Sergeant James Wrench is deep in a game of whist with his mates when the Corporal appears.

Lieutenant Morant wants to see you in his quarters right now.

There is something in the way the Corporal says it, the glint in his eyes, which brings to mind that wretched sing-song playground taunt, 'You're in TRUB-ull!'

Well, we'll see. Wrench heads off to Morant's tent, a little like the kid called to the headmaster's office – while still determined not to kow-tow to the brute – only to be hailed on approach by the still recumbent commander.

'Wrench, you've made a fool of yourself.'

What?

Morant holds up the paper he is writing on.

'This is the letter reporting you. It will very likely mean a court martial for you.'[48]

Oh, really? YOU are reporting *me*? *Court martial? For what?*

Well, it concerns those Boer prisoners that you were supposed to be guarding. Morant gravely shakes his head as he points out Wrench's sad deficiencies, for all the world as if he is personally well known for insisting that prisoners have their rights, and all those who do not recognise those rights will answer to him personally.

Wrench reddens. This is beyond outrageous. Everyone in the BVC knows that Morant shot those prisoners down like dogs, and yet now he wants to court-martial Wrench for not guarding them properly while on their way to be murdered by him. The sheer, shameless and galloping *gall* of the man!

'Don't let us beat about the bush,' says Morant with such a thin-lipped smile it fits perfectly with the distinct and menacing edge in his voice. For let's get to the matter at hand shall we, Wrench, you cur?

'From what I can see of it, there are several men here who don't agree with this shooting.'[49]

Well Morant doesn't care, and follows up hard, his red face now glowing, glowering, even more than usual.

'I want *you* to go round to the men and find out those who are willing to [shoot Boers like this] and those who are not, and then we will soon *get rid* of those who don't agree. I had orders to weed out the Fort, which you know I did, but I still find there are a lot of sentimental [soldiers] left.'[50]

Sorry, what? 'Sentimental?' If it's sentimental to frown on murder, then you can pass Wrench a violin and some handkerchiefs.

One who is not remotely sentimental is Lieutenant Handcock, who simply glares menacingly at Wrench as Morant continues.

'I have had several letters of congratulation from headquarters over the last fight, and now I've started I mean to go on with it,'[51] Morant says.

A *fight*, you say? Didn't our mothers tell us it takes two to start a fight? Where was the fight in the eight Boers? They had given up. They had surrendered, however much you no doubt wrote it up as a 'skirmish'. Still, the point of what Morant is implying is that HQ are not only in the know on this, they are encouraging him to go further, and to do away with softies like, well, like Wrench. But now Morant seems to soften himself, and perhaps even give Wrench another chance.

'From what I can see of it,' the Lieutenant says, 'you had a rotten lot of men, but we will give you another chance. I shall send out a small patrol in a few days; I shall pick my own men this time, and send you with them.'[52]

But now think on it, Wrench. Am I softening, or am I sending you out in the Spelonken, alone with my hand-picked killers? Will they perhaps put you to the test, giving you some murders to do, and if you don't do them, leave you somewhere in a shallow grave? You will have to prove yourself to them, or . . . die.

Wrench's own blood runs cold as he is lectured to by this cold-blooded killer who commands him.

'I'll find the men who are agreeable,' Morant finally finishes, 'and the men who are . . . not.'[53]

Do you follow, Sergeant Wrench? Are you 'agreeable'? What shall it be? Would you like to apologise and fully co-operate? Or, will I try to work out whether to continue with your court martial, or . . . send you out on Handcock's left flank?

'If I could get only ten men,' Handcock breaks in darkly, 'that would be sufficient for my purpose.'[54]

No doubt. Wrench is dismissed by Morant and walks off in something of a daze.

•

Let us see now . . .

This is all a tad difficult. In Major Lenehan's life to date, there has been nothing to besmirch his good name. But these rather unsavoury allegations that have been made about his friend Lieutenant Morant? Having the men shoot down in cold blood an unarmed prisoner? If proven, it is not just Morant's reputation which will be damaged. It will be also that of the entire BVC *and* their Commanding Officer. Him, Major Robert Lenehan! This is something that must be quickly nipped in the bud and he comes to the reluctant conclusion that to do so he must venture north to Sweetwaters Farm itself. At least he has the solemn words of both Lieutenant Morant and Captain Taylor that it is all nonsense, and that is something.

CHAPTER FOURTEEN

TROUBLE BUILDS

If I were not an eyewitness to the sickening scenes of plunder and incendiarism committed by our troops I should decline to believe them capable of such atrocities. And yet these Boers have not injured an English subject in the Transvaal. In England and Australia one only hears a garbled ... account of the war. They see their country in ruins, their fields and crops destroyed, their cattle driven away by the enemy, and the flames from their burning houses rising sky high. I have known instances in which our troopers did not leave in a house one morsel of bread for the women and children. Is it any wonder that among a people so independent a spirit of hatred consumes them?[1]

Father Francis Timoney, Catholic Chaplain
with the NSW Citizens' Bushmen

27 August 1901, Sweetwaters Farm, who has rid us of this turbulent priest?

George Witton sits, transfixed, hanging on every word coming from Captain Taylor as the Intelligence man presides over the latest of his weekly meetings for his officers. Huddled around Taylor, they pore over myriad maps and plan their patrols, the likely targets, estimating how many they will get in their bag, while working out how to cut off the Boers' most likely avenues of retreat and respite. Taylor is the fat spider at the centre of this great dark web, using each titbit of information from one of his Intelligence operatives as a delicious morsel to bring the Breaker ever deeper, bound to trust him totally, to do exactly what he says. And the Breaker is completely caught in turn. Usually so loquacious, so garrulous, he is silent in the presence of Taylor, struck mute by his calculation and cunning. For Witton, watching it closely, Taylor is terrifying in his feverish focus, speaking softly and so bending Morant to his will that it is like watching a knife-thrower readying his superbly sharpened blade. Taylor knows it will go wherever he wishes, flying through the air to slice and dice today's target, whenever Taylor decides to release the Breaker with a quick, sharp flick of his wrist.

Witton cannot help but feel that, for all the dangers from the Boers who surround them, the most lethal threat to the men of the BVC lurks here, among them. The Breaker and Taylor are more than rough men. They are *ruthless* men, men who would not think twice before cutting a throat to steal a purse. But even as Witton falls ever deeper into this web of thought, he is brought to by a knock at the door.

It is the owner of Sweetwaters Farm, Charlie Bristow, reporting a rumour abroad that a missionary has been murdered by the track at Bandolier Kopjes – a couple of hours ride from Fort Edward, and perhaps the most isolated and dangerous spot on the way to Pietersburg. He had been missing for nearly a week, and they have now apparently found him.

The reaction of both Captain Taylor and Lieutenant Morant is surprisingly muted, but at least George Witton is quick to volunteer: 'I will take out a patrol and investigate?'[2]

Taylor and Morant agree, on the strict proviso set by Lieutenant Morant that Witton and the half-dozen men he will go with do not go as far as Bandolier Kopjes – restricting themselves instead to stopping at a farmhouse just five miles from Fort Edward to make inquiries. It is curious. Patrols of half-a-dozen frequently go as far as 30 miles from the fort, but suddenly they must stop within five miles?

Alas, the patrol finds nothing and Witton is soon reporting that Taylor and Morant say: 'In my opinion it is only a Kaffir yarn.'[3]

Two days later, however, Lieutenant Handcock is sent out to Bandolier Kopjes with a strong patrol to make a further search, and – wouldn't you know it? – discovers some distance off the road the bodies of the missionary and the driver by their buggy, the mules nearby.

Handcock reports to Morant, with regret, it looks very much as if the two men had been murdered. The missionary had been shot 'through his left hand and left breast',[4] the driver in the back of the head, and both had fallen from the buggy, which was found jammed between some trees, with the pole broken. The mules, still bound to each other, were grazing nearby. Clearly these poor innocent men had been shot while fleeing the bloody Boers. And one a man of God too!

Are there no limits to what these bastards will do? And to think we were only talking to him such a short time ago. Only to be murdered by Boers. Another sad case closed by the BVC.

Though not all in the corps have come to the same conclusion. Not that you would dare speak a word of your suspicions around the Lieutenants

Handcock and Morant. For the moment at least, it is time to keep your head down, or risk having it shot off.

•

In his HQ in Pretoria, Captain de Bertodano is aghast.

He has just been informed by a wire from Major Lenehan of the BVC that a predicant – a German missionary by the name of Heese – 'has been shot by Boers'.[5]

This is unthinkable. This is madness. This is . . . *evil*.

Why would the Boers shoot a German missionary, who was practically one of them? What did they have to gain by it? Clearly, nothing. The good Captain does not believe it for an instant and is overcome with an enormous sense of guilt, as it feels like he was the one who sent Heese to his death. He should have realised the danger, should have realised that, with Captain Taylor in the BVC command structure, there was always a danger of this occurring.

Yes, of course he had heard rumours about BVC prisoners going missing, only to turn up . . . *dead*. But not for a minute did he think this would happen to a priest! And that had been his mistake, he knows now. Put Taylor in any pond and the risk is that it will be poisoned. But when the pond is so far removed from other authority? It is practically guaranteed. That is why he had been quick to warn HQ about Taylor, but that is no excuse. Taylor had still been there, and de Bertodano had sent an innocent man, a man of God, right into his clutches!

Furious, de Bertodano remarks to his colleague, Major George Milne, 'The Ball has commenced!'[6]

Oh yes, Taylor's dance of death – with the Grim Reaper on the fiddle and the Devil on drums – is underway. Only God knows when it will cease.

From the first moment he hears the news of the murder of Reverend Heese, Captain de Bertodano is intent on getting to the bottom of it, and briefs two of his best Native scouts, Hans and Kaffirland, whom he has already closely worked with on matters of intelligence since near the beginning of the war.

Hans is a cautious and reserved lad, an image of innocence that belies his uncanny canniness when it comes to actual intelligence gathering. He lies so well he probably learnt as soon as he could talk. He is ever alert, and remembers everything, the perfect spy. And then there is Kaffirland, a bold 'boy' with a bravado that can steer any conversation in the direction he chooses. There is a confidence to him that Hans lacks, a bravery that, for Kaffirland, may be as much a liability as an asset.

For in de Bertodano's experience, a confident spy is a doomed one, an agent who will one day bite off more than he can chew. But, for now, they are promising young agents who he can trust, and he will never say no to another set of eyes and ears.

Here are your orders.

'I want you to go up to Fort Edward, approaching from the east or south-east, anywhere except from Pietersburg and arrive at the native [camps] about dusk. Leave your horses some distance away so you don't look like scouts and get all the information possible from the BVC boys. The most important thing: on *no* account remain longer than a couple of hours and under *no* circumstances stay the night.'[7]

De Bertodano is under no illusions about just what will be their fate if it gets out just what his scouts are up to.

•

Cochrane! Have you heard? Have you seen it? *Proof!* Headquarters have *approved* the shooting of Boer prisoners!

What?

Trooper Robert Cochrane has been among the loudest whisperers who have accused Lieutenant Morant of making up orders, well, he must feel a bloody fool now. For here is the written proof! A letter from Colonel Hall himself.

Cochrane, a bloke who has been around the block a time or two, cannot believe it. A *public* letter? Well, not quite. A private letter that has been stolen. For, well, you know how careless Morant is with documents and such, and how nosy certain Troopers can be; well, just now one of the Troopers spied and pried this letter from the scraps that surround Morant's camp bed; and it is a letter worth reading!

For while it is a missive with a massive reprimanding of the Breaker, concerning the eight Boers who were shot, the problem Hall has is not the shooting, it is that *he wants the Breaker to make up a better lie!*

Have a look, Cochrane.

The Trooper does exactly that, grabbing the proffered letter, and sees with a sinking heart that it is true.

> This report will not do. How could disarmed men assume the offensive. Send something more probable . . . Hall.[8]

After all, Boers with no guns can hardly be a threat enough to justify executing them. Just like Major Lenehan, it seems that Colonel Hall wants a story that has a better chance of passing muster, not this risible nonsense.

Cochrane gasps, just to read it. Could it possibly get any worse? Decidedly, yes. For as Cochrane reads on, he sees another purported cause of Colonel Hall's annoyance – *the Colonel is not getting his cut of the loot!* Yes, according to the letter, 'profits of the cattle thefts were participated in at headquarters'.[9]

Cochrane can scarcely make sense of it. It can't be . . . can it? There's only one explanation, it must be. The letter . . . was *meant* to be stolen, that's why Morant *forged it* to begin with!

It is no less than the perfect excuse, an attempt to forge a ticket to freedom.

Lieutenant George Witton, on the other hand, is now surer than ever that HQ is right behind Morant.

'This [letter] tended to convince me,' he will note, 'that the orders and the interpretation of the orders regarding prisoners as transmitted to me by Lieutenant Morant were authentic, and that such proceedings were not only permitted, but were approved of by the headquarters authorities.'[10]

And besides that, Witton knows about the whole racket going on whereby enormous numbers of Boer cattle have been, well, *encouraged* onto Captain Taylor's land. Of course, it makes sense that Colonel Hall would be in on it too. That explains everything!

So, there you have it, on Kitchener's orders, Boer Commandos are to be shot, while Boer cattle are to be commandeered, by order of the brass who would like to make some brass themselves before this war is soon over.

Quickly, the two competing views spread around camp. The wide view is that *the fix is in. HQ is onside.* Morant is in control, his actions sanctioned if not sanctified. The smaller view is that of the doubters, led by Cochrane, left to whisper and wonder; who can they trust?

For most the answer is not clear – but the safest way to proceed really is to obey every order given.

After all, they all know about the penalty for mutiny, and that means for many that if you are told by an officer to cold-bloodedly kill a prisoner, you had better say, 'Yes, sir,' or the best you could hope for would be a spell in military prison.

'Many men,' Cochrane will recount, 'believed that they would have no support at headquarters in refusing, and could have been sent to the Breakwater for two or three years penal servitude for mutiny.'[11]

But enough discussion for now. You must put that letter back where you found it, before the Breaker knows it's gone!

Cochrane watches the carry-on with a strange cross between bemusement and disgust. For he is certain that the Breaker not only knows the letter is gone, but actively wants it circulated as much as possible – as pleased as ever that yet one more of his preposterous fictions has been taken for Gospel Truth. Why, the Devil himself would be hard pressed to lie better than Harry Morant!

'Who was the author of this forgery I cannot say,' Cochrane will later recount. 'The presumption is that if the idea did not originate with Lieutenant Morant, the endorsement was written by him, as Lieutenant Handcock could not write or spell the simplest sentence without disclosing his authorship.'[12]

For yes, Lieutenant Handcock is only as educated as a mid-sized rock, but the Breaker, well there is a smart fellow indeed who uses his pen to profit himself in war and peace.

How far the conspiracy goes Trooper Cochrane is not sure – he will tell King Edward if he has to – but *somebody* must still care that British soldiers have become murdering mercenaries in the BVC.

Early days, but Cochrane resolves to watch, learn, chronicle and then inform. He just has to work out who he can inform, and who amongst the BVC will back him up. Having Christie and Browne with him is a very good start.

Late August 1901, Fort Edward, injury time

Sergeant James Wrench must be careful these days. He must stick like shit to an army blanket to his solid BVC friends who he can trust, and avoid Breaker Morant and Peter Handcock like two plagues. Never, under any circumstances, can he be alone with them because he is under no illusions – his life will be in danger.

After all, given that there has been no more talk of his 'court martial' it can only mean that they have likely come up with another option – and it will probably be a swift and bloody one and . . .

And God help us all.

Here is Lieutenant Morant, after just receiving fresh 'intelligence' from Captain Taylor. Some more Boers are on their way in, about a day's ride out on the Transvaal veldt, and they need an escort. And, of course, he is as unsurprised as he is disgusted to hear from Morant that he is 'to go out with the object of shooting them'.[13]

That is, if there *are* any Boers.

Wrench is already wary but then some friendly fellow BVC men quietly warn him that he is not imagining a danger.

'Several men warned me if I went out on that patrol my life would probably be attempted,'[14] he notes.

Orders are orders, however, and he cannot directly disobey one. And so, even as Morant watches him closely, Sergeant Wrench upsaddles and heads out on a patrol filled with a bevy of the Breaker's hand-picked men – none of whom appears to be in a chatty mood right now. But wouldn't you know it? Only a short distance from Fort Edward, Wrench suddenly falls from his horse while on a brief canter.

And he has badly hurt his back in the fall. Blast it! *Alas*, he can no longer go on patrol and instead must slowly trudge his way back to camp. Riding would hurt his back too much, don't you see? Look at the way poor Wrench must limp along, trying as he might to walk upright. It was such an unfortunate fall, you know?

(In fact, as he will later recount, 'I threw myself off my horse purposely.'[15])

With his rifle at the ready, always on the lookout for anyone coming for him from any direction, Wrench sends his horse and servant on ahead, to tell Captain Taylor what has happened.

And here is a rider now!

Wrench grips his rifle tightly, his finger on the trigger, ready for trouble but – oh the relief – it proves to be his own servant, returning with a furious message from Captain Taylor: 'It is imperative that you are to go at all costs.'[16]

Well, not at the cost of his life. Taylor's message 'confirmed my suspicions that my life would have been none too safe on that patrol'.[17]

And Wrench would have loved to, really.

But now his injury becomes even worse. Why, his back is giving him such agony, he can barely walk at all! He sends the servant back to Captain Taylor with the bad news and with his abject apologies. In the meantime, Wrench leaves the open track to sit under a tree, which guards his back while he surveys all before him, still with his rifle at the ready. He will take his time getting back to Fort Edward and get there by a different path – to send more apologies to Captain Taylor, but this time surrounded by Troopers that he trusts. He has the feeling this terrible twist in his back will trouble him for some time.

•

Today's orders from Taylor are simple. There are some wagons of Boers coming in to surrender. Send a patrol to intercept them. And then you know what to do.

Of course, Morant is not foolish enough to give such direct orders himself, at least not to men he is not sure he can trust yet.

So the job falls to a pliable Corporal who, in this early evening, approaches a group of soldiers to propose a mission that must be . . . spoken of discreetly. The right sort of chaps are needed to do a job, to do with some surrendering Boers.

Yes, so?

Trooper Christie and a few other idle Troopers lean in close to hear the Corporal's hushed tones as he explains: 'Eight of you are to go out and bring in three wagons with four men with them, and some women and children.'[18]

Is that all? More pointless 'patrolling', as this is called, in fact merely escorting a beaten people to a concentration camp?

'Leave them alone,' Christie says on behalf of them all, 'they are trekking up this way out of fever country, and will come in.'

After all, not only is the duty tedious but if the Boers have the fever – the dreaded typhoid, which seems to be running rampant among the starving Boers at the moment – then the Troopers will catch it! Why go out with an armed escort to bring them in when they are coming in of their own accord?

'No,' the Corporal replies, '*we* are to go out. None are to be brought in.'

'What do you mean?' asks Christie, somewhere between bemused and confused.

'Oh,' says the Corporal casually, 'we've got to blot the lot out.'

Blot the lot out? What? There is a stunned rumbling, before one outraged Trooper asks the obvious.

'What! Shoot *kids*?'

You cannot be serious!

'Yes, of course,' answers the Corporal, matter-of-factly.

'Whose orders are those?' asks Christie.

'Never mind, that's orders,' responds the Corporal.

Are you having a lend?

'I am telling you, seriously, that such is the case,' the Corporal says, his expression hard enough to crack granite, immediately returned in kind by the looks of the BVC Troopers. It is James Christie who speaks for them all now as he steps forward, menacingly, and looks the Corporal in the eye.

'What sort of men do you take us for?' Christie asks with a softness that belies his own hardness; the question soon backed by the dangerous rumbling of the Troopers behind him.

Still the Corporal stands his ground. The orders are to *Blot the lot*, do you get that? These are *orders*.

And now the rumbling is so strong, the Corporal finally gets it and backs off, offering just one thing which, Christie incredulously notes, seems to be put forth as an inducement to listen to him.

'If you bring the Boers in you shall have to feed them,' the Corporal says menacingly. Yes, kill women and children or feed them? It is not quite the dilemma the Corporal imagines. Trooper Christie's choice is made immediately.

'I am for no such duty,' he says in a manner which conveys this discussion is closed.

The Corporal shrugs, the plight of the innocent clearly not weighing as heavily on him as it does Christie.

'I can get plenty more,' he says and shortly rides off.[19]

Plenty more? Who would do such a thing? And who would have been behind that order in the first place? Who could seriously *propose*, let alone actually *do* such a thing?

Good *God*. You don't have to tell Trooper Christie what dead children look like. Every night when he closes his eyes, he sees his own – after they'd been burned alive.

It was a tragedy he will never overcome, a horror that will haunt him to his final days.

And now, in the very place he had come to get away from all that, he has been ordered to murder children?

It is so deeply shocking that James Christie can barely credit it. How did it come to this? The murder of a child is reserved for the great villains of novels or the theatre, the likes of a Moriarty or a Macbeth – it is inconceivable that it should be planned in real life. At least not by British troops. It is madness. Appalling madness. And it is for good reason the men are uneasy on this night. Somewhere out there, in the darkness, a Corporal is riding, looking for others to join his darkness. Orders are orders, he said. *I can get plenty more.*

5 September 1901, five miles from Modjadji, suffer the little children to come unto me

In the late afternoon, Lieutenant Charles Hannam, a notably well-heeled chap from Queensland – with no less than 'gentleman' as his profession on his enlistment papers – gathers his men to him.

Listen here. Three wagons with Boers aboard will be coming down this road within the hour. You, Troopers Hampton and Gibbald, will stick with me and my two armed Native 'boys' to the right *of the road. And you, Corporal Ashton, Troopers Hatfield and Maynard, must conceal yourselves on the* left, *along with ten Natives, with your .303s loaded and safety catches off.*

You will all await my signal shot, and on that shot just keep firing into them and . . .

And now they hear it!

It is the unmistakable creak and clunk of wagon wheels coming down the rutted track. In their secreted spots, the soldiers grip their rifles tightly, their knuckles white and pale, their trigger fingers curled and ready. And there they are, in the distance! A couple of Boers are walking along just in front of the covered wagons. It is impossible to tell how many Boers are concealed within, and just what arms they bear. But now Trooper Hampton – a decent family man from London – hears something that deeply disturbs him. And no, it is not gunfire, nor the menacing *click-click* of a rifle being cocked.

No, it is something far more alarming than that. For it is *laughter* . . . there it is again! . . . The laughter of *children*! And now listen, as those laughs are backed by the melodic sounds of women talking gaily . . .

Good God, there are women and children in those wagons, so don'–

BANG![20]

The shattering crack of Lieutenant Hannam's rifle to Hampton's right is the very signal the others have been waiting for and now nearly all the rifles of the BVC ring out, their fusillade of bullets bursting through the evening air to smash into the wagons and Boers alike. And now Trooper Hatfield, firing on the other side of the road, hears something too – a remarkably high-pitched screaming. A woman? Yes!

For God's sake, Ashton, that is a woman!

Corporal Ashton doesn't care. It might or might not be. All he knows is what he yells back, even as he reloads to keep on firing: 'My orders are to keep on firing until I get the order to stop!'[21]

Ah, but now Ashton hears another, most welcome yell: '*Ons ge orr!* We surrender!'[22] He ceases firing and runs to Lieutenant Hannam to tell him.

More cries now, more loud male voices: 'We surrender! We surrender!'[23] On the right side of the road, Trooper Hampton looks over expectantly at Lieutenant Hannam, only to be astonished to see his Commanding Officer still firing. The Dutch have fired no shots at all. Hannam's own servant leaps up now and calls out: '*De Dootcheman* say they surrender, sir!'[24]

Lieutenant Hannam takes no notice.

'Gibbald, Hampton, keep firing!'[25] he orders his disbelieving men. Corporal Ashton charges towards Hannam, thinking he could not have heard him the first time about there being women and children in the wagons, but he is dismissed before a word leaves his mouth. *Keep firing!* Trooper Hampton's disgust grows, he will recount, as 'the women and children were shrieking all the time'.[26]

Hampton's response? 'I fired every shot deliberately wide of the wagon ... as I could not bear to fire on women and children.'[27]

Ashton returns to tell Trooper Hatfield the order: 'Continue firing'.[28] Trooper Hatfield, disgusted, aims his rifle at the sky and pulls the trigger, squeezing off a single shot. Order fulfilled. Ashton understands, and issues no reprimand. Both men now wait, neither firing for a full five minutes. Finally, all the shooting dies away and Lieutenant Hannam gives his next order. *Close in on the wagons.*

Slowly, carefully, the BVC Troopers arise from their ditches and approach the wagons, fearful of what they will find ... There proves to be just one groaning and wounded Boer still inside, while all of the other occupants have run for the shelter of a riverbed about 200 yards back up the road.

'Hatfield, Gibbald,' Lieutenant Hannam gives his orders in a strangely strangled voice, 'take the Dutchman to tell the other Dutchmen to come in.'[29]

While some of them tend to the wounded Boer – an odd thing to help stem the very bleeding you and yours have caused, but there it is – Lieutenant Hannam and his men do not have to wait long.

But it is not a Dutchman who comes in. It is a weeping, nay *wailing*, woman, holding a limp boy in her arms. It is Aletta Grobler, and the boy is her son, Jacobus.

He is only five years old, and he is dead. But she refuses to be parted from him.

Right behind her is a Boer man, also holding a lad, though this one is bleeding badly from the neck and clearly does not have long to live. The two boys fatally shot are brothers, the 12-year-old Jan Grobler had been carrying his exhausted sibling Jacobus on his back, and one of the first bullets had passed through them both.

An eight-year-old girl, who also has a bleeding neck, is the last to be led in, with Troopers Hatfield and Gibbald on either side of her, both men glaring at Lieutenant Hannam.

You bastard. This is what you have had us do. Proud of yourself, now? Take a bow, the British Empire, the BVC and our commander Lieutenant Hannam.

For his part, Hannam seems to be realising only now the enormity of what has happened, his face pale, his voice stale. His orders come slowly, mechanically, as the wounded Boers are put back into one of their original wagons and they are underway once more, back to the nearest outpost, Blas' store.

In the wagon, Trooper Hatfield does his best to save the dying boy who, alas, as he will recount, 'was suffering horribly. He died in about an hour.'[30]

The shattered bodies of Jan and Jacobus Grobler, 12 and five years old respectively, lie side by side, while their eight-year-old sister, Elizabeth, is badly wounded and it is only their widowed mother, Aletta, who is alive and unharmed, physically.

How strange and sad and sombre a procession they are, as they make their morbid march to the nearest outpost. Silent Troopers, weeping Boer families, and two dead lads. As they go, the thoughts of Trooper Hatfield, still holding the cold child, are darker than the night that envelops them now. How *did* it come to this? The shooting by the men of the BVC had been for no reason at all!

'I can positively say,' he will affirm, 'that neither the Boer in the wagon or the Boers in the *donga* fired a single shot from first to last.'[31]

Trooper Richard Innes feels the same, and will acidly record: 'A glorious victory, killing two children and wounding another.'[32]

This has been a disgrace, a war crime. But who can he report it to? Certainly none of the BVC officers at Fort Edward. They are the bastards who ordered it!

6 September 1901, Medingen, ill met by daylight

Morant passes his orders to Corporal Browne, then rides on to join Handcock.

Trooper Christie.

Yes, Corporal Browne?

'Go to the Koodoo River and take over wagons from Corporal Ashton, and take them to the fort.'[33]

Yes, sir.

And with that, Christie heads off, deeply troubled. What horrors will come from this new leg of the journey, what sort of a 'mission' will it really be? What fresh havoc do his ne'er-do-well commanders have in mind? Sure enough, on arrival he is greeted by something else, a fog of grim tidings and darker doings. The men of the BVC are in *shock*.

And they are not alone, for with them are a large and shattered group of Boers in the midst of grief and mourning.

What is going on? What *has happened*?

Well, explain the Troopers, coming to their senses as they try to speak, we opened fire when the wagons were some 250 yards away, and well ... 'the sequel was that two children were shot dead ... and a girl of nine was shot through the neck and the lobe of her ear taken off'.

Christie cannot believe what he is hearing, while the Troopers who are telling him cannot believe they have done it.

'The Boers never fired a shot,'[34] Christie is told. Lieutenant Hannam, who gave the order to fire, is shocked to see the 'extent of the damage'.

'My God,' he said, 'I didn't think this would happen?'

'What the hell did you *think* would happen,' Trooper Hampton snaps, 'if you fire at women and children?'[35]

And *now* the penny drops for Christie at last. The Corporal who'd been looking for murderers to 'blot the lot' had not found the 'plenty more' he'd threatened to find. He'd found one, just one, but that was all he needed. He'd found Lieutenant bloody Hannam, who had agreed to order the atrocity only to now be shaking and quaking as he is confronted with the consequences of his agreement. He had followed orders and given orders to do the shooting and this is the grim harvest they now reap: dead children.

He is clearly a soul in torment, and Christie is glad to see it – the bastard should be tormented, and then shot.

Many of Christie's comrades feel the same.

Trooper Hampton exclaims, 'You won't get me in an outfit like this again.'[36]

Trooper Hatfield, a former sailor from Nova Scotia, is equally disgusted and expresses it clearly to Christie.

'I've seen some sights in my time,' he breathes in a raspy voice, even over the unearthly wails of the parents howling over their dead children, 'but I feel more sick over this business than anything I've ever been mixed up in.'[37]

Christie feels precisely the same, and makes an inventory of the contents of their disgust: 'The three wagons now contained four men, four women and twenty-two children (all of tender years), and two bodies.'

The uncle of the dead boys, Piet Grobler, has a question for his captors: 'May I have leave to bury them?'[38]

Yes, of course.

And so it goes, with the men who made the corpses – a few of the BVC Troopers – now making a coffin from some planks they find lying about. Meanwhile some of the Africans set to digging a grave. All is done by dusk and as Christie lifts the bodies of the brothers into their one wooden encasement, one Boer man sobs out a prayer in Dutch, while some of his Boer brethren chant what sounds like a psalm, as the coffin is carefully lowered into the grave. More prayers follow with the only words recognised by the shaken Christie – the whole thing being so close to his own experience of burying his own children almost two years before – being 'Louis Botha' and 'Kitchener'. (Afterwards it will be explained to Christie that the bereaved Boer was lamenting to the Lord that Botha had not accepted Kitchener's peace terms, as that would have prevented such unnecessary bloodshed.)

In the morning they must begin their sad trek to Fort Edward, and at lunch, at a farmhouse, Christie considers the situation over his soup. *If Boer prisoners are a target, then the Boers he is escorting are at risk.* It is now a matter of urgency to get them safely to an army camp, where they can be protected by the safety of having many witnesses.

Trooper, lunch is over.

Get everyone back on the road. And we will not stop at dusk, but trek on into the night.

Late that night, they finally do make camp, fires are lit and all of them bar one gets some sleep.

Trooper Christie keeps a silent vigil; everything about what has happened in recent weeks whirling in his mind, putting together all the broken pieces, the sad stories and wild whispers.

'I remembered how six Boers had surrendered and were said to have attacked our men, had all been shot. I remember van Buuren, one of our own men, being shot while out flanking. He was supposed to know too much. Now, here were eight blotted out. And the same old yarn – that they had grabbed at a rifle and fired at our men and in the melee, all were shot – no casualties on our side; and here was me coming in with another lot.'[39]

The sandman will not take Trooper Christie tonight. He is forced to endure the horrors he has witnessed in the waking world, not even afforded the luxury of a restless nightmare.

Dawn breaks and who should appear 'at a full gallop in a buggy and pair',[40] but Captain Taylor! Trooper Christie knows that he is called 'Killer' by the Natives, but Captain Taylor is all smiles and charm this morning.

'How are your men?'[41] the Englishman asks the Kiwi, for all the world as if they are just returning from a couple of days' leave in Pretoria.

You mean, apart from shocked, and disgusted, at having to murder children?

Now, however, is not the time for a reckoning.

'I have a wounded girl in the wagon,' Christie replies tightly.

'How did that happen?' asks Taylor, just as if he doesn't already know precisely what has happened because he had *ordered* it.

Christie can barely bear it.

'*Our* men opened fire on the women and children and two little boys have been killed,' replies Christie evenly.

'Indeed?' queries Captain Taylor, interested but unconcerned. 'You had better keep that quiet.'[42]

Still, Taylor looks at the girl's wound, and orders Christie to get her to the local Elim Hospital near Sweetwaters Farm.

'You had better get on as quickly as possible,' warns Taylor 'There is a convoy waiting to go to Pietersburg.'

Taylor drives off in his buggy and Christie heads to the hospital, where the injured child is attended to, as well as a fellow he knows well from the BVC, Trooper Alfred Petrie, who had taken a bullet to the leg in a minor action. Can Christie trust him, and share what's truly on his mind – the horror of the eight men being blotted out? He decides he can, and after Petrie expresses equal shock, he tells Christie something he has heard.

'It was about a German missionary . . . ? After coming to this hospital with a patient, he was shot dead on his return at Bandolier Kopjes. See, the missionary had been present just before or immediately after the eight men had been shot, and one of our lieutenants secretly left the fort after the missionary, but was seen by the guard to go in the direction the missionary had taken. The lieutenant returned to the fort late . . .'[43]

And the missionary was later found dead.

This Lieutenant's name? Peter Handcock.

Christie is not surprised. Something about Handcock has always troubled him – starting with his slavish devotion to Captain Taylor and Lieutenant Morant. For now, Christie must get back to Fort Edward, with his men and wagons, and soon departs, only to hear the thunder of hooves coming hard from behind. And who would this be?

Why, speak of the *Devil*.

It is Lieutenant Peter Handcock, with two Troopers!

What a coincidence. Christie brings in Boer prisoners, expresses his disgust to Captain Taylor at what has happened and now here is Taylor's preferred executioner, galloping towards him, a henchman on each side. And yes, of course, the New Zealander recognises both henchmen as soldiers who follow orders, come what may.

Christie takes an immediate decision and works the bolt of the .303 in his lap, slipping a round from the magazine into the chamber.

'My mind was made up,' he will recount, 'that . . . I should shoot that lieutenant if he opened fire on the men in my charge, or else get shot, according to who might have the advantage.'[44]

And so Trooper Christie waits to shoot or be shot. Lieutenant Handcock will not be gunning down all unarmed men today.

Handcock has no sooner brought his horse to a slightly skidding halt than – with what he surely thinks passes for guile – he offers first salutations and now a suggestion.

Why not come on ahead with me? We can travel to the fort together?

'Very good,' replies Christie, 'but I have my orders from Captain Taylor.'[45]

Handcock looks confused, most likely because he has been sent here on a murderous mission by one and the same Captain Taylor. But the bottom line remains, Christie is declining to be separated from the group, the way van Buuren had been.

All together thus, they move on, towards Fort Edward some 10 miles away, until Lieutenant Handcock again rides up, whereupon Christie broaches the appalling subject of the Boer women and children who had been shot while surrendering.

'Oh, they had no business there,' replies Handcock, for all the world as if it was all their fault for being in the wagons in the first place. As a matter of fact, Handcock is very free with his views that, when it comes to Boers, 'They should all be shot.'[46]

Christie can only just manage to contain his anger, glaring and grunting, but at least allowing Handcock, who senses his fury, to continue.

'We are justified in shooting everything in sight,' Handcock insists with a menace that he, too, is struggling to contain.

Each man eyes the other.

Whose move?

'All this time I held my rifle across my saddle bow,' Christie will recount, 'and if he had dared to put his hand to his revolver I would have dropped him like a buck. The man I found to be an ignorant and cowardly bully.'

But Handcock makes no such move, and only a suggestion.

'I want you to go back and see the donkey wagon,' he says lightly, referring to the wagon and donkey in the rear which carries much of their food.

Of course you do. But that would place me away from the sight of the others, and at your mercy. So, no thanks.

'Oh, it's all right,' Christie replies.

'It's *not* all right,' replies Handcock sharply, still intent on getting him on his own.

'Well,' answers Christie evenly, 'it's come about 100 miles, and no one has looked after it, and it's not likely to run away now.'

It is the way that Christie says it, which gives Handcock pause. The Trooper's words are on the calm side of things, but the tone is unmistakable. *I will* not do as you ask, and will not be the easy kill you hoped for. And now to emphasise that he means it, Christie calls out to a fellow Trooper, 'Cootzee, wait for the donkey wagon!'

Trooper Christie and his loaded rifle are staying right here with the Boers.

His exact thoughts are clear: 'My fine fellow, if you think to get me away from these wagons you have struck the wrong party. That was how the others were always "done in" – "Oh, you can go home: we'll take the wagons in". Result: Every one of those who have surrendered butchered. Not me I'm going to take those refugees in, or there will be a scene.'[47]

And take the Boer prisoners in Christie does, every one of them delivered alive and kicking to Fort Edward, just as he was charged to do, and despite the glares of the likes of Handcock. The orders of Captain Alfred Taylor be damned, the prisoners now have the added safety of that which murderers and monsters most abhor – multiple independent witnesses.

And yet, the storm brewing now is not just the clash that inevitably must come between the decent and the evil. For now it is a genuinely dark and stormy night, with the thunder clapping and the wind howling around the wagons, the wounded, the women and the children as they all make their way to where they must sleep for the night. At least the water running down the faces of the children is genuine rain, not tears, but it is now urgent to get them in the shelter provided. Lieutenant Handcock nods a wordless if grim farewell, off into the darkness, likely for dark purposes, Christie suspects – and a visit to report to Captain Taylor the most likely. Still, Christie at least takes some satisfaction in seeing all the prisoners all formally received and catalogued, this very paperwork providing them with protection; proof that they are in *British* custody now – and that has to count for something, particularly when it is all signed, stamped and filed? He desperately hopes so anyway.

'I got my lot in,' Christie proudly records.

Not that the tears are over for the night as, while the wives and children are free to find shelter where they can in some of the tents provided, the regulations insist that the men be segregated from them, imprisoned, 'in a cage barb wire enclosure about 20 feet by 10 feet, with an iron roof'.[48]

Yes, there are more howling women and children as a result, the children clinging to the outstretched hands of their fathers, but Christie has satisfaction. This, *this* is the sort of prison Christie likes, where at least the prisoners can be seen by all, and not gunned down on the quiet, out on the veldt, away from all. And yet, perhaps a sixth sense makes him still fret. *Are they really safe?* Will Taylor and Handcock be defeated by the fact they are now in camp? Or try something desperate?

It is with this in mind that he makes the offer to guard the surrendered Boers through the night, first putting them back in the wagons they were captured in, where they would be more comfortable. But the offer is declined.

At least Christie takes some comfort from the man who is left in charge of the whole shebang, a 'cage and a guard with fixed bayonets put round them',[49] Corporal Ernest Browne, a good and decent fellow with a warm heart. If Cochrane, or anyone, decides to act to stop the killings, Corporal Browne will back them to the hilt.

And yet, what now?

He has a visitor.

Not surprisingly, Lieutenant Hannam has been keeping his distance from the 30 surviving prisoners since their arrival, either from guilt, shame or the hope of avoiding public recriminations, but now approaches the nearest sentry and asks in brisk tones: 'Who is in charge of the guard?'

'*I* am,' replies Browne evenly. Yes, Hannam outranks him by a huge amount. But the man in charge of the guard has real authority, on matters pertaining to that guard.

'Be careful,' warns Hannam. 'The prisoners might attempt to escape.'[50]

What?

Family men wanting to charge off in the night, leaving behind their wives and children? What complete and utter rot. And did Lieutenant Hannam still not bloody hear? As they kept screaming repeatedly, they have *surrendered*. These are not fighters from a Commando they have captured, these are non-fighting Boer farmers who had come in, in the hope the British would offer what they had promised – sanctuary, even if it is in a concentration camp or a prison. They are willing vassals, men who have forgone their freedom in the vain hope of *safety*. Something in Browne's lack of concerned reply clearly irks the Lieutenant.

'Does your sentry have his bayonet fixed?' asks Hannam.

Yes.

'And is his rifle loaded?'

Yes, of course it is, why would . . .

But Hannam now pulls Corporal Browne aside, clearly to have a very quiet word with . . . no witnesses.

'Remember you are responsible for the prisoners,' Hannam says. 'As they must know we are shorthanded they may attempt something.'

The chill down Corporal Browne's back has nowt to do with the pouring rain that has already drenched him. This is not a friendly warning being offered by Hannam, this has the air of a man tilling the ground – *this is the story we shall tell, yes?* – to commit an unspeakable act. As monstrous as it seems, Lieutenant Hannam might be wanting to eliminate, *tonight*, all these bitter Boers with their wild and damaging lies about having surrendered to British troops, with their wives and children, only to be fired on, whereupon two of those children had been killed. Browne is fully of the view that Hannam must be murderously mad, but that is hardly an identifying feature when it comes to the men of the BVC.

Well, Corporal Browne refuses to play along.

'It is not possible to hunt them out of the birdcages,' he says, 'they are too contented.'

In other words, if you are thinking of shooting these men in their cage, you are on your own. You may tell HQ escaping prisoners were coming right at you, but it is absurd, and I will not be backing you up.

I am in charge of this guard, not you, and I do not accept these men are either dangerous, or have any desire to escape.

'That's true,' Hannam concedes as the rain and wind continue to smack the ground around them. 'But we can't be *sure* and we can't take *any* chances. Anyhow, if they do make any move *you know what to do*. At the first chance fire into them at once and *shoot the lot*, only be careful you don't shoot any of our own fellows.'

Corporal Browne, who has a gift for understatement as well as handling crazed officers, observes that, 'I understood this to be a broad hint to shoot the lot.'[51]

The Lieutenant leaves, Corporal Browne staring at him as he goes. How *has* it come to this? Either way, Browne has no doubt where his duty lies. Yes, it is to stop the Boers escaping. But it is also to defend those Boers from those who would do them any harm, and that starts with Lieutenant Hannam.

•

In his own tent, Trooper Christie lies staring at the peak of the canvas roof, just a couple of feet above his nose. The wind surges back and forth outside, the rain hammers down like a thousand tiny drummers, each and every drop a tear of his conscience. For here he is dry, warm and safe, while those men in the cage out there, those poor bereaved Boers, will be soaked from the rain coming in sideways with the wind.

It is true, he had not only saved those Boers to get them here alive, but he had also tried to get word to a patrol of his BVC mates bringing in another lot of Boers that, under no circumstances, were they to let them out of their sight until delivered safe and sound back here – only to be thwarted as he and his friends in camp were 'watched like hawks by officers and their minions'[52] which had prevented them sending a messenger out.

But are such actions enough when the poor bastards are now out there freezing, wet and hungry, while he is still in here?

The hell with it – he must get up and check on them. It is not as if he will be missing out on a good sleep by doing so, just delaying the nightmare surely to come about dead Boer children on his watch.

Waking a couple of groggy and reluctant chums, and insisting they help, all together they grab some sacks and cavalry cloaks so – with Corporal Browne's grateful blessing – the Boers can use them for some protection from the rain, and for warmth. Just looking at the still-shaking prisoners now, however, sets off Christie's rage once more.

The aristocratic impersonator. A studio portrait of Harry Morant taken while he was in England in late 1901.

(National Archives, UK)

Members of E Company, 5th Contingent, Victorian Mounted Rifles about to see action against the Boers in the Transvaal. (AWM P01866.006)

A stone blockhouse fort, one of up to 8000 constructed and garrisoned by the British to guard rail lines and other key infrastructure during the war. (Alamy)

Recruitment notice for the Bushveldt Carbineers. Notices like this were put up all over Pretoria, Bloemfontein, Cape Town and Durban . . . at ports, train stations and bars. The British needed soldiers who could play the Boers at their own game. (Hennie Heymans)

Major Robert Lenehan, the Australian lawyer and officer appointed to command the Bushveldt Carbineers. To fill out his unit, he needed British Empire soldiers who had finished their term of enlistment, but who could be persuaded to stay on; men who could ride, shoot and survive in sparse scrub. Breaker Morant fitted the bill perfectly. (AWM P00854.002)

Studio portrait of Peter Handcock, taken in Sydney prior to his departure for South Africa. (AWM 05816)

Studio portrait of 2nd Lieutenant James Francis Thomas, A Squadron, NSW Citizens' Bushmen. (AWM A05817)

Photo of B Squadron, Bushveldt Carbineers, 1901. Left to right: Peter Handcock; Harry Morant; Dr Thomas Johnston, civil surgeon; Captain Percy Hunt; Captain Alfred Taylor and Lieutenant Henry Picton. (Newspix)

An often-reproduced studio portrait of Breaker Morant, taken just prior to his departure for South Africa with the 2nd Mounted Rifles from South Australia. (AWM A05311)

Fort Edward, the pre-fabricated collapsible steel fort used by the BVC as a base in the Northern Transvaal. This photo was taken by H.F. Gros, c. 1888, prior to the war, when the fort was known as Fort Hendrina.

Sweetwaters Farm and Hotel, as it is today. (Hennie Heymans)

The Reverend Daniel Heese and his wife, Johanna. (Cape Archives)

Melrose House, Kitchener's headquarters in Pretoria. (Wikimedia Commons)

Participants in the peace conference at Middelburg, Transvaal, 1901. Front row, left to right: General Christiaan de Wet, General Louis Botha, Lord Kitchener, Colonel Hamilton. (Alamy)

Major Thomas stands over the freshly dug graves of Morant and Handcock.
(Alamy)

Portrait of George Witton, taken in 1930. His book, *Scapegoats of the Empire*, first published in 1907 after he was released from prison, set out his version of events.
(AWM A04434)

In April 2016, a chance find at a Tenterfield rubbish tip uncovered a cache of artefacts thought to have once been in the possession of Major James Thomas. They included a bullet-damaged British penny etched with the name 'Edwin Henry Morant', and a faded red ensign flag inscribed with the names of Morant and Handcock, the dates of their birth and death, and the words 'This flag bore witness to II scapegoats of the Empire'. These extraordinary finds now rest in the Tenterfield Museum. (Photos © Peter Reid Tenterfield 2020)

'They sat and shivered in the rain all night, and these were the men who had come in and voluntarily surrendered, and whom we had escorted for five days through the veldt without a guard.'[53]

In the silent watch of the night, with the rain still falling, another man approaches Corporal Browne. It is a very worried and very wet Sergeant John Baker. You are not going to believe this, Browne, but, 'I have been sounded out as to whether I would give tabloids [to the prisoners].'[54]

Tabloids? Yes, pills.

'Arsenic *and* strychnine,' Baker goes on, incredulous, 'each of which I have heard the doctor say by way of warning is capable of killing four men, to the Boer prisoners to wipe them out!'[55]

Well, to Corporal Browne it is obvious then. In for a penny in for a pound, after Lieutenant Hannam had organised the murder of two of his Boer prisoners, he has decided to murder all the rest who can stand witness to his crimes in one fell and foul swoop. Sergeant Baker continues, shaking with nerves as he tells Browne he had only been sounded out so far, but he is nigh on certain that will not be the end of ending the lives of the Boer prisoners.

'I fear that I will be directly ordered to do it, and that if I refuse I will be shot!'

Corporal Browne rises to the moment and offers a hasty solution.

'I advise you,' he tells the Sergeant, 'to substitute harmless tabloids for the poisonous ones and so save your skin by seeming to comply.'[56]

Baker grunts and shuffles off in the darkness, the rain still pouring, both of them aware that the wet night likely has eyes and they are being watched in this dark downpour.

It is a living nightmare, the epitome of hell on earth, and all Corporal Browne can do is pray to the good Lord above that he can find a way out before the next atrocity occurs. For now, he keeps a close watch on the Boers through the night, not to keep them from escaping, but to protect them from whatever murderous plan Lieutenant Hannam might have come up with.

●

No sooner has Trooper Christie woken than he goes to see the prisoners, all of them still drenched and dazed in the dawn's early light.

'It turned some of us sick to see the treatment meted out to them,' he will recount. Amazingly, they have been told they are to be taken under armed escort to the concentration camp at nearby Pietersburg, but despite asking, Christie is refused permission to accompany them.

Dismayed, he goes to bid farewell to the Boers who, recognising him as the solid beacon of humanity to them through all of the last five days, reach through the wire to shake his hand, even as the rain continues to fall.

'You can take the sacks,' Christie tells them, only to be confronted by a storming Lieutenant Hannam who proves to be 'in a tearing passion',[57] as he confronts him.

Something on your mind, sir?

'What right have you,' Hannam barks, 'to give Government property to prisoners?'

'Some of the sacks are mine, sir,' Christie answers evenly. 'But if I have given away any Government property inadvertently I will get them back.'

As good as his word, Christie does apologetically get a couple of sacks back. Not quite three bags full, but two sacks empty will have to satisfy that sod, Hannam.

And now what? It is Corporal Browne approaching, seeking to blow the shitter out of Christie for taking back the sacks when any fool can see it is still raining. He can only be placated when Christie tells him the truth of it, at which point the good Corporal's fury turns on Hannam.

'If he wants to get you and me into a row, let him,' says Browne. 'I'll put him up as high as a kite.'[58]

Punch him? No, *string him up*! Not, courtesy of a lynch mob, *necessarily*, but ideally, officially, after a court martial. Justice *will* be done, come hell or high water.

It is a telling moment, when two men of the BVC realise for the first time just how outraged they are by their BVC officers, and their own preparedness to do something about it.

'And so,' Christie will record, 'we took comfort in the fact that together we would help to hang him before we were much older, unless we shot him.'[59]

But how to get justice? They cannot go up the chain of command at the BVC, for that chain is already slick with blood, inclined to brutally strangle any voice raised against it, and always on the lookout for even a peep of protest.

'We swore,' Christie will note, 'that if anything came over . . . we would "hands up" the officers and put them in irons, or, if necessary, take the law into our own hands and shoot them. The trouble was to get a sufficient force of our view to take a step. One had to move warily in the matter.'[60]

For yes, that is the key. They now must survive long enough, themselves, to bring these bastards to justice. At least Christie now knows he is not alone in the endeavour.

•

Darkness falls, the moon rises and a weary wind whispers across the veldt.

Approaching the Native kraal right by the BVC tents, Captain de Bertodano's 'Native boys' are easily welcomed into the flickering light of the fire by the BVC 'boys', just preparing for their evening meal, the evening filled with that most exquisite waft of African stew.

All Africans together, in a world dominated by the white men, there is an immediate bond between them all, and the BVC 'boys' take the scouts at their word, that they are passing through on their way to a distant camp. And they talk easily, of the affairs of the BVC, the things they have done, the things the Africans have seen. Still, are the scouts a little *too* inquisitive?

Perhaps, for after a time one of the Africans heads up to the white men's quarters and returns with an officer, a Lieutenant Morant, though he is dressed casually in shirt sleeves and slacks.

(Typically, Taylor has placed his own spies among the Africans, to report on precisely this kind of thing. Always be on the lookout for people asking questions.)

'Who are these two strange boys?'[61] Morant asks the others sharply, almost as if Hans and Kaffirland are not there.

Hastily, the newly arrived 'boys' explain who they are, and why they are here.

We are just passing through, Boss, on our way to Pietersburg.

Morant nods, and leaves them to it, adding, with slightly narrowed eyes, 'You can stay the night.'

Which is fine, but Hans, who has a mind as sharp as Morant's tongue, is himself suspicious about this inquisitive and suddenly friendly white man.

'Does he usually come to your camp?' Hans asks.

'No,' the others reply, clearly surprised and even a little suspicious themselves, 'it is unusual.'[62]

Very well then.

'Let us get our blankets,' Hans says to Kaffirland, who agrees to come with him.

As they leave, one of the Native 'boys', clearly alarmed, whispers to them, that it is important for them 'not to return'.[63]

Something is up, and they are not safe here.

Hans does not have to be told twice.

But Kaffirland is of a different view.

Once they get to the horses, he is insistent.

'I am tired. I will stay at the camp.'

'But we have orders – "on *no* account remain longer than a couple of hours and under *no* circumstances stay the night".'[64]

Kaffirland does not care. He outright refuses to obey.

He will be fine at the camp. He is tired, and that is that.

•

They can say what they like about Breaker Morant. But they can't say he is anything other than sentimental and kind . . . at least when it comes to horses. For gather round, mates, and let's hear some more verse from the Breaker around the fire, the flames casting a flickering glow on his face as, *basso profundo*, his voice rings out upon the veldt:

> *They are mustering cattle on Brigalow Vale*
> *Where the stock-horses whinny and stamp,*
> *And where long Andy Ferguson, you may go bail,*
> *Is yet boss on a cutting-out camp.*
> *Half the duffers I met would not know a fat steer*
> *From a blessed old Alderney cow.*
> *Whilst they're mustering there I am wondering here –*
> *Who is riding brown Harlequin now?*[65]

And poetry soon begets prose as the Breaker goes through his favourite bush tales of stockmen and deeds on steeds that would make the Man from Snowy River turn green with envy, that would make a brown dog weep with laughter!

Yes, most of the men laugh, but these days there appears something forced in the Breaker's performance, something contrived.

The laughter rings out in the night, loud and brash, but there is a faint echo to it, a ringing that suggests it comes from a hollow place.

It is like he is trying to prove he is still the Breaker of old. Before Captain Hunt died. Before the killing began.

But nothing alters the truth: the BVC are a long way from the Brigalow Brigade, and the Breaker far from the buccaneer who once filled the pages of *The Bulletin* . . .

CHAPTER FIFTEEN

THE LAW CLOSES

Faith, I have been a truant in the law
And never yet could frame my will to it;
And therefore frame the law unto my will.[1]

William Shakespeare,
Henry IV, Part 1, Act 2, Scene 4

7 September 1901, Fort Edward, three for the road

The odd thing about murder is that while the first one is hard, if you just keep at it, the whole thing can become an easy habit with astonishing speed.

The Breaker himself is a man at ease today, as he hand-picks three accomplices – well, two actually as Lieutenant Handcock is always automatically his right-hand murderer of choice – as a new mission is announced. They are to relieve the escorting party of some Boers (and then relieve these Boers of their lives, though he doesn't tell his men that yet).

It is a deathly procession, Lieutenants Morant, Handcock and a posse of pale riders, but they are in good spirits. For now.

Presently they see the escort up ahead coming towards them, and Morant trots on ahead, to give the walking corpses they are escorting the once-over.

They prove to be a farmer by the name of Roelf van Staden and his two sons, 16-year-old Roelf Jnr and 12-year-old Chris, who is very sick with the fever. Returning from a hunting trip across the border in Rhodesia they are on their way to register with the British authorities as 'neutrals', trusting the promise that thereafter they will be allowed to go straight home.

Once Morant is certain that the escorting party is well out of earshot, he gives his orders, *sotto voce*.

'When I say "Lay down your arms" then shoot them.'[2]

Yes, there is shock. But no-one dares protest.

Before they even quite realise it is upon them, they have come to a secluded spot on the veldt, whereupon Morant brings out a dusty bottle of brandy and offers it to the sick lad. The father, appreciative, thanks Morant in his simple way, as the lad takes a swig and chases it down with a shiver and a shudder.

And now Morant barks at the other men, who have remained on their horses: 'Dismount!'

The two Troopers and Handcock do it, and, following another pre-arranged signal, ready their rifles to fire.

The Boers look at them, confused, and with growing horror, the sick young boy looking to his father for solace, for comfort, for assurance that they are not actually going to . . . ?

'Lay down your arms!' Morant commands, for all the world as if he wishes his Troopers to genuinely put their rifles on the ground.

The father relaxes just a little, only for the Troopers and Handcock to suddenly swing their rifles up, take aim through the cold iron sights and . . .

Three shots are fired.

Three Boers fall dead.

They are left where they lie.

●

Well, fancy meeting you here!

The boisterous bonhomie of good old Major Bob Lenehan is cut short this September morning. There is something strange afoot, namely these stragglers on foot. They are prisoners, but their captors look guilty! What had happened here? Or do I not want to know, Witton? For it is indeed an ashen Lieutenant George Witton in charge of a shamefaced troop of Troopers escorting the grieving Boers 'captured' while committing the act of surrender, their children slaughtered and then buried, while Lieutenant Hannam and his BVC men watched. Witton tells the tale as best he can, the way he has been told to tell it, the way he wished it was. But his own men listen in disbelief as they trudge south to the concentration camp at Pietersburg with the BVC Commanding Officer Major Robert Lenehan. The Major was coming the other way with his own escort and, by God, he wishes he had gone another way instead of stumbling into yet another scandal to sweep under the rug.

Lenehan had thought Pietersburg was rough country. It is harsh, stony and unforgiving, yes, but nowhere near so harsh, stony and unforgiving as the looks he is receiving from the Boer women. There's such sheer *contempt* and fury in their eyes. Something wicked has this way come. Had Witton been telling the truth about what truly happened here?

Lenehan hears something of what has really happened from men less delicate or discreet than Witton, and that it involves Boer children being shot by the men of the BVC, the men he is responsible for, whose actions he is accountable for.

Major Lenehan and his escort leave Witton and his escort behind as they ride on, with the Major having a great deal to think about. The stricken expressions on the faces of the women and children, the fact that kids as young as five were killed at the hands of his own men, would have occasioned incandescent rage in many an officer. In the case of Major Lenehan, however, the greater issue is how to keep what has happened hidden.

●

When Morant and Handcock and their cohort arrive back at Fort Edward in the late afternoon it is to find they have a distinguished visitor, the BVC's Commanding Officer, Major Lenehan. It is something of a shock, as he has been so rarely seen.

But Lenehan in turn is shocked when he gets a close look at Morant for the first time in many weeks. That man he had known back in Sydney only a few short years ago, and in the early part of the war, is long gone.

In his stead is an embittered shell of a man, still deeply grieving over the death of his dear friend, Captain Hunt. He just wants to kill Boers, and doesn't particularly care who knows it.

As Lieutenant Witton will recount, 'The Major thought, as did others, that Morant's mind had become unhinged with grief.'[3]

As unaccustomed as members of the BVC are to seeing their Commanding Officer in these remote parts, all proprieties must be observed, including providing him with a suitably commodious tent, showing him around their quarters, inviting him to informally 'inspect' the men and their quarters – and of course hosting him to dinner in the Sweetwaters dining room on the night of his arrival. Of course, the redoubtable Olivia Bristow outdoes herself to put on the best meal she can, tailoring her Boer instincts to put on as British a dinner as possible – a *Potjiekos*, slow-cooked stew in a small cast-iron pan – as she has learnt through 30 years of marriage to her English husband, Charles.

As the Major manages to intimate without saying it, he is not here to knock heads together, and call them to account, so much as to do his bit to protect the BVC's reputation, concerning the 'methods' of

Captain Taylor and Lieutenant Morant. A man of the world of war, he understands that, in these parts, not everything can be done by the book, least of all when up against Commandos whose founding principle was to throw the book away in the first place.

It is extremely important to Lenehan, however, that his purpose be entirely unstated, as any acknowledgement in the public domain is dangerous. That much is apparent when the conversation over the rum – led by Taylor and Morant – turns to the reliability or otherwise of those members of the BVC who are disaffected Boers, and whether or not they can be counted on to actually kill their countrymen.

On the spot, Morant calls forth his interpreter, Theunis Botha, who that very morning had accompanied him on this *errand*.

'Well, Botha,' Morant says, 'did you shoot the . . . Dutchman today?'

'Yes, sir,' Trooper Botha replies, 'I shot him.'[4]

At this point, however, things have really gone too far for the lawyerly and urbane sensibilities of Major Lenehan.

'I do not want such things talked of at mess,' he says sharply. 'Botha, you can go.'[5]

And that is the extent of the 'investigation' of the BVC. Just like ladies' names, war crimes are *not* to be mentioned in the mess. For you see, it is one thing for such things to go on. But to be openly discussed like this in *front of Major Lenehan?* It changes everything, makes him complicit in such activities and he will not have it.

But it is too late.

Among those in earshot in the mess, there is . . . pause. Major Lenehan is in on this! Morant feels comfortable enough to discuss atrocities in front of him, and the only complaint of the Commanding Officer of the BVC is that, effectively, it should not be mentioned in earshot of potential witnesses.

Further evidence of Major Lenehan's notable lack of interest in the truth is soon in view. For the Troopers who are called in to report to Lenehan the next day are in for a rude awakening. Rather than digging for the truth, it is soon clear that Lenehan is reaching for a 'truth' of his own choosing and their role is to put their name to backing him up on the lie.

Let's start with the court martial of the prisoner Visser, one of the Boers who had mutilated Captain Hunt before dressing himself up in the late Captain's uniform, something that no doubt inflamed your passions, gentlemen?

Well, no, *our* passions were not inflamed, it was all Lieutenant Morant and Captain Taylor.

Well, let Major Lenehan put it another way, asking these future witnesses to agree to the statement he has, after talking to Breaker Morant, already drafted.

'Will you swear that the wounded Boer prisoner Visser, shot on Aug 11th, was wearing the tunic of the late Captain Hunt?'[6]

No, the Major has got it wrong, one Trooper helpfully explains: 'The clothes of Captain Hunt have been continuously worn by Lt Morant, he's wearing them at this moment.'[7]

What? Oh yes, another Trooper adds, who, to Lenehan's infinite chagrin, peers out of the tent and, while looking at Lenehan, starts to list just what items of clothing the lawyer officer is after: 'Morant is wearing Captain Hunt's British Warm, riding breeches, tunic and leggings.'[8]

Good God!

All right, leaving Lieutenant Morant out of it, can we at least agree that when captured, Visser *was wearing* Hunt's uniform.

No, the naïve Troopers correct him, we need to be clear on this. When we got him, Visser *wasn't* wearing anything of Hunt's.

'I will swear,' one Trooper offers, seemingly trying to be helpful, 'that Visser was wearing an old British Warm.'[9]

'And,' another Trooper adds, 'the water bottle belonging to Hunt I found in a Cape cart, and not in the possession of Visser . . .'[10]

Major Lenehan does some swearing of his own now.

'Out!'[11] he barks at the men.

('As if we had been dogs!'[12] remarks one Trooper.)

'*That* kind of evidence is no good to us,'[13] yells Lenehan as they depart. For what is ever more clear is that if the *truth* is presented as evidence, then this whole mess is likely to get a whole lot messier. So, in fact, this exercise is less at getting to the truth than putting together a *cordon sanitaire* to prevent others, higher up, getting to it. Already Lenehan knows of the interest of Captain de Bertodano in this whole affair, and is worried by it.

•

Rumours from beyond the eastern horizon say that the famed Boer leader, Commandant Tom Kelly, is leading a select group of Commandos, and they have artillery with them.

Kelly, again!

'A . . . splendid fighter,' one contemporary account describes him, 'and one of the most hated [and feared by the British] of the Boer irregular leaders.'[14]

A war correspondent on the ground regards Kelly even more highly.

'He ranks among the first of the latter-day leaders,' he reports. 'He is in charge of the Zoutpansberg division, and has 20,000 Kaffirs under him. He is a rampant Boer agitator, and as fond of fighting as a Matabele warrior. It will not be hard to understand this when it is known that he is an Irish–Boer descendant of the old stock that finds its way so strangely into all lands and under all flags, but is still ever proud of its Irish blood. Tom Kelly speaks only Dutch and Kaffir. All the present leaders are up to the old standard of the fighting Boer. They care nothing for life – their own or that of their enemy; in fact, they go into a fight with the determination to die sooner than accept defeat.'[15]

Lieutenant Morant knows he will never get a better opportunity to strike a real blow and entreats Major Lenehan to allow him to take 30 men, and go out after Kelly. Let's not wait for him to attack us, let us go to him, and attack him, when he is least expecting it!

After some reflection – it is a question of balancing the need for Fort Edward itself to be sufficiently defended, against the need to strike at the Boers, all of it qualified by concerns at Morant's mental state – Major Lenehan agrees to the request.

'But,' says Lenehan sternly, in a caution that he trusts the Breaker will take as a commandment from his Commanding Officer, 'we particularly want this man brought in alive.'

'*Alive?*' interjects Morant, for all the world as if the idea never occurred to him. 'Don't you know what a bloody scoundrel he is?'[16]

Yes, Lenehan does. But, in the first place, it would be useful to interrogate Kelly. And, in the second place, not only will it be a good challenge for Morant, but it will also spare Lenehan the endless paperwork that inevitably comes with dead prisoners.

In the company of 30 Troopers and Lieutenant Witton, Morant leaves Fort Edward bound for the last reported sighting of Kelly, near the Birthday Mine some 40 miles to the east, near the headwaters of the Shingwedzi River.

7 September 1901, Sweetwaters Farm, Lenehan's Law

In quiet groups around Fort Edward, many of the Troopers gloomily reflect on the meetings they have just had with their Commanding Officer. Their collective summation of the situation, as later expressed, is that:

'Major Lenehan . . . endeavoured to bounce the troopers into giving evidence which would exonerate the officers.'[17]

When it is clear that their own Commanding Officer is in on it, what are they to do, how can they set things to rights? For if nobody is going to help these Troopers, it is ever more obvious that they have to help themselves – not to a second serve of murder – but to get out of this mess, and bring to justice their corrupt and murderous officers who have brought the BVC to this. They will write up their own evidence and find a way to get it to that rarest of all things, a British officer in South Africa that they can *trust*!

The key breakthrough is that, in a series of hushed, if rushed, conversations, a critical mass of critical Troopers agree to bring official complaint about the murders. Yes, that's it, they will write a report listing the atrocities that have been perpetrated on the orders of their officers – some of them committed personally by the officers themselves – sign it and get it to someone high up.

The soldier who takes carriage of the affair is their own 'bush lawyer', Trooper Robert Mitchell Cochrane, who was also, of course, the former editor of the Charters Tower paper, *The Eagle*. Though only a Trooper and his actual legal training extending no more than being a Justice of the Peace, Cochrane has a good grasp of the law, and more importantly still a good grasp of what is wrong and right. A substantial figure in the BVC, the fact that he has a moral compass with a bearing of true north makes him the natural leader of this affair, backed by the two Kiwis, Trooper James Christie and Corporal Ernest Browne – both of whom have seen Morant's atrocities up close. All put together, Cochrane can carefully frame a *j'accuse* letter that is startlingly comprehensive. It will be a fatal document; the fatalities will depend on who reads it first, HQ or Captain Taylor.

In the meantime, James Christie can help carefully corral those fellow Troopers who might co-operate with them, while leaving in the dark those complicit.

•

After completing his own inquiries, the new Native Commissioner for Zoutpansberg, Francis Enraght Moony, is now more alarmed than ever about the activities of Captain Alfred Taylor, and writes to the Minister of Native Affairs on 11 September 1901, in very stark terms: 'From all reports I have heard regarding the actions of this man, in his dealings with the Natives, the more I am convinced that he should be removed without delay . . . Some of the charges are so serious as to practically amount to murder . . . Taylor is very rough and arbitrary in his treatment of the Natives and flogs freely. From all I can hear, the Natives of the Spelonken and Zoutpansberg were very friendly disposed towards the British upon our occupation . . . but I fear Taylor's administration is fast dispelling this friendly feeling and will in its place sow sullen antipathy . . . I hope that you will be able to arrange with the Commander in Chief for the removal of Taylor from the District at the earliest possible date . . .'[18]

Moony also writes to the Secretary of Native Affairs, Sir Godfrey Lagden, and letter begets letter until, on 24 September 1901, Lagden is informed that:

> The Chief wishes to remove Taylor, who is making trouble in the North. Lord K. thinks it is time for your department to take over native control of the Zoutpansberg . . . [19]

•

News for Captain de Bertodano!

One of the two native scouts, Hans, has returned from Fort Edward. There is no sign of brave Kaffirland.

Eagerly, Captain de Bertodano makes his way to him, to hear the full story.

But first Hans has one urgent question for *him*.

Kaffirland! Has Captain de Bertodano seen him, or heard from him? Where *is* he?

No, no sign, no word.

Hans is devastated, and fears the worst.

His story comes tumbling out. Kaffirland had gone back to the camp, despite Hans telling him not to, that it was dangerous there, that the white men had seemed to know they might be asking too many questions.

Yes, yes, yes, but what happened? What did the BVC 'boys' TELL you?

Captain de Bertodano is also concerned about Kaffirland, but relieved that at least Hans is back, and eager to hear what he knows.

His account is staggering. For yes, he had managed to talk directly to Morant's 'boy', who had told him everything. Pursuing Reverend Heese, Lieutenant Morant had followed Lieutenant Handcock out of Fort Edward by a different route, and met up with him further down the track.

'When the Cape cart [with Reverend Heese] had travelled about five miles from Headquarters,' Hans recounts, 'Morant and Handcock appeared out of the bush. They . . . had some conversation with the Rev. Heese, said they were very sorry he was leaving them and to come back again, shook hands with him and said goodbye.'[20]

'How did the boy know,' de Bertodano wants to know, 'what was said?'

The answer is, the 'boy' spoke English well, and was standing close enough, holding the Lieutenants' horses, that he could hear it all. Extraordinary!

And what happened then?

'As the driver was just starting the mules, Handcock shot him through the back of the head. At the report, the Reverend Heese turned to see what was the cause of the shot and Morant shot him through the side of the head. There was a third shot . . . but he was so terrified that he could not be sure.'

At this point the terrified mules tried to bolt, only to find that the death grip of the dead driver on the reins held them back, as his dead body on the bottom of the cart had those reins held fast. It had given Handcock time to jump to the head of the mules and hold them.

Morant, in turn, had turned to the 'boy' and said, 'If you ever breathe a word about this, we will shoot you too.'[21]

By this, the 'boy' had assumed he meant to white people. He had no problem telling Hans, a fellow African, because he, too, had no doubt suffered at the hands of whites in this manner. It was what the 'boys' do – frequently talking about the cruelty of the whites.

After the murders, the 'boy' tells Hans, 'Handcock got into the driver's seat and took the reins and drove the Cape cart. Morant and I followed on horseback for some miles until they were near a place called Bandolier Kopjes.'[22]

It is at this point, well away from the scene of the actual murder – and more in Boer territory – they abandoned the dray and the bodies and returned to Fort Edward by separate routes, at separate times.

'Morant's boy,' Hans reports to Captain de Bertodano, 'was terrified and there was some discussion as to whether all the natives should not clear out but it was decided not to do so owing to their fear, not only of "Bulala" Taylor but of Morant himself.'[23]

It is a staggering tale, confirming all of de Bertodano's worst fears, and then some.

'This story,' de Bertodano will recount, 'gave [me] much cause for anxiety.'[24]

Still, while a tale *of* a tale of a Native 'boy' is one thing, proving it will be quite another. The most urgent thing for now is trying to stop Morant and Taylor committing their next murders . . .

•

Come in, Captain de Bertodano, Major Lenehan will see you now.

The two are cut from the same cloth, the same private schools and the same university, two former apprentices of the Sydney legal world who now find themselves thrown together on the other side of the world – about to be thrown apart, if not blown apart. For yes, they have been raised on the virtues of the law, on how its observance marks the difference between civilised beings and savages, but . . .

But the problem is that de Bertodano is fast coming to the conclusion that he and Lenehan are now on opposite sides of the law, and that Lenehan is complicit in the outrages committed by the BVC.

Lenehan wishes to report that not only had the bodies of Reverend Heese and his driver been buried, but 'every effort is being made to capture the Boers, his murderers!'[25]

De Bertodano keeps his own counsel. Though completely stunned at just how wide this conspiracy of killers and their cohort runs, now is not the time to be raising it. Instead, he decides to report to General Lord Kitchener directly, and seek his support.

It does not take long. Within 24 hours, de Bertodano has secured an audience with the great man at his Pretoria HQ and tells him everything that Hans has told him.

Kitchener's response is swift as he immediately orders de Bertodano to '[investigate the alleged atrocities] at any cost: it occurred in your territory'.[26]

This, at least, is heartening. To have support from the very top is no small thing.

Now going to see Colonel Hall, who is commanding at Pietersburg, he again tells all, and is gratified that this fine officer is so appalled he wishes to make immediate arrests. But de Bertodano insists otherwise.

'Our only chance of obtaining the necessary information,' he tells the Colonel, 'is to let the matter die down and show no further interest in it. I will arrange this with HQ Pretoria.'[27]

Colonel Hall finally agrees and de Bertodano gets to work. It will not be easy. It is clear that all of 'Lenehan, "Bulala" Taylor, Morant chiefly, and perhaps one or two others were a certain coterie which apparently had no respect for life.'[28]

And yet, Hall has no jurisdiction over Captain Taylor whatsoever, as the Intelligence man is a civilian appointment, not military – even though he holds a military rank and is far and away the most influential figure on the affairs of the BVC around Fort Edward. Removing him and holding him to account is an administrative nightmare.

The first task is to get a secret message to the agent they have within the BVC, Leonard Ledeboer, the agent attached to the Carbineers, and this is done by sending a tightly worded letter.

You must find out the characters of the Native 'boys' employed at the Fort and to what extent they could be trusted. You are particularly to find out how far Morant's boy's statement could be relied upon as evidence in a possible court martial.[29]

•

It is a letter that makes for unpleasant reading for Ledeboer. How to move now?

For while he is, effectively, a double agent – working for Taylor, while also reporting back to Captain de Bertodano in Pietersburg – so too is he aware that Captain Taylor has instituted a system whereby a couple of the African 'boys' have been assigned to watch the other 'boys'. As Ledeboer knows only too well, it is the way Taylor does things, to always be ahead of what is happening, before it actually happens. The problem Ledeboer has is that he doesn't know which 'boys' are which, who is watching, and who is being watched. All he knows is that he must, very carefully, get to Morant's 'boy' to talk to him about what he knows.

It takes some doing, but finally he is able to get the lad alone, and indeed get some scant details from him. But the lad is so terrified, Ledeboer pulls back. Now is not the time to crack him for every bit of information he has, and he reports both his scant confirmation of the story Hans had told, and his terror, in his report back to de Bertodano.

De Bertodano moves quickly, getting a message back to Ledeboer that under the circumstances 'no further attempt should be made to question him until we could get him safely away'.[30]

In the meantime, the cautious but keen spy chief sends more 'boys' – who in fact are his agents – towards Fort Edward. There are no fewer than half-a-dozen of them and they are instructed on the methods by which they should follow up on 'any clue that came to light, not an easy business . . .'

Any Fort Edward Native 'boy' who gives information is given five or ten shillings, depending on how good the information is, and de Bertodano's own 'boys' are also rewarded accordingly.

'It worked remarkably well. Our boys took a keen interest in getting information . . .'[31]

The intelligence is precise and detailed, with the only problem being that it is coming from Africans only, and as a rule their testimony is never given much weight in court or courts martial as it is always too difficult to take the sworn word of a black man over the sworn word of a white man, particularly when the latter is more likely to be a Christian and swear his word on the Bible.

•

The work of the Bushveldt Carbineers goes on, much of it now involved with rounding up remaining Boer families and escorting them to the newly constructed burgher camps at Pietersburg.

Witton has little sympathy for them, regarding them as several rungs below what he would call civilised.

'This is the class of people that predominates in South Africa, and in my opinion, there must be generations of purging, educating, and civilising before they will be capable of taking part in national life. They appear habitually to shun water, and never undress; as they go to bed, so they get up again – dirty, untidy, and unwashed.'[32]

And yes, of course Lieutenant Witton hears reports of how terrible and unsanitary the conditions in the concentration camps are, but he will record his views very firmly. It is their fault:

'The task [of having a clean camp] would be, I think, an impossible one, as most of the camp inmates had lived all their lives without even knowing what sanitation or cleanliness meant . . . A few who had lived a sort of gipsy life previously were discontented, and anxious to start roving again; otherwise there was no cause for complaint.'[33]

All up, the situation in the concentration camps is now beyond critical. As Boers have given up all over the countryside, with now some 30,000 farms and farmhouses destroyed, the numbers in the concentration camps have grown by 50 per cent in just the last two months, with now a net total of 94,000 whites and 24,000 blacks incarcerated.

How to feed that many people when, by definition, they are incapable of feeding themselves as the camps have no means of producing the sustenance required? The short answer is only with great difficulty, and the mortality rate lifts accordingly.

•

Shattered with an exhaustion that nearly approaches that of their horses, after three days of panting pursuit, Morant and his men at last arrive in the vicinity of Birthday Mine, and are quickly rewarded for their efforts. African scouts who've been sent ahead have good news. They know where Kelly's laager is to be found, just 25 miles away.

Onwards! *Onwards.* ONWARDS!

By very late on Sunday evening the BVC Troopers have carefully pushed to within two miles of Kelly's laager, some 150 miles from Fort Edward. Quietly dismounting – anxious that their stirrups not clank against their rifles to send out a warning of their presence in the damp night air – they go forward on foot.

They soon make contact with the local Natives, who inform Morant that Kelly had been here just a couple of hours earlier, drinking wine with them, while boasting that, 'If even a thousand Englishmen come to my laager I will wipe them all out.'[34]

The Natives are warned, under penalty of death, to stay tightly within their kraal while Morant and his men carefully make their way to Kelly's stronghold on the banks of the Thsombo River, right by the Portuguese East African border, arriving very quietly at midnight. Keenly aware of what had happened last time when he had attacked too hastily – when he had gone after the murderers of Captain Hunt – Morant, this time, is caution itself. Leaving Lieutenant Witton in charge of the exhausted men, he and Trooper Constantin of the Intelligence Department go forward in the freezing cold on an exceedingly careful reconnaissance mission.

And there they are in the soft and misty moonlight. In a clearing in the bush up ahead, Morant can see the Boer wagons arranged in their protective circle, a small fire going in the middle and one or two sentries on duty while most of the others sleep, though they can see a woman nursing a child there.

Instinctively, Morant wants to fire on the camp right away, to go in right behind a blizzard of bullets. However, as Trooper Silke – once again in the thick of it, and alarmed by hot-headed officers – will note, 'Constantin, a Swiss intelligence scout, restrained him and induced him to wait till morning.'[35]

Very well, then. Carefully returning to the main body of men, Morant divides them into three 'troops' to prepare to attack from three sides – with no-one to take any action until Morant and his troop do, likely at dawn if they all remain undiscovered.

'Refrain from shooting,'[36] orders Morant reluctantly. A touch of luck and pluck and this camp can be captured without the sound of a gun fired.

Again Sergeant Major Hammett takes one troop off to the right flank, while the Lieutenants Morant and Witton each take their troop along the riverbed, which Morant knows goes right to a point near the wagons, at the ready to block the Boers' most obvious line of retreat.

It doesn't take long for all three groups to be in position, at which point there is nothing they can do but wait till the dawn. All is calm bar one incident when, in the wee-est of all wee hours – perhaps around 3 am, a dog picks up the scent of intruders nearby and starts barking; they all freeze . . . just a little more than their current frozen state. Mercifully one of the Boers is seen to rise from his swag and, with great annoyance at being so awoken, gives the dog a kick to shut it up.

'A man never knows his luck in South Africa,' Morant breathes to Witton in appreciation. An hour later again, one of the African men in the laager arises to get the fire going and put the coffee on.

It's time . . .

Morant signals his men to follow him and suddenly charges forward, shouting, '*Handen omhoog!*' Hands up![37]

With the slightest sign of resistance, Morant and his men really would have opened fire with everything they had in them, but not only is not a shot fired against them, nor even a fist raised, but they immediately hear women wailing, which means shooting is out of the question for the Boers, they fear a stray British shot tearing through kinder and kin more than capture. It has gone better than any could hope.

On the reckoning that Kelly's tent is the grandest, Morant dispatches his men accordingly, and it is Trooper John Silke who tackles it, later recounting, 'I got to a tent door when Kelly himself poked his head out and I put the muzzle of my rifle under his chin and told him hands up. He opened his mouth so wide I thought I would fall into it so I stepped back a pace but he never showed fight at all.'[38]

The rest of Kelly's men – his sons among their number, closer to boys than they are men – have no chance. By the time they have all come out from under the wagons, where most of them had been sleeping, they are surrounded by the Bushveldt Carbineers, and have no choice but to sulkily put their hands up, while their rifles are gathered up. As the light of the early morning strengthens, the Carbineers are able to get a good look at the notorious Boer leader, and Lieutenant Witton, for one, is impressed.

'Kelly was a fine type of a man,' he will note, 'over six feet in height, and about 55 years of age; his father was an Irishman and his mother a Dutch woman. When I saw him again he was sitting in a Boer chair beside the fire; it had completely staggered him to realise that he was a prisoner, he who had boasted so often that he would give every Englishman a warm reception who came after him, and he had been taken without an opportunity of making the slightest resistance. The talk about the guns was all bluff.'

'Where are the big guns?' one of Morant's men asks.

'Don't talk to me, young man,' Kelly replies quite snappishly, in easy English. 'I'm a prisoner.'[39]

The Breaker is more interested in the fact that all of Kelly's gear seems to have been supplied by Her Majesty: 'His rifles, with exception of one Mauser, and his saddle gear, are all British, which his people have captured early in the war.'[40]

The weapons and saddles now return to British and Australian hands.

Corralling all the other Boer fighters and their wives around Kelly so they can be put under guard by just a few men, Morant sends a small party back to the kraal to bring back their horses and, once settled, begin their trek to get back to the Birthday Mine, before pushing on once more to Fort Edward, over the next three days.

Finally arriving back at Fort Edward, the Boer men, of course, are kept prisoner so they can be sent in a convoy to the burgher camp at Pietersburg while, for the moment at least, the women are free to go. These include two of Tom Kelly's daughters, who jump out of the wagon as soon as Fort Edward is reached.

'Where are you going?' Lieutenant Witton asks.

'Home to get the house ready,' they reply gaily.

Of course, their house, just a few miles down the road, has long been destroyed but Witton cannot bring himself to tell them the agony that awaits them when they arrive to see it.

For their part, those at Fort Edward are relieved first to see the safe return of their patrol, and soon enough delighted to see who they have brought to ground – the infamous Commandant Tom Kelly with nine of his best men! A dispatch rider is quickly sent to Pietersburg with the tidings. He returns promptly with a congratulatory message from Colonel Hall: 'Very glad to hear of your success, and should like to have an account of what must have been a good bit of work.'[41]

Breaker meantime has composed a carefully crafted capture report on Kelly, which makes clear (*cough*), if still in passing, that, well, he personally was actually the one who got the Boer leader. Yes, this would be surprising news to the man who actually did, Trooper Silke, but for the Breaker, why gild just one lily when you can order a dozen tied with a ribbon and have them sent to yourself? Why not make your great triumph, just a little greater?

> 25/9/01
> 25 Miles E, by S. of the Birthday Mine
>
> To O.C. BVC. Pietersburg
> SIR, – I have the honor to report the capture of the Boer Veldt Cornet Tom Kelly and nine (9) other Boers . . . . The whole camp was taken completely at a surprise. I took Kelly's rifle whist he was still in bed, and the camp put their hands up sulkily as the B.V.C. collected their rifles, etc . . .'[42]

And given such a personal triumph, could Morant perhaps make a small request?

> As the country is now clear, I should like permission to escort these prisoners personally to Pietersburg, leaving Lieut. Handcock in charge of the fort, as if possible I would like very much to go to Pretoria for a couple of days to settle up the affairs of my friend, the late Captain Hunt, as he wished me to. I will write you upon my arrival at Spelonken.
> I have the honor to be, Sir, yours obediently,
> HARRY MORANT, Lieutenant
> O.C.BVC, Spelonken.[43]

Of course, Morant's request is quickly granted and he and his 'boy' are soon on their way, the Breaker in high spirits as never before. Taking Tom Kelly down with nary a shot fired, well, if that is not worthy of a medal or a promotion, he doesn't know what is.

For now, the Breaker is the man of the hour, a commander in full command, a scallywag turned saviour, a chancer made good, a rogue redeemed. One never knows how their luck may twist and turn in this war.

True, he has some worries over the tension in camp, a growing sense that there might be some troubles down the track over the Visser and Heese business, but he has some ideas on how to eliminate at least some of his worries on that account.

Boy, get the horses, and some scoff. We are moving out.

•

It has been many tense weeks now of hard work, but Captain de Bertodano is now satisfied with the evidence he has assembled in order to convict Morant and Handcock for the murder of the missionary. The only problem is the failure to get Morant's lad away from Morant. It is the way of these things that the army itself has no formal relationship with the 'boys', they are more the 'property' of the officers, and so the army can't order them to move about. And when Morant is keeping such a strong eye on the lad – the reports are that he barely lets him out of his sight – they simply cannot get him away 'without rousing suspicion'.[44] But wait a moment. Has the Breaker cottoned on to de Bertodano's goal? Has Morant the mind to realise that the lad is a liability, that he has seen too much to be let loose, lest his lips bring ruin? This is a troubling thought, but . . . either way, de Bertodano's instructions remain clear: tread carefully, and . . .

Get. That. 'Boy'.

•

It has taken many drafts, and even more discreet discussions in remote spots – see you down by the clump of buffalo thorn in ten minutes – but at last it is completed.

The letter put together by Robert Cochrane is *written*. Corporal Browne insists on being the first man to sign. Then, one by one, each Trooper who has agreed steps forward to this quiet spot by Fort Edward to read it, and now reach for the quill of justice, putting their signatures to something which stands to be either Morant's death warrant . . . or their own, if he gets wind of it. Yes, it is a momentous act. But all of them have seen things that have haunted them and will likely haunt them for the rest of their lives unless they take action and do their best to bring the perpetrators to justice. Troopers McMahon and Lucas sign with the helpless Native in mind, whose last words were '*I konna*,' before Taylor brutally murdered him; Christie thinks of the dead children; Duckett has no hesitation in putting his name as he is still completely gutted at what Morant had made him do in being part of the firing party to kill the eight Boer prisoners. Every man has his reasons, every man signs solemnly in turn. Soon enough, it is done. The letter, with signatures, is ready to be delivered to the one man who can take swift action.

To Colonel Hall
O. C. Line of Communications
Pietersburg

We the undersigned non-commissioned officers and men of the Bushveldt Carbineers recently returned from the Spelonken district feel it is our imperative duty to ask you to kindly hold an exhaustive and impartial inquiry into the following disgraceful incidents which have occurred in the Spelonken district in order that the exact truth may be elicited and the blame attributed to those responsible.

The disgraceful incidents in question, the letter asserts, are:

the shooting of six surrendered Boer prisoners who had been entirely disarmed and who offered no resistance whatsoever ... the shooting of Trooper van Buuren BVC by Lt Handcock BVC ... the shooting of a surrendered and wounded Boer prisoner, Visser ... shooting eight surrendered Boer prisoners and one German missionary ... Lt Hannam BVC and party fired on wagons containing women and children ... killing 2 children of tender years and wounding one little girl ... shooting 2 men and a boy who were coming in to surrender.

Each alleged atrocity is gone into in some detail, before Cochrane closes out the letter.

We cannot return home with the stigma of these crimes attached to our names therefore we humbly pray that a full and exhaustive inquiry may be made by impartial Imperial officers in order that the truth may be elicited and justice done.

We are, sir
Your obedient servants
[Sgd]
ERNEST G. BROWNE, Cpl;
J.A. SKELTON Trooper
A.W.M. THOMPSON Trooper
J. HATFIELD Trooper
F.C. SHERIDAN Trooper
J.W.H. PENN Trooper
A. DUCKETT Trooper
JAS CHRISTIE Trooper
E. STRATTON Trooper
GEO D. LUCAS Trooper

F.C. HAMPTON Trooper
H.Y. COX Trooper
A. VAN DER WESTHUIZEN Trooper
A.R. MC CORMICK Cpl
JOHN SILKE Trooper

The signatures of many other men now absent on patrol can also
be obtained.
Witness to all the above signatures
R. M. Cochrane
Justice of the Peace, W. Australia
4 October 1901[45]

The main thing is that it is done. Actually getting the letter to Hall is
quite another. So dark is the mood among the officers like Morant and
Handcock – not to mention the omnipresent Captain Taylor – so wary do
they now seem of news getting out, that anything that involves contact
with the outside world is watched very closely.

'We could see they were afraid anything would leak out, and you may
be sure we were the very pictures of innocence.'[46]

They will have to wait for their opportunity.

•

After painting the Spelonken crimson with the blood of surrendered
Boers, Breaker Morant, now arrived in Pretoria, paints the town red
with endless reunions with old chums. A few of them are surprised that
Breaker is without his 'boy' – previously never more than spitting distance
away from him, and always fetching more grog – but apparently, he has
gone missing. You know how it is. They can be good lads one moment
and good and gone the next, usually with some of your kit.

Never mind. He does not seem overly concerned.

He is a newly minted war hero, his currency the fact that he is the
sole capturer of Tom Kelly, did he mention, and only a short time left to
gather his rosebuds while he may, before heading back to Fort Edward.
The young maidens of Pretoria receive his particular attention, which
begins with a courtly bow as the Breaker presents himself, with compliments, dash and flattery.

•

It is a strange thing to be your own kind of turncoat in the midst of your own unit. For James Christie is now indeed turning on his own criminal officers, and carries a secret missive that will surely destroy the BVC if he can just get it to the right authorities in Pietersburg. Both Morant and his senior men are now so buoyed with the triumph of Tom Kelly's capture Christie knows that there will never be a better time to make his move. After all, they have to get Kelly himself and his wagons down to Pietersburg and will need an escort of Troopers to do so in full security.

It takes some doing as he is knocked back several times, but after getting some of the other signatories to stand down to create vacancies in the escort, Christie is given his chance, as is Corporal Browne who will ride shotgun.

With the signed letter firmly inside his breast pocket atop his beating heart and the redoubtable Corporal Browne riding on his shoulder – both of them tingling with nervous energy, ready for any kind of interference – they set off.

Prisoner Kelly is duly delivered to headquarters, and *so are they*.

'We got in without mishap, and there laid our complaint before the Provost Marshal.'[47]

The Provost Marshal cannot believe what he is reading. *God Almighty.* Aware of the strict protocol in place on such occasions, the wheels of justice begin to move, as they must, formally. The letter is handed to Colonel Hall late on the afternoon of 8 October, and signed for.

He reads it, for much the same reaction.

GOD ALMIGHTY.

And they are going to have to tell one and the same! Yes, Lord Kitchener himself must hear of this at once. But who shall tell him? It falls to the Transvaal Colony's Assistant Provost Marshal, Major Wilfred Nash Bolton – better known in England before the war as 'Baby' Bolton, the giant rugby winger at over six feet tall and thirteen stone, who played rugby for England in 11 internationals.

This hulk of a fellow shuffles into the grand halls of Melrose House, where he is greeted by a smaller – albeit far grander – fellow, none other than the right-hand man to Lord Kitchener himself, one Provost Marshal Poore.

As officially noted with careful vagueness by Poore, Bolton has arrived 'with some papers about some rather bad things which have been taking place N. of Pietersburg'.[48]

In fact, 'rather bad' doesn't remotely cover it. The Provost Marshal begins his report in a proper and professional fashion, detailing the broad allegations, though Kitchener is unable to match the mood, simmering and bubbling with each new fact, each fresh atrocity he must listen to. This is *precisely* what de Bertodano had raised several months earlier, the dangers of that vicious beast Taylor and the scoundrel Morant. They are a mob of monsters those men in the BVC, they have raved and raided, they have murdered and maimed, and now they cause Lord Kitchener to lose his temper. His orders to Poore are delivered with some heat: get to the bottom of it. *Quickly*. Find the men responsible, and then we can get their accounts, before settling accounts.

Lord Kitchener will not rest until they are *shot*. But of course, due process must be observed, even in the case of swine such as this. A trial will have to come first.

As soon as the following day, Major Poore, ably assisted by a junior officer, orders depositions to be taken, starting, if they can, with Christie and Browne. If there are uniformed murderers at large in the Transvaal, the most urgent thing now is to gather the evidence that will bring them to justice.

One by one, from this point on, those soldiers who have served with the BVC and who are in Pietersburg for whatever reason – on leave, or running errands from Fort Edward – continue to be quietly interviewed about what has occurred, with their depositions taken down, before they sign them.

Albert van der Westhuizen affirms he witnessed Morant talking to Reverend Heese and, shortly afterwards, loudly order Lieutenant Handcock to ride out, before leaning in to whisper something to him for several minutes, whereupon Handcock had galloped out after the missionary, and . . . 'Shortly afterwards we heard the missionary was shot.'[49]

Trooper James Hampton details the horrific shooting of the women and children, that had continued even after the shouts of 'we surrender', and how 'the cries of surrender were ignored by Hannam who ordered that firing continue. I can positively swear that from the first to last not one of the Dutchmen . . . made the slightest attempt to fire a shot. The first to arrive was a woman with a dead boy in her arms between five and six years of age.'[50]

Corporal Ernest Garnett Browne details the shooting of the six Boers, and the suggested poisoning of 30 others.

Quickly, quietly, Provost Marshal Poore is able to confirm that the appalling allegations contained in the letter signed by the 16 BVC

Troopers are true. That does not yet mean they can be proved true in a court martial, but it does mean that action must be taken.

•

Captain de Bertodano paces the floor of his office in rough synchronicity with his mind going forth and back between what he knows and what he suspects. His informants tell him that Morant has indeed arrived in Pretoria. His 'boy' has not. That 'boy' is the sole witness to two murders, all de Bertodano has is inadmissible hearsay unless the 'boy' himself can testify about the fate of Reverend Heese and his driver. Morant is now reported to have left Pretoria and now be in Pietersburg. But there is still no sign of his 'boy'. De Bertodano's network of spies and informers are set to work, the time for subtlety has passed – find that 'boy'. But each inquiry leads to the same spot . . . Breaker Morant, arriving in Pietersburg, on his own, despite having left Fort Edward in the company of the 'boy'.

'We were never able to find any trace of the unfortunate lad and came to the conclusion that he had been shot.'[51]

That conclusion will be no sure thing until they have a body and a smoking gun, but Captain de Bertodano *is* sure about one thing. He will see Breaker Morant dead before this is through.

21 October 1901, Fort Edward, arresting officers

Move out.

Their time in these parts is up for the foreseeable future, and on this morning the convoy of those relieved by the new contingent – which has just arrived the previous day – moves out with Major Lenehan and the Lieutenants Witton and Handcock in the lead, together with another 40 men who have also finished their tour of duty. Troopers Christie and Cochrane, two of the men responsible for writing the secret *j'accuse* letter to Colonel Hall, stick so closely together each always has one flank of the other covered. It is not just the beating sun that makes them perspire freely today, it is the fact that their greatest danger lies in the very remoteness they must pass through to get from Fort Edward to Pietersburg. *Stick tightly together.* That has been their motto ever since the idea of writing the letter had come up, and it is never so urgent as right now. And whatever else, do *not* get on the left flank of Peter Handcock with no witnesses. In the two days and nights to come before they arrive, there can be no relaxing, on the reckoning that if Taylor or Morant have become aware of the letter and ordered their murder, they must always be on the lookout for something out of the ordinary, and . . .

And what's *that*?

Just three miles out of Pietersburg on the morning of 23 October comes the first sign that something is afoot. Well ahead, they can see two mounted horsemen approaching at a fair clip.

With the advance guard, Lieutenant Witton is the first to meet them.

'Are you Lieutenant Witton?'[52] one of them asks him in the officially clipped tones of one who is not offering salutations, but is here on important business.

'Yes,' answers the surprised Witton.

'The garrison commandant wishes to see you.'[53]

What?

Witton is puzzled. What on earth can this be about, particularly when it is less in the way of a request, and more in the way of an order – enforced by the fact that he is accompanied by one of the officers for the rest of the way, that officer staying just a little behind him?

Meanwhile, behind him the sun continues to shine down on the rest of the convoy, which remains unaware of what has just happened until . . .

Until the 20th Mounted Infantry troops swoop down from all sides upon the convoy! Similar conversations to the one had with Lieutenant Witton take place and, within minutes, all of Major Lenehan, Captain Taylor, Lieutenants Handcock, Picton, Hannam, and Sergeant Major Hammett have been relieved of their weaponry and advised that they are now under arrest and must accompany them back to the garrison. Oh yes, as Christie notes, 'nominally every man with the convoy was a prisoner'[54] but it is clear who is *really* under arrest. The officers of the BVC are being taken to the nearest fort – humiliation of all humiliations – 'under escort right before their own men!'[55]

Oh, and just in case anyone might be thinking of going for a short ride, their arresting officers announce, 'We have orders to shoot anyone leaving the convoy.'[56]

(Shoot an unarmed prisoner? Heavens!)

Trooper James Christie can scarcely conceal his delight and his *relief*.

'No message is to be sent by your Natives to Spelonken,' the arresting officer goes on, likely with 'Bulala' Taylor specifically in mind, for he can be given no warning. 'Under pain of court martial all communications must go through the authorities.'[57]

Christie knows at once what it all means. *The letter has got through and action is being taken.* Prisoners! It is the first time he has felt free in weeks. The only pity is that Morant is not here too, as he is still on leave in Pretoria, but his time will surely come.

For the moment, Christie now sees something that shows him that Colonel Hall and the authorities have some idea of the nature of the men they are up against.

For as extraordinary as it may seem, the arresting officers have with them . . . carrier pigeons! They are but three miles from Pietersburg, but there are to be no chances taken. Who knows how many in the BVC are brigands? Why, if there is a battle then these pigeons will be immediately released, 'so that the authorities at Pietersburg could be advised if any hitch occurred'.[58]

Colonel Hall has received a letter signed by only 16 men out of a possible 50 Troopers at Fort Edward; he has no idea if the entire BVC are desperadoes who will die before capture. James Christie is delighted to record that, 'the men of the BVC were only too pleased to see the officers off; they had endured things long enough'.[59]

And now as they ride, the word spreads of just how big this particular 'bag' is: 'The arrests comprise one major, one captain, five lieutenants, and one Sergeant Major.'[60]

The Major would be Major Lenehan, sent out to investigate rumours of a crime, now arrested as a criminal in uniform himself! The Captain is Alfred Taylor, while the Lieutenants are Witton, Handcock, Picton and Hannam, with Sergeant Major Hammett bringing up the rear – Morant is still free for the moment, on leave, but it won't be long. As they arrive in Pietersburg the soldiers they pass watch, mouths open, agog – officers and soldiers with their guns trained on the disarmed officers before them – and who can blame them? As Christie gleefully notes: 'Such a spectacle has never, I hear, taken place in the annals of the British Army.'[61]

When George Witton arrives under guard at the commandant's office, still ignorant as to what is happening, what he has done, he is met by Major Kenneth Neatson, staff officer to the commandant Colonel Hall. Witton can feel his heart making the slow climb up to his throat with every passing moment. This is not good.

Again, the question of identity is put, and rather sharply at that.

'Are you Lieutenant George Witton?'

'Yes.'

Major Neatson turns to the guard, and snaps off an order.

'Accompany Lieutenant Witton to the Garrison Artillery Fort.'[62]

Accompany? Well that is one word for it. 'Frogmarch' might be another term employed.

Things are turning ever more queer – and cold.

There is a chill to these officers, a remoteness entirely unbecoming to the way they might be expected to greet a brother officer returning from three months on the front line of the war on the Boer. But they will not tell him what the issue is. It is almost as if he has done something *wrong*? For the life of him, Witton cannot think what it might be.

Arriving at the fort, he is left in the charge of a Lieutenant Beattie, who is equally remote and declines to reveal what is going on. But here now is Major Neatson suddenly arriving, all business-like with a distinct air of *all-right-now-let-us-get-on-with-this*.

'Lieutenant Witton,' he says in coldly officious tones, 'you are under close arrest pending a court of inquiry.'

The officer commanding the fort, Colonel Hall, now approaches with more shocking words for Witton.

'You are a military prisoner under my charge, and if you attempt to escape, or go outside the wire entanglements, you will be shot. You are *not* to communicate with anyone outside, and all correspondence is to go through me.'[63]

Lieutenant Witton remonstrates, demanding to know for what possible offence he has been arrested, but receives no answers.

All around Pietersburg at much the same time, similar scenes are taking place for Major Lenehan, Captain Taylor, Lieutenants Handcock, Picton, Hannam, and Sergeant Major Hammett.

Lieutenant Morant quickly joins them the instant he returns to Pietersburg from Pretoria – displaying enough *sang-froid* that nothing he says or does is remarkable enough for any around him to chronicle.

In short order, and in close order, each one of them is placed under strict military guard in confined areas, with Morant 'under guard in lines', meaning his own spot is in the actual barracks, making him completely surrounded by Troopers with guns.

Even while under guard, Morant has a consistent story, carefully tailored to promote the idea that it is all a terrible misunderstanding, that he is innocent, that it all began when brave Captain Hunt attacked a Boer stronghold and was wounded.

'We had to retire and leave him there,' Morant lies fluently, 'but after getting reinforcements we again went out to capture the Boers who had wounded our captain. One of the native servants of Captain Hunt then came running up to me and said the captain has his neck

386 • BREAKER MORANT

broken. This upset me a good deal, and I immediately inquired where he was. The servant took me to where he lay, and there we found another native servant by the mutilated body crying like a child. We asked him what was the matter, and he then told us that the Boers had first tied a rope around the captain's neck and had drawn it lightly against a tree to break it, but finding they could not do so by this means one of the fellows jumped on his head with his heels. Captain Hunt and I were engaged to two sisters in Kent, England.'[64]

Well, under such circumstances, who *wouldn't* lose their mind a little and wreak havoc on those who had so mutilated their best friend and brother-in-law-to-be? It would be practically a matter of family duty, and surely a crime committed in the crucible of war such as this could be understood, if not condoned? Ever and always Morant goes on, emphasising the point.

'Seeing the captain, my chum, there in that awful state, after we had left him with only a wound in the thigh, was too much for me. I felt most horribly angry. In fact, I felt savage, and some little time afterwards we captured a Boer wearing Captain Hunt's uniform. We shot him, after trying him by court martial.'[65]

His account is filled with lies, of course. But they are also classic Morant lies – for there is just enough truth to them that they can pass muster from a distance of five yards, but any closer and the falsehood is obvious. The only question is whether that will still be the case on close inspection, and that is what the coming Court of Inquiry – perhaps followed by a court martial – will seek to establish.

•

The arrest of Lieutenant Breaker Morant is more than just a little pleasing to some. Corporal Herbert Sharp, for example – who had been booted from the BVC for being caught trying to sell his boots and uniform to the Boers – well, he is positively gleeful. In fact, he is even overheard to say in a Pietersburg bar that 'I would be willing to walk barefooted from Spelonken to Pietersburg, ninety miles, to be in a firing party to shoot Morant and Handcock.'[66]

Nothing perhaps that drastic is required, but Sharp *is* quick to sign as an assistant to Major Bolton in collecting evidence for this investigation. He tracks down potential witnesses, talks to them, determines their willingness to give evidence and even takes down their depositions before having them sign.

Bit by bit, day by day, written depositions come in, with detailed allegations building the case against the likes of Taylor and Morant.

October 1901, Pretoria, the Court of Inquiry

The Court of Inquiry – more inquiry than a court, a blizzard of hard questions with fast answers expected to determine if the disgrace of a court martial is warranted – is 'convened', as they are pleased to call it, on 16 October. Colonel Herbert Carter of the Wiltshire Regiment presides as President of the Court, assisted by Captain Edward Evans and Major Wilfred N. Bolton, the Assistant Provost Marshal.

And while he may not be present, Colonel James St Clair is following events closely. As the Deputy Judge Advocates General, and Kitchener's senior legal man in Pretoria, he will be the arbiter on which charges are laid and which will be left.

As it happens, 'convened' is indeed a rather grand word, for an affair held in a tent hastily erected near the Commandant's quarters. But inquire and enquire they do. On and on. The truth will out or they will pass out, one or the other.

It is a gruelling process. By Witton's account, at least, 'when the men of the Carbineers were being examined they were questioned in a most high-handed manner, and in some cases questions and answers would be taken down in writing without their knowledge; a day or so later they would be sent for again, and a long statement read over to them which they were ordered to sign'.[67]

There are upsets along the way, the most significant of which is Lieutenant Handcock, who is shocked to find himself seemingly accused of, as Witton will put it, 'the murder of every Dutchman that had been shot in South Africa, as well as that of a German missionary. He was so completely ignorant of military law and court proceedings that he asked the president what would be the best course for him to pursue; he was advised to make a clean breast of everything ...'[68]

Pursuing that course, the Bathurst man opens up, telling all, even if, as Witton will also claim, Handcock's 'confession', most particularly to the murder of Reverend Heese, was 'unwittingly done while in a high shivery nervous state'.[69]

When, however, only a short time later, Handcock, even more lugubrious than usual, tells Morant what he has done, the Breaker comes up with the solution. Claim 'duress'! Less a bush lawyer than a prison version of the same, Morant – who had worn the broad arrow all over Australia – knows more than he ever wanted to about the legal loopholes available after making confessions to the law, and the major one is claiming 'duress', insisting you were *bullied* into making a false statement. That's it, Peter. You had *no* legal representation, you were *exhausted* and *confused*, and you only said what you said under *duress*. Practise saying the word, it will stick. *Duress* rolls around on Breaker's tongue, the vicious poet loving the feel of it, implying a level of legal learning that he has not remotely reached, and so all the more enjoyable just for saying it.

'Upon being made aware of his position,' Witton will recount, 'he [Handcock] refuted his previous statement, and said that he had only made it to please Colonel Carter.'[70]

(It will take Morant and Taylor some time to get Handcock to understand and stick to an alternative story, what he was 'actually' doing instead of killing Reverend Heese, but eventually he has it down pat.)

When Lieutenant Picton starts to be questioned about the shooting of the Reverend Heese, he is quick to protest his innocence, before adding, 'I shrink to tell you all that really has taken place. If everything comes out it will be a shock to the world, and unless some step is taken we shall be at war with Germany within a month.'[71]

27 October 1901, Table Bay, SS *Avondale Castle*, under Hobhouse arrest

Well she never.[72]

Emily Hobhouse has no sooner arrived back in Cape Town aboard the *Avondale Castle* than she sees a steam tug pulling alongside filled with men in khaki. Soldiers. Trouble. Once they are on board that is confirmed, as things get organised.

An officer sets himself up on board in the smoking room, and proceeds to examine the papers of every one of the 450 passengers.

When the time comes for Miss Hobhouse, she has no sooner handed over her papers than he looks her up and down and informs her quietly that he prefers to talk to her alone, once he has completed the examination of everyone else.

Miss Hobhouse agrees to speak to him, but only in the presence of the Captain, 'for I had an instinctive turning to the Captain at the moment as the only man to stand by me'.[73]

It is as well, for Miss Hobhouse has no sooner made her way to the Captain's cabin, to be joined by the officer, than she is told: 'You are under arrest, and you will not be allowed to land in South Africa. You can have no communication with anyone on shore by word or letter . . . Captain, she is in your charge, and you are held responsible for her. You are to see she does not leave the ship, or communicate with anyone.'[74]

He is acting under the authority of Colonel H. Cooper, the Military Commandant of Cape Town, whose own orders are coming from the highest level.

Needless to say, Miss Hobhouse refuses to co-operate in any way and the stand-off will continue for five days while she – still in her cabin, afloat on a sea of discontent and lost in a mist of rage – pens a couple of letters to important people that will enter the public domain.

Starting with you, Lord Kitchener: 'You have forgotten so to be a patriot as not to forget that you are a gentleman. I hope in future you will exercise greater width of judgement in the exercise of your high office. To carry out orders such as these is a degradation both to the office and the manhood of your soldiers. I feel ashamed to own you as a fellow-countryman.'[75]

And, as for *you*, British High Commissioner Lord Milner, well where does she start? 'Your brutal orders [to put women and children in concentration camps] have been carried out and thus I hope you will be satisfied. Your narrow incompetency to see the real issues of this great struggle is leading you to such acts as this and many others, staining your own name and the reputation of England . . .'[76]

Finally, my Lords Kitchener and Milner order her *forcible* removal to the ship that will take her back to England.

A Colonel arrives in the company of two burly soldiers.

'Will you yield of your own free will,' he asks Miss Hobhouse, 'otherwise there are the soldiers.'

'Sir, I cannot and will not give other reply than what I have said from the beginning . . . I am weak and ill – unfit to take this voyage.'

'Madam,' he says archly, 'do you wish to be taken like a lunatic?'

'Sir, the lunacy is on your side and with those whose commands you obey. If you have any manhood in you, you will go and leave me alone.'[77]

One of the soldiers, clearly shamed by her words, decides to do exactly that, and appears to be about to leave the room until the Colonel barks at him, whereupon he returns and they get to the job at hand.

Miss Hobhouse suffers the indignity of having her shawl wound tightly round her arms, and she is *carried* on board the *Roslin Castle*, which will return her to England – where the great debate over the concentration camps goes on, with the clergy becoming particularly involved.

On the one hand, you have the likes of the very Reverend John Knox exulting: 'Among the unexampled efforts of kindness and leniency made throughout this war for the benefit of the enemy, none have surpassed the formation of the Concentration Camps.'[78]

On the other hand, you have leading Baptist minister, Dr Charles Aked, thundering from his pulpit in Liverpool, 'Great Britain cannot win the battles without resorting to the last despicable cowardice of the most loathsome cur on earth – the act of striking a brave man's heart through his wife's honour and his child's life. The cowardly war has been conducted by methods of barbarism . . . the concentration camps have been Murder Camps.'[79]

He is followed home by a large crowd and they smash the windows of his house.

Nevertheless, in the face of such damaging accusations at home and abroad, it is hard for the British establishment to know how to react.

Lord Milner's starting point is to exculpate himself, noting archly in a cable to Colonial Secretary Joseph Chamberlain, 'I did not originate this plan,'[80] before noting the tragic truth: '. . . even if the war were to come to an end tomorrow, it would not be possible to let the people in the concentration camps go back to their former homes. They would only starve there. The country is, for the most part, a desert . . .'[81]

Which is true.

But still they must end this war, as the British themselves are beyond exhausted. Attrition has turned to atrophy.

'I wish I could find some way of finishing the war,' Lord Kitchener writes to Secretary of State for War, William Brodrick '. . . Milner asked me about Mrs Hobhouse being allowed to land at Cape Town and we argued that considering the attention she had taken up and the untruths she had published that it would not be desirable in the present state of the colony to allow her to do so. I enclose copies of her letters on the subject to Milner and myself. I daresay if they were published in the papers it might give the public a clearer insight into the sort of lady she is.'[82]

In the meantime, another small sign of just how tired of it all Lord Kitchener himself is, how *desperate* he is to see the war finished quickly, comes in many reports carried in the British press, even while Emily Hobhouse is on the high seas heading back to England.

KHAKI-CLAD BOERS.
ORDERED TO BE SHOT.

LONDON, Nov. 12.

The. 'Daily Mail' states that Lord Kitchener has issued an order that all Boers who are captured dressed in khaki, and disguised as British soldiers are to be at once shot.[83]

23 November 1901, Pietersburg, Court of Inquiry, stunned by statements

Breaker Morant is no stranger to composing his own poems and polemics, but for now the words of an Irish poet by the name of Wilde are apposite:

> *I never saw a man who looked*
> *With such a wistful eye*
> *Upon that little tent of blue*
> *Which prisoners call the sky,*
> *And at every drifting cloud that went*
> *With sails of silver by.*[84]

How prescient. Minutes pass like hours and hours like days as the spectre of dark eternity hovers ...

It has been a month so far of captivity for himself, George Witton, Peter Handcock, Henry Picton, Robert Lenehan, Alfred Taylor, Ernest Hammet and Charles Hannam, and the lot of them are starting to go mad. They know that the Court of Inquiry continues apace, that they are likely being torn apart by unseen accusers, and it is *infuriating*.

The men had not expected anything on so black a Christmas as this one approaching, but they are finally blessed with the gift of information on their planned future.

They are brought from their cells to a tent close to the Commandant's HQ. Standing to attention before the judges, led by Colonel Carter in the middle, George Witton feels a strange elation, certain of his innocence and confident he will not be returned to a prison cell.

'Morant,' on the other hand, Witton himself will note, 'appeared gloomy and irritable. The past months of close confinement had greatly impaired his health, physically and mentally, and he looked upon current events from a very pessimistic standpoint.'[85]

As for Peter Handcock, well, he is 'even more silent than usual, and looked much worried and dejected'.[86]

'We were informed by the president that we would be tried by court martial at an early date, and the statements of the witnesses for the prosecution were read over to us.'[87]

Notwithstanding that Colonel Carter reads each word of the statement in a careful, deliberate tone, each sentence for the prisoners has an eerie echo as the shocking accusations bounce about.

Take this one. How does this statement strike your ears? This is what your supposed friend Trooper Sidney Staton has to say about you.

Sid, turned?

Oh yes. Listen well.

> I, Sidney Allen Staton, hereby make oath and swear as follows:
> I remember the second of July when the Six Boers were shot.
> The patrol was drawn up at Sweetwaters Farm and I saw there
> Captain Taylor, Captain Robertson and Lt Handcock. Then we
> rode on until we came across five Boers lying in the road dead
> and one lying dead in the wagon under his blankets never having
> left his bed . . .
> I remember the shooting of the captured Boer prisoner F. Visser
> who was severely wounded when captured . . . I heard Lieutenant
> Morant tell Trooper Botha to translate to the Boer this sentence:
> 'You might tell me something about the Boers for as your doom is
> sealed anyhow you needn't tell any lies.' The words were to that
> effect. Before the wounded Boer was shot, Lt Picton called for
> volunteers to shoot him. The men murmured and Lt Picton said
> 'it was no crime to shoot him as he was outlawed'.
> I saw Trooper Gill volunteer . . . Shortly after either Lt Handcock
> or Lt Picton went up with a revolver and blew out his brains . . .
> Signed: Sidney Allen Staton
> Witness: R. M. Poore
> Provost Marshal
> Army Headquarters
> Pretoria
> 11 October 1901.[88]

It makes for grim reading and grimmer listening, but as George Witton will note, it has a surprise effect on the Breaker: 'Morant listened in austere silence to the end, then, springing to his feet, exclaimed, "Look here, Colonel, you have got us all here now; take us out and crucify us at once, for as sure as God made pippins, if you let one man off he'll yap."'[89]

Colonel Carter – leaning forward, a little bemused and a little intrigued at the suggestion of a grand conspiracy put in such theatrical terms by the red-hued accused – declines the offer, merely suggesting that the men would be wise to seek counsel before the inevitable court martial.

A lawyer? George Witton doesn't really know any. Uncertainly, he asks the advice of Captain Evans, who acted as the secretary for the Court of Inquiry, who has a reassuring response: 'I've gone into your case thoroughly, and I consider that you have taken such a subordinate part that it is not necessary for you to go to the trouble of bringing counsel or witnesses from Capetown.'

But what of those damning statements! All that incriminating evidence?

Never you mind, Mr Witton, it's no more than pomp and fancy.

'You have nothing to fear or trouble about,' Evans replies, 'you are bound to be exonerated!'[90]

Yes, this court martial is a formality, for chaps understand how things were and how things went.

Lawyers are for the lawless, for men who have committed monstrosities, not for good honest soldiers. Just by consulting a lawyer, wouldn't they look as though they had something to hide?

Speaking of which . . .

Captain Taylor? He may be many things, but he is no fool. He knows the ways of his army and he knows himself. He will require no counsel as he has always kept his own. Taylor will rely on his own wits to defend his actions; or rather, to point out that the actions were all taken by others. He has no fewer than eight charges pending, most of them murder, and is detained like all of them until those charges can be formalised.

One thing General St Clair does not agree with is continuing to pursue Lieutenant Hannam for ordering the attack on Boer wagons containing women and children, which had seen the killing of two young brothers. The Boer men in those wagons had never surrendered, and were still armed at the time. Such is war, such is the law.

Ideally, Lord Kitchener's own opinion on the matters at hand should have no sway one way or another, as he is not a formal part of the legal process and justice must be blind.

This does not stop the Lord, however – as 'Convening Officer' of the courts martial – looking very closely at the Taylor case in particular, and drawing a line through all bar two of the eight charges the Deputy Judge Advocates General wishes to bring against him. He will face court martial for inciting the murder of the six Boers and shooting a black man. Justice may try her hardest to remain blind, but, as Lord Kitchener will attest, in this war she does peek from underneath the blindfold every now and then.

CHAPTER SIXTEEN

COURT MARTIAL

The first thing we do, let's kill all the lawyers.

William Shakespeare,
Henry IV, Part 2, Act 4, Scene 2

Early December 1901, Pietersburg, dishonoured, dismembered, dissolved[1]

The ultimate indignity for the one-time proud members of the Bushveldt Carbineers? It is that on this day they are no more, without even a name to cling to.

So shameful are the charges that have been levelled against them, so embarrassing for all of the British forces, it has been judged better to bury them entirely so that no-one will be even reminded of their one-time existence. From now, early December 1901, their corps will be called the Pietersburg Light Horse, and such few members of the original BVC who remain – only one officer of whom was with the original command – will be well advised to never mention their previous connection.

As a matter of fact, it is not in name only that they are diminished. So weak has their presence been in the northern Transvaal that from December onwards the Boer leader General Beyers moves back into the Sweetwaters Farm hotel, reclaiming the room so recently occupied by Captain Taylor!

Olivia Bristow makes him most welcome, as ever.

4 December 1901, Cape Colony, concentrated blame

The grim truth is that, despite the best intentions of the British to keep the Boer women and children safe, things had quickly spiralled out of control as a variety of viruses had felled the innocent like a scythe through wheat. The challenge is to constrain an illness while containing a populace. Who will be blamed is obvious. For who can lay blame on those in fresh graves? No, in such circumstances it is the captors not the captive who will most likely be judged poorly by the public and history alike.

Alarmed, the Governor of Cape Colony and High Commissioner for Southern Africa, Lord Milner, writes to one of his officials, the Commissioner for Bechuanaland, Major Sir Hamilton John Goold-Adams: 'It is impossible not to see that, however blameless we may be in the matter, we shall not be able to make anybody think so, and I cannot avoid an uncomfortable feeling that there must be some way to make the thing a little less awfully bad if one could only think of it.'[2]

Perhaps on the reckoning of 'lies, damned lies and statistics', they could put together some statistics that might, if looked upon in the right light as the wind blows from the east, and given to a sympathetic English press, not look *quite* so bad? All options must be examined but, right now, all things and all the damned statistics look very bad indeed.

To Lord Milner, the problem is now simply insoluble. In response to the likes of Emily Hobhouse and the outcry in Britain, they have done what they can – medical care, hygiene and rations have all been improved – with what result? More deaths!

'The theory that, all the weakly children being dead,' Milner continues, 'the rate would fall off, is not so far borne out by the facts. I take it the strong ones must be dying now and that they will all be dead by the spring of 1903!'[3]

In a subsequent letter to Joseph Chamberlain, Milner is frank. This procession of unintended death that still 'continues is no doubt a condemnation of the camp system. The whole thing, I now think, has been a mistake . . . a sad fiasco . . . I should never have touched the thing if, when the "concentration" first began, I could have foreseen that the soldiers meant to sweep the whole population of the country higgledy-piggledy into a couple of dozen camps . . .'[4]

But as far as doing something about the deaths in camp? They have not so much turned over a new leaf as they have poisoned the whole tree.

'I thought,' Milner wrote, 'that we had begun to turn the corner and that after having reached unparalleled heights of mortality in October we should now show a heavy decline. Unfortunately, the figures have risen again alarmingly.'[5]

No fewer than 2380 die in December and the new year brings no new hope, just fresh graves and the same old terrors.

•

With the formal court martial of the BVC men approaching, on 15 January 1902 – just a week before it is to begin – on this day all of the accused are served with their formal charge sheets with a list of the cold facts and even colder acts they are accused of committing. In dry, emotionless tones, the offence, the date and the place of each alleged crime is read out, and the accused listen in the full knowledge that they only need to be found guilty of one of these grave charges to head to their own early grave after being shot by a firing party.

When George Witton mentions in passing to Morant that he is being charged with a total of nine murders – the eight Boers and Visser – the one-time horse-riding champion can't help himself.

'Only nine!' the Breaker bursts out blackly, 'that is nothing; I am charged with twelve, and an infanticide.'[6]

Lieutenant Handcock is charged with the murder of Trooper van Buuren, as well as Visser, Reverend Heese, the eight Boers on 23 August, and the three Boers on 7 September.

On the killing of the six Boers on 2 July, Captains Robertson, Taylor, and Sergeant Major Morrison, are charged with 'committing the offense of murder while on active service'. For his lack of action on that matter, Major Lenehan is charged with 'failing to make a report which it was his duty to make'.[7]

•

He may have, for the moment, lost his liberty, but nobody will ever accuse Breaker Morant of having lost his *nerve*. And bloody cheek, come to think of it. The first to attest to that at this point, is Captain Thomas Purland, Pretoria's Director of Prisons and therefore Lieutenant Morant's gaoler, who on this day opens a letter from his most infamous prisoner of the moment, Morant.

Captain Purland, I would be honoured if you would act as my counsel, in my upcoming court martial?

The sheer *hide* of the man!

Nevertheless, a written request deserves a formal reply, and Purland gives it in the most detached third person way he can muster, two days later.

> I am astonished that Lieut. Morant shall have made such a request. I have only the slightest acquaintance with him and he should be aware that my official position prevents my undertaking such a duty as he suggests – even if I had the inclination.[8]

One legal eagle familiar with the case suggests he should 'plead insanity for the defence'.[9]

Such counsel is firmly *rejected* by Morant as is this counsel, as are all other prospective legal counsellors.

And Morant is not the only one without counsel. They are all in the same boat. As it happens, not surprisingly, it is the only lawyer among the accused, Major Robert Lenehan, who comes up with the one Australian lawyer with military background who is in South Africa, and with so little else to do that he might be tempted . . .

(Of course, Lenehan could represent himself, but the old adage stands – 'A lawyer who represents himself has a fool for a client.')

Mid-January 1902, Cape Town, no doubting Thomas, Major for martial

A cable for you, Major Thomas.

Thomas, the Tenterfield lawyer who, after a second stint in South Africa with the NSW Bushmen, is again about to return home, opens it with interest and is taken aback by the contents. It is from his old acquaintance from the University of Sydney legal fraternity, Bob Lenehan, about to face court martial in Pietersburg, and urgently needing counsel. Is Major Thomas interested?

Major Thomas does not have to consider for long. With his military skills no longer in demand, it is propitious that there suddenly be a call for his legal skills.

'I did not like to refuse,' Thomas will recount, 'so I got a permit . . . and proceeded to Pietersburg where I was engaged for about five weeks upon as difficult task as I suppose ever fell to an advocate.'[10]

Difficult?

Rather.

For no sooner has Thomas arrived in Pietersburg than it turns out that while Taylor has chosen indeed to represent himself, none of Morant, Handcock, Witton or Picton has been able to secure legal representation of their own. Under such extreme circumstances, Thomas is prevailed upon to represent them all, which sees him 'briefed' for a few frantic hours by a breathless Bob Lenehan, who leads him through the byzantine plots and copious charges he will have to cope with. Thomas then meets briefly with Morant and Handcock; their encounters fleeting as they greet their fresh counsel, who is completely fresh to the peculiarities of a court martial or the minutiae of military law. As one would expect, Morant is all bluff bravado and charm, Handcock silent and stoical.

Hands are shaken, good luck is wished and by God they shall need it and a good lawyer to end this trial as free men. As for George Witton, well, he will only manage to meet with his lawyer in a flash, the last to be counselled by this counsel on the very morning of their trial.

'He paid me a hurried visit,' Witton will recount, 'which lasted for a few minutes only. In this time I briefly detailed to him the part I had been compelled to take, which had resulted in the charges now preferred against me. I was then escorted to the court-house in the town.'[11]

16 January 1902, Pietersburg public court, trial of error

All rise.

The assembled military men do indeed rise in this unmistakably British courtroom, transplanted to a far-flung foreign field of the Empire – the Old Bailey, this is not. The constant trickle of sweat which drips from every oily hide in the room is proof enough of that. Today, there will be a total of six judges, a jury of justices with the power of life in one hand and death in the other.

The judges appointed for this court martial sit either side of the President of the Court, Lieutenant Colonel Henry Cuthbert Denny – an English officer with a superior air and a moustache ideally trimmed to bristle with indignation – and survey the prisoners as they are led in.

Morant, Handcock, Witton and Picton stand before the court charged with the murder of Floris Visser.

A pack of scallywags? Murderers? Monsters? Or dutiful soldiers doing what had to be done to survive and win this war out in the badlands; doing what had to be done far from the comforts of those who would presume to sit in judgement of them?

There is no doubt that is what one of the accused thinks.

There stands the Breaker, his chest puffed out and his back upright, the very picture of defiant and completely self-assured importance. Handcock, removed and reserved, is harder to read, while Witton and Picton wobble and sweat like cadets on a humid parade ground. Lenehan seems simply deflated, humiliated. No, not to be in a court – but to be here as *defendant*, not *advocate*.

Counsel for the accused, Major Thomas, looks at them all warily.

Is he, alone, really to defend these five Australians, against six judges who would clearly like nothing more than to deliver six guilty verdicts?

It would seem so.

It is for good reason that the Scottish prosecutor, Captain Robert Burns-Begg, a former Intelligence man on Lord Kitchener's staff as it so happens, seems full of easy confidence as, with practised ease – for this man really does know his way around a courtroom – he calls his first witness. It proves to be a very nervous Sergeant Samuel Robinson, a member of the BVC who was present for much of the action described. It is no small thing for a man of such low rank as a Sergeant to stand and testify about such momentous matters, but Robinson affirms he is prepared to do so, and only tell the truth so help him God.

Captain Burns-Begg wastes no time in getting to the matter that sparked this whole affair: the bloody night that Captain Hunt died . . .

'Do you remember the fight at Devil's Kloof?' he asks in his light Scottish lilt.[12]

'I do,' replies Robinson firmly. 'That was when Captain Hunt and Sergeant Eland were killed. We found Captain Hunt's body . . . stripped.'

And then?

'I took the bodies back to Reuter's farm, where our party was reinforced by Lieutenant Morant, Handcock, Picton and Witton. The next morning we went in pursuit of the Boers, overtook them, and captured their laager.'

And were there any prisoners taken?

'We found one wounded Boer there.'

And what happened to this Boer?

'The next day he accompanied our forces some distance.'

Did Morant speak to the prisoner?

'Yes, during the dinner hour he had a conversation in which the Boer prisoner, who was in a Cape cart six yards away, appeared to take no part.'

A conversation in which one party does not speak? To somebody six yards away? What was said?

'Well, Morant and an intelligence officer . . . went to Visser and told him "We're sorry, but you have been found guilty of being in possession of the late Captain Hunt's clothing, and also of wearing khaki".'

What else was said?

'I didn't catch what else was said, but I was told to warn two men for duty.'

And that 'duty' was . . . ?

Preparing a firing party for the prisoner.

What did you say to this?

'I refused. I asked Lieutenant Picton, "By whose orders is this man to be shot?" He replied the orders were by Lord Kitchener.'[13]

Do tell? When were these orders issued?

Sergeant Robinson cannot help him on that one, affirming only that Picton at the time had given a specific date.

Very well then, what was Lord Kitchener's order, such as you were told?

'It was to the effect that all Boers wearing khaki from that date were to be shot.'

Have you ever seen such an order written down?

'I have never seen any such orders.'

What is the usual case with new orders of such a magnitude?

'They should have been posted or read regimentally.'

But they were not, because there were no such orders, Captain Burns-Begg's point is clear. Major Thomas now rises to cross-examine the Sergeant.

'Did Captain Hunt's body bear marks of ill-treatment?' asks Thomas.

'Yes,' replies Robinson.

'And was the Boer prisoner wearing khaki?' continues Thomas.

'He had a kind of khaki jacket on,' Robinson says, an answer that clearly gives Major Thomas some satisfaction, for in this grim, dim courtroom the evidence that the Sergeant is giving is akin to a distant lighthouse on an exceedingly dark and stormy night. It does not guarantee salvation, but it is certainly to be found in this direction.

Now Major Thomas is curious about Robinson's apparent surprise to be given the order to shoot a Commando prisoner. Because Lieutenant Picton was not the first or highest officer to tell him of such an order, was he?

No, Robinson admits.

'Captain Hunt had previously told me that he had direct orders that no prisoners were to be taken.'

Indeed? And was that the only occasion Captain Hunt spoke of this order?

No, it wasn't.

'On one occasion Captain Hunt abused me for bringing in three prisoners against orders,'[14] Robinson says.

As for Captain Morant, had he ever hurt a prisoner before taking command?

'Morant was previously considerate to prisoners,' Robinson confirms. But that changed with the death of Hunt.

'Lieutenant Morant was in charge of the firing party that executed Visser.'[15]

This is a claim that Morant has never denied and Major Thomas does not dispute. No further questions, Sergeant Robinson, the next witness may be called.

Trooper Theunis Botha is a Boer, a 'joiner', as he is known to the British, though a 'traitor' to the Boers. Whatever he is, he is a man with a troubled conscience, eager to unburden himself of the thing he has struggled with for the last six months.

'I was one of the firing party who carried out the sentence on Visser! He was carried down to a river and shot. I had lived with Visser on the same farm!'

So, you declined to be in the firing party?

'I did object,' Botha says.

(This is not how Breaker Morant and others recall it, Trooper Botha was not only one of the firing party, but eager to be there.) Ultimately, however, it is neither here nor there for these proceedings whether the Boer was a part of it. All that counts here is to establish whether in giving the orders to form up a firing party and then ordering the men to fire upon Visser, Morant was himself following orders. As Botha can shed no light on that, or at least not the light that Thomas is looking for, the Tenterfield lawyer has no further questions for Botha, and the next witness enters the box.

Captain Burns-Begg asks Corporal Herbert Sharp the same questions he has been asking witnesses all day. Was the prisoner shot? Was there a firing party? Who was in command? The tedium of asking so repetitiously is matched only by the tedium being answered so repetitiously. Yes. Yes. Morant was in command, sir. This monotony continues till the last, when Captain Burns-Begg – with courtly calm perfect for the occasion, as it heightens the shock of what is to come – asks if the Corporal in the box has anything else to add. Actually, yes he does.

Oh?

'After the firing party had fired, Picton discharged his revolver,' Sharp says.

At what, precisely?

'It appeared to me to be at the dead man's head,' Sharp finishes.

The court shudders as one.

And yet the defence is not without recourse. Yes, Major Thomas? The bush lawyer rises to speak, first citing the deposition of Intelligence Officer Leonard Ledeboer.

'On August 10 last year,' the Major reads portentously, 'I translated the sentence of a court martial that condemned Visser to be shot. Morant, Picton, Handcock, and Witton formed the *court martial*.'[16]

So you see, my good gentlemen of this court, there *was* a 'court martial' – a drum-head court martial to be sure – but it handed down a sentence which Ledeboer then translated into Dutch for the silent Boer who awaited his fate.

Better still, however, let us hear from the man who presided over the said drum-head court martial. Major Thomas now motions towards Lieutenant Harry Harbord Morant.

As he rises, the Major pauses. He has not wanted to put Morant on the stand, has actively argued against it, but the Lieutenant himself has insisted so vociferously there had been no choice. Very well, then. I cannot stop you. And so, on this very morning, just an hour before he had given Morant his last instruction: now is not the time to *be* the Breaker, it is time to be Harry Harbord Morant, if you please. Yes, Harry, no doubt a litany of quips and witticisms will occur to you, each one more barbed than the last, but for your own sake if not ours, would you mind keeping them to yourself? To win over this court, you're going to have to pretend that you *aren't* Breaker Morant.

Lieutenant, what was your position prior to the events that led to the death of the prisoner Visser?

'I was under Captain Hunt, with the force charged with clearing the northern district of Boers,' says Morant, with the clipped tone and steely speed of a man used to using his words as weapons.

It was regular warfare?

'It was regular *guerrilla* warfare.'

The question of orders has been brought up in this court, of taking no prisoners. What is your understanding of where these orders originated?

'Captain Hunt acted on orders he brought from Pretoria,' answers Morant carefully but pointedly. He is not saying that the orders came from Lord Kitchener, but that is the inference the court will draw. And Morant is happy to tell the court how he did not follow these orders, not at first, not until Hunt himself died.

'On one occasion I brought in thirty prisoners, then Captain Hunt reprimanded me for bringing them in at all. "Don't do it again," he told me.'

Fine. Well, when was it that you became the presiding field officer for the BVC?

'I took command after Captain Hunt was killed, I went with reinforcements,' Morant tells the court. 'When I learnt the circumstances of Captain Hunt's death, and the way he had been maltreated . . .'

The Lieutenant pauses, and slips a little. Major Thomas can see the Breaker stirring beneath. The recollection of Hunt's demise troubles

Morant in a way that nothing else could. Yet his voice steadies as he speaks, rising to this grave occasion when he can talk of *justice* served:

'I followed the Boers and attacked their laager. The Boers cleared, leaving Visser, he had on a soldier's shirt. He was using Captain Hunt's trousers as a *pillow*!'

Morant bites off each word, doing what he can to maintain a veneer of composure. His anger at what happened to Hunt is matched only by his disgust at the Boers. They have no *rules*, no *honour*.

'Visser was court-martialled and shot on this account,' Morant declares.

And were his men reluctant to shoot the prisoner?

'The others knew of Captain Hunt's orders.'

Everyone understood, don't you see? *There are to be no prisoners brought in, and if they are wearing khaki, they are to be shot at once.*

But certainly, the men were initially hesitant. Why, he had resisted Captain Hunt's orders himself, at first.

'I told the men I had previously disregarded the orders, but after the way the Boers had treated Captain Hunt, I would carry out the orders,' Morant finishes.

Did you regard the orders as lawful?

'I did.'

Major Thomas leaves it at that, handing over to Captain Burns-Begg to begin his cross-examination.

What precisely were the orders given by Captain Hunt?

'Captain Hunt's orders were to clear Spelonken and take no prisoners.'

Have you ever seen these orders in *writing*? (As in, the way orders of such moment would usually be given.)

'No, but Captain Hunt quoted the action of Kitchener's and Strathcona's Horse as precedents,' says Morant, the latter referring to a widespread rumour of a unit that had trusted a Boer white flag as a sign of genuine surrender, only to be shot for their trouble. They had then strung up their Boer prisoners on the spot, in a brutal retaliation that went unpunished – and practically uncriticised.

Once again, the implication is an accusation: our actions were not unprecedented and you know it. Would the court like to explore those precedents?

No, the court would not.

The Scottish Captain continues the cross-examination. Lieutenant Morant, you said that you had previously disregarded these orders to shoot prisoners. Why?

'I did not carry out the orders previously because my captures were a good lot. I shot no prisoners prior to Visser.'

This 'court martial' you held for Visser, did you call any witnesses?

'No witnesses were called as we were *all* eye-witnesses,' replies Morant acidly. They could see the man with their dead Captain's clothing, they knew he was a party to Hunt's death.

Was there no formal objection from the men to shooting a prisoner?

'Yes,' replies Morant. 'Picton raised an objection to Visser being shot, on the grounds that he should have been shot *the night before*.'

Morant's black wit is lost on the court, particularly Captain Burns-Begg who has no time for japes right now. Without even raising a smile, the Captain returns to the 'orders'.

'Captain Hunt told me not to take prisoners,' replies Morant, 'I never questioned the validity of his orders.'[17]

The court is adjourned.

Major Thomas and the Breaker are pleased. Today went well, and provided a valuable lesson. There is evidently an answer that this court will not hear, a name that must remain unsaid.

This revelation aside, when the trial resumes the next morning, the court has . . . reconsidered.

Again, Captain Burns-Begg asks the question. *Who was it* that gave Captain Hunt his orders? It has to have been somebody.

'Colonel Hamilton, Military Secretary, was the one who had given Captain Hunt the orders that no prisoners were to be taken,' Morant replies coolly. There is a suppressed gasp. Colonel Hamilton, of course, is Chief-of-Staff to the Commander-in-Chief himself! It does not take a genius then to work out who Morant is saying gave Colonel Hamilton this order.

A thrown Captain Burns-Begg continues his cross: Your 'court martial' of Visser, was that ever reported to any authority?

'Yes, it was reported to Colonel Hall within a fortnight after it was held,' replies Morant evenly. 'A report was also sent to Captain Taylor.'

But Captain Burns-Begg's mind is clearly still on a previous sensational answer.

What *evidence* did you have that Colonel Hamilton gave such an order to Captain Hunt?

'I have Captain Hunt's word,'[18] replies Morant simply, with an added sombre note for the deceased. Colonel Hamilton might need further evidence than that, but for Lieutenant Morant that was always enough.

More than a brother officer, he was practically a brother in fact, and it never would have occurred to Lieutenant Morant to question that word.

Moving on, then.

This 'report' that you gave of what you are pleased to call your 'court martial'. Where is the evidence of that?

'I have made no attempt to get my report of the court martial *as* evidence,' answers Morant simply.

And yet many questions do remain. The next one is from President of the Court, Lieutenant Colonel Denny. And what of the so-called 'trial' of Visser? He is anxious to know if the military rules of the 'Red Book' of British soldiers' regulations were followed. Did they follow the *rules*?

'Was your court at the trial of Visser constituted like this?' asks the President. 'And did you observe paragraph six of the seventh section of the King's Regulations?'[19]

'Was it like *this*?' snaps Morant. 'No; it was not quite so *handsome*. As to rules and sections, we had no Red Book, and knew nothing about them. We were out *fighting* the Boers, not sitting comfortably behind barb-wire entanglements.'

Morant's words curl with contempt, in rough tandem with his upper right lip. And so the 'President' in this farce of a legal action wants to know, from the comfort of the bench, just which regulation he, as a fighting man on the front line risking his life every hour he was out there, had followed in killing Boers?

Very well, then. Morant will create chapter and verse for him:

'We *got them* and we *shot them* under Rule 303!'[20]

As God is their witness, out there on the front line the .303 rifle is the BVC's judge, jury and executioner all in one, and the Breaker will be damned if he is not going to make this point to one who would presume to judge *him*. Seated in front of him, Major Thomas does not groan – at least not out loud – but it is a close-run thing. What might have been a brilliant quip in a bar-room is murder in a court martial, and in fact very close to an admission of murder. With his eyes alone, Major Thomas implores the Breaker to stop, but like the Man from Snowy River himself, at the climax of the saga, there is just no stopping him now.

When they reached the mountain summit, even Clancy took a pull, but not the Man from Snowy River, nor Morant.

'My *defence*? I openly *admit* the charges. I take *all* responsibility upon myself. I plead custom of war and orders from headquarters. I have *no* regret and *no* fear as to what my fate will be.'[21]

No, the Breaker does not abate, his bravado and rage growing to a climax.

'You can't blame the young'uns, they only did as I told them. They just carried out orders, and that they had to do. They were obeying MY orders and thought they were obeying LORD KITCHENER'S.'[22]

Well, it can't be unsaid now. Morant doesn't seem to care about being acquitted anymore, but damned if he won't bring down Lord Kitchener with him. 'I alone was responsible!'[23] says Morant.

'I ALONE,' he repeats in a bellow. He is unhinged, a man come unstuck from good sense and sensibility, repeating his declaration no fewer than *ten* times. But the Breaker is not finished, oh no, his coherent cacophony is only just getting started.

Yes, to you in all your comfort of this court martial, my actions may well 'stagger humanity'.[24] But *I* was not the one who gave the order to do this, and now is as good a time as any – *Major Thomas' eyes plead to the point of popping, 'No, no, no, don't do it!'* – to put on the record who actually *did* give this order, so you can judge *him*, as well!

'I vow,' the accused thunders, 'I will have *Lord Kitchener* put into the box and cross-examined as to the orders given to officers, and *his* methods of conducting the war!'[25]

Major Thomas slumps back, nearly broken. George Witton cannot believe he is watching the Breaker talk himself to death. Every word is another cobblestone on the path to damnation, and Morant seems determined to lay each one himself, never mind the prosecution.

Their only hope if found guilty is clemency, and the only man who can grant clemency is Lord Kitchener.

'The folly of all this was apparent to everyone,' Witton will record, 'as Lord Kitchener held Morant's life in his hands; but Morant would not be restrained, and was prepared to suffer.'[26]

And while he's at it, Lieutenant Morant decides the time is right to bring something else about Lord Kitchener into the open as well. For you see, the highest-ranking officer in the British Army had a very particular reason for handing out the deadly orders given to Captain Hunt. Hunt told Morant himself. Listen:

'He told me that they had said at headquarters that they didn't want prisoners to *flood the concentration camps.*'[27]

Do you see? These were Kitchener's camps. And these were Kitchener's orders to kill, to prevent them overflowing, and to sap the will of the Boers to fight on.

'I did *not* carry out those orders until my best friend was brutally murdered. Then I resolved to carry out *orders*. But if anybody is to blame it is *me*.'[28]

And with that Morant finally stops, the silence of a shocked court smashing over him as he stands. Major Thomas asks if Morant may step down from the witness box. The court is only too happy to oblige.

Please, dear God, yes.

Lieutenant Picton now takes the stand to defend himself with Major Thomas' questioning to help him.

How long have you previously served in this war?

'Two years.'

And you have been decorated, have you not?

'I gained a D.C.M. under Le Gallais.'

Honour and record established, Major Thomas then asks what Lieutenant Morant told him after the capture of Visser?

'He said that he was perfectly justified in shooting him. I said it would be hard lines to shoot him, and asked Morant to call the other officers together.'

And did he?

'Yes, a meeting was held, and it was decided to shoot Visser.'

Did you also receive orders from Captain Hunt not to take prisoners?

'Yes.'

Did you ever question the order?

'No. I was reprimanded by Hunt for bringing in prisoners.'

Did Lieutenant Picton ever wonder why Captain Hunt gave such an order?

'Captain Hunt was very bitter about the death of a friend of his, a Lieutenant in the Gordon Highlanders, who had been killed in a train wrecked by Boers,' Picton replies. Much as the death of Hunt brought out the worst in the Breaker, the loss of Hunt's own friend spurred on his bloody determination. Revenge begets more of the same and takes no prisoners.

But was the report of Visser's execution passed onward and upward?

'Yes, verbally to Major Lenehan immediately after, and then to Colonel Hall.'

Did you notice any change in Lieutenant Morant at this time?

'Yes,' replies Picton readily. 'Morant and Hunt were old friends, and after Hunt's death Morant was inclined to be more severe on the enemy.'

Had you ever previously shot a prisoner?

'No, and I've never seen one shot.'

Captain Burns-Begg now cross-examines. Regarding this 'court martial', was the prisoner Visser even informed of the nature of the trial taking place?

'No.'

Did you approve of the verdict of the court martial?

'No, I opposed the shooting.'

And why had you never before obeyed your 'orders' not to take prisoners?

'I did not like the idea.'

But you *were* in command of the firing party that shot Visser?

'I was merely obeying orders.'

But come now, did Visser even know he was being 'charged' with a crime? Did he realise what was at stake?

Picton considers, scratching his chin before answering in as convincing a manner as he can muster.

'On the whole, Visser would be aware of the charge against him, as I previously told him of the seriousness of his position.'

Why did Captain Hunt never shoot any prisoners?

'Hunt never had any chance to carry out his own orders,' the court hears.

But Captain Burns-Begg repeats Picton's answer sceptically.

'Captain Hunt never had the chance to carry out his own orders?' Seriously? The most likely explanation for that, surely, is that Captain Hunt never gave any such orders, and you and your murderous cohorts are simply loading up a dead man with your own sins to give yourself an alibi. How ostentatiously convenient. And it is also true that after Captain Hunt died many more Boer prisoners were gunned down, which is why you are all here. But when he was alive and in command, no prisoners at all were killed. *This* is the man who is the source of all your ills?

Captain Burns-Begg makes compelling points, but the accused will not budge from their common insistence: Captain Hunt gave the order, and they merely obeyed them as the British Army had always insisted they must. Move on, sir.

Major Thomas now brings forth his equal in rank, Major Neatson. Staff Officer to Colonel Hall and the officer commanding lines of communication, Major Thomas has one *specific* communication he is interested in. *What*, Major, was passed on to you? Simply put, was the chain of command kept informed? Did they know what the BVC were doing with their captives?

Neatson's reply is delivered with calculated caution.

'I received certain reports from Captain Taylor with regard to engagements with Boers,' he says. Major Thomas is content to let the ambiguity speak for itself. Captain Burns-Begg has his own question though: What about the 'court martial' of Visser?

'I remember nothing about a summary of a court martial,' replies Major Neatson, clearly more comfortable with both this question and the answer he can provide.

Lieutenant Peter Handcock is next to defend himself in the stand. Speaking slowly, in his ever-lugubrious manner, he agrees with the account of the Breaker.

'I attended the trial of Visser at Morant's request,' he states, making the drum-head court martial sound as formal an affair as this very proceeding. Visser was wearing khaki, British uniform, and he was carrying parts of Hunt's uniform. He was sentenced to death.

And in any case: 'I had orders *not* to take prisoners.'

(Don't you see? Under the circumstances, Visser was lucky to get the courtesy of a trial!)

Lieutenant Witton takes the stand now, and Major Thomas wants him to cast his mind to the news of Hunt's death; how did he hear, and what did he make of it?

'I was present at a conversation with a Mr Reuter. From what he said, I gathered that Hunt had been murdered.'

Not 'killed' in a fair fight, but, specifically, *murdered*. A wounded man who had been tortured. What basis did you have to think Hunt had been murdered? asks Major Thomas.

'Reuter said Hunt's neck was broken, and his eyes gouged out,' Witton answers.[29]

Captain Burns-Begg cross-examines as coolly as ever. Did you want to shoot Visser? Witton's reply is careful and formal. He has known the question was coming, and this is clearly the answer he has formulated . . . while contemplating the consequences if he dares speak the truth.

'I was guided by my superior officers in regard to the finding of the court martial.'[30]

Did Visser even know he was being tried?

'I believe he knew,' answers Witton, equally carefully.

Was he given any opportunity to speak or defend himself?

'No,' says Witton simply. And his own opportunity to defend himself ceases. No further questions.

Major Thomas' next witness swears on the Bible to tell the truth, but as he is a Reverend this seems a redundant action. Please tell the court your name and position.

'My name is F. L. Reuter and I am the missionary in charge of the German Berlin Mission station,' he says.

The bodies of Captain Hunt and Sergeant Eland were brought to your station?

'Yes, they were brought.'

And so to the key question. Major Thomas must establish that what happened to Visser was because Morant et al were provoked. On this principle, the *Manual of Military Law* is very clear:

> It must be clearly established in all cases where provocation is put forward as an excuse [for murder], that at the time when the crime was committed the offender was actually so completely under the influence of passion arising from the provocation that he was at that moment deprived of the power of self-control . . .[31]

And so to the question of provocation, of presenting the key evidence for what might have seized the accused with such passion, they cannot be held responsible for their actions – even if the timing is a little off, as Visser was killed four days after the battle at the Viljoen house.

Can you describe the condition of Captain Hunt's body?

'It was . . .' the German pauses, wondering how to best express the grim sight in English, before continuing in his thick accent. 'It was much mutilated.'

How so?

'His neck appeared to have been broken, and his face . . . bore marks of boot heels.'[32]

This is no wild imagining, no second-hand gossip; this is the testimony of a man of God who saw this corpse himself and examined it in horror.

Major Thomas knows each judge is picturing the scene that would have caused this effect: a bleeding officer, lying and dying as Boers kick him, jumping on his head for sport, before gouging his eyes out. Is it any wonder that his second-in-command swore vengeance? Any wonder there was blood for blood?

Up next is a civil surgeon by the name of Dr Thomas Johnston. Will the witness take the stand? Major Thomas begins his questioning.

Did Captain Hunt ever reprimand Lieutenant Morant? Did you ever hear anything to this effect, Dr Johnston?

'Yes, for bringing in prisoners,' says Johnston.

But soldiers have already testified to this fact. Major Thomas is actually far more interested in a medical question addressed to a medical man.

Was Captain Hunt's body maltreated pre- or post-mortem? The civil surgeon – though not present when Hunt's body was repatriated to the mission, and operating only on hearsay – has no doubt.

'It is my opinion from the evidence that the injuries to Hunt's body were caused *before* death.'[33]

Which, it might be construed, is a tad fanciful, owing to the fact that Hunt was fatally shot through the heart. Such an intervention would have necessitated implausible haste on the part of the Boers.

Following Dr Johnston to the stand is a cool customer indeed, Captain Taylor, who proceeds calmly. Carefully cognisant of the fact that the court martial for his *own* charges of murder are looming, he remains resolute. Taylor is so certain of his testimony it almost seems as if he is giving it as an unnecessary chore – as if even being here in the first place and going through all this is such a waste of time over what was always a trivial matter.

And in all this, what of the Boers? How do they treat their own captives? Would it be above the Boers to torture a man?

'Well,' Taylor replies calmly, 'I did receive a message from the Boers, through natives, that if I were caught I would be given four days to die. That means torture.'

Four days of torture before being given the mercy of death. Christ alive. Whatever happened to Captain Hunt, every man present would rather that than half a week of torture. Being kicked to death seems a blessing when compared to . . . *that*.

But why, Captain Taylor, would a man such as yourself be marked for such a hideous fate? Why you?

'Because I had previously been hunting in the country,' Taylor replies. No man in the court is entirely sure whether Taylor means hunting boars or hunting Boers, but none care to ask as he continues with more remarks on these savage Boers.

'The Boers in this part of the country are more outlaws than part of a legal Commando.'

In other words, they are wild brigands not disciplined soldiers. Is it not obvious that the rules of war don't apply to bandits who obey no rules themselves?

Again, Major Thomas must return to the crux of his case, that the death of Visser, while perhaps regrettably hasty, was the *direct result* of an order being followed. What more can be done when one is given a mandatory instruction from a British officer?

Did Captain Taylor know that these orders were handed down? Did he know that they had been ordered to *shoot* prisoners? How could such a thing have happened?

Well, yes. Captain Taylor knows such orders well because, more often than not, he was the man who gave the orders. Wary of his surroundings, however, he is wise to remain quiet on that matter in front of a court martial. His words are plucked and picked with the utmost care when he responds.

'I had heard Captain Hunt reprimand Morant for bringing in prisoners.'

But was Visser the first? Had Morant done the same to other hapless souls to cross his path?

'No, Morant had always behaved well to the Boers,' Taylor states flatly.

Captain Burns-Begg knows that the same cannot be said for Captain Taylor, but Taylor is not on trial here. However, his next question on the 'trial' of Visser involves a neat trap for Taylor. Now, Morant has testified that a report of the killing of Visser was sent to you, Captain Taylor. Was that the case? (Both Captains know that if Taylor knew a prisoner had been executed and did not either notify a superior or reprimand a lesser, he is culpable.) Captain Taylor has another clever and careful answer at the ready:

'I did transmit a report of the expedition in which Hunt was killed, but I didn't know what was in it.'[34]

Alas, you see, the uncurious Captain Taylor did not *read* the report, so of course he cannot be held to blame for not acting on its contents. Yes, it was indeed remarkably uncurious for the Intelligence operative in command of the entire district not to read such a report, but you must understand how busy it sometimes gets.

So it seems Morant wrote a report for Taylor, who did not read it. Taylor sent it on to Colonel Hall, who is presently out of reach, having been posted to India. It is all as convenient as it is unlikely as it is . . . impossible to disprove.

Regardless, Captain Burns-Begg remains sceptical of these third-hand messages. The Boers wanted to torture this Captain to death? Surely not. Did Taylor even receive any direct communication from the Boers themselves?

Well . . .

Yes, yes, in fact he did.

'Commandant Tom Kelly sent me a message saying that the first Englishman who came near his wagon would be shot,' replies Taylor.

The next to take the stand is the 'Commander' of the Bushveldt Carbineers, Major Lenehan, though most of the court knows that is more a nominal title than the reality.

Major Lenehan squirms and shifts uncomfortably in the stand while trying to put on a respectable face. Just as is the case with Captain Taylor, Lenehan knows he has his own court martial to come, in his own case charged with falsifying the BVC military reports. A man who has turned a blind eye to the atrocities he knew were occurring, he now has the manner of one who would shut both eyes if he could, to block out the horror, the humiliation of being involved in this whole disaster in any way at all. And did he mention that he was *not* involved?

'I had no direct control over the corps,' he says firmly in response to the first question, 'they acted under headquarters at Pretoria.'

That is neither here nor there. The BVC were at Fort Edward, not Pretoria. *Who* was in command?

'Captain Hunt. He took over the command from Robertson and got orders from the officer commanding the line of communication.'

Of course, Captain Taylor is the one *really* in charge of the 'line of communication', he has his own intelligence, reports and requests.

Well, Major Lenehan, Major Thomas asks, do you really believe that Lieutenant Morant is a murderer?

'From my knowledge of Morant, I wouldn't think him capable of murder,' replies Lenehan remarkably mildly. 'Or inciting it.'

Perish the thought.

And yet Captain Burns-Begg wishes to know who exactly told him about the shooting of Visser?

'Lieutenant Picton reported the shooting to me and I reported it to Colonel Hall,' replies Lenehan.

'Did you know of any order not to take prisoners?' asks Burns-Begg.

'No,' replies Lenehan.

It seems this is the modus operandi of the BVC. Every soldier stationed at Fort Edward has heard the order to take no prisoners, they have heard the Captains discuss it, they have even heard a Lieutenant severely abused over a failure to follow it. And yet, despite how common knowledge it all is, the commander's commander has never heard anything about it?

Surely not.

Major Thomas pauses, his eyebrow raised. Come now, Major, this is surely too absurd an answer even for you. The pause creates a verbal vacuum that Major Lenehan feels obliged to fill, as he, too, is struck by the sheer absurdity of what he just said under oath.

'I have never heard of orders that *no* prisoners were to be taken.'[35]

And so it proves enough for this day, for now the court and the prisoners must move to Pretoria. Questioning the men available will only lead so far, and some of the most important witnesses are absent. Indeed, the court martial is in need of a witness so grand that he could not possibly come to court. No, the court must go to him. Colonel Hamilton, the right hand of Lord Kitchener, has agreed to give evidence and bear witness, so help him God.

•

Now, when it comes to giving evidence, Captain de Bertodano is still searching for a witness who has eluded him. And his key fear remains that while the lad may have escaped the questions of the court, he may not have escaped the Breaker, a far worse fate. The courts martial have not yet reached the case of Reverend Heese and there is still time to find the 'boy' who saw the Reverend murdered.

'When the trial took place, enquiries were made at all locations,' he will recount, 'and a reward offered, with no effect.'[36]

No, not for love, fear or money can the 'boy' be found and de Bertodano comes to the view that yet another murder can be chalked up to Breaker Morant. But his search continues; he'll be damned if Morant will escape charge or sentence for this particular crime. For it is very personal to Captain de Bertodano. He cannot *help* but feel responsible.

If he had not offered that sick man Craig a wagon for hospital, well then Reverend Heese would not have offered to accompany the wagon, and then he would not have wandered across the Breaker shooting eight Boers. There is an old saying: 'For want of a nail the shoe was lost, for want of a shoe the horse was lost, for want of a horse a message was lost, for want of a message the battle was lost, for want of a battle the kingdom was lost, and all for want of a horseshoe nail.' De Bertodano applies this logic in reverse; he gave a man a horse and a carriage and all that led to a murder. Alive or dead, that 'boy' must be found. For want of a witness, the case could be lost . . .

•

How do you get the British guards on the Boer burgher camp just outside Pietersburg to leave their posts for a short time – at exactly the right moment?

Well, not to put too fine a point on it, some of the Boer women accomplish the *complete* distraction of the guards in the time-honoured manner.

It means that General Beyers and some 300 of his fighters face practically no resistance when, just before midnight on 21 January 1902, they take over the entire camp at Pietersburg after making the superintendent and his guards – some still pulling up their trousers – prisoners. The food and drink stores are raided and an all-night party ensues as many of the men are reunited with their wives and children for however brief a time. Beyers and his men release their British prisoners at the first crack of dawn and ride off with the departing night. As they go, they take with them 150 Boer men who had also been in camp, who have decided to join Beyers.

But where can Beyers get the horses and guns he needs to fit out their new recruits? Beyers' Boers will be useless without munitions.

Well, that would be from the very outpost from which the 150 Boers have just been liberated. At dawn two days later, Morant wakes to the sound of gunfire – getting closer. Sure enough it is Beyers and his men launching a full-blown attack on the blockhouses that ring the town. With Pietersburg under attack from several hundred men, it needs every man that can hold a rifle to get into position and start firing against them.

And yes, that does mean *every* man, including those in prison cells. When it is a matter of life and death, even those on trial for their lives under threat of death must be called in to service. And so Morant, Handcock and Witton, on trial for shooting Boers, are released from their cells, given rifles and told to shoot Boers! From a prisoner of His Majesty to a soldier for His Majesty in the turning of a key, the Breaker and Handcock are armed, and as dangerous as only they can be.

Both men soon position themselves atop the flat roof of the prison and are in it with the best of them.

'They fought as only such brave and fearless men can fight,' Witton records. 'Handcock in particular, in his cool and silent manner, did splendid work, one of his bullets finding its billet in Marthinus Pretorius, Beyers' fighting leader.'[37]

For his part, Witton will chronicle, 'I espied a party making round the foot of [a] kopje, about one mile and a half from the fort. I drew the attention of the cow-gun officer to them, and he hurriedly had the gun loaded, and sent a 50-lb. lyddite shell after them.'[38]

The Boers are beaten off, and everyone resumes their customary positions, with Morant and Handcock back to fighting for their lives, albeit without weaponry.

•

With the Boer battle over, the legal battle resumes, now in Pretoria with the whole court moved for one man too important to travel.

And who is this distinguished officer now standing before the court – now convened in the Artillery Barracks – and warily taking the oath to tell the truth, the whole truth and nothing but the truth, so help him God?

Of course, it is the very man they have journeyed here to hear evidence from, Colonel Hubert Hamilton, General Kitchener's Military Secretary.

It is a delicate matter to have an officer of such high rank and singular importance being taken through the legal process by officers of inferior rank. Still, they have the weight of the law behind them, and the mere fact that the entire court has come so far means that due deference has to a certain extent already been paid, allowing them to proceed.

'He was,' Witton will chronicle, 'stern and hard-featured, and looked just then very gaunt and hollow-eyed, as though a whole world of care rested on his shoulders. He was apparently far more anxious than those whose fate depended on the evidence he was to give.'

And yet, though Colonel Hamilton may look under strain, his answers are easy and short. The court has come a long way to hear very little. Colonel Hamilton will give them precisely four sentences. As a courtesy to his rank, the first question comes not from counsel, but from the President of the Court:

'Lieutenant Morant, in his evidence, states that the late Captain Hunt told him that he had received orders from you that no prisoners were to be taken alive. Is this true?'

The Colonel answers in two words: 'Absolutely untrue.'

Major Thomas is allowed to ask the witness a question. It is a question with a peculiar amount of detail.

'Do you remember Captain Hunt taking two polo ponies early in July last, up to Lord Kitchener's quarters; at which time you came in, and had a conversation with Captain Hunt?'[39]

Colonel Hamilton does not care about details. His memory is not jogged; it is fixed and unrelenting.

'No. I have no recollection whatever. I have *never* spoken to Captain Hunt with reference to his duties in the Northern Transvaal.'[40]

Well, to Major Thomas, the whole idea of getting Colonel Hamilton in the dock had seemed like a good idea at the time. But, perhaps in a sign that the fact it had taken him seven years to do his five-year degree at Sydney University had been a fair indication of his base legal skills, the whole plan has come unstuck. With such a definitive answer, from such a high-ranking officer and gentleman, that whole line of defence is shot to pieces and all he can do is flounder forward.

'As regards the evidence of Colonel Hamilton,' Major Thomas says, if it please the court (which it doesn't for they all clearly resent this colossal waste of time), 'I wish to state that the defence do not regard his evidence, one way or the other, as having any real bearing on the defence; in fact, I submit to the court that it is really illegal evidence. It really amounts to this: a certain conversation is stated to have taken place between Colonel Hamilton and the deceased, Captain Hunt, which conversation was mentioned by Captain Hunt to Lieut. Morant, apparently in a confidential or private way. This, having been obtained by the court from the prisoner Morant, is then sought to be contradicted by the evidence of Colonel Hamilton, which, I submit, is quite contrary to the laws of evidence.'[41]

Which may be the case. But with a slide-rule, a comfortable chair and a bottle of port needed to understand such a rebuttal, it makes little impact.

The court will spend the remainder of their day hearing the closing address of the two counsel. Major Thomas begins his closing address as he intends to finish it – furiously, throwing every argument he can summon against the very *idea* that the defendants might be guilty as charged.

After all, there is an old lawyers' aphorism: 'If you don't have the law on your side, cite the facts. If you don't have the facts on your side, cite the law. If you have neither the facts or the law on your side . . . pound the table!'

In the desperation of his situation, Major Thomas decides to do all three in turn and often at once.

'It really does not matter much, from the point of view of the defence,' Major Thomas thunders, '*where* Captain Hunt got his instructions. The fact is clear from the evidence that Captain Hunt *did* tell his subordinates, not once, but many times, that prisoners were not to be taken. This fact is admitted by witnesses for the prosecution. The chief value of these instructions, as given by Captain Hunt, is that they go to show that he, being a man of some standing, and a personal friend of Lieut. Morant, they were entitled to weight, and go to remove any question of malicious intent.'[42]

Major Thomas now notes that all the Troopers who *actually* killed the prisoners have not been charged.

'Now, has the prosecution attempted to show that the murder was committed by these troopers? I submit the contrary. Two were brought as witnesses by the prosecution. They were not even warned to be careful lest they should incriminate themselves, and, really, I submit to the court that the assumption that these troopers are murderers is simply monstrous, and cannot by any possible means be substantiated. Clearly, they only obeyed the orders of a superior officer, and formed a firing party for the execution of Visser after their officers had held a summary court martial and convicted him. There is not the slightest evidence that these troopers were in any way a party to the shooting of Visser, except that they obeyed their orders as soldiers. They are, therefore, not murderers.'

But if the Troopers themselves are not murderers, how can his clients be accessories to murder or instigators of a crime that did not occur?

It is a cunning argument, it is a conniving argument, but unfortunately for the accused, it is not a terribly *convincing* argument. Nevertheless, the court will humour the bush lawyer.

We are listening, Major Thomas, continue.

'Lieutenant Morant, no doubt, is primarily responsible, being senior officer at the time when the trial took place, and the court has to be satisfied in his case, as in that of the others, that he deliberately and feloniously ordered the men to commit murder.'

But how could that be?

'There is no doubt that Captain Hunt did give certain very definite orders to Lieutenant Morant, and on his death Mr. Morant took over command. There is no doubt that his conduct was largely influenced by the treatment of the body of his friend, showing circumstances of barbarity.'

And Morant responded to that barbarity, with a revenge that is understandable, surely. It is the way of war, the way of this war, for barbarity to prompt barbarity in turn. An eye for an eye, a bullet for a bullet, and a life for the notion that it is sin enough to be part of a people Britain is at war with when no quarter is being given.

'In war retaliation is justifiable, revenge is justifiable. Rules applicable in times of peace are quite inapplicable in times of war. In the Manual of Military Law it is stated, "Retaliation is military vengeance"; it takes place when an outrage committed on one side is avenged by a similar act on the other. I am free to admit that this maltreatment of his friend did exercise an influence over him when he came to deal with this man Visser, and it is natural he should be so influenced. He pursues these Boers, which ends in the capture of Visser, whom he finds wearing clothing the property of the late Captain Hunt. I go so far as saying that under the circumstances Mr. Morant would have been perfectly justified in shooting Visser straight away. The fact of wearing British uniform is altogether against the customs of war, and I know that this man Visser was present when Captain Hunt was killed from the evidence.'

Major Thomas is clear, a court martial was held on the field of war, rough and ready as such courts martial are. But as to the result? 'At the request apparently, of Mr. Picton, it was decided to give Visser a court martial, such a court martial as is frequently held in the field. Informal, no doubt, [but] how can we expect formality in the field, in the immediate vicinity of the enemy . . . ? All this is provided for in the Manual of Military Law. We claim that substantial justice was done, and I submit that there is nothing whatever to satisfy the court that Mr. Morant ordered a wilful or felonious murder. On the contrary, under the Rules of War, I consider that he was quite justified in confirming the sentence. The evidence of Captain Taylor shows that these men were the offshoots of commandos and mere outlaws.'[43]

These Boers are not soldiers – they are brigands, looters, murderers! Are they even men?

'Such men forfeit all rights to be treated as prisoners of war.'

Much as they'd like to apply them, the court knows that the old standards of disciplined military units are of no help when it comes to these thieves and ne'er-do-wells, these 'Commandos'. The BVC dished out rough justice, and it was no more or less than the rough Boers deserved. When a gentleman is in a street fight in a back alley, and the thug opposite him pulls a knife, it is not right to punish him for not bowing to the rules of the Marquess of Queensbury.

And yet, speaking of devastating blows, Captain Burns-Begg starts his closing address by destroying Major Thomas' opening argument:

'The defence has made a good deal of the fact that the court must hold the four troopers guilty of murder before they can hold the four prisoners now before them guilty of accessories. That is perfect nonsense. The Manual of Military Law says that where a person has been guilty of killing another the law presumes the killer to be guilty of murder, and on that the court must necessarily rest content, in so far as the guilt or innocence of the troopers is concerned. This is borne out by the statute law of England, which enables an accessory to be tried before, after, or with a principal felon, irrespective of the guilt or innocence of the latter.'

It couldn't be more simple. Captain Burns-Begg has in his corner two powerful allies: the law and the truth. There is no need for anachronistic arguments, all that remains is to repeat the evidence and highlight the prisoners' own admissions.

'As regards the so-called court martial, the court cannot hold that it was a court martial in any sense of the word. It was anything that the court pleases except a tribunal, martial or otherwise. It was a consultation, a conspiracy, a measure to mature a criminal purpose, but it was not a court.'[44]

As to Major Thomas claiming that Morant's actions were an outcome of revenge and retaliation, an outburst of grief and rage? Well, good Major, that is *precisely* the point. There was no court martial, there was only a revenge killing. No legal sentence was administered. What happened was a premeditated killing with unmistakably malicious intent.

The prosecutor's contempt blows through the room like a chilly wind. It extends beyond the accused and their foolishness, and with an only just restrained sneer encompasses their clearly inept counsel.

'[It is clear that] every one of the prisoners, as well as the counsel for the defence, admits that the real reason for shooting Visser was because Hunt had been killed. Could proof of malice conceivably be clearer? Counsel for the defence urges that retaliation is recognised as legitimate by the Manual of Military Law. That is a mere twisting of words, and I think it is hardly necessary for me to urge on a body of military men the danger of acknowledging the right of subaltern officers to avenge their private grievances on prisoners of war who happen to fall into their hands. Retaliation has a perfectly definite meaning in military law, and means the deliberate and authoritative taking of measures of reprisal, as answer to some action on the part of the enemy contrary to the customs of war, but it certainly does not mean that subordinate officers are entitled to shoot prisoners who fall into their hands because an officer of their regiment has been killed.'

Captain Burns-Begg reiterates that Lieutenant Morant and his men had no right to answer injustice with their own crude form of justice, asking 'could anything be more preposterous than to say that minor officers are entitled to make war on principles of barbarity approved only by themselves? If they do so they must abide by the consequences.'[45]

His points are well made, at least from the point of view of those presiding. For as the President of the Court Lieutenant Colonel Denny delivers his summary of the events and arguments of the day, it seems obvious that his own views and those of Captain Burns-Begg are, if not brothers, at least very good friends.

'The essence of the crime of murder is malicious intent. I would point out that the prisoners did not carry out the order they allege to have received re the shooting of Boers in khaki until after the death of Captain Hunt, which they admit biased their minds.'

Visser was their prisoner only, he should not have become their victim.

'The right of killing an armed man exists only so long as he resists; as soon as he submits he is entitled to be treated as a prisoner of war.'[46]

Granted, a key fact in this grisly charade has been Visser's possession of some of Hunt's uniform, an admittedly damning condemnation.

Yet the Judge Advocate makes little of it.

'As regards the treatment of an enemy caught in the uniform of his opponent, it would have to be shown that he was wearing such uniform at the time with the deliberate intention of deceiving.'[47]

Had Visser souvenired a British uniform? Quite possibly, it was certainly not uncommon. Was he impersonating a British officer in an attempt to trick enemy forces? Certainly not. The treatment of Visser was therefore disgraceful and an affront to the law: 'Enemies rendered harmless by wounds must not only be spared; but humanity commands that if they fall into the hands of their opponents the care taken of them should be second only to the care taken of the wounded belonging to the captors.'[48]

Yes, it sounds more like a verdict than a summation. But the Judge Advocate is but one man, the judges themselves are like a jury. The majority shall hold sway, and crucially they may convict but recommend mercy for their comrades in arms. The court will now consult with itself and so the prisoners, their armed escorts, and the counsel must all awkwardly wait outside the court in a corridor.

'In a little over half an hour,' Witton will recount, they are recalled. 'Glancing round the court, I noticed one of the members in tears. My attention was arrested, but I did not then attach any significance to it.'[49]

It is unique to the nature of these trials, with so many repeated and revolving witnesses and defendants, the verdicts may not be announced until the very end of *all* the trials. It is a bizarre way of conducting justice, but a necessary one. The defendants have said their piece and stood their trial, but they will not know the result of the matter for weeks yet. For now, they are in limbo.

CHAPTER SEVENTEEN

TRIAL AND ERROR

NOW this is the Law of the Jungle – as old and as true as the sky; And the Wolf that shall keep it may prosper, but the Wolf that shall break it must die.

Rudyard Kipling,
The Jungle Book

January 1902, leaving Pretoria for Pietersburg

All aboard! For the next case, the court will take place at Pietersburg, reconstituted after their extraordinary excursion to question Colonel Hamilton, and yet while all of the judges and counsel take their place in comfort aboard one of the carriages, such is not the case for the accused.

'When we entrained,' Lieutenant Witton will recount, 'it was evident our social status had undergone a decided change . . . This time we were not permitted to enter a carriage.'[1]

Good enough for the accused on this boiling hot day is a filthy sheep truck attached to the rear of the carriages and into this they must crowd like those very sheep off to the abattoir, complete – mind the sheep dung – with their escorts, servants and baggage. Could anything be more uncomfortable, more desperate?

Only if they had to suffer all that, while also being under attack from the Boers.

And here they are now!

On the approach to Warm Baths Station, about 105 miles on the way to Pietersburg, the train stops on the report that there are Boers up ahead, and for the second time in this terrible time of being on trial for their lives, the prisoners are also asked to fight for their lives, as a member of the court comes back and they are ordered to stand to arms.

Yes, they are given guns.

'Morant prayed,' Witton notes, 'as I am sure he never prayed in his life before, that we might get into action.'[2]

As it happens, the train simply stays sweltering in the sun for an entire hour while those up front use their field glasses to scan the country for any sign of the Boers, before 'moving on slowly from blockhouse to blockhouse, we safely passed the point of danger'.[3] Morant and Handcock hand back their weapons as an oyster might hand over its pearl – with extreme reluctance, and a sense that this is against nature. Nevertheless, from that moment they become mere prisoners once more, and are no longer soldiers.

Such is the tension of the situation, and the extreme discomfort of the sheep truck, even the prisoners are relieved when they finally arrive back at Pietersburg the next day, to be hustled into the garrison's makeshift solitary cells. As appalling as their new confined digs are, at least it is not a sheep truck burning up in the blasting sun, and at least they can lie down on a bunk.

21 January 1902, Pietersburg, Major mistakes

Nerves. Sweat, trickling down the small of your back, as your breath comes in small gasps. It is a depth of *fear* that grips your very soul. Now, while it has been one thing to experience that feeling while taking on the Boers on the high veldt of the Transvaal, knowing that with one bullet you are done for, this is different.

For the accused, the staggering thing is to be experiencing much the same thing, while sitting like a proper gentleman in a safe trial in Pietersburg. As the court has been noting, however, not all members of the BVC have exactly behaved as gentlemen, including the man who stands now to face them. Hark now, as Lieutenant Colonel Denny's stately voice rings out with the formal accusation:

'Major Robert Lenehan, you are charged with failure to report that a trooper of the Bushveldt Carbineers had been shot by Lieutenant Handcock. How do you plead?'

'Not guilty.'[4]

'The second charge against you is that, being on active service, you culpably neglected your duty by failing to report the shooting by men of your regiment, the Bushveldt Carbineers, of one man and two boys, these being prisoners and unarmed. How do you plead?'

'Not guilty,' replies Lenehan, standing defiant if nervous.

Major Lenehan is, of course, well aware of the van Buuren tragedy, his life cut short with a bullet to the body while out on patrol. He was told it was from the gun of a sniper, and though many suspect it may have been a pistol shot from Handcock, he had no reason for any such suspicion – and resents the suggestion that he did!

But what are now suggestions will soon be accusations, and it won't be long before those accusations are reinforced with the defendant's worst nightmare: *evidence*.

Right then, Lieutenant Edwards, up to the stand with you.

Edwards, the adjutant of Major Lenehan, rises and makes his way forward, readying himself for the tale he must tell about a tail removed.

'I received a confidential letter from Captain Hunt, I made a copy of it and forwarded the original to Pretoria.'

And did this letter arrive intact in Pretoria? No.

'The postscript to the original was torn off.'

And what did this now missing PS say in the original document?

'It read: "Will also write details of death of van Buuren; Handcock shot him".'[5]

But did Pretoria receive details of van Buuren's demise?

'No details of van Buuren's death were ever received. Major Lenehan sent word by me that he would make a confidential report.'

Then who actually reported his death?

'It was Handcock.'

Oh, Handcock reported it all right, but he certainly neglected to mention that he'd fired a bullet into his own man. It is no surprise to Major Thomas. This still leaves the question of quite who it was that tampered with the letter to begin with.

Major Bolton, please take the stand.

'I searched Major Lenehan's kit and found the letter, minus the footnote.'[6]

Begging your pardon? *Minus* the *footnote*? The same footnote that would have read 'Handcock shot him'? A pregnant pause grows in the courtroom, as all take in the implications.

So Major Lenehan had the wherewithal not only to keep Hunt's letter, but rip off the postscript and then . . . copy the non-incriminating parts of it and send it on to HQ as though it were the original? Good God, *what* is happening in the BVC?

Lenehan winces, barely able to believe that Lieutenant Edwards had made a copy of the bloody report! For goodness sake, how was *he* to know? Did Lieutenant Edwards not trust him?

God forbid.

The next witness summoned to the stand by Captain Burns-Begg is a surprise, none other than . . . . . . Captain Robertson!

Yes, one and the same. The very man removed by Colonel Hall to preserve the good name of the BVC – sent back to England in disgrace – has now returned to do his bit to bury it for good, and throwing on top for good measure the man he holds responsible for his own fall, Captain Taylor. And Robertson's intent is clear from the first: to show that 'Killer' is not so much a nickname as a way of life for his former compadre in crime.

Robertson is rather frank, as he will not be prosecuted and shall be brief and blunt.

'I knew van Buuren, he was shot on July 4 last.'

And how was van Buuren regarded by the BVC?

'I'd been warned about him. He was one who was not to be trusted. Van Buuren was suspected of stealing whisky from an officer and money from Kaffirs. Men refused to go on duty with him. He was always creating disturbances and abusing khakis.'

So what was the way forward with van Buuren, what did you do?

'Myself, Captain Taylor, and Handcock had a talk over the man. It was decided he was to be shot.'[7]

The once steady tick-tick of the clock becomes infrequent, each second passing slower than the one before, until . . . tick- . . . it stops.

Everything, all of it, has come to this. Everything is now laid bare. This is what happened! I was *there*.

All eyes turn to Captain Taylor, who appears to be only vaguely interested, if that. It is as if instead of sworn testimony that directly implicates him in a murder, he has just heard some half-baked tall tale told around a campfire, and as he sets no store by it, well, why should anyone else?

Lieutenant Peter Handcock, by contrast, looks as if he will explode. This is damning, irrefutable evidence from an impeccable source, and if Robertson has already gone this far, there can be little doubt what is to come.

And how was that accomplished?

'Handcock,' Captain Robertson begins to set the scene, 'and four men went out on the left flank.'

Yes, we understand that Captain Robertson, but only *three* of those men actually returned. Did you find the time to alert anyone in a position of authority? Why, yes.

'I told Major Lenehan I was prepared to stand a court martial,' replies Robertson, cheerfully defending himself as he implicates Lenehan. 'I had thirty prisoners with me, the Boers were near, and van Buuren might have given us the slip and given us away.'[8]

So that's how it was, Trooper van Buuren had been viciously killed, in cold blood no less, a murder over a mere matter of maybes.

And had you written your own report of these events?

He had not, he explained, but with good reason.

'I was superseded by Hunt. *He* made a report of this occurrence and of the shooting of six men to Major Lenehan.'

Yes, but that's besides the *real* point. Was the 'official' report of van Buuren's death legitimate, Captain Robertson? Was it accurate?

'It was not a true one. Hunt concealed the true facts in the interests of the corps.'

'True Facts'. Only in the BVC is the phrase not a tautology. Captain Robertson is quite fond of this revealing phrase: 'Captain Taylor also knew the true facts. I reported the true facts to Hunt.'[9]

The Breaker's lip curls in complete contempt, his mouth twisting to a snarl. Fancy besmirching the good name of a dead man for your own alibi! (How *dare* Robertson horn in on his act! The number of things Captain Hunt was told and did not act on, the number of atrocities he ordered, makes him far and away the busiest of any of the corpses this court martial has dealt with.)

But Robertson goes on, giving his own version of the true facts. Handcock and the Breaker throw silent daggers with their eyes at Captain Robertson. What they would do to that man if only they could get him on their left flank in some isolated spot on the veldt.

Captain Burns-Begg finishes for now, passing the baton to Major Thomas, who begins by requesting that the court discharge the prisoner this instant.

Why, Major Thomas?

On what grounds?

'On the ground that it has not been shown *who* was the superior authority to whom Major Lenehan should have reported, and it was not shown, therefore, that a report had not been sent.'[10]

It is a technical yet flimsy defence, and the court pays it no mind. Much like Major Thomas' twisting and teasing with the Visser case, this court martial has not the time for empty sophistry.

Proceed.

'Did Robertson ever inform you of the manner of van Buuren's death?'

'No,' answers Lenehan flatly.

But what of this missing postscript found in his possession?

Lenehan pauses and then offers a response that would kill a brown dog let alone a defence attorney.

'It never occurred to me that the postscript in Hunt's letter indicated anything suspicious.'

It never . . . *what*? The words 'Handcock shot him' didn't send any alarm bells ringing?

It is fair to say that Arthur Conan Doyle, who had left South African shores so recently, did not base any of his character Sherlock Holmes on Major Lenehan. Captain Burns-Begg does not ask any questions as there is no need when the witness is so determined to condemn himself with such answers.

Now, once more, Captain Taylor takes the stand. He is a man who never gives a foolish response; his answers are careful and credible, if not, well, quite . . . honest.

'Were you party to the conversation when it was agreed van Buuren must be shot?' asks Thomas.

'I was not,' Taylor replies. 'Captain Robertson mentioned casually that he would have to shoot van Buuren.'

Casually? A passing remark about assassination?

'I never heard till afterwards that van Buuren was shot,' Taylor continues.

Perhaps Robertson and Handcock agreed, but Captain Taylor is no more than a bystander, a man who just happens to eavesdrop on remarks.

Major Lenehan is incredulous and, as his own counsel, is able to cross-examine.

'Captain Taylor, did you know *anything* about van Buuren's death?'

Taylor's reply is masterful in its evasion.

'Not personally.'

Sigh. You may step down.

And so, after a little more blustering from Major Thomas, the trial of Major Lenehan draws to a close, and the gentlemen of the court, led by Lieutenant Colonel Henry Cuthbert Denny, retire to consider their verdict – which they will keep to themselves until the final trial is over. Like Morant, thus, Lenehan is left in legal limbo, obliged to wait while the rolling trials slowly roll on.

3 February 1902, Pietersburg, one over the eight

The accused of the BVC do not have their charges dropped, but they do have a prosecutor dropped. Only shortly after the Visser case had been concluded, prosecutor Captain Robert Burns-Begg had been recalled to England. It is a slightly surprising turn of events given there are still cases to come, but George Witton will later put up a theory as to why this occurs: 'It seemed as though he was required at the War Office to give particulars personally of the trial and of the disclosures that had been made there.'[11]

Either way, his place as prosecutor is taken by Major Wilfred Nash Bolton, the former England rugby champion and now Assistant Provost Marshal from Pietersburg.

Examining his brief for the case against Morant and Handcock for murdering the Reverend Heese, Bolton comes to one quick conclusion, and he puts it in a cable to the Judge Advocate General in Cape Town:

> In case of missionary I can obtain no further evidence stop Can I
> withdraw charge against Morant absolutely no evidence in his case.[12]

The short answer is, if the trial has already begun you must proceed. If it has not, you may drop Morant but under no circumstances drop the charges against Handcock on the missionary case. He must be pursued.

As the case has indeed technically begun, in that charges have been read in court, though not yet tried, Bolton must indeed go on with it.

In truth, if Bolton had a choice in the matter, he would not be on the case himself and had applied before his appointment to be removed from it, as he felt he lacked the requisite experience, and in any case had wanted to get back to his regular work as Assistant Provost Marshal at Pietersburg.

As it happens, both Breaker Morant and Peter Handcock would love nothing more than to get back to their own regular work too, but first they must throw themselves into their new occupation: defending themselves like lower order batsmen against an unending array of fast bowlers as the barrage of charges continue.

Now that they have been conveyed safely back to Pietersburg, all is in order for the proceedings against them to resume, and they face their final charges of murdering the eight Boers who had surrendered.

Lieutenant Colonel Denny begins by reading – flatly, and with no hint of emotion – the charges.

'Lieutenant H. H. Morant you are charged with having murdered, or instigated others to murder, eight men whose names were unknown. How do you plead?'

The Breaker rises to repeat what will become his mantra: 'Not guilty.'

Well, be that as it may, the prosecution has a number of reliable men who will *beg* to differ. First up, Officer Ledeboer with an honest account of his delivery to the Breaker; eight, count 'em, *eight* Boers.

'I do not know what happened to them after,'[13] he tells the court. Well, then, who might know?

Trooper Thompson! The jaws of those watching in judgement slowly drop as Thompson relates his memory of a mad Morant, a rabid dog insatiable for the kill.

'Those who take up the sword shall *perish* by the sword!' he mimics Morant's biblical outburst. 'The *Lord* has delivered eight Boers into our hands and *we are going to shoot them!*'[14]

If only Morant weren't so eloquent, so gifted with words! Thompson may have forgotten it had it been spoken by a lesser orator. But not only is it that orders were orders, but orders given so theatrically under such circumstances could never be forgotten, and could be so credibly recounted because you just couldn't make up the things that he said.

Thank you, Trooper, that will be all.

Sergeant Major Hammett now rises. Yes, if it pleases the court, those were Morant's words exactly: *'we are going to shoot them!'*. And not only that, but the Sergeant Major even questioned the Breaker directly.

'I said, "Lt. Morant, are you sure you are not *exceeding* orders?"'[15]

To which Morant said what?

'I have hitherto disregarded my orders, I shall do so no longer!'[16]

Major Thomas can hardly believe it. Had Captain Morant ever acted like this before? Hammett pauses and furrows his brow before his face drops. He replies quietly.

'No, Lieutenant Morant always treated prisoners well, till Hunt's death. Then he became a different man altogether.'[17]

This much is beyond doubt to the court, Hunt's death was the catalyst. The new prosecutor, Major Wilfred Bolton, calls his next witness.

Sergeant Wrench has compelling testimony to give about bringing in prisoners, only to be greeted by an agitated Morant and sent away on a contrived 'patrol'; of the whole absurd theatre contrived to make them think they had been fired on by Boers; of his own refusal to play along with Captain Taylor and the danger this clearly put him in. It is all so very extraordinary, just one more piece in this graphic puzzle which points to a unit that has descended to evil, run by murderously Machiavellian monsters.

And, yes, the intrigued court hears the tale of Lieutenant Morant's invented court-martial 'letter' written for Wrench, as, irony of ironies, he sits in his own court martial now! Unfortunately for the Breaker, each phrase Wrench utters sounds exactly like the sort of cutting and sarcastic things Morant has unleashed upon this very court, more than once.

'Mr. Morant said, "Don't let us beat about the bush. From what I can see of it, there are several men here who don't agree with this shooting. I want you to go round to the men and find out those who are willing to do it and those who are not, and then we will soon get rid of those who don't agree" . . .'[18]

Major Thomas tries to question the veracity of Wrench's memory, but once again the Breaker's gift for memorable expression comes to haunt any attempt for his defence. Is Wrench sure he understood what Lieutenant Morant was saying about the death of these eight Boers? Quite sure. In fact, Morant told him 'that he had been congratulated by headquarters over the last affair, and meant to go on with it'.[19]

No further questions, and no wonder.

Major Thomas rises, only to *again* begin his defence with a legal technicality.

'I claim the discharge of the prisoners on the ground that the charge is not proven. They should, if charged with anything, be charged with conspiracy.'

The court, effectively, sighs. Yes, Major Thomas, we have no doubt that Morant and Handcock are conspirators, but the charges *remain*. You must present a legitimate defence.

Fine then.

'I do not propose to put the prisoners in the box,' Thomas boldly begins, 'as the main facts are not in dispute. Rather, I will table statements from them, and the evidence I call will be confined to three things. Firstly, the orders received. Secondly, the prevailing customs of the war. Thirdly, the practices adopted by other irregular corps against an enemy breaking the usages of war.'[20]

Major Thomas has decided that those three defendants will independently submit a *written* statement of defence.

After Breaker's 'got them and shot them' testimony during the Visser case, Major Thomas will take no chances. The statements are handed to the court, who immediately notice a marked difference in their respective styles. In his fashion, the Breaker's testimony is bold and boastful. He *thrives* with the written word, his statement is as daring as it is determined, as full of detail as it is dense with denial. It is a speech, a song, a soliloquy, a lecture, a valedictory and a defence all at once.

I do not feel called upon, nor am I advised by my counsel, that it is necessary for me to enter the witness-box in this case . . . I was distinctly and repeatedly told by Captain Hunt . . . that 'no Boer prisoners were in future to be taken' . . . and he reprimanded me for not carrying out this order . . . Until Captain Hunt's body was found stripped and mutilated I shot no prisoners . . . After Captain Hunt's death and the brutal treatment of him, alive or dead, I resolved as his successor and survivor to carry out the orders he had impressed upon me, orders which other officers have in other places and in other corps carried out, with the provocation we had received. The Boers had left my friend's body, the body of an Englishman and officer, lying stripped, disfigured, and not buried – thrown into a drain like a pariah dog . . .

I was Senior Officer of the BVC in the Spelonken, and for the ordering of the shooting of these Boers I take full and entire responsibility. I admit having sent in an 'edited' report, but I did so for reasons which have actuated higher military authorities than myself. I have been told that I was never myself after the death of Captain Hunt, and I admit that his death preyed upon my mind when I thought of the brutal treatment he had received.

The alleged conversation between myself and Sergeant Wrench is absolutely untrue; No such conversation ever occurred. It is an entire fabrication.[21]

•

For his part, Lieutenant Picton gives evidence about being on a patrol towards the settlement of Scinde, when Captain Hunt personally 'Gave me instructions not to bring back any prisoners.'

Expanding, Picton notes how on this patrol, 'I got some prisoners on this patrol and brought them back to Fort Edward, and was reprimanded for doing so.'[22]

Very well, then.

Captain Taylor to the stand, please.

As ever, the contrast of his demeanour with that of Morant could not be greater.

For this is no simmering melting pot of emotions, full of wild accusations mixed with one part wit to two parts bile. He is calm, eager to help, wanting to explain how these unfortunate things occurred to those who, unlike him, have had no experience on the front lines of the badlands. Today there is no sign of 'Bulala' Taylor. Rather, he is calculated and very considered – each answer practised and always diverting the finger of blame away from himself to one figure in particular.

Do you recall, Captain Taylor, an occasion when Morant brought in prisoners?

Why yes, he remembers it well. No sooner had Lieutenant Morant brought in the prisoners than he was asked by Captain Hunt why he brought them in? Captain Hunt was quite insistent that they should have been shot. Captain Taylor was personally surprised at Captain Hunt's reaction, but it was not in his bailiwick of operations, so it was not for him to interfere in military matters. That was a matter for . . . you are surely way ahead of me, Major Bolton . . . Captain Hunt.

Baby Bolton the prosecutor is incredulous.

'Were you not,' he asks pointedly, 'Officer Commanding of the Spelonken?'

'Yes,' Taylor replies helpfully, eager to clear up any misunderstanding, 'of the *district*.'[23]

And therein lies the key to it all. Despite the fact that Captain Taylor is just that, a Captain, he does not actually have even a scintilla of military authority. The killing of Boers, either legally or illegally, was nothing to do with him, and all he could really do was to sometimes offer counsel, and act as an observer, an unwitting witness to military decisions.

On the issue of Captain Hunt, many witnesses echo the words of one Trooper who insists that Hunt once publicly reprimanded Morant for bringing in Boers alive saying, 'What the hell do you mean by bringing these men in? We have neither room nor rations for them here.'[24]

Major Thomas now transitions to what he thinks will be his *coup de grâce*. He will attempt to embarrass not only the court, but the British military itself. For what he knows is that, if we are honest with ourselves, shooting prisoners is not exactly limited to the BVC in this underhanded war. Under Thomas' guidance, Lieutenant Hannam gives brief and startling evidence: 'When I was a trooper in the Queensland Mounted Infantry on one occasion at Bronkhorst Spruit in 1900 my squadron took some prisoners. We were reprimanded by Colonel Craddock for taking them.'[25]

His point is clear. Their commanding officers had one view: no prisoners. We only want dead Boers.

Major Thomas now calls to Sergeant Waller Ashton of 'Brabant's Horse', another of the roving British militias:

'We received orders to take no prisoners in consequence of specific acts of treachery on the part of the Boers.'[26]

The Judge Advocate, Major C. S. Copeland, speaks from the bench. 'I object to such evidence as irrelevant.'[27]

The objection is noted and Major Thomas calls his witnesses regardless. Man after man tells of their secret orders and customs.

Sergeant McArthur, what say you?

'I saw one Boer summarily shot for being caught in khaki.'[28]

Lieutenant Colin Philip of the Queensland Mounted Infantry?

'We were in disgrace on one occasion for bringing in prisoners caught sniping.'[29]

Were all Boers shot?

'Boers caught breaking the customs of war were shot summarily. Instructions were published in the orders in Colonel Garrett's column that Boers caught in khaki were to be shot.'[30]

Captain King, of the Canadian Scouts?

'Boers guilty of wearing British uniforms, train wrecking, or murdering soldiers were dealt with summarily.'[31]

That is to say, shot immediately.

Now the court is cleared, and upon its resumption none other than Major Lenehan is recalled to give evidence on the character of the accused men. He proves to be full of praise for the pluck and devotion to duty of Morant, focusing particularly on his stunning capture of Tom Kelly. As to Handcock, well, he was a simple-minded man who obeyed orders without question, and also had a very strong sense of duty and strong record. Witton was a fine soldier and officer. None of them had ever given him cause for concern.

Major Thomas forgoes a plea of guilt or innocence, choosing instead to focus on 'justification'.

'On the ground that the Boers in this district were gangs of train wreckers without a head, and their conduct had brought reprisals.'

Damn the law, Major Thomas will not argue it. He is going to argue sense, because the prisoners – rather unlike *certain* witnesses – have been truthful.

'The main facts, as adduced by the evidence for the prosecution, are not denied by the defence.'

But surely the court will see the reality of the situation they were in?

'That which would be a crime, a felony, or a malicious act in time of peace may be quite justifiable in time of war, and doubly so in guerrilla warfare, waged against men who cannot be regarded as lawful belligerents, but only as lawless bands of marauders, who carry on desultory hostilities, combined with train wreckings and other uncivilised practices.

Upon such an enemy I maintain our troops are justified in making the severest reprisals, and are entitled to regard them, not as lawful belligerents at all, but as outlaws.'[32]

And what were the BVC?

'A small body, about 100 strong, they had to work over a vast area of difficult country, where, in small patrols and parties they had literally to hunt down the shifting bands of the enemy, in kloofs and almost inaccessible places, taking their lives in their hands. And sufficient evidence has come out during these cases to show how excellently their work was done. Practically they cleared the Spelonken district of Boers, many of whom found harbour there after their exploits against trains on the Pietersburg line. Even the prosecution admit that these Boers were of a bad class, and that this was the character of some, if not of all, of the eight men alleged to have been murdered.'

The court is again reminded of Captain Hunt's vicious orders, and how his own undignified death had spurned his men into hideous acts of brutality.

'It was not until Hunt himself was killed, with rather brutal surrounding circumstances, that his directions were fulfilled. After this, his successor, Lieutenant Morant, as he says, resolved to carry out previous orders. Up to this Morant had been particularly lenient towards prisoners, and there is no proof (but the very opposite) of his being of a malicious or cruel nature. It is true that after Hunt's death he changed a good deal, and adopted the sternest measures against the enemy. In civil life, and if trying a civil offence, under civil and peaceful conditions, it might be said that he became revengeful, but in time of war revenge and retaliation are allowable. It would be cant and hypocrisy to maintain otherwise. War makes men's natures both callous and, on occasions, vengeful. After all,' Major Thomas asks rhetorically, 'what is the object of war? Surely, it is simply to kill and disable as many of the enemy as possible. In pursuing these objects, soldiers are not to be judged by the rules of citizen life, and often, as soldiers, they do things, which, calmly regarded afterwards or in time of peace, appear, and are, unchristian and even brutal.'

Major Thomas closes with a none too subtle reminder of just where this case might lead, if one followed its logic and its directions all the way to the top.

'If in every war, especially guerrilla war, officers and men who committed reprisals were to be brought up and tried as murderers, courts martial might be kept going all the year. Such might be the case in the present war, if all the reprisals, summary executions, slaughters,

were dragged before formal courts, argued over by counsel and prosecutor as to points of law, and all the gruesome details exposed to the
light of day.'[33]

Major Bolton does not bother to argue.

His case is simple: 'The evidence is not denied. The eight men were
shot.'[34]

•

Lieutenant Peter Handcock tables his own statement along similar lines
to Morant, adding only that in the case of the shooting of van Buuren,

> Captain Robertson said it was right to shoot traitors. As to
> Robertson's successor, Captain Hunt told us when he came out
> that no Boers were to be taken. I had often heard that Boers were
> to be shot if they sniped or wore khaki or smashed up trains. I do
> not know what the rule under such things is, but we all thought
> that Captain Hunt knew the correct thing. I did not much believe
> in Captain Robertson, and when he ordered the man to be shot
> I told Captain Hunt all about it. When he came to Spelonken,
> Captain Hunt did not say it was wrong; he said we were not to
> take prisoners any more, so I thought he was doing his orders.
> I did what I was told to do, and I cannot say any more.[35]

Bolton remains silent as the statement is recited. There is no need to
speak when your quarry is so eager to confess in writing.

The Judge Advocate does not pass judgement; but his summation
indicates clearly where his sympathies lie.

'In the case now under consideration the prisoners practically admit
having committed the offence with which they stand charged, but maintain that they had justification for the course they pursued, and that there
was palliation for their action owing to the fact, as alleged by them, that
similar occurrences have taken place during the course of this war, and
have been ignored or condoned. I would point out that two wrongs do
not make a right, and that the commission of a wrongful act can scarcely
be urged as a justification for the repetition of that act.'[36]

•

It is no simple thing to make sense of the letter of the law. It is a burden-
some duty that bears down on the shoulders of President of the Court

Lieutenant Colonel Denny. After thinking on it deeply, sitting to consider all the outcomes, he pauses . . . and up goes his finger! LBW is the call!

Trials are important, yes, but they can wait for an appropriate afternoon. There is cricket to be played. The great unifying game of a fracturing Empire, boys from distant continents forget their differences and see only the pluck and luck of one another out on the field. The men do what they can to don some white by way of khaki mixes with flannel and the game is on. An impromptu Ashes between Australian Troopers and their British brethren has proved more important today than the court martial, or at least more enticing.

Certainly, these court-martial proceedings are a matter of life and death, deciding the guilt or innocence of soldiers for which the likely sentence for guilt will be execution by firing party.

But does that mean you can't enjoy a game of cricket in the middle of it? Of course not!

The members of the court are having a wonderful time. It is a nice change from days and days spent slouched and surly, growing weary of war crimes. See them as they are, hunched and bunched in the slips, backsides in the air, squatting with cupped hands.

As Oscar Wilde once remarked: 'I never play cricket. It requires one to adopt such indecent postures.'

It is hot, sweaty fun with swearing kept to a minimum as would-be Fred Spofforths and W. G. Graces show off their paces and graces. But a cloud appears over President Denny's face. He has spotted a bounder on the boundary; for here strides George Witton, bat in hand, ready to try his luck at the crease. Although the other cricketers of the court give him a welcome, Witton cannot help but notice 'a surprised kind of stare from the haughty president'.[37] Ah well, he will not be the last Englishman to look down his nose at a lout from Down Under on a cricket field. The game goes on, the defendant defending his wicket, the prosecutor pressing him with a leg cutter, and Lieutenant Colonel Denny just waiting for an opportunity to send Witton to the dressing room for good.

The point remains, however, that the President of the Court has seen him at the cricket and accepts it. Despite Denny's steely stare, Witton will recount, 'my presence there was unheeded. Incidents such as these tended to convince me that the penalty hanging over me could not be a very serious one. We were often provided with horses, and permitted to take riding exercise in the morning before breakfast.'[38]

5 February 1902, Pietersburg, trial for a trio

The court has heard many claims against the men of the BVC but this next claim is one set to turn any stomach, no matter how hardened – the murder of a boy.

Once more President of the Court Lieutenant Colonel Denny rises and faces Breaker Morant. He says his piece:

'Lieutenant Morant you are charged with murder in instigating the killing of two Boers and one boy, names unknown. How do you plead?'

'Not guilty,' answers the Breaker. Handcock stands and enters the same plea.

The first witness please, Major Bolton.

Sergeant Major Hammett?

'I was one of the patrol which Lieutenant Morant and Lieutenant Handcock accompanied in search of three Boers,' Hammett begins a little nervously, clearly starting to relive some of the horror. There was no doubt these three men intended to surrender, nor that Lieutenant Morant wanted them dead.

'It was agreed that when Morant asked, "Do you know Captain Hunt?" that was to be the signal for shooting them.'

And did they shoot the Boers when Morant said this?

'It was done,' answers Hammett chillingly.

And how old were the victims?

'The youngest Boer was about seventeen.'[39]

More members of the patrol appear in the box and all say the same thing. The Boers were first found, 'at a native kraal, were sent on, and at the signal shot. It was understood that no prisoners were to be taken.'[40]

What choice does Major Thomas have?

Yes, Morant's last speech to the court – 'we got them and we shot them under rule 303' – had been such a disaster he had doubly resolved not to put him in the box again. But two things persuade him to put Morant back there now.

Firstly, there is nothing to lose, as the testimony of the other witnesses to this point has been so damaging.

And secondly, Morant *insists*. As ever, he will not take no for an answer. Very well then.

Lieutenant Morant, please give us your account of what happened.

Morant, glowing more red than ever now that he is where he is always at his best – the centre of attention once more – begins.

'I went out to look for the three Dutchmen,' he says coolly. 'I found them, and never asked them to surrender. As they were Dutchmen with whom we were at war and belonged to a party which had stripped and mutilated a brother officer, who was a friend of mine, I had them shot.'[41]

Yes, he goes on to give *much* more detail, but that is what it boils down to. There is no hint of nervousness to his presentation, no sign that he realises his life is on the line. He simply presents the facts as he sees them, and makes no apology for any of them.

Major Thomas has no more questions, other than wondering why Breaker won't stop talking. Doesn't he understand the damage he's doing to himself? Major Bolton now rises, only to receive a spirited welcome from the Breaker in the box.

'Look here, Major, you are just the Johnnie I have been waiting to be cross-examined by! Cross-examine me as much as you like, but let us have a straight gallop.'[42]

A straight gallop it is, but Major Bolton is trampled by the Breaker's sarcasm and rejoinders. As Witton records: 'In the cross-examination Morant's retorts were so straight and so bitter that they resulted in the collapse of the Prosecutor after a very few questions had been asked.'[43]

Now, Major Bolton may have been bested back to his bench in a match of brains with the Breaker, but he knows that Morant only incriminates himself further. When Handcock comes to speak, he only repeats that Hunt had ordered that no prisoners be taken.

And again, Major Thomas argues that the Boers do not qualify as organised soldiers, and as such the rules of decent war should not apply to them. Thank you, Major, we have heard that song and dance before and we are quite sick of it. Major Bolton need not conclude things with a closing argument, he need only repeat the facts and charges as they stand.

And again, a case is closed and a verdict voted on. That verdict, like those before them, will not be announced to the accused until the entire cavalcade of calumny has been concluded.

7 February 1902, Pietersburg, Taylored defence

On this day the court has the refreshing change of hearing a couple of murder cases that, for once, do *not* involve Breaker Morant.

'Captain Alfred Taylor, you are accused of murder in inciting Sergeant Major Morrison, Sergeant Oldham, and others to kill and murder six men, names unknown. How do you plead?'

'Not guilty.'

Now while to the eye it might look like this court is made up of the same men as the last one, it has now transitioned from a 'Court Martial' to a 'Military Court'. A distinction *with* a difference it would seem. This body of legality has so transformed because Captain Taylor, testing a technicality, has successfully argued he is no soldier, he is but a Native Commissioner, and he cannot be court-martialled. Captain Taylor has also had the good fortune to lean on the best possible man for his defence counsel, *himself*.

Major Bolton calls the first witness for the prosecution of Taylor: Sergeant Major Morrison of the BVC. The grumpy and grizzled Sergeant Major – described by a contemporary as a man whose 'face generally wears a sly, unpleasant expression',[44] which is never more apparent than right now – was under the impression that he was in the service of the British Military; however, one day he found that the reality was a little different:

'I paraded my patrol and reported to Captain Robertson. Captain Taylor was present. Captain Taylor said, "I have intelligence that six Boers with two wagons are coming in to surrender, but I would have no prisoners".'

And your response was?

'I asked Captain Robertson if I should take orders from Taylor. Captain Robertson said, "Certainly, as he is commanding officer at Spelonken".'

The trouble, as Major Bolton knows, is that Taylor is a tremendously careful man. *He* never outright stated that he was Morrison's commanding officer, he left that to Robertson. Captain Robertson is wrong, but Taylor chose not to contradict or correct. This is precisely the sort of thing a cunning lawyer would do.

'I would have no prisoners,' Taylor said, but a wish is not a command. Major Bolton hopes the court will see what Taylor did; rather than the deliberate ambiguity of his words.

Morrison proceeds with his damning recollection.

'I asked Captain Taylor to repeat his order, which he did. He said, "If the Boers showed the white flag, Morrison, you are not to see it".'

And we presume you passed these on?

'I repeated these orders to Sergeant Oldham, and I warned six men and a corporal to accompany Oldham as an advance party.'

And did you kill the Boers?

'Six Boers were shot by the advance guard,' Morrison replies.

'And were these the only Boers met with that day?' asks Bolton.

'Yes.'[45]

Captain Taylor thinks better of cross-examining Morrison, so it is now Sergeant Oldham's turn. So, what did Sergeant Major Morrison say to you then?

'He warned me about six Boers, and told me I was to *make* them fight, and on no account bring them in alive.'

Which led to what sort of an interaction with the Boers?

'They were ambushed. There was a man in front of a wagon holding a white flag, and a great noise in the wagon. I stopped the fire, thinking there might be women and children, but since I found only six men, as described in the orders, they were taken out and shot.'

Orders are what they say on the tin: orders. Were these Boers flying a white flag? Had they surrendered?

Oldham's brow furrows as thinks on it.

'I believe the flag was put up after the firing commenced.'

They were armed?

'They were armed, and their rifles loaded.'

And you reported what to Captain Taylor?

'I addressed my report of the affair to Captain Taylor, by Morrison's orders,' says Oldham.

This is a sealed fate. Precisely the answer a prosecutor would pray for, but there is more. Never mind the prayer, Captain Taylor seems to have the luck of the Devil as Oldham continues with a twist that may yet save him:

'Captain Robertson complained, and the report was readdressed to him.'

Once more Captain Taylor remains uninformed when it comes to the doings and dealings of the BVC.

'Were Captain Taylor or Captain Robertson present at the shooting of the Boers?' asks Major Bolton hopefully.

'No.'[46]

The Crown's most useful witness, Captain Robertson, is ready to take the stand and do that rarest of all things for a one-time BVC commander. He will tell the truth!

'I told Morrison he must take his orders from Captain Taylor.'

And did Oldham make a report to you?

Oh yes.

'Oldham reported, "All correct; they are all shot".'

A hideous correction.

'I saw the bodies,' Robertson notes.

It is Taylor's turn to cross-examine. He has left the other witnesses as they were, but he will not do so for Captain Robertson. Perhaps the court should know a thing or two about *his* character. So, Captain Robertson, are you currently serving with the BVC?

'I have had to resign my commission in that corps.'

And have you a new corps?

'I have been refused admission to any other corps.'

To your knowledge, has Sergeant Major Morrison been arrested while with the BVC?

'Morrison reported he was threatened with arrest.'

Actually, not just threatened – the Sergeant Major *was* arrested by none other than . . . Lieutenant Picton, another of the accused. Behind the table of the accused, the shade of a smile crosses Captain Taylor's face, confident that the court will now tie itself in knots questioning and criticising the reliability of both Morrison and Robertson. Surely they are the *real* conspirators here, and it is nothing to do with Captain Taylor?

Go on please, Captain Robertson, what happened with this 'arrest'?

'Morrison demanded an inquiry, but broke his arrest and went to Pietersburg.'

So not only was Morrison under arrest, but he *broke arrest*, and went absent without leave? To Pietersburg? Under the command, no less, of a disgraced Captain that no good soldier would stand to serve with? This is preposterous! Taylor's examination continues:

'Did I ask for a patrol?'

'Yes, as six armed Boers with two wagons were reported,' answers Robertson.

'Did Sergeant Major Morrison receive any instruction from me in your presence?'

'No,' replies Roberston. (Technically, this is true, and Taylor is careful to leave it at that.)

'Was it usual for patrols to get orders from me?' asks Taylor.

'Yes,' replies Robertson.[47]

Captain Taylor now takes the stand to give evidence in his own defence, making a statement given that he can't ask himself questions.

'During July last year I was in charge of natives and intelligence work. No part of my instructions authorised me not to take prisoners. I had no military command . . .'[48]

Do you see? I simply didn't like to interfere on BVC matters. It was not my place, it was not . . . *proper.*

'I received intelligence of certain Boers coming in to surrender, but never of the party of six. I never gave Morrison any orders, and knew nothing about the six Boers, nor had I asked for a patrol to meet them

. . . The first intimation I received of the charge of six Boers having been shot was made yesterday in court.'[49]

Again Captain Taylor makes clear just how appalled he was at the very *idea* of . . . killing prisoners!

Taylor is finished for the moment, preparing to plead the next charge.

'Captain Alfred Taylor, you are charged with the murder of a native. How do you plead?'

'Not guilty.'

Corporal McMahon is called forth as the first witness, and provides a graphically vivid account:

'I was on patrol when I sighted some Boers, but they evidently had wind of my coming, for when the place where they had been seen was rushed no Boers were there. Some of them opened fire from a Kaffir kraal. The Boers were driven off.'

And then it had happened . . .

'I heard a report and somebody said, "Taylor's shot a n . . . ger." I walked over and saw a Kaffir, and Taylor standing by with a pistol in his hand.'[50]

A *literal* smoking gun.

Captain Taylor will not examine this witness, what would be the point? Major Bolton now calls for Trooper Lucas' recollection.

'After the engagement with the Boers I rode to the kraal. Captain Taylor questioned a native, who said "I *konna*." I heard a report, and the native fell dead. Taylor had a pistol in his hand.'[51]

There are no more questions from Captain Taylor, none directed to Trooper Sheridan who backs up this account. Taylor will defend himself in the box.

'I received this appointment as Native Commissioner in the north on account of my knowledge of the natives, and went on condition that I should have a free hand. On this occasion the natives had warned the Boers of the approach of the party, and one native was brought in and recognised as one of those who had been assisting the Boers. This native refused to give any information and was threatened with trial as a spy. He refused to show or say anything, and was going off when I called him back, but he would not return. I then fired, meaning to frighten him, but unfortunately fired too low, and the native was killed. The shooting of this native had a salutary effect.'[52]

Oh we see, Captain Taylor *meant* to fire a warning shot, but fired just a little too low. Look, it was a dashed unfortunate error, and he really hadn't meant to put a bullet in his head, but it still had a 'salutary effect'!

With that explained, proceedings draw to a close, allowing those sitting in judgement to make their deliberations – they don't take long – at the conclusion of which the verdict can now be disclosed immediately, for Captain Taylor is not part of the BVC collectively, where the verdicts will only be announced at the end of all proceedings.

All rise . . .

Taylor stands alone as he awaits the announcement.

President of the Court, Lieutenant Colonel Henry Cuthbert Denny, you have the floor.

'Captain Alfred Taylor,' Denny says, in portentous tones, 'you are acquitted of both charges.'[53]

A self-contained and utterly self-assured man, Captain Taylor still permits himself a small courtly smile and a subdued nod of thanks to the bench. For he is cunning enough to know that a guilty man like him ought never to look *too* thankful and relieved. No, much safer to do what he does now and take this declaration of innocence as his due.

Right now, as is made clear by his own expression, Sergeant Major Morrison can scarcely believe what he has just heard and that the court can have heard the evidence he just gave. He was there! He witnessed it! He knows what happened. But they have found Taylor innocent? How can that be?

The prosecutor, Major Bolton, knows the answer better than most.

For Taylor has been the only accused so far clever enough not to admit to his crimes, the first one therefore who had a shot at creating reasonable doubt – and the court has obliged by reaching a *conclusion* on something. It is the first the court has delivered, and they choose to provide Taylor with an acquittal. It will be enough to give Witton, Handcock and the Breaker some heart. After all, if Captain Taylor can go free, why shouldn't they?

•

The morning sun is perfect and piercing as Captain de Bertodano strides into the parade grounds of Pietersburg. Yet clouds loom in the approaching distance, dark clouds in the form of Breaker Morant, supervised by a young officer, who, despite having the duty of guarding him, seems already less a guard than a star-struck fan, thrilled to be hearing the stories of such a famous man.

Spotting the Captain in the yard, the Breaker breaks away from his guard and approaches, clearly wanting to have a word – and not a quiet one at that.

Walking right up to him, Morant brings his face to within an inch of de Bertodano's – close enough to bite his nose off if he chose, and it really looks like he might – before launching.

'My "trial" for the shooting of this Missionary is a scandal and a disgrace to the Army,'[54] Morant begins. Heads are turning, Troopers cocking an ear to catch the show. 'I am innocent!' the Breaker proclaims to his audience. 'I have been *selected* as a victim because I shot a few damned Boers!'[55]

The Breaker knows how to draw a crowd and how to play to it. He now has a *j'accuse* to deliver to the silent Captain de Bertodano.

'You are the man who has worked up all the evidence and you ought to be ashamed of yourself for the betrayal of your *brother officers*.'[56]

Do tell? Well, Captain de Bertodano does not want to play Portia to his Shylock, no desire to be the foil for his theatrical display of innocence. Instead, he will play to an audience of one – just Morant. Lowering his voice, the Captain has a little soliloquy for the Breaker's ears alone.

'Morant, I am very *proud* of having been the cause of bringing you to trial,' de Bertodano whispers. 'You know in your heart that you and Handcock murdered poor old Heese because you were afraid that he would report the shooting of the Boers in cold blood. But you were such damned fools as not to realise that we had all the evidence without calling on him. We know who is behind it and he's led you by the nose, but we haven't got him yet.'[57]

De Bertodano does not mention 'Bulala' Taylor's name, Morant knows who he means, and de Bertodano knows he knows. The soldiers scattered around the parade ground watch as for once Breaker Morant is that rarest of all things – – – – – – – – – silent. *What is de Bertodano saying to him?* The Captain continues calmly and coolly, each soft sentence another body blow to the deflating Morant, each phrase another punch to end the Punch and Judy show.

'I don't recognise you and that poor fool Handcock *as "brother officers"*. You are guilty as Hell, and I am glad to help to send you there.'[58]

But de Bertodano is just warming up. For now he has a quiet question, a calculated one to let Morant know exactly how much he knows. He leans in close to hiss it: 'Where is your boy?'

Yes, that's right. Where is your African servant, Morant, the one who saw you shoot Heese in the back of the head, just as Handcock shot and killed his driver? That one! *That* 'boy'. You think everyone has forgotten about him, that you got away with that one, too? Well, you haven't.

'Your boy has *disappeared*. Have you murdered him too?'[59]

His eyes darting wildly like frenzied small fish in a bottle, Morant remains in a shocked silence, a silence that speaks all.

Has Captain de Bertodano broken the Breaker? Probably not. But he has had the satisfaction of telling him what he thinks of one who has disgraced the uniform and the flag in this manner, and that is something. To mark the victory he now raises his voice so everyone can hear, and chooses his words carefully, as he addresses the young armed officer who 'guards' Morant.

'Your *prisoner*,' he says, lingering on that particular word for the said prisoner's benefit, and all those listening, 'is not allowed to speak to anyone.'[60]

Harry Harbord Morant, the Breaker, does not deserve a name or an audience. He is a prisoner and he is to stop talking. So sayeth Captain de Bertodano, before he turns on his polished heel, and walks away with the strut of a *free* man. If he never sees Breaker Morant again that will be fine with him.

The prisoner is led back to his cell.

•

As it happens, Breaker Morant is not the only man who shall proclaim that he is being wrongfully accused of the murder of Reverend Heese. The other is . . . well, this is a bit awkward, but it's the prosecutor, Major Bolton. For in fact, he wants to . . . *drop* the charges. All right, Breaker?

But Morant will not let them fall, catching the charges before Bolton can drop them.

'I will stand my trial,'[61] he states, flatly.

Again, Major Bolton presses, surely Lieutenant Morant would prefer not to be charged with conspiracy to murder?

'I *will* stand my trial,'[62] Morant repeats, declaring the discussion and negotiation over.

Although Peter Handcock and George Witton are gobsmacked at what Morant is saying, Major Bolton is not. For after all the to-ing and fro-ing, it is obvious that Morant is canny enough to have realised the truth – the only reason the prosecutor does not wish to proceed with that particular charge is because his key evidence has *disappeared*. For the truth is, just as de Bertodano had hissed at him, Morant's 'boy', really is 'disappeared', read 'dead', meaning Morant and Handcock are the only ones living who can attest to what happened. As Handcock had withdrawn his 'duress' confession, it means the chances of getting a conviction are nearly nothing. Which is *precisely* why the Breaker wants the case to proceed – handing your enemy a rifle that you know is loaded with blanks not only does you no harm, it weakens him. And so it shall proceed, to the chagrin of Major Bolton.

Meanwhile the Breaker's charm has worked its charms on Major Thomas with extraordinary effect. For, from a standing start, the Major has moved from being a mere legal advocate to being a *believer* in their innocence. Who could not see that the *Boers* killed that poor priest? Certainly Lieutenant Handcock was seen riding off in a similar direction, but now Major Thomas understands the delicate truth – one that involves the reputation of good women, and it is clear the Breaker *would rather be shot* than put a lady's name in peril in some sordid witness box, by divulging what had happened. Major Thomas is enormously impressed by such selfless sacrifice.

Now when it comes to the shooting of the other Boer prisoners, Thomas equally accepts Morant's explanation: we were on the front line of a war, winning it the best way we knew how. When orders come from Kitchener himself to take no prisoners, who are we to question them? Besides which, after what the Boers did to my friend Captain Hunt, the Boers *all* had it coming!

Major Thomas feels angry now on Morant's behalf. This is not a trial, it is a vendetta! Why, these men are scapegoats of the Empire, not murderers!

Few things are more dangerous for a defendant than a lawyer who believes *everything* he says. Major Thomas has become such a danger; he cannot see anything except the 'truth' that Morant dazzles him with on a daily basis.

17 February 1902, Pietersburg, so help me God, God help you

And so once again the court is assembled. This time not for war or transgressions within, but for a far more civilian if equally uncivil accusation of murder. It is that rarest of things in these whole proceedings – a genuine mystery. Who killed Reverend Heese, and for that matter, *why?*

The session begins, and it only remains to be seen what kind of an innings the BVC men will have.

Two men are being charged and tried in today's court martial. They are more than familiar to the court.

'Lieutenant Handcock, when on active service you are charged with committing the offence of murder, in that you, at or near Bandolier Kop, in the district of Zoutpansberg, Transvaal, on or about the 23rd day of August, 1901, when on active service, wilfully, feloniously, and of malice aforethought, did kill and murder one C. A. D. Heese, a missionary. How do you plead?'[63]

'Not guilty.'

'Lieutenant Morant, you are charged with the offence of inciting to murder. How do you plead?'

'Not guilty.'

So be it.

Proceed, Major Bolton.

'Witnesses will be called to prove that on 23 August 1901, Missionary Heese left Fort Edward for Pietersburg. The motive for killing him was that he had got to know of the killing of eight Boers, and was on his way to Pietersburg to report the occurrence when he was shot by Handcock under orders from Morant.'

Our first witness is Corporal Joseph Phillips.

Blinking warily, Trooper Phillips is called, swears to tell the truth, and gives his account, carefully questioned by Major Bolton.

'On 23rd August last,' he begins tentatively, 'I was on duty on Cossack Post when a Cape cart containing the missionary and a Cape boy was going in the direction of Pietersburg.'

And did you question Reverend Heese about his business, given that all foreigners who pass are inspected?

Yes, indeed.

'The missionary showed a pass signed by Captain Taylor.'

And what was his demeanour?

'He was greatly agitated. He said there had been a fight that morning and several had been killed.'

Objection! Major Thomas wishes to know, did Reverend Heese tell you whether those killed were *British* or *Boers*?

'He did not say.'[64]

Which speaks, of course, to reasonable doubt, and that is all it needs to speak to. No further questions.

And now to Corporal Herbert Sharp.

'I saw Morant addressing Heese, and afterwards I saw Handcock riding in the same direction as the missionary.'

What time was this?

'It was about 10 or 11 am when the missionary went past, and Handcock went about 12.'

Was Handcock armed?

'He had a carbine. Handcock did not take the same road as the missionary.'

No, not the same road, but as Major Bolton is quick to point out, the fact that the Reverend took the high road and Handcock took the low road does not mean that Handcock's route did not quickly merge with that of Heese's once out of sight of Fort Edward.

In any case, your witness, Major Thomas.

As the Tenterfield lawyer rises to cross-examine, he surveys the Corporal with a gimlet eye. For yes, we know about you Corporal Sharp, don't we? You are not merely a witness here, but the recruiter of other witnesses? Not merely an uninvolved observer called into this prosecution, but someone who has been actively involved in organising that prosecution!

'I admit I did go a long way to fetch Mr van Rooyen, who, I thought, was an eye-witness of the killing of the missionary.'

Which proves my point. Corporal Sharp is not just a witness, he is an *advocate*. And Major Thomas has some more evidence to this effect?

'Did you not tell Trooper Hodds: "I would walk barefooted from Spelonken to Pietersburg to be in the firing party to shoot Morant"?'

Clearly shaken that this is known, Corporal Sharp carefully concedes that is possible.

'And did Lieutenant Handcock not issue an order against soldiers selling their uniforms in consequence of your having done so?'

Selling his uniform? In a war where Boer Commandos have disguised themselves in khaki, so as to better be able to KILL BRITISH SOLDIERS?

A shamefaced Corporal Sharp admits that it is true. Well then, does it not appear he had something of a vendetta against Lieutenant Handcock and Lieutenant Morant? Corporal Sharp does not look at it like that.

'I made it my business to collect notes of what was going on at Spelonken.'[65]

Major Thomas is disgusted, and has nothing more to say to such a creature as this. But his point is obvious. Sharp is a disgrace to the very uniform he has sold, and his testimony on anything cannot be trusted.

Two further witnesses are now called by Major Bolton, both of whom confirm that Handcock left the fort on horseback, carrying a rifle.

The next witness in the court is not given a name, only being described as 'a native'.[66] But even if denied the dignity of a name like everyone else, Silas has a short story to tell.

'I saw an armed man on horseback following the missionary. The man was on a brown horse.'

And what happened then?

'Afterwards I heard shots, and then I saw the dead body of a coloured boy. I was frightened and fled.'

Trooper Thompson testifies that: 'I saw the missionary speaking to the eight Boers who were shot.'

And now Mr Hendrik van Rooyen – a farmer in the area where Reverend Heese was murdered – the witness that Corporal Sharp had gone to the ends of the earth to find, gives evidence for the prosecution.

So, do tell us, Mr van Rooyen, about the day in question?

'I spoke to the Reverend Mr Heese on the road.'

At what time?

'About 2 pm.'

And then?

'I trekked on with my wagon till sundown, when I saw a man on horseback coming from the direction of Pietersburg. The man turned off the road. Afterwards a man came on foot [towards me].'

Was it the same man?

Van Rooyen pauses, hesitant.

'I could not say if it was the *same* man I saw on horseback.'

Then who was the man on foot?

'It was Lieutenant Handcock. He advised me to push on, as Boers were about.'[67]

Major Bolton closes his case.

Major Thomas can barely contain his exasperation. Poor Handcock, he muses, has no recourse but to sit and endure these blatant lies.

Breaker Morant will speak in his own defence and, as a man who has been telling lies his entire life, he is the picture of composed confidence. To tell a lie is little different for the Breaker than telling the time. It is but a menial task that must be done now and again. And just as he winds his watch, so he winds another story, careful to keep the mechanism of murder ticking over without detection.

What occurred on the 23rd of August last?

'Eight Boers guilty of train wrecking and other crimes were shot by my orders. Reverend Heese spoke to these Boers and I told him not to do so.'

Then what occurred?

'Afterwards, I saw Heese in a cart. He produced a pass signed by Captain Taylor. I advised him not to go on to Pietersburg because of the Boers. Heese said, "I'll chance it". I advised him to tie a white flag to the cart.'

And Morant is absolutely firm on what happened then.

'I returned to the fort and then went to Taylor's, and I afterwards saw Handcock at Bristow's. Handcock went on to Schiel's.'[68]

Major Bolton now leans in close, to ask the question they all know must be asked, the key question of this case.

Did you tell Handcock to shoot Reverend Heese?

The Breaker reels in seeming shock – obviously mortally offended at the very idea of such a thing.

'I never made any suggestion about killing the missionary. I was on good terms with him.'[69]

You may stand down.

Morant is replaced in the dock by the glowering Lieutenant Handcock, who insists he wasn't even riding a horse at all on the afternoon in question, and then proceeds to place his itinerary for the morning in exactly the opposite order to that of Morant's recollection.

'I left on foot for Schiel's in the morning. I took the road which branched off to the Pietersburg road, and then across country. I lunched at Schiel's, and then went to Bristow's till dusk, then back to the fort.'

Yes, well.

It is all a bit delicate.

Lunch at Schiel's? Then to Bristow's?

And who might they be?

Well, they are the next two witnesses – two Boer women of notably attractive form, whose husbands are away. And, while home alone, both attest to having received a 'visit' from Lieutenant Handcock on that day, a man whose own wife is thousands of miles away in Australia.

George Witton records the delicate details for posterity: Mrs Schiel is first to the stand. With an air of light discretion, Major Thomas, having prepared the ground for what he hopes will be a faultless recital, asks Madame if she would care to make a statement to the court? She would.

'I live on a farm about three miles from Fort Edward. I am the wife of Colonel Schiel, an artillery officer, who fought with the Boers, and has been captured and sent as a prisoner to St Helena. Lieutenant Handcock had lunch at my house on the 23rd August, and left during the afternoon.'[70]

There are no questions from Major Bolton. For we are not only gentlemen in this court, we are men of the world. We all understand what a lady admitting she received a man in her house who was not her husband or her relative actually means, and what the main course on the menu actually was. Let us, ahem, leave it at that.

Mrs Bristow is next to give evidence. She wishes to make one point clear: 'I am not on speaking terms with Mrs Schiel.'

Though this court does not say it, it is not surprised – and the fact that they have Lieutenant Handcock in common on the one afternoon in question is not going to bring them closer together.

'I live about a mile from Fort Edward,' she attests. 'I am the wife of an old settler in the district who had not taken any part in the war. Lieutenant Handcock had been at our place on the afternoon of the 23rd August, and had returned to the fort in the evening.'[71]

It is compelling testimony, and hard to refute. (Well, one man in particular won't be refuting it. And that is the old settler himself, Mr Charles Bristow, husband of the lady 'visited' by Lieutenant Handcock. It is true, he had assured Trooper Cochrane weeks ago that he would give evidence against the 'veritable reign of terror' launched by Morant and Handcock. But somehow, someone has got to him since, and he is not available. Nor is Captain Alfred Taylor. Cochrane may draw his own conclusions and speculate at 50 yards if he pleases, but it changes nothing. While Mrs Bristow gives testimony to exculpate Handcock, her husband is not available to refute it, or to tell what he knows.)

And so it is locked in, as the court report chronicles: 'Further witnesses proved that Handcock was at Schiel's and Bristow's when the missionary was shot.'[72]

After all, these two women are trashing their own reputation to swear on oath that each one of them had 'entertained' him, alone in their houses on the afternoon in question. This, clearly, is . . . surprising. But it is not for this court to pass judgement on Handcock's morality, and whether or not he has been faithful to his wife. Their appointed task is to determine whether or not he has murdered the Reverend Heese and it seems obvious that, given that gentleman met his end at much the same time that Handcock was with the women, the glowering Lieutenant cannot be guilty.

The court retires to consider its verdict. These long trials are over; all that is left is for the verdicts to be revealed.

CHAPTER EIGHTEEN

'SHOOT STRAIGHT, YOU BASTARDS'[1]

... Some day I'll be on the ground
And the van will hurry round!
Doc. will gravely wag his head:
'No use now! the poor chap's dead! ...'

... Carve in stone above his head
Words that some old Christian said:
'Grace he sought, and grace he found,
Twixt the saddle and the ground![2]

'Short Shrift', the last poem of the Breaker
published, in *The Bulletin*, 1902

Poor beggar, how well I remember him: outcast, boon comrade,
drunken beast, and brave man. It seems but yesterday we trekked,
starved, stole and fought together – what a mate in those long
hours of night watch or day march – what tales he could tell,
what merry rhymes recite. And there were days before, too, down
in great sunny Australia: days of racing, of begging and starving,
days of wine and women, rags, drunkenness and disgrace – Poor
old Breaker![3]

Major Victor Marra Newland,
a friend of the Breaker's present at the final scene

18 February 1902, Pietersburg, the waiting is the hardest part

And now, nothing ...

The next day and the next and the next pass with no word.

The sun rises, the sun falls, the darkness presses ... always the darkness presses. And yes, as far as we know, we will make sunrise tomorrow, but just how many more sunrises might be left to us before the eternal night falls upon us? Is it really possible that we are now living the last days of our lives and that we are soon to die? Oddly, for he has been so brave throughout, so unyielding in his contempt for the whole legal process, it is Breaker Morant who seems to feel most closely the horror of what might now await.

Witton on this afternoon is allowed to spend time with Morant, Handcock and Picton in their cell.

Morant's mood is sombre.

'What do you think they will do with us?' he asks Witton, even as he clutches at the penny on the string around his neck as if it were a rosary bead, almost as if trying to reactivate it after a long run of outs. 'Do you think they will shoot us?'[4]

Witton is non-committal for he simply has no clue, and has worries enough of his own without concerning himself with cheering up the Breaker.

All they can do is pass the time the best they can, and with that in mind they spend the afternoon in the prison garden where some peach trees grow, regrettably with fruit not yet ripe enough to pick or eat. No matter, when they see anyone they know well passing by, they eagerly send a shower of hard peaches their way. When one of these proves to be a deposed 'Kaffir chief', Magato, an African who had worked with Intelligence, and with whom the Breaker had previously fallen out – for the fact that Morant considered that Magato had tried to swindle Hunt – *Hunt!* – out of a rug of skins, the old man does not take the flurry of fruit well.

Storming off in all directions, in short order and high dudgeon he immediately files an official complaint with the Garrison Adjutant, and that letter is just as quickly presented to Morant himself.

Rising to the occasion, and with no little *elan*, the Breaker – for he's back, just for a short while – simply turns the letter over and dashes off his thoughts:

> An Intelligence N . . . r named Magato
> Has been singing a sad obligato,
> And begs to complain
> He suffered much pain
> By being struck with a squashy tomato.
> [P.S. – For 'tomato' read 'peach' – exigency of verse.][5]

Ah, how the good fellows in the officers' mess of the Pietersburg garrison gaol laugh that evening when the letter is passed around. Typical Breaker! How capital of him!

•

'Not guilty!'

For Major Thomas, those two words are like twin beams of sunlight breaking through the clouds of a cold and dark morning. They are so sweet that he doesn't just hear them, he can feel them. On those rare times he has been able to sleep in the last five weeks, he has dreamt of such a verdict. But these aren't the ethereal machinations of a tired mind looking for comfort, this is *real*.

Not guilty!

Though by nature a buttoned-down man, in other circumstances than a formal legal environment, he might have unbuttoned and actually leapt for joy. For now he is content to smile beatifically. Christ knows there were days when he had felt like a man drowning in a bloody sea of his own making, but by God, and thank God, salvation has come.

It takes the Major a moment to compose himself as he gathers his transcripts and documents together. He had expected to be launching an appeal right now, not trying to hear himself think over a chorus of congratulations from uniformed observers. Someone will have to get the word to Breaker and Handcock. No, not someone. The Major will do it himself, he will tell the lads that they are officially and legally NOT guilty of the murder of the Reverend Heese. He relishes the opportunity to be the bearer of such glad tidings.

•

But Captain de Bertodano, when he hears shortly afterwards, is disgusted.

'I do not think that there was a man on the court martial,' he will recall, 'who did not but believe that they were guilty.'[6]

In the meantime, the law is an ass, Morant is a swine and this is a dog of a day.

20 February 1902, Pietersburg, champagne Charlies

And so it is not just in the courtroom that those wonderful words are heard, but here in the cells tonight . . .

'Not guilty!' 'Not guilty!' 'NOT GUILTY!'

Besides themselves with joy, Morant and Handcock do not bother to hide it and this evening their cells are a place of riotous revelry, of uproarious laughter, hand-pumping and back-slaps, never more than when half-a-dozen bottles of champagne arrive with the compliments – can you believe it? – of a member of the court! Well, well, well . . . they are not without friends on the bench! Tonight is their first celebration of a Not Guilty verdict, may there be many more to come!

And here, friends, is a toast to Captain Taylor! Why, what a good man! And if only the court had known that two of Mrs Schiel's sons work for Captain Taylor. Now isn't that a coincidence? Oh, and Mrs Bristow? She was, of course, the matron of Sweetwaters Farm, and dependent on the patronage of Captain Taylor and his senior officers to stay afloat. What a small and helpful world it is when one is a friend of Captain Taylor!

And now who is this, suddenly come on a visit? It proves to be an orderly with some news. Now, it is totally unofficial of course, but he has overheard a staff officer boasting he knows what verdict the court martial will deliver for Morant and his subordinates on the remaining charges pertaining to the Visser case, the Eight Boers case and the Three Boers case.

And that verdict will be ... *innocent of all charges*!

Hurrah! *Hurrah! HURRAH!*

If true – and they are sure it is – it means they will likely be set free as soon as the following day. The champagne and the laughter flow freely once more, as does the poetry and salacious stories, until nearing midnight the party breaks up. And yet here is something a little strange.

Just as Witton is returning to his quarters near the cow-gun, he is met by the garrison's commanding officer, who informs him rather coldly that 'I have orders to remove you to the garrison prison right here and now.'[7]

How very peculiar? It seems a very odd order to give to a man who is about to be set free on the morrow, but the officer insists, despite Witton's protest. Soldiers soon arrive to carry his bedding and few possessions to Handcock's cell, where he must doss down for the night. Well, never mind. Witton is at least heartened by the fact that this is likely his last night of imprisonment.

The following morning at dawn Major Bob Lenehan appears at the cells of Morant and Handcock to wish them well, and farewell – he, personally, is to be taken by armed escort to Cape Town and sent home in disgrace – when suddenly the officer in charge of the guard, Captain Brown of the 2nd Wiltshire Regiment, appears and asks to speak to the Major outside. There is something in his voice that bodes ill, and Lenehan exits, fearing bad news. Sure enough, wordlessly, Brown shows Lenehan the cable that had come from Army HQ the evening before:

> Send prisoners Major Lenehan, Lieutenants Morant, Picton, Handcock and Witton to Pretoria under an adequate escort commanded by a competent officer. They are all to be handcuffed except Major Lenehan. Every precaution must be taken against possibility of escape . . .[8]

Brown's voice breaks as he begs: 'Lenehan, you must tell them that they are to be sent down to Pretoria in irons. I cannot.'[9]

Lenehan gulps and nods, accepting that his final duty for the BVC will be his toughest ever.

He enters the cell to tell the men he once commanded what is to happen to them. Now, given there is no easy way to say it, he just says it: 'Gentlemen, you are to be put in irons and sent down to Pretoria.'[10]

They are just a few words, but they manage to instantly pop the bubble of joyous optimism that had lingered from the night before. For yes, right up to this moment they thought they might 'be reprimanded; or, at the worst, would lose their commissions'.[11]

But this?

This is very grave indeed. No sooner have they packed their kits and had a rough breakfast than the Provost Sergeant arrives with four pairs of handcuffs for all four of them: Morant, Handcock, Witton and Picton.

It is all so contrary to their expectations of the night before.

As George Witton will recount, 'they recognised for the first time that death or penal servitude awaited them'.[12]

This time, the Breaker really is broken. George Witton watches closely as the irons are placed around the Englishman's wrists in preparation for leaving the cells. And now Morant turns to him and says in a strangled voice, 'George, this is what comes of Empire building.'[13]

And now tears, real tears, roll down his red face.

Witton is stunned. The only other time he had witnessed the Breaker crying was just after Captain Hunt had been killed and the new commanding officer had broken down while trying to tell the men they were going out after the Boers who did it. But now, just moments after a dry quip has sprung from his lips, those lips tremble and Morant is actually sobbing.

This is no jape or jest; this is the croaking dark raven of consequence come home to roost. And so fold the wings of Harry Morant's freedom, broken and bent as he weeps for the life that is no longer his.

This is only a taste of what is to come, as George Witton would later relate, 'While waiting on the platform to entrain, Major Bolton came up to us, as though to gloat over the successful consummation of his labours. Picton turned to him, and exposing the irons on his hands, called out, "I have to thank you for these, Major Bolton."'[14]

Major Bolton seems pleased to hear it.

In the meantime Major Thomas, stunned at the rapid turnaround in fortunes of his clients, goes in search of one of the judges he knows to find out what on earth is going on, and receives some key assurance.

'You have nothing to fear,' he is told. 'None of the prisoners will be shot.'[15]

For yes, although some of his clients have indeed been found guilty – because there had been no other choice on the overwhelming evidence presented – the good news for Thomas is that the court had such sympathy for the circumstances they had added a 'strong recommendation to mercy',[16] and had little doubt but that those recommendations would be acted upon. You see, Major, it is the form that must be followed. They have to be found guilty and sentenced to be shot, but if the court explains the provocation they were under, and formally recommends mercy, Lord Kitchener could grant mercy and they would be spared.

•

Which is as maybe.

In the here and now, for Morant and his companions, it soon gets even worse. For in short order they are in two open carriages heading to Pretoria. Witton and Morant are handcuffed in one carriage with the uncuffed Lenehan. Picton and Handcock are in similar circumstances in another, each carriage under the guard of an officer and six armed Troopers.

That verdict now seems certain, with the chains that bind them just a prelude. As Witton bitterly remarks: 'They made up their minds to shoot us before we were sent down to Pretoria.'[17]

A strong escort of military police are waiting to greet the men when they arrive at Pretoria Station. They are led to a military van and locked inside.

And now, as Witton will recount, 'with armed men on either side of us, and with mounted police armed with revolvers and swords riding in the front and rear, and on both flanks, [we started moving]. There were quite enough to form a bodyguard for the Commander-in-Chief himself.'[18]

When they arrive at the heart of Pretoria, all of them bar Major Lenehan are marched straight into the cells of old Pretoria Gaol without ceremony, with the cell doors slammed behind them.

For his part, Major Lenehan makes his way to the office of a friend who he thinks might be able to help. Arriving, he sends in his card, whereupon he is shortly afterwards ushered forth.

Captain de Bertodano can see by Lenehan's face that *words* are about to be had!

Without preamble, Lenehan bursts forth.

'I have come to complain bitterly about the indignity put upon three of my officers,' says Lenehan. 'They have been sent to Pretoria in handcuffs!'[19]

De Bertodano looks at him with frozen countenance and his reply is even colder.

'You are speaking of three men [guilty] of murder: they are not officers.'[20]

In other words, you may be complicit with these monsters, but I am not. They are a disgrace, and so are you! To yourself, your legal profession, your uniform and your country. You presided over these murders, and did nothing!

Lenehan is shocked as he realises that there is to be no quarter. Making no reply, he turns on his heel and leaves de Bertodano's office. They will never speak again.

•

What now?

At eight o'clock on the morning of 26 February a warder arrives at Morant's cell to advise him that he is required at the office of the prison Governor. Witton watches him pass with his usual cocky strut, and a few minutes later sees him . . .

Wait, what's this?

'His face was deathly pale,' Witton will recall. 'He looked as though his heart had already ceased to beat.'

Stunned at the transformation, Witton exclaims through the bars of his cell: 'Good God, Morant, what is the matter?'

'Shot tomorrow morning!' Morant replies with a reedy, broken voice as if the life is already leaving him. All up, Morant has been found guilty of murdering 12 men. Still reeling, the words and the sentence clearly echoing in his mind – *can this be really happening?* – Breaker Morant is led away white-faced to his cell.

A short time later, the morose figure of Lieutenant Handcock also looms, taking the same path back and forth as Morant, and also passing Witton's cell both ways.

What news, Peter?

'Same as Morant,'[21] he gurgles to Witton. He is to be shot. Guilty three times over.

There is barely time to contemplate the horror of it all when the guard detail arrives outside Witton's cell.

Lieutenant George Witton, you are to accompany us.

In the Governor's office he is confronted by Captain Henry Hutson, Provost Marshal of Pretoria, the man in charge of all military police.

'George Ramsdale Witton,' he says without preamble, and with much the same tone of voice as he might read out a laundry list, 'you have been found guilty of murder and sentenced to death.'

Hutson pauses, clearly to make sure the sentence of his sentence has sunk in, before going on . . .

'Lord Kitchener has been pleased to commute your sentence to penal servitude for life.'[22]

Strangely, Witton feels no relief, and instead – as he is marched back to his cell – feels resentful.

'I felt that death a thousand times would be preferable to the degradation of a felon's life,' he will explain. 'I had already suffered a dozen times over pangs worse than death.'

The parade goes on, with Lieutenant Picton the next called and he, too, is soon on his way back to his cell.

'Well, what luck?' Witton asks as he passes.

'Found guilty of manslaughter and cashiered!' comes the quick reply.

For his part, Major Lenehan is found guilty only of 'neglecting to report knowledge acquired after the fact'.[23] It is enough to warrant his removal from South Africa in disgrace, but not quite enough to land him in a cell. In his case, the Provost Marshal receives the instruction on Lenehan: 'he is . . . to be despatched to Cape Town and embarked for Australia as soon as practicable. Will you be so good as to have him carefully supervised until he actually sails.'[24]

And Captain Taylor? The cunning conductor of the whole catastrophe, the one who has presided and even ordered much of the murderous mayhem of those deadly three months of the BVC? He has resigned his commission, and is now living on his farm in Rhodesia, one singularly well stocked with cattle.

And so it is done, their fates foretold. In the near distance they can soon hear two carpenters in the nearby prison workshop, banging together a couple of rough coffins. A short time later, without comment or any attempt to hide them, those coffins are placed in the prison courtyard in full view of those in the prison cells.

Charmed, we're sure.

George Witton, in the meantime, is told that he will be taken to Pretoria Station at five the following morning, to catch the train to Cape Town where the ship *Canada* will deliver him and Picton to Britain so he can serve his time in a military prison.[25]

And so the men shuffle in silence in what will be the final BVC parade in the courtyard. Witton struggles to find words that will be of any comfort, and the men are instead left with the quiet drumbeat made by the sounds of their boots echoing from the pressing cold walls.

When, just a little later, two of the warders come round to lock them in their cells, Morant, true to form, makes the first of several 'last requests'.

Could he and Handcock be moved into just the one cell?

That request is quickly granted – and it doesn't hurt that one of those warders is, as happenstance has it, none other than John Morrow, once a member of the Second South Australian Contingent, with whom Morant had travelled to South Africa on the *Surrey*, some two years earlier. They have barely seen each other since the first months of the war – but Morrow had made his way into the Provisional Transvaal Constabulary, and now to this position on what is due to be the final evening of Morant's life.

The next request is for writing material, which is also quickly provided, whereupon Morant personally petitions Lord Kitchener himself for a reprieve, while Handcock takes the opportunity to write to the Australian government in his untidy scrawl, requesting that provision be made to look after his three children.

Morant turns to a familiar refuge, poetry. Yes, his pen flies as he dashes off a pre-posthumous poem for the lads at *The Bulletin*. Death awaits? What of it? His work will live:

> *What tho' my life be filled with many crimes!*
> *Death hurts but once – Life a thousand times.*
> *If thou should'st come to me with tales of Hell,*
> *Pshaw! – I will go bravely, and say "Tis well!!'*
> *But if thou should'st come to me with tales of love,*
> *With chant and songs of kindness from above,*
> *And kiss away my scalding tears of pain –*
> *Then – oh, God, perhaps I'd wish to live again!*
> BRING ON YOUR GUNS![26]

They can take his life, they can take his freedom, but his wit will be his until he breathes his last. Byron and Shelley revelled in their tragedies, works of fiction born from restless minds. But the Breaker? His tragedy is his reality, and he revels in spite of it.

The doomed man continues to scrawl as words come to him. But before he can finish the next thought, the devastated Major Thomas arrives, all hustle and bustle, shock and heartbreak, completely floored at the news. What of the promise that they would be shown *mercy*?

But he cannot tarry long.

For he, too, must do his best to reach the only man who can stop this outrage – the execution of two innocent men by firing party – Lord Kitchener. Their lawyer appears resolute and undone at once.

'The terrible news had almost driven him crazy,'[27] Witton chronicles.

After promising the two condemned men he will do what he can, Thomas is on his way to Melrose House.

As he waits, Morant decides to write a letter to Major Lenehan, who has been a wonderful support throughout.

MY DEAR MAJOR,

Hell to pay! (Isn't it? *You* are all right and will live to go hunting again.) If anything happens to me you write to my governor and to my girl ... Also see *Bulletin* people in Sydney town and tell 'em all the facts. How Hunt was shot by Boers, and how I carried on same as he would have done – had I been shot that night at Viljoen's. Had I tumbled into Boer hands, I'd have gone on whilst I had a cartridge left, and then used the butt, and then have been wiped out. That's what I'd expect if I had fallen into Boer lines – wouldn't have 'groused' either – it would have been just part of the programme – War! But it is damned rough this treatment! from our own British(?) side!

However, put my faith in the Lord and Headquarters, Pretoria, and hope to see a fox killed and kiss a Devon girl, again.

Buck-up, old man. Had I known as much two months ago as I know today – there would be a lot of Dutchmen at large that are now in Hell, or the Bermudas.

I've starved and trekked, and done my work tolerably success-fully – from the Buck River to the Portuguese Border – and the result is:

D. S. O...

(Damn Silly Officer)

Hope we go home together, if not,
>   Write to:
>>   My Guvnor
>>   Girl
>>   And *Bulletin*.
>   Thine,
>>   TONY LUMPKIN[28]

Someone now at the cell door.

It is the Provost Marshal, Captain Hutson, with a question.

Would you like an Army padre to be present to help ease your passage to the next world?

'No, thank you, I'm a pagan,' Breaker Morant replies blithely.

'What's a pagan?' asks Handcock.

A pagan, the Breaker gently explains, is one who does not believe in any organised religion.

That is enough for Handcock.

'Right, I'm a pagan too,'[29] says Handcock.

•

Rarely in this war has the generally imperturbable Lord Kitchener been more upset, more under pressure, more distracted by a single issue at hand than at this time. Even at Paardeberg, when a thousand men had died due to his ludicrous orders, there was no obvious change to his demeanour, no sign that it was getting to him.

But this is different. This matter is all consuming, an engulfing fog.

His pet starling – a beautiful, glossy bird, of black metallic sheen that he had kept in a cage in his office – has somehow escaped, Lord Kitchener is completely beside himself, organising his staff to search for it high and low. It is nearing dusk when finally the little fellow is at last found in a neighbour's chimney, 'but not before the Chief himself was covered in mud having repeatedly fallen prone in wet flower-beds'.[30]

The relief from his staff is palpable.

When it comes to the suggestion that he might commute the death sentences of Morant and Handcock, however, Kitchener – in contrast to his timely intervention on behalf of George Witton – has so little interest he has already made clear to his staff that he will not change his mind, and then left Pretoria for Harrismith, where no fewer than 700 Boers have been captured, his biggest bag since the war began.

After all, how could he commute sentences when some 20 surrendered Boers and one Reverend were shot, far and away the worst atrocity of the war? Beyond everything else, at the next peace conference that is being mooted, it is important that the British be *seen* to be serious when it comes to severely disciplining British soldiers who shoot unarmed Boers.

The Secretary of State for War, Sir William Brodrick, is almost fully in support of his stance, with the only rider being that perhaps the Lord might have been even more severe:

> My Dear Lord Kitchener. Your report of the court martial of Bushveldt Carbineers came to hand last night. It is a most deplorable performance and, if it gets out, as I fear it will, even the strong measures we are taking will not undo the shame it inflicts on the colonial forces. I should myself have been inclined to shoot all of the three officers, but you are in the best position to judge.[31]

•

The closest Major Thomas can get to Lord Kitchener is Major William Kelly, the Adjutant-General for General Commanding-in-Chief South African Field Forces, the senior legal man in Pretoria.

The conversation is brief.

'I implore you,' Thomas says, 'to defer the execution to enable me to cable to England to the King on behalf of the Australian people for mercy.'[32]

No.

'The order came from England,' he says gravely, 'and grave political trouble has been roused over the Heese murder in particular.'

But surely Handcock, especially, 'who was merely present as a veterinary lieutenant when Morant ordered the Boers to be shot for outrages [can be spared]. Think of his want of education and military knowledge.'[33]

But Major Kelly will have none of it. He has his orders, and they will stand.

For Major Thomas there is nothing for it but to leave, and head back to the cells to give Handcock and Morant the grim news.

Major Thomas is filled with bitter regret.

'Poor Handcock, a brave, true, simple man; and Morant, brave but hot-headed.'[34]

He returns to the cells, desperately despondent, and arrives at much the same time as Major Kelly's formal reply to Morant's petition arrives bearing the same news: No.

•

It is now Morrow's job to ensure that Morant makes the morrow still as a prisoner, so he can be satisfactorily shot dead.

Morant calls for more paper. No more begging, more poetry. Morrow, if you could fetch the necessities? Words whirl like a storm in the Breaker's mind, more aware than ever that these words may well be his last. While his heart may stop on the other morrow, there's no reason his thoughts can't survive him. The pen may be mightier than the sword – and the British firing party trumps both – but Breaker knows that words are his only chance at an immortal legacy.

Meanwhile Lieutenant William Press,[35] a friend from the old days with the Second South Australian Contingent, is bracing for the tough time he suspects he has ahead of him this evening. Frankly, he'd rather be in a pitched battle with the Boers than where he is now, walking with two Troopers on the same errand to visit those sorry fellows, Harry Morant and Peter Handcock. They will wake tomorrow, but not the day after, for they are to be shot. Those grisly details aside, there is no reason everything must be all doom and gloom. Lieutenant Press is determined to 'cheer them up a bit'[36] and so he and his escorts fix smiles to their faces and enter George Witton's larger cell, where the condemned men have been allowed some level of camaraderie on what will be their final night – including receiving visitors. Press finds Morant and Handcock preparing to eat their final meal, and . . .

And what? This is not the maudlin atmosphere Lieutenant Press had been expecting!

'Not to be blasphemous, lads,' Morant greets them, 'but this is "The Last Supper"!'[37]

And this evening, appearing for one night only, he is the Breaker of old, sparkling with vivacity! Come what may tomorrow, tonight Breaker Morant is alive, a whirlwind of wit and whimsy, spinning yarns and telling tales as though he were the same free man he had always been. Just give this man a fresh audience – in this case including some fresh warders drawn to the death cell – and he performs like never before . . . and never again. Everyone assembled is thrilled with the meal they have in front of them. George Witton notes with as much surprise as pleasure that 'a hamper was sent in containing a nicely got-up dinner for four'.[38]

The food is laid out formally and looks delectable, though the portions are a little shy. Thankfully it matters not, as the men are more concerned with drinking the beer and wine that came with the hamper and telling tales of the lives they have lived until now. The Breaker holds court as the court now holds him, the centre of attention and the lynchpin of the last social occasion he will attend. He tells of the women he has loved, the horses, noses, conventions and hearts he has broken, the men he has known and the bets he has won. He talks of everything under the sun, everything he will never get to experience again. He could talk a leg off a table, this man. The men's faces are wet with tears but they are not the tears of men who await their doom. They are tears of laughter, the tears of men who are still free in their hearts. But all good things must pass, and so must the night. The warden appears. You are out of time. Leave Witton in peace. Morant and Handcock, back to your cells if you would. Thank you, Lieutenant, you must go too.

Morant clasps Lieutenant Press' hands in his hands and grins as he says, 'Remember me to all South Australians who knew me.'[39]

Lieutenant Press is ready to leave but curiosity keeps him. Say, Breaker … *What happened?* Rumours abound in the outside world, each one more outlandish than the last, but nobody can say for sure. Why are they going to shoot you? Morant sighs and conjures vague facts about the only tale he has chosen not to recount tonight.

'An officer of the corps, a friend of mine and Peter's, was shot in cold blood by Boers. We fellows caught some Boers who did it, and we instantly shot eleven of them. I admitted that fact at the trial.'[40]

There was nothing else? I heard tell of a missionary getting involved somehow?

Oh yes, that.

'In the meantime a German missionary came up and heard of the affair.'[41]

The fellow was shot by somebody, not us. And yet here we are. *Goodbye, gentlemen.*

Oh, Morant has a last wish for Lieutenant Press, a last favour:

'I have one desire; to be buried outside, decently.'[42]

Press nods. Back in England, executed prisoners are buried in unmarked graves, in unconsecrated ground. Their bodies are covered in quicklime to dissolve them. Morant wants his corpse to be treated with more respect. He wants a headstone, he wants … to be remembered.

Farewell, good Press.

George Witton must go too.

'Goodbye, Harry,'[43] he says with hand outstretched. Morant shakes it and consoles the young man, who he can see is on the verge of tears.

'It's hard lines and a sideways ending,' the Breaker says with a smile and a mock flourish. 'Thus being sacrificed as an atonement to pro-Boer sentiments. Goodbye, Witton.'[44]

Witton heads for the door but pauses as Breaker begins his parting words.

'Goodbye, Witton. Tell *The Bulletin* people The Breaker will write no more verse for them. I'm going into "laager" in the morning!'[45]

Witton breaks into a sad smile, and exits. He has just heard Breaker's last lie and he doesn't even realise it. For in fact, the Breaker has one last poem, his magnum opus. As Dr Johnston said, there's nothing quite like 12 hours to live to sharpen one's mind and hone one's focus. And concentrate he will, so much so that he is even willing to *edit* some of his work. Breaker revises his lines, polishing it into a radiant piece of poetry. It is no mournful farewell; that would be too obvious for a man like the Breaker. It must be full of power and pride, vim and vigour, the sweet of life as well as the sour. The words pour forth, with the only pause being the odd shock when the waves of pleasurable creativity ebb for a moment, and he realises anew he is to *die tomorrow at dawn* . . . before he embarks once more on the next verse. It shan't be long until the Breaker is food for the worms, rotting away until he is no more than dirt. But the poem? It is a piece of stoicism, bravery, fury, charm, wit, and romance, and unlike the Breaker himself – it shall live on.

BUTCHERED TO MAKE A DUTCHMAN'S HOLIDAY
by The Breaker

In prison cell I sadly sit,
A dammed crestfallen chappie,
And own to you I feel a bit –
A little bit – unhappy!

It really ain't the place nor time
To reel off rhyming diction;
But yet we'll write a final rhyme
While waiting crucifixion.

No matter what end they decide
Quick-lime? Or boiling oil, sir?
We'll do our best when crucified
To finish off in style, sir!

But we bequeath a parting tip
For sound advice of such men

Who come across in transport ship
To polish off the Dutchmen.

If you encounter any Boers
You really must not loot 'em,
And, if you wish to leave these shores,
For pity's sake, DON'T SHOOT 'EM!

And if you'd earn a D.S.O.,
Why every British sinner
Should know the proper way to go
Is: ASK THE BOER TO DINNER!

Let's toss a bumper down our throat
Before we pass to heaven,
And toast: *The trim-set petticoat*
We leave behind in Devon.[46]

Morant now takes a photograph he has of himself, Handcock, Hunt, Taylor and Picton, and on the back of it writes:

To the Reverend Canon Fisher, Pretoria. The night before we're shot. We shot the Boers who killed and mutilated <u>our</u> friend (the best mate I had on Earth)
Harry Harbord Morant
Peter Joseph Handcock.[47]

His last will and testament?

Writing it as quickly as he can think of it, he promises all his worldly goods – chains and rings and shiny stones and all the things that ladies like – to a variety of women he has loved and left over the course of his too short life. One of them is even the 'trim-set petticoat' he mentions in his final comic poem. The remnants and reminders of his time in the military are left to the lads, with a special mention to Surgeon Johnston who'd done his very best during the trial. The surgeon had testified about an event he'd never seen – the finding of Captain Hunt's body – all for the sake of the Breaker. A good man.

Dawn, 27 February 1902, Pretoria, last words and testament

All is quiet now. With all non-prisoners gone, and Handcock snatching a little sleep before the long sleep of eternity that awaits them in that deep sorrow of a morrow, the Breaker sits down to compose himself once more. His pen cannot stop; now *this* shall be his last verse.

Taking pen in hand and the piece of paper left by the guard, the lines come to him easily, just as they always have, flowing from his pen with a cool cadence that less skilled writers might have to mull over for days to come up with something half as good.

> The days of the Breaker are over
> The days of the Buccaneer.
> He lived the life of a Rover
> And now lies buried here.
>
> And Peter lies within the grave.
> And Percy rests on the hill.
> And though their lives I could not save
> I love their memory still.
>
> The reckless one, 'The Breaker'
> Sleeps beneath this sod
> The bravest one, True Peter,
> Went with him to God.
>
> **Envoi.**
>
> When the last rousing gallop is ended,
> And the last post-and-rail has been jumped,
> And a cracked neck that cannot be mended
> Shall have under the yew tree been 'dumped';
> Just you leave him alone – in God's acre –
> And drink, in wine, whisky or beer:
> 'May the saints up above send "The Breaker"
> A horse like good old Cavalier!'[48]

The contrast with Handcock could not be greater. No flights of fancy for him. No burst of creativity. No rapiers of wit to give him the last word. For he has no 'public' to write for, he can barely think of any who want to hear from him. Rather, in this darkest soul of the night, when the last dawn of this dark soul is nigh – Handcock puts down a few sad words to his sister . . . while ignoring any last communication to his wife, the mother of his three children.

> Dear Sister,
>   I have but an hour or so longer to exist and altho my brain
>   has been harassed for four long weary months I can't refrain
>   from writing you a few last lines. I am going to find out the

grand secret. I will face my God with the firm belief I am innosent of murder. I obeyed my orders and served my King as I thought best . . .

From your fond Brother,
P.J. Handcock
Australia for ever. Amen.[49]

•

All is dark now, all is quiet.

Some 30 minutes before dawn, a highly ranked English officer suddenly appears unannounced in the gloom, walking between the tents of a Scottish outfit, the Cameron Highlanders, about a mile from their fatal destination. He rouses their Commanding Officer, Major Thomas Souter, who in turn rouses 13 soldiers, who are soon parading bleary-eyed before the English officer.

You have a specific task today. Not an easy one, but it must be done. There is a reason no roll call is being taken this morning, and no record taken of your names. You will do what you must, what I order, and then return to your regular soldierly duty.

Aye, sir.

Good men. Now, go to the Quartermaster who will give you the rifles you will need for this specific job. They have been loaded for you – some with blanks so you will never know if the shots you fired were the fatal ones.

Aye, sir.

In short order and in tight order, the 13 soldiers are tramping up the grey road in the cool morning, their way lightly illuminated now by the dull lustre to the east, as they push towards the menacing monoliths of the old Pretoria forts up ahead, until they come to the old prison.

•

The clang of the key in the lock rouses George Witton in his cell a little, and he is soon shaken awake. It is a warder informing him that his time has come. He is to go to Pretoria Station, to catch the train which will take him to Cape Town.

Quickly pulling his boots on and throwing his few possessions into his kit, Witton is soon tramping down the darkened corridors of the prison, asking permission as he goes to say goodbye to Morant and Handcock.

I was allowed to see them only through the small trap-door. I clasped their hands through this for the last time, and could scarcely stammer a good-bye. I was more unnerved at the thought of their hateful death than they were themselves. They were calmly prepared to meet their death, as they often had been before at times during the war.[50]

Goodbye, Breaker.
Goodbye, Handcock.
Goodbye, George.

Witton is now marched to the office of the Chief Warder, where he is handcuffed in preparation for being taken beyond the prison walls before an escort starts marching him towards the gates, where, as he passes through, he spies red and black skirts, the kilts of the Cameron Highlanders, each man waiting in solemn silence.

'It was unnecessary to ask why or what they were there for. It was a heart-breaking sight.'[51]

Walk on, George. On and away.

•

Firing Party . . . halt!

There is the sound of a heavy bolt being drawn back, and now the creak of protesting hinges cracks the dawn as the gate is opened, and the Cameron Highlanders make their way into the main prison square.

In a tone of voice perfectly attuned to the low light and grievously grave occasion, the Highlanders' commander breathes his orders in a low, sad rumble of a voice: 'Halt. Riiiight face. Stand aaaaat . . . ease.'[52]

Their 'ease' is also in tune with the times – their rifle butts do not echo on the paving stones as they bring them down gently.

Around and about the courtyard, as the light begins to strengthen just a little, there are growing signs of life, as warders appear from their barracks, as do various officers.

•

And so it has come. The Breaker and Handcock have dozed off a little here and there through the night, always waking with a start as the realisation hits them anew – they are about to be shot dead at dawn, and the only thing that still protects them is that very darkness. That dull lustre in the east spells their doom, and now it has come they are hit as never before by the very bleakness of their situation, as the shocking realisation comes that the end of the road is nigh, and there is nothing that can be done.

It means that, just after footsteps ring out on the stone floor with the first streaks of dawn, the warder who has come to get them finds, as he opens the cell door, the Breaker quietly weeping while Handcock sits glumly.

Nevertheless, within less than a minute, Morant goes from open misery to extraordinary *sang-froid*. If these are to be his last minutes on life's stage, let him, one more time for the road, put on a good show as his final audience gathers.

'Are you ready?' the warder asks.

'Yes,' the Breaker replies, having composed himself. 'Where is your shooting party?'[53]

Not far away.

By the riiiiight . . . quick march!

The tramp of boots on prison floors echoes down the corridor and off the stone walls as the condemned traipse outside. But as they go, Breaker pauses at the sight of someone he did not expect, the adjutant of Major Lenehan, one Lieutenant James Edwards.

'Remember the Boers mutilated my friend Hunt,' Morant instructs him as he passes. 'I shot those who did it. We had our orders; I only obeyed them when Hunt was murdered. I did it. Witton and Picton had nothing to do with it; I told them so at the court-martial.'[54]

Edwards nods in acknowledgement but the Breaker does not slow his stride. He can keep Edwards waiting, but not Death.

Seeing the Cameron Highlanders for the first time, the Breaker hails them heartily. *Good morning, gentlemen!* It is a greeting that chills with its cheerfulness, and none will forget the gallantry of this man they are about to shoot. Say what you like about the Breaker, he knows how to die with panache.

And here now are the two chairs by the wall, some 20 yards in front of the Scots. Without hesitation, or reservation, the two men hold hands as they walk towards the chairs. It is a strangely intimate thing to know you are about to have your life ended within a split instant of each other, and holding hands somehow gives a shred of comfort.

Taking their place on the chairs – Morant on the right, Handcock on the left, as the squad faces them – the Sergeant begins to place blindfolds on both men, but the Breaker won't have it.

'Take this thing off,'[55] the Breaker barks, and his wish is immediately observed. Morant rubs the lucky penny hung about his neck for the last time, the talisman has failed him but the habit remains. And speaking of habits . . .

The other tradition of a last cigarette?

Of course. With great elan, Morant takes out his cigarette case from the inside pocket of his service jacket, removes a thin white stick, lights it, and makes a gift of his case to Major Souter with a cheery, 'I shan't be smoking any more of these!'[56]

Dragging deeply on the cigarette several times, he now flicks it away with a practised flourish, to lie and smoke offended on the stones – though it is every chance to still have life in it longer than the man who just threw it.

Let us get on with this.

Bring on your guns.

Crossing his arms, he stares straight at his executioners, as they stare nervously back at him.

(It is one thing to shoot a man in the hurly-burly of battle. And quite another to do it cold-bloodedly, like this.)

There is a moment's pregnant pause. And now the order.

'Firing party . . . aim.'

Now it is Major Thomas Souter who hesitates, but again the Breaker won't have it, knowing he must break this impasse measured in microseconds.

Still the firing party stare, clearly hesitant to follow each command, fearful of what they are about to do. Obviously, they need some encouragement.

'If you don't fire,' Morant calls out mockingly, 'I will look down the barrels of your rifles for the bullets!'[57]

They squint down their barrels, aghast.

'Shoot straight, you bastards!'[58] the Breaker orders. 'Don't make a mess of it!'[59]

Another pause, and now one word is spoken softly but intensely: 'Fire!'[60]

The volley of shots echoes off the prison walls and instantly angry splotches of red appear on their chests and they slump backward.

'Morant,' John Morrow will recount, 'got all in the left side, and died at once. With his arms folded and his eyes open you would have thought he was alive.'[61]

At Pretoria railway station, just 500 yards away, George Witton hears the shots in the distance and shudders. It seems impossible to believe that they are gone.

'I distinctly heard in the clear morning air the report of the volley of the firing party,' he will recall, 'the death knell of my late comrades, and I knew they had gone to that bourne from whence no traveller returns. So went out two brave and fearless soldiers, men that the Empire could ill afford to lose.'[62]

•

Among those in the barracks, it does not take long for the news to get out that it has finally happened and the reaction is strong.

'A great deal of bitter feeling is raging here against the execution,' one of the Troopers writes home. 'It was two years yesterday since the Second Contingent landed at the Cape, and it seems strange that Morant should receive his death exactly two years from the date of his landing in South Africa.'[63]

John Morrow writes to a mutual friend, giving an account of Morant's last hours, and is proud to report: 'They faced their doom as brave as men could do. Everyone said it was a pity to shoot two such brave men.'[64]

•

Most shocked at the news?

Oddly, it is the very men who had sat in judgement, who found them guilty and sentenced them to death. For despite that, just as Major Thomas had been told, there really had been an addendum to the verdicts and sentences, reading, in the case of Morant for example:

RECOMMENDATION TO MERCY.
The court strongly recommend the prisoner to mercy on the following grounds:–
1. Extreme provocation by the mutilation of the body of Capt. Hunt, who was his intimate personal friend.
2. His good service during the war, including his capture of Field-Cornet T. Kelly in the Spelonken.
3. The difficult position in which he was suddenly placed, with no previous military experience and no one of experience to consult.
Signed at Pretoria the 29th day of January, 1902.
H. C. DENNY, Lt.-Col.[65]

Lord Kitchener had rejected the recommendation, simply signing above the sentences:

> Confirmed–
> KITCHENER, General. President.
> 25th February, 1902.[66]

And that had been that.

'We were,' one of the members of the court will later write to Major Thomas, 'astounded.'[67]

•

In the still of a hot afternoon, the gatehouse of the Old Pretoria Gaol rattles open. A hearse followed by soldiers and officers goes through, to be greeted by an assemblage of Australians. So many have come to pay their respects to the Breaker.

The cathedral has sent a parson post-haste, whose first job it is now to guide the cortege – at the centre of which are the two rough coffins being carried by Australian officers, one of whom is Lieutenant Charles Hannam – to Church Street Cemetery while a Pretorian watches on with only a faint interest.[68]

'There were about twenty persons at the graveside and all of these were Australians, both soldiers and civilians, all big-boned men they are, and I must say some of them looked the sons of deported sheep stealers or convicts, or worse.'[69]

As the two bodies are lowered into their earthen chamber, the padre dutifully intones a special and especially pointed preamble to the burial service, leaving his audience in no confusion about the distinction between *consecrated* ground and the detached grave gaping before them. The message is plain. These men don't deserve to spend eternity in sacred ground blessed by the Lord. They are merely buried in the dirt, food for the worms, no better than mangy dogs rotting in the soil. Look, Morant wouldn't mind, what matter would it be to him? He isn't so pious and pompous to think that there might be room for him up among the clouds in any case. He has come from the dirt, and he will return to the dirt . . .

One onlooker will write shortly after, 'We were informed at the grave that both condemned officers kept up bravely right to the last, and died like men.'[70]

Morose, mournful, morbid even, but the funeral is largely uneventful, certainly compared with everything that led to it. They are at rest, and so is the evening.

•

His epitaph, beyond the stark details on his tombstone? There will be many.

But perhaps the last words must go to his friend, the Reverend Gordon Tidy, a one-time jackaroo and mate of the Breaker back in Australia, who was in something of a triumvirate of poets with Breaker and Will Ogilvie.

When the Reverend Tidy hears the news, the words pour out of him . . .

A GAOL-WALL INSCRIPTION
by 'Mousquetaire', AKA Gordon Tidy

A volley-crack, a puff of smoke,
And dead the Murderer grins,
– Come, cover with the Charity-cloak
That multitude of sins.
And though some blame and count it shame
I won't withhold the tear
For the cold heart, the bold heart,
That ceased its beating here.

They say his debts he oft forgot,
– But one he settled up!
They say he used to drink a lot
– His last was a bitter cup.
And right or wrong, or weak or strong,
I can't keep back the tear
For the Devil-heart, the revel-heart
That ceased its beating here.

I know he went from bad to worse,
I know what ill he wrought,
But I have seen him on a horse,
And heard of how he fought;
And, fool or wise, I own my eyes
Are troubled with a tear
For the rough heart, the tough heart,
That ceased its beating here.

A sorry life of drink and debt
That finished with the shrift
Men give the murderer, and yet
Was his the singer's gift;
A scrap of song 'gainst a world of wrong!
I know – but here's a tear
For the Crime-heart, the Rhyme-heart
That ceased its beating here.

Some heels may spurn 'The Breaker's' grave,
Some mouths thereon may spit,
But some have owned to hands that gave
A wreath to even it;
And here's a meed of poor word-weed
Would fain express the tear
For that Other-heart, that Brother-heart
That ceased its beating here.[71]

THE END

EPILOGUE

There is lots more one could write about poor Harry Morant and his doings, if there was any end to be gained by it. He is gone, like many a worse man, to answer for his deeds in this world before a harsher tribunal than ours. He gave many a woman a golden hour to dream over, and many a man a chum to remember with keenest pleasure. Poor old chap! He acted according to his lights. He sowed the whirlwind and reaped the storm, and though he lies in a dishonoured grave in that far-off strange country, we, who knew him at his best, can afford to forget his last great crime, and, while sorrowing for his untimely death, think kindly of him, and trust that 'After life's fitful fever, "The Breaker" sleeps well.'[1]

Wilhelmina (Mina) Rawson, Australian author

He was a good fellow at heart, but a reckless daredevil, who saw danger in nothing, and allowed nothing to trouble him. He wrote a heap of capital verse, some of which was first published in the Gazette. Everyone who knew him will regret to hear of the sad end of the genial, good-hearted, but misguided Harry Morant.[2]

Windsor and Richmond Gazette

Within weeks of the executions of Morant and Handcock, the Boer War begins to sputter, stutter and putter to a close, before finally the great machine of war comes to a dead stop. With barely a homestead left standing, many thousands dead, and 115,000 of the Boer population incarcerated in concentration camps, even the bitter-enders could see that if it got any more bitter there would be just about no-one left standing.

'It is my holy duty to stop this struggle now that it has become hopeless,' Acting President Schalk Burger of the Southern African Republic of Transvaal would note, 'and not to allow the innocent, helpless women and children to remain any longer in their misery in the plague-stricken concentration camps . . .'

As for the British, they were physically and morally exhausted. The Boer War was causing ever more trenchant criticism in Westminster and the press, and if the war did indeed get any more bitter it would start to look as though they were actually wiping out an entire population.

By this time, 30,000 Boer homesteads had been destroyed, as well as those of tens of thousands of their African labourers, 40 Boer towns had been razed, 28,000 white civilians had lost their lives. Probably more of their African slaves had also died. (For the latter, no-one was particularly counting.)

In sum, it was time for both sides to parley, and emissaries soon meet to discuss terms. The meeting takes place in the Transvaal town of Vereeniging, with 30 officials from Orange Free State and the South African Republic, led by Jan Smuts, meeting with a British contingent led by Lord Kitchener. The result is the Treaty of Vereeniging, which will be made official once Burger and de Wet make their way to the Transvaal town. They had come on the first train from Pretoria after such sudden and unexpected agreement was reached between all parties. And so it came to pass that at 11 pm on the night of 31 May 1902, twin quills are dipped, lifted, and dropped to the parchment, two signatures in wet ink. It is done.

While the Boer republics agreed to lay down the last of their arms and cede their sovereignty to Britain, the British agreed to an amnesty for all remaining combatants; the return of all their prisoners-of-war from the overseas internment camps; the closing of the concentration camps; the rendering void of all the current death sentences against Boer combatants. The following morning, the concentration camps began to empty as surviving burghers come to claim surviving wives and children, and the shattered shards of the Boer population slowly head back to what were mostly burnt farmhouses and destroyed farms.

As they begin to rebuild, so too, slowly, does the new nation of South Africa, initially a self-governing Dominion of the Crown established in 1910, with the Boer and English languages accorded equal status but eventually self-governing and equal standing for the two languages, Dutch and English.

The treaty was signed, and it all came to pass.

•

But what is the view like from Australia?

Well, despite British attempts through censorship to keep the story of the court martial and subsequent executions out of the public domain for as long as possible – as Boer resolve would be hardened should they learn details of the atrocities against their people – the news of the executions broke in Australia on 10 March 1902.

It came in the form of a small cablegram appearing in the *Adelaide Advertiser*, together with other papers:

> TWO MURDERERS SHOT
> London March 9
> Two troopers belonging to the irregular forces operating with the British army, having been tried by court martial and convicted on a charge of shooting Boers who had surrendered, have been shot at Pretoria.[3]

That tiny report was, however, but a small ember that started a spotfire – as in succeeding days the news soon spreads far and wide, generating an enormous amount of angry heat.

The idea that an Australian soldier, Peter Handcock, together with Breaker Morant – a well-known figure who had been in Australia for 20 years – had been court-martialled and shot, *mostly for shooting Boers*, without any reference to the Australian government caused widespread outrage.

We are no longer a colony.

We have rights.

We have a national dignity that has been trampled upon.

We have sent you 16,000 Australian soldiers – of whom we lost about 600 to battle and the ravages of disease – as part of our colonial units who have served with distinction, killing many Boers, and you have now executed one without reference to us? We demand an explanation.

A cable was sent with that very demand and on 5 April 1902 Lord Kitchener himself replies with a cable of his own, sent to the Australian Governor-General John Hope and subsequently published in most of the major Australian newspapers:

> Morant, Handcock, and Witton were charged with twenty separate murders, including one of a German missionary, who had witnessed other murders. Twelve of these murders were proved. From the evidence it appears that Morant was the originator of the crimes which Handcock carried out in cold-blooded manner ... The prisoners were convicted after most exhaustive trial, and were defended by counsel.[4]

Broadly, the first Prime Minister of the recently federated Australia, Edmund Barton, accepted both the verdict and punishment, noting in passing to the press that, while Handcock and Witton were Australians, 'Lieutenant Morant, was the son of an English admiral'.[5] But his soothing remarks did nothing to allay the popular outcry, much of which now focused on at least securing a pardon for the last man left standing, **George Witton**, then rotting in an English military prison.

Efforts were soon under way to pardon him,[6] led by George Witton's brother and enlisting the aid of one of Australia's most eminent lawyers Isaac Isaacs KC – later to be Chief Justice of the High Court and then Australia's first home-grown Governor-General. Together they composed and launched a petition. With a legal sharpness that completely escaped Major Thomas, Isaac Isaacs positioned Witton for what he was: a very inexperienced subaltern who had never even met the dead commander Captain Hunt, whose orders he thought he was enacting. Isaacs also raises a stirring stratagem which Major Thomas had likely never thought of – the matter of 'Condonation' concerning prisoners who are given arms when the collective is under attack and fight honourably. Back in 1832, no less than the Duke of Wellington had decreed that such an act could be used as grounds for pardon, and given that Witton had indeed been given arms and helped to direct the return fire when the Boers had attacked while he had been in the Pietersburg garrison with Morant and Handcock, he should indeed be pardoned now.

The petition received 80,000 signatures and was personally presented to the Governor-General, Lord Tennyson. Still, as noted by Frank Shields and Margaret Carnegie in their seminal work *In Search of Breaker Morant*, 'The petition for his release languished in the War Office until Mrs George Keppel, a close friend of King Edward VII, took a sympathetic interest. She interceded with the King on Witton's behalf.'[7]

As Mrs Keppel was indeed a *very* close friend – she was his mistress – her lobbying counted for more than most and, in a twist to the story that has a nice symmetry, it was a certain well-known someone who first put the question in the public domain.

For on the night of 10 August 1904, it was none other than Winston Churchill who rose in the House of Commons to ask the then Secretary of State for War, Hugh Oakeley Arnold-Foster, whether he could now state the intention of His Majesty's Government in respect to George Witton?

'His Majesty the King,' Mr Arnold-Foster replies portentously, 'has been pleased to order that Witton be released.'[8]

The very next morning Witton was called to the Prison Governor's office, where he was informed that he was to be released at 3 pm that afternoon, so . . . get packing. In short order he was on a ship on its way to Australia, settling initially in the Victorian town of Lancefield, working as a dairy farmer. It was here that he wrote his memoir on the whole affair, *Scapegoats of the Empire*, published in 1907 – an account with a relatively even mix of detail, self-serving falsehoods and outright lies. We are asked to believe, for example, that the Boers who had their children shot by Lieutenant Hannam bore him no ill will.

'I afterwards escorted these prisoners to Pietersburg,' Witton recounted, 'and in conversation with the parents of the children they told me that they in no way reproached Lieutenant Hannam or his men for what had happened; they were themselves to blame . . . This is the only foundation for the wicked reports as to the wholesale shooting of women and children by the Carbineers.'[9]

(Right. Clive James and your *Unreliable Memoirs*, eat your heart out.)

Witton settled at Biggenden in Queensland and, in 1913, married Mary Louise Humphrey. He went on to become a Justice of the Peace and director of the Biggenden Cheese Factory. He married twice, and in August 1942 died following a heart attack, aged 68.

•

Major James Francis Thomas arrived back in Australia in August 1903, having tried, and failed, over the previous 18 months to convince authorities to release George Witton. Exhausted and demoralised, he had only just got back to Tenterfield when he received a cable from London advising that his own petition to His Majesty, pleading for King Edward VII's intervention, had been declined.

Although Thomas tried hard to resume his old life as a respected Tenterfield solicitor, actually leaving behind the drama of what had happened to Morant, Handcock and Witton, and his failure to stop the execution of the first two, proved beyond him.

That trial was the defining episode in his life and he was haunted by the thought that the world at large didn't understand 'the real story' of what had gone on.

'Thomas would not let go,' author Greg Growden noted in his 2018 book *Major Thomas*. 'He could not get rid of that dreaded feeling he had let his fellow soldiers down. He felt unfairly cast as a failure, a victim of politics, diplomacy, mistruths and circumstances. He gradually became bitter. He would tell any willing listener his account of the proceedings; it was usually a passionate, painful admission of frustration.'[10]

After ending his proprietorship of the *Tenterfield Star* and selling his law practice in 1919, he first plunged into farming and, when that failed, headed to Sydney in 1921 to try his luck as a solicitor.[11]

It did not go well, and in one contempt of court case, he was actually sent to Long Bay Gaol. To add insult to injury, and insolvency to incarceration, Thomas was declared bankrupt while in there! Through it all, still he was haunted by the memories of Morant and Handcock, believing their cries of innocence until the last. He would regale people – rant and rave if you ask some – with the tale of those Scapegoats of the Empire. Speaking of which, he writes to the author of that book in 1928 and receives a reply from George Witton that kills the soul of Major Thomas as it includes this passage:

'I saw Handcock shortly after [the Court of Inquiry] and asked him about the Heese business, he said, "Why wasn't you standing beside Morant when he asked me if I was game to follow the missionary and wipe him out" . . . Had there been no Heese case the shooting of prisoners would not have worried them much. But the shooting of Heese was a premeditated and most cold-blooded affair. Handcock with his own lips described it all to me.'[12]

For Thomas it was a shattering blow. For a quarter of a century he had fought for his famous clients, the gallant Breaker and poor, simple Handcock. And now he had discovered the last of Harry Morant's confidence tricks, to know that he has wasted so much of his life, efforts and earnest arguments to try to exonerate two murderers . . . No, he could not believe it, he would not believe it, still he proclaimed the innocence of the Breaker in any pub that would take him or credit him. But Thomas ceased writing the book about the whole affair he had been well launched on – which was likely the point of Witton's reply in the first place. Witton wanted the book killed off because he did not want the truth of what happened 30 years ago stirred up once more. Among other things, there was always the matter of the Handcock statement, later ruled inadmissible, which he feared was in the British archives. Who knew what it said about Witton? He, for one, did not want anyone to know and never wanted to see it re-emerge.

'But you must not forget Kitchener held Handcock's confession in which he implicated me as an accessory,' Witton writes to Thomas, '(no doubt unwittingly done in a high strung nervous state) but that accounts for the reason why only Morant, Handcock and myself were punished and the War Office so adamant in my case.'[13]

Well, at the risk of seeming a little suspicious, Thomas, would you mind sending over *all* of the papers on the Heese trial?

'I would very much like to peruse the evidence of the Heese trial although I took no part in it nor was present. If you have a copy and would care to send it to me I would take particular care of it and return it safely.'[14]

We can't make guesses as to whether Major Thomas indeed sent the papers to Witton, but we *do know* that nobody ever saw them again!

James Francis Thomas died at his Boonoo Boonoo property in November 1942, just a few months after George Witton. His body was discovered on Armistice Day by an old friend who had gone to check up on him. He was 81 years of age, and had never married.

His younger brother, William Beach Thomas, who was the executor of Thomas' estate, discovered the letter from Witton and, realising its significance, sent it to the Mitchell Library in Sydney with a covering note, instructing that – in deference to Handcock's wife, who he erroneously believed was still alive – it not be released until 1970.[15]

As to what became of all of the rest of Thomas' papers concerning the Morant trial, therein lies a tale with a certain beginning and end, but indeterminate middle. At the time he died – in the middle of the Second World War – there was so little interest in the Morant case it seems little effort was made to secure Thomas' body of work on the case for posterity. It is not clear what was initially done with those papers, though obviously the attic of his brother might have been a fair starting point.

Whatever the case, all of his papers and mementos disappeared until one day in April 2016 a man was poking around a tip not far from Tenterfield, when he notices something odd – a stuffed hessian bag, inside which he could see an old . . . *what's this?* . . . Royal Mail bag. And what a treasure trove inside! Opening it up, he finds dozens of documents – letters, legal memorandums, contracts, old invoices, notifications and the like. But now look. For when he turns the bag upside-down to give it a good shake something falls out.

What's this?

Why, it's a British penny etched with the name of Edwin Henry Morant . . . and there is a chunk of the penny missing in one spot which looks like it must have been caused by a bullet! Could this be, *the* Morant, *Breaker* Morant, the one people still talk about a fair bit in Tenterfield, because his lawyer, James Francis Thomas, came from this town?

He looks closer. The penny is attached to the loop of a leather thong, like it is designed to hang around a neck, maybe like some form of dog tag.

Perhaps, the graze on the penny's edge is from one of the bullets that killed him? And yes, now that he looks closely there are many objects marked either with the name *Henry Morant*, or the initials *HM*, including a cartridge bandolier, a bayonet scabbard, a piece of an old trumpet, several brass drinking cups and a Boer War medallion.

Nearby is an Australian red ensign with the name of Morant and Peter Handcock, together with what seem to be the dates of their birth and death, written on the white part of the Southern Cross stars, together with the declaration:

> This flag bore witness [to] II scapegoats of the Empire Feb 27 1902 Pretoria.
> Signed J F Thomas.
> Lt Peter J Handcock Feb 17 1868 Feb 27 1902 RIP.
> Lt Henry H Morant Dec 9 1864 Feb 27 1902 Pretoria RIP.

The provenance of the cache is obvious – William Thomas – as is their destination: the Sir Henry Parkes School of Arts, encompassing the Tenterfield Museum. What would be wonderful to know is if there might possibly be more out there, most particularly including the memoir that Thomas was writing.

I live in hope!

•

Captain Alfred Taylor returned to an uneventful life on his farm in Plumtree, Rhodesia, before becoming a local Native Commissioner. He returned to service at the outset of the First World War, serving as an officer in the South African Native Labour Corps.

In the corollary to the aphorism that only the good die young, he died in October 1941, aged 79,[16] and is buried in the Bulawayo cemetery. Of all the guilty, in my view, he was the most guilty, the one most responsible for the many atrocities that occurred.

•

Upon his return to Australia, **Major Robert Lenehan** initially denied that he had *anything* to do with the charging of the Bushveldt Carbineers, labelling it libellous and rejecting it outright.

'I venture the opinion which I hope will one day be justified,' he blithely told the press, 'that this charge was brought against me because, having been locked up for a long while, I had to be charged with something ... It was plain I had no complicity in any unlawful killing, and no control of the district where the outrages occurred. The court martial showed its opinion of the character of my innocence by subjecting me to a simple reprimand.'[17]

None of which, of course, was true.

For all his fanciful retellings and questionable recollections, the Australian Army always knew the truth. After a poorly received series of lectures, Lenehan decided that his only recourse was to rejoin his unit, something the army was reluctant to allow. They denied him a war gratuity and *insisted* he must resign, but Lenehan refused to accept it, leading to an official inquiry to clear his name, aided by one Edmund Barton, Prime Minister. Lenehan had given his account of the story – and his account really was a *story* – to everybody who would take it. Regardless, Barton believed him, and soon became an advocate for poor Lenehan. Perhaps he had been punished and disgraced and his unit disbanded, but that was another war, another country, another time. The War Office finally concluded that, for whatever misdeeds he may be guilty of while serving the British Army, he shouldn't be barred from again serving Australia.

He once again returned to the active military lists, whereupon he was promoted to Lieutenant Colonel commanding the 4th Field Artillery Brigade in January 1913. It was not long before he was serving on the home front during the First World War. He retired in August 1918, and died in Sydney in May 1922.

•

Lieutenant Charles Hannam returned to Australia and assured the press that nothing much had happened.

'Undoubtedly,' he said frankly, 'the action of Morant and Handcock was high-handed, and certainly cannot be championed. But it can be truly said that the men thought they were acting within their rights. There was not the least idea of cruelty. To be acquainted with Morant and Handcock was to know that there was not a cruel bone in either of their bodies. But apart from the shooting, the men were accused of a great deal that is entirely without foundation. Any charges of drunkenness or want of consideration to women and children are absolutely false.'[18]

It was a strange comment from one whose own order had directly led to the death of two small children, and who had wanted to poison the rest.

After a business career in Taiwan as a trader, Hannam returned to Brisbane, to the life of a 'gentleman', and died of a stroke in November 1923 at the age of 46.

•

Upon his return to England, **Lieutenant Henry Picton** ran into a slew of problems. Once news of the Carbineers' actions became apparent in London, Picton began feeling the full brunt of criticism. Because he was cashiered, he could never again work in a government position. On 6 May 1902, the *London Gazette* published that, 'The grant of the DCM to Corporal H G Picton (Loch's Horse) who afterwards became lieutenant in the BVC awarded in the LG 27 September 1901 is cancelled.'[19]

After a few years, Picton had had enough of Great Britain, and decided to travel around Europe, holding various odd jobs along the way – working at one point with horses at the Potocki Stud in Poland.[20]

In the early 1920s, he married a Hungarian woman named Theodora Knechtsberger, and they had two sons together, Harold and Patrick. He died in May 1952 in Brighton, aged 72.

•

James Christie stayed on in South Africa dealing with the flotsam and jetsam of war's aftermath. Eventually he returned to his home in the Clutha district in New Zealand in December 1904, before embarking on a career change which saw him become headmaster of the Loburn School. Christie suffered a devastating blow in November 1918 when his only surviving daughter, Monica – born three months after the fire that had killed four of his other children – died of Spanish flu at just 18 years old. He never recovered from the loss and died less than two years later in February 1921, aged 58.[21]

•

In 1916, **Trooper Muir Churton** enlists in the New Zealand Defence Forces with the Machine Gun Corps, eager to serve his country in the field of battle. Churton is granted his wish, deploying to France and becoming a Corporal before honourable discharge in 1919. He spends the rest of his days in the Waikato district, taking odd jobs and hard labour to earn himself a crust. It takes until the age of 66, but Churton finds love, marrying an older woman, a widow by the name of Fanny O'Sullivan.

In 1973, one Frank Shields is inquiring into the life and times of Breaker Morant. Shields is a director, putting together a documentary about the extraordinary case of Breaker and the Bushveldt Carbineers. Striving for as much accuracy and insight as he can find, Shields wonders who he might speak to who knew something of the time, when he discovers that, against all odds, there is a member of the Bushveldt Carbineers who is still alive. It is none other than Mr Muir Churton, now aged 91.

Shields travels to New Zealand, astonished that this once in a lifetime opportunity has presented itself. To speak to someone who was actually *there*, who actually *took part* in it all? Churton proves an open book, happy to divulge everything he knows and recount the events as though they had happened not a day before.

Churton explains that he had been among the patrol that shot Visser, and 70 years of time and distance hasn't been enough to dull the pain it has left him with. He remains terribly overcome with emotion even after all this time; 'those men had surrendered under a white flag and had given up their arms when they were shot'.[22] Delicately, careful not to overstep the mark, Shields asks if the Trooper thought Lieutenants Morant and Handcock were deserving of their dark fate. Feeble in his age, but resolute in his response, Churton is bold when he speaks.

'They were guilty as sin!' he cries.

Muir Churton died in May 1977 at the tremendous age of 95. Living 75 years past his service, Muir was the last surviving Trooper of the Bushveldt Carbineers.

•

Frederick Ramon de Bertodano remained in the Transvaal for two years as an administrator, before becoming an unsuccessful gold prospector and leaving for England in 1905. Serving with the Nottinghamshire Yeomanry in the First World War, Major de Bertodano was mentioned in dispatches and after the war settled in Spain where, in 1921, he became the Marquis of Morel following the death of his uncle. He went on to father eight children to two wives, and moved to London during the Spanish Civil War as a representative of General Franco.

In 1928, while in London, he ran into his old Sydney law lecturer, by now a Judge, Laurens Armstrong. While swapping stories of old Sydney Uni cronies, the subject of Robert Lenehan comes up, whereupon the whole saga of Lenehan's involvement with Breaker Morant tumbles out, including the nefarious role played by the evil Captain Taylor. Transfixed, Judge Armstrong insists that de Bertodano writes it all down. This is *history*, Armstrong insists, and must be chronicled before all the lies become concrete. De Bertodano proceeds to do exactly that, and the dossier ends up among remnants of his old Intelligence files where it will sit in a dusty cabinet until – long after de Bertodano's death in 1955 in Harare – it is, wonderfully, retrieved from the archives by Margaret Carnegie in 1976. Arthur Davey's book, *Breaker Morant and the Bushveldt Carbineers*, includes a short comment de Bertodano made to a Lady Henderson in 1954 where he commented he had been reading his old diary from the Boer War and 'I have still got all my intelligence and secret service reports.' Why had he taken them with him? Well, he had been ordered to take them! Yes, at the end of the Boer War his superiors had decided that files such as his, documenting the BVC atrocities in graphic detail, 'were too dangerous if the Boers got control in S.A. [as they eventually did]. If they were known what a shemozzle there would be!'[23]

In short, what happened with the BVC under Taylor and Morant was a stain on the name of British arms, and needed to be hidden. But the fact that de Bertodano still had all his original files with him is a fair answer to those who have essayed to discredit de Bertodano's recollections over the years on the grounds that he had written them so long after the events he described.

•

Frederick Harper Booth returned to Australia in May 1901, and went on to marry Mary Finlay Towt, known as 'Pollie', the sister of one of his Boer War comrades, Charles Towt. He entered the wool trade, became a substantial Sydney business figure, and did so well he was able to build the nine-storey 'Booth House', which still stands at 44 Bridge Street, Sydney. He and Pollie had six children, one of whom was my mother. He was my only surviving grandparent; I was the youngest of his 27 grandchildren, and I was very glad to get to know him enough to remember him well and fondly, before he died when I was 12, in Wahroonga, Sydney, in 1974 at the age of 93.

As a family we are proud of his inclusion on the Boer War Memorial in Canberra. On a personal note, I am proud he fought honourably in a war where honour was too often in short supply, and proud too of his prose that brings the dark truth and stark bravery of battle alive for us to ponder.

•

In late December 1900, the widow of **James Annat** received a letter from Queen Victoria, requesting a photograph of the hero of Elands River be sent to her. The request was obliged. The gesture by Queen Victoria was just one of many tributes made to Lieutenant Annat's bravery, and they all helped give his widow solace. In response to one letter from the Commanding Officer of the Queensland Rifles, she replied with sentiments that summed up her gratitude.

'Dear Major Plant, I must thank you very kindly for the sympathetic and comforting letter you sent me on the loss of my dear husband. Although I know he died a noble death, it is very hard for me, for he was both a loving husband and father.'[24]

She never remarried, raised her five children alone and remained in the family home at 55 Lewis Street in the Brisbane suburb of Woolloongabba for the rest of her life. Two of her sons served in the First World War.

She died on 29 June 1946, aged 80.

One of her granddaughters, 'Pixie' Annat, MBE OAM, an office bearer of the Royal Australian Nursing Federation, would travel to Elands River to preside at the unveiling of a plaque in memory of her grandfather; and in Brisbane, a plaque for him hangs on the west wall of Warwick Uniting Church.

Though Annat was posthumously awarded medals for his service in the Boer War, there was no specific clasp for the Battle of Elands River – effectively Australia's Gallipoli before Gallipoli, in terms of capturing the popular imagination – because it was not regarded as a big enough battle to have individual recognition.

The Elands River flag is in the Zimbabwe archives in Harare. Captain Ham had it, but it was stolen, reportedly by a Rhodesian soldier.

•

After the death of her husband Frank, **Dora Eland** never married again. She died in South Africa in 1938 at the age of 76. Their baby daughter, Dora Maude Eland, died in 1981 in England. Frank Shields filmed some of his 1974 documentary *The Breaker* at Dora Eland Jnr's house.

•

Paul Kruger settled in Holland, where he remained for the rest of the war. Devastated after hearing that the Treaty of Vereeniging had been signed, he refused to believe it.

As long as those bold flags fluttered in wind outside his home in Holland, the war wasn't over. It just *couldn't* be. And yet at sunset on the 14th of June 1902, two weeks after hostilities ceased, the flags fell still, were taken down and folded neatly for now.

'My grief,' Kruger noted, 'is beyond expression.'[25]

The new country that emerged from the war would never claim him as a citizen. He refused to swear allegiance to King George and he died in July 1904. His body was first interred in The Hague, but, with British permission, was soon repatriated to Pretoria and laid to rest in the Church Street Cemetery, just 500 yards from the house he lived in and 100 yards from the grave of Breaker Morant.

•

After the war, **Deneys Reitz** spent a period of exile in Madagascar, where he wrote down many of his experiences with his Commando during the war. Returning to South Africa, he became a successful lawyer before serving in the First World War for the Union of South Africa as an officer in the British Army. Marrying upon his return to South Africa, he returned to his life as a lawyer and in 1929 published his masterpiece *Commando: A Boer Journal of the Boer War* to deserved great acclaim. Reitz then turned to politics, rising to be the Minister for Agriculture, and in 1939, Minister for Native Affairs and Deputy Prime Minister. In 1943, he was appointed South African High Commissioner to London. Reitz died in 1944.

•

After being shipped to a concentration camp in St Helena for the duration of the war, **Tom Kelly** and his two sons – like all Boer prisoners of war who wanted to return home – were asked to sign an Oath of Allegiance to the British monarch, King Edward VII. Tom Kelly resisted, despite pleas from former Boer leaders, but eventually signed nearly 18 months after the conclusion of the war, and finally made it back to his farm.

He died in March 1923, aged 74.

•

In 1902 **Louis Botha**, then 40, travels to London, aspiring to become the sort of politician who cares more about peace than pennies. He hopes to secure enough loans to rebuild his shattered country and while there meets at a private lunch with the newly elected Member for Oldham, Winston Churchill, who at this time was 28. By Churchill's account, the subject of the Boer War naturally arose quickly and shortly thereafter turned to the episode on the train where the young war correspondent had been captured.

'We talked of the war,' Churchill will recount, 'and I briefly told the story of my capture. Botha listened in silence; then he said, "Don't you recognise me? I was that man. It was I who took you prisoner. I, myself," and his bright eyes twinkled with pleasure. Botha in white shirt and frock coat looked very different in all save size and darkness of complexion from the wild war-time figure I had seen that rough day in Natal. But about the extraordinary fact there can be no doubt.'[26]

Botha died of the Spanish Flu in Pretoria, 27 August 1919. He, too, is buried in the Church Street Cemetery in Pretoria, not far from Breaker Morant and Peter Handcock.

•

The fame of **Banjo Paterson** only grew upon his return to Australia in 1900, after shortly taking up poetry full-time, with the only interregnum being a stint serving in France in the First World War, where he served not as a soldier, but as the driver of an ambulance for the Australian Voluntary Hospital. He rose to the rank of Major, commanding a squadron of the 2nd Remount Unit. In 1939 he wrote about Breaker Morant, who he was careful to now frame as a rather glancing acquaintance, rather than a friend and fellow poet.

'Somehow, I seemed to see the whole thing,' Banjo recounted, 'the little group of anxious-faced men, the half-comprehending Dutchman standing by, and Morant, drunk with his one day of power. For years he had shifted and battled and contrived; had been always the underdog, and now he was up in the stirrups. It went to his head like wine.'[27]

Banjo Paterson died on 5 February 1941 after a brief illness. His plot is in the Northern Suburbs Memorial Gardens and Crematorium in Sydney.

•

Lord Kitchener's military career continued to prosper after the Boer War, which had again turned him into such a national hero that, upon landing in England, he was driven through the streets in an open carriage as the people cheered, before receiving a formal welcome at St James's

Palace by King Edward VII. He was shortly thereafter created Viscount Kitchener of Khartoum and of the Vaal in the Colony of Transvaal.

At the beginning of the First World War, as Secretary of State for War, he was persuaded by none other than Winston Churchill to invade the Dardanelles, which of course included the landing at Gallipoli. The subsequent disaster saw the career of both men take something of a downturn and Kitchener's powers were severely curtailed. It all ended very badly indeed when, on 5 June 1916, he was aboard HMS *Hampshire*, travelling to the Russian port of Archangel, with a mission of negotiating ways with the Tsar's government to better co-ordinate the Allies' military operations, when the ship hit a mine and sank. Twelve survived, but 737 men lost their lives, including Lord Kitchener.

•

Lord Roberts only just made it to the First World War. In November 1914, while visiting St Omer in France to meet with some of the Indian troops with whom he had served in previous campaigns on the subcontinent, he fell ill with pneumonia and died on the night of 14 November.

'Lord Roberts died as he would have wished to die,' *The Times* reported, 'at the headquarters of the greatest army England has ever placed on foreign soil, amongst the troops he so often led to victory, and within the sound of their guns.'[28]

•

David Lloyd George, one of the most notorious opponents of the Boer War, would famously go on to become British Prime Minister at the height of the First World War, staying in the post until 1922. He served in the House of Commons for a total of 55 years, before dying in 1945, aged 82.

•

After her successful campaign against the concentration camps in the Boer War, **Emily Hobhouse** threw all of her weight against the First World War and tried to unite the women of Britain, Germany and Austria into having it stopped. When the war finished, she equally led the campaign to raise money to buy food and get it to the devastated areas of central Europe. Hobhouse died in England in 1926, aged 66, and her ashes were put in the National Women's Monument in Bloemfontein which stands in memorial to the nigh on 30,000, mostly women and children, who died in the concentration camps. (Another 14,000 Africans died in the segregated camps.)

•

Another monument worthy of mention in these pages is the Zoutpansberg Commando Monument at Vliegenpan, which was unveiled in 2005. At the opening, the great-grandson of Charles and Olive Bristow said, 'I'm not sure which side my great-grandfather was on.'[29]

I wish I could help!

•

The idea that Morant and Handcock were wrongly convicted and shot is a wish that becomes a truth too strong to ever be torn back by facts. In the first wave, the push was powered by accounts that glossed over the atrocities, and gave particularly lurid accounts of their execution, which portrayed them in courageous, heroic light. Here, for example, is a quick burst from a contemporaneous article published about the final minutes:

> Morant broke out into a song about Australia . . . The lieutenant yelled for them to be tied and put with their faces towards the wall.
>
> 'No,' called Morant, 'we will die as Australians should, with our faces to our enemies.' And Handcock said, 'We will show you bastards how Australians can die. You may murder us now, you brutes, because you are cowards, but as there is a God we will be avenged.' Morant called out to the soldiers: 'Kill us quickly, boys, we know you must do your duty, do not wing us, make it a quick thing.' Then he flung down his cigarette, and holding up his hand, exclaimed, 'Some day Australia will avenge our murder! It is a pity someone is not here to take the news to show those at home how Australians can die,' and as Morant broke out again into song, 'Fire, Fire!' screamed the frantic Afrikander Englishman. The firing line wavered. Some of the men's eyes were filled with tears. The corporal said in a voice husky with emotion, hesitatingly, 'Fi-fi-re.'[30]

You get the drift.

Witton's book, *Scapegoats of the Empire*, added further fuel to the flames, with an account that also minimised the horror, and largely exculpated them.

Most of the popular accounts that have appeared also see Morant elevated to the position of wronged Australian hero.

In the modern era, the story saw an enormous resurgence of interest in the early 1970s after the author Kit Denton was down in South Australia helping with the Don Dunstan election campaign. He was having a counter lunch at a North Adelaide pub one day, with four companions who had also been in the services, it was just before Anzac Day 1970 and they were telling their own version of war stories when they were interrupted by a raspy voice from the corner.

'*Youse* jokers don't know what you're *talkin*' about . . .'[31]

They turned . . . and there he was. At the corner table, drinking on his own, sat a 'little old man' from Central Casting, about 90 years old, with 'a face like a crinkled walnut',[32] skin like hard leather and opinions that were all of the above. The only *real* soldiers, he said, were those who had their own horses and went off to war. Blokes like him. And his mates. Like when they had gone to the Boer War.

The other blokes went back to work. But Denton stayed on – there was something about this bloke – and as the afternoon went on, out came the story of his unit, the Second South Australian Contingent and his mate, Breaker Morant, you know the one . . . the one the British shot, even though he was an innocent man. Put up against the wall and shot, after being convicted by a Pommy kangaroo court, you know?

No, Kit Denton didn't know it, but was fascinated to hear it, and encouraged the old fellow to keep speaking.

The bee released from his bonnet was the bug that bit Denton, for as soon as he started digging into it he became completely obsessed by the whole story – something I can entirely understand! – and went on to write a semi-fictional account of the affair, titled *The Breaker*. A bestseller and the jumping-off point for the iconic film in 1980 by Bruce Beresford, *Breaker Morant*, starring Jack Thompson as Major Thomas, Edward Woodward as the Breaker, and Bryan Brown as Lieutenant Handcock. It is a film that holds up well, even 40 years on, portraying the shade and light of Morant, though perhaps allowing Major Thomas to shine more brightly in a fictional court than he did in reality.

Still, it was the fine detail of Witton's original account in *Scapegoats of the Empire*, particularly, which has allowed people of serious legal pedigree – particularly those steeped in the rigorous standards of twenty-first century civil and criminal trials, as opposed to the rough and tumble of a court martial in the middle of a brutal war – to proclaim the men were wrongly convicted as a matter of law.

Few were stronger in this field than Geoffrey Robertson QC.

'Breaker Morant's trial,' he told author Nick Bleszynski in 2002, 'was a particularly pernicious example of using legal proceedings against lower ranks as a means of covering up the guilt of senior officers and of Kitchener himself, who gave or approved their unlawful "shoot to kill" order. Morant may have been all too happy to obey it, of course, in which case he deserved some punishment. But it was wrong to use him as a scapegoat for an unlawful policy. I regard the convictions of Morant and Handcock as unsafe.'[33]

I strongly disagree, my learned friend, Geoffrey.

I bow to no-one in my disdain for Kitchener's actions in the Boer War – starting with the hideous concentration camps and the policy of burning down 30,000 Boer homesteads. But there is no established link of Kitchener giving orders to kill surrendering Boer prisoners – and it defies common sense. How could that be when at the time of the Morant/Handcock atrocities, Boers were surrendering at the rate of 1000 prisoners a month? Moreover, the BVC themselves took over 100 prisoners in the same period.

Were there, then, problems with the overall legal process?

No doubt. The prisoners were not allowed to seek or see counsel until 12 weeks of solitary confinement had been endured; and were not even told what they were accused of for over a fortnight after their arrest; the Court of Inquiry was supposed to be *in camera*, but instead was openly discussed by participants in mess, which led to corruption of process, etc. When Witton asked for counsel, he was told there was no need. Morant, Handcock and Witton didn't even see the counsel they eventually secured until the night before the first court martial.

We may put those flaws down as regrettable, even though they fit within the broad parameters of such courts martial, as defined by the *Manual of Military Law* 1899. (We can also bitterly regret that as the transcripts of the courts martial have been lost, it frequently sees Morant advocates pointing to Witton's account as if it is Holy Writ of what happened, which it is not.)

But, all up, do even the undisputed flaws in the legal process mean you offer a pardon a century later to men who actually *did* commit such brutal murders, including the murder of a civilian witness?

Of course, it doesn't. For when you cut through it all, in terms of judging guilt, you need focus only on the murder of that non-combatant, the Reverend Daniel Heese. At the very least we know that Peter Handcock did it, on the orders of Lieutenant Breaker Morant. Why?

Not just because that is what fits with every other shred of evidence, but because George Witton left a first-hand account of Handcock's *confession* to it.

I repeat. A pardon for men who did that? The full bench of my researchers and myself, who have been buried in this material for the last 12 months, give a very firm and unanimous decision: NO.

Beyond everything else, such a pardon would dishonour the true heroes of the piece, the men like James Christie, Cochrane and Browne, who had the wherewithal, the decency, and the sheer *courage* to speak up, corral the honourable and help bring Morant to justice.

Nevertheless, the push to posthumously pardon Morant, with no less a figure than the former Deputy Prime Minister of Australia, my late friend Tim Fischer, backing it, going so far as to refer to Morant and Handcock in the Foreword he wrote for Nick Bleszynski's *Shoot Straight, You Bastards!* as, 'two brave Australians', who were 'shot dead on the altar of political expediency'.

He went on: 'It is essential that honour be restored to Morant and Handcock because they did not deserve to die . . . Even if Breaker Morant killed Boer prisoners in cold blood, even if he dealt with and killed Heese, undeniably there were mitigating circumstances whereby at no stage should they have been sentenced to death by firing party.'

It all happened, he insisted, because 'Kitchener wanted a hanging court martial and nothing too much should be allowed to interfere with that result.'[34]

I wish I could have raised this with Tim before he passed away, but my gentle point would have been my certainty that Josef (Floris) Visser must have felt the same way when faced with his own firing party. So, too, the eight Boers; two more Boers and a boy; and of course, the Reverend Daniel Heese, mourned by his wife and, in turn, by his descendants to this day, as were all those so cruelly shot down at the hands of Morant and Handcock.

Nevertheless, in 2009, petitions were presented to Queen Elizabeth II to review and posthumously overturn both the convictions and sentences of Morant, Handcock and Witton.

In the midst of the attendant publicity, famed Australian television journalist Ray Martin took the cameras of Channel Nine's *Sixty Minutes* into the fray in May 2010, journeying to South Africa for a week to interview descendants of some of the key players, including Ronnie Visser, a descendant of Josef (Floris) Visser, the first man murdered on Morant's orders. Mr Visser was appalled by the very idea of Morant being granted a pardon, and so intent on stopping it he engaged a law firm to formally protest to the Australian Attorney-General.

The South African historian whom I consulted on this book, Charles Leach, is aggrieved at the very suggestion of a pardon. His point is that the murders were beyond question, and any legal revision of the original judgements should not see a turning over of the guilty verdicts, but an expansion of them. If done properly, he maintains, 'the court martial would have found Captain A. Taylor to have been extremely influential and deeply implicated in many killings that, regrettably, were never dealt with. This would certainly have led to his own guilty verdict and for far more than only 12 convictions of murder!'

At the conclusion of writing this book, I must say I entirely agree with Mr Leach.

He further feels the movement to pardon Morant and Handcock entirely disrespectful of the descendants of those who were murdered by them.

'Despite proponents of the "Pardon" movement having visited the far north where the BVC was deployed, not once did any of them request meeting any of the descendants of the Boer victims in order to gauge their feelings!'

In any case, the British Ministry of Defence, on behalf of the Queen, addressed the petition in November 2010, stating: 'After detailed historical and legal consideration, the Secretary of State has concluded that no new primary evidence has come to light which supports the petition to overturn the original courts-martial verdicts and sentences.'[35]

On Monday, 27 February 2012, the 110th anniversary of the execution of Morant and Handcock, the LNP member for Mitchell, Alex Hawke, a conservative firebrand, rose in the House to make a claim for their pardon.

'I rise once again in this parliament to say that it is timely for the Australian government to do everything it can to assist the modern-day descendants of these men to access a judicial review of this case. It is the case that the executions were conducted with extreme haste and without appeal.'

(A point of order, Mr Speaker, if I may. An appeal is something they had in civilian courts, but did not exist with courts martial. There are things to criticise in the legal process for Morant and Handcock, but lack of appeal is not one of them.)

'The Australian government was not informed until some two months after the events. At the same time around 80,000 Australians signed a petition to release George Witton and to pardon Morant and Handcock. Given that the men who were executed – Morant and Handcock – led to the saving of hundreds of Australian soldiers' lives in World War I because they were unable to be executed by the British because of what had happened in the Boer War, I think it is important that we seek the British government's assistance in [getting] a judicial review and pardon. It is an episode that appeals greatly to every Australian because of the doctrine of fairness which says that no-one should be treated differently because of their birth, rank or status. We do know that these men were treated differently because of their birth, rank and status. We certainly need legends in Australian history.'[36]

You're right. It was a tepid argument with so little foundation it could not stand in even a mild breeze, and the Federal Parliament was not disposed to petition the British Parliament to petition the Queen to grant a pardon itself.

All up?

All up I think Breaker Morant and Peter Handcock got exactly what they deserved. The one who didn't – the guiltiest man of all – is Captain Alfred Taylor, the *scoundrel* who was ever and always slinking his way through the whole dreadful episode, and who was never properly held to account for being the one ultimately responsible for much of it.

There can be no doubt that Breaker Morant would love the fact that people are still quarrelling over him 120 years later, and that there remain so many romantics who cannot reconcile the poet with the killer that he still has people arguing his case well into the twenty-first century.

But a killer he was.

Still, let us leave Morant with the last words, for he was a poet too, one much obsessed by death, and wrote many memorable odes upon it before he went to his own:

> *This night is near! Are you waiting friend,*
> *That Night? – we're drawing nigh it –*
> *When we to the Restful Land shall wend,*
> *And leave life's feverish riot –*
> *When the gods to each tired soul shall send*
> *Eternal, dreamless quiet.*[37]

'When the Light is as Darkness'
Harry 'Breaker' Morant

ENDNOTES

Introduction

1 Conan Doyle, *The Great Boer War*, Smith, Elder and Co., London, 1900, p. 244.
2 Wilhelmina (Mina) Rawson in *Sunday Times (Sydney)*, 27 April 1902, p. 5. https://trove.nla.gov.au/newspaper/article/126420866

Dramatis Personae

1 Jarvis is quoted in Walker, 'A Man Never Knows His Luck in South Africa: Some Australian Literary Myths of the Boer War', *The English in Africa*, Vol. 12, No. 2, p. 14.
2 'The Breaker Again', H.R. in *Windsor and Richmond Gazette*, 5 March 1904, p. 12. https://trove.nla.gov.au/newspaper/article/85890555

Prologue

1 Burchell, *Travels in the Interior of Southern Africa, Vol. II*, Longman, Hurst, Rees, Orme, Brown and Green, London, 1824, p. 443.
2 Ash, *Kruger, Kommandos and Kak: Debunking the Myths of the Boer War*, 30 Degrees South Publishers, Pinetown, 2014, p. 67.
3 Ash, *Kruger, Kommandos and Kak*, p. 76.
4 Genesis 9:25, Christian Standard Bible.
5 Author's note: The Bechuanaland Protectorate was established on 31 March 1885 by the United Kingdom. On 30 September 1966 it became the Republic of Botswana.
6 Ash, *Kruger, Kommandos and Kak*, p. 76.
7 Iwan-Muller, *Lord Milner and South Africa*, Heinemann, London, 1902, p. 154.
8 'Famous People in the Diamond Industry', *Erasmus Stephanus Jacobs 1851 – 1933*, Cape Town Diamond Museum https://www.capetowndiamondmuseum.org/about-diamonds/famous-people/
9 'Famous People in the Diamond Industry', Cape Town Diamond Museum.
10 Kruger, *The Memoirs of Paul Kruger*, The Century Co., New York, 1902, p. 179.
11 Davis, *With Both Armies in South Africa*, Scribner, New York, 1900, pp. 101–102.
12 Lines from Rudyard Kipling's poem, 'If –'.
13 *Times Law Reports*, Vol. XII, G E Wright, London, 1896, p. 586.

Chapter One

1 Paterson, *Singer of the Bush, Complete Works: 1885–1900*, Lansdowne, Sydney, 1983, p. 686.
2 *Windsor and Richmond Gazette*, 5 March 1904, p. 12. https://trove.nla.gov.au/newspaper/article/85890555
3 'Freaks of Harry Harbord Morant, "The Breaker"', *The World's News*, 12 April 1902, p. 22. https://trove.nla.gov.au/newspaper/article/128448859
4 *Upper Murray and Mitta Herald* and quoted from: Bleszynski, *Shoot Straight, You Bastards!*, Random House, Sydney, 2003, p. 95.
5 Bleszynski, *Shoot Straight, You Bastards!*, p. 95.

6   West and Roper, *Breaker Morant: The Final Roundup*, Amberley Publishing Limited, Gloucestershire, 2016, p. 27.

7   'The Freaks of Harry Harbord Morant', *The World's News*, 12 April 1902, p. 22. https://trove.nla.gov.au/newspaper/article/128448859

8   *Windsor and Richmond Gazette*, 5 March 1904, p. 12. https://trove.nla.gov.au/newspaper/article/85890555

9   *Windsor and Richmond Gazette*, 5 March 1904, p. 12. https://trove.nla.gov.au/newspaper/article/85890555

10 Morant, 'A Night Thought', *The Bulletin*, Vol. 11, No. 603, 5 September 1891.

11 *Sunday Times (Sydney)*, 27 April 1902, p. 5. https://trove.nla.gov.au/newspaper/article/126420866

12 West and Roper, *Breaker Morant*, pp. 60–61.

13 *Windsor and Richmond Gazette*, 5 June 1897, p. 7. https://trove.nla.gov.au/newspaper/article/72552053

14 *Windsor and Richmond Gazette*, 5 June 1897, p. 7.

15 *Windsor and Richmond Gazette*, 5 June 1897, p. 7.

16 *Windsor and Richmond Gazette*, 5 June 1897, p. 7.

17 *Western Champion*, 22 January 1889, p. 2.

18 West and Roper, *Breaker Morant*, p. 61.

19 *Morning Bulletin* (Rockhampton), 5 January 1889, p. 5. https://trove.nla.gov.au/newspaper/article/52274456

20 *Sydney Morning Herald*, 25 February 1939, p. 21. https://trove.nla.gov.au/newspaper/article/17564428

21 Readers will recognise the lines from Banjo Paterson's 'Clancy of the Overflow'.

22 *Windsor and Richmond Gazette*, 15 May 1897, p. 11. https://trove.nla.gov.au/newspaper/article/72551891

23 *Windsor and Richmond Gazette*, 15 May 1897, p. 11. https://trove.nla.gov.au/newspaper/article/72551891

24 *Hawkesbury Herald*, 26 September 1902, p. 6. https://trove.nla.gov.au/newspaper/article/66352374

25 'Freaks of Harry Harbord Morant, "The Breaker"', *Windsor and Richmond Gazette*, 26 April 1902, p. 14. https://trove.nla.gov.au/newspaper/article/86216522

26 'Advertising', *Nepean Times*, 6 November 1898, p. 4. https://trove.nla.gov.au/newspaper/article/101310119

27 'Town Gossip', *Windsor and Richmond Gazette*, 17 December 1898, p. 10. https://trove.nla.gov.au/newspaper/article/66439773

28 Carnegie and Shields, *In Search of Breaker Morant*, Graphic Books, Armadale, 1979, p. 22.

29 'Freaks of Harry Harbord Morant, "The Breaker"', *Windsor and Richmond Gazette*, 26 April 1902, p. 14. https://trove.nla.gov.au/newspaper/article/86216522

30 'Freaks of Harry Harbord Morant, "The Breaker"', *Windsor and Richmond Gazette*, 26 April 1902, p. 14. https://trove.nla.gov.au/newspaper/article/86216522

31 'Freaks of Harry Harbord Morant, "The Breaker"', *Windsor and Richmond Gazette*, 26 April 1902, p. 14. https://trove.nla.gov.au/newspaper/article/86216522

32 *Sydney Morning Herald*, 25 February 1939, p. 21. https://trove.nla.gov.au/newspaper/article/17564428

33 *Sydney Morning Herald*, 25 February 1939, p. 21. https://trove.nla.gov.au/newspaper/article/17564428

34 *Sydney Morning Herald*, 25 February 1939, p. 21. https://trove.nla.gov.au/newspaper/article/17564428

35 *Sydney Morning Herald*, 25 February 1939, p. 21. https://trove.nla.gov.au/newspaper/article/17564428

36 *Sydney Morning Herald*, 25 February 1939, p. 21 [reported speech].

37 Paterson, *The Man From Snowy River and Other Verses*, Angus & Robertson, Sydney, 1917, p. 179.

38 'Mostly about the "Breaker"', *Windsor and Richmond Gazette*, 18 June 1898, p. 5. https://trove.nla.gov.au/newspaper/article/66438135

39 'Mostly about the "Breaker"', *Windsor and Richmond Gazette*, 18 June 1898, p. 5. https://trove.nla.gov.au/newspaper/article/66438135

40 *Windsor and Richmond Gazette*, 6 March 1897, p. 9. https://trove.nla.gov.au/newspaper/article/72551256

41 West and Roper, *Breaker Morant*, p. 69.

42 Reitz, *God Does not Forget: The Story of a Boer War Commando*, Fireship Press, 2010, p. 8.

43 'Australian Troops Will Be Accepted If Required', *Sunday Times* (Sydney), 16 July 1899, p. 9. https://trove.nla.gov.au/newspaper/article/127378878

44 'A Battle at Sunnyside', *The West Australian*, 4 January 1900, p. 5. https://trove.nla.gov.au/newspaper/article/3241705

45 Rintala, 'Made in Birmingham: Lloyd George, Chamberlain, and the Boer War', *Biography*, Vol. 11, No. 2, 1988, p. 124.

46 Rintala, 'Made in Birmingham', p. 124.

47 Author's note: See Joshua Slocum's *Sailing Alone Around the World*, Bloomsbury, London, pp. 237–239.

48 Davis, *With Both Armies in South Africa*, p. 108.

49 Reitz, *God Does not Forget*, p. 10 [reported speech].

50 Reitz, *God Does not Forget*, p. 10.

51 Reitz, *God Does not Forget*, pp. 10–11.

52 Reitz, *God Does not Forget*, p. 14.

53 'The Australian Contingent', *The Bendigo Independent*, 21 September 1899, p. 2. https://trove.nla.gov.au/newspaper/article/173153823

54 Conan Doyle, *The Great Boer War*, p. 54.

55 Conan Doyle, *The Great Boer War*, p. 78.

56 Conan Doyle, *The Great Boer War*, p. 79.

57 Conan Doyle, *The Great Boer War*, p. 80.

Chapter Two

1 Green, *The Story of the Australian Bushmen*, William Brooks and Co., Limited, Sydney, 1903, p. 2.

2 'The Shooting of "The Breaker"', *Windsor and Richmond Gazette*, 19 March 1904, p. 9. https://trove.nla.gov.au/newspaper/article/85895697

3 *Port Macquarie News and Hastings River Advocate*, 14 October 1899, p. 4.

4 *The Mount Lyell Standard*, 9 October 1899, p. 3.

5 *The South Australian Register*, 13 October 1899, p. 5.

6 *Newcastle Morning Herald and Miners' Advocate*, 13 October 1899, p. 5.

7 Reitz, *God Does not Forget*, p. 17.

8 Reitz, *God Does not Forget*, p. 18.

9 'The Transvaal National Anthem', *Northern Territory Times and Gazette*, 8 December 1899, p. 3. https://trove.nla.gov.au/newspaper/article/4253559 Translated in 1890 by J. Edward Clennell.

10 Reitz, *God Does not Forget*, p. 18.

11 Reitz, *God Does not Forget*, p. 18.

12 Randolph Churchill, ed., *Winston S. Churchill, Companion Volume 1, Part 2*, Heinemann, London, 1967, p. 839.

13 Churchill, *My Early Life 1874–1908*, Collins and Son, Glasgow, 1985, p. 236.

14 Baillie, *Mafeking: A Diary of a Siege*, Archibald Constable & Company, Westminster, 1900, http://www.gutenberg.org/files/41511/41511-h/41511-h.html

15 Ferguson, *Empire: How Britain Made the Modern World*, Penguin Books, Australia, 2004, pp. 277–278.

16 Baillie, *Mafeking: A Diary of a Siege*, Archibald Constable & Company, Westminster, 1900.

17 Ferguson, *Empire*, p. 277.

18 Viljoen, *My Reminiscences of the Anglo Boer War*, Hood, Douglas & Howard, London, 1902, p. 19.

19 Viljoen, *My Reminiscences of the Anglo Boer War*, p. 39.

20 Morris, *Soldier, Artist, Sportsman: The Life of Lord Rawlinson of Trent*, Pickle, London, 2017, p. 54.

21 *Evening News*, 8 November 1899, p. 4. https://trove.nla.gov.au/newspaper/article/113689308

22 *Evening News*, 1 January 1900, p. 3. https://trove.nla.gov.au/newspaper/article/117035739

23 'Mr A. B. Paterson', *The Sydney Mail and New South Wales Advertiser*, 28 October 1899, p. 1049. https://trove.nla.gov.au/newspaper/article/163701066

24 'To The Front', *Truth*, 29 October 1899, p. 3. https://trove.nla.gov.au/newspaper/article/168084243

25 Ash, *Kruger, Kommandos and Kak*, p. 385.

26 Davis, *With Both Armies in South Africa*, pp. 40–41.

27 Davis, *With Both Armies in South Africa*, p. 41.

28 Churchill, *My Early Life: A Roving Commission*, Thornton Butterworth, London, 1931, p. 258.

29 Churchill, *My Early Life: A Roving Commission*, pp. 257–258.

30 Hussey, 'The Boer War Armoured Train Incident and Churchill's Escape, 1899', Churchill Project, 30 September 2019, https://winstonchurchill.hillsdale.edu/boer-escape/

31 Candace Millard, *Hero of the Empire: The Making of Winston Churchill*, Penguin, UK, 2016.

32 Churchill, *My Early Life: A Roving Commission*, p. 251.

33 Churchill, *My Early Life: A Roving Commission*, p. 259.

34 Churchill, *My Early Life: 1874–1908*, p. 248.

35 Churchill, *My Early Life: 1874–1908*, p. 258.

36 Winston Churchill, *London to Ladysmith via Pretoria*, Longmans, Green & Co., London, 1900, p. 134. http://www.gutenberg.org/cache/epub/14426/pg14426.txt

37 'With The S.S. Kent Contingent', *Sydney Morning Herald*, 28 December 1899, p. 5. https://trove. nla.gov.au/newspaper/article/14216858

38 *Sydney Morning Herald*, 28 December 1899, p. 5. https://trove.nla.gov.au/newspaper/article/14216858

39 Semmler, *The Banjo of the Bush: The Life and Times of A. B. 'Banjo' Paterson*, University of Queensland Press, St Lucia, 1984, pp. 104–105.

40 Reitz, *God Does not Forget*, p. 38 [reported speech].

41 Reitz, *God Does not Forget*, p. 38 [reported speech].

42 *The Warwick Argus*, 13 January 1900, p. 4. https://trove.nla.gov.au/newspaper/article/76633967

43 Drooglever, *From the Front: A. B (Banjo) Paterson's Dispatches from the Boer War*, Pan Macmillan, Sydney, 2000, p. 31.

44 *The Warwick Argus*, 13 January 1900, p. 4. https://trove.nla.gov.au/newspaper/article/76633967

45 Paterson, *Happy Dispatches*, Angus & Robertson, Sydney, 1934, p. 3.

46 Paterson, *Happy Dispatches*, p. 3.

47 Drooglever, *From the Front*, p. 31.

48 Paterson, *Happy Dispatches*, p. 9

49 Paterson, *Happy Dispatches*, p. 10.

50 Paterson, *Happy Dispatches*, p. 16.

51 'Mr Banjo Paterson's Letters', *The Australasian*, 3 February 1900, p. 7. https://trove.nla.gov.au/newspaper/article/139774397

52 *The Australasian*, 3 February 1900, p. 7. https://trove.nla.gov.au/newspaper/article/139774397

53 *The Australasian*, 3 February 1900, p. 7. https://trove.nla.gov.au/newspaper/article/139774397

54 William Shakespeare, *Julius Caesar*, Act 1, Scene 3.

55 'Incidents of The War', *The West Australian*, 3 March 1900, p. 10. https://trove.nla.gov.au/newspaper/article/23830438

56 Churchill, *London to Ladysmith via Pretoria*, p. 78.

57 Churchill, *My Early Life: A Roving Commission*, p. 288.

58 Churchill, *My Early Life: A Roving Commission*, p. 289.

59 Churchill, *My Early Life: A Roving Commission*, p. 296.

60 Churchill, *My Early Life: A Roving Commission*, p. 296.

61 Churchill, *My Early Life: A Roving Commission*, p. 303.

62 Churchill, *My Early Life: A Roving Commission*, p. 307.

63 Churchill, *My Early Life: A Roving Commission*, p. 310.

64 Churchill, *My Early Life: A Roving Commission*, p. 310.

65 Churchill, *My Early Life: A Roving Commission*, p. 310.

66 Churchill, *My Early Life: A Roving Commission*, p. 311.

67 Churchill, *My Early Life: 1874–1908*, p. 312.

68 Churchill, *My Early Life: 1874–1908*, p. 313.

69 Pakenham, *The Boer War*, Futura, London, 1988, p. 307.

Chapter Three

1 *Queanbeyan Age*, 24 February 1900, p. 2. https://trove.nla.gov.au/newspaper/article/31370977
2 Conan Doyle, *Memories and Adventures*, Little, Brown and Company, Boston, 1924, p. 174.
3 *Windsor, Richmond and Hawkesbury Advertiser*, 12 January 1899, p. 2.
4 *The Bulletin*, 5 August 1899.
5 'The Breaker Again', *Windsor and Richmond Gazette*, 5 March 1904, p. 12. https://trove.nla.gov. au/newspaper/article/85890555
6 Leach, *The Legend of Breaker Morant is Dead and Buried*, self-published, 2012. p. 203.
7 Lines from Banjo Paterson's poem, 'The Geebung Polo Club'.
8 West and Roper, *Breaker Morant*, p. 77.
9 'City Chatter', *Port Pirie Recorder and North Western Mail*, 2 April 1902, p. 3. https://trove.nla. gov.au/newspaper/article/95244327
10 'The Mounted Contingent', *The Advertiser*, 15 January 1900, p. 7. https://trove.nla.gov.au/ newspaper/article/29526876
11 'The Members Of The Contingent', *The South Australian Register*, 27 January 1900, pp. 9–10. https://trove.nla.gov.au/newspaper/article/54425674/4107386
12 Morant, 'A Departing Dirge', *The Bulletin*, 5 August 1899.
13 *Adelaide Observer*, 7 April 1900, p. 14. https://trove.nla.gov.au/newspaper/article/162391666
14 Booth family collection.
15 Booth family collection.
16 *Manual of Military Law*, War Office 1899, Her Majesty's Stationery Office, London, Part 1, p. 287.
17 Booth family collection.
18 Barnard, 'General Botha and the Spion Kop Campaign', *Military History Journal of South Africa*, Vol. 2, No. 1, June 1971, p. 1.
19 Gale and Polden Limited, *A Handbook of the Boer War*, Buller and Tanner, London, 1910, p. 105.
20 Gale and Polden Limited, *A Handbook of the Boer War*, pp. 105–106.
21 Barnard, 'General Botha and the Spion Kop Campaign', p .1.
22 Reitz, *God Does not Forget*, p. 62.
23 Churchill, *My Early Life: 1874–1908*, p. 319.
24 Droogleever, *Thorneycroft's 'Unbuttoned': The Story of Thorneycroft's Mounted Infantry in the Boer War 1899–1902*, Apple Print, Melbourne, 2014, p. 82.
25 Pemberton, *Battles of the Boer War*, Pan Books, London, 1964, pp. 175–176.
26 Author's note: Though at this point Mahatma Gandhi was known as Mohandas Gandhi, for ease of narrative I have left it as Mahatma.
27 Churchill, *My Early Life: A Roving Commission*, p. 329.
28 Churchill, *The Boer War*, Bloomsbury, London, 2002, p. 123.
29 Reitz, *God Does not Forget*, p. 63.
30 Reitz, *God Does not Forget*, p. 63.
31 Reitz, *God Does not Forget*, p. 63 [reported speech].
32 Reitz, *God Does not Forget*, p. 63.
33 Reitz, *God Does not Forget*, p. 65.
34 Payne, *The Life and Death of Mahatma Gandhi*, Brick Tower Press, New York, 1997, p. 51.
35 Sandys, *Churchill Wanted Dead or Alive*, Texas A&M University Press, College Station, 2013, p. 145.
36 Davitt, *The Boer Fight For Freedom*, Funk & Wagnalls, London, 1902, p. 582.
37 *Baltimore Sun*, 6 February 1900, p. 2.
38 Lane (ed.), *The War Diary of Burgher Jack Lane*, Van Riebeeck Society, Cape Town, 2001, p. 68.
39 Hales, *Campaign Pictures of the War in South Africa*, Cassell, London, 1900, p. 55.
40 'The Slingersfontein Skirmish', *Western Mail*, 31 March 1900, p. 53. https://trove.nla.gov.au/ newspaper/article/33182109
41 *Western Mail*, 31 March 1900, p. 53. https://trove.nla.gov.au/newspaper/article/33182109
42 Hyslop, *The Plough, the Gun and the Glory*, self-published, 2007, p. 256.
43 Hales, *Campaign Pictures of the War in South Africa*, p. 56.
44 Hales, *Campaign Pictures of the War in South Africa*, p. 56.
45 *Western Mail*, 31 March 1900, p. 53.
46 'The Slingersfontein Affair', *The West Australian*, 26 June 1900, p. 3. https://trove.nla.gov.au/ newspaper/article/23838542

47 *The West Australian*, 26 June 1900, p. 3.
48 *The West Australian*, 26 June 1900, p. 3.
49 *The West Australian*, 26 June 1900, p. 3.
50 *The West Australian*, 26 June 1900, p. 3.
51 *The West Australian*, 26 June 1900, p. 3.
52 *The West Australian*, 26 June 1900, p. 3.
53 *The West Australian*, 26 June 1900, p. 3.
54 *The West Australian*, 26 June 1900, p. 3.
55 Hales, *Campaign Pictures of the War in South Africa*, p. 73 [reported speech]. https://archive.org/details/campaignpictures00hale/page/68
56 *Western Mail*, 31 March 1900, p. 53.
57 'Australian Heroes', *Daily Telegraph* (Tas.), 14 June 1900, p. 3. https://trove.nla.gov.au/newspaper/article/153629694
58 *Bunbury Herald*, 21 June 1900, p. 3. https://trove.nla.gov.au/newspaper/article/87133301
59 Green, *The Story of the Australian Bushmen*, pp. 5–6.
60 Green, *The Story of the Australian Bushmen*, pp. 5–6.
61 Booth family collection.
62 Booth family collection.

Chapter Four

1 Pakenham, *The Boer War*, pp. 311–312.
2 Paterson, *Happy Dispatches*, pp. 19–20 [reported speech].
3 Paterson, *Happy Dispatches*, pp. 19–20.
4 'Banjo Paterson', *Examiner* (Tas), 18 September 1900, p. 3. https://trove.nla.gov.au/newspaper/article/35371407
5 Booth family collection.
6 West and Roper, *Breaker Morant*, p. 107.
7 Booth family collection.
8 *Barrier Miner*, 5 April 1900, p. 2. https://trove.nla.gov.au/newspaper/article/44254064
9 *Barrier Miner*, 5 April 1900, p. 2.
10 *Barrier Miner*, 5 April 1900, p. 2.
11 *Barrier Miner*, 5 April 1900, p. 2.
12 *Barrier Miner*, 5 April 1900, p. 2.
13 *Barrier Miner*, 5 April 1900, p. 2.
14 *Barrier Miner*, 5 April 1900, p. 2.
15 'The Boer War', *The Warwick Argus*, 7 April 1900, p. 3. https://trove.nla.gov.au/newspaper/article/76635035
16 Conan Doyle, *The Great Boer War*, p. 234.
17 'Banjo Paterson', *Bathurst Free Press and Mining Journal*, 27 April 1901, p. 2. https://trove.nla.gov.au/newspaper/article/64454170
18 de Wet, *Three Years War*, Scribner, New York, 1902, p. 30.
19 'Banjo Paterson', *Bathurst Free Press and Mining Journal*, 27 April 1901, p. 2. https://trove.nla.gov.au/newspaper/article/64454170
20 'Go Now!', *Table Talk*, 10 April 1902, p. 11. https://trove.nla.gov.au/newspaper/article/145706480
21 'The Surrender Of Cronje', *Barrier Miner*, 9 April 1900, p. 2. https://trove.nla.gov.au/newspaper/article/44254208
22 'War Correspondents', *Truth*, 30 September 1900, p. 6. https://trove.nla.gov.au/newspaper/article/200507944
23 Paterson, *Happy Dispatches*, p. 27.
24 *Bathurst Free Press and Mining Journal*, 27 April 1901, p. 2. https://trove.nla.gov.au/newspaper/article/64454170
25 Ziegler, *Omdurman*, Book Club Associates, London, 1973, p. 186.
26 Ziegler, *Omdurman*, pp. 185–186.
27 Michelle Gordon, 'British Colonial Violence in Sierra Leone, Perak and Sudan', PhD, University of London, August 2017, p. 145.
28 Gordon, 'British Colonial Violence in Sierra Leone', p. 147.

29 'Banjo Paterson's Lectures', *Evening Journal*, 24 October 1900, p. 3. https://trove.nla.gov.au/newspaper/article/199970702

30 Hobhouse, *The Brunt of the War, and Where it Fell*, Methuen & Co., London, 1902, pp. 7–8.

31 Conan Doyle, *The Great Boer War*, p. 187.

32 Kieza, *Banjo*, HarperCollins Publishers, Sydney, 2018, p. 316.

33 *Gympie Times and Mary River Mining Gazette*, 27 February 1900, p. 4. https://trove.nla.gov.au/newspaper/article/177737532/19126642

34 *Gympie Times and Mary River Mining Gazette*, 27 February 1900, p. 4.

35 *Manual of Military Law*, p. 294.

36 'Interesting Letters', *Singleton Argus*, 1 March 1900, p. 4. https://trove.nla.gov.au/newspaper/article/78885726

37 Cornelissen and Grundlingh (eds), *Sport Past and Present in South Africa*, Routledge, New York, 2012, p. 69.

38 Baillie, *Mafeking: A Diary of a Siege*, p. 241.

39 Wilcox, *Australia's Boer War: The War in South Africa 1899–1902*, Australian War Memorial, Canberra, 2002, p. 72.

40 Paterson, 'The Entry into Bloemfontein', *Barrier Miner*, 26 April 1900, p. 2 [reported speech]. https://trove.nla.gov.au/newspaper/article/44255122

41 *Sydney Morning Herald*, 17 April 1900, p. 5. https://trove.nla.gov.au/newspaper/article/14306241

42 *Sydney Morning Herald*, 17 April 1900, p. 5. https://trove.nla.gov.au/newspaper/article/14306241

43 'The "Ignorant Boers" Banjo Paterson's Picture', *The Catholic Press*, 2 June 1900, p. 4. https://trove.nla.gov.au/newspaper/article/104659629

44 'The "Ignorant Boers" Banjo Paterson's Picture', *The Catholic Press*, 2 June 1900, p. 4. https://trove.nla.gov.au/newspaper/article/104659629

45 Paterson, *Happy Dispatches*, p. 36.

46 Paterson, *Happy Dispatches*, p. 38.

47 Paterson, *Happy Dispatches*, p. 38.

48 Paterson, *Happy Dispatches*, p. 38.

49 Paterson, *Happy Dispatches*, p. 38 [reported speech].

50 Paterson, *Happy Dispatches*, p. 38.

51 Paterson, *Happy Dispatches*, p. 39.

52 Davis, *With Both Armies in South Africa*, p. 99.

53 Viljoen, *My Reminiscences of the Anglo Boer War*, p. 27.

54 de Wet, *Three Years War*, p. 43.

55 de Wet, *Three Years War*, p. 43.

56 de Wet, *Three Years War*, p. 44.

57 de Wet, *Three Years War*, p. 44.

58 de Wet, *Three Years War*, p. 44.

59 Pretorius, *Life on Commando During the Anglo-Boer War 1899–1902*, Human and Rousseau, Cape Town, 2000, p. 212 [reported speech].

60 Pretorius, *Life on Commando During the Anglo-Boer War 1899–1902*, p. 212.

61 Paterson, *Happy Dispatches*, p. 129.

62 Paterson, *Happy Dispatches*, p. 34.

63 'Banjo Paterson Meets Kipling', *Barrier Miner*, 17 May 1900, p. 3. https://trove.nla.gov.au/newspaper/article/44256457

64 *Adelaide Observer*, 25 March 1899, p. 13. https://trove.nla.gov.au/newspaper/article/162358040

65 *The Argus*, 24 May 1900, p. 7. https://trove.nla.gov.au/newspaper/article/9542191

66 *The Argus*, 24 May 1900, p. 7.

67 *The Argus*, 24 May 1900, p. 7.

68 Booth family collection.

69 Booth family collection.

70 Drooglever, *From the Front*, p. 305.

71 Paterson, *Happy Dispatches*, p. 17.

72 Ash, *Kruger, Kommandos and Kak*, p. 170.

Chapter Five

1 'Letters From The Front', *The Argus*, 8 June 1900, p. 5. https://trove.nla.gov.au/newspaper/article/9543828

2 Green, *The Story of the Australian Bushmen*, pp. 1–2.

3 Shakespeare, *Julius Caesar*, Act 3, Scene 1.

4 Drooglever, *Colonel Tom's Boys: Being the Regimental History of the 1st and 2nd Victorian Contingents in the Boer War*, Printbooks, South Melbourne, 2013, p. 155.

5 'The Royal Horse Artillery', *The Border Watch*, 22 August 1900, p. 3. https://trove.nla.gov.au/newspaper/article/81041536

6 'Drawing Fire', *Critic* (SA), 11 August 1900, p. 5. https://trove.nla.gov.au/newspaper/article/212144794

7 *The Hawkesbury Advocate*, 13 April 1900, p. 6. https://trove.nla.gov.au/newspaper/article/66369013

8 *The Hawkesbury Advocate*, 13 April 1900, p. 6. https://trove.nla.gov.au/newspaper/article/66369013

9 Booth family collection.

10 Booth family collection.

11 Booth family collection.

12 Booth family collection.

13 Booth family collection [reported speech].

14 Booth family collection.

15 Booth family collection.

16 Booth family oral history.

17 Booth family collection.

18 Reitz, *God Does not Forget*, p. 78.

19 Reitz, *God Does not Forget*, p. 78.

20 Reitz, *God Does not Forget*, p. 78.

21 Reitz, *God Does not Forget*, p. 78 [reported speech].

22 Reitz, *God Does not Forget*, p. 109.

23 Reitz, *God Does not Forget*, p. 114.

24 Hobhouse, *The Brunt of the War*, p. 12.

25 Hobhouse, *The Brunt of the War*, p. 10.

26 Hobhouse, *The Brunt of the War*, p. 10.

27 Reitz, *God Does not Forget*, p. 78.

28 Reitz, *God Does not Forget*, p. 79.

29 Reitz, *God Does not Forget*, p. 79.

30 Reitz, *God Does not Forget*, p. 79.

31 Reitz, *God Does not Forget*, p. 79.

32 Reitz, *God Does not Forget*, p. 79.

33 Reitz, *God Does not Forget*, p. 80.

34 Reitz, *God Does not Forget*, p. 80.

35 Reitz, *God Does not Forget*, p. 80.

36 Reitz, *God Does not Forget*, p. 81.

37 Reitz, *God Does not Forget*, p. 81.

38 Reitz, *God Does not Forget*, p. 82.

39 Booth family collection.

40 Booth family collection.

41 Booth family collection.

42 Fletcher, *Baden-Powell of Mafeking*, Methuen & Co., London, 1900, p. 120.

43 Fletcher, *Baden-Powell of Mafeking*, Methuen & Co., London, 1900, p. 120.

44 Ferguson, *Empire*, p. 278.

45 Ferguson, *Empire*, p. 278.

46 Pretorius, *Life on Commando During the Anglo-Boer War 1899–1902*, p. 147.

47 Reitz, *God Does not Forget*, p. 82.

48 'Taking Johannesburg', *The Argus*, 18 July 1900, p. 11. https://trove.nla.gov.au/newspaper/article/9548475

49 Leslie Stuart, 'Soldiers of the Queen', 1898.
50 'Taking Johannesburg', *The Argus*, 18 July 1900, p. 11. https://trove.nla.gov.au/newspaper/article/9548475
51 Viljoen, *My Reminiscences of the Anglo Boer War*, pp. 50–51.
52 Paterson, *Happy Dispatches*, p. 29 [reported speech].
53 Paterson, *Happy Dispatches*, p. 30.
54 Paterson, *Happy Dispatches*, p. 30.
55 Liddle Hart Centre for Military Archives, HAMILTON: 2/5/15; 1900 Jun 1–1900 Jun 18.
56 Reitz, *God Does not Forget*, p. 88.
57 Booth family collection.
58 Booth family collection.
59 Viljoen, *My Reminiscences of the Anglo Boer War*, p. 148.
60 Reitz, *God Does not Forget*, p. 109.
61 De Lisle papers, Kings College Archives, 3B 40/4, p. 69.
62 Creswicke, *South Africa and the Transvaal War*, TC and EC Jack, 1900, Edinburgh, Vol. V, p. 177.
63 Churchill, *My Early Life*, p. 358.
64 Booth family collection.
65 Christie, 'With the Bush Veldt Carbineers', *Clutha Leader*, Vol. XXVIII, Issue 1564, 25 October 1901.
66 Paterson, 'At The Front', *Sydney Morning Herald*, 21 April 1900, p. 10. https://trove.nla.gov.au/newspaper/article/14307012/1351284
67 Drooglever, *From the Front*, pp. 373–374.
68 Conan Doyle, *Memories and Adventures*, p. 176.
69 Churchill, *My Early Life*, p. 362.
70 *Barrier Miner*, 19 June 1900, p. 2.

Chapter Six

1 'Our Light Horse', *Sydney Morning Herald*, 1 October 1910, p. 5. https://trove.nla.gov.au/newspaper/article/15180556
2 Conan Doyle, *Memories and Adventures*, p. 165.
3 'With The Second Contingent', *Adelaide Observer*, 1 September 1900, p. 4. https://trove.nla.gov.au/newspaper/article/162400824
4 Wilcox, *Australia's Boer War*, p. 86.
5 Bolsman, *Winston Churchill: The Making of a Hero in the South African War*, Galago, Bromley, 2008, p. 240.
6 Churchill, *My Early Life: A Roving Commission*, p. 366.
7 Booth family collection.
8 'At The Front', *Warwick Argus*, 11 August 1900, p. 4. https://trove.nla.gov.au/newspaper/article/76636820
9 Hobhouse, *The Brunt of the War*, p. 14.
10 Drooglever, *From the Front*, p. 377.
11 Gordon, *Chronicles of a Gay Gordon*, Cassell, London, 1921, p. 257.
12 'Mr. Bennet Burleigh', *Sydney Morning Herald*, 19 June 1914, p. 9. https://trove.nla.gov.au/newspaper/article/15517174
13 'Freaks of Harry Harbord Morant, "The Breaker"', *Windsor and Richmond Gazette*, 26 April 1902, p. 14. https://trove.nla.gov.au/newspaper/article/86216522
14 'Freaks of Harry Harbord Morant, "The Breaker"', *Windsor and Richmond Gazette*, 26 April 1902, p. 14.
15 'At Elands River', *Australian Town and Country Journal*, 1 September 1900, p. 21. https://trove.nla.gov.au/newspaper/article/71389036
16 Drooglever, *Colonel Tom's Boys*, p. 223.
17 Drooglever, *Colonel Tom's Boys*, p. 223.
18 Booth family collection.
19 Booth family collection.
20 Reitz, *God Does not Forget*, p. 87.
21 Pretorius, *Life on Commando*, p. 72.

22 'Boers And Bushmen', *The Australian Star*, 7 September 1900, p. 5 [reported speech]. https://trove. nla.gov.au/newspaper/article/230633106

23 'With The Bushmen', *The Inquirer and Commercial News*, 19 October 1900, p. 12. https://trove. nla.gov.au/newspaper/article/670ctl 67824

24 'With The Bushmen', *The Inquirer and Commercial News*, 19 October 1900, p. 12.

25 'With The Bushmen', *The Inquirer and Commercial News*, 19 October 1900, p. 12.

26 'With The Bushmen', *The Inquirer and Commercial News*, 19 October 1900, p. 12.

27 'With The Bushmen', *The Inquirer and Commercial News*, 19 October 1900, p. 12.

28 'With The Bushmen', *The Inquirer and Commercial News*, 19 October 1900, p. 12.

29 'Death of Sergeant-Major Mitchell', *Glen Innes Examiner and General Advertiser*, 26 October 1900, p. 2. https://trove.nla.gov.au/newspaper/article/217835367

30 Green, *The Story of the Australian Bushmen* , p. 82.

31 'Our Boys', *Darling Downs Gazette*, 24 October 1900, p. 3. https://trove.nla.gov.au/newspaper/article/185587676

32 'No Surrender', *The Express and Telegraph*, 27 October 1900, p. 7. https://trove.nla.gov.au/newspaper/article/209544771

33 'Death of Sergeant-Major Mitchell', *Glen Innes Examiner and General Advertiser*, 26 October 1900, p. 2.

34 'Letter from Trooper W. J. Smith', *Cootamundra Herald*, 17 October 1900, p. 4. https://trove.nla.gov.au/newspaper/article/144344868

35 Rintala, 'Made in Birmingham', p. 126.

36 Rintala, 'Made in Birmingham', p. 126.

37 Rintala, 'Made in Birmingham', p. 126.

38 Spender, *The Prime Minister*, George H. Doran Company, New York, 1920, p. 117.

39 Rintala, 'Made in Birmingham', p. 128.

40 Rintala, 'Made in Birmingham', p. 127.

41 'Letters from The Front', *The Ballarat Star*, 24 October 1900, p. 5. https://trove.nla.gov.au/newspaper/article/206979352

42 'The Siege of Elands River Camp', *Sydney Morning Herald*, 9 October 1900, p. 3. https://trove.nla.gov.au/newspaper/article/14373662

43 'The Elands River Fight', *Mount Alexander Mail*, 7 November 1907, p. 2. https://trove.nla.gov.au/newspaper/article/200389870

44 'The Elands River Fight', *Mount Alexander Mail*, 7 November 1907, p. 2.

45 'The Siege of Elands River Camp', *Sydney Morning Herald*, 9 October 1900, p. 3.

46 Frederick Younge Gilbert, 'The Man Who Broke the Bank at Monte Carlo', composed 1891. Baker, *British Music Hall – an illustrated history*, Pen & Sword Social, Barnsley, 2014.

47 'The Bare Belled Ewe', *Bacchus Marsh Express*, 5 December 1891, p. 5. https://trove.nla.gov.au/newspaper/article/89280995

48 'The Siege of Elands River Camp', *Sydney Morning Herald*, 9 October 1900, p. 3.

49 'The Siege of Elands River Camp', *Sydney Morning Herald*, 9 October 1900, p. 3.

50 'No Surrender', *The Express and Telegraph*, 27 October 1900, p. 7.

51 'The Siege of Elands River Camp', *Sydney Morning Herald*, 9 October 1900, p. 3.

52 'The Siege of Elands River Camp', *Sydney Morning Herald*, 9 October 1900, p. 3.

Chapter Seven

1 Buchan, *The African Colony*, William Blackwood and Sons, London, 1903, p. 107.

2 Conan Doyle, *The Great Boer War*, p. 484.

3 'Eland's River', *The Argus*, 3 August 1901, p. 13. https://trove.nla.gov.au/newspaper/article/10564541?

4 Green, *The Story of the Australian Bushmen*, p. 95.

5 Green, *The Story of the Australian Bushmen*, p. 95.

6 Green, *The Story of the Australian Bushmen*, p. 96.

7 Green, *The Story of the Australian Bushmen*, p. 95.

8 'No Surrender', *The Express and Telegraph*, 27 October 1900, p. 7.

9 'Death of Sergeant-Major Mitchell', *Glen Innes Examiner and General Advertiser*, 26 October 1900, p. 2.

10 'The Siege of Elands River Camp', *Sydney Morning Herald*, 9 October 1900, p. 3.

11 'Elands River Siege', *The Capricornian*, 20 October 1900, p. 43.

12 'No surrender', *The Express and Telegraph*, 27 October 1900.

13 'Siege of Elands River Camp', *Glen Innes Examiner and General Advertiser*, 14 December 1900. p. 4. https://trove.nla.gov.au/newspaper/article/217835676

14 Green, *The Story of the Australian Bushmen*, pp. 97–98.

15 'The Siege of Elands River Camp', *Sydney Morning Herald*, 9 October 1900, p. 3.

16 'The Fight Against Fearful Odds', *The Catholic Press*, 13 October 1900, p. 22. https://trove.nla.gov.au/newspaper/article/104658555

17 'No Surrender', *The Express and Telegraph*, 27 October 1900, p. 7.

18 'No Surrender', *The Express and Telegraph*, 27 October 1900, p. 7.

19 'From Walter J. Smith', *Cootamundra Herald*, 21 November 1900, p. 3. https://trove.nla.gov.au/newspaper/article/144344669

20 'No Surrender', *The Express and Telegraph*, 27 October 1900, p. 7.

21 'With The Third Queensland Contingent', *The Northern Miner* (Qld), 26 October 1900, p. 6. https://trove.nla.gov.au/newspaper/article/79795642

22 'Letter from Lieutenant Zouch', *Goulburn Evening Penny Post*, 18 October 1900, p. 4. https://trove.nla.gov.au/newspaper/article/98699859

23 Personal papers of Lieutenant Robert Gartside, AWM 3DRL 7274.

24 'No Surrender', *The Express and Telegraph*, 27 October 1900, p. 7.

25 'No Surrender', *The Express and Telegraph*, 27 October 1900, p. 7.

26 'No Surrender', *The Express and Telegraph*, 27 October 1900, p. 7.

27 'No Surrender', *The Express and Telegraph*, 27 October 1900, p. 7.

28 'No Surrender', *The Express and Telegraph*, 27 October 1900, p. 7.

29 'No Surrender', *The Express and Telegraph*, 27 October 1900, p. 7.

30 'Death of Sergeant-Major Mitchell', *Glen Innes Examiner and General Advertiser*, 26 October 1900, p. 2.

31 'The Late John Wadell', *The Sydney Mail and New South Wales Advertiser*, 27 October 1900, p. 999. https://trove.nla.gov.au/newspaper/article/163695999

32 'Death of Sergeant-Major Mitchell', *Glen Innes Examiner and General Advertiser*, 26 October 1900, p. 2.

33 'Death of Sergeant-Major Mitchell', *Glen Innes Examiner and General Advertiser*, 26 October 1900, p. 2.

34 'Death of Sergeant-Major Mitchell', *Glen Innes Examiner and General Advertiser*, 26 October 1900, p. 2.

35 'Eland's River Siege', *The Telegraph* (Qld), 9 October 1900, p. 2. https://trove.nla.gov.au/newspaper/article/175286485

36 'The Fight Against Fearful Odds', *The Catholic Press*, 13 October 1900, p. 22. https://trove.nla.gov.au/newspaper/article/104658555

37 'The Story of Elands River', *South Bourke and Mornington Journal*, 20 June 1912, p. 4. https://trove.nla.gov.au/newspaper/article/66180795

38 'Hero Of Elands River', *Weekly Times* (Vic), 19 January 1901, p. 19. https://trove.nla.gov.au/newspaper/article/223797265

39 'The Siege of Elands River Camp', *Sydney Morning Herald*, 9 October 1900, p. 3. https://trove.nla.gov.au/newspaper/article/14373662

40 'The Siege of Elands River Camp', *Sydney Morning Herald*, 9 October 1900, p. 3.

41 'The Siege of Elands River Camp', *Sydney Morning Herald*, 9 October 1900, p. 3.

42 'The Siege of Elands River Camp', *Sydney Morning Herald*, 9 October 1900, p. 3.

43 'The Siege of Elands River Camp', *Sydney Morning Herald*, 9 October 1900, p. 3.

44 'The Siege of Elands River Camp', *Sydney Morning Herald*, 9 October 1900, p. 3.

45 'Australian Soldiers in South Africa', *The Cobden Times and Heytesbury Advertiser*, 5 August 1914, p. 3. https://trove.nla.gov.au/newspaper/article/122875320

46 'With The Third Queensland Contingent', *The Northern Miner*, 26 October 1900, p. 6 [reported speech]. https://trove.nla.gov.au/newspaper/article/79795642

47 'The Elands River Fight', *Mount Alexander Mail*, 7 November 1907, p. 3. https://trove.nla.gov.au/newspaper/article/200389870

48 'The Fight Against Fearful Odds', *The Catholic Press*, 13 October 1900, p. 22.

49 Hubert Murray, quoted in Australian Boer War Memorial. https://www.bwm.org.au/warcourse/Elands_River.php

50 AWM 3DRL 7274, Personal papers of Lieutenant Robert Gartside, 5 August 1900 [reported speech].

51 AWM 3DRL 7274, Personal papers of Lieutenant Robert Gartside, 5 August 1900.

52 'Elands River Camp', *The Week*, 19 October 1900, p. 11. https://trove.nla.gov.au/newspaper/article/182860605

53 'The Story of Elands River', *South Bourke and Mornington Journal*, 20 June 1912, p. 4 [reported speech].

54 'To The Editor Of The Herald', *Sydney Morning Herald*, 16 February 1904, p. 6. https://trove.nla.gov.au/newspaper/article/14600063

55 'No Surrender', *The Express and Telegraph*, 27 October 1900, p. 7.

56 'The Siege of Elands River Camp', *Sydney Morning Herald*, 9 October 1900, p. 3.

57 'The Siege of Elands River Camp', *Sydney Morning Herald*, 9 October 1900, p. 3.

58 Wilcox, *Australia's Boer War*, p. 124.

59 Reitz, *God Does not Forget*, p. 107.

60 'With the Bushmen's Contingent', *The Braidwood Dispatch and Mining Journal*, 22 September 1900, p. 4. https://trove.nla.gov.au/newspaper/article/100201633

61 Green, *The Story of the Australian Bushmen*, p. 107.

62 Green, *The Story of the Australian Bushmen*, p. 107.

63 Green, *The Story of the Australian Bushmen*, p. 107.

64 Green, *The Story of the Australian Bushmen*, p. 108 [reported speech].

65 Green, *The Story of the Australian Bushmen*, p. 108.

66 'Siege of Elands River Camp', *Glen Innes Examiner and General Advertiser*, 14 December 1900, p. 4.

67 National Archive WO 105/10 12067197, p. 7.

68 'With The Third Queensland Contingent', *The Northern Miner*, 26 October 1900, p. 6. https://trove.nla.gov.au/newspaper/article/79795642

69 'The Elands River Fight', *Mount Alexander Mail*, 7 November 1907, p. 2. https://trove.nla.gov.au/newspaper/article/200389870

70 *Cootamundra Herald*, 17 October 1900, p. 4. https://trove.nla.gov.au/newspaper/article/144344868

71 'The Elands River Fight', *Mount Alexander Mail*, 7 November 1907, p. 2.

72 'Elands River Siege', *The Capricornian*, 20 October 1900, p. 43. https://trove.nla.gov.au/newspaper/article/68244938/6792325

73 'Elands River Siege', *The Capricornian*, 20 October 1900, p. 43.

74 'The Diary Of A Siege', *The Queenslander*, 20 October 1900, p. 823. https://trove.nla.gov.au/newspaper/article/21249834

75 'Trooper F. Craig's Story', *The Week*, 19 October 1900, p. 12. https://trove.nla.gov.au/newspaper/article/182860914

76 Baden-Powell, Diary, Aug 1900, NAM Archives 6411-1-7 7.

77 Green, *The Story of the Australian Bushmen*, p. 119.

78 Green, *The Story of the Australian Bushmen*, p. 118.

79 'No Surrender', *The Express and Telegraph*, 27 October 1900, p. 7.

80 'Elands River', *The Brisbane Courier*, 21 May 1901, p. 14. https://trove.nla.gov.au/newspaper/article/19108314

81 'The Elands River Battle', *Warwick Examiner and Times*, 17 October 1900, p. 2. https://trove.nla.gov.au/newspaper/article/82161031

82 'Elands River Siege', *The Capricornian*, 20 October 1900, p. 43.

83 'No Surrender', *The Express and Telegraph*, 27 October 1900, p. 7.

Chapter Eight

1 'The Birth of a Tradition', *The Canberra Times*, 19 January 1974, p. 11. https://trove.nla.gov.au/newspaper/article/110757352

2 'The Fight at Rustenburg', *Bathurst Free Press and Mining Journal*, 24 September 1900, p. 2. https://trove.nla.gov.au/newspaper/article/63874866

3 Roberts to Hamilton, 6 August 1900, National Archive, WO105/37, S19.

4 Green, *The Story of the Australian Bushmen*, p. 115.

5 'Death of Sergeant-Major Mitchell', *Glen Innes Examiner and General Advertiser*, 26 October 1900, p. 2.

6 'The Diary Of A Siege', *The Queenslander*, 20 October 1900, p. 823. https://trove.nla.gov.au/newspaper/article/21249834

7 'Australian Soldiers in South Africa', *The Cobden Times and Heytesbury Advertiser*, 5 August 1914, p. 3. https://trove.nla.gov.au/newspaper/article/122875320

8 'Siege of Elands River Camp', *Glen Innes Examiner and General Advertiser*, 14 December 1900, p. 4.

9 Green, *The Story of the Australian Bushmen*, pp. 116–117.

10 'A Credit To Their Country', *The Daily Telegraph*, 29 October 1900, p. 7. https://trove.nla.gov.au/newspaper/article/237119596

11 'The Elands River Battle', *Warwick Examiner and Times*, 17 October 1900, p. 2 [reported speech]. https://trove.nla.gov.au/newspaper/article/82161031

12 'The Elands River Battle', *Warwick Examiner and Times*, 17 October 1900, p. 2.

13 'The Elands River Battle', *Warwick Examiner and Times*, 17 October 1900, p. 2.

14 'The Fight Against Fearful Odds', *The Catholic Press*, 13 October 1900, p. 22. https://trove.nla.gov.au/newspaper/article/104658555

15 'Colonel Hore At Elands River', *Sydney Morning Herald*, 25 October 1900, p. 7. https://trove.nla.gov.au/newspaper/article/14343456

16 'Elands River', *Examiner*, 16 October 1900, p. 3. https://trove.nla.gov.au/newspaper/article/35374778

17 'No Surrender', *The Express and Telegraph*, 27 October 1900, p. 7.

18 Green, *The Story of the Australian Bushmen*, p. 118.

19 'The Fight Against Fearful Odds', *The Catholic Press*, 13 October 1900, p. 22.

20 'The Siege of Elands River Camp', *The Sydney Morning Herald*, 9 October 1900, p. 3.

21 Odgers, *Army Australia: An illustrated history*, Child & Associates, Frenchs Forest, 1988, p. 41.

22 'Battle Ballad', *The Beverley Times*, 4 September 1958, p. 6. https://trove.nla.gov.au/newspaper/article/202787582

23 'The Fight Against Fearful Odds', *The Catholic Press*, 13 October 1900, p. 22.

24 'Siege Of Elands River', *Darling Downs Gazette*, 22 October 1900, p. 3. https://trove.nla.gov.au/newspaper/article/185585232

25 'A Cairns Hero', *Morning Post*, 27 November 1900, p. 3. https://trove.nla.gov.au/newspaper/article/42943952

26 'Letter from Trooper W. J. Smith', *Cootamundra Herald*, 17 October 1900, p. 4 [reported speech]. https://trove.nla.gov.au/newspaper/article/144344868

27 'The Fight Against Fearful Odds', *The Catholic Press*, 13 October 1900, p. 22.

28 Letter from Trooper W. J. Smith', *Cootamundra Herald*, 17 October 1900, p. 4 [reported speech].

29 'The Fight Against Fearful Odds', *The Catholic Press*, 13 October 1900, p. 22.

30 'No Surrender', *The Express and Telegraph*, 27 October 1900, p. 7.

31 'Death of Sergeant-Major Mitchell', *Glen Innes Examiner and General Advertiser*, 26 October 1900, p. 2.

32 'Letters From Camp', *The Kerang Times*, 16 October 1900, p. 3. https://trove.nla.gov.au/newspaper/article/221118610/23306243

33 'Letters From Camp', *The Kerang Times*, 16 October 1900, p. 3.

34 'Letters From Camp', *The Kerang Times*, 16 October 1900, p. 3.

35 Banjo Paterson, *Happy Dispatches*, pp. 34–35.

36 *The Clarence River Advocate*, 31 August 1900, p. 8. https://trove.nla.gov.au/newspaper/article/120224543

37 Correspondence, Kitchener to Brodrick, Kitchener Papers, NA WO 30 57 22 (1), p. 65.

38 'Elands River Siege', *The Telegraph* (Qld), 10 October 1900, p. 2.

39 'Home From The War', *Sydney Morning Herald*, 20 October 1900, p. 10. https://trove.nla.gov.au/newspaper/article/14345754/1345046

40 'Elands River', *Daily Mercury*, 25 June 1912, p. 2. https://trove.nla.gov.au/newspaper/article/168628612

41 'The Fight Against Fearful Odds', *The Catholic Press*, 13 October 1900, p. 22.

42 Telegram, Roberts to Hamilton, 14 August 1900, Hamilton Papers, King's College, 2/6/8 14.

43 de Wet, *Three Years War*, p. 104.

44 'The Story of Elands River', *South Bourke and Mornington Journal*, 20 June 1912, p. 4. https://trove.nla.gov.au/newspaper/article/66180795

45 Green, *The Story of the Australian Bushmen*, p. 121.

46 Green, *The Story of the Australian Bushmen*, p. 121.

47 'Elands River', *Daily Mercury*, 25 June 1912, p. 2.

48 'Eland's River Siege', *The Week*, 12 October 1900, p. 23. https://trove.nla.gov.au/newspaper/article/182860215

49 'The Birth of a Tradition', *The Canberra Times*, 19 January 1974, p. 11. https://trove.nla.gov.au/newspaper/article/110757352

50 'No Surrender', *The Express and Telegraph*, 27 October 1900, p. 7.

51 'At Elands River', *The Age*, 13 October 1900, p. 9. https://trove.nla.gov.au/newspaper/article/188649458

52 'Letters from the Front', *The Scrutineer and Berrima District Press*, 17 October 1900, p. 2. https://trove.nla.gov.au/newspaper/article/125084354

53 'The Siege of Elands River Camp', *Sydney Morning Herald*, 9 October 1900, p. 3.

54 Green, *The Story of the Australian Bushmen*, p. 126.

55 Green, *The Story of the Australian Bushmen*, p. 126.

56 'Siege of Elands River Camp', *Glen Innes Examiner and General Advertiser*, 14 December 1900, p. 4. https://trove.nla.gov.au/newspaper/article/217835676

57 Smuts, *Memoirs of the Boer War*, Jonathon Ball, Johannesburg, 1994, p. 102.

58 'The Elands River Battle', *Warwick Examiner and Times*, 17 October 1900, p. 2. https://trove.nla.gov.au/newspaper/article/82161031

59 'Abide With Me', hymn written by Henry Francis Lyte in 1847.

60 'The Siege of Elands River Camp', *Sydney Morning Herald*, 9 October 1900, p. 3.

61 'No Surrender', *The Express and Telegraph*, 27 October 1900, p. 7.

62 Green, *The Story of the Australian Bushmen*, p. 127.

63 'Story of Elands River', *Dungog Chronicle: Durham and Gloucester Advertiser*, 15 March 1901, p. 5. https://trove.nla.gov.au/newspaper/article/137935597

64 Smuts, *Memoirs of the Boer War*, p. 102.

65 Conan Doyle, *The Great Boer War*, p. 484; 'The Real Australians', *The Queenbeyan Observer*, 3 June 1902, p. 3. https://trove.nla.gov.au/newspaper/article/237941768

Chapter Nine

1 Morant, *The Poetry of Breaker Morant*, Golden Press, Hong Kong, 1980, p. 27.

2 Trooper Muir Churton, interviewed by Frank Shields in the mid-1970s.

3 Meiring, *Against the Tide: A Story of Women in War*, iUniverse, USA, 2009, p. 213.

4 Burnett, *The 18th Hussars in South Africa*, Warren & Son, Winchester, 1905, p. 309.

5 Burnett, *The 18th Hussars in South Africa*, p. 310.

6 Hobhouse, *The Brunt of the War*, p. 29.

7 *Morning Bulletin* (Rockhampton), 24 September 1900, p. 6. https://trove.nla.gov.au/newspaper/article/52584041

8 *South African Journal of Military Studies*, Vol. 11, No. 3, 1981, p. 24.

9 *Sydney Morning Herald*, 7 September 1900, p. 5. https://trove.nla.gov.au/newspaper/article/14334892

10 Liddle Hart Centre for Military Archives, HAMILTON: 2/6/13.

11 Hobhouse, *Report of a Visit to the Camps of Women and Children in the Cape and Orange River Colonies*, Friars Printing Association Limited, London, 1901, p. 3.

12 Harbord, *Froth And Bubble*, E. Arnold, London, 1915, p. 196.

13 Booth family collection.

14 Booth family oral history.

15 *Adelaide Observer*, 29 December 1900, p. 4. https://trove.nla.gov.au/newspaper/article/162423318/19010539

16 Hobhouse, *The Brunt of the War*, p. 214 [reported speech].

17 Hobhouse, *The Brunt of the War*, p. 214 [reported speech].

18 'Banjo's Estimate of the Boers', *The Cumberland Argus and Fruitgrowers Advocate*, 25 August 1900, p. 12. https://trove.nla.gov.au/newspaper/article/85824785

19 'War Correspondents', *Truth* (Qld), 30 September 1900, p. 6. https://trove.nla.gov.au/newspaper/article/200507944

20 'War Correspondents', *Truth* (Qld), 30 September 1900, p. 6.

21 '"Banjo" Paterson', *The Clipper* (Tas), 10 November 1900, p. 3. https://trove.nla.gov.au/newspaper/article/83082968

22 'War Correspondents', *Truth* (Qld), 30 September 1900, p. 6.

23 Paterson, 'Now Listen To Me And I'll Tell You My Views', *The Bulletin*, 29 March 1902.

24 Hobhouse, *The Brunt of the War*, p. 20.

25 Hobhouse, *The Brunt of the War*, p. 93.

26 Storey, *Great British Adventurers*, Casemate Publishers, 2012, p. 58.

27 The South African Military History Society, Tyrrell, 'Melrose House', *Military History Journal*, Vol. 1, No. 2, June 1968, http://samilitaryhistory.org/vol012at.html

28 'Letter from Trooper Oakes, Burning the Homesteads', *The Grafton Argus and Clarence River General Advertiser*, 23 November 1900, p. 4. https://trove.nla.gov.au/newspaper/article/234783514

29 Booth family collection.

30 'The Horrors Of War', *Barrier Miner*, 25 May 1901, p. 5 [reported speech]. https://trove.nla.gov.au/newspaper/article/44322490

31 'The Horrors Of War', *Barrier Miner*, 25 May 1901, p. 5.

32 Raath and Louw, *Vroueleed, Die Lotgevalle van die vroue en kinders buite die konsentrasiekampe 1899–1902*, p. 106. https://www.labuschagne.info/scorched-earth.htm#.Xwa5SucRVPY

33 Pakenham, *The Boer War*, p. 429.

34 Reitz, *God Does not Forget*, p. 113 [reported speech].

35 Reitz, *God Does not Forget*, p. 113.

36 Reitz, *God Does not Forget*, p. 113.

37 Reitz, *God Does not Forget*, p. 114.

38 Viljoen, *My Reminiscences of the Anglo Boer War*, p. 76.

39 Magnus, *Kitchener: Portrait of an Imperialist*, John Murray, London, 1958, p. 177.

40 Rintala, 'Made in Birmingham', p. 56.

41 Jewell, 'Using Barbaric Methods in South Africa: The British Concentration Camp Policy During the Anglo-Boer War', *Scientia Militaria*, Vol. 31, No. 1, 2003, p. 11.

42 Hobhouse, *The Brunt of the War*, p. 45.

43 Ash, *Kruger, Kommandos and Kak*, p. 353.

44 *The Bulletin*, 5 January 1901, p. 10.

45 Aitken, 'Guerrilla Warfare, October 1900 – May 1902: Boer attacks on the Pretoria–Delagoa Bay Railway Line', *Military History Journal*, Vol. 11, No. 6, The South African Military History Society, December 2000. http://samilitaryhistory.org/vol116da.html

46 Aitken, 'Guerrilla Warfare, October 1900 – May 1902: Boer attacks on the Pretoria–Delagoa Bay Railway Line', *Military History Journal*, Vol. 11, No. 6, The South African Military History Society, 2000 [reported speech].

47 Reitz, *God Does not Forget*, p. 134.

48 Reitz, *God Does not Forget*, p. 134 [reported speech].

49 Reitz, *God Does not Forget*, p. 134.

50 Hobhouse, *Report of a Visit to the Camps*, p. 4.

51 Hobhouse, *Report of a Visit to the Camps*, p. 4.

52 Hobhouse, *The Brunt of the War*, p. 214.

53 Hobhouse, *The Brunt of the War*, p. 215 [reported speech].

54 Hobhouse, *Report of a Visit to the Camps*, p. 4.

55 Ferguson, *Empire*, p. 280.

56 Letter, Kitchener to Roberts, 25 January 1901, NA WO 9609-48-1.

57 Kitchener papers, NA WO 9609-48-1, 8 Feb 1901.

58 Spender, *General Botha*, Houghton Mifflin Company, New York, 1916, p. 114.

59 Spender, *General Botha*, p.114.

60 Ash, *Kruger, Kommandos and Kak*, p. 699.

61 Lee, *General Sir Ian Hamilton: A Soldier's Life*, Pan, London, 2000, p. 69.

62 West and Roper, *Breaker Morant*, p. 43.

63 Kitchener to Roberts, Letter, 25 January 1901, Kitchener Papers NA WO 9609-48-1.

64 'Colonial Soldiers in London', *Chronicle*, 23 March 1901, p. 18. https://trove.nla.gov.au/newspaper/article/87718647

65 'Colonial Soldiers in London', *Chronicle*, 23 March 1901, p. 18.

66 Kitchener to Brodrick, 1 February 1901, Kitchener papers, Correspondence William St John Brodrick and Lord Kitchener, PRO 30 57 22 (1) p. 64.

67 Kitchener to Brodrick, 1 February 1901, p. 65.

68 West and Roper, *Breaker Morant*, p. 87.

69 Kitchener to Roberts, November 1901, Kitchener Papers, WO 9609-48-1 K to R 22.

70 Davey, *Breaker Morant and the Bushveldt Carbineers*, Van Riebeeck Society, Cape Town, 1987, preface xviii.

71 NA WO 126/100 Attestation form for BVC.

72 *Hawkesbury Herald*, 15 August 1902, p. 5. https://trove.nla.gov.au/newspaper/article/66352110

73 'Statement by a Carbineer', *The Scone Advocate*, 11 April 1902, p. 3. https://trove.nla.gov.au/newspaper/article/156370892

74 Denton, *Closed File*, Rigby, Adelaide, 1983, p. 67.

75 'Complimentary Supper', *Otago Witness*, Issue 2654, 25 January 1905 [reported speech].

76 'Complimentary Supper', *Otago Witness*, Issue 2654, 25 January 1905 [reported speech].

77 West and Roper, *Breaker Morant*, p. 94.

78 Carnegie and Shields, *In Search of Breaker Morant*, p. 55.

79 Kitchener papers, Kitchener to Brodrick, NA 30 57 22 (1), 29 March 1901, p. 125.

80 Arthur, *Life of Lord Kitchener*, MacMillan and Co., Limited, London, 1920, p. 24.

81 Hobhouse, *The Brunt of the War*, p. 100.

82 Ash, *Kruger, Kommandos and Kak*, p. 325 [reported speech].

83 Conan Doyle, *The War in Africa: Its Causes and Conduct*, McClure, London, 1902, p. 140 [reported speech].

84 Hobhouse, *The Brunt of the War*, p. 66.

85 Ash, *Kruger, Kommandos and Kak*, p. 325.

86 Ash, *Kruger, Kommandos and Kak*, p. 516.

87 'Women and Children in White Concentration Camps During Anglo-Boer War 1900–1902', South African History Online, https://www.sahistory.org.za/article/women-and-children-white-concentration-camps-during-anglo-boer-war-1900-1902

88 Spender, *General Botha*, p. 113.

89 Reitz, *God Does not Forget*, p.147.

90 Reitz, *God Does not Forget*, p. 148.

91 Creswicke, *South Africa and the Transvaal War*, p. 196.

92 'Stonewall Kitchener's Blockhouses', *Evelyn Observer and South and East Bourke Record*, 30 May 1902, p. 4. https://trove.nla.gov.au/newspaper/article/64029064

93 'Stonewall Kitchener's Blockhouses', *Evelyn Observer and South and East Bourke Record*, 30 May 1902, p. 4.

94 'Stonewall Kitchener's Blockhouses', *Evelyn Observer and South and East Bourke Record*, 30 May 1902, p. 4.

95 Kitchener Papers, PRO 30 57 22 (1), 22nd 1901 March, Kitchener to Brodrick, p. 119.

Chapter Ten

1 *Macquarie Advocate*, 10 February 1900, p. 6.

2 *The Argus*, 11 April 1901, p. 5. https://trove.nla.gov.au/newspaper/article/10544966

3 Changuion, *Pietersburg. Die eerste eeu – 1886–1986*.

4 Changuion, *Pietersburg: Die eerste eeu – 1886–1986*, p. 55.

5 Witton, *Scapegoats of the Empire*, Oxford City Press, 2010, p. 35.

6 *The Argus*, 11 April 1901, p. 5.

7 'Boer War Leaders', *The Inquirer and Commercial News*, 8 December 1899, p. 11. https://trove.nla.gov.au/newspaper/article/67195170

8 West and Roper, *Breaker Morant*, p. 225 [reported speech].

9 West and Roper, *Breaker Morant*, p. 225.

10 Davey, *Breaker Morant and the Bushveldt Carbineers*, pp. 8–9.

11 Fox, *Breaker Morant – Bushman and Buccaneer*, H.T. Dunn & Co., 1902, p. 49.

12 Christie, 'With the Bush Veldt Carbineers', *Clutha Leader*, Vol. XXVIII, Issue 1572, 22 November 1901. https://paperspast.natlib.govt.nz/newspapers/CL19011011.2.10

13 Bleszynski, *Shoot Straight, You Bastards!*, p. 194.

14 Christie, 'With the Bush Veldt Carbineers', *Clutha Leader*, Vol. XXVIII, Issue 1560, 11 October 1901.

15 'Complimentary Supper', *Otago Witness*, Issue 2654, 25 January 1905 [reported speech].

16 Davey, *Breaker Morant and the Bushveldt Carbineers*, pp. 9–12.

17 Christie, 'With the Bush Veldt Carbineers', 11 October 1901. https://paperspast.natlib.govt.nz/newspapers/CL19011011.2.10

18 Carnegie and Shields, *In Search of Breaker Morant*, p. 58.

19 Christie, 'With the Bush Veldt Carbineers', 11 October 1901.

20 Christie, 'With the Bush Veldt Carbineers', 11 October 1901.

21 Davey, *Breaker Morant and the Bushveldt Carbineers*, p. xxvi.

22 Davey, *Breaker Morant and the Bushveldt Carbineers*, p. xxvi.

23 'To Thomas Moore', Byron, *The Works of Lord Byron*, A.&W. Galignani, Paris, 1826, p. 541.

24 *Newcastle Herald*, 17 September 1904, p. 7. https://trove.nla.gov.au/newspaper/article/250936699

25 Hobhouse, The *Brunt of the War, and Where it Fell*, p. 214.

26 Hobhouse, *Report of a Visit to the Camps of Women and Children*, p. 4.

27 Hobhouse, *Report of a Visit to the Camps of Women and Children*, p. 5.

28 Hobhouse, *Report of a Visit to the Camps of Women and Children*, p. 10.

29 Hobhouse, *Report of a Visit to the Camps of Women and Children*, p. 9.

30 Carnegie and Shields, *In Search of Breaker Morant*, p. 53.

31 Carnegie and Shields, *In Search of Breaker Morant*, p. 53.

32 West and Roper, *Breaker Morant*, p. 128.

33 Davey, *Breaker Morant and the Bushveldt Carbineers*, pp. 12–13.

34 'The Vlakfontein Murders', *The Walcha Witness and Vernon County Record*, 14 September 1901, p. 2. https://trove.nla.gov.au/newspaper/article/194098880

35 'The Vlakfontein Murders', *The Walcha Witness and Vernon County Record*, 14 September 1901, p. 2.

36 'The Vlakfontein Murders', *The Walcha Witness and Vernon County Record*, 14 September 1901, p. 2.

37 'The Battle Of Vlakfontein', *Queensland Times*, 9 July 1901, p. 5. https://trove.nla.gov.au/newspaper/article/122952898

38 Hobhouse, *Report of a Visit to the Camps of Women and Children*, p. 5.

39 Spender, *The Prime Minister*, p. 120. http://www.gutenberg.org/files/60179/60179-h/60179-h.htm

40 Hobhouse, *The Brunt of the War, and Where it Fell*, p. 140.

41 Hewison, *Hedge of Wild Almonds: South Africa, the Pro-Boers & the Quaker Conscience, 1890–1910*, James Curry Publishers, Suffolk, 1989, p. 197.

42 Krebs, *Gender, Race, and the Writing of Empire: Public Discourse and the Boer War*, Cambridge University Press, Cambridge, 2004, p. 73.

43 Speech at the Holborn Restaurant (14 June 1901), quoted in John Wilson, *C.B.: A Life of Sir Henry Campbell-Bannerman*, Constable, London, 1973, p. 349.

44 Armstrong, *Judge Not*, Xlibris, London, 2017, p. 235.

45 Leach, *The Legend of Breaker Morant is Dead and Buried*, p. 16.

46 'The Three Mutineers', *Geelong Advertiser*, 18 December 1901, p. 4. https://trove.nla.gov.au/newspaper/article/150297926

47 Droogleever, *Colonel Tom's Boys*, p. 94.

48 'The Three Mutineers', *Geelong Advertiser*, 18 December 1901, p. 4 [reported speech].

49 'The Fifth Victorians', *The Daily Telegraph* (NSW), 28 October 1901, p. 5. https://trove.nla.gov.au/newspaper/article/237364119

50 'The Three Mutineers', *Geelong Advertiser*, 18 December 1901, p. 4.

51 'The Three Mutineers', *Geelong Advertiser*, 18 December 1901, p. 4.

52 'The Three Mutineers', *Geelong Advertiser*, 18 December 1901, p. 4.

53 *The Age*, 28 October 1901, p. 5. https://trove.nla.gov.au/newspaper/article/192210809

54 'The Three Mutineers', *Geelong Advertiser*, 18 December 1901, p. 4.

55 'The Three Mutineers', *Geelong Advertiser*, 18 December 1901, p. 4.
56 *The Sydney Mail and New South Wales Advertiser*, 2 November 1901, p. 1105. https://trove.nla.gov.au/newspaper/article/165238310/17334470
57 Lines from Robert Louis Stevenson's poem 'Requiem'.
58 Growden, *Major Thomas*, Affirm Press, Melbourne, 2019, p. 113.

Chapter Eleven

1 'The Breaker again', *Windsor and Richmond Gazette*, 5 March 1904, p. 12. https://trove.nla.gov.au/newspaper/article/85890555
2 *Kalgoorlie Western Argus*, 3 June 1902, pp. 2, 43. https://trove.nla.gov.au/newspaper/article/32611356
3 *Kalgoorlie Western Argus*, 3 June 1902, pp. 2, 43.
4 *Kalgoorlie Western Argus*, 3 June 1902, pp. 2, 43.
5 *Sydney Morning Herald*, 22 May 1902, p. 4. https://trove.nla.gov.au/newspaper/article/14464470
6 *Sydney Morning Herald*, 22 May 1902, p. 4.
7 *Sydney Morning Herald*, 22 May 1902, p. 4.
8 *Sydney Morning Herald*, 22 May 1902, p. 4.
9 Davey, *Breaker Morant and the Bushveldt Carbineers*, p. 92 [reported speech].
10 'The Bushveldt Carbineers', *The Advertiser* (Adelaide), 8 May 1902, p. 3. https://trove.nla.gov.au/newspaper/article/4917213
11 Davey, *Breaker Morant and the Bushveldt Carbineers*, p. 95 (from George Heath deposition).
12 Davey, *Breaker Morant and the Bushveldt Carbineers*, p. 95 [reported speech].
13 Davey, *Breaker Morant and the Bushveldt Carbineers*, p. 95.
14 Davey, *Breaker Morant and the Bushveldt Carbineers*, p. 96.
15 Davey, *Breaker Morant and the Bushveldt Carbineers*, p. 96.
16 Leach, *The Legend of Breaker Morant is Dead and Buried*, p. 20.
17 Davey, *Breaker Morant and the Bushveldt Carbineers*, p. 83.
18 West and Roper, *Breaker Morant*, p. 125.
19 'Court-Martialled Australians', *The Argus*, 21 May 1902, p. 7 [reported speech]. https://trove.nla.gov.au/newspaper/article/9059750
20 *Sydney Morning Herald*, 22 May 1902, p. 4.
21 Witton, *Scapegoats of the Empire*, 2010, p. 90.
22 Green, *The Story of the Australian Bushmen*, p. 46.
23 Green, *The Story of the Australian Bushmen*, p. 47.
24 Carnegie and Shields, *In Search of Breaker Morant*, pp. 56–58.
25 West and Roper, *Breaker Morant*, p. 125.
26 West and Roper, *Breaker Morant*, p. 126.
27 Leach, *The Legend of Breaker Morant is Dead and Buried*, p. 26.
28 Bleszynski, *Shoot Straight, You Bastards!*, p. 136.
29 'A Chaplain at the Front', *The Mercury*, 28 May 1902, p. 6. https://trove.nla.gov.au/newspaper/article/9582968
30 Davey, *Breaker Morant and the Bushveldt Carbineers*, pp. 21–22 [reported speech].
31 Davey, *Breaker Morant and the Bushveldt Carbineers*, pp. 21–22.
32 Davey, *Breaker Morant and the Bushveldt Carbineers*, pp. 21–22.
33 Davey, *Breaker Morant and the Bushveldt Carbineers*, p. 24.
34 Witton, *Scapegoats of the Empire*, 2010, p. 34.
35 'Fort Hendrina Makhado', http://www.theheritageportal.co.za/thread/fort-hendrina-makhado and van Zyl, Anton, 'The Story of the Zoutpansberg's last three forts', *Zoutpansberger*, 29 September 2017. https://www.zoutpansberger.co.za/articles/news/44226/2017-09-29/the-story-of-the-zoutpansbergas-last-three-forts
36 Christie, 'With the Bush Veldt Carbineers', *Clutha Leader*, Vol. XXVIII, Issue 1580, 20 December 1901.
37 West and Roper, *Breaker Morant*, p. 132.
38 Carnegie and Shields, *In Search of Breaker Morant*, p. 65.
39 Carnegie and Shields, *In Search of Breaker Morant*, p. 63.
40 Davey, *Breaker Morant and the Bushveldt Carbineers*, pp. 28–30.

41 'With The Bushveldt Carbineers', *The Express and Telegraph*, 30 April 1902, p. 3. https://trove.nla.gov.au/newspaper/article/209146026
42 'With The Bushveldt Carbineers', *The Express and Telegraph*, 30 April 1902, p. 3.
43 'With The Bushveldt Carbineers', *The Express and Telegraph*, 30 April 1902, p. 3.
44 Hannam, 'The Bushveldt Carbineers', *Manawatu Standard*, Vol. XL, Issue 7329, 24 June 1902.
45 'The Bushveldt Carbineers', *Queensland Times, Ipswich Herald and General Advertiser*, 12 April 1902, p. 12. https://trove.nla.gov.au/newspaper/article/122553344
46 Hannam 'The Bushveldt Carbineers', *Manawatu Standard*, Vol. XL, Issue 7329, 24 June 1902.

Chapter Twelve

1 'With The Bushveldt Carbineers', *The Express and Telegraph*, 30 April 1902, p. 3. https://trove.nla.gov.au/newspaper/article/209146026
2 Hobhouse, *The Brunt of the War, and Where it Fell*, p. 180.
3 West and Roper, *Breaker Morant*, p. 140.
4 West and Roper, *Breaker Morant*, p. 140.
5 West and Roper, *Breaker Morant*, pp. 138–40.
6 Davey, *Breaker Morant and the Bushveldt Carbineers*, p. 31.
7 Author's note: There are various spellings for this in sources; for ease and consistency in the narrative I have standardised to Modjadji.
8 Carnegie and Shields, *In Search of Breaker Morant*, p. 72.
9 Carnegie and Shields, *In Search of Breaker Morant*, p. 72.
10 West and Roper, *Breaker Morant*, p. 140.
11 Carnegie and Shields, *In Search of Breaker Morant*, p. 72.
12 Witton, *Scapegoats of the Empire*, 2010, p. 43.
13 Witton, *Scapegoats of the Empire*, 2010, p. 43.
14 West and Roper, *Breaker Morant*, p. 141.
15 West and Roper, *Breaker Morant*, p. 141.
16 West and Roper, *Breaker Morant*, p. 141.
17 West and Roper, *Breaker Morant*, p. 141.
18 West and Roper, *Breaker Morant*, p. 141.
19 Leach, *The Legend of Breaker Morant is Dead and Buried*, p. 43.
20 West and Roper, *Breaker Morant*, p. 142.
21 West and Roper, *Breaker Morant*, p. 143.
22 West and Roper, *Breaker Morant*, p. 143.
23 *Evening Journal* (Adelaide), 5 April 1902, p. 4. https://trove.nla.gov.au/newspaper/article/200784442
24 'An Old Sore Re-Opened', *Murchison Advocate*, 7 June 1902, p. 3. https://trove.nla.gov.au/newspaper/article/213884920
25 'An Old Sore Re-Opened', *Murchison Advocate*, 7 June 1902, p. 3. https://trove.nla.gov.au/newspaper/article/213884920
26 Witton, *Scapegoats of the Empire*, Angus & Robertson, London, 1907, p. 53.
27 Witton, *Scapegoats of the Empire*, 1907, p. 54.
28 Witton, *Scapegoats of the Empire*, 2010, p. 44 [reported speech].
29 Witton, *Scapegoats of the Empire*, 1907, p. 54.
30 Witton, *Scapegoats of the Empire*, 1907, p. 54.
31 Witton, *Scapegoats of the Empire*, 2010, p. 44.
32 West and Roper, *Breaker Morant*, p. 143.
33 West and Roper, *Breaker Morant*, p. 143.
34 West and Roper, *Breaker Morant*, p. 143.
35 Witton, *Scapegoats of the Empire*, 2010, p. 44.
36 West and Roper, *Breaker Morant*, p. 144.
37 West and Roper, *Breaker Morant*, p. 144.
38 Robert Lowry, 'Shall We Gather At The River', hymn written in 1864.
39 West and Roper, *Breaker Morant*, pp. 144–145.
40 West and Roper, *Breaker Morant*, pp. 144–145.
41 Witton, *Scapegoats of the Empire*, 2010, p. 44.

42 Witton, *Scapegoats of the Empire*, 2010, p. 45.

43 West and Roper, *Breaker Morant*, p. 145.

44 West and Roper, *Breaker Morant*, p. 146.

45 Witton, *Scapegoats of the Empire*, 2010, p. 45.

46 Witton, *Scapegoats of the Empire*, 2010, p. 45.

47 Witton, *Scapegoats of the Empire*, 2010, p. 46.

48 Witton, *Scapegoats of the Empire*, 2010, p. 47.

49 Witton, *Scapegoats of the Empire*, 2010, p. 46.

50 Witton, *Scapegoats of the Empire*, 2010, p. 47.

51 'The Witton Case,' *The Northern Miner*, 29 September 1904, p. 2. https://trove.nla.gov.au/newspaper/article/79037957

52 'The Witton Case,' *The Northern Miner*, 29 September 1904, p. 2.

53 Witton, *Scapegoats of the Empire*, p. 47.

54 Witton, *Scapegoats of the Empire*, p. 47.

55 Witton, *Scapegoats of the Empire*, p. 47 [reported speech].

56 Witton, *Scapegoats of the Empire*, 2010, p. 47.

57 Davey, *Breaker Morant and the Bushveldt Carbineers*, p. 101.

58 West and Roper, *Breaker Morant*, p. 150.

59 West and Roper, *Breaker Morant*, p. 150.

60 West and Roper, *Breaker Morant*, p. 151.

61 West and Roper, *Breaker Morant*, p. 151.

62 Christie, 'Outrages on the Bush Veldt', *Patea Mail*, Vol. XV, Issue 42, 14 April 1902.

63 West and Roper, *Breaker Morant*, p. 151.

64 West and Roper, *Breaker Morant*, p. 199.

65 Davey, *Breaker Morant and the Bushveldt Carbineers*, p. 102.

66 Davey, *Breaker Morant and the Bushveldt Carbineers*, p. 102.

67 Davey, *Breaker Morant and the Bushveldt Carbineers*, p. 102.

68 Davey, *Breaker Morant and the Bushveldt Carbineers*, p. 102.

69 Davey, *Breaker Morant and the Bushveldt Carbineers*, p. 102.

70 Davey, *Breaker Morant and the Bushveldt Carbineers*, p. 102.

71 Davey, *Breaker Morant and the Bushveldt Carbineers*, p. 102.

72 Davey, *Breaker Morant and the Bushveldt Carbineers*, p. 102.

73 West and Roper, *Breaker Morant*, p. 199.

74 West and Roper, *Breaker Morant*, p. 151.

75 Christie, 'Evidence in New Zealand, An Eye-Witness Account of a Brutal Deed', *Evening Post*, Vol. LXIII, Issue 85, 10 April 1902.

76 Witton, *Scapegoats of the Empire*, p. 47.

77 Christie, 'Evidence in New Zealand, An Eye-Witness Account of a Brutal Deed', 10 April 1902.

78 Davey, *Breaker Morant and the Bushveldt Carbineers*, p. 99.

79 Davey, *Breaker Morant and the Bushveldt Carbineers*, p. 98.

80 Davey, *Breaker Morant and the Bushveldt Carbineers*, p. 98.

81 Davey, *Breaker Morant and the Bushveldt Carbineers*, p. 98.

82 Davey, *Breaker Morant and the Bushveldt Carbineers*, p. 98.

83 Christie, 'Evidence in New Zealand, An Eye-Witness Account of a Brutal Deed', 10 April 1902.

84 Christie, 'Evidence in New Zealand, An Eye-Witness Account of a Brutal Deed', 10 April 1902.

85 Christie, 'Evidence in New Zealand, An Eye-Witness Account of a Brutal Deed', 10 April 1902.

86 Author's note: This fact is confirmed by this newspaper article, *Truth*, 13 March 1904, p. 6. https://trove.nla.gov.au/newspaper/article/167902992

87 Davey, *Breaker Morant and the Bushveldt Carbineers*, p. 98.

88 Davey, *Breaker Morant and the Bushveldt Carbineers*, p. 99.

89 West and Roper, *Breaker Morant*, p. 153.

90 Witton, *Scapegoats of the Empire*, 2010, p. 47.

91 West and Roper, *Breaker Morant*, p. 199.

Chapter Thirteen

1 *Manual of Military Law*, p. 287.
2 Fox, *Breaker Morant – Bushman and Buccaneer*, pp. 36–37.
3 de Wet, *Three Years War*, p. 248.
4 de Wet, *Three Years War*, p. 248.
5 Armstrong, *Judge Not*, p. 298.
6 West and Roper, *Breaker Morant*, pp. 238–239.
7 Davey, *Breaker Morant and the Bushveldt Carbineers*, p. 105.
8 'The Bush Veldt Carbineers', *The Age*, 6 May 1902, p. 5. https://trove.nla.gov.au/newspaper/article/199398844
9 West and Roper, *Breaker Morant*, p. 156.
10 West and Roper, *Breaker Morant*, p. 156.
11 Davey, *Breaker Morant and the Bushveldt Carbineers*, p. 55.
12 Davey, *Breaker Morant and the Bushveldt Carbineers*, p. 55.
13 Davey, *Breaker Morant and the Bushveldt Carbineers*, p. 55.
14 Davey, *Breaker Morant and the Bushveldt Carbineers*, p. 55.
15 Davey, *Breaker Morant and the Bushveldt Carbineers*, p. 103.
16 Witton, *Scapegoats of the Empire*, 2010, p. 50 [reported speech].
17 Witton, *Scapegoats of the Empire*, 2010, pp. 50–51 [reported speech].
18 Witton, *Scapegoats of the Empire*, 1907, p. 62.
19 Davey, *Breaker Morant and the Bushveldt Carbineers*, p. 105.
20 Davey, *Breaker Morant and the Bushveldt Carbineers*, p. 105.
21 Davey, *Breaker Morant and the Bushveldt Carbineers*, p. 105.
22 Davey, *Breaker Morant and the Bushveldt Carbineers*, p. 105.
23 Carnegie and Shields, *In Search of Breaker Morant*, pp. 95–96.
24 Carnegie and Shields, *In Search of Breaker Morant*, pp. 95–96.
25 Davey, *Breaker Morant and the Bushveldt Carbineers*, p. 132.
26 Davey, *Breaker Morant and the Bushveldt Carbineers*, p. 132.
27 Fox, *Breaker Morant – Bushman and Buccaneer*, p. 40.
28 Leach, *The Legend of Breaker Morant is Dead and Buried*, p. 68.
29 Witton, *Scapegoats of the Empire*, 2010, p. 51.
30 Author's note: Witton's account is that he was not part of the firing squad, but given the other self-serving lies in his book, I do not believe it. The South African historian Charles Leach's account says indeed Smit was only wounded in the first shots, then rushed at the man who had shot him, and that man was almost certainly Witton. See Leach, *The Legend of Breaker Morant is Dead and Buried*, p. 68.
31 'The Bushveldt Carbineers', *Bairnsdale Advertiser and Tambo and Omeo Chronicle*, 22 May 1902, p. 2. https://trove.nla.gov.au/newspaper/article/86234570
32 Witton, *Scapegoats of the Empire*, 1907, p. 63.
33 Davey, *Breaker Morant and the Bushveldt Carbineers*, p. 104.
34 Davey, *Breaker Morant and the Bushveldt Carbineers*, p. 105.
35 Davey, *Breaker Morant and the Bushveldt Carbineers*, p. 105.
36 Davey, *Breaker Morant and the Bushveldt Carbineers*, p. 105.
37 Davey, *Breaker Morant and the Bushveldt Carbineers*, p. 105.
38 'The Bushveldt Carbineers', *Bairnsdale Advertiser and Tambo and Omeo Chronicle*, 22 May 1902, p. 2 [reported speech].
39 Carnegie and Shields, *In Search of Breaker Morant*, pp. 95–96.
40 Davey, *Breaker Morant and the Bushveldt Carbineers*, p. 106.
41 West and Roper, *Breaker Morant*, p. 327 [reported speech].
42 Davey, *Breaker Morant and the Bushveldt Carbineers*, p. 106.
43 West and Roper, *Breaker Morant*, p. 161.
44 Denton, *Closed File*, p.111.
45 West and Roper, *Breaker Morant*, p. 163.
46 West and Roper, *Breaker Morant*, p. 163.
47 Denton, *Closed File*, pp. 111–112.
48 Witton, *Scapegoats of the Empire*, 2010, p. 99 [reported speech].

49 Witton, *Scapegoats of the Empire*, 2010, p. 99.
50 Witton, *Scapegoats of the Empire*, 2010, p. 99.
51 Witton, *Scapegoats of the Empire*, 2010, p. 99.
52 Witton, *Scapegoats of the Empire*, 2010, p. 99.
53 Witton, *Scapegoats of the Empire*, 2010, p. 99.
54 Witton, *Scapegoats of the Empire*, 2010, p. 99 [reported speech].

Chapter Fourteen

1 'Graphic Letter from Fr. Timoney', *Advocate* (Vic.), 15 December 1900, p. 24. https://trove.nla.gov.au/newspaper/article/169869932. 'Francis Timoney, Fighting Padre and Whistle Blower', The Australian Boer War Memorial. https://www.bwm.org.au/soldiers/Francis_Timoney.php
2 Witton, *Scapegoats of the Empire*, 2010, p. 52 [reported speech].
3 Witton, *Scapegoats of the Empire*, 2010, p. 52 [reported speech].
4 Colonial Secretary Confidential papers 1907, National Archive, Pretoria.
5 Carnegie and Shields, *In Search of Breaker Morant*, p. 98.
6 Davey, *Breaker Morant and the Bushveldt Carbineers*, p. 56.
7 Carnegie and Shields, *In Search of Breaker Morant*, pp. 92–97 [reported speech].
8 Davey, *Breaker Morant and the Bushveldt Carbineers*, p. 89.
9 Davey, *Breaker Morant and the Bushveldt Carbineers*, p. 89.
10 Witton, *Scapegoats of the Empire*, 2010, p. 49.
11 Davey, *Breaker Morant and the Bushveldt Carbineers*, p. 89.
12 Davey, *Breaker Morant and the Bushveldt Carbineers*, p. 89.
13 Davey, *Breaker Morant and the Bushveldt Carbineers*, p. 104.
14 Davey, *Breaker Morant and the Bushveldt Carbineers*, p. 104.
15 Davey, *Breaker Morant and the Bushveldt Carbineers*, p. 104.
16 Davey, *Breaker Morant and the Bushveldt Carbineers*, p. 104.
17 Davey, *Breaker Morant and the Bushveldt Carbineers*, p. 104.
18 West and Roper, *Breaker Morant*, p. 167.
19 West and Roper, *Breaker Morant*, p. 167.
20 Christie, 'Evidence in New Zealand, An Eye-Witness Account of a Brutal Deed', *Evening Post*, Vol. LXIII, Issue 85, 10 April 1902; Christie, 'The Bushveldt Horrors', *Evening Post*, Vol. LXIII, Issue 88, 14 April 1902. https://paperspast.natlib.govt.nz/newspapers/EP19020414.2.6
21 Davey, *Breaker Morant and the Bushveldt Carbineers*, p. 110.
22 Davey, *Breaker Morant and the Bushveldt Carbineers*, p. 110.
23 Davey, *Breaker Morant and the Bushveldt Carbineers*, p. 109.
24 Davey, *Breaker Morant and the Bushveldt Carbineers*, p. 109.
25 Davey, *Breaker Morant and the Bushveldt Carbineers*, p. 110.
26 Davey, *Breaker Morant and the Bushveldt Carbineers*, p. 109.
27 Leach, *The Legend of Breaker Morant is Dead and Buried*, p. 84.
28 Davey, *Breaker Morant and the Bushveldt Carbineers*, p. 110.
29 Davey, *Breaker Morant and the Bushveldt Carbineers*, p. 109 [reported speech].
30 Davey, *Breaker Morant and the Bushveldt Carbineers*, p. 110.
31 West and Roper, *Breaker Morant*, p.168.
32 Leach, *The Legend of Breaker Morant is Dead and Buried*, p. 84.
33 *Sydney Truth*, 27 July 1902, p. 8. https://trove.nla.gov.au/newspaper/article/167894844
34 *Sydney Truth*, 27 July 1902, p. 8.
35 Christie, 'The African Horror', *Auckland Star*, Vol. XXXIII, Issue 89, 16 April 1902.
36 Christie, 'The African Horror', 16 April 1902.
37 Christie, 'The African Horror', 16 April 1902.
38 Christie, 'The African Horror', 16 April 1902.
39 Christie, 'The African Horror', 16 April 1902.
40 West and Roper, *Breaker Morant*, p. 171.
41 West and Roper, *Breaker Morant*, p. 171.
42 Christie, 'The African Horror', 16 April 1902.
43 Christie, 'The African Horror', 16 April 1902 [reported speech].
44 Christie, 'The African Horror', 16 April 1902.

45 Christie, 'The African Horror', 16 April 1902.

46 West and Roper, *Breaker Morant*, p. 172.

47 Christie, 'The African Horror', 16 April 1902.

48 West and Roper, *Breaker Morant*, p. 173.

49 Christie, 'The African Horror', 16 April 1902.

50 Davey, *Breaker Morant and the Bushveldt Carbineers*, p. 93.

51 Davey, *Breaker Morant and the Bushveldt Carbineers*, p. 93.

52 Christie, 'The Australian Sensation', *Clutha Leader*, Vol. XXVIII, Issue 1508, 11 April 1902.

53 Christie, 'The African Horror', 16 April 1902.

54 Davey, *Breaker Morant and the Bushveldt Carbineers*, p. 93.

55 Davey, *Breaker Morant and the Bushveldt Carbineers*, p. 93.

56 Davey, *Breaker Morant and the Bushveldt Carbineers*, pp. 91–93.

57 West and Roper, *Breaker Morant*, p. 173.

58 Christie, 'The Australian Sensation', 11 April 1902.

59 *Sydney Truth*, 27 July 1902, p. 8. https://trove.nla.gov.au/newspaper/article/167894844

60 *Sydney Truth*, 27 July 1902, p. 8.

61 Carnegie and Shields, *In Search of Breaker Morant*, pp. 92–97 [reported speech].

62 Carnegie and Shields, *In Search of Breaker Morant*, pp. 92–97 [reported speech].

63 Carnegie and Shields, *In Search of Breaker Morant*, pp. 92–97.

64 Carnegie and Shields, *In Search of Breaker Morant*, pp. 92–97 [reported speech].

65 From Morant, 'Who's Riding Old Harlequin Now?', *The Poetry of Breaker Morant*, pp. 39–40.

Chapter Fifteen

1 William Shakespeare, *Henry IV*, Part 1, Act 2, Scene 4.

2 Davey, *Breaker Morant and the Bushveldt Carbineers*, p. 92.

3 Witton, *Scapegoats of the Empire*, 2010, p. 55.

4 Carnegie and Shields, *In Search of Breaker Morant*, p. 124.

5 Bleszynski, *Shoot Straight, You Bastards!*, p 191.

6 West and Roper, *Breaker Morant*, p. 319.

7 West and Roper, *Breaker Morant*, p. 319.

8 West and Roper, *Breaker Morant*, p. 319.

9 West and Roper, *Breaker Morant*, p. 319.

10 'Bushveldt Buccaneers', *Truth*, 13 March 1904, p. 8. https://trove.nla.gov.au/newspaper/article/167902992

11 West and Roper, *Breaker Morant*, p. 319.

12 West and Roper, *Breaker Morant*, p. 319.

13 West and Roper, *Breaker Morant*, p. 319.

14 Fox, *Breaker Morant – Bushman and Buccaneer*, p. 44.

15 *The Inquirer and Commercial News*, 8 December 1899, p. 11. https://trove.nla.gov.au/newspaper/article/67195170

16 Fox, *Breaker Morant – Bushman and Buccaneer*, p. 41.

17 West and Roper, *Breaker Morant*, p. 319.

18 West and Roper, *Breaker Morant*, p. 182.

19 West and Roper, *Breaker Morant*, p. 184.

20 Davey, *Breaker Morant and the Bushveldt Carbineers*, p. 58.

21 Carnegie and Shields, *In Search of Breaker Morant*, p. 98 [reported speech].

22 Carnegie and Shields, *In Search of Breaker Morant*, p. 98 [reported speech].

23 Carnegie and Shields, *In Search of Breaker Morant*, pp. 92–97.

24 Carnegie and Shields, *In Search of Breaker Morant*, pp. 92–97.

25 Carnegie and Shields, *In Search of Breaker Morant*, pp. 92–97.

26 Carnegie and Shields, *In Search of Breaker Morant*, p. 98.

27 Carnegie and Shields, *In Search of Breaker Morant*, p. 98 [reported speech].

28 Carnegie and Shields, *In Search of Breaker Morant*, p. 98.

29 Carnegie and Shields, *In Search of Breaker Morant*, p. 98 [reported speech].

30 Carnegie and Shields, *In Search of Breaker Morant*, p. 98 [reported speech].

31 Carnegie and Shields, *In Search of Breaker Morant*, p. 98.

32 Witton, *Scapegoats of the Empire*, 2010, p. 53.

33 Witton, *Scapegoats of the Empire*, 2010, p. 54.

34 Witton, *Scapegoats of the Empire*, 2010, p. 56.

35 West and Roper, *Breaker Morant*, p. 179.

36 Fox, *Breaker Morant – Bushman and Buccaneer*, p. 43.

37 Witton, *Scapegoats of the Empire*, 2010, p. 57.

38 West and Roper, *Breaker Morant*, p. 179.

39 Witton, *Scapegoats of the Empire*, 2010, p. 57.

40 Fox, *Breaker Morant – Bushman and Buccaneer*, p.44.

41 Witton, *Scapegoats of the Empire*, 2010, p. 58.

42 Fox, *Breaker Morant – Bushman and Buccaneer*, pp. 43–44.

43 Fox, *Breaker Morant – Bushman and Buccaneer*, pp. 43–44.

44 Davey, *Breaker Morant and the Bushveldt Carbineers*, p. 61.

45 Leach, *The Legend of Breaker Morant is Dead and Buried*, pp. 100–101.

46 West and Roper, *Breaker Morant*, p. 179.

47 West and Roper, *Breaker Morant*, pp. 179–180.

48 NAM GB0099 KCLMA Poore, Correspondence. Vol. 2/4, 28 Jun 1901–12 Jan 1902, Letter dated Monday 07 Oct 1901 Pretoria. Provost Marshal Poore's diary entry; Davey, *Breaker Morant and the Bushveldt Carbineers*, p. 74.

49 West and Roper, *Breaker Morant*, p. 160.

50 West and Roper, *Breaker Morant*, p. 168.

51 Carnegie and Shields, *In Search of Breaker Morant*, p. 99.

52 Witton, *Scapegoats of the Empire*, 2010, p. 59 [reported speech].

53 Witton, *Scapegoats of the Empire*, 2010, p. 59 [reported speech].

54 West and Roper, *Breaker Morant*, p. 180.

55 West and Roper, *Breaker Morant*, p. 180.

56 West and Roper, *Breaker Morant*, p. 180.

57 West and Roper, *Breaker Morant*, p. 180.

58 West and Roper, *Breaker Morant*, p. 180.

59 West and Roper, *Breaker Morant*, p. 180.

60 West and Roper, *Breaker Morant*, p. 180.

61 West and Roper, *Breaker Morant*, p. 180.

62 Witton, *Scapegoats of the Empire*, 2010, p. 59 [reported speech].

63 Witton, *Scapegoats of the Empire*, 2010, p. 59 [reported speech].

64 *The Blayney Advocate*, 5 April 1902, p. 4. https://trove.nla.gov.au/newspaper/article/144296437

65 *The Blayney Advocate*, 5 April 1902, p. 4.

66 Witton, *Scapegoats of the Empire*, 2010, p. 60.

67 Witton, *Scapegoats of the Empire*, 2010, p. 62.

68 Witton, *Scapegoats of the Empire*, 2010, p. 62.

69 Denton, *Closed File*, p. 133.

70 Witton, *Scapegoats of the Empire*, 2010, p. 63.

71 *The Northern Miner*, 12 April 1902, p. 4. https://trove.nla.gov.au/newspaper/article/79031927

72 'Emily Hobhouse: Writings', Charter for Compassion, https://charterforcompassion.org/emily-hobhouse/emily-hobhouse-writings

73 Hobhouse, *Boer War Letters: Arrest and Deportation*, Rykie van Reenen (ed.), Human & Rousseau, Cape Town, 1984, pp. 137–142.

74 Hobhouse, *Boer War Letters*, pp. 137–142 [reported speech].

75 Seibold, *Emily Hobhouse and the Reports on the Concentration Camps during the Boer War 1899–1902*, Ibidem, Stuttgart, 2014, p. 91.

76 'Women and Children in White Concentration Camps During Anglo-Boer War 1900–1902', South African History Online, https://www.sahistory.org.za/article/women-and-children-white-concentration-camps-during-anglo-boer-war-1900-1902

77 'Miss Hobhouse's Deportation', *The Tocsin* (Vic.), 16 January 1902, p. 3. https://trove.nla.gov.au/newspaper/article/197525846

78 Letter to *The Times*, October 1901.

79 'Women and Children in White Concentration Camps During Anglo-Boer War 1900–1902', South African History Online, https://www.sahistory.org.za/article/ women-and-children-white-concentration-camps-during-anglo-boer-war-1900-1902
80 Milner, Correspondence to British Colonial Secretary, Joseph Chamberlain, 7 November 1901.
81 Milner, Correspondence to British Colonial Secretary, Joseph Chamberlain, 15 November 1901.
82 Kitchener papers, Kitchener to Brodrick, NA 30 57 22 (1), 8 November 1901.
83 'Khaki-Clad Boers', *Kalgoorlie Miner*, 13 November 1901, p. 15. https://trove.nla.gov.au/ newspaper/article/88723875
84 Lines from Oscar Wilde's poem 'The Ballad of Reading Gaol'.
85 Witton, *Scapegoats of the Empire*, 2010, p. 63.
86 Witton, *Scapegoats of the Empire*, 2010, p. 63.
87 Witton, *Scapegoats of the Empire*, 2010, p. 64.
88 Davey, *Breaker Morant and the Bushveldt Carbineers*, pp. 99–100.
89 Witton, *Scapegoats of the Empire*, 1907, pp. 79–80.
90 Witton, *Scapegoats of the Empire*, Angus & Robertson, Hong Kong, 1982, p. 80.

Chapter Sixteen

1 Unkles, 'An Infantry Officer In Court – A Review of Major James Francis Thomas as Defending Officer for Lieutenants Breaker Morant, Peter Handcock and George Witton – Boer War', 2010, http://breakermorant.com/new/wp-content/documents/short_article_thomas_final_doc_Jun_10x.pdf
2 Harris, '"Spin" on the Boer Atrocities', *The Guardian*, 9 December 2001. https://www.theguardian. com/world/2001/dec/09/paulharris.theobserver
3 Harris, '"Spin" on the Boer Atrocities', 9 December 2001.
4 Harris, '"Spin" on the Boer Atrocities', 9 December 2001.
5 Harris, '"Spin" on the Boer Atrocities', 9 December 2001.
6 Witton, *Scapegoats of the Empire*, 2010, p. 65.
7 Leach, *The Legend of Breaker Morant is Dead and Buried*, p. 203.
8 Growden, *Major Thomas*, p. 143.
9 'The Executed Officers', *Queensland Times, Ipswich Herald and General Advertiser*, 7 June 1902, p. 12. https://trove.nla.gov.au/newspaper/article/122545303
10 Bleszynski, *Shoot Straight, You Bastards!*, p. 318.
11 Witton, *Scapegoats of the Empire*, 2010, p. 65.
12 *Sydney Morning Herald*, 22 May 1902, p. 4.
13 'That Court Martial', *The Herald*, 20 May 1902, p. 2. https://trove.nla.gov.au/newspaper/ article/241896086
14 'That Court Martial', *The Herald*, 20 May 1902, p. 2.
15 'That Court Martial', *The Herald*, 20 May 1902, p. 2.
16 'That Court Martial', *The Herald*, 20 May 1902, p. 2.
17 Witton, *Scapegoats of the Empire*, 2010, p. 66 [reported speech].
18 Witton, *Scapegoats of the Empire*, 2010, p. 66 [reported speech].
19 Witton, *Scapegoats of the Empire*, 2010, p. 67 [reported speech].
20 Witton, *Scapegoats of the Empire*, 2010, p. 67.
21 *Sydney Morning Herald*, 22 May 1902, p. 4. https://trove.nla.gov.au/newspaper/article/14464470
22 Fox, *Breaker Morant – Bushman and Buccaneer*, p. 35.
23 Fox, *Breaker Morant – Bushman and Buccaneer*, p. 52.
24 Witton, *Scapegoats of the Empire*, 2010, p. 84.
25 *Sydney Morning Herald*, 22 May 1902, p. 4.
26 Witton, *Scapegoats of the Empire*, 2010, p. 67.
27 Fox, *Breaker Morant – Bushman and Buccaneer*, p. 53.
28 Fox, *Breaker Morant – Bushman and Buccaneer*, p. 53.
29 'The Sensational War Incident', *Kalgoorlie Miner*, 22 May 1902, p. 2 [reported speech]. https:// trove.nla.gov.au/newspaper/article/88711487
30 'The Sensational War Incident', *Kalgoorlie Miner*, 22 May 1902, p. 2 [reported speech].
31 *Manual of Military Law*, p. 126.
32 Witton, *Scapegoats of the Empire*, 2010, pp. 67–68.
33 Witton, *Scapegoats of the Empire*, 2010, p. 68.

34 *Sydney Morning Herald*, 22 May 1902, p. 4.
35 West and Roper, *Breaker Morant*, p. 225 [reported speech].
36 Carnegie and Shields, *In Search of Breaker Morant*, p. 99.
37 Witton, *Scapegoats of the Empire*, 2010, p. 71.
38 Witton, *Scapegoats of the Empire*, 2010, p. 71.
39 West and Roper, *Breaker Morant*, p. 226.
40 West and Roper, *Breaker Morant*, p. 226.
41 Witton, *Scapegoats of the Empire*, 2010, p. 75.
42 West and Roper, *Breaker Morant*, pp. 226–227.
43 West and Roper, *Breaker Morant*, pp. 229–230.
44 West and Roper, *Breaker Morant*, pp. 229–230.
45 Witton, *Scapegoats of the Empire*, 2010, p. 81.
46 Witton, *Scapegoats of the Empire*, 2010, p. 83.
47 Witton, *Scapegoats of the Empire*, 2010, p. 83.
48 Witton, *Scapegoats of the Empire*, 2010, p. 83.
49 Witton, *Scapegoats of the Empire*, 2010, p. 83.

Chapter Seventeen

1 Witton, *Scapegoats of the Empire*, 2010, p. 87.
2 Witton, *Scapegoats of the Empire*, 2010, p. 88.
3 Witton, *Scapegoats of the Empire*, 2010, p. 88.
4 West and Roper, *Breaker Morant*, p. 241.
5 West and Roper, *Breaker Morant*, p. 243.
6 West and Roper, *Breaker Morant*, p. 243 [reported speech].
7 Witton, *Scapegoats of the Empire*, 2010, p. 106.
8 *Sydney Morning Herald*, 22 May 1902, p. 4.
9 *Sydney Morning Herald*, 22 May 1902, p. 4.
10 *Sydney Morning Herald*, 22 May 1902, p. 4 [reported speech].
11 Witton, *Scapegoats of the Empire*, 2010, p. 87.
12 Davey, *Breaker Morant and the Bushveldt Carbineers*, p. 122.
13 Davey, *Breaker Morant and the Bushveldt Carbineers*, p. 132.
14 Davey, *Breaker Morant and the Bushveldt Carbineers*, p. 132
15 Davey, *Breaker Morant and the Bushveldt Carbineers*, p. 132.
16 Davey, *Breaker Morant and the Bushveldt Carbineers*, p. 132.
17 Davey, *Breaker Morant and the Bushveldt Carbineers*, p. 132.
18 Witton, *Scapegoats of the Empire*, 2010, p. 99.
19 Witton, *Scapegoats of the Empire*, 2010, p. 157.
20 Witton, *Scapegoats of the Empire*, 2010, p. 88 [reported speech].
21 Witton, *Scapegoats of the Empire*, 2010, p. 90.
22 Witton, *Scapegoats of the Empire*, 2010, p. 91 [reported speech].
23 Witton, *Scapegoats of the Empire*, 2010, p. 91.
24 Witton, *Scapegoats of the Empire*, 2010, p. 91.
25 *Sydney Morning Herald*, 22 May 1902, p. 4.
26 *Sydney Morning Herald*, 22 May 1902, p. 4.
27 *Sydney Morning Herald*, 22 May 1902, p. 4.
28 *Sydney Morning Herald*, 22 May 1902, p. 4.
29 *Sydney Morning Herald*, 22 May 1902, p. 4.
30 *Sydney Morning Herald*, 22 May 1902, p. 4.
31 *Sydney Morning Herald*, 22 May 1902, p. 4.
32 Witton, *Scapegoats of the Empire*, 2010, p. 118.
33 Witton, *Scapegoats of the Empire*, 2010, p. 95.
34 *Sydney Morning Herald*, 22 May 1902, p. 4.
35 George Witton, *Scapegoats of the Empire*, 2010, p. 90. Author's note: In the actual document, Handcock says Robinson – an error compounded by Witton making the same mistake in his book *Scapegoats*. For the sake of clarity, I have corrected it to Robertson.
36 Witton, *Scapegoats of the Empire*, 2010, p. 103.

37 Witton, *Scapegoats of the Empire*, 2010, p. 134.
38 West and Roper, *Breaker Morant*, p. 265.
39 'That Court Martial', *The Herald*, 20 May 1902, p. 2. https://trove.nla.gov.au/newspaper/article/241896086
40 'That Court Martial', *The Herald*, 20 May 1902, p. 2.
41 Witton, *Scapegoats of the Empire*, 2010, p. 107.
42 Witton, *Scapegoats of the Empire*, 2010, p. 107.
43 Witton, *Scapegoats of the Empire*, 1982, p. 187.
44 Davey, *Breaker Morant and the Bushveldt Carbineers*, p. 90.
45 *Sydney Morning Herald*, 22 May 1902, p. 4.
46 *Sydney Morning Herald*, 22 May 1902, p. 4.
47 *Sydney Morning Herald*, 22 May 1902, p. 4.
48 Witton, *Scapegoats of the Empire*, 2010, p. 109 [reported speech].
49 Witton, *Scapegoats of the Empire*, 2010, pp. 109–110.
50 *Sydney Morning Herald*, 22 May 1902, p. 4.
51 *Sydney Morning Herald*, 22 May 1902, p. 4.
52 *Sydney Morning Herald*, 22 May 1902, p. 4.
53 Witton, *Scapegoats of the Empire*, 2010, p. 40 [reported speech].
54 Carnegie and Shields, *In Search of Breaker Morant*, p. 100.
55 Carnegie and Shields, *In Search of Breaker Morant*, p. 100.
56 Carnegie and Shields, *In Search of Breaker Morant*, p. 100.
57 Carnegie and Shields, *In Search of Breaker Morant*, p. 100.
58 Carnegie and Shields, *In Search of Breaker Morant*, p. 100.
59 Carnegie and Shields, *In Search of Breaker Morant*, p. 100.
60 Carnegie and Shields, *In Search of Breaker Morant*, p. 100.
61 *The Age*, 5 August 1903, p. 5. https://trove.nla.gov.au/newspaper/article/197215837
62 *The Age*, 5 August 1903, p. 5.
63 Parliament of Australia, South African War, *Sentences on Officers in South Africa – Despatches from the Commander-in-Chief in South Africa, and Extracts from Proceedings of two General Courts-Martial relating thereto*, House of Representatives, April 1902.
64 *Sydney Morning Herald*, 22 May 1902, p. 4.
65 *Sydney Morning Herald*, 22 May 1902, p. 4.
66 *Sydney Morning Herald*, 22 May 1902, p. 4.
67 Witton, *Scapegoats of the Empire*, 2010, p. 112.
68 Witton, *Scapegoats of the Empire*, 2010, p. 113 [reported speech].
69 Witton, *Scapegoats of the Empire*, 2010, p. 113 [reported speech].
70 Witton, *Scapegoats of the Empire*, 2010, p. 113.
71 Witton, *Scapegoats of the Empire*, 2010, p. 113 [reported speech].
72 'Murders by Officers', *Clarence and Richmond Examiner*, 27 May 1902, p. 8. https://trove.nla.gov.au/newspaper/article/61388108

Chapter Eighteen

1 Cutlack, *Breaker Morant: A Horseman Who Made History*, Ure Smith, Sydney, 1962, p. 99.
2 *The Bulletin*, 5 April 1902.
3 Carnegie and Shields, *In Search of Breaker Morant*, p. 2.
4 Witton, *Scapegoats of the Empire*, 2010, p. 114.
5 Witton, *Scapegoats of the Empire*, 2010, p. 115.
6 Carnegie and Shields, *In Search of Breaker Morant*, p. 99.
7 Witton, *Scapegoats of the Empire*, 2010, p. 115 [reported speech].
8 Pretoria Archive, PMO 47 PM 3198-02.
9 *The Argus*, 31 March 1902, p. 5. https://trove.nla.gov.au/newspaper/article/9633985
10 *The Argus*, 31 March 1902, p. 5.
11 *The Argus*, 31 March 1902, p. 5.
12 *The Argus*, 31 March 1902, p. 5.
13 Fox, *Breaker Morant – Bushman and Buccaneer*, p. 54.
14 Witton, *Scapegoats of the Empire*, 2010, pp. 115–116.

15 *The Age*, 5 August 1903, p. 5.

16 *The Age*, 5 August 1903, p. 5 [reported speech].

17 *The Argus*, 31 March 1902, p. 5.

18 Witton, *Scapegoats of the Empire*, 1982, p. 158.

19 Davey, *Breaker Morant and the Bushveldt Carbineers*, p. 62.

20 Davey, *Breaker Morant and the Bushveldt Carbineers*, p. 62.

21 Witton, *Scapegoats of the Empire*, 2010, p. 117.

22 Witton, *Scapegoats of the Empire*, 2010, p. 118.

23 West and Roper, *Breaker Morant*, p. 280.

24 Denton, *Closed File*, p. 135.

25 Witton, *Scapegoats of the Empire*, 2010, p. 130.

26 *Windsor and Richmond Gazette*, 17 September 1920, p. 10. https://trove.nla.gov.au/newspaper/article/85874127

27 Witton, *Scapegoats of the Empire*, 2010, p. 119.

28 Fox, *Breaker Morant – Bushman and Buccaneer*, p. 38.

29 Witton, *Scapegoats of the Empire*, 2010, p. 119.

30 Pakenham, *The Boer War*, p. 539.

31 Brodrick to Kitchener, letter, Kitchener papers PRO 30 57 22 (1)-22 Feb 1902 [photo no 216].

32 'Harry Morant', *Townsville Daily Bulletin*, 10 December 1954, p. 9. https://trove.nla.gov.au/newspaper/article/62543001

33 'Harry Morant', *Townsville Daily Bulletin*, 10 December 1954, p. 9 [reported speech].

34 'Harry Morant', *Townsville Daily Bulletin*, 10 December 1954, p. 9 [reported speech].

35 Author's note: Having examined all officers named Press who served in the war, this cannot be Captain A. E. Press, as claimed by 'a comrade' of Morant's in a letter published in 1902, and as other sources have it. It must be Lieutenant (perhaps temporary captain) William Press of South Australia.

36 'The Execution of Lieut. Morant', *The Narracoorte Herald*, 8 April 1902, p. 4.

37 Witton, *Scapegoats of the Empire*, 1982, p. 152.

38 Witton, *Scapegoats of the Empire*, 1982, p. 152.

39 'The Execution of Lieut. Morant', *The Narracoorte Herald*, 8 April 1902, p. 4.

40 'The Execution of Lieut. Morant', *The Narracoorte Herald*, 8 April 1902, p. 4.

41 'The Execution of Lieut. Morant', *The Narracoorte Herald*, 8 April 1902, p. 4.

42 'The Execution of Lieut. Morant', *The Narracoorte Herald*, 8 April 1902, p. 4.

43 Witton, *Scapegoats of the Empire*, 1982, p. 152.

44 Witton, *Scapegoats of the Empire*, 1982, p. 152.

45 Witton, *Scapegoats of the Empire*, 1982, p. 152.

46 Witton, *Scapegoats of the Empire*, 2010, pp. 119–120.

47 Denton, *Closed File*, p. 126.

48 Morant, 'Envoi', *The Bulletin*, 12 April 1902, p. 15; Bleszynski, *Shoot Straight, You Bastards!*, pp. 296–297.

49 Part of a letter from Peter Joseph Handcock to his sister, 27 February 1902, Australian War Memorial, Collection number 3DRL/3834.

50 Witton, *Scapegoats of the Empire*, 2010, p. 120.

51 Witton, *Scapegoats of the Empire*, 2010, p. 120.

52 Author's note: Generic orders.

53 'The Bravery of Morant', *National Advocate*, 4 April 1902, p. 2. https://trove.nla.gov.au/newspaper/article/157253146

54 Witton, *Scapegoats of the Empire*, 2010, p. 120.

55 'The Bravery of Morant', *National Advocate*, 4 April 1902, p. 2.

56 Cutlack, *Breaker Morant*, p. 99.

57 'How Morant And Handcock Died', *Examiner* (Tas), 7 April 1902, p. 5. https://trove.nla.gov.au/newspaper/article/35481629

58 Cutlack, *Breaker Morant*, p. 99.

59 'The Bravery of Morant', *National Advocate*, 4 April 1902, p. 2.

60 *Murray Pioneer*, 17 January 1930, p. 7. https://trove.nla.gov.au/newspaper/article/109443200

61 'The Bravery of Morant', *National Advocate*, 4 April 1902, p. 2.

62 Witton, *Scapegoats of the Empire*, 2010, p. 121.
63 'The Execution of Lieut. Morant', *The Narracoorte Herald*, 8 April 1902, p. 4.
64 'The Bravery of Morant', *National Advocate*, 4 April 1902, p. 2.
65 Witton, *Scapegoats of the Empire*, 1907, p. 158.
66 Witton, *Scapegoats of the Empire*, 1907, p. 158.
67 *The Age*, 5 August 1903, p. 5 [reported speech].
68 Hannam, 'The Bushveldt Carbineers', *Manawatu Standard*, Vol. XL, Issue 7329, 24 June 1902.
69 Davey, *Breaker Morant and the Bushveldt Carbineers*, p. xxiv.
70 'The Execution of Lieut. Morant', *The Narracoorte Herald*, 8 April 1902, p. 4.
71 *The Bulletin*, 26 April 1902, p. 14.

Epilogue

1 *Sunday Times (Sydney)*, 27 April 1902, p. 5. https://trove.nla.gov.au/newspaper/article/126420866
2 *Windsor and Richmond Gazette*, 29 March 1902, p. 4. https://trove.nla.gov.au/newspaper/article/86218566
3 'Two Murderers Shot', *The Express and Telegraph*, 10 March 1902, p. 3. https://trove.nla.gov.au/newspaper/article/209142191
4 'The Boer War', *The Sydney Stock and Station Journal*, 8 April 1902, p. 3. https://trove.nla.gov.au/newspaper/article/121562402
5 'Statement by Mr Barton', *Weekly Times* (Vic.), 5 April 1902, p. 23. https://trove.nla.gov.au/newspaper/article/221226938
6 *The Herald*, 19 September 1902, p. 3. https://trove.nla.gov.au/newspaper/article/241999057\
7 Carnegie and Shields, *In Search of Breaker Morant*, p. 168.
8 Witton, *Scapegoats of the Empire*, 1982, p. 236.
9 Witton, *Scapegoats of the Empire*, 2010, p. 50.
10 Growden, *Major Thomas*, pp. 201–209.
11 Growden, *Major Thomas*, p. 226.
12 https://www.lieutpjhandcock.com/2014/04/wittons-letter-to-thomas-21-october-1929.html
13 Growden, *Major Thomas*, p. 250.
14 Growden, *Major Thomas*, p. 250.
15 https://www.lieutpjhandcock.com/2014/04/wittons-letter-to-thomas-21-october-1929.html
16 West and Roper, *Breaker Morant*, p. 335.
17 'Lecture by Major Lenehan', *Evening News* (NSW), 30 July 1902, p. 8. https://trove.nla.gov.au/newspaper/article/112780053
18 *Northern Star*, 11 June 1902, p. 8. https://trove.nla.gov.au/newspaper/article/72061921
19 West and Roper, *Breaker Morant*, p. 341.
20 West and Roper, *Breaker Morant*, p. 341.
21 West and Roper, *Breaker Morant*, p. 337.
22 Frank Shields, interview with Muir Churton, 1973.
23 Davey, *Breaker Morant and the Bushveldt Carbineers*, p. 64.
24 'Late Lieutenant Annat', *The Telegraph* (Qld), 16 October 1900, p. 2. https://trove.nla.gov.au/newspaper/article/175298114
25 Meintjes, *President Paul Kruger*, Cassell, 1974, p. 260.
26 Sandys, *Churchill: Wanted Dead or Alive*, p. 59.
27 'Banjo Paterson Tells His Own Story', *The Sydney Morning Herald*, 25 February 1939, p. 21. https://trove.nla.gov.au/newspaper/article/17564428
28 'Death of Lord Roberts', *The Avon Gazette and Kellerberrin News* (WA), 21 November 1914, p. 3. https://trove.nla.gov.au/newspaper/article/210985821
29 Leach, *The Legend of Breaker Morant is Dead and Buried*, caption on photograph after page 141.
30 *Windsor and Richmond Gazette*, 27 February 1904, p. 9.
31 'Kit Denton and the old man "with a face like a walnut"', *The Canberra Times*, 24 June 1980, p. 16. https://trove.nla.gov.au/newspaper/article/110963977
32 'Kit Denton and the old man "with a face like a walnut"', *The Canberra Times*, 24 June 1980, p. 16.
33 Bleszynski, *Justice or Murder*, The Australian Light Horse Association, http://www.lighthorse.org.au/the-bushveldt-carbineers/

34 Bleszynski, *Shoot Straight, You Bastards!*, pp. ix–xiii.
35 *Sydney Morning Herald*, 11 November 2010 https://www.smh.com.au/world/uk-govt-rejects-morant-pardon-20101111-17pkm.html
36 Speech by Alex Hawke MP, 'Lieutenants Morant, Handcock and Witton', House of Representatives, 27 February 2012. https://parlinfo.aph.gov.au/parlInfo/genpdf/chamber/hansardr/dfa1725a-aa28-48db-ba56-7995bad31f8c/0195/hansard_frag.pdf;fileType=application/pdf
37 *The Bulletin*, 27 August 1892, p. 17. http://www.middlemiss.org/lit/authors/moranth/poetry/whenlight.html

BIBLIOGRAPHY

Books

Armstrong, Charles, *Judge Not*, Xlibris, London, 2017.

Arthur, Sir George, *Life of Lord Kitchener*, MacMillan and Co., Limited, London, 1920.

Ash, Chris, *Kruger, Kommandos and Kak: Debunking the Myths of the Boer War*, 30 Degrees South Publishers, Pinetown, 2014.

Baillie, F. D., *Mafeking: A Diary of a Siege*, Archibald Constable & Company, Westminster, 1900.

Bleszynski, Nick, *Shoot Straight, You Bastards!*, Random House, Sydney, 2003.

Bolsman, Eric, *Winston Churchill: The Making of a Hero in the South African War*, Galago, Bromley, 2008.

Buchan, John, *The African Colony*, William Blackwood and Sons, London, 1903.

Burchell, William J., *Travels in the Interior of Southern Africa, Vol. II*, Longman, Hurst, Rees, Orme, Brown and Green, London, 1824.

Burnett, Major Charles, *The 18th Hussars in South Africa*, Warren & Son, Winchester, 1905.

Byron, *The Works of Lord Byron*, A. & W. Galignani, Paris, 1826.

Carnegie, Margaret and Frank Shields, *In Search of Breaker Morant*, Graphic Books, Armadale, 1979.

Cornelissen, Scarlett and Albert Grundlingh (eds), *Sport Past and Present in South Africa*, Routledge, New York, 2012.

Changuion, Louis, *Pietersburg. Die eerste eeu – 1886–1986*, Die Stadsraad, Pretoria, 1986.

Churchill, Randolph S. ed., *Winston S. Churchill, Companion Volume 1, Part 2*, Heinemann, London, 1967.

Churchill, Winston, *The Boer War*, Bloomsbury, London, 2002.

Churchill, Winston, *My Early Life: 1874–1908*, Collins and Son, Glasgow, 1985.

Churchill, Winston, *My Early Life: A Roving Commission*, Thornton Butterworth, London, 1931.

Churchill, Winston, *London to Ladysmith via Pretoria*, Longmans, Green & Co., London, 1900.

Conan Doyle, Arthur *The War in Africa: Its Causes and Conduct*, McClure, London, 1902.

Conan Doyle, Arthur *Memories and Adventures*, Little, Brown and Company, Boston, 1924.

Conan Doyle, Arthur *The Great Boer War*, Smith, Elder and Co., London, 1900.

Creswicke, Louis, *South Africa and the Transvaal War*, Vol. V, TC and EC Jack, 1900, Edinburgh.

Cutlack, F.M., *Breaker Morant: A Horseman Who Made History*, Ure Smith, Sydney, 1962.

Davey, Arthur, *Breaker Morant and the Bushveldt Carbineers*, Van Riebeeck Society, Cape Town, 1987.

Davis, Richard, *With Both Armies in South Africa*, Charles Scribner's Sons, New York, 1900.

Denton, Kit, *Closed File*, Rigby, Adelaide, 1983.

de Wet, Christiaan, *Three Years War*, Scribner, New York, 1902.

Drooglever, Robin, *Colonel Tom's Boys: Being the Regimental History of the 1st and 2nd Victorian Contingents in the Boer War*, Printbooks, South Melbourne, 2013.

Drooglever, Robin, *From the Front: A. B. (Banjo) Paterson's Dispatches from the Boer War*, Pan Macmillan, Sydney, 2000.

Drooglever, Robin, *Thorneycroft's 'Unbuttoned': The Story of Thorneycroft's Mounted Infantry in the Boer War 1899–1902*, Apple Print, Melbourne, 2014.

Ferguson, Niall, *Empire: How Britain Made the Modern World*, Penguin Books, Australia, 2004.

Fletcher, J. S., *Baden-Powell of Mafeking*, Methuen & Co., London, 1900.

Ford, Carl, *Fighting Words: Australian War Writing*, Lothian, Melbourne, 1986.

Fox, Frank, *Breaker Morant – Bushman and Buccaneer*, H.T. Dunn & Co., 1902.

Gale and Polden Limited, *A Handbook of the Boer War*, Buller and Tanner, London, 1910.

Gordon, General Jose, *Chronicles of a Gay Gordon*, Cassell, London, 1921.

Green, James, *The Story of the Australian Bushmen*, William Brooks and Co. Limited, Sydney, 1903.

Growden, Greg, *Major Thomas*, Affirm Press, Melbourne, 2019.

Hales, A. G., *Campaign Pictures of the War in South Africa*, Cassell, London, 1900.

Hewison, Hope Hay, *Hedge of Wild Almonds: South Africa, the Pro-Boers & the Quaker Conscience, 1890–1910*, James Curry Publishers, Suffolk, 1989.

Hobhouse, Emily, *Boer War Letters: Arrest and Deportation*, Rykie van Reenen (ed.), Human & Rousseau, Cape Town, 1984.

Hobhouse, Emily, *The Brunt of the War, and Where it Fell*, Methuen & Co., London, 1902.

Hobhouse, Emily, *Report of a Visit to the Camps of Women and Children in the Cape and Orange River Colonies*, Friars Printing Association Limited, London, 1901.

Hyslop, *The Plough, the Gun and the Glory*, self-published, 2007.

Iwan-Muller, Edward, *Lord Milner and South Africa*, Heinemann, London, 1902.

Kieza, Grantlee, *Banjo*, HarperCollins Publishers, Sydney, 2018.

Krebs, Paula M., *Gender, Race, and the Writing of Empire: Public Discourse and the Boer War*, Cambridge University Press, Cambridge, 2004.

Kruger, Paul, *The Memoirs of Paul Kruger*, The Century Co., New York, 1902.

Lane, William, (ed.), *The War Diary of Burgher Jack Lane*, Van Riebeeck Society, Cape Town, 2001.

Leach, Charles, *The Legend of Breaker Morant is Dead and Buried,* self-published, 2012.

Lee, John, *General Sir Ian Hamilton: A Soldier's Life*, Pan, London, 2000.

Magnus, Philip, *Kitchener: Portrait of an Imperialist*, John Murray, London, 1958.

Manual of Military Law, War Office, Her Majesty's Stationery Office, London, Part 1, 1899.

Meintjes, Johannes, *President Paul Kruger*, Cassell, London, 1974.

Meiring, Jane, *Against the Tide: A Story of Women in War*, iUniverse, USA, 2009.

Morant, Harry, *The Poetry of Breaker Morant*, Golden Press, Hong Kong, 1980.

Morris, Frederick, *Soldier, Artist, Sportsman: The Life of Lord Rawlinson of Trent*, Pickle, London, 2017.

Odgers, George, *Army Australia: An Illustrated History*, Child & Associates, Frenchs Forest, 1988.

Pakenham, Thomas, *The Boer War*, Futura, London, 1988.

Paterson, A. B., *Happy Dispatches,* Angus & Robertson, Sydney, 1934.

Paterson, A. B., *The Man From Snowy River and Other Verses*, Angus & Robertson, Sydney, 1917.

Paterson, A. B., *Singer of the Bush, Complete Works: 1885–1900,* Lansdowne, Sydney, 1983.

Payne, Robert, *The Life and Death of Mahatma Gandhi*, Brick Tower Press, New York, 1997.

Pemberton, W. Baring, *Battles of the Boer War*, Pan Books, London, 1964.

Postma, M. M., *Stemme Uit Die Verlede*, (Voices from the Past), Johannesburg and Pretoria, Voortrekkerspers Beperk, 1939.

Pretorius, Fransjohan, *Life on Commando During the Anglo-Boer War 1899–1902*, Human and Rousseau, Cape Town, 2000.

Reitz, Deneys, *God Does not Forget: The Story of a Boer War Commando*, Fireship Press, 2010 (first published as *Commando: A Boer Journal of the Boer War* in 1929).

Sandys, Celia, *Churchill Wanted Dead or Alive*, Texas A&M University Press, College Station, 2013.

Seibold, Birgit, *Emily Hobhouse and the Reports on the Concentration Camps during the Boer War 1899–1902*, Ibidem, Stuttgart, 2014.

Semmler, Clement, *The Banjo of the Bush: The Life and Times of A. B 'Banjo' Paterson*, University of Queensland Press, St Lucia, 1984.

Smuts, Jan Christiaan, *Memoirs of the Boer War*, Jonathan Ball, Johannesburg, 1994.

Spender, Harold, *General Botha: The Career and the Man,* Houghton Mifflin Company, New York, 1916.

Spender, Harold, *The Prime Minister*, George H. Doran Company, New York, 1920.

Storey, Nicholas, *Great British Adventurers*, Casemate Publishers, 2012.

Times Law Reports, Vol. XII, G. E. Wright, London, 1896.

Viljoen, Ben, *My Reminiscences of the Anglo Boer War*, Hood, Douglas & Howard, London, 1902.

West, Joe and Roger Roper, *Breaker Morant: The Final Roundup*, Amberley Publishing Limited, Gloucestershire, 2016.

Wilcox, Craig, *Australia's Boer War: The War in South Africa 1899–1902*, Australian War Memorial, Canberra, 2002.
Wilson, John, *C.B.: A Life of Sir Henry Campbell-Bannerman*, Constable, London, 1973.
Witton, George, *Scapegoats of the Empire*, Angus & Robertson, London, 1907.
Witton, George, *Scapegoats of the Empire*, Angus & Robertson, Sydney, 1982.
Witton, George, *Scapegoats of the Empire*, Oxford City Press, 2010.
Ziegler, Philip, *Omdurman*, Book Club Associates, London, 1973.

Periodicals/Journals

Aitken, D. W., 'Guerrilla Warfare, October 1900 – May 1902: Boer attacks on the Pretoria–Delagoa Bay Railway Line', *Military History Journal*, Vol. 11, No. 6, The South African Military History Society, 2000.
Barnard, C.J., 'General Botha and the Spion Kop Campaign', *Military History Journal of South Africa*, Vol. 2, No. 1, June 1971.
Gordon, Michelle, 'British Colonial Violence in Sierra Leone, Perak and Sudan', PhD, University of London, August 2017.
Jewell, James, 'Using Barbaric Methods in South Africa: The British Concentration Camp Policy During the Anglo-Boer War', *Scientia Militaria*, Vol. 31, No. 1, 2003.
Rintala, Marvin, 'Made in Birmingham: Lloyd George, Chamberlain, and the Boer War', *Biography*, Vol. 11, No. 2, 1988, pp. 124–139. *JSTOR*, www.jstor.org/stable/23539369.
South African Journal of Military Studies, Vol. 11, No. 3, 1981

Newspapers

Adelaide Observer
The Advertiser
The Age
The Argus
Auckland Star
The Australasian
The Australian Star
The Ballarat Star
Baltimore Sun
Barrier Miner
The Bendigo Independent
The Border Watch
The Brisbane Courier
The Beverley Times
The Bulletin
Bunbury Herald
The Capricornian
The Catholic Press
The Clarence River Advocate
The Clipper
Clutha Leader
The Cobden Times and Heytesbury Advertiser
Cootamundra Herald
Daily Mercury
The Daily Telegraph (Sydney)
Daily Telegraph (Tas.)
Darling Downs Gazette
Evelyn Observer and South and East Bourke Record
Evening Journal (Adelaide)
Evening News
Evening Post
Examiner (Tas.)

The Express and Telegraph
Geelong Advertiser
Glen Innes Examiner and General Advertiser
Goulburn Evening Penny Post
The Hawkesbury Advocate
Hawkesbury Herald
The Herald
The Inquirer and Commercial News
Kalgoorlie Western Argus
The Kerang Times
Manawatu Standard
The Mercury
Morning Bulletin (Rockhampton)
Morning Post
Mount Alexander Mail
The Mount Lyell Standard
Murchison Advocate
Murray Pioneer
The Narracoorte Herald
Narromine News and Trangie Advocate
National Advocate
Nepean Times
Newcastle Herald
Newcastle Morning Herald and Miners' Advocate
The Northern Miner
Northern Territory Times and Gazette
Otago Witness
Patea Mail
Port Macquarie News and Hastings River Advocate
Port Pirie Recorder and North Western Mail
Queanbeyan Age
The Queenslander
The Scone Advocate
Singleton Argus
The South Australian Register
South Bourke and Mornington Journal
Sunday Times (Sydney)
Sydney Morning Herald
Sydney Truth
Table Talk
The Telegraph (Qld)
The Times (London)
Townsville Daily Bulletin
Truth
Truth (Qld)
The Warwick Argus
Warwick Examiner and Times
The Week
Weekly Times (Vic)
The West Australian
Western Champion
Western Mail
Windsor and Richmond Gazette
Windsor, Richmond and Hawkesbury Advertiser
The World's News

Papers/Archives

Baden Powell, Diary, Aug 1900, NAM Archives 6411-1-7 7, National Army Museum, Chelsea.

Colonial Secretary Confidential papers 1907, National Archives of South Africa, Pretoria.

De Lisle Papers, Kings College London Archives, 3B 40/4.

Hamilton Papers, King's College London Archives, 2/6/8 14.

Kitchener Papers, NA WO 30 57 22 (1), NA WO 9609-48-1, National Archives, Kew, London.

Lord Roberts Papers, NA WO 9609-48-1, National Archives, Kew, London.

Letter from Peter Joseph Handcock to his sister, 27 February 1902, Australian War Memorial, Collection number 3DRL/3834.

Milner, Correspondence to British Colonial Secretary, Joseph Chamberlain, 7 and 15 November 1901, Viscount Alfred Milner; Papers, National Archives PRO 30/30.

National Archives, Kew, London, WO 105/10 12067197, p. 7.

Personal papers of Lieutenant Robert Gartside, AWM 3DRL 7274, Australian War Memorial.

Songs

Gilbert, Frederick Younge, 'The Man Who Broke the Bank at Monte Carlo', composed 1891. Baker, R.A., *British Music Hall – an illustrated history*, Pen & Sword Social, Barnsley, 2014.

Lowry, Robert, 'Shall We Gather at the River', 1864.

Lyte, Henry Francis, 'Abide With Me', 1847.

Stuart, Leslie, 'Soldiers of the Queen', 1898.

'The Bare Belled Ewe', *Bacchus Marsh Express*, 5 December 1891, p. 5. https://trove.nla.gov.au/newspaper/article/89280995

Articles/Websites

Bleszynski, Nick, *Justice or Murder*, The Australian Light Horse Association, http://www.lighthorse.org.au/the-bushveldt-carbineers/

Cape Town Diamond Museum, https://www.capetowndiamondmuseum.org/about-diamonds/famous-people/

'Fort Hendrina Makhado', http://www.theheritageportal.co.za/thread/fort-hendrina-makhado

Harris, '"Spin" on the Boer Atrocities', *The Guardian*, 9 December 2001.

Hussey, 'The Boer War Armoured Train Incident and Churchill's Escape, 1899', Churchill Project, 30 September 2019, https://winstonchurchill.hillsdale.edu/boer-escape/

https://www.lieutpjhandcock.com/2014/04/wittons-letter-to-thomas-21-october-1929.html

South African War, *Sentences on Officers in South Africa – Despatches from the Commander-in-Chief in South Africa, and Extracts from Proceedings of two General Courts-Martial relating thereto*, House of Representatives, April 1902. https://parlinfo.aph.gov.au/parlInfo/search/display/display.w3p;adv=yes;orderBy=customrank;page=0;query=PPYear:1902%20PPNumber:A34%20Dataset:ppSeries;rec=0;resCount=Default

Speech by Alex Hawke MP, 'Lieutenants Morant, Handcock and Witton', House of Representatives, 27 February 2012. https://parlinfo.aph.gov.au/parlInfo/genpdf/chamber/hansardr/dfa1725a-aa28-48db-ba56-7995bad31f8c/0195/hansard_frag.pdf;fileType=application/pdf

Unkles, James, 'An Infantry Officer In Court – A Review of Major James Francis Thomas as Defending Officer for Lieutenants Breaker Morant, Peter Handcock and George Witton – Boer War', 2010. http://breakermorant.com/new/wp-content/documents/short_article_thomas_final_doc_Jun_10x.pdf

van Zyl, Anton, 'The Story of the Zoutpansberg's last three forts', *Zoutpansberger*, 29 September 2017.

Walker, Shirley, 'A Man Never Knows His Luck in South Africa: Some Australian Literary Myths of the Boer War', *The English in Africa*, Vol. 12, No. 2, October 1985.

'Women and Children in White Concentration Camps During Anglo-Boer War 1900–1902', South African History Online, produced 21 March 2011, https://www.sahistory.org.za/article/women-and-children-white-concentration-camps-during-anglo-boer-war-1900-1902

Interviews

Trooper Muir Churton, interviewed by Frank Shields in the mid-1970s.

INDEX

AUSTRALIA

If you would like to find out more about Hachette Australia,
our authors, upcoming events and new releases you can visit
our website or our social media channels:

hachette.com.au

 HachetteAustralia

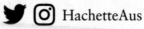 HachetteAus